PUBLIC AND PRIVATE FAMILIES

A Reader

SEVENTH EDITION

Andrew J. Cherlin

Johns Hopkins University

Mc Graw Hill

Connect
Learn
Succeed™

The McGraw-Hill Companies

Connect
Learn
Succeed™

PUBLIC AND PRIVATE FAMILIES: A READER, SEVENTH EDITION

Published by McGraw-Hill, a business unit of The McGraw-Hill Companies, Inc., 1221 Avenue of the Americas, New York, NY, 10020. Copyright © 2013 by The McGraw-Hill Companies, Inc. All rights reserved. Printed in the United States of America. Previous editions © 2010, 2008, and 2005. No part of this publication may be reproduced or distributed in any form or by any means, or stored in a database or retrieval system, without the prior written consent of The McGraw-Hill Companies, Inc., including, but not limited to, in any network or other electronic storage or transmission, or broadcast for distance learning.

Some ancillaries, including electronic and print components, may not be available to customers outside the United States.

This book is printed on acid-free paper.

1 2 3 4 5 6 7 8 9 0 DOC/DOC 1 0 9 8 7 6 5 4 3 2

ISBN: 978-0-07-802668-3
MHID: 0-07-802668-7

Senior Vice President, Products & Markets: *Kurt L. Strand*
Vice President, General Manager, Products & Markets: *Michael Ryan*
Vice President, Content Production & Technology Services: *Kimberly Meriwether David*
Managing Director: *Gina Boedeker*
Development Editor: *Amy Mittelman*
Marketing Specialist: *Alexandra Schultz*
Director, Content Production: *Terri Schiesl*
Editorial Coordinator: *Adina Lonn*
Lead Project Manager: *Jane Mohr*
Buyer: *Laura Fuller*
Cover Designer: *Studio Montage, St. Louis, MO.*
Cover Image: *Royalty-Free / CORBIS*
Typeface: *10.5 / 12 TimesLTStd*
Compositor: *Laserwords Private Limited*
Printer: *R. R. Donnelley*

All credits appearing on page or at the end of the book are considered to be an extension of the copyright page.

Library of Congress Cataloging-in-Publication Data
Public and private families : a reader/[edited by] Andrew J. Cherlin.—7th ed.
    p. cm.
  Includes bibliographical references.
  ISBN 978-0-07-802668-3 (alk. paper)
  1. Families—United States. 2. Families. 3. Family policy. I. Cherlin,
Andrew J., 1948–
    HQ536.C44 2013
    306.850973—dc23   2012033281

The Internet addresses listed in the text were accurate at the time of publication. The inclusion of a website does not indicate an endorsement by the authors or McGraw-Hill, and McGraw-Hill does not guarantee the accuracy of the information presented at these sites.

www.mhhe.com

ABOUT THE AUTHOR

(Courtesy of Will Kirk,
Johns Hopkins University)

ANDREW J. CHERLIN is Benjamin H. Griswold III Professor of Public Policy in the Department of Sociology at Johns Hopkins University. He received a B.S. from Yale University in 1970 and a Ph.D. in sociology from the University of California at Los Angeles in 1976. His books include *The Marriage-Go-Round: The State of Marriage and the Family in America Today* (2009), *Marriage, Divorce, Remarriage* (revised and enlarged edition, 1992), *Divided Families: What Happens to Children when Parents Part* (with Frank F. Furstenberg Jr., 1991), and *The New American Grandparent: A Place in the Family, A Life Apart* (with Frank F. Furstenberg Jr., 1986). In 1989–1990, he was Chair of the Family Section of the American Sociological Association. In 1999, he was President of the Population Association of America, the scholarly organization for demographic research.

In 2003, Professor Cherlin received the Distinguished Career Award from the Family Section of the American Sociological Association. In 2009, he received the Irene B. Taeuber Award from the Population Association of America for "an accumulated record of exceptionally sound and innovative research." He also has received the Olivia S. Nordberg Award for Excellence in Writing in the Population Sciences and a MERIT (Method to Extend Research in Time) Award from the National Institutes of Health for his research on the effects of family structure on children. In 2005–2006, he was a recipient of a John Simon Guggenheim Memorial Foundation Fellowship. His articles include "The Deinstitutionalization of American Marriage," in the *Journal of Marriage and Family* (2004);

"American Marriage in the Early Twenty-First Century," in *The Future of Children* (2005); and "The Influence of Physical and Sexual Abuse on Marriage and Cohabitation," in *American Sociological Review* (2004). He also has written many short articles for *The New York Times, The Washington Post, The Nation, Newsweek,* and other periodicals. He has been interviewed on *ABC News Nightline,* the *Today Show,* network evening news programs, National Public Radio's *All Things Considered,* the BBC, and other news programs and documentaries.

CONTENTS

v

PREFACE

The metaphor of public and private families in the title of this Reader reflects my sense that families matter in two senses. First, they perform activities of great importance to the public interest— most notably raising the next generation and caring for the frail elderly. Second, as the main site of our personal lives, they provide the private satisfactions of love, intimacy, and companionship. Many textbooks and readers focus more on the private family; they mainly describe how people manage their personal relationships as they proceed through their life course. I include this perspective, too; but I attempt to balance it with a consideration of the important public issues raised by the great recent changes in family life. Indeed, hardly a week goes by without some family issue—gay marriage, government programs to promote marriage, teenage childbearing, child care, domestic violence, and so forth—appearing on the front page of the newspapers. Consequently, it's crucial that students studying the sociology of the family encounter not just studies of the individual life course but also of the ways that family life affects our society. I have attempted to provide both the public and private perspectives on the family in this Reader.

ORGANIZATION

This book consists of 28 readings that are keyed to the 14 chapters of the seventh edition of the textbook that I have written for courses in the Sociology of the Family, *Public and Private Families: An Introduction.* Two readings are presented for each chapter. Nevertheless, this book can be used with other textbooks or no textbook at all. The readings represent a broad sampling of new ideas and older insights from the literature on families. After introductory and historical material, I introduce readings on gender, class, race, and ethnicity. I then turn to readings on sexuality, cohabitation, marriage, the work of caring for others, children, and older people. After that, the readings cover issues of conflict, disruption, and reconstitution such as domestic violence, divorce, and remarriage. The volume concludes with readings on family policy.

NEW TO THE SEVENTH EDITION

Eight of the 28 readings are new to this edition. Here is a guide to what's new:

- *Chapter 1.* The readings are unchanged from the previous edition.
- *Chapter 2.* The readings are unchanged from the previous edition.
- *Chapter 3.* I have included an article by Barbara Risman and Elizabeth Seale about changes in the gendered expectations for middle-school girls and boys. The article by Doucet on fathers has been deleted.
- *Chapter 4.* I have included an excerpt on differences in family formation between college-educated and less educated young adults, taken from my 2009 book, *The Marriage-Go-Round.* The 1995 *New Yorker* article, "Ain't No Middle Class," has been deleted.
- *Chapter 5.* I have added a 2009 article on black marriage by Shirley Hill. The reading on transnational motherhood has been deleted (but see the new reading by Dreby in Chapter 9).
- *Chapter 6.* The readings are unchanged from the previous edition.
- *Chapter 7.* The readings are unchanged from the previous edition.
- *Chapter 8.* I have replaced the well-known but more than 20-year-old example of Evan and Nancy Holt from Arlie Hochschild's *The Second Shift* with an article on work–family balance, public policy, and social class, by Joan Williams.
- *Chapter 9.* I have replaced both readings in this chapter, Wilcox on religion and men and Stacey on gay fatherhood, with two articles: Sara McLanahan on instability and complexity in the lives of low- and moderate-income families and Joanna Dreby on a Mexican family divided by the United States–Mexico border.
- *Chapter 10.* The readings are unchanged from the previous edition.
- *Chapter 11.* The readings are unchanged from the previous edition.
- *Chapter 12.* The readings are unchanged from the previous edition.
- *Chapter 13.* I have replaced the 2001 Nelson et al. study with an article on the many types of relationships that stepdaughters have with their nonresident stepmothers.

- *Chapter 14.* I have included an article about "disconnected" single mothers who neither receive welfare benefits nor work for pay. I have deleted an article about the effects of welfare reform.

ACKNOWLEDGMENTS

To write a book this comprehensive requires the help of many people. At McGraw-Hill, sponsoring editor Lisa Pinto provided initial support, freelance development editor Nadia Bidwell provided valuable editorial guidance, and Jane Mohr smoothly managed the production process. In addition, the following people read the sixth edition and provided me with helpful suggestions for this revision:

Kiran Cunningham, Kalamazoo College
Catherine Fobes, Alma College
Michael Grimes, Louisiana State University
Jonathon Varhola, Wright State University

Andrew J. Cherlin

Part One

Introduction

CHAPTER 1

Public and Private Families

The state of the American family—indeed, the state of the family in all industrialized nations—is a controversial issue, much debated by social commentators, politicians, and academic experts. A half century ago, few observers seemed concerned. But since the 1960s, family life has changed greatly. Many users of this reader will have experienced these changes in their own families. Divorce is more common; at current rates, 40 to 50 percent of marriages would end in divorce. Young adults are postponing marriage and often living with a partner prior to marrying. A growing number of children—currently about 40 percent—are born to mothers who are not married (but who may be cohabiting). And many more married women are working outside the home.

These trends aren't necessarily negative. For instance, married women's jobs often give them an improved sense of self-worth and boost their families' standards of living. Young adults may use living with a partner as a way to search for a more compatible spouse. In fact, some commentators hail the decline of the 1950s middle-class family in which wives usually stayed home and specialized in housework and child care. These breadwinner-homemaker families, it is alleged, restricted the lives of women and supported the continuation of conflict-ridden marriages that may have been worse for children than a parental divorce would have been. But the overall tone of the public commentary on family change has been one of concern.

To develop your own views on the subject, you first need to know the basic facts about changes in American families. In the first selection, sociologists Claude S. Fischer and Michael Hout present a series of charts that show the demographic changes that occurred in the American family in the twentieth century. Their information comes mainly from the U.S. Census of Population, which the Constitution requires the federal government to conduct every ten years. Scholars now have access to Census records going back a century or more. Taking a long view, the authors find that, in some respects, the most unusual and distinctive period of family life occurred in the middle of the twentieth century rather than at the end. They examine the extent to which trends during the century support the widespread belief that "family troubles" have increased.[1]

But more than the demographics of family life changed during the twentieth century. At midcentury marriage was a partnership in which fulfilling one's roles—being a good homemaker, earning the family's income—provided the highest satisfactions. Much of a person's gratifications, then, occurred through activities external to the self. But after the 1950s, marriages, and the rising numbers of heterosexual and homosexual nonmarital partnerships, came to be defined more in terms of individual growth and development than in terms of fulfilling prescribed roles. Sociologist Francesca Cancian, in a selection from her book *Love in America: Gender and Self-Development,* calls this a transition "from role to self" in the focus of personal rewards in marriages and partnerships.

Cancian maintains that love itself was "feminized" under the older kinds of marriage because emotion was seen as the domain of women. Now, love is more "androgynous," meaning that both women and men are concerned about expressing love and emotional support. Correspondingly, autonomy and self-development were emphasized more for men, whereas now these goals are put forth for both genders. To provide evidence for her view of the evolution of marriage, she studied articles on marriage in popular magazines between 1900 and 1979. Their shifting content, she argues, demonstrates the shift from role to self.

---

[1]The authors presented a more thorough examination of changes during the century in their book, *Century of Difference: How America Changed in the Last One Hundred Years* (New York: Russell Sage Foundation, 2006).

READING 1-1

The Family in Trouble
Since When? For Whom?

Claude S. Fischer

Michael Hout

OVERVIEW OF FAMILY CHANGES

American family life changed in many ways in the twentieth century, but the severity of a change and the severity of the conversations about that change

did not often match. As we shall see, some of the greatest changes involved the demography of the family and affected the elderly, while the much-discussed matters, such as family dissolution and family intimacy, were much more stable.

Major Changes

Let us highlight the "big" changes in the American family over the century. The first one to note is basic and critical: Americans live a lot longer than they used to.[1] Figure 1.1 shows the average life expectancy of white women and men who had already made it to the age of twenty.[2] A twenty-year-old white woman in 2000 could expect seventeen more years of life than could her ancestor in 1900; a twenty-year-old white man today could expect thirteen years more than a twenty-year-old man a century ago. (In addition to this change, there was an even greater expansion in the life expectancy of infants.) There are, as we shall see, profound implications to this greater longevity.

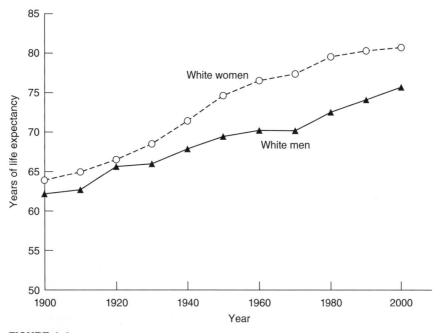

FIGURE 1.1

Years of life expected at age 20, white men and women, 1900–2000. (*Source:* National Center for Health Statistics via http://www.infoplease.com/ipa/A0005140.html.)

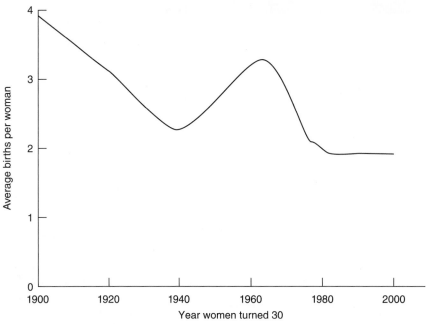

FIGURE 1.2
Number of births over a woman's lifetime by year of her 30th birthday, for women born 1870–1970. (*Source:* Steven Ruggles, Matthew Sobek, Trent Alexander, Catherine A. Fitch, Ronald Goeken, Patricia Kelly Hall, Miriam King, and Chad Ronnander, *Integrated Public Use Microdata Series: Version 3,* machine-readable database [Minneapolis: Minnesota Population Center, 2004], available at http://www.ipums.umn.edu/usa/.)

Add to this another major change—the reduction in the birthrate. The average number of births per woman, dated at the age she turned thirty, dropped steeply from 1900 to the 1940s, as shown in Figure 1.2; if we could push back the view here to 1800, we would see a tilted line starting from about seven or eight births per woman in 1800 down to about two in 1940.[3] The 1950s and early 1960s were unusual. Take out the anomalies—the drop in births during the Depression and World War II and the Baby Boom afterward—and we would see a smoothly declining curve from 1800 on; the last thirty years are right on track. Women who were thirty years old around 1900 averaged four children apiece; women who were thirty years old around 2000 averaged two children apiece.

Extensions of life and reductions in births drove two other major changes: A large increase in the proportion of people fifty and older living in an "empty nest" (with just a spouse) and an increasing proportion of elderly Americans living alone. In 1900, about one in four of the elderly lived in one of these two circumstances; in 2000, more than three in four elderly people did so. These are enormous reversals in family life, shown in Figure 1.3. Note that the biggest changes in family life, in Americans' living arrangements, during the twentieth century occurred for the elderly. The elderly today end their parenting much earlier in life, they have fewer children, and they live longer than the elderly a few generations ago. They also have more money and better health. They may also cherish their independence more than did the elderly of earlier eras.[4] Consequently, the elderly now live on their own instead of with their children. Ironically, during the past thirty years,

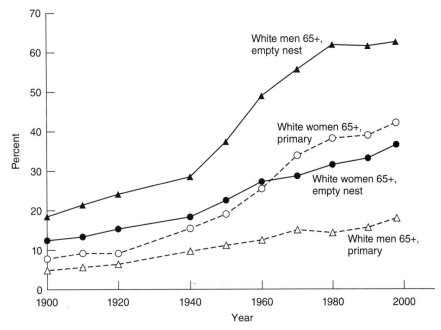

FIGURE 1.3

Percent of elderly who live either as "primary individuals" [alone or with nonrelatives only] (dashed lines) or in an "empty nest" (solid lines), for white men (triangles) and white women (circles), 1900–98. (*Source:* Steven Ruggles, Matthew Sobek, Trent Alexander, Catherine A. Fitch, Ronald Goeken, Patricia Kelly Hall, Miriam King, and Chad Ronnander, *Integrated Public Use Microdata Series: Version 3,* machine-readable database [Minneapolis: Minnesota Population Center, 2004], available at http://www.ipums.umn.edu/usa/; Current Population Survey.)

Americans have increasingly told pollsters that they think the aged should not live independently but should live with their children, but that trend emerged only because younger generations, not the elderly themselves, endorsed co-living.[5]

The next big change is the enormous increase in the proportion of married women, and the proportion of mothers with children under six, working outside the home, shown in Figure 1.4. In 1920, about 10 percent of married women officially worked; in 2000, more than 60 percent did. Note that the low percentages in the early part of the century are serious underestimates.[6] Nonetheless, the "real" trend is still a fundamental and sharp change. This trend, by the way, accelerated through the 1950s without pause. This transformation, too, had immense ramifications for our families, our children, and our culture—ramifications we have not yet fully absorbed.

These family changes, we submit, were the greatest in scale and probably in consequence. But there were also other noteworthy changes.

Modest Changes

One such change is the fluctuation in the age at which Americans married. First it dropped. American women marrying around 1900 tended to be about twenty-two years old; those marrying around 1950 tended to be about twenty, meaning that in the 1950s, about half of all brides were teenagers. This helps to explain the baby boom. Those marrying at the end of the century averaged twenty-four years of age on their wedding day, and a growing subgroup was marrying in their thirties.

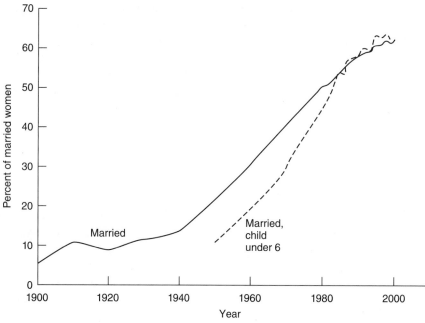

FIGURE 1.4
Percent of married women (and married women with a child under 6) in the labor force, 1900–2000. (*Sources:* U.S. Bureau of the Census, *Historical Statistics* and *Statistical Abstracts.*)

Also, of course, the divorce rate increased. At the beginning of the century, there was roughly one divorce issued for every ten marriages performed. By the early 1990s, it was about one for every two, although the divorce rate has been dropping since roughly 1980.[7] This is a fivefold increase in divorce, but we do not call it a "big change." One reason is that rates of marriage dissolution did not change nearly as much. Early in the century, marriages broke up because a spouse died. If one combines dissolution by death with dissolution by divorce, the total stayed pretty constant to 1970, as rising divorce balanced out declining mortality. By 1980, rising divorce pushed the total dissolution rate about one-fourth over its historical level, but it has subsided some since then.[8] Another reason we do not stress divorce is that most divorced people remarry. The proportion of adults living unmarried did not increase nearly as much as the

dramatic rise in the divorce rate would suggest. Many of those who do not remarry, it turns out, cohabit instead.

The increasing delay of marriage, in turn, contributed to higher rates of premarital sex. So, for example, about half of women who were teenagers in the 1950s were virgins at marriage, compared with under one-third of women who were teens in the 1970s.[9] The drop in virgin brides is, in part, simply the result of a longer time between puberty, which is now arriving earlier, and marriage, which is now arriving later. This change, by the way, also stopped or reversed in the 1990s.

Cohabitation, both before and after the first marriage, has increased significantly in the last few decades, as has popular tolerance of it. The proportion of American households at any one time with a cohabiting couple rose from under 1 percent in 1960 to a still low 5 percent in 2000.

More important, half of married couples now begin their conjugal lives by cohabiting.[10]

A consequence of both delaying marriage and increasing divorce is the increase in children living with a single parent. We shall look more closely at this below, but the simple fact is that for the first half of the century, about 5 percent of American children were recorded as living with only a single parent, and more than 20 percent were doing so in 2000.

Finally in this list, survey data, which do not go back further than about 1960, show that Americans became in recent decades increasingly tolerant of these and related changes—of smaller families, of women working, of premarital sex, of cohabitation, and of single-parent families. That is, Americans increasingly accepted wider ranges of individual choices in how to form a family.

Minor or Minimal Changes

Many other aspects of the family changed little, as far as we can tell. Both marriage and children continue to be valued. Americans still say they want to marry. For example, in a 2001 Gallup survey, more than nine in ten teenagers said that they wanted to marry and to have children, an increase over a generation.[11] Single adults age twenty through twenty-nine fully endorsed marriage; 78 percent said that being married was a very important life goal, 88 percent said that they were confident of finding a suitable spouse when they are ready to marry, and 88 percent answered yes when asked if there was a unique "soul mate" for them "out there."[12]

Moreover, Americans do get married. The latest estimates are that 90 percent of women now about forty years old have married or will eventually marry, even if later in life. This is a marriage rate notably higher than that in the early part of the twentieth century or, for that matter, the mid–nineteenth century.[13] Another indicator of how Americans value marriage is that, despite increasingly tolerating premarital sex, Americans in recent decades have become less tolerant of extramarital sex. The thread connecting American attitudes on these subjects seems to be an increasing emphasis on freedom of choice combined with insistence on personal responsibility: Have premarital sex as you wish, marry as you wish, but if you marry, stay faithful.[14]

Finally, sociologists and historians have perused as many tea leaves as possible to see if they can spot a trend in familial intimacy, affection, and commitment. We can make no solid case one way or the other. What scholars can say with some confidence is that the standards and expectations for intimacy, affection, and commitment have increased. Whether in responses to survey data or in the complaints people list when filing for divorce, Americans during the twentieth century demanded more companionship, warmth, and happiness in marriage.

What can we generalize about family change over the century? Here are a few defensible statements:

- Americans always preferred the household of a married couple with children.
- During the twentieth century, it became increasingly possible to have such a nuclear family. In the earlier years, many external events blocked that goal: premature death, ill health, economic dislocation, unplanned pregnancies, and infertility. These disturbances became less important. People have more control now. So more people spend more of their lives in marriage than was true a few generations ago.
- The second choice after a married-couple household has changed. In the first half of the century, people who could not—because they were spinsters or widows or orphans—be in a married-couple household lived instead with other relatives, or in institutional settings like poorhouses and orphanages. In recent decades, this has changed. People have been more able and perhaps more willing to choose other alternatives—if the married-couple arrangement was not available—to live alone, cohabit, or be a single parent.
- Other values such as personal attainment and independence, especially for women, increasingly

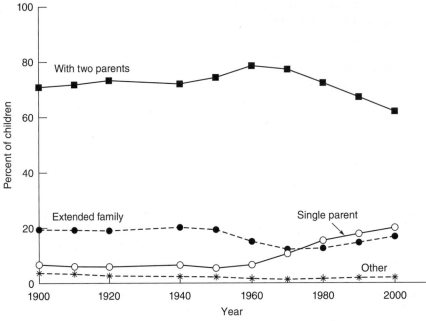

FIGURE 1.5

Percent of children (birth to age 17), by living arrangement, 1900–2000. (*Source:* Steven Ruggles, Matthew Sobek, Trent Alexander, Catherine A. Fitch, Ronald Goeken, Patricia Kelly Hall, Miriam King, and Chad Ronnander, *Integrated Public Use Microdata Series: Version 3,* machine-readable database [Minneapolis: Minnesota Population Center, 2004], available at http://www.ipums.umn.edu/usa/.)

competed with the goal of the married-couple household. Women's alternatives have expanded. Standards for a good marriage rose, and escapes from bad ones became easier. As a result, marriages are increasingly delayed or broken by choice rather than by external disruptions.

One consequence of these decisions can be trouble for the children. Children increasingly are living with a single parent outside a nuclear or an extended household. This is what we will look at more closely now.

FAMILY TROUBLE: THE SINGLE-PARENTED CHILD

It is generally understood that children have easier lives and do somewhat better when they live with two parents instead of one.[15] Figure 1.5 shows the distribution of children, age birth to seventeen years, by their living arrangements across the century.[16] On top, we see the percentage who lived just with two parents and siblings (if any), the ideal nuclear family. In 1900, about 70 percent of children lived that way; another roughly 20 percent lived in an extended family that often included both parents.[17] The proportion in the nuclear family then rose to 78 percent by 1960 and then dropped down to 64 percent at the end of the century, a bit lower than it was 100 years before. (If we add cohabiting parents to married parents, then the 2000 figure is 66 percent.) These numbers unfortunately do not distinguish between children living with their original parents from those living in a stepfamily, and some literature suggests that stepparent families are less conducive to child welfare than having both original parents.[18] The long-term data we draw upon cannot distinguish biological from stepparents, but stepparents surely formed a larger portion of two-parent households recently than they did in the 1950s; whether stepparents were more common recently than in the early part of the century is not clear.

Until thirty years ago, children who were not in a nuclear family were likely to be in extended-family households, perhaps with a grandparent, uncle, or cousins—shown in Figure 1.5 by a dashed line. Most of those households included both the child's two parents, at least early in the century, or one parent, more often now. Whether the extended household experience was better, the same, or worse than the two-parent household can be argued. The category of "other," shown at the bottom, refers to children living on their own or in some kind of group setting. Finally, we see—along a line connecting circles—the rise since 1960 in the proportion of children living with only one parent and no other relatives besides siblings. It had been under 10 percent for most of the century, took off in 1970, and reached 20 percent in 2000. This group and this last period is the subject of greatest public concern.[19]

The first question we have been raising is "Since when?" And we see here that the "when" is the 1950s. Indeed, if we were to push our view before 1900 back into the nineteenth century, we would quite likely see the bottom line, "other," keep going up and up as we move backward—backward into the era when children under eighteen, even many under twelve, were sent out of their homes to be farmhands, apprentices, and servants in other people's homes and thus lived with neither parent nor extended kin but with "others." The 1950s may have been the decade with the least disruption to Victorian ideals of childhood in American history.

If comparing a couple of centuries is too long a period to make the point that we need to be specific about "when," then consider the last decade alone. The proportion of children living with fewer than two parents topped out at 32 percent in the mid-1990s (67 percent in 1995 for blacks) and dropped to 31 percent in 2002 (61 percent for blacks).[20] Other data also point to a recent decline in the behaviors that produce single-parent families, such as teen pregnancy and divorce, suggesting that we may have already seen the peak of one-parent households. So, again, we need to ask what we are using as historical comparisons and what is a reasonable comparison. Since when?

The other question we have been asking is "For whom?" Figure 1.6 focuses on the category of children living with only a single parent only or in one of those anomalous "other" settings. Then Figure 1.7 shows us that the rise in such children is disproportionately among black children. The black/white differential opened up in 1940 and then widened. Before 1940, white children were about 60 percent as likely as black children to be in a single-parent household; by the 1990s, they were about 40 percent as likely.[21] Single parenting has become disproportionately a "trouble" of the black community.

Sociologists believe that the trouble for black children, which accelerated in the 1950s and 1960s, coincides with increasing difficulties of black men in northern cities, which began with the loss of well-paying blue-collar jobs and then were compounded by rising drug use and crime. The result is that, though blacks and whites equally value the aspiration of getting married, blacks have become more disappointed with or even cynical about marriage.[22] That response may have taken on a life of its own, although there were signs in the late 1990s of marriage starting to rebound among African Americans. . . .

CONCLUSION

The effort we have gone through to look at who was affected when by family troubles is more than an accounting exercise. The numbers help us understand why these changes occurred and, potentially, what levers of influence exist.

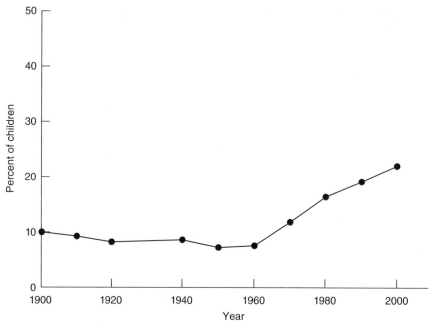

FIGURE 1.6
Percent of children (birth to age 17) living with one parent only or in "other" nonfamily arrangement, 1900–2000. (*Source:* Steven Ruggles, Matthew Sobek, Trent Alexander, Catherine A. Finch, Ronald Goeken, Patricia Kelly Hall, Miriam King, and Chad Ronnander, *Integrated Public Use Microdata Series: Version 3,* machine-readable database [Minneapolis: Minnesota Population Center, 2004], available at http://www.ipums.umn.edu/usa/.)

For example, the historical data going back to the early part of the twentieth century make it difficult to explain family change as a linear consequence of "modernity." Classic sociological theories of the family, notably those of the 1950s, claim that the family lost its functions to the state and other institutions and therefore became weaker. But the nonlinear changes in the family cast doubt on such an explanation; for example, people are as or more likely to marry now as they were a century ago. The internal variations we have tracked also lead us to question such explanations. It is, after all, the most advantaged among us who have most embraced nonfamilial opportunities, sending children off to college and purchasing family services such as food, cleaning, child care, and parenting advice.

Yet the most advantaged have been the least affected by family troubles. The data also cast doubt on simple economic explanations of family patterns. For example, the notion that people have children to serve as their old-age insurance runs up against the contradiction that Americans indulged in a huge baby boom just after the U.S. government set up public old-age insurance.[23] History speaks to us.

When we put "family troubles" in historical perspective, we learn a few broad lessons. One is that troubles with marriage and parenting are concentrated among Americans with disadvantages. These Americans would live the 1950s ideal if they could, but they often cannot. In this way, they are like many Americans a century ago, whose family aspirations were blocked by death, disease,

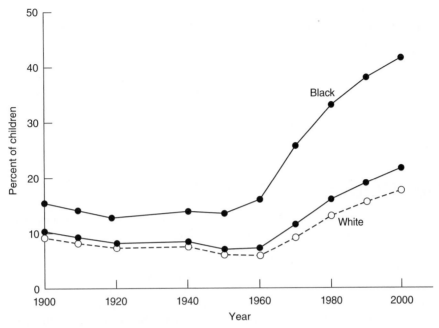

FIGURE 1.7

Percent of children (birth to age 17) living with one parent only or in "other" nonfamily arrangement, by race, 1900–2000. (*Source:* Steven Ruggles, Matthew Sobek, Trent Alexander, Catherine A. Fitch, Ronald Goeken, Patricia Kelly Hall, Miriam King, and Chad Ronnander, *Integrated Public Use Microdata Series: Version 3,* machine-readable database [Minneapolis: Minnesota Population Center, 2004], available at http://www.ipums.umn.edu/usa/.)

and disaster. Not many advantaged Americans have such problems. In 2000, only one in ten white children with a college-educated parent as head of household lived in a single-parent home.

Another lesson is that, for more advantaged Americans, being unwed, childless, or divorced is less a matter of malign fate and more a matter of new opportunities. Increasing affluence and improving health have made more choices more available to more people. These people choose to delay marriage, to have fewer children, and to live apart from those children when they age. These choices are not "family troubles," except insofar as one assumes that people not living in a nuclear family are ipso facto troubled. To be sure, trouble in the form of divorce or single parenting does occasionally visit such people these days. We might best understand

the family troubles that some of the advantaged face as a by-product of cultural shifts, such as the increasing freedom that individuals have to make personal, self-expressive choices in sex, marriage, and the family. And these are cultural shifts we typically approve. For example, vastly more wives work than before and vastly more Americans approve. In 1938, about one in four Americans said that it was okay for a wife to work if her husband could support her; by the 1990s, more than three in four did.[24] Yet such expansions of personal autonomy for the well-off can carry costs, one of which is increasing divorce and another is increasing numbers of children being single parented. Our moral burden, then, is to deal with the side effects, such as single parenting, of the changes we desire, such as more options for women.

Finally, we learn that America's social history is more complex and nuanced than many a simple gloss would have it. For example, every year the Bureau of the Census announces and newspapers report that a smaller percentage of American homes are occupied by nuclear families. True, but what does that mean? It largely means that more homes are occupied by still-vibrant older couples or singles whose youngest child left home before the parents turned fifty and who have thirty years of life to go. Increasing life spans have also meant that Americans spend more years knowing their aging parents, watching their children grow up, and sharing the company of a spouse.[25] So with regard to family troubles, we do need to ask "Since when?" and "For whom?"

■ Review Questions

1. Why do the authors consider the rise in divorce during the twentieth century not to be a major change?
2. Why do the authors say that people have more control over their family lives than they did a century ago?

ENDNOTES

1. Our data largely come from the U.S. censuses for 1900 through 2000—except for 1930, which has only just been released. These raw files have been compiled and made available as the Integrated Public Use Microdata Series; see Steven Ruggles, Matthew Sobek, Trent Alexander, Catherine A. Fitch, Ronald Goeken, Patricia Kelly Hall, Miriam King, and Chad Ronnander, *Integrated Public Use Microdata Series: Version 3,* machine-readable database (Minneapolis: Minnesota Population Center, 2004), available at http://www.ipums.umn.edu/usa/.

2. These numbers are from the National Center for Health Statistics, available at http://www.infoplease.com/ipa/A0005140.html.

3. That longer line is unavailable because earlier data use the number of children under five per the number of women age fifteen to forty-four. See U.S. Census Bureau, *Historical Statistics of the United States* (Washington, D.C.: U.S. Government Printing Office, 1977), 54; and subsequent *Statistical Abstracts.*

4. Frances E. Kobrin, "The Fall in Household Size and the Rise of the Primary Individual in the United States since 1940," *Journal of Marriage and the Family* 38 (May 1976): 233–39.

5. Authors' analysis of the General Social Survey (GSS) item "AGED," http://csa.berkeley.edu:7502/archive.htm.

6. For one, many wives worked informally in family businesses—farms, in particular. Others "took in" work, such as laundry, that they may not have reported. Also, we have reason to suspect that "respectable" families underreported the wives' work.

7. The gross divorce rate in 1979 was 5.3 per 1,000 Americans; it was 4.1 in 2000 (http://www.cdc.gov/nchs). Joshua R. Goldstein, "The Leveling of Divorce in the United States," *Demography* 36 (August 1999): 409–14, finds that this was a meaningful social change, not a statistical fluke.

8. These calculations are summarized in Andrew J. Cherlin, *Marriage, Divorce, Remarriage,* rev. ed. (Cambridge, Mass.: Harvard University Press, 1992), 25. The rate of dissolution from the 1860s through 1970 was about 33 to 34 dissolutions per 1,000 marriages; it rose to a peak of 41 around 1980 and declined to 39 by 1989.

9. Edward Laumann, John H. Gagnon, Robert T. Michael, and Stuart Michaels, *The Social Organization of Sexuality* (Chicago: University of Chicago Press, 1994), 197–99, 213–14; see also Sandra L. Hofferth, Joan R. Kahn, and Wendy Baldwin, "Premarital Sexual Activity among American Teenage Women over the Past Three Decades," *Family Planning Perspectives* 19 (March 1987): 46–53. On early-twentieth-century premarital sexuality, see, e.g., Daniel Scott Smith, "The Dating of the American Sexual Revolution" in *The American Family in Social-Historical*

Perspective, 2nd edition, ed. Micahel Gordon (New York: St. Martin's Press, 1978), 426–38; Amara Bachu, "Trends in Marital Status of U.S. Women at First Birth: 1930 to 1994," *Current Population Reports,* Special Studies (Washington, D.C.: U.S. Bureau of the Census, 1999), 23–197; and Stuart N. Seidman and Ronald O. Rieder, "A Review of Sexual Behavior in the United States," *American Journal of Psychiatry* 151 (March 1994): 330–41.

10. Lynne M. Casper and Suzanne M. Bianchi, *Continuity and Change in the American Family* (Thousand Oaks, Calif.: Sage Publications, 2002), chap. 1.

11. Linda Lyons, "Kids and Divorce," Gallup Online, http://www.gallup.com.

12. Kelley Maybury, "I Do? Marriage in Uncertain Times," Gallup Online, http://www.gallup.com.

13. Joshua R. Goldstein and Catherine T. Kenny, "Marriage Delayed or Marriage Forgone? New Cohort Forecasts of First Marriage for U.S. Women," *American Sociological Review* 66 (August 2001): 506–19. Goldstein and Kenny project current women's experiences into the twenty-first century. On longer historical comparisons, see Catherine A. Fitch and Steven Ruggles, "Historical Trends in Marriage Formation: The United States 1850–1990," in *The Ties That Bind: Perspectives on Marriage and Cohabitation,* ed. Linda J. Waite (New York: Aldine de Gruyter, 2000), 59–89. The percentage of never-married women in Charleston and Boston circa 1845 was higher than now; see Jane H. Pease and William H. Pease, *Ladies, Women, and Wenches: Choice and Constraint in Antebellum Charleston and Boston* (Chapel Hill: University of North Carolina Press, 1990).

14. On this and other attitude items, see Arland Thornton and Linda Young-Demarco, "Four Decades of Trends in Attitudes toward Family Issues in the United States," *Journal of Marriage and the Family* 63 (November 2001): 1009–38.

15. Sara McLanahan, "Life without Father: What Happens to the Children?" *Contexts* 1 (spring 2002): 35–44, provides an overview. The literature is large and controversial, but we assume that, other things being equal, a one-parent family is less desirable for children.

16. The numbers exclude from the base the few zero- to seventeen-year-olds who were in married couples with no children households—i.e., young brides and grooms. "Other" includes the very tiny fraction who were on their own and a small percentage who were in some form of "shared quarters."

17. Census data show that 84 percent of children in 1900 lived with two parents, suggesting that most of the children in extended households (seven of ten) had both parents there. U.S. Bureau of the Census, "Historical Living Arrangements of Children," http://www.census.gov/population/socdemo/child/p70-74/tab02.xls.

18. E.g., Andrew J. Cherlin and Frank F. Furstenberg Jr., "Stepfamilies in the United States: A Reconsideration," *Annual Review of Sociology* 20 (1994): 359–81; McLanahan, "Life without Father."

19. Census Bureau calculations show that the percentage of children living with one or neither parent was 13 to 17 percent from 1900 through 1970, then rose to 31 percent by 2000. U.S. Bureau of the Census, "Historical Living Arrangements of Children"; plus 2000 Current Population Survey.

20. These figures are based on slightly different data, "Table CH-1: Living Arrangements of Children under 18 Years Old: 1960 to Present," http://www.census.gov, drawn from the *Current Population Survey* and more recent data from the same source. These data count children living in extended households with a parent or two as living with a parent or both.

21. On this point, see also Fitch and Ruggles, "Historical Trends," 65.

22. This summary statement is supported by the many ethnographies of poor African Americans. It also shows up in survey data. The GSS asked unmarried people in the 1990s, "If the right person came along, would you like to be married?" There was no difference between blacks and whites (either a raw difference, or after statistical controls). Blacks were even slightly more likely to say that a bad marriage was better than no marriage. But on questions such as whether married people were happier than unmarried people, whether personal freedom was more important than marriage, whether people who want children should wait to get married, and whether single mothers can raise children as well as married couples, blacks were noticeably more skeptical about the marriage option. Authors' analysis of the GSS.

23. Similarly, scholars of the fertility decline that began in the nineteenth century have found simple economic explanations insufficient.

24. The GSS asked Americans whether the women's movement had improved, worsened, or not affected the lives of particular groups. Moderate pluralities to large majorities said "improved" in answers referring to questions about effects on "homemakers," working-class women, professional women, and even children. People were evenly split as to whether men benefited or lost from the women's movement (authors' analysis).

25. Susan Cotts Watkins, Jane A. Menken, and John Bongaarts, "Demographic Foundations of Family Change," *American Sociological Review* 52 (June 1987): 346–58.

READING 1-2

From Role to Self: The Emergence of Androgynous Love in the 20th Century

Francesca M. Cancian

In the long run, the social changes that began in the 19th century destroyed Victorian family patterns. The ideal of masculine independence spread to women and the private sphere, undermining people's willingness to be restricted by narrow family and gender roles. Wives became less subordinate and absorbed by mothering, as they had fewer children and increasingly joined the labor force, and many husbands became less consumed by their work as leisure time expanded and jobs became bureaucratized. Through most of the 20th century, there has been a trend toward more fluid, androgynous family roles and more involvement in self-development and personal life. Americans have become more concerned with individual happiness and pleasure, more tolerant of alternative lifestyles, more committed to equality for women and men, and more prone to divorce.

The trend to androgynous love has been discontinuous. In eras that emphasized personal liberation like the 20s and the late 60s, the trend accelerated, while in the 50s the long-range trend reversed as gender roles became more rigid and tolerance declined. These discontinuities can be used to identify different periods in the social organization of marriage, each dominated by a different family blueprint, or a different mix of blueprints.[1] Each blueprint combines a cultural image of the ideal marriage with expectations for daily life that guide behavior.

Figure 1.8 presents the major blueprints of marriage since the 19th century. First is the Victorian blueprint of family duty in which love is the woman's responsibility. Then come the three blueprints that dominate contemporary marriage: the more traditional companionship blueprint that first evolved in the 20s, and the newer blueprints of independence and interdependence in which the woman and the man share the obligation to work on their relationship, and the goal of self-development replaces conformity to roles. This reading gives a general description of these changes in blueprints of marriage, and then presents quantitative data on the major trends.

Francesca M. Cancian, "From Role to Self: The Emergence of Androgynous Love in the 20th Century," from *Love in America: Gender and Self-Development*, pp. 30–45. Copyright © 1987 by Cambridge University Press. Reprinted with the permission of Cambridge University Press.

	Who is responsible for love?	What is love?
Feminized love		
Family duty (19th century)	woman	fulfill duty to family
Companionship (1920–)	woman	intimacy in marriage
Androgynous love		
Independence (1970–)	woman and man	individual self-development and intimacy
Interdependence (1970–)	woman and man	mutual self-development, intimacy, and support

FIGURE 1.8
Blueprints of Love

THE DECLINE OF THE FAMILY DUTY BLUEPRINT

The family duty blueprint was the first solution to the problem of maintaining family bonds in an increasingly individualistic society. According to this image of family life, as we have seen, the ideal family was a nuclear household consisting of a father who left home every day to make the money to support the family, a loving mother who was the center of family life, and the children. Marriage was forever, and a man had considerable authority over his wife and children. The relation between husband and wife began with falling in love and might develop into companionship, although intimacy and sexual relations between spouses were not central and both spouses had important ties with relatives and friends of their own sex. The key relation was an intense, emotional tie between mothers and children, and raising moral, respectable, and healthy children was a woman's major task.

This ideal dominated in the United States from about 1840 to 1880 and then began to show signs of decline.[2] The divorce rate was increasing at the end of the century, and it doubled between 1900 and 1920. The proportion of women remaining single was rising, and so many affluent women were childless that some social critics raised the spectre of "race suicide" and "race sterility." Others criticized the family as an oppressive institution that deprived Americans of freedom and equality. Feminists attacked the tyranny of husbands over wives; plays like Ibsen's *A Doll's House* attacked the childlike position of women; advocates of free love protested against sexual repression; and sociologists viewed the difficulty of divorce as an unnecessary impediment to self-development.

By the turn of the century there was widespread debate in government, churches, and the mass media on the future of the family, the decline of sexual morality, and especially divorce. Opponents of divorce believed that it would destroy the family, which they saw as the basis of civilization. Divorce was attributed to "dangerous individualism," especially individualism in women, and women were charged with being spoiled, romantic, "jealous of men and usurpers of the male's time-honored functions." But by 1910, the opposition was overwhelmed and divorce was accepted.[3]

The 1920s witnessed the dissolution of Victorian family patterns. Social commentators believed that a "revolution in manners and morals" was sweeping the country, and, according to William Chafe, "almost all agreed that the age was one of unprecedented personal liberation."[4] The historian of the family, Arthur Calhoun, writing in 1917, believed he was witnessing the passing of patriarchy and devotion to the family, as people became more and more individualistic.

In the Roaring Twenties, college students and other young people cast aside Victorian clothes and pursued sexual liberation and exciting personal experiences.[5] The institution of dating developed—the pattern of young men and women seeing each other without chaperones, and without any intention of marriage, to "have a good time." High school students in Muncie, Indiana, in 1924 went to necking and petting parties and only with difficulty could be persuaded to be home for dinner three nights a week. On college campuses, dedication to social reform gave way to social activities organized by sororities and fraternities.[6] Women from respectable families smoked in public, wore short skirts and cosmetics, worked as secretaries before they married, and modeled the new image of a woman with an expensive wardrobe and sex appeal. The response of many older, more conservative Americans to all this was horror at the decline of morality and the sexual orgies (real and imagined) of the young.[7]

The causes of the decline of the family duty blueprint include changes in the sexual division of labor and an increasing value placed on self-fulfillment. Women's daily activities shifted away from motherhood and toward more participation in the public sphere. The ideal of the free, self-made man was spreading, and women were beginning to be seen as similar and equal to men, as persons who should develop themselves. The declining birthrate reduced the burdens of motherhood, although many housewives were busier than ever as standards for a clean and attractive home rose. Employment opportunities for women expanded through the growth of respectable jobs such as being a secretary or a saleswoman. "Nowadays," said suffragist Frances Willard in 1897, "a girl may be anything from a college president down to a seamstress or a cash girl. It depends only upon the girl what rank she shall take in her chosen calling."[8] In fact, most working women were segregated in a few low-paying jobs, and it remained shameful for married women to work, but being a single career woman was becoming a respected way of life.[9]

The Victorian ideal that woman's place was in the home was also challenged by women's participation in the temperance movement and in other social reform movements of the early 20th century. The movement for women's suffrage, which obtained the vote for women in 1920 and involved an estimated two million women, most directly undermined the family duty blueprint.[10] The suffragists used the rhetoric of separate spheres and argued that women needed the vote because they were more moral and altruistic than men, but women's suffrage removed a major barrier to women's participation in public life.[11]

Men's lives also changed as routine white-collar jobs expanded with the growth of large corporations, and the 40-hour workweek became more common. Men's work became more sedentary and regimented, and less heroic. According to several social historians, as many men found less validation for their masculinity in work, their personal identification with their jobs diminished and they became more involved with their personal lives, their families, and leisure activities.[12] Work probably continued to be the center of life for men pursuing challenging and prestigious careers, but personal life became increasingly important for men as the 20th century advanced.[13]

The increasing focus on personal life and self-development and decreasing commitment to traditional roles was fueled by several changes. Security—experiencing the world as safe and abundant—seems to promote a concern with self-development, and the average person's sense of security probably rose in the early 20th century because of gradual improvements in the standard of living and the widespread economic boom during the early 20s.[14] The growth of consumerism and advertising also encouraged people to develop new personal needs and try to fulfill them. "The American citizen's first importance to his country," editorialized the Muncie newspaper in the 1920s, is "that of consumer."[15] Valuing self-development and independence over conformity to roles was also encouraged by public education, which expanded enormously for both sexes.[16] In 1924, high-school diplomas were awarded to 213,000 men and 281,000 women, an increase since 1900 of about 500 percent for both sexes, while the population had only increased by 50 percent.[17] Finally, the social reform movements of the Progressive Era challenged traditional roles and political institutions, and the unpopularity of World War I further undermined established authority, leading people to seek direction and meaning in their own personal lives.[18]

THE COMPANIONSHIP BLUEPRINT

As the Victorian blueprint of duty to family roles was disintegrating, a new ideal was being articulated in academia and the mass media: the companionship family. This blueprint identified the family with marriage, not parenthood, and emphasized emotional and sexual intimacy between husband and wife.

Sociologists proposed a new family ideal focused on affection and supporting each other's personalities, now that families had lost their traditional economic and social functions. The modern family was "a unity of interacting personalities" in the famous phrase of sociologist Ernest Burgess, and had evolved "from institution to companionship."[19] The first principles of family life, according to Burgess, are "that the highest personal happiness comes from marriage based on romantic love" and "that love and marriage are essentially personal and private and are, perhaps, even more than other aspects of life to be controlled by the individual himself."[20] Marriage, in this view, is a private arena of self-fulfillment, not duty. With the spread of the companionship blueprint, affective individualism and a more androgynous self became part of mainstream American culture.

For the first time, popular advice books suggested that having children might weaken a family, and in 1931, for the first time, there were more advertisements for cosmetics than for food in the *Ladies' Home Journal*. Being an attractive companion was becoming more important than being a competent homemaker. Dorothy Dix, in her syndicated newspaper column for women, advised: "The old idea used to be that the way for a woman to help her husband was by being thrifty and industrious . . . but a domestic drudge is not a help to her husband, she is a hindrance. . . . The woman who cultivates a circle of worthwhile people, who belongs to clubs, who makes herself interesting and agreeable . . . is a help to her husband."[21]

The companionship family blueprint emphasized the similarity of husband and wife much more than the family duty blueprint. Both partners were expected to need and to give affection and understanding, and increasingly, both were expected to enjoy sexual intimacy. But love was still feminized, and wives were still expected to be economically dependent and submissive to their husbands. Marriage was to be all of a woman's life but only part of a man's. There was no column by Dorothy Dix instructing a man on how to be a help to his wife, and the magazines of the period consistently told women that it was their responsibility to create successful marriages.[22] Despite some changes towards androgyny, gender roles remained fairly polarized in the companionship blueprint.

The reality of family life in the 20s, according to Robert and Helen Lynd's study of Muncie, is more similar to the family duty blueprint than to the world of companionship marriage and libertine flappers. In the business class (the top 30 percent of the families), wives did not work, and the social status of the family was a primary concern to both husband and wife. Most couples did not place a very high value on companionship in marriage, and frankness between spouses was not encouraged. Husbands described wives as purer, morally better, and more emotional and impractical than men, and their wives agreed. The motto of one of the women's clubs was "Men are God's trees; Women are his flowers."[23] Social life was organized primarily around couples, although men and women were also active in sex-segregated clubs and friendships were important to the women. Wives were very child-centered, while husbands had little contact with their children beyond meals and family auto trips. Husbands were, however, beginning to share in the housework. In the working class, a substantial minority of the wives worked, but marital relations were even farther from the companionship ideal. Husbands and wives rarely talked, and in the absence of other methods of birth control wives kept away from their husbands sexually. Only the beginnings of the companionship family were observable in Muncie; an intimate emotional and sexual bond between two developing personalities was seldom achieved or even strongly desired. Contrary to what many historians have suggested, marital intimacy was rare, as late as the 20s.

The Great Depression from 1929 to 1941 was probably the major force in reversing the trend towards individual freedom of the 20s. As the economy collapsed, people faced an insecure, hostile environment, and adopted a rigid version of the companionship ideal that emphasized traditional family and gender roles more than personal development. Although domestic politics became more radical in the 30s, with the growing power of labor unions and the social programs of the New Deal, family life became more conservative.

College students in the early 30s expressed less approval of divorce and extramarital sex than in the 20s, and there was a rise in the proportion of students who intended to marry and have children.[24] Opposition to women's entering the labor force reappeared as more and more men lost their jobs, and employers increasingly denied married women the right to work. A survey of 1,500 school systems in 1930 reported that 77 percent refused to hire wives and 63 percent fired women teachers if they married. When the Gallup Poll asked Americans in 1936 whether wives should work if their husbands were employed, 82 percent said "no."[25] Women's magazines "urged their readers to return to femininity and constructed an elaborate

ideology in support of the home and marriage to facilitate the process," according to historian William Chafe.[26] The *Ladies' Home Journal* told its readers that "the creation and fulfillment of a successful home is a bit of craftsmanship that compares favorably with building a beautiful cathedral," while *McCall's* observed that only as a wife and mother could the American woman "arrive at her true eminence."[27]

The effects of economic insecurity on commitment to traditional family roles is documented by Glen Elder's study of people who grew up during the Depression. Compared with people whose families had not suffered economically, men and women from families that had suffered substantial economic losses in the Depression placed a greater value on family life as opposed to work and leisure, and were more interested in raising children and less interested in husband–wife companionship. The deprived men actually had a larger number of children, on the average, than men from nondeprived backgrounds. Another finding that supports the link between economic deprivation and traditionalism is that working-class people have more traditional attitudes about family and gender than middle-class people.[28]

World War II ended the Depression and interrupted normal life for many families as men went off to war and women to work. Between 1940 and 1944, the proportion of married women in the labor force rose from 17 percent to 20 percent.[29] Although there was an effort to push women workers back into the home after the war, married women continued to enter the workforce in growing numbers, radically changing the division of labor between husbands and wives that had persisted since the 19th century.

The postwar decades were a period of extreme commitment to the family and to split gender roles. People married earlier, had more children, and avoided childlessness, causing the famous baby boom. The divorce rate stayed unusually steady,[30] and new suburban tracts provided a setting for a family-centered way of life. There was a resurgence of antifeminism and a revival of the 19th-century theme of separate spheres. Thus the head of one women's college advocated that preparing women for "the task of creating a good home and raising good children" be made the primary purposes of women's colleges.[31] Women's magazines described the joys of femininity and togetherness, and public opinion, which had supported wives working during the war, once again opposed their working if their husbands could support them. Most people also supported a traditional division of labor in which men determined where a family lived and how it spent its money.[32] Yet all the while, more and more wives were working.

The blueprint for family life was a revised version of the companionship family of the 20s and 30s.[33] The companionship ideal of the 50s was based on intimate affection between husband and wife. Although the relation between mother and children was vitally important, a woman was warned not to let motherhood weaken her relation with her husband or to smother her children with too much attention. The couple was expected to lead an active social life but not to have close ties outside the nuclear family. The Victorian ideology of separate spheres was still partly intact; it was the husband's job to support the family, while the wife was the center of home life. But the authority of the husband had declined—he was to be more of a pal to his children and more of a companion to his wife. The concept of family togetherness—of mom, dad, and the kids barbecuing dinner together in the backyard—softened the separation of men's and women's spheres. Marriage began with falling in love and developed into companionship; but if love died, divorce might be the best solution.

This family ideal was endorsed by most intellectuals and social scientists in the postwar era. Talcott Parsons provided a theoretical justification with his argument that a well-functioning family required an instrumental father and an expressive mother. Other sociologists obscured the gender differentiation in the companionship

model by emphasizing its equality and flexibility in comparison with the patriarchal Victorian family or the marriages of conservative Americans. Few observers noted that as long as marriage was defined as the wife's responsibility and love was feminized, emphasizing companionship increased her dependency on her husband.[34] The Victorian wife at least had her separate sphere of children and women friends. For the wife in a companionship marriage, her husband was her sphere, and her life was focused on getting the right emotional response from him. The price of companionship marriage was high, especially for the educated, middle-class women who valued their independence the most.[35]

The strong commitment to traditional family roles throughout the 50s and early 60s is somewhat puzzling since many social conditions encouraged androgyny and self-development. A growing number of wives had jobs and became less economically dependent on their husbands. By 1965, 45 percent of married women with school-age children worked, compared with 26 percent in 1948. There was an unprecedented economic prosperity in the postwar era, and a very large expansion of public higher education. One would expect these conditions to accelerate the trend from role to self, but this did not happen until the late 60s, when a wave of protest movements and the Vietnam War produced a counterculture that rejected traditional roles and beliefs, including the companionship family blueprint.[36]

THE DECLINE OF THE COMPANIONSHIP BLUEPRINT

Another period of personal liberation began in the sixties. This time many observers felt that a major boundary of social organization had been crossed—that we had passed from an era in which people's private lives were regulated by the obligations of family roles into a new era of the self.[37] There was a rapid reversal of the familism of the 50s. Divorces accelerated sharply and fertility declined to an all-time low. The rate of couples living together without being married doubled between 1970 and 1979, and there was a large increase in the number of persons living alone. Premarital sexual experience, which had been increasing since the 20s, became much more frequent; for example, the percentage of single 17-year-old girls who had experienced sex rose from 27 to 41 percent between 1971 and 1976.[38]

The trend toward wives working for money was probably the underlying cause of the decline of the companionship family. But the immediate cause was the antiestablishment social movements of the 60s and 70s. The 60s began a period of "revolution in manners and morals" similar to the twenties, literally a "counterculture."[39] The civil rights movement, the antiwar movement, and the women's movement involved a large minority of Americans in demonstrations, drug trips, petition campaigns and consciousness-raising groups, all of which undermined the patriotism and devotion to family of the postwar era.

The women's movement, in particular, attacked the companionship family blueprint. Conservative feminists endorsed the "two-career family," in which both husband and wife were equally committed to glamorous careers and to childrearing and homemaking. Radical feminists rejected the family as the preferred living arrangement and developed images of homosexual households or socialist collectives. By the early 70s, ideas about gender equality diffused throughout the nation as the women's movement received a great deal of media coverage and achieved a rapid series of legislative victories supporting expanded opportunities for women in the labor force and in education.[40]

Once again, a strong women's movement had undermined traditional family roles. As long as family blueprints emphasized self-sacrifice and polarized gender roles, women's freedom conflicted with family bonds. Thus Carl Degler concludes his history of women and the family in America by observing that "the great values

for which the family stands are at odds . . . with those of the women's movement."[41]

Companionship family roles were also attacked by the human potential movement. Popular psychology books like Gail Sheehy's *Passages* rejected the role of successful provider and cheerful housewife as hypocritical and deadening. They urged people to free themselves from restrictive obligations, get in touch with their feelings, and experience their full potential. New therapies and growth centers sprung up—encounter groups, Esalen, Primal Scream, EST—all of them encouraging adult men and women to develop themselves and reject traditional roles. In contrast to the orthodox therapies of previous decades that had urged patients to adjust to traditional family and gender roles, the new therapies preached androgyny, and urged men and women to reject the expectations of others and develop their own true selves.[42]

The decline of the companionship blueprint was welcomed by some groups and opposed by others. Not surprisingly, women supported the new flexibility in gender roles more than men, especially highly educated professional women.[43] These women valued independence the most and could benefit the most from improved career opportunities. Thus, in the political struggle over abortion, the "pro-choice" activists were mostly well-educated, career-oriented women who placed a high value on individual freedom and self-development. The "pro-life" women were primarily less educated housewives with a deep commitment to religion and to the traditional roles of the loving housewife and the strong husband who provides for her.[44] For these women and for many other Americans, the companionship family continued to be their ideal.

THE NEW BLUEPRINTS: INDEPENDENCE AND INTERDEPENDENCE

By the middle of the 70s, new androgynous images of close relationships were beginning to crystallize. A prolonged economic recession dampened people's aspirations for freedom, and academics and the mass media began to criticize the human potential movement as selfish and narcissistic.[45] The need for intimacy began to seem more pressing than the need to combat oppressive family and gender roles.

The new blueprints emphasize three sets of qualities that I label *self-fulfillment, flexible roles,* and *intimacy and open communication.* First, in the new images of love, both partners are expected to develop a fulfilled and independent self, instead of sacrificing themselves for the other person. Second, family and gender roles are flexible and are continually renegotiated. Third, the relationship centers on intimate communication of needs and feelings, and on openly confronting problems. Self-development and love are integrated in these blueprints, and love is the responsibility of the man as well as the woman. The independence and the interdependence blueprints both emphasize these qualities; they differ on the issue of self-sufficiency and independence versus mutual support and commitment.

The new blueprints of relationships began to emerge in the middle of the 60s, according to a study of women's magazines. Women were advised that they must develop an independent self in order to be loving, and they were told to build a vital, spontaneous relationship without fixed rules, by communicating openly about feelings and working through conflicts. In contrast, in the 50s, "putting aside of self was defined as loving behavior," and women were advised to sacrifice themselves for their families, follow traditional sex roles, and strive for harmony and togetherness.[46]

When Ann Swidler interviewed 60 residents of an affluent California suburb around 1980, she found that most of them emphasized self-fulfillment and accepted the "therapeutic ideal" of love promoted by psychologists and the human potential movement. They believed that love is partly expressed by sharing oneself and one's feelings; therefore, a person must develop a somewhat independent self in order to

be loving. For example, a young wife explained that she had had problems with her husband, Thomas, because "I was doing things just for him and ignoring things for myself." Now, since her therapy, she feels more independent and self-confident. "The better I feel about myself, I feel I have a whole lot that I can contribute to Thomas."[47]

Good communication is crucial in the new blueprints, both to express one's self, and to negotiate a unique, flexible relationship in the absence of definite family and gender roles. Verbal communication is also part of being intimate and working on the relationship. As a college man commented, "You have to work at your marriage, it's like a job." A poll conducted for *Playboy* magazine in 1976 indicates the importance of communication to contemporary American men. "Someone to be totally open and honest with" was the most frequently mentioned quality for an ideal lover.[48]

The new blueprints are radically androgynous and anti-institutional. The themes of self-fulfillment and intimate communication resemble the companionship blueprint, and its concern with personality development and marital interaction. But unlike the companionship ideal, the new blueprints do not legitimate predetermined roles or a sexual division of labor; they are blueprints for relationships, not marriages. Both partners are expected to work on the relationship, communicate openly and develop themselves. Wives are advised to cultivate independent interests and goals, while husbands are encouraged to express their feelings. Love is no longer part of women's special sphere.

The independence blueprint adds to these themes a strong emphasis on being self-sufficient and avoiding obligations. Developing an independent self and expressing one's needs and feelings is seen as a precondition to love. In contrast, couples who follow the interdependence blueprint believe that they owe each other mutual support and affection, and that love is a precondition to full self-development.

Sociologists disagree about the relative importance of these two blueprints. Robert Bellah and his associates conclude that independence is becoming the dominant image of love in America. People are increasingly avoiding commitments, they argue and support their interpretation by quoting from Swidler's interviews. For example, a counselor commented: "I guess, if there is anyone who needs to owe anybody anything, it is honesty in letting each other know how they feel about each other, and that if feelings change, to be open and receptive, to accept those changes, knowing that people in a relationship are not cement."[49]

In contrast, my study of 133 adults in 1980 indicates that Interdependence, not Independence, is the dominant blueprint of love. The respondents, who came from diverse social backgrounds, were asked about the "qualities that are most important for a good marriage or love relationship." . . . Contrary to the argument of Bellah et al., the second most frequently mentioned quality was "support and caring." "Good, open communication" was most frequently mentioned, while "tolerance, flexibility and understanding" was third, "honesty" was fourth, and "commitment" was fifth. Individuals who emphasized "support and caring" usually talked about the obligation to be nurturant and attentive, and many of them connected support and caring with self-development. For example, when a 30-year-old minister in San Diego was asked what he most valued in his wife, he replied:

> I trust her to react in a reaffirming way to me when I share with her. . . . I know that she will respond to me in a positive way. She will share the pain or frustration or triumph of the day with me, and I feel like what I have to say about me is very important, because it's me in a sense.

Although there is disagreement about the importance of mutual support and commitment in contemporary relationships, researchers agree on the growing importance of self-fulfillment, flexible roles, and intimate, open communication.

With the decline of the companionship blueprint, the trend from role to self accelerated, producing new, more androgynous images of love.

It is possible that another shift back to traditional roles has begun, partly as a result of the continued economic difficulties of the 70s and 80s. The slight drop in the divorce rate and the reversal of feminist gains in affirmative action and abortion rights may be signs of such a shift. But the evidence that would document this change is not yet available.

EVIDENCE FROM POPULAR MAGAZINES

The changes in family blueprints that I have just described are clearly reflected in magazine articles that give advice on how to have a happy marriage. I analyzed a sample of articles from 1900 to 1979 and measured the proportion of articles in each decade that endorsed the traditional family duty and companionship blueprints versus the modern themes of self-fulfillment, flexible roles, and intimacy. The results confirm the long-range trend from role to self during the 20th century, and also show that the 20s and 60s were unusually modern while the 50s were unusually traditional. Studies by other researchers show this same pattern of change.

I examined 128 articles on marriage from high circulation magazines like the *Ladies' Home Journal, McCall's,* and the *Reader's Digest.* The articles are addressed primarily to women, and advise them on how to produce a happy, loving marriage and how to overcome feelings of disappointment and loneliness. For each five-year period, I randomly selected eight articles listed in the *Readers' Guide to Periodicals* under the topic "Marriage." The content of each article was coded according to the dominant message that the article seemed to communicate to readers.[50]

The categories used to analyze the articles focused on self-fulfillment, flexible roles, and intimacy and open communication. One category that measured self-fulfillment was "self-sacrifice versus self-fulfillment." An example of endorsing self-sacrifice is a 1909 editorial in *Harper's Bazaar* that advised: "Marriage means self-discipline. Marriage is *not* for the individual, but for the race. . . . Marriage is the slow growth of two persons into one—one person with one pursuit, one mind, one heart, one interest . . . one ideal."[51] In contrast, a *Ladies' Home Journal* article in 1978, illustrating the self-fulfillment theme, warned that it was a myth to believe that marriage should "meet all the emotional needs of both spouses," that it "is an all-encompassing blend of two personalities fused into one. A marriage like this leaves no breathing space for two individuals to retain their own personalities."[52]

A category for measuring flexible roles was "rigid versus flexible female gender role." The traditional side of this category is illustrated by a 1940s article which comments that, compared to men, "women have much less time for action, being absorbed, consciously or unconsciously, by their preoccupation with love and maternity."[53] Intimate communication was measured by the category "avoid conflict, and keep up a front versus communicate openly and confront problems." Illustrating the modern view of communication, an article in the *Reader's Digest* in 1974 asserted that "if spouses are thoughtful toward each other on *all* occasions, they probably have a sick marriage."[54]

Table 1.1 shows the number of articles in each decade that support traditional versus modern themes in these three categories. The percent of modern themes—combining the three categories—gradually rises, as shown at the bottom of the table. There are also discontinuities; for instance, there are more articles endorsing flexible gender roles in the 1920s than in the next three decades. Thus a 1925 article in the *Ladies' Home Journal* proclaimed: "The woman of today acknowledges no master." Women now regard marriage as "a social partnership, an adventure, an experiment even, but it must always be on a fifty-fifty basis."[55] And in every decade, there is considerable variation in what the magazines

are saying, and a substantial number of both traditional and modern themes.

The trend from role to self and the discontinuities in this trend are more clearly displayed in the graph in Figure 1.9. The graph shows the percent of themes in each decade that support self-fulfillment, flexible roles, and intimate communication, combining eight categories that include the three already discussed. For example, "flexible roles" is measured by the previously discussed category about the female role, as well as categories about the male role and the acceptability of divorce. . . .

The graph shows a trend to modern themes over the 20th century. In the first two decades of the century, about 30 percent of the themes are modern, compared to about 70 percent in the 1970s. There is also a clear up-and-down pattern of change, with modern themes predominating in the 20s and again in the 60s and 70s.

The causes of the trend from role to self, as I have discussed, probably include economic prosperity, increasing leisure and education, and the tendency of women as well as men to work for individual wages. The discontinuities can partly be explained by the same factors; in particular, economic hard times apparently reversed the trend in the 30s. Other researchers have emphasized demographic shifts in explaining discontinuities in American family life, and unpopular wars may also be important.[56]

The intriguing association between the women's movement and images of marriage suggests other explanations of the discontinuities—explanations that point to the great importance of gender roles in understanding the American family. A strong women's movement accompanied or preceded the extreme emphasis on personal freedom and self-fulfillment in the 20s and again in the late 60s. The women's movement, as measured by the amount of coverage of women in the *New York Times* and popular magazines, was strongest between 1905 and 1920. It reached its low point between 1950 and the early 60s, and then rose again in the late sixties. . . . The rise

TABLE 1.1

TRENDS IN MAGAZINE ARTICLES ON MARRIAGE, 1900–1979: NUMBER OF ARTICLES SUPPORTING TRADITIONAL VERSUS MODERN THEMES

Traditional [T]		Modern [M]	1900–1909		1910–1919		1920–1929		1930–1939		1940–1949		1950–1959		1960–1969		1970–1979	
			T	M	T	M	T	M	T	M	T	M	T	M	T	M	T	M
1 self-sacrifice compromise	vs.	self-fulfillment individuality	7	1	4	3	5	1	7	2	10	0	11	0	7	7	5	2
2 rigid female role	vs.	flexible female role	10	7	14	4	8	10	11	7	8	9	13	5	8	10	6	13
3 avoid conflict, keep up a front	vs.	communicate openly, confront problems	1	2	2	0	3	2	5	3	4	0	4	6	4	8	3	10
Percent of modern themes			36%		26%		45%		34%		29%		28%		57%		64%	

FIGURE 1.9
Modern themes in magazine articles on marriage, 1900–1979: Percent
of themes supporting self-fulfillment, flexible roles, and intimacy.

and fall of the women's movement thus parallels the rise and fall of modern images of marriage, as shown in Figure 1.9, except that the high point of the movement around 1910 preceded the change in marital images by about a decade.

This relationship between the women's movement and the trend from role to self is not surprising, and has been noted by social historians. The women's movement usually has urged women to avoid self-sacrifice and traditional gender roles, and participating in the movement probably made women more powerful and independent of their families as they acquired new skills and friends, and new ideas about women's proper place.

The conflict between traditional family roles and women's rights may also produce a self-generating cycle of change. When there is a strong commitment to a traditional family blueprint (i.e., the family duty or companionship blueprint), individual freedom and self-development are suppressed, especially for women. But freedom and self-development are highly valued in America, leading to a conflict that eventually undermines the blueprint and produces a period of personal liberation like the 1920s. Greater freedom to develop oneself, especially for women, then threatens people's needs for attachments, creating a readiness to accept a new family blueprint. This cyclic tendency, if it exists, will be weakened by the diffusion of the interdependence blueprint, which combines stable attachments and self-development.

Whatever the causes of the changing images of marriage, two patterns of change emerge clearly from my analysis of magazine articles. There has been a gradual trend toward self-fulfillment, flexible roles, and intimate communication, as well as some major discontinuities.

■ Review Questions ■

1. In what ways do the changing themes of magazine articles reflect a shift "from role to self"?
2. What does the author mean by "androgynous love"?

ENDNOTES

1. Fixing the date of these periods is only approximate, and is based on the sources quoted in this and the previous reading.
2. The Civil War occurred in the middle of this period, but, surprisingly, most historians do not attribute great social consequences to it. Eleanor Flexner's history of women is an exception.
3. O'Neil, 1978, pp. 143–44.
4. Chafe, 1972, p. 49.
5. Fass, 1977.
6. Rothman, 1978.
7. Fass, 1977; Newcomb, 1937.
8. Quoted in Rothman, 1978, p. 43.
9. For a poignant description of how respectable but poor married women had to hide the fact that they were working see Rothman, 1978, Chapter 2. Single life was not unattractive, given the close bonds among women, especially for the privileged few with a college education. The women born between 1865 and 1874 "married later and less frequently than any group before or since," and by the turn of the century "nearly one in five married women was childless" (Ryan, 1979, p. 142).
10. Ryan, 1979, p. 140.
11. Many of its supporters and opponents believed that women's winning the vote would change their role in the family and drastically alter electoral politics. The large amounts of money spent by the liquor industry and urban political machines to fight women's suffrage are an indication of the importance they attributed to it. On the high hopes of many suffragists about the changes that would occur after women got the vote, see Flexner, 1974; and O'Neil, 1978. O'Neil documents the conservative and occasionally racist rhetoric of the suffrage movement.
12. The eight-hour day became common during World War I and the 40-hour week was mandated by New Deal legislation in the thirties (Harris & Levy, 1975, pp. 1, 511). On the declining masculinity of work, see Hantover, 1980, pp. 285–302, and also Filene, 1974.
13. For a supporting argument, see Zaretsky, 1976, and for supporting evidence see Pleck, 1985; and Veroff et al., 1981.
14. On the economic changes, see U.S. Bureau of the Census, 1976, pp. 164–165. On the relation of security and self-development, see Maslow's theory of the hierarchy of needs, 1970.
15. The quotation is from Lynd & Lynd, 1937, p. 80. For a description of this period, also see Chafe, 1972, and Rothman, 1978.
16. Educated people, according to many studies, are more likely to believe that they control their lives and to question authority and traditional rules. See Kohn, 1969.
17. U.S. Bureau of the Census, 1976, pp. 379 and 380. In 1924 B.A.s or first professional degrees were awarded to 55,000 men and 28,000 women, an increase since 1900 of about 200 percent for men and 500 percent for women.
18. I am indebted to Thomas Kemper for this observation.
19. Quoted in Lasch, 1977, p. 31.
20. These quotes are taken from Rothman, 1978, p. 180.
21. Quoted in Lynd & Lynd, 1937, p. 116.
22. See the thought-provoking analysis of magazines from 1921 to 1940 by Johns-Heine and Gerth, 1949.
23. Lynd & Lynd, 1937, p. 118.
24. Newcomb, 1937. In contrast, the Lynds report that high school students in Muncie became more accepting of premarital sex and women's working between 1924 and 1935. This may be an instance of a lag in changes among working-class and provincial people compared to college students.
25. Chafe, 1972, Chapter 4. The proportion of college teachers who were women began to fall in the 30s and continued to decline until the late 50s.
26. Chafe, 1972, p. 105.
27. Quoted in Chafe, 1972, p. 105.

28. Elder, 1974, analyzes the effects of the depression. Virtually all researchers find that middle-class people tend to be more modern. They value companionship between husband and wife more and having children less, and place more emphasis on self-fulfillment, tolerance of diversity, and flexible gender roles. This pattern confirms the hypothesis that economic security, prosperity, and education promote the shift from role to self. The classic study of class and child-rearing values is Melvin Kohn's *Class and Conformity,* 1969. The preference of middle-class people for self-actualization and esteem, and working-class people for belonging and security, is shown in an interesting British study using Abraham Maslow's theory of the hierarchy of needs by Gratton, 1980. Duncan et al., 1973, document the greater importance of job security for working-class people. Also see Gurin et al., 1960; Mason et al., 1976; Gecas, 1979; and Rubin, 1976.

29. U.S. Bureau of the Census, 1976, p. 133.

30. Cherlin, 1981.

31. Chafe, 1972, p. 208.

32. Ibid., p. 178.

33. For a similar interpretation, see Rothman, 1978, p. 218.

34. For an example, see Hicks and Platt's widely quoted and basically sound review of the literature on marital adjustment, published in 1970. Even Komarovsky (1962), usually very sensitive to issues of gender, took for granted the superiority of companionship marriage. She criticized the blue-collar pattern of restricted communication and separate social activities for husbands and wives as a form of "social disorganization," failing to see that the husband's buddies and the wife's close ties with relatives and friends might provide a valuable counterbalance to the tendency of women to be overdependent on their husbands in companionship marriages. Evidence on the role of relatives and friends in limiting wives' dependency on husbands comes from a study of British working-class families by Michael Young and Peter Willmott. They found that wives became more dependent after they moved away from their old community into a suburb.

35. Evidence of the discontent of college-educated wives with their marriage is presented in Campbell et al., 1976. Also Pahl & Pahl, 1971.

36. See Cherlin, 1981, for data on changes in women working and an analysis of how the fifties interrupted many long-term demographic and family trends. For quantitative data on the postwar boom, see U.S. Bureau of the Census, 1976, and Lebergott, 1976. Generation and politics may explain the unusual familism of the 1950s. Perhaps the generation that raised their families in the 50s had too many frightening memories of depression and war to feel secure, despite their new prosperity. And perhaps American politics of cold war and McCarthyism diminished people's sense of self-direction and the importance of their personal lives by enhancing the significance of government actions and patriotic values.

37. The phrase "from role to self " was suggested to me by Almond's essay (1977) on the transitions from character to role to self since the 19th century. Also see Turner's influential paper (1976).

38. For more detailed information on these trends see Cherlin, 1981, and U.S. Bureau of the Census, 1982. The survey on premarital sex is reported in Zelnik and Kantner, 1980.

39. Several studies document substantial shifts of public opinion toward personal liberation and away from the standards of the companionship family between the middle of the sixties and the middle of the seventies. See, for example, Yankelovich, 1974. Cherlin, 1981, also suggests that the acceptance of divorce accelerated in the late 60s and early 70s.

40. For a history of the women's movement, see Carden, 1974; and Hole and Levine, 1971. Freeman, 1975, gives an excellent account of its legislative victories. For an analysis of media coverage of the movement, see Cancian and Ross, 1981.

41. Degler, 1980, p. 471.

42. See Friedan, 1963, on the conservative message of Freudian and other therapists in the 1950s.

43. See, for example, Osmond & Martin, 1975.

44. Luker, 1984.

45. Clecak, 1983, reviews this criticism. Christopher Lasch's book, *The Culture of Narcissism,* 1978, is the critical book that had the greatest impact. On the need for commitment, see Yankelovich, 1981.

46. Kidd, 1974 and 1975. Zube's study (1972) of changing concepts of morality in the *Ladies' Home Journal* from 1948 to 1969 comes up

with an interpretation similar to Kidd's. Her quantitative analysis shows a clear shift from values oriented to the future and active "doing," to values oriented to "being" in the present.

47. Bellah et al., 1985, pp. 93 and 100; and Swidler, 1982, pp. 7–8. Similar findings are reported by Quinn, 1982, who did intensive interviews with eleven couples in North Carolina.

48. Harris, 1979.

49. Bellah et al., 1985, p. 101.

50. Here is more detail in the methodology. The high circulation magazines that were included were taken from a list in Kidd, 1975. In the early decades, I also selected articles listed in the *Readers' Guide* from *Harper's* and *Atlantic.* Because of the ease of obtaining articles from *Reader's Digest,* I randomly selected four articles from *Reader's Digest* and four from other magazines, after *Reader's Digest* began publication in the early 1920s. The coding system was originally developed to study changes in magazines between 1950 and 1970; therefore the categories are progressively less applicable as we move toward the beginning of the century, and the earlier articles receive fewer codes in any of the categories. The categories about gender roles are an exception; every article was coded as traditional or modern on these categories. A few articles contained very contradictory messages and were "double-scored," or counted as both traditional and modern on some categories; however, double-scoring was avoided whenever possible. The category system was refined until I reached a criterion of two coders agreeing on 85 percent of the coding for a particular article. This method of measuring changes in popular images of marriage has several problems. The intended audience of the magazines seems to come from a higher social class in the earlier decades, and the content of the articles partly reflects the policies of editors and advertisers and the attitudes of the writers. Nonetheless, the magazines seem to provide a fairly valid measure, since my findings are consistent with the other sources of data described in this chapter.

51. *Harper's Bazaar,* September 1909.

52. Vahanian & Olds, 1978.

53. Maurois, 1940.

54. Lederer & Jackson, 1974.

55. Miller, 1925.

56. Easterlin, 1980, emphasizes the changing size of birth cohorts. He sees very little change in family blueprints and gender roles since World War II. What has changed, in his view, is young people's income relative to the standard of living they grew up with. When their income was relatively high, they lived according to their family ideals, and wives stayed home and had many children as happened in the 50s. When the baby boom generation (or cohort) reached the labor market in the late 70s, wages were relatively low because the cohort was so large that wages were depressed. As a result, they were unable to live according to their ideals and had fewer children. When their children reach the labor market, their income will be relatively high because their cohort is so small, and the cycle will repeat. The relative merits of his theory and mine will be clarified by changes in the family during the recession that began in the 70s. Easterlin predicts a decline in family attachments as relative income declines. I predict a rise because hard times lower people's aspirations for freedom. See Cherlin, 1981, for an excellent analysis and critique of Easterlin. Although I agree with Easterlin that the changes in gender roles are often exaggerated, he exaggerates the stability. For evidence of major changes in women's goals since the late 60s, see Parelius, 1975; Roper & Labeff, 1977; Duncan et al., 1973; Thornton et al., 1983. Cherlin argues that the pattern of family change is not cyclical; rather, there have been gradual changes since 1900 interrupted by the peculiar 50s. Another explanation sociologists have developed is the marriage squeeze argument advanced by Oppenheimer, 1973, and others. They argue that, because women marry men about three years older than themselves, it will be difficult for women to find attractive husbands in historical periods following a rise in fertility, since there will be more younger women on the marriage market than older men. This situation occurred in the 70s, following the baby boom. According to Heer and Grossbard-Schechtman's interpretation (1981), the unfavorable marriage market for women in the 70s helps explain why a growing proportion of women did not marry, why they turned to employment instead and became involved in a women's movement to improve their situation at work.

CHAPTER 2

The History of the Family

Whether feminized or androgynous, love was part of late-nineteenth- and twentieth-century marriage. It is certainly central to marriage today. But it has not always been so. What we recognize as love seems to have played a smaller role in marriage in the past. It was not that people in the past were unfeeling but rather that they had more important things to worry about. A farm husband needed a wife who would be healthy and sturdy, bear many children, and tend the vegetable garden. A farm wife needed a man who would grow and harvest the crop. When men began to earn wages, a woman needed a husband who was a steady provider of income rather than a no-good who couldn't keep a job or who would drink up his pay. Whom to marry was too important a decision to leave to the whims of romantic love, which could fade away, revealing an unreliable or dishonest spouse.

Stephanie Coontz, in the book from which the first reading in this chapter is adapted, *Marriage, A History: From Obedience to Intimacy, or How Love Conquered Marriage,* tells the story of the rise of love as the central force of marriage. Prior to the 1700s, love was seen as separate from marriage. But great changes such as the introduction of wage labor and the migration of young laborers from rural areas to the city undermined parental control over their children. Young adults had more freedom to choose a spouse, and they began to value love. All this happened gradually, over the course of a century or two, and it did not occur among all classes at the same time. But Coontz argues that it eventually produced a profound change in the meaning of marriage that led to the kinds of marriages and relationships we see today.

History is not only about bygone eras; it is also about changes in the recent past and in our lifetimes. Here is an example of a historic change in which you, the reader, most likely will play a role: the emergence of a new life stage between being an adolescent and being fully adult. It is a stage that scholars are calling "early adulthood." It barely existed a half century ago, when people tended to marry young (half of all young women in the 1950s married by age 20), have children quickly, and move into the workforce—in other words, leap from childhood to adolescence to adulthood. Such a quick transition to adulthood is much rarer today. Young adults stay in school longer, cohabit more, and delay childbearing much longer than their parents or grandparents did. Sociologists who study the "life course" of individuals today have noticed this change, labeled it, and thought about its implications for young adults and for the larger society around them. The second reading in this chapter provides an overview of this newly emerging stage of life.

READING 2-1

What's Love Got to Do with It?
A Brief History of Marriage

Stephanie Coontz

It's remarkable to realize that no one under the age of 30 is old enough to actually remember the fairy-tale wedding of Lady Diana Spencer to Prince Charles back in 1981. Yet almost everyone knows about the disillusion and drama that set in a few years later, when it became clear that they weren't going to live "happily ever after." As soon as Diana had the two sons the monarchy needed to serve as "an heir and a spare," Charles returned to his longtime lover, and Diana, bitterly angry, went on to take a series of lovers of her own. As Diana famously complained to a television interviewer, she hadn't known at the time of her wedding that there'd be three persons involved in her marriage. Many individuals still identify so much with the disappointed princess that they've reacted with fury to the announcement that Prince Charles will finally marry the woman with whom he's had a 35-year relationship.

But having only three people involved in a marriage would have seemed downright lonely to most people of the past, and for thousands of years it would have seemed strange for anyone to have entered a marriage with such high expectations for personal happiness as Diana and the millions of her admirers had.

George Bernard Shaw once described marriage as an institution that brings two people together under the influence of the most violent, delusive, and transient of passions, and requires them to

Stephanie Coontz, "What's Love Got to Do with It?" from *Psychotherapy Networker*, May/June 2005, Vol. 29, No. 3, pp. 56–61, 74. Based on her book *Marriage, A History: From Obedience to Intimacy, or How Love Conquered Marriage*, Viking Press. Used by permission of the author.

swear they'll remain in that abnormal, exhausting condition until death do them part. His comment pokes fun at the unrealistic expectations attached to the cultural ideal that marriage should be based on true love. But for thousands of years, people would not have gotten the joke, because almost no one believed that people should marry for love. When individuals did advocate such a bizarre belief, it was no laughing matter, but a serious threat to social order.

In ancient India, falling in love before marriage was considered a disruptive, antisocial act. In some Chinese dialects, a term for *love* didn't traditionally apply to feelings between husband and wife: It was used to describe an illicit, socially disapproved relationship. Both the ancient Greeks and medieval Europeans thought lovesickness was a type of insanity, and that it was almost indecent to love a spouse too ardently. The Greek philosopher Plato did hold love in high regard, because he felt that it led men to behave honorably; however, he was referring not to the love of women, "such as the meaner men feel," but to the love of a man for another man, which was the Greek ideal for the purest form of love.

Once the Greeks became Christians, they got far less tolerant of same-sex relationships. But for the first thousand years of Christianity, the church didn't like heterosexual love much better than it liked homosexual love. "It's better to marry than to burn," said Paul, but it's better still to remain single and celibate. Right up until the 16th century, the Christian church taught that married love was only one step above unmarried fornication: The Virgin Mary was the most admired woman; the widow the next. The wife occupied the lowest rung of respectable womanhood.

The hierarchy of good things was different for the aristocracy, but for them, too, the pleasures of marriage were way down on the totem pole. The courtly love poems and songs that have so influenced our own sense of what romance is all about were originally based on the notion that adultery was the purest form of love. In 12th-century France, the author of the first treatise on courtly love wrote that marriage is no excuse for not loving. By this he meant that marriage was no excuse for not loving someone *outside* the marriage!

In most cultures of the past, it was inconceivable that young people would choose their spouse on the basis of an unpredictable feeling like love. Marriage wasn't about the happiness of two individuals—it was a political and economic arrangement between two families. For the propertied classes, marriage was a way of consolidating wealth, merging resources, forging political alliances, and even concluding peace treaties.

Marriage was also an economic and political transaction in the lower classes. Farms or businesses could rarely be run by a single person, so prospective partners' skills, resources, tools, and useful in-laws were more important than their attractiveness. For a farmer or artisan, getting married was like picking your most crucial employee, and it was a foolish man indeed who would choose her for her looks, or fire her because he didn't love her anymore.

Certainly, people fell in love in the ancient and medieval world—sometimes even with their own spouse. But marriage was far too vital an economic and political institution to be entered into solely on the basis of something as irrational as love, and too important to be left to the whims of two young people. For thousands of years, the theme song for most courtships and weddings could have been "what's love got to do with it?"

Married love began to get a better reputation with the Protestant Reformation in the 16th century. Protestants argued that the clergy should be allowed, even encouraged, to marry, and that Roman Catholics were wrong to call marriage a necessary evil or a second-best existence to celibacy. Rather, said Luther, marriage was "a glorious estate."

But Protestants were just as suspicious of ardent love between husband and wife as were Roman Catholics, and they were even more hostile toward young people's right to freely choose their own mate. Protestants insisted that a marriage wasn't valid unless the parents agreed to it, even if the couple had gone through a ceremony and later had children together. Luther argued that parents didn't have the right to force a child into a loveless match, but they were totally justified in forbidding a match, no matter how much the couple loved each other, or in annulling a match for which they hadn't given permission. Both Catholic and Protestant theologians criticized women who used endearing nicknames for their husbands, because such familiarity undermined the lines of authority that ought to govern marriage.

It wasn't until the 18th century that a decisive change began to occur in popular attitudes toward love and marriage, spurred by two seismic social revolutions. First, the spread of wage labor made young people less dependent on their parents to get a start in life. A man didn't have to delay marriage until he inherited land or took over a business from his father. A woman could earn her own dowry. This made it harder for parents to control their children's courting.

Second, the freedoms afforded by the market economy had their parallel in new philosophical ideas. During the 18th-century Enlightenment and the age of revolution, influential thinkers across Europe began to champion individual rights and insist that the pursuit of happiness was a legitimate goal. They advocated marrying for love, rather than for wealth or status.

By the end of the 1700s, personal choice of partners had replaced arranged marriage as a social ideal, and individuals were encouraged to make that choice on the basis of love. For the first time in 5,000 years, marriage came to be seen as a private relationship between two individuals, rather than one link in a larger system of political and economic alliances. The measure of a successful marriage was no longer how big a financial settlement was involved, how many useful in-laws were acquired, or how many children were produced, but how well a family met the emotional needs of its individual members.

But these new ideas, conservatives immediately complained, posed a crisis of social order. If marriage was suddenly to be about love and lifelong intimacy, they worried, what would hold a marriage together if love and intimacy disappeared? And how could household order be maintained if marriages were based on love, rather than power?

Traditionalists had good cause to fret. The 1780s and 1790s saw a crisis over these questions, especially in regions influenced by the radical ideas of the American and French revolutions. In America, New Jersey gave women the vote, and several states enacted measures that made it easier for young people to choose their own partners. Most states began to liberalize divorce laws.

The French revolutionaries went further. They redefined marriage as a freely chosen civil contract, made divorce more accessible than it would be again until 1975, and decriminalized homosexual acts, on the grounds that such penalties violated the principle that the state should respect people's private choices. They mandated that families couldn't favor boys over girls in inheritance. Traditionalists thought the world was coming to an end.

At the end of the 18th century, however, the most radical innovations were rolled back. In France, Napoleon repealed the no-fault divorce laws and struck down equal inheritance for women. In America, New Jersey revoked the right of women to vote, and most states adopted restrictions on women's political activity. At the same time, women lost access to many occupations that had formerly been open to them.

But the ideas fostered by these revolutions had made it impossible to fall back on the old saying that women had to obey their husbands as subjects had to obey the king. So people cast about for a new understanding of the relationship between men and women and the nature of marriage—one that didn't unleash the "chaos" of equality, but didn't insist too much on women's subordination or raise uncomfortable parallels between the right to rebel against political tyrants and women's right to rebel against domestic ones.

The result was a compromise between egalitarian and patriarchal views of marriage. There was a new outrage against forcing women into loveless marriages, reflected in the art and literature of the day. But women, in or out of marriage, weren't extended the same rights as men. Instead, women were said to possess such a unique moral worth and such a delicate constitution that they shouldn't be exposed to the risks that men had to take by participating in business or politics. The exclusion of women from politics, in this new theory, wasn't an assertion of male privilege, but a mark of deference to women's talents and needs.

And those needs began to be defined in totally new ways. In the Middle Ages, popular culture had painted women as the lusty sex, more prone to passion and sexual excess than men. Suddenly this was turned on its head. It became accepted wisdom in the 19th century that the "normal" woman lacked any sexual drives at all—another reason to protect her from too much freedom.

By the early 19th century, idealization of love, marriage, home, hearth, and female purity was the bedrock of popular culture. Poems were written about the "angel in the house" and the sanctity of home, completely overturning an older popular culture that focused on community rather than family celebrations.

When Queen Victoria walked down the aisle wearing white instead of the multicolored costumes of the past, a new "tradition" was instantly invented, and people began to lose the memory of a time when female purity, loving marriage, and domesticity weren't the most cherished subjects of popular culture. One author summed up the new view by saying that if you had just four letters with which to express all the affection and morality and meaning in life, you would simply spell out H-O-M-E.

In the late 18th century, conservatives had warned that unions based on love and the desire for personal happiness were inherently unstable. If love was the most important reason to marry, how could society condemn people who stayed single rather than enter a loveless marriage? If love disappeared from a marriage, why shouldn't the couple be allowed to go their separate ways? If men and women were true soulmates, why should they not be equal partners in society?

In the 19th century, the doctrine that men and women had innately different natures and occupied separate spheres of life seemed to sidestep these problems by allowing people to romanticize love and marriage without unleashing the radical demands that had rocked society in the 1790s. The doctrine of separate spheres held back the inherent individualism of the "pursuit of happiness" by making men and women dependent upon each other, insisting that each party was incomplete without marriage. It justified women's confinement to the home without having to rely on patriarchal assertions about men's right to rule. Men were protecting women, it was said, not dominating them, by reserving political and economic roles for themselves, and women in return would rescue men from material corruption because of their own pure, sexless natures. For a while, the doctrine of female purity seemed to resolve the problem of how to justify women's exclusion from political, economic, and sexual rights without returning to the naked patriarchal controls of the past.

But there were two serious problems with the compromise between the radical implications of love and the traditional constraints of marriage. First of all, the idealized home was out of reach for most of the population, and in fact, middle-class women's domesticity and seclusion depended on the denial of domesticity to the working-class women, men, and children who took over the chores that had formerly taken up the bulk of middle-class wives' time. In the southern United States, slaveholders had no respect for the "sanctity" of marriage, motherhood, or protected childhood when it came to their slaves, and even after emancipation, most African Americans had neither the time nor the resources for wives to be full-time homemakers and children to stay home to be nurtured by their mothers.

In the North, women and children who couldn't survive on their husbands' or fathers' wages worked as domestic servants in other people's homes and provided cheap factory labor. Without their work, middle-class homemakers would have had scant time to minister to the emotional needs of their husbands and children. In mid-19th-century cities, providing enough water to maintain what advice writers called "a fairly clean" home required a servant to lug the equivalent of 100 bottles of water from the public pipe every day.

Even for those who could afford to practice the new ideals of domesticity and gender segregation, there was a problem. The doctrine of difference said that men and women were complementary figures who could be completed only by marriage, but it also drove a wedge between the sexes by emphasizing their differences. Women began to see men as a threat to their pure nature and their more refined friendships. In letters and diaries, women often referred to men as "the grosser sex." For their part, men found it easier to worship an angel in the abstract than to constantly curb their manners and restrain their own enjoyments to put up with the conventions of ladylike behavior on a daily basis.

If the doctrine of difference inhibited emotional intimacy between men and women, the cult of female purity made physical intimacy even more problematic, creating a huge distinction in men's minds between good sex and "good" women. Many men couldn't think about a woman they respected in sexual terms; they often went to prostitutes for sexual relief, and frequently passed venereal diseases on to their wives. For many women, marital sex was a source of anxiety, guilt, or disgust, yet Victorian women suffered from an epidemic of ailments that were almost certainly associated with sexual frustration. They flocked to hydrotherapy centers, where strong volleys of water sometimes relieved their symptoms. Physicians regularly massaged women's pelvic areas to alleviate "hysteria." In fact, the mechanical vibrator was invented at the end of the 19th century to relieve physicians of this time-consuming chore!

No wonder there was a revolt against Victorian prudery and the doctrine of separate spheres. The sexual revolution of the early 20th century wasn't a revolt against marriage—it was an attempt to make marriage more satisfying and to make married love more central to people's identity. And it succeeded dramatically. In the early 20th century, the age of marriage fell, the proportion of men and women who remained single all their lives fell, and the same-sex bonds and intense extended-family ties that had once coexisted with marital ties were devalued, or even labeled deviant. This was when marriage became the happy ending for every story, and when expectations of emotional and sexual satisfaction in marriage led people to elevate marriage above all other personal and family ties. Marriage became a much more important goal, especially for women, and more people reported themselves happy in marriage, than in the past. But the more that people expected to find love and sexual satisfaction in marriage, the more discontented they became when a marriage proved unsatisfying. Divorce rates tripled during the early 1900s. By the end of the 1920s, hundreds of books and articles worried about *The Bankruptcy of Marriage; The Revolt of Women;* and *The Marriage Crisis* and asked, "Is Marriage on the Skids?"

The crisis was put on the back burner during the 1930s and 1940s by the Great Depression and World War II, and in the 1950s, it was almost completely forgotten, as the love-based, male-breadwinner family swept aside all other family forms and values. The reaction against the hardship and turmoil of the '30s and '40s combined with postwar prosperity and unprecedented government subsidies for male-breadwinner families during the 1950s to create what many people see as the Golden Age of Marriage.

By the 1960s, marriage had become nearly universal in North America and Western Europe, with 95 percent of all persons marrying. And as people married at a younger age, life spans lengthened, and divorce rates fell or held steady, individuals were spending much more of their lives in marriage than ever before or since. By 1959, almost half of all American women were married by age 19, and 70 percent were married by age 24. There were also more full-time housewives in society than ever before or since.

Never before had so many people shared the experience of courting their own mates, getting married when they wanted to, and setting up their own households. And never before had married couples been so independent of community groups and extended family ties. The postwar period was characterized by the overwhelming dominance of the nuclear family, male-breadwinner model of marriage. Any departure from this model—whether late marriage, non-marriage, divorce, single motherhood, or even delayed childbearing—was considered deviant.

A 1957 survey in the United States reported that four out of five people believed that anyone who preferred to remain single was "sick," "neurotic," or "immoral." Even larger majorities agreed that, once married, the husband should be the breadwinner and the wife should stay home. As late as 1961, one survey of young women aged 16 to 21 found that almost all expected to be married by age 22, most wanted to have four children, and they expected to quit work permanently when their first child was born.

But under the surface of that placidity, disillusion and discontent were mounting, for both sexes. Hugh Hefner founded *Playboy* magazine in 1953 as a voice of revolt against male family responsibilities. He urged men to "enjoy the pleasures the female has to offer without becoming emotionally involved"—or, worse yet, financially responsible. *Playboy*'s first issue, in April 1953, featured the article "Miss Gold-Digger of

1953," assailing women who expected husbands to support them.

Housewives had their own discontents. In poll after poll, women who married in the 1950s said that they didn't want their daughters to have the same life that they'd had. Instead, they wanted their daughters to marry later in life and get more education. The limits that these wives and mothers had experienced in their marriages had led them to encourage behaviors in their children that, in combination with the new economic and political trends of the 1960s and 1970s, overturned prior gender roles and marriage patterns. As African Americans, young people, and women challenged the restrictions they'd faced in social life and the economy brought more women into the workforce on new terms, all the old contradictions of the love-based, male-breadwinner marriage reemerged, and this time they exploded.

It took more than 150 years to establish the love-based, male-breadwinner marriage as the dominant model in North America and Western Europe. It took less than 25 years to dismantle it. In barely two decades, marriage lost its role as "the master event," which governed young people's sexual initiation, their assumption of adult roles and work patterns, and their transition into parenthood. People began marrying later. Divorce rates soared. Premarital sex became the norm. Acceptance of gay and lesbian relations increased. The division of labor between husband as breadwinner and wife as homemaker, which sociologists in the 1950s had believed was vital for industrial society, fell apart. And many of the mores that once governed why people marry, what predicts marital satisfaction, who divorces, and how cohabitation affects future marital behavior began to change in fundamental and unexpected ways.

Today researchers chase a moving target as they study the new dynamics and relationships of married life. And all of us struggle to understand and come to terms with these changes in our own families. It doesn't help when the mass media and political pundits assure us that if we just tried harder, we could recapture a Golden Age of "traditional" marriage. Such illusions merely burden us with unrealistic nostalgia for what love and marriage "used to be," feeding our guilt and our fears about family change, instead of showing us the grounds for hope: the fact that many people are now discovering how to sustain commitments and make deeper connections both inside and outside marriage. Our challenge today is to reject romanticized views of the past, which make us feel guilty for not living in a sit-com marriage, and to find ways to help all peoples—whatever kind of family they live in, whether they're currently married or not—build healthier relationships and meet their obligations to dependents.

■ Review Questions

1. Why is it "inconceivable," according to Coontz, that young people in most cultures in the past would have chosen a spouse based on love?
2. How might the rise of marriage based on love have affected the amount of divorce in a society?

Growing Up Is Harder to Do

Frank F. Furstenberg Jr.

Sheela Kennedy

Vonnie C. McLoyd

Rubén G. Rumbaut

Richard A. Settersten Jr.

In the years after World War II, Americans typically assumed the full responsibilities of adulthood by their late teens or early 20s. Most young men had completed school and were working full-time, and most young women were married and raising children. People who grew up in this era of growing affluence—many of today's grandparents—were economically self-sufficient and able to care for others by the time they had weathered adolescence. Today, adulthood no longer begins when adolescence ends. Ask someone in their early 20s whether they consider themselves to be an adult, and you might get a laugh, a quizzical look, a shrug of the shoulders, or a response like that of a 24-year-old Californian: "Maybe next year. When I'm 25."

Social scientists are beginning to recognize a new phase of life: early adulthood. Some features of this stage resemble coming of age during the late 19th and early 20th centuries, when youth lingered in a state of semi-autonomy, waiting until they were sufficiently well-off to marry, have children, and establish an independent household. However, there are important differences in how young people today define and achieve adulthood from those of both the recent and the more distant past.

This new stage is not merely an extension of adolescence, as has been maintained in the mass media. Young adults are physically mature and often possess impressive intellectual, social and psychological skills. Nor are young people today reluctant to accept adult responsibilities. Instead, they are busy building up their educational credentials and practical skills in an ever more demanding labor market. Most are working or studying or both, and are developing romantic relationships. Yet, many have not become fully adult—traditionally defined as finishing school, landing a job with benefits, marrying and parenting—because they are not ready, or perhaps not permitted, to do so. For a growing number, this will not happen until their late 20s or even early 30s. In response, American society will have to revise upward the "normal" age of full adulthood, and develop ways to assist young people through the ever-lengthening transition.

Among the most privileged young adults—those who receive ample support from their parents—this is a time of unparalleled freedom from family responsibilities and an opportunity for self-exploration and development. For the less advantaged, early adulthood is a time of struggle to gain the skills and credentials required for a job that can support the family they wish to start (or perhaps have already started), and a struggle to feel in control of their lives. A 30-year-old single mother from Iowa laughed when asked whether she considered herself an adult: "I don't know if I'm an adult yet. I still don't feel quite grown up. Being an adult kind of sounds like having things, everything is kind of in a routine and on track, and I don't feel like I'm quite on track."

CHANGING NOTIONS OF ADULTHOOD

Traditionally, the transition to adulthood involves establishing emotional and economic independence from parents or, as historian John Modell described it, "coming into one's own." The life events that make up the transition to adulthood are accompanied by a sense of commitment, purpose and identity. Although we lack systematic evidence on how adulthood was defined in the past, it appears that marriage and parenthood represented important benchmarks. Nineteenth-century American popular fiction, journalism, sermons and self-help guides rarely referred to finishing school or getting a job, and only occasionally to leaving home or starting one's own household as the critical turning point. On the other hand, they often referred to marriage, suggesting that marriage was considered, at least by middle-class writers, as the critical touchstone of reaching adulthood.

By the 1950s and 1960s, most Americans viewed family roles and adult responsibilities as nearly synonymous. In that era, most women married before they were 21 and had at least one child before they were 23. For men, having the means to marry and support a family was the defining characteristic of adulthood, while for women, merely getting married and becoming a mother conferred adult status. As Alice Rossi explained in 1968: "On the level of cultural values, men have no freedom of choice where work is concerned: they must work to secure their status as adult men. The equivalent for women has been maternity. There is considerable pressure upon the growing girl and young woman to consider maternity necessary for a woman's fulfillment as an individual and to secure her status as an adult."

Research conducted during the late 1950s and early 1960s demonstrated widespread antipathy in America toward people who remained unmarried and toward couples who were childless by choice. However, these views began to shift in the late 1960s, rendering the transition to adulthood more ambiguous. Psychologists Joseph Veroff, Elizabeth Douvan, and Richard Kulka found that more than half of Americans interviewed in 1957 viewed someone who did not want to get married as selfish, immature, peculiar or morally flawed. By 1976, fewer than

one-third of a similar sample held such views. A 1962 study found that 85 percent of mothers believed that married couples should have children. Nearly 20 years later, just 40 percent of those women still agreed, and in 1993 only 1 in 5 of their daughters agreed. Arland Thornton and Linda Young-Demarco, who have studied attitudes toward family roles during the latter half of the 20th century, conclude that "Americans increasingly value freedom and equality in their personal and family lives while at the same time maintaining their commitment to the ideals of marriage, family, and children." While still personally committed to family, Americans increasingly tolerate alternative life choices.

To understand how Americans today define adulthood, we developed a set of questions for the 2002 General Social Survey (GSS), an opinion poll administered to a nationally representative sample of Americans every two years by the National Opinion Research Center. The survey asked nearly 1,400 Americans aged 18 and older how important each of the following traditional benchmarks was to being an adult: leaving home, finishing school, getting a full-time job, becoming financially independent from one's parents, being able to support a family, marrying and becoming a parent.

The definition of adulthood that emerges today does not necessarily include marriage and parenthood. As shown in Figure 2.1, the most important milestones are completing school, establishing an independent household and being employed full-time—concrete steps associated with the ability to support a family. Ninety-five percent of Americans surveyed consider education, employment, financial independence and the ability to support a family to be key steps on the path to adulthood. Nonetheless, almost half of GSS respondents do not believe that it is necessary to actually marry or to have children to be considered an adult. As a young mother from San Diego explained, having a child did not make her an adult; instead she began to feel like an adult when she realized that "all of us make

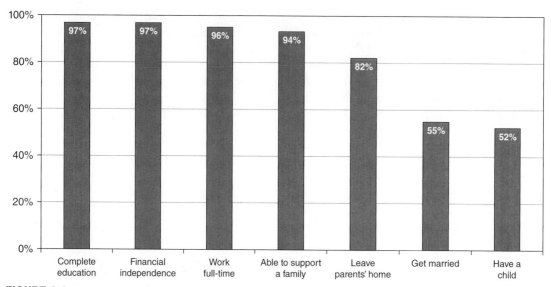

FIGURE 2.1

Percent of Americans who say that an event is at least somewhat important to being considered an adult. (*Source:* General Social Survey 2002. Reprinted by permission.)

mistakes, but you can fix them and if you keep yourself on track . . . everything will come out fine." Compared with their parents and grandparents, for whom marriage and parenthood were virtually a prerequisite for becoming an adult, young people today more often view these as life choices, not requirements.

THE LENGTHENING ROAD TO ADULTHOOD

Not only are the defining characteristics of adulthood changing, so is the time it takes to achieve them. To map the changing transitions to adulthood, we also examined several national surveys that contain information on young adults both in this country and abroad. Using U.S. Census data collected as far back as 1900, we compared the lives of young adults over time. We also conducted about 500 in-depth interviews with young adults living in different parts of the United States, including many in recent immigrant groups.

Our findings, as well as the work of other scholars, confirm that it takes much longer to make the transition to adulthood today than decades ago, and arguably longer than it has at any time in America's history. Figure 2.2, based on the 1960 and 2000 U.S. censuses, illustrates the large decline in the percentage of young adults who, by age 20 or 30, have completed all of the traditionally defined major adult transitions (leaving home, finishing school, becoming financially independent, getting married and having a child). We define financial independence for both men and women as being in the labor force; however, because women in 1960 rarely combined work and motherhood, married full-time mothers are also counted as financially independent in both years. In 2000, just 46 percent of women and 31 percent of men aged 30 had completed all five transitions, compared with 77 percent of women and 65 percent of men at the same age in 1960.

Women—who have traditionally formed families at ages younger than men—show the

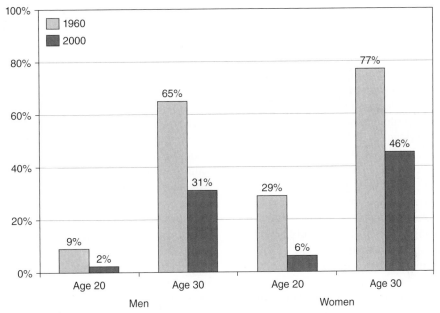

FIGURE 2.2
Percent completing transition to adulthood in 1960 and 2000 using traditional benchmarks
(leaving home, finishing school, getting married, having a child, and being financially
independent). (*Source:* Integrated Public Use Microdata Series extracts [PUMS] of the 1960
and 2000 U.S. Censuses.)

most dramatic changes at early ages. Although
almost 30 percent of 20-year-old women in 1960
had completed these transitions, just 6 percent
had done so in 2000. Among 25-year-olds (not
shown), the decrease is even more dramatic:
70 percent of 25-year-old women in 1960 had
attained traditional adult status, in 2000 just
25 percent had done so. Yet, in 2000, even as
they delayed traditional adulthood, 25-year-old
women greatly increased their participation in
the labor force to levels approaching those of
25-year-old men. The corresponding declines for
men in the attainment of traditional adult status
are less striking but nonetheless significant. For
both men and women, these changes can largely
be explained by the increasing proportion who
go to college and graduate school, and also by
the postponement of marriage and childbearing.

If we use the more contemporary definition
of adulthood suggested in Figure 2.1—one that

excludes marriage and parenthood—then the
contrasts are not as dramatic. In 2000, 70 percent
of men aged 30 had left home, were financially
independent, and had completed their schooling,
just 12 points lower than was true of 30-year-old
men in 1960. Nearly 75 percent of 30-year-old
women in 2000 met this standard, compared to
nearly 85 percent of women in 1960. Nonetheless,
even these changes are historically substantial,
and we are not even taking into account how
many of these independent, working, highly educated young people still feel that they are not yet
capable of supporting a family.

The reasons for this lengthening path to
adulthood, John Modell has shown, range from
shifting social policies to changing economic
forces. The swift transition to adulthood typical after World War II was substantially assisted
by the government. The GI Bill helped veterans
return to school and subsidized the expansion of

education. Similarly, government subsidies for affordable housing encouraged starting families earlier. At the same time, because Social Security was extended to cover more of the elderly, young people were no longer compelled to support their parents. The disappearance or reduction of such subsidies during the past few decades may help to explain the prolongation of adult transitions for some Americans. The growing cost of college and housing forces many youth into a state of semi-autonomy, accepting some support from their parents while they establish themselves economically. When a job ends or they need additional schooling or a relationship dissolves, they increasingly turn to their family for assistance. Thus, the sequencing of adult transitions has become increasingly complicated and more reversible.

However, the primary reason for a prolonged early adulthood is that it now takes much longer to secure a full-time job that pays enough to support a family. Economists Timothy Smeeding and Katherin Ross Phillips found in the mid-1990s that just 70 percent of American men aged 24 to 28 earned enough to support themselves, while fewer than half earned enough to support a family of three. Attaining a decent standard of living today usually requires a college education, if not a professional degree. To enter or remain in the middle class, it is almost imperative to make an educational commitment that spans at least the early 20s. Not only are more Americans attending college than ever before, it takes longer to complete a degree than in years past. Census data reveal that from 1960 to 2000, the percentage of Americans aged 20, 25, and 30 who were enrolled in school more than doubled. Unlike during the 1960s, these educational and work investments are now required of women as well as men. It is little wonder then that many young people linger in early adulthood, delaying marriage and parenthood until their late 20s and early 30s.

Those who do not linger are likely those who cannot afford to and, perhaps as a result, views on how long it takes to achieve adulthood differ markedly by social class. Less-educated and less-affluent respondents—those who did not attend college and those at the bottom one-third of the income ladder—have an earlier expected timetable for leaving home, completing school, obtaining full-time employment, marriage and parenthood. Around 40 percent of the less well-off in the GSS sample said that young adults should marry before they turn 25, and one-third said they should have children by this age. Far fewer of the better-off respondents pointed to the early 20s, and about one-third of them said that these events could be delayed until the 30s. These social class differences probably stem from the reality that young people with more limited means do not have the luxury of investing in school or experimenting with complex career paths.

NEW DEMANDS ON FAMILIES, SCHOOLS, AND GOVERNMENT

The growing demands on young Americans to invest in the future have come at a time of curtailed government support, placing heavy demands on families. Growing inequality shapes very different futures for young Americans with more and less privileged parents.

Early adulthood is when people figure out what they want to do and how best to realize their goals. If they are lucky enough to have a family that can help out, they may proceed directly through college, travel or work for a few years, or perhaps participate in community service, and then enter graduate or professional school. However, relatively few Americans have this good fortune. Youth from less well-off families must shuttle back and forth between work and school or combine both while they gradually gain their credentials. In the meantime, they feel unprepared for marriage or parenting. If they do marry or parent during these years, they often find themselves trying to juggle too many responsibilities and unable to adequately invest in their future. Like the mother from Iowa, they do not feel "on track" or in control of their lives.

More than at any time in recent history, parents are being called on to provide financial assistance (either college tuition, living expenses or other assistance) to their young adult children. Robert Schoeni and Karen Ross conservatively estimate that nearly one-quarter of the entire cost of raising children is incurred after they reach 17. Nearly two-thirds of young adults in their early 20s receive economic support from parents, while about 40 percent still receive some assistance in their late 20s.

A century ago, it was the other way around: young adults typically helped their parents when they first went to work, if (as was common) they still lived with their parents. Now, many young adults continue to receive support from their parents even after they begin working. The exceptions seem to be in immigrant families; there, young people more often help support their parents. A 27-year-old Chinese American from New York explained why he continued to live with his parents despite wanting to move out, saying that his parents "want me [to stay] and they need me. Financially, they need me to take care of them, pay the bills, stuff like that, which is fine."

As young people and their families struggle with the new reality that it takes longer to attain adulthood, Americans must recognize weaknesses in the primary institutions that facilitate this transition—schools and the military. For the fortunate few who achieve bachelor's degrees and perhaps go on to professional or graduate training, residential colleges and universities seem well designed. They offer everything from housing to health care while training young adults. Likewise, the military provides a similar milieu for those from less-privileged families. However, only about one in four young adults attends primarily residential colleges or joins the military after high school. The other three-quarters look to their families for room and board while they attend school and enter the job

market. Many of these youth enter community colleges or local universities that provide much less in the way of services and support.

The least privileged come from families that cannot offer much assistance. This vulnerable population—consisting of 10 to 15 percent of young adults—may come out of the foster care system, graduate from special education programs, or exit jails and prisons. These youth typically lack job skills and need help to secure a foothold in society. Efforts to increase educational opportunities, establish school-to-career paths, and help students who cannot afford postsecondary education must be given higher priority, even in a time of budget constraints. The United States, once a world leader in providing higher education to its citizens, now lags behind several other nations in the proportion of the population that completes college.

Expanding military and alternative national service programs also can help provide a bridge from secondary school to higher education or the labor force by providing financial credit to those who serve their country. Such programs also offer health insurance to young adults, who are often cut off from insurance by arbitrary age limits. Finally, programs for the vulnerable populations of youth coming out of foster care, special education, and mental health services must not assume that young people are fully able to become economically independent at age 18 or even 21. The timetable of the 1950s is no longer applicable. It is high time for policy makers and legislators to address the realities of the longer and more demanding transition to adulthood.

RECOMMENDED RESOURCES

Furstenberg, Frank F., Jr., Thomas D. Cook, Robert Sampson, and Gail Slap, eds. *Early Adulthood in Cross-National Perspective*. London: Sage Publications, 2002. The contributors describe the emergence of this life stage across countries and the wide variation between them in the patterns of adult transitions.

Larson, Reed W., Bradford B. Brown, and Jeylan T. Mortimer, eds. *Adolescents' Preparation for the Future: Perils and Promises.* Ann Arbor, MI: The Society for Research on Adolescence, 2002. The articles in this interdisciplinary book consider how well adolescents in different societies are being prepared for adulthood in a rapidly changing and increasingly global world.

Modell, John. *Into One's Own: From Youth to Adulthood in the United States 1920–1975.* Berkeley, CA: University of California Press, 1989. Modell documents dramatic 20th-century changes in the transition to adulthood and places these shifts within the context of larger economic, political, and technological changes.

Portes, Alejandro, and Rubén G. Rumbaut. *Legacies: The Story of the Immigrant Second Generation.* Berkeley, CA: University of California Press, 2001. This book includes findings from the Children of Immigrants Longitudinal Study on the adaptation of second-generation immigrants during adolescence.

Schoeni, Robert, and Karen Ross. "Material Assistance Received from Families during the Transition to Adulthood." In *On the Frontier of Adulthood: Theory, Research, and Public Policy,* eds. Richard Settersten Jr., Frank Furstenberg Jr., and Rubén Rumbaut. Chicago: University of Chicago Press, 2004. This study estimates the amount of financial assistance given to young adults by their families at different points during early adulthood.

Settersten, Richard A., Jr., Frank F. Furstenberg Jr., and Rubén G. Rumbaut, eds. *On the Frontier of Adulthood: Theory, Research, and Public Policy.* Chicago: University of Chicago Press, 2004. This book describes prolonged and complex patterns of school, work, and family transitions for young adults in America and Western Europe.

Smeeding, Timothy, and Katherin Ross Phillips. "Cross-National Differences in Employment and Economic Sufficiency." *Annals of the American Academy of Political and Social Science* 580 (2002): 103–133. This article examines the economic independence of young adults in seven industrialized countries.

Thornton, Arland, and Linda Young-DeMarco. "Four Decades of Trends in Attitudes toward Family Issues in the United States: The 1960s through the 1990s." *Journal of Marriage and the Family* 63 (2001): 1009–37. The authors review survey data showing changes in Americans' attitudes toward the family.

■ Review Questions

1. What does it mean to be "fully adult" in contemporary American society?
2. Why does it typically take longer to become an adult today than it did in the mid-twentieth century?

Part Two

Gender, Class, and Race-Ethnicity

CHAPTER 3

Gender and Families

Over the past half century, scholarship on gender has grown in substance and stature so much that gender studies is now one of the core areas of inquiry in sociology. The advances have occurred in two stages. In the first stage, roughly the period from 1965 to 1985, sociologists relied heavily on the concept of gender roles. Some demonstrated ways in which parents, the media, and peer groups influenced children's ideas of the proper role for a girl or boy. Other sociologists studied ways in which society reinforced the roles of breadwinner and homemaker. The second stage began in the mid-1980s, when a new wave of gender scholars became dissatisfied with the concept of gender roles. They argued that the simple dichotomy between men's roles and women's roles shouldn't be taken for granted. Instead, argued the revisionists, scholars should examine the tenuous, changing, socially constructed nature of the very idea of a "male role" and a "female role." They also maintained that gender is a master identity, far too broad to be considered just one of life's roles, like the role of professor or student. They argued instead for an approach that focuses on the continual construction and maintenance of gender differences throughout adulthood.

These second-stage scholars drew upon symbolic interaction theory[1] and its offshoot, ethnomethodology.[2] In 1987, Candace West and Don H. Zimmerman put forward the interactionist approach in "Doing Gender," perhaps the most influential article on the sociology of gender in the past 25 years. "We argue," West and Zimmerman wrote, "that gender is not a set of traits, nor a role, but the product of social doings of some sort." These social doings occur through "situated conduct"—interactions between men and women in particular settings (such as a kitchen or a job interview). Gender is an achieved property that is created through countless social interactions that reinforce gender differences. The first selection in this chapter is an excerpt from "Doing Gender."

---

[1]H. Blumer, "Society as Symbolic Interaction," in *Human Behavior and Social Processes,* ed. A. M. Rose (Boston: Houghton Mifflin, 1962).

[2]H. Garfinkel, *Studies in Ethnomethodology* (Englewood Cliffs, NJ: Prentice Hall, 1967).

Over the past several decades, the expectations for how women and men should behave have changed greatly. It is much more acceptable for a married woman to work outside the home than it was in the past. It is also more acceptable for a father to be the primary caregiver to his children, although it is still unusual. In some ways, the family and work lives of women have changed more than have the family and work lives of men. For example, women have moved into formerly men's jobs such as physician or lawyer, but men have not moved into women's jobs such as nurse or child care aide. This asymmetry is even visible among middle-school students, argue Barbara J. Risman and Elizabeth Seale, in the second reading of this chapter. They show that it's more acceptable for girls to act like boys than for boys to act like girls.

READING 3-1

Doing Gender

Candace West

Don H. Zimmerman

In the beginning, there was sex and there was gender. Those of us who taught courses in the area in the late 1960s and early 1970s were careful to distinguish one from the other. Sex, we told students, was what was ascribed by biology: anatomy, hormones, and physiology. Gender, we said, was an achieved status: that which is constructed through psychological, cultural, and social means. To introduce the difference between the two, we drew on singular case studies of hermaphrodites (Money 1968, 1974; Money and Ehrhardt 1972) and anthropological investigations of "strange and exotic tribes" (Mead 1963, 1968).

Inevitably (and understandably), in the ensuing weeks of each term, our students became confused. Sex hardly seemed a "given" in the context of research that illustrated the sometimes ambiguous and often conflicting criteria for its ascription. And gender seemed much less an "achievement" in the context of the anthropological, psychological, and social imperatives we studied—the division of labor, the formation of gender identities, and the social subordination of women by men. Moreover, the received doctrine of gender socialization theories conveyed the strong message that while gender may be "achieved," by about age five it was certainly fixed, unvarying, and static—much like sex.

Since about 1975, the confusion has intensified and spread far beyond our individual classrooms. For one thing, we learned that the relationship

between biological and cultural processes was far more complex—and reflexive—than we previously had supposed (Rossi 1984, especially pp. 10–14). For another, we discovered that certain structural arrangements, for example, between work and family, actually produce or enable some capacities, such as to mother, that we formerly associated with biology (Chodorow 1978 versus Firestone 1970). In the midst of all this, the notion of gender as a recurring achievement somehow fell by the wayside.

Our purpose in this article is to propose an ethnomethodologically informed, and therefore distinctively sociological, understanding of gender as a routine, methodical, and recurring accomplishment. We contend that the "doing" of gender is undertaken by women and men whose competence as members of society is hostage to its production. Doing gender involves a complex of socially guided perceptual, interactional, and micropolitical activities that cast particular pursuits as expressions of masculine and feminine "natures."

When we view gender as an accomplishment, an achieved property of situated conduct, our attention shifts from matters internal to the individual and focuses on interactional and, ultimately, institutional arenas. In one sense, of course, it is individuals who "do" gender. But it is a situated doing, carried out in the virtual or real presence of others who are presumed to be oriented to its production. Rather than as a property of individuals, we conceive of gender as an emergent feature of social situations: both as an outcome of and a rationale for various social arrangements and as a means of legitimating one of the most fundamental divisions of society.

To advance our argument, we undertake a critical examination of what sociologists have meant by *gender*, including its treatment as a role enactment in the conventional sense and as a "display" in Goffman's (1976) terminology. Both *gender role* and *gender display* focus on behavioral aspects of being a woman or a man (as opposed, for example, to biological differences between the two). However, we contend that the notion of gender as a role obscures the work that is involved in producing gender in everyday activities, while the notion of gender as a display relegates it to the periphery of interaction. We argue instead that participants in interaction organize their various and manifold activities to reflect or express gender, and they are disposed to perceive the behavior of others in a similar light.

To elaborate our proposal, we suggest at the outset that important but often overlooked distinctions be observed among *sex, sex category,* and *gender. Sex* is a determination made through the application of socially agreed upon biological criteria for classifying persons as females or males.[1] The criteria for classification can be genitalia at birth or chromosomal typing before birth, and they do not necessarily agree with one another. Placement in a *sex category* is achieved through application of the sex criteria, but in everyday life, categorization is established and sustained by the socially required identificatory displays that proclaim one's membership in one or the other category. In this sense, one's sex category presumes one's sex and stands as proxy for it in many situations, but sex and sex category can vary independently; that is, it is possible to claim membership in a sex category even when the sex criteria are lacking. *Gender,* in contrast, is the activity of managing situated conduct in light of normative conceptions of attitudes and activities appropriate for one's sex category. Gender activities emerge from and bolster claims to membership in a sex category.

We contend that recognition of the analytical independence of sex, sex category, and gender is essential for understanding the relationships among these elements and the interactional work involved in "being" a gendered person in society. While our primary aim is theoretical, there will be occasion to discuss fruitful directions for empirical research following from the formulation of gender that we propose.

We begin with an assessment of the received meaning of gender, particularly in relation to the roots of this notion in presumed biological differences between women and men.

PERSPECTIVES ON SEX AND GENDER

In Western societies, the accepted cultural perspective on gender views women and men as naturally and unequivocally defined categories of being (Garfinkel 1967, pp. 116–18) with distinctive psychological and behavioral propensities that can be predicted from their reproductive functions. Competent adult members of these societies see differences between the two as fundamental and enduring—differences seemingly supported by the division of labor into women's and men's work and an often elaborate differentiation of feminine and masculine attitudes and behaviors that are prominent features of social organization. Things are the way they are by virtue of the fact that men are men and women are women—a division perceived to be natural and rooted in biology, producing in turn profound psychological, behavioral, and social consequences. The structural arrangements of a society are presumed to be responsive to these differences.

Analyses of sex and gender in the social sciences, though less likely to accept uncritically the naive biological determinism of the view just presented, often retain a conception of sex-linked behaviors and traits as essential properties of individuals (for good reviews, see Hochschild 1973; Tresemer 1975; Thorne 1980; Henley 1985). The "sex differences approach" (Thorne 1980) is more commonly attributed to psychologists than to sociologists, but the survey researcher who determines the "gender" of respondents on the basis of the sound of their voices over the telephone is also making trait-oriented assumptions. Reducing gender to a fixed set of psychological traits or to a unitary "variable" precludes serious consideration of the ways it is used to structure distinct domains of social experience (Stacey and Thorne 1985, pp. 307–8).

Taking a different tack, role theory has attended to the social construction of gender categories, called "sex roles" or, more recently, "gender roles" and has analyzed how these are learned and enacted. Beginning with Linton (1936) and continuing through the works of Parsons (Parsons 1951; Parsons and Bales 1955) and Komarovsky (1946, 1950), role theory has emphasized the social and dynamic aspect of role construction and enactment (Thorne 1980; Connell 1983). But at the level of face-to-face interaction, the application of role theory to gender poses problems of its own (for good reviews and critiques, see Connell 1983, 1985; Kessler, Ashendon, Connell, and Dowsett 1985; Lopata and Thorne 1978; Thorne 1980; Stacey and Thorne 1985). Roles are *situated identities*—assumed and relinquished as the situation demands—rather than *master identities* (Hughes 1945), such as sex category, that cut across situations. Unlike most roles, such as "nurse," "doctor," and "patient" or "professor" and "student," gender has no specific site or organizational context.

Moreover, many roles are already gender marked, so that special qualifiers—such as "female doctor" or "male nurse"—must be added to exceptions to the rule. Thorne (1980) observes that conceptualizing gender as a role makes it difficult to assess its influence on other roles and reduces its explanatory usefulness in discussions of power and inequality. Drawing on Rubin (1975), Thorne calls for a reconceptualization of women and men as distinct social groups, constituted in "concrete, historically changing—and generally unequal—social relationships" (Thorne 1980, p. 11).

We argue that gender is not a set of traits, nor a variable, nor a role, but the product of social doings of some sort. What then is the social doing of gender? It is more than the continuous creation of the meaning of gender through human actions (Gerson and Peiss 1985). We claim that gender itself is constituted through interaction.[2] To develop the implications of our claim, we turn to Goffman's (1976) account of "gender display." Our object here is to explore how gender might be exhibited or portrayed through interaction, and thus be seen as "natural," while it is being produced as a socially organized achievement.

GENDER DISPLAY

Goffman contends that when human beings interact with others in their environment, they assume that each possesses an "essential nature"—a nature that can be discerned through the "natural signs given off or expressed by them" (1976, p. 75). Femininity and masculinity are regarded as "prototypes of essential expression—something that can be conveyed fleetingly in any social situation and yet something that strikes at the most basic characterization of the individual" (1976, p. 75). The means through which we provide such expressions are "perfunctory, conventionalized acts" (1976, p. 69), which convey to others our regard for them, indicate our alignment in an encounter, and tentatively establish the terms of contact for that social situation. But they are also regarded as expressive behavior, testimony to our "essential natures."

Goffman (1976, pp. 69–70) sees *displays* as highly conventionalized behaviors structured as two-part exchanges of the statement-reply type, in which the presence or absence of symmetry can establish deference or dominance. These rituals are viewed as distinct from but articulated with more consequential activities, such as performing tasks or engaging in discourse. Hence, we have what he terms the "scheduling" of displays at junctures in activities, such as the beginning or end, to avoid interfering with the activities themselves. Goffman (1976, p. 69) formulates *gender display* as follows:

> If gender be defined as the culturally established correlates of sex (whether in consequence of biology or learning), then gender display refers to conventionalized portrayals of these correlates.

These gendered expressions might reveal clues to the underlying, fundamental dimensions of the female and male, but they are, in Goffman's view, optional performances. Masculine courtesies may or may not be offered and, if offered, may or may not be declined (1976, p. 71). Moreover, human beings "themselves employ the term 'expression,' and conduct themselves to fit their own notions of expressivity" (1976, p. 75). Gender depictions are less a consequence of our "essential sexual natures" than interactional portrayals of what we would like to convey about sexual natures, using conventionalized gestures. Our *human* nature gives us the ability to learn to produce and recognize masculine and feminine gender displays—"a capacity [we] have by virtue of being persons, not males and females" (1976, p. 76).

Upon first inspection, it would appear that Goffman's formulation offers an engaging sociological corrective to existing formulations of gender. In his view, gender is a socially scripted dramatization of the culture's *idealization* of feminine and masculine natures, played for an audience that is well schooled in the presentational idiom. To continue the metaphor, there are scheduled performances presented in special locations, and like plays, they constitute introductions to or time out from more serious activities.

There are fundamental equivocations in this perspective. By segregating gender display from the serious business of interaction, Goffman obscures the effects of gender on a wide range of human activities. Gender is not merely something that happens in the nooks and crannies of interaction, fitted in here and there and not interfering with the serious business of life. While it is plausible to contend that gender displays—construed as conventionalized expressions—are optional, it does not seem plausible to say that we have the option of being seen by others as female or male.

It is necessary to move beyond the notion of gender display to consider what is involved in doing gender as an ongoing activity embedded in everyday interaction. Toward this end, we return to the distinctions among sex, sex category, and gender introduced earlier.

SEX, SEX CATEGORY, AND GENDER

Garfinkel's (1967, pp. 118–40) case study of Agnes, a transsexual raised as a boy who adopted a female identity at age 17 and underwent a sex reassignment operation several years later, demonstrates how gender is created through interaction and at the same time structures interaction. Agnes, whom Garfinkel characterized as a "practical methodologist," developed a number of procedures for passing as a "normal, natural female" both prior to and after her surgery. She had the practical task of managing the fact that she possessed male genitalia and that she lacked the social resources a girl's biography would presumably provide in everyday interaction. In short, she needed to display herself as a woman, simultaneously learning what it was to be a woman. Of necessity, this full-time pursuit took place at a time when most people's gender would be well-accredited and routinized. Agnes had to consciously contrive what the vast majority of women do without thinking. She was not "faking" what "real" women do naturally. She was obliged to analyze and figure out how to act within socially structured circumstances and conceptions of femininity that women born with appropriate biological credentials come to take for granted early on. As in the case of others who must "pass," such as transvestites, Kabuki actors, or Dustin Hoffman's "Tootsie," Agnes's case makes visible what culture has made invisible—the accomplishment of gender.

Garfinkel's (1967) discussion of Agnes does not explicitly separate three analytically distinct, although empirically overlapping, concepts—sex, sex category, and gender.

Sex

Agnes did not possess the socially agreed upon biological criteria for classification as a member of the female *sex*. Still, Agnes regarded herself as a female, albeit a female with a penis, which a woman ought not to possess. The penis, she insisted, was a "mistake" in need of remedy (Garfinkel 1967, pp. 126–27, 131–32). Like other competent members of our culture, Agnes honored the notion that there *are* "essential" biological criteria that unequivocally distinguish females from males. However, if we move away from the commonsense viewpoint, we discover that the reliability of these criteria is not beyond question (Money and Brennan 1968; Money and Ehrhardt 1972; Money and Ogunro 1974; Money and Tucker 1975). Moreover, other cultures have acknowledged the existence of "cross-genders" (Blackwood 1984; Williams 1986) and the possibility of more than two sexes (Hill 1935; Martin and Voorheis 1975, pp. 84–107; but see also Cucchiari 1981, pp. 32–35).

More central to our argument is Kessler and McKenna's (1978, pp. 1–6) point that genitalia are conventionally hidden from public inspection in everyday life; yet we continue through our social rounds to "observe" a world of two naturally, normally sexed persons. It is the *presumption* that essential criteria exist and would or should be there if looked for that provides the basis for sex categorization. Drawing on Garfinkel, Kessler and McKenna argue that "female" and "male" are cultural events—products of what they term the "gender attribution process"—rather than some collection of traits, behaviors, or even physical attributes. Illustratively they cite the child who, viewing a picture of someone clad in a suit and a tie, contends, "It's a man, because he has a pee-pee" (Kessler and McKenna 1978, p. 154). Translation: "He must have a pee-pee [an essential characteristic] because I see the *insignia* of a suit and tie." Neither initial sex assignment (pronouncement at birth as a female or male) nor the actual existence of essential criteria for that assignment (possession of a clitoris and vagina or penis and testicles) has much—if anything—to do with the identification of sex category in everyday life. There, Kessler and McKenna note, we operate with a moral certainty of a world of two sexes. We do not think, "Most persons with

penises are men, but some may not be" or "Most persons who dress as men have penises." Rather, we take it for granted that sex and sex category are congruent—that knowing the latter, we can deduce the rest.

Sex Categorization

Agnes's claim to the categorical status of female, which she sustained by appropriate identificatory displays and other characteristics, could be *discredited* before her transsexual operation if her possession of a penis became known and after by her surgically constructed genitalia (see Raymond 1979, pp. 37, 138). In this regard, Agnes had to be continually alert to actual or potential threats to the security of her sex category. Her problem was not so much living up to some prototype of essential femininity but preserving her categorization as female. This task was made easy for her by a very powerful resource, namely, the process of commonsense categorization in everyday life.

The categorization of members of society into indigenous categories such as "girl" or "boy," or "woman" or "man," operates in a distinctively social way. The act of categorization does not involve a positive test, in the sense of a well-defined set of criteria that must be explicitly satisfied prior to making an identification. Rather, the application of membership categories relies on an "if-can" test in everyday interaction (Sacks 1972, pp. 332–35). This test stipulates that if people *can be seen* as members of relevant categories, *then categorize them that way*. That is, use the category that seems appropriate, except in the presence of discrepant information or obvious features that would rule out its use. This procedure is quite in keeping with the attitude of everyday life, which has us take appearances at face value unless we have special reason to doubt (Schutz 1943; Garfinkel 1967, pp. 272–77; Bernstein 1986).[3] It should be added that it is precisely when we have special reason to doubt that the issue of applying rigorous criteria arises, but it is rare, outside legal or bureaucratic contexts, to encounter insistence on positive tests (Garfinkel 1967, pp. 262–83; Wilson 1970).

Agnes's initial resource was the predisposition of those she encountered to take her appearance (her figure, clothing, hair style, and so on), as the undoubted appearance of a normal female. Her further resource was our cultural perspective on the properties of "natural, normally sexed persons." Garfinkel (1967, pp. 122–28) notes that in everyday life, we live in a world of two—and only two—sexes. This arrangement has a moral status, in that we include ourselves and others in it as "essentially, originally, in the first place, always have been, always will be, once and for all, in the final analysis, either 'male' or 'female'" (Garfinkel 1967, p. 122).

Consider the following case:

> This issue reminds me of a visit I made to a computer store a couple of years ago. The person who answered my questions was truly a *salesperson.* I could not categorize him/her as a woman or a man. What did I look for? (1) Facial hair: She/he was smooth skinned, but some men have little or no facial hair. (This varies by race, Native Americans and Blacks often have none.) (2) Breasts: She/he was wearing a loose shirt that hung from his/her shoulders. And, as many women who suffered through a 1950s' adolescence know to their shame, women are often flat-chested. (3) Shoulders: His/hers were small and round for a man, broad for a woman. (4) Hands: Long and slender fingers, knuckles a bit large for a woman, small for a man. (5) Voice: Middle range, unexpressive for a woman, not at all the exaggerated tones some gay males affect. (6) His/her treatment of me: Gave off no signs that would let me know if I were of the same or different sex as this person. There were not even any signs that he/she knew his/her sex would be difficult to categorize and I wondered about that even as I did my best to hide these questions so I would not embarrass him/her while we talked of computer paper. I left still not knowing the sex of my salesperson, and was disturbed by that unanswered question (child of my culture that I am). (Diane Margolis, personal communication)

What can this case tell us about situations such as Agnes's (cf. Morris 1974; Richards 1983) or the process of sex categorization in general? First, we infer from this description that the computer salesclerk's identificatory display was ambiguous, since she or he was not dressed or adorned in an unequivocally female or male fashion. It is when such a display *fails* to provide grounds for categorization that factors such as facial hair or tone of voice are assessed to determine membership in a sex category. Second, beyond the fact that this incident could be recalled after "a couple of years," the customer was not only "disturbed" by the ambiguity of the salesclerk's category but also assumed that to acknowledge this ambiguity would be embarrassing to the salesclerk. Not only do we want to know the sex category of those around us (to see it at a glance, perhaps), but we presume that others are displaying it for us, in as decisive a fashion as they can.

Gender

Agnes attempted to be "120 percent female" (Garfinkel 1967, p. 129), that is, unquestionably in all ways and at all times feminine. She thought she could protect herself from disclosure before and after surgical intervention by comporting herself in a feminine manner, but she also could have given herself away by overdoing her performance. Sex categorization and the accomplishment of gender are not the same. Agnes's categorization could be secure or suspect, but did not depend on whether or not she lived up to some ideal conception of femininity. Women can be seen as unfeminine, but that does not make them "unfemale." Agnes faced an ongoing task of *being* a woman—something beyond style of dress (an identificatory display) or allowing men to light her cigarette (a gender display). Her problem was to produce configurations of behavior that would be seen by others as normative gender behavior.

Agnes's strategy of "secret apprenticeship," through which she learned expected feminine decorum by carefully attending to her fiancé's criticisms of other women, was one means of masking incompetencies and simultaneously acquiring the needed skills (Garfinkel 1967, pp. 146–47). It was through her fiancé that Agnes learned that sunbathing on the lawn in front of her apartment was "offensive" (because it put her on display to other men). She also learned from his critiques of other women that she should not insist on having things her way and that she should not offer her opinions or claim equality with men (Garfinkel 1967, pp. 147–48). (Like other women in our society, Agnes learned something about power in the course of her "education.")

Popular culture abounds with books and magazines that compile idealized depictions of relations between women and men. Those focused on the etiquette of dating or prevailing standards of feminine comportment are meant to be of practical help in these matters. However, the use of any such source *as a manual of procedure* requires the assumption that doing gender merely involves making use of discrete, well-defined bundles of behavior that can simply be plugged into interactional situations to produce recognizable enactments of masculinity and femininity. The man "does" being masculine by, for example, taking the woman's arm to guide her across a street, and she "does" being feminine by consenting to be guided and not initiating such behavior with a man.

Agnes could perhaps have used such sources as manuals, but, we contend, doing gender is not so easily regimented (Mithers 1982; Morris 1974). Such sources may list and describe the sorts of behaviors that mark or display gender, but they are necessarily incomplete (Garfinkel 1967, pp. 66–75; Wieder 1974, pp. 183–214; Zimmerman and Wieder 1970, pp. 285–98). And to be successful, marking or displaying gender must be finely fitted to situations and modified or transformed as the occasion demands. Doing gender consists of managing such occasions so that, whatever the particulars, the outcome is seen and seeable in context as gender-appropriate or, as the case may be, gender-*in*appropriate, that is, *accountable*.

GENDER AND ACCOUNTABILITY

As Heritage (1984, pp. 136–37) notes, members of society regularly engage in "descriptive accountings of states of affairs to one another," and such accounts are both serious and consequential. These descriptions name, characterize, formulate, explain, excuse, excoriate, or merely take notice of some circumstance or activity and thus place it within some social framework (locating it relative to other activities, like and unlike).

Such descriptions are themselves accountable, and societal members orient to the fact that their activities are subject to comment. Actions are often designed with an eye to their accountability, that is, how they might look and how they might be characterized. The notion of accountability also encompasses those actions undertaken so that they are specifically unremarkable and thus not worthy of more than a passing remark, because they are seen to be in accord with culturally approved standards.

Heritage (1984, p. 179) observes that the process of rendering something accountable is interactional in character:

> [This] permits actors to design their actions in relation to their circumstances so as to permit others, by methodically taking account of circumstances, to recognize the action for what it is.

The key word here is *circumstances*. One circumstance that attends virtually all actions is the sex category of the actor. As Garfinkel (1967, p. 118) comments:

> [T]he work and socially structured occasions of sexual passing were obstinately unyielding to [Agnes's] attempts to routinize the grounds of daily activities. This obstinacy points to the *omnirelevance* of sexual status to affairs of daily life as an invariant but unnoticed background in the texture of relevances that compose the changing actual scenes of everyday life. (italics added)

If sex category is omnirelevant (or even approaches being so), then a person engaged in virtually any activity may be held accountable for performance of that activity as a *woman* or a *man,* and their incumbency in one or the other sex category can be used to legitimate or discredit their other activities (Berger, Cohen, and Zelditch 1972; Berger, Conner, and Fisek 1974; Berger, Fisek, Norman, and Zelditch 1977; Humphreys and Berger 1981). Accordingly, virtually any activity can be assessed as to its womanly or manly nature. And note, to "do" gender is not always to live up to normative conceptions of femininity or masculinity; it is to engage in behavior *at the risk of gender assessment.* While it is individuals who do gender, the enterprise is fundamentally interactional and institutional in character, for accountability is a feature of social relationships and its idiom is drawn from the institutional arena in which those relationships are enacted. If this be the case, can we ever *not* do gender? Insofar as a society is partitioned by "essential" differences between women and men and placement in a sex category is both relevant and enforced, doing gender is unavoidable.

RESOURCES FOR DOING GENDER

Doing gender means creating differences between girls and boys and women and men, differences that are not natural, essential, or biological. Once the differences have been constructed, they are used to reinforce the "essentialness" of gender. In a delightful account of the "arrangement between the sexes," Goffman (1977) observes the creation of a variety of institutionalized frameworks through which our "natural, normal sexedness" can be enacted. The physical features of social setting provide one obvious resource for the expression of our "essential" differences. For example, the sex segregation of North American public bathrooms distinguishes "ladies" from "gentlemen" in matters held to be fundamentally biological, even though both "are somewhat similar in the

question of waste products and their elimination" (Goffman 1977, p. 315). These settings are furnished with dimorphic equipment (such as urinals for men or elaborate grooming facilities for women), even though both sexes may achieve the same ends through the same means (and apparently do so in the privacy of their own homes). To be stressed here is the fact that:

> The functioning of sex-differentiated organs is involved, but there is nothing in this functioning that biologically recommends segregation; that arrangement is a totally cultural matter . . . toilet segregation is presented as a natural consequence of the difference between the sex classes when in fact it is a means of honoring, if not producing, this difference. (Goffman 1977, p. 316)

Standardized social occasions also provide stages for evocations of the "essential female and male natures." Goffman cites organized sports as one such institutionalized framework for the expression of manliness. There, those qualities that ought "properly" to be associated with masculinity, such as endurance, strength, and competitive spirit, are celebrated by all parties concerned—participants, who may be seen to demonstrate such traits, and spectators, who applaud their demonstrations from the safety of the sidelines (1977, p. 322).

Assortative mating practices among heterosexual couples afford still further means to create and maintain differences between women and men. For example, even though size, strength, and age tend to be normally distributed among females and males (with considerable overlap between them), selective pairing ensures couples in which boys and men are visibly bigger, stronger, and older (if not "wiser") than the girls and women with whom they are paired. So, should situations emerge in which greater size, strength, or experience is called for, boys and men will be ever ready to display it and girls and women, to appreciate its display (Goffman 1977, p. 321; West and Iritani 1985).

Gender may be routinely fashioned in a variety of situations that seem conventionally expressive to begin with, such as those that present "helpless" women next to heavy objects or flat tires. But, as Goffman notes, heavy, messy, and precarious concerns can be constructed from *any* social situation, "even though by standards set in other settings, this may involve something that is light, clean, and safe" (Goffman 1977, p. 324). Given these resources, it is clear that *any* interactional situation sets the stage for depictions of "essential" sexual natures. In sum, these situations "do not so much allow for the expression of natural differences as for the production of that difference itself" (Goffman 1977, p. 324).

Many situations are not clearly sex categorized to begin with, nor is what transpires within them obviously gender relevant. Yet any social encounter can be pressed into service in the interests of doing gender. Thus, Fishman's (1978) research on casual conversations found an asymmetrical "division of labor" in talk between heterosexual intimates. Women had to ask more questions, fill more silences, and use more attention-getting beginnings in order to be heard. Her conclusions are particularly pertinent here:

> Since interactional work is related to what constitutes being a woman, with what a woman *is*, the idea that it *is* work is obscured. The work is not seen as what women do, but as part of what they are. (Fishman 1978, p. 405)

We would argue that it is precisely such labor that helps to constitute the essential nature of women *as* women in interactional contexts (West and Zimmerman 1983, pp. 109–11; but see also Kollock, Blumstein, and Schwartz 1985).

Individuals have many social identities that may be donned or shed, muted or made more salient, depending on the situation. One may be a friend, spouse, professional, citizen, and many other things to many different people—or, to the same person at different times. But we are always women or men—unless we shift into another sex category. What this means is that

our identificatory displays will provide an ever-available resource for doing gender under an infinitely diverse set of circumstances.

Some occasions are organized to routinely display and celebrate behaviors that are conventionally linked to one or the other sex category. On such occasions, everyone knows his or her place in the interactional scheme of things. If an individual identified as a member of one sex category engages in behavior usually associated with the other category, this routinization is challenged. Hughes (1945, p. 356) provides an illustration of such a dilemma:

> [A] young woman . . . became part of that virile profession, engineering. The designer of an airplane is expected to go up on the maiden flight of the first plane built according to the design. He [sic] then gives a dinner to the engineers and workmen who worked on the new plane. The dinner is naturally a stag party. The young woman in question designed a plane. Her co-workers urged her not to take the risk—for which, presumably, men only are fit—of the maiden voyage. They were, in effect, asking her to be a lady instead of an engineer. She chose to be an engineer. She then gave the party and paid for it like a man. After food and the first round of toasts, she left like a lady.

On this occasion, parties reached an accommodation that allowed a woman to engage in presumptively masculine behaviors. However, we note that in the end, this compromise permitted demonstration of her "essential" femininity, through accountably "ladylike" behavior.

Hughes (1945, p. 357) suggests that such contradictions may be countered by managing interactions on a very narrow basis, for example, "keeping the relationship formal and specific." But the heart of the matter is that even—perhaps, especially—if the relationship is a formal one, gender is still something one is accountable for. Thus a woman physician (notice the special qualifier in her case) may be accorded respect for her skill and even addressed by an appropriate title. Nonetheless, she is subject to evaluation in terms of normative conceptions of appropriate attitudes and activities for her sex category and under pressure to prove that she is an "essentially" feminine being, despite appearances to the contrary (West 1984, pp. 97–101). Her sex category is used to discredit her participation in important clinical activities (Lorber 1984, pp. 52–54), while her involvement in medicine is used to discredit her commitment to her responsibilities as a wife and mother (Bourne and Wikler 1978, pp. 435–37). Simultaneously, her exclusion from the physician colleague community is maintained and her accountability *as a woman* is ensured.

In this context, "role conflict" can be viewed as a dynamic aspect of our current "arrangement between the sexes" (Goffman 1977), an arrangement that provides for occasions on which persons of a particular sex category can "see" quite clearly that they are out of place and that if they were not there, their current troubles would not exist. What is at stake is, from the standpoint of interaction, the management of our "essential" natures, and from the standpoint of the individual, the continuing accomplishment of gender. If, as we have argued, sex category is omnirelevant, then any occasion, conflicted or not, offers the resources for doing gender.

We have sought to show that sex category and gender are managed properties of conduct that are contrived with respect to the fact that others will judge and respond to us in particular ways. We have claimed that a person's gender is not simply an aspect of what one is, but, more fundamentally, it is something that one *does*, and does recurrently, in interaction with others. . . .

■ Review Questions

1. What do the authors mean when they say that gender is not a property of individuals but rather a feature of social situations?
2. Can you give an example of a setting you have experienced in which gender differences were assumed to be natural but were really socially created?

ENDNOTES

1. This definition understates many complexities involved in the relationship between biology and culture (Jaggar 1983, pp. 106–13). However, our point is that the determination of an individual's sex classification is a *social* process through and through.
2. This is not to say that gender is a singular "thing" omnipresent in the same form historically or in every situation. Because normative conceptions of appropriate attitudes and activities for sex categories can vary across cultures and historical moments, the management of situated conduct in light of those expectations can take many different forms.
3. Bernstein (1986) reports an unusual case of espionage in which a man passing as a woman convinced a lover that he/she had given birth to "their" child, who, the lover, thought, "looked like" him.

READING 3-2

Betwixt and Be Tween: Gender Contradictions among Middle Schoolers

Barbara J. Risman and Elizabeth Seale

This research is based on interviews with middle-school children in a southeastern city of the United States. In this paper, we ask whether the gender revolution has freed these children from being constrained by stereotypes. We find that both boys and girls are still punished for going beyond gender expectations, but boys much more so than girls. For girls, participation in traditionally masculine activities, such as sports and academic competition, is now quite accept-able and even encouraged by both parents and peers. We find, indeed, that girls are more likely to tease each other for being too girly than for being a sports star. Girls still feel pressure, how-ever, to be thin and to dress in feminine ways, to "do gender" in their self-presentation. Boys are quickly teased for doing any behavior that is traditionally considered feminine. Boys who deviate in any way from traditional masculinity are stigmatized as "gay." Whereas girls can and do participate in a wide range of activities with-out being teased, boys consistently avoid activi-ties defined as female to avoid peer harassment. Homophobia, at least toward boys, is alive and well in middle school.

Today parents and educators tell children that they can be whatever they want to be. Children are taught that women and men and whites and blacks are equal.[1] Changes in gender norms have created opportunities for girls that never before existed. For instance, in school, Title IX has encouraged girls' participation in athletics. But are boys and girls actually free to construct personal identities that leave behind gender ste-reotypes, even when their parents and teachers encourage them to do so?

How free are middle-school boys and girls to form identities outside the constraining gender expectations that have traditionally disadvan-taged girls in the public sphere and repressed boys from exploring their emotions? We approached this subject by interviewing forty-four middle-school children in a mid-sized southeastern city. They were not yet teenagers but were already adapting to pressures to view the world through the eyes of their peers. Middle school is a time when peers become a crucial reference group. Conformity to group norms becomes central to popularity, fitting in, and self-image.[2] What do the experiences and perceptions of these preado-lescent kids (tween-agers) tell us about growing up in contemporary society? How much have their expectations and self-images transcended traditional gender norms?

Peers become centrally important as tween-agers face new and complicated situations in which they must negotiate friendships, issues of sexuality, self-image, conflict, stratification, cliques, and the like. In this so-called "tween" culture, these kids try to make sense of things in their daily lives by using new tools as well as old ones taken from "cultural tool kits." The lives of tween-agers provide a glimpse into how contem-porary definitions of race and gender are shaping the next generation, and what new realities the children themselves may be creating at a time when their core identities are developing.

Our data suggest that American middle-school children, at least in the midsized south-eastern city we examined, have adopted an ideal of equality. Nearly all the kids say that men and women are equal, and that race no longer matters, or at least that it shouldn't. These children have been raised in a society that posits the ideals of gender and racial equal-ity, and the kids seem to accept and believe in those ideals, at least when you scratch the sur-face of their opinions. But that ideal of equality is not what they experience in their real lives, and at least half of them recognize and iden-tify contradictions between what should be and what is.

Despite their acceptance of the rhetoric of gender equality, these tween-agers hold very gender-stereotypical beliefs about boys, although not about girls. Any male gender nonconformity, where boys engage in behaviors or activities traditionally considered female, is taken as evidence that the boy is "gay." As a result, boys are afraid to cross any gender boundaries for fear of having that stigma attached to them. By contrast, the lives of girls are much less constricted by stereotypes about femininity. In fact, girls are more likely to be teased for being "too girly," than for being a tomboy. Girls still police each other's behavior, but the rules of femininity that they enforce now seem to focus almost exclusively on clothes, makeup, diet, and bodily presentation. The girls in our study still "do gender,"[3] but mostly by how they look.

RESEARCH ON GENDER AND YOUTH

Research on how traditional femininity constrains girls is contradictory. Some studies suggest that girls are viewed as less feminine if they participate in sports. Others argue that athleticism is no longer seen as incompatible with femininity and may indeed be part of the "ideal girlhood" package.[4]

In their study of middle-school cheerleaders, Adams and Bettis also point to fundamental contradictions in the contemporary ideal of girlhood. Traditional feminine characteristics like passivity and docility, they argue, have been replaced by independence, assertiveness, and strength, and participation in sports is considered an "essential component of girl culture today."[5] At the same time, when it comes to popularity, attractiveness trumps all other attributes. Cheerleading, in keeping up with changing gender expectations, has incorporated the new ideals of girlhood, including "confidence, rationality, risk-taking, athleticism, independence, and fearlessness."[6] But it continues to attract girls who value feminine looks and who are interested in attracting boys. Becoming a cheerleader is one

way to cope with the contradictions of girlhood because it allows girls to be athletic and adopt some desired masculine traits, while retaining feminine characteristics that the girls enjoy and that make them desirable to boys.[7]

A few studies address how race and class differences among young women affect their standards of femininity. Bettie found class- and race-specific versions of femininity among high-school girls.[8] Lower-class white and nonwhite girls adopted a more sexualized style of femininity than white middle-class girls. Bettie suggested that "las chicas," the Latina girls, adapted a style of femininity that emphasized their ethnicity, preferring darker and more visible makeup and tight-fitting clothes. Working-class white girls also generally wore more makeup than middle-class students. While school officials and middle-class peers commonly interpreted these bodily expressions as evidence of "looser" sexual morals, Bettie found that these girls were less interested in romantic attachments than outsiders supposed, and that their styles of bodily presentation had more to do with incorporating racial and community markers into their gender displays. For example, working-class white girls expressed resistance to middle-class culture by "dressing down" in torn jeans, whereas Mexican-American girls, feeling that their brown skin was already perceived as a "dressed down" appearance, would dress "up" in an effort to deny any link between color and poverty. Bettie also found that although these girls presented a very sexualized version of femininity, they did not want to or expect to lead traditional lives as at-home mothers and wives and they were in favor of gender equality for adults.

Many studies of middle- and high-school girls find strong evidence of pressures to be attractive to boys.[9] Lemish finds that widely different modes of femininity are acceptable among preadolescent girls, as long as the girl is also "pretty." One of the paradoxes of contemporary girlhood is that there are confusing and conflicting messages about what a girl should be like, as well as what type of girl should be (de)valued.

There is very little latitude or tolerance for boys to behave in ways that have been traditionally labeled as girlish. Engaging in any traditionally feminine activity, from dancing well, to knitting, to playing the piano opens boys up to being taunted as "gay." Usually it is boys who tease other boys, but sometimes girls do as well. Researchers suggest that homophobia is not merely antihomosexual prejudice. It also reinforces sharp gender divisions through the deployment of fear. This is seen particularly at the high-school level, but some research suggests it is also evident in elementary school and in middle school.[10] Thorne found that by the fourth grade "fag" is sometimes used as an insult. But Plummer points out that homophobic insults used in grade school do not actually carry sexual meaning.[11] Rather they are used to tease boys who are different, including boys viewed as effeminate. The use of homophobic terms as insults, Plummer maintains, increases with adolescence. Eder and her coauthors discuss homophobic insults among middle-school boys as a ritualistic way to assert masculine dominance, as a way to insult and further isolate the lowest on the peer hierarchy, and as a self-defense mechanism in identifying oneself as heterosexual and normal.[12] Their research illustrates the intense anxiety over peer approval and acceptance, and how that fosters bullying in middle school for both girls and boys, although more so for boys. By middle school, any sign of gender boundary crossing by boys is taken as signifying homosexuality, and elicits strong homophobic teasing.

As boys grow older, the gender expectations appear to become more rigid and regulated. Among high-school youth, masculinity is defined as toughness: a potential if not an inclination for violence, lack of emotion, and sexual objectification of girls. By high school, it is a major insult for a boy to be called gay, and the label may be applied to any boy who is different from his male peers in some way, any boy who is considered feminine or unpopular, any boy who is a target for being bullied. Among

young people, the word "gay" has acquired such a negative connotation that it is commonly used to describe anything that is bad, undesirable, or "lame."[13]

Pascoe (2005) identifies a "fag" discourse through which high-school boys use the term as an epithet on a daily basis. Any boy, she notes, may be temporarily labeled a "faggot," and so all boys continually struggle to avoid being stigmatized. With the possibility of being called a "faggot" only an insult away, constant work is required to be sufficiently masculine to avoid the label. In fact, the primary use of homophobia in policing the activities of boys is not to root out, expose, or punish potential homosexuals, but rather to regulate gender behavior and narrowly channel boys toward accepted activities and away from others.

It is not clear whether or how this use of homophobia to police boys' gender varies according to race. In Pascoe's (2007) study of "fag" discourse among high-school boys in a working-class California school, she found that behaviors that incur a "fag" stigma for white boys, such as attention to fashion, or dancing with another man, are accepted as normal by nonwhite boys. She suggests that the use of homophobic insults is more common among white than nonwhite teenagers.

Froyum studied an underclass African-American summer program in a large East Coast city, however, and found heavy policing of heterosexuality among both boys and girls.[14] She argues that these impoverished urban kids use heterosexuality to carve out some self-esteem from the only stratification in which they can feel superior to someone else, that they take solace in the fact that "at least they aren't gay."

METHODS

The authors and several graduate students interviewed forty-four middle-school students. We asked the children a set of questions, told them stories and solicited their responses, and had them draw pictures and write poems in order to find out what these boys and girls thought about their own lives, their friends, and their interactions with peers at school. We wanted to delve into middle-school students' expectations around gender, to examine how it feels to grow up in a society that proclaims gender equality and encourages "girl power."

We wanted to find out if children today still see limitations based on their sex, or if they really feel they live in a post-feminist world. We asked about family life, friendship, popularity, cliques, pressures to conform to stereotypes around being a boy or a girl, what "girl power" means, and attitudes regarding racial inequality. This was a diverse group of children, mostly white and African-American, and we paid careful attention to whether the answers to our questions differed by race and/or ethnicity.

The interviews took place between the fall of 2003 and the summer of 2004. They typically lasted between one and two hours and were recorded. Respondents were in the sixth, seventh, and eighth grades and ranged in age from eleven to fourteen. The children were recruited at a racially integrated magnet middle school, a diverse YWCA after-school program and summer camp, and an urban, mostly black Girls' Club. All attended public middle schools in a mid-sized city in the southeastern United States. Because we did not get data on many topics of interest from two of the middle schoolers, we reduced our sample to be discussed here to forty-two. Most were middle class, although a few were from working-class or upper middle-class professional families. We paid careful attention to any racial differences in the responses. But having only four nonwhite boys, two of whom were black, hampered our ability to examine racial or ethnic differences among boys. We hoped to learn something about what it is like to grow up in today's world. Interviewers asked the children many questions. How are you similar to other boys/girls? How are you different from other girls/boys? We also asked about likes and dislikes, activities, friendship groups, cliques

at school, and favorite subjects. Many of our questions dealt specifically with the children's perceptions of gender. What does it mean when someone is called a "girly-girl"? What does it mean when a girl is called a tomboy? Is there a word (like "girly" for prissy boys) that refers to boys who are really tough or macho? Is there a word for a boy who is quiet and thoughtful and likes to do arts and crafts, one who likes the kinds of activities that girls more often like to do?

Using a hypothetical scenario to draw them out, we asked students to describe what their lives would be like as the opposite sex. We asked: "If an alien with supernatural powers came into your bedroom one night and turned you into a boy/girl, how would your life be different in the morning?" We also asked: "How would your life be different if an alien made you gay?"

We asked students to write a poem or paragraph beginning with "If I were a boy/girl . . ." If they preferred they could draw a picture elaborating on that theme. We also explored their acceptance of nontraditional gender behavior by using vignettes and asking how they or their peers would react to a person who crossed a gender boundary.

To understand the boundary of female behavior, we used this hypothetical story: "Pretend for a moment that there is a girl in your grade named Jasmine. Jasmine is very athletic and loves competition. She decides that she wants to start an all-girls football club at your school. She places posters all over student lockers and the hallways promoting the girls' club and asking for players. Then she approaches the principal and asks if she can start the team." For male gender nonconformity, we constructed this story: "Imagine that there is a boy in your grade named Marcus. He loves to dance. He has taken gymnastics since he was little, and is very good. Now that he is older, he wants to be a cheerleader. He knows that [Name of University] has male cheerleaders and he wants to join that squad when he goes to college." Students who seemed mature enough were asked about homosexuality, including how they and their peers would react to a gay student.

Due to time constraints, variations in maturity levels, and the occasional tape malfunction, we do not have responses to all of these questions from every student. Although we do have a wealth of information from almost every student to utilize for analysis, with such open-ended qualitative data it is very challenging to compare responses across kids for interpretation.

There were several limitations to the methods we employed. Because we did not directly observe interactions between the middle schoolers, we had to rely on what they told us, and how they explained their thoughts on boys, girls, gender nonconformity, gender expectations, homosexuality, heterosexuality, and life in general. Nonetheless, we believe the method is useful because the thoughts and feelings of these preadolescents help us understand how they experience and react to peer pressure. Moreover, in one-on-one interviews, children and adults may reveal more about their thoughts and feelings than they would if others were present.

CONTRADICTIONS AND EQUALITY RHETORIC

When we asked these students questions about gender or race, their responses indicated that most have assimilated both the feminist-inspired ideology that women and men are equal and the post-civil rights ideology that all races are equal. Nine out of twelve male students and seventeen of twenty-two female students (for whom we have appropriate data) professed some belief in gender equality. For example, Molly finished the phrase "If I were a boy" in a poem that read: "If I were a boy, / Nothing should be different, / Because all people are equal." For the same exercise, another student, Marney, wrote that "I think I would be treated mainly the same by parents, friends, teachers." Brady similarly argued that "all people should be treated the same," although he felt life would be "very freaky" if

he were turned into a girl. Micah told us that girl power means that girls now have every right that men do. The kids appeared to believe that males and females either were equal in reality or ought to be.

Despite this equality rhetoric, there were serious inconsistencies in their responses. For example, when the kids answered questions about what would happen if they were turned into the opposite sex, most expressed a belief that gender stereotypes were based in biology, despite earlier declarations that "we are all the same." With these questions, we found that many kids were well aware of the consequences for not conforming to gender norms.

This contradiction between the rhetoric of equality and more experience-biased appraisals of gender inequality was further revealed when we asked the children to place cards with occupations written on them under the categories "men," "women," and "both." They were first asked to place their cards according to whether men or women are more likely to hold each job, and afterward according to how they think it *should* be. This activity showed us whether students felt there was occupational segregation by sex and how they judged it. None of the boys and only five out of twenty-three girls thought that men and women were equally distributed among all occupations. Six of twelve boys and ten of twenty-two girls told us that all occupations *should* be distributed equally among men and women. The others, who believed gender segregation was appropriate, usually explained that men and women were different. In most cases, when asked how it should be versus how it really is, students put more occupations under the category of "both." Nurse, secretary, and librarian were commonly thought to be women's jobs, whereas police officer, firefighter, mechanic, and engineer were often seen as men's jobs. Sixteen out of thirty-four students expressed the belief that men and women were or should be "equal" and that girls and women should be able to do anything they want.

These children, even those consistently committed to equality in theory, however, often expressed contradictory views in other parts of the interview, displaying a belief in the essential differences between boys and girls or holding their peers to gendered expectations. In many cases, advances in ideology were not consistently guiding reported behavior.

BETWEEN TOMBOY AND GIRLY-GIRL

We asked boys and girls to answer questions about what girly-girls and tomboys are like, how girls think they are similar to and different from other girls, and what boys thought would be different if they were "turned into a girl."

Nearly all the students could describe a typical girly-girl and a tomboy. Many boys and girls alike defined girly-girls as preoccupied with appearances, in contrast to tomboys. One female student, Kay, described girly-girls in these terms: "'Oh my gosh!' totally into stuff like that. Always having their hair, you know, down like that, you know, kind of prissy. Want to wear high-heeled shoes all the time. Laughing and flirting and stuff like that." Marney, who stated that she did not consider herself a girly-girl, responded that "they're afraid to get dirty, you're obsessed with your hair, you like to wear makeup a lot." Kay indicated that girly-girl meant being obsessed with boys or talking about boys. Although this description was less common than references to appearance in characterizing girly-girls, romance-centered behavior (e.g., being "boy-crazy" or obsessed with boys, flirting, talking about boys, or gossiping about relationships) was mentioned by four girls and two boys as characterizing "girly-girls." Several more mentioned such behavior when discussing "typical" girls in general.

Nearly 80 percent of those who responded provided what we interpret as a "negative" description of a girly-girl, and the rest gave neutral responses. Of the nine males, five gave negative descriptions and four gave neutral descriptions of girly-girls. A neutral response, for instance, might refer to girly-girls as wearing pink often, without indicating that wearing a lot of pink is objectionable.

There was not a single overtly positive definition of a girly-girl. No one told us, for instance, that girly-girls are kind, looked up to, or even desirable to boys. We did not count the suggestion that girly-girls are the most popular as being positive in itself, because such comments were often paired with expressions of disdain for the "popular" kids.

Common descriptions of girly-girls included fear of getting dirty, breaking a nail, or getting sweaty. Seven girls and two boys used the word "prissy." Samantha suggested that a girly-girl is "prissy," wears makeup everyday, and is obsessed with hair. She mimics such a person: "'Oh my gosh, it has to be perfect. I have to put hairspray in it.' Glitter, gel, whatever. Like, always running around screaming [high-pitched], 'Oh my God, a spider! Oh my gosh, my nail broke!' Just little things that are like your nail breaking. Crying over it or something. That's a girly-girl."

Girls were, overall, more censorious, but boys sometimes described girly-girls in a similarly contemptuous fashion. With a disgusted expression on his face, Jason told his interviewer that, "To me, it means makeup and a whole lot of other girlie perfumes and . . . lipstick and mascara and eye shadow and other makeup that they put on that I don't even want to mention."

At the same time, when researchers asked explicitly whether "being a girly-girl is a good or bad thing" the kids were divided. Karlin, for example, initially portrayed girly-girls in a contemptuous fashion, saying that they are girls who would say, "'Guys are better. I don't do sports. I might get my shoes wet.' Or like, 'I can't kick a ball. I try to look good but I don't have any specific talent.'" But when asked directly whether being a girly-girl is a bad or good thing, her response was that it depends on the person. If they are selfish, that is bad, but if this is just how they were brought up, then "it's fine."

Several kids indicated that being girly made a girl popular, whereas others (and sometimes even the same respondents) suggested that it was annoying, or that they themselves did not like these people. Mona talked about the "bad preps"—girls who dye their hair blonde, wear too much makeup, wear revealing clothes, and draw their eyebrows in after waxing them. She reported that she and her friends despise this group and frequently make jokes about them. But in other parts of the interview she associated girl preps with playing a lot of sports. Girly-girls were often defined in the abstract as girls who do not play sports, but in actual references to peers, being a girly-girl and playing sports were not always incompatible.

Although students tended to associate girly-girls with being popular and being more feminine, stereotypical girls were subject to substantial ridicule by girls and boys alike in these interviews. None of the female respondents identified themselves to the interviewer as exclusively girly-girl. And all three of the girls who did say they thought of themselves as at least part girly, also described themselves as partly or occasionally tomboyish (and none of these girls considered herself a "typical girl"). This reflects the negative connotations associated with being a girly-girl, which was usually defined contemptuously or with reference to activities and concerns generally seen as narcissistic and trivial (e.g., wearing too much makeup too often, afraid of breaking a nail, excessive shopping).

These disdainful descriptions of what it means to be a girly-girl tell us that too much emphasis on femininity is looked down upon at this age level. No matter where they fell on the girly-girl/tomboy continuum, the girls saw themselves as different from the category of the prototypical feminine girl, who was seen as narcissistic, vain, and silly. They did not want to be identified as that type of girl. But in the process of rejecting this stereotype for themselves, they sometimes conferred it upon others as the prototypical teenage girl.

The girls in our study also felt that girls should display *some* level of femininity, especially when it comes to looks. Several girls, black and white, indicated that being too much of a tomboy could be a bad thing. Karlin, for instance, chastised tomboys who fail to "recognize the fact that they're a girl." According to her, playing sports should not get in the way of "being a girl."

Kerri indicated that it is okay to be girlish if one is athletic as well. She asserted that "there are a lot" of girly-girls, although she did not personally *know* very many:

> Yeah, there are a lot. I don't know a lot of girly-girls. I know I don't mind wearing skirts and I don't mind wearing makeup but I'm not a girly-girl. And I know what a girly-girl is. It's when you're all obsessed with makeup and looking good and I mean all the girls I know play at least two sports and they own makeup, and they're, I mean, my room is blue and pink and yellow but you'd have to look around and see all my soccer pictures and all my basketball trophies. And I mean if you just looked in my room, didn't see any trophies, you'd think I was a really big girly-girl.

At least five kids indicated that being a tomboy was positive in some respects, but no one indicated that tomboys were considered the popular or privileged girls. One female middle schooler suggested a tomboy might have difficulty getting a boyfriend. In the interviews, being a tomboy was associated with being athletic, although girls could be athletic without being seen as a tomboy. It is also noteworthy that only three girls identified themselves as tomboys but not at all girly, although this was more than the number who considered themselves "girly-girls."

Most girls clearly do not place themselves in either of these two extreme categories, although they often suggest that they have characteristics associated with both. These two extremes bracket the entire spectrum of gender meanings for girls, but do not represent the majority of identities. Some girls embraced the label of tomboy (often while simultaneously embracing aspects of bodily femininity) as a strategy to avoid negative associations with being female. For example, one girl told us "we've actually made up, like those ten girls, we've made up the tomboy club because we don't mind competing against the guys for stuff, and we, I mean I actually liked being called a tomboy because then I knew people didn't just look at me as a girl. That they could actually see me as doing something more than being just a ballet dancer."

Most girls do adopt some aspects of traditional femininity. They wear makeup or lip gloss, enjoy shopping for and dressing up in gendered clothes, or like talking about boys. This became apparent in the interviews where girls discussed how they were similar to other girls, what they liked to do, and how they spent their time. It was also apparent in some of the field notes written by interviewers, who noted details about how the students dressed and presented themselves.

The female middle schoolers criticized only extreme forms of this femininity, such as wearing lots of makeup everyday, dressing in too revealing a fashion, worrying about looking good all of the time, and especially having a "girly-girl" identity. Jamie, for example, said she is similar to other girls in that she likes clothes and guys, but says she is not girly like the ones who are "prim" and "afraid to get dirty, to get down and goof around."

When it comes to untangling the gender expectations that these middle schoolers hold and perceive, contradictions abound. In one part of her interview, Lola said that "there's just some traits that all girls have in common. . . . Ability to accessorize [laughs]. Just stuff. You can always tell who's a boy and who's a girl. It's different. Like boys like video games and girls like makeup. . . . Boys are rougher. Girls are more into sitting and talking. And boys are more into going outside and playing Frisbee or something." But she also asserted that girls would love to have their own football team. It is clear that girls perceive pressures both to be identifiably feminine and to take on some traditionally masculine characteristics like assertiveness, fearlessness, rationality, and independence in order to be taken seriously.

While girls face less restrictive norms for gender-appropriate behavior, there still seem to be limitations, especially in regard to ideals of beauty. Girls are still expected to demonstrate a type of femininity, although one that is no longer threatened by participation in traditionally male-dominated activities. Our story about a girl who wants to start a football team elicited a few worries that she might be teased because she did not play well, but there was little concern that Jasmine would be teased for violating norms of femininity. As Malcom pointed out in her study of softball players, girls who play sports run the risk of being seen as or teased for being incompetent as athletes rather than for displaying behavior inappropriate for girls.[15]

The girls in this study felt a girl can ignore many gender boundaries (in fact playing sports is no longer even considered a gender boundary). But in their view, girls are still expected to display some markers of traditional femininity. Put another way, appropriate femininity does not require avoidance of traditionally masculine activities, but it is accomplished through attention to how the girl displays her body. Femininity has become very body-centered and many respondents simply equate femininity with "looks." But it is interesting that even on this dimension, girls tend to look down on and avoid extreme femininity. For example, several girls criticized pop stars for dressing in tight, revealing clothing, although they also saw this as a requirement for celebrity.

We only have very suggestive data in our sample on how gender norms varied by race. But in three interviews, white girls criticized black girls for overly emphasizing the sexualized aspects of femininity—dressing in tight, revealing clothing, wearing inappropriate makeup, and engaging in inappropriate bodily display. Kerri related the following story about a black peer:

> And the girls, we won't really make fun of her but we just "why? Why is she wearing that?" Because like if she combed her hair and put on some makeup and wore pants she'd be very pretty. But

she doesn't. She has to wear the tightest skirts. She never combs her hair. She'll put on makeup but she doesn't put it on right. She'll put on like this dark blue and like gold mascara and she doesn't look right and she's trying, but she's not using the right stuff. So all of us got together one recess and we, not to be mean, but to say okay we could give her a makeover and this one girl, who could really draw. We said okay, we're gonna give her—if we could give her a makeover this is what we'd do. Some girl said okay. I'd pick out all her makeup and I'd tweeze her eyebrows and I'd like shave her legs or something. And one girl said, I'd get her on Slim-Fast. And all this stuff. And like she drew a picture of what she'd look like if we all worked with her and she looked kind of looked a lot like me, but kinda, it looked like all the girls had given a part of themselves to her so that was really fun and we thought if she did all of those things she'd look like that.

We also have suggestive data that African-Americans girls sometimes try to adapt "white" beauty norms. Three black or biracial girls indicated that they wished they had physical traits more often seen in Caucasian women. For example, Joleesa, an African-American sixth grader, wished she had long, soft, smooth hair and blue eyes. We do not have a large enough sample to have strong evidence of racialized femininity, but we do find suggestions that white and black girls value white markers of femininity, and that black girls are criticized by white girls if they exhibit more sexualized forms of femininity.

When boys were asked how they would be different if turned into a girl, several indicated they would act the way girly-girls are described. Four boys thought they would act "girly" in some way. Boys spoke of girls with stereotypical language. Tyrone drew a picture of a woman's makeup table and explained that "I drew a vanity, which is a mirror with bulbs around it, and it usually has makeup and perfume around it, and then I drew a little girl stretching since it's been a long day and she's about to go out to the movies with her friends. . . . I drew the vanity because they like wearing tons of makeup."

By referring to an exaggerated, abstract notion of femininity when asked to imagine themselves as a girl or to describe girls in general, boys are implicitly defining masculinity as the opposite of this girly-girl femininity. Girls as well as boys distance themselves from this feminized, stereotypical "other" when they try to construct valued images of themselves.

POLICING MASCULINITY

Our respondents described preadolescent masculinity in very narrow and uniform ways. The most common response was that boys like sports (sometimes specific sports like football and basketball were emphasized). Other responses included competitiveness, hating losing to a girl, playing video games, general rowdiness, and being different from girls in that girls want to "really impress people and boys want to have their own way." When boys talked about their interests, they commonly emphasized sports, video games, and competing with male friends. But they almost never mentioned "liking" girls, flirting with girls, or talking about girls. It appears that at this age, romantic interests figure prominently among girls, but not among boys.

A boy who is perceived as too feminine is subject to much more ridicule than a girl who is seen as either overly masculine or overly feminine. If a boy tends to be quiet, shy, bookish, artistic, and/or nonassertive, his sexuality is called into question and he loses respect among other boys. We saw this in the way students made sense of our hypothetical story about Marcus, the boy who wants to be a cheerleader. We asked students whether Marcus should be allowed to join a cheerleading squad when he gets to high school, whether he would be teased by others, and whether the student her/himself would remain friends with Marcus, even if he were teased.

Many pointed out that Marcus would be the target of substantial ridicule because not many boys are cheerleaders.[16] In Lorenzo's opinion, "yeah [Marcus should be allowed to join a cheerleading squad], but um, he's probably gonna get made fun of by like a lot of boys." Asked what the boys would say, Lorenzo responded, "Like um, they're like homosexual or something." Krista told us that "people think that a male cheerleader is always gay, and, I mean, people would make fun of him. Or if he does stuff that people only think girls should do." Deirdre replied that the kids would call Marcus a sissy, and the boys especially would "call him gay." She also suggested that even if they had been friends, she would not stay "close friends" with him because "everyone [would be] calling him gay, and if I hang around him, they'd be like, ew you're gay too." Other questions also revealed the middle-schoolers' fear of peer disapproval. For instance, when we asked Samantha if she would still dance if she were turned into a boy, she responded "probably not" because she would be "made fun of."

Deviating from masculine norms inevitably led to teasing, according to student reports. While only two kids suggested that a tomboy might have her heterosexuality questioned, many suggested that a boy who liked girl-type activities would be called gay. Some of the terms the students applied to girlish boys were "wimps," "tomgirls," "weird," "geeks," "weak," and "punk." Because of the stigma associated with being considered feminine in any way, it is not surprising that some girls described themselves as tomboys, but not a single boy described himself in any way as "girly." A few female students, however, indicated that some of the girls would appreciate such a boy, even though other boys would make fun of him. The threat of being stigmatized as "gay" or a "faggot" plays a big part in policing and enforcing masculinity.

POLICING HETEROSEXUALITY

Antigay sentiment is widespread among these youth, although there was a total confusion between sexual preference and gender behavior, which led to very low tolerance for gender

nonconformity among boys. Usually we broached the topic of homosexuality toward the end of the interview and only with those students who seemed relatively mature or comfortable enough with the topic. Typically the researcher asked how the student would respond if a friend revealed to him/her that he or she was gay. They were also usually asked how their own life would change or how they would feel if they woke up one morning and found out they were gay.

In all, thirty-four students answered one or both of these questions (twenty-two girls and twelve boys). Most of these children expressed opposition to homosexuality in general, although white girls were more accepting of homosexuality than others. Most of the boys who discussed homosexuality in any way were clearly homophobic, although one boy seemed unsure and another indicated some acceptance of gays. Jason was adamant that "guys should go with girls and girls should go with guys." "It shouldn't be the same sex . . . that is eeww." Micah thought "it's nasty to be gay." When Dante was asked what would happen if he found out he were gay, he replied, "It would be extremely different and I would hate myself."

None of three nonwhite boys felt comfortable about homosexuality. The two African Americans, Marc and Tyrone, told interviewers that they thought being gay was wrong and "nasty." Lorenzo, a Latino American, did not condemn homosexuality, but neither did he indicate much tolerance for it.

In many instances, a feeling of disgust was cited as a rationale for judging gays, as in Jason's interview. This was especially common among boys, somewhat common among nonwhite girls, and the least common among white girls. Marc said, "I think they would be like, 'Stay away from me, I don't want you doing this and this,' and some people, when they go to the bathroom they would always be looking over their shoulder." Cynthia claimed that teachers might "pay close attention" to a gay student "just to make sure he doesn't do anything nasty around other kids and stuff."

Several of the respondents were horrified at the suggestion of being gay. Jason claimed he would shoot himself if he woke up gay, and Micah said "I would be suicidal. I know that's wrong, but I would." Deirdre responded that if she were gay "I would like girls, which would be nasty." And Kay would be too embarrassed even to go to school. Prejudice by heterosexuals against gays appears to be very much internalized by most of the kids.

A substantial minority, however, expressed tolerant views. Katie felt that people should love who they want to love. When Jack, a seventh grader, was asked what life would be like if he were gay, he said nothing would really be different. He also claimed that he would remain friends with a gay boy, as long as the friend did not "like" him. But even the eleven tolerant youths expressed concern over the reactions of other people, especially peers, toward any indication of homosexuality. The fear of associating with gay peers was quite strong, even among the otherwise tolerant girls, who exhibited some sense of discomfort to the idea of a friend coming out as gay.

This confusion of sexuality and gender stereotypes feeds into the fear boys have about crossing gender boundaries. Responses to the hypothetical scenario about Marcus, the boy who wanted to be a cheerleader in high school, often raised doubts about his sexuality, even though there was absolutely no reference to sexuality in the scenario. All these responses were volunteered by the kids themselves.

Nearly all of the children told the interviewers that Marcus would be teased. Forty-one percent of boys and 43 percent of girls suggested that other students would call Marcus gay, but more girls voiced support for the hypothetical Marcus. None of the respondents believed that Marcus *must* be gay if he wants to be a cheerleader. Rather, responses focused on the idea that he would be called gay and would have to prove his heterosexuality.

There was a widely held conviction that Marcus' peers would verbally abuse him. Jason admitted he would directly taunt Marcus: "I'd

go up to his face and say, 'You are a little fruitcake, do you know that?'" But most students seemed to want to protect Marcus from taunts and bullying, especially from *other boys*. Ten girls and three boys who discussed Marcus getting teased mentioned boys as the primary teasers. Some students recommended that Marcus should "keep it hush-hush" or even reconsider his decision, because of the negative peer reaction it would invite. Jack said "if I were him I would choose not to say anything about it or else everyone would make fun of me."

Most students acknowledged that if a boy wants to be a cheerleader in high school it does not necessarily mean he is gay, but 40 percent suggested their peers would operate on such an assumption. A few students thought that Marcus might not face much disapproval—that it would not be a big deal. But most kids told us that their peers severely tease male gender nonconformity. No one policed girls' sports behavior by insinuating girl athletes must be gay.

HOMOPHOBIC TAUNTS AND ENFORCEMENT OF MASCULINITY

The Marcus scenario was not the only part of the interview that brought out the *gender nonconformity = gay* assumption for boys. When we asked students to give us a word to describe boys who are shy, quiet, maybe artistic or creative, and who like activities that girls usually do, four students asserted that such a boy is or would be called gay or some variant thereof. Jeffrey, for example, volunteered that there is no word for boys who act like girls, the way tomboy describes girls who act like boys, but he has heard such boys called "fruit." When we asked Marshall for a term to describe boys who like to do the kinds of activities girls usually do, he responded that "a lot of people call 'em gay." Similarly, without hesitation Deidre gave us the word "fag." Other responses to this particular question indicated that such a boy would be teased in some way, even if he were not called gay.

Just as kids interpret boys' gender nonconformity as evidence of homosexuality, the flip side is that they also consistently associate homosexuality with gender nonconformity. Middle-school students assume that someone who is gay will violate gender norms. One male student told us that if he were gay, he would no longer like sports. In general, the kids assumed that gay males are more feminine than straight members of their sex. Jeffrey thought that if he were gay he "might like to hang around with girls a little more. Not like flirting, but acting like a girl or around girls."

Such presumptions lend legitimacy to the regulation of male gender nonconformity through antigay remarks. The stigmatizing of Marcus was in sharp contrast to responses to the hypothetical scenario about Jasmine, the girl who wanted to start a girls' football club. None of the students suggested that Jasmine's sexuality would be suspect, although a few suggested she might be teased or thought "weird" by other students. It seems that gender nonconformity is less policed among girls than boys, and is much less likely to be presumed as a marker of sexuality for girls.

Kids fear being labeled gay by their peers, which makes this a powerful tool for policing gender. In general, when the kids were asked "what if you found out you were gay?," their first response was to discuss the reaction of their peers, rather than their parents or family members, providing further evidence that, for preadolescents, peers form a critical reference group. In fact, eighteen of twenty-one girls referred to peer disapproval when responding to hypothetical questions about being gay themselves or having a gay friend. Seven of nine boys did the same. Boys and girls consistently suggested that their peers would react negatively to them if they came out as gay. In several cases, respondents acknowledged that they might react negatively or would apply some type of sanction to a gay student.

Being called gay is evidently the worst insult and the most effective way to shame another student. When Cynthia spoke of a male friend of hers who is frequently bullied, she claimed that "most of the time he ignores it but if somebody ends up calling him 'gay' or something, he takes it really bad." Interestingly, Cynthia and others do not consider this friend to be particularly feminine, although they describe him as "scrawny" and "short." Rather, she believes that he is called gay because it is a dependable way for his attackers to insult him.

Branding nonconformists as gay in this middle-school context constitutes a primary form of regulation as well as harassment. When a boy is labeled as gay, it is not necessarily about his sexuality, but it is rather a surefire way to insult him. The gay stigma is not primarily used to tease someone as homosexual, but to deprive a boy of the status that comes with masculinity.[17]

Paradoxically, we have some very suggestive evidence that if a person actually does embrace a gay identity, he or she is freer to cross gender boundaries and to enjoy activities usually limited to the other sex. Mallory and several of the other children told us that a male gay student they knew was taunted by peers for a while, but the bullying leveled off substantially with time. Jamie told us that she has a gay female friend who had some problems with other students, "but people kind of just got over it, and said, 'hey, so what?'" Jamie claimed that other people were initially standoffish with her gay female friend, but they forgot about it by the next year.

In some cases, when discussing other students who are openly gay or lesbian, a student would claim that the teasing was not that bad. Cynthia said that her gay male friend is called names by "like two or three" of the girls in her class, but the boys do not really make fun of him. She thought that is because although he's told all the girls, he probably has not told the boys. When asked if the boys would make fun of him if they knew, she replied: "No, I think he has told them but they probably really don't consider it something big."

In response to the story about Marcus the cheerleader, Mallory described her gay friend, Jo, as an exception to the gender rules. She said, "Now, I know for a fact that [Marcus would] be made fun of for that. Except Jo. Everybody knows Jo's going to do something like that, so nobody really cares if Jo did something like that. But if that boy is not Jo, he will probably get made fun of." When asked why people do not make fun of Jo, Mallory explained that he's friends with half of the seventh grade, even though there are *some* people who "hate him." Jo, as openly gay, seems accepted by most of his peers. Mallory indicated that Jo enjoys some girl-typed activities like dancing, but it is accepted because he is gay.

It is not possible to conclude from our data that openly gay students are not harassed precisely in ways similar to male gender nonconformists, but further research would do well to investigate the possibility. It is notable that all three examples of exempting gays and lesbians from sustained harassment in this study related to a specific person that the respondent knew, whereas most of the respondents who thought a gay person would be subject to significant harassment were dealing with an imaginary scenario. Since stereotypes about gay people being gender nonconformist were common among our respondents, it makes sense that gay peers are not harassed for gender nonconformity in the same ways that heterosexuals are. Openly gay kids, having already acknowledged they are gay, face different challenges than their peers who are anxious to avoid the taunt of being a "faggot" or gay.

The data clearly show that most middle-school children in our sample still hold stereotypical views about gay people. For boys, no distinction is made between same-sex attraction and gender nonconformity. The children expect that boys who break gender norms will be teased and called gay. But the children in this study are quite diverse in their own opinions and many feel that although harassment would occur, it should not.

DISCUSSION AND CONCLUSION: FEMININITY ON THE BODY, MASCULINITY AS THE BOY

Our findings confirm other studies about the narrow confines in which boys need to stay in order to avoid being teased by peers. What is perhaps more unexpected in our findings is that girls are now stigmatized for displaying some of the traditional markers of femininity. Girls look down on peers who are ultra-feminine, "wimpy," and afraid to get dirty or be competitive. The responses from girls in this study suggest that the way girls now "do gender" is restricted to "looks" and the body.

Girls have come to expect and take advantage of access to traditionally masculine arenas such as sports, and they display heightened expectations of academic success in all subjects, and are willing to compete with boys in those arenas. None of the girls discussed personally shying away from competition with boys, or worrying about their popularity if they did well in school, and no mention at all was made of fear of math and science. Girls in this study took for granted that they can be involved in different sports, and they rarely mentioned any constraints in their academic pursuits or their career plans.

The girls consistently expressed disdain for exaggerated notions of femininity and looked down on other girls who were seen as too passive, too prissy, or too vain. Girls who are good at sports and still exhibit a feminine bodily presentation are looked upon with favor. The traditional aspects of girlhood most related to subordination to boys are no longer revered or even accepted aspects of femininity. In a world where most mothers work for pay and all the girls expect to do so themselves, it makes sense that they've adopted the means to develop strong bodies and competitive minds.

In our view, the new concept "undoing gender" offered recently by Deutsch is the best framework for understanding contemporary girlhood.[18] These girls do not "do gender" the way generations before them did. They compete with other girls on the field and with boys in the classroom. They get dirty, and they expect to be taken seriously by teachers, parents, and boys.

While these girls have begun to "undo gender" as we knew it, they have not undone it completely. Their focus on femininity seems to have narrowed to concern and attention, even if sporadic, to their looks. For most girls, being feminine means wearing nice clothes, applying lip gloss, and paying attention to hairstyles. While girls are allowed, and perhaps even encouraged, to "undo gender" in how they behave, they still face pressures to be attractive, to be good looking.

But the norms are contradictory. Most girls we questioned believe they should do gender with their body display. But if they concentrate too much on this aspect, they risk being looked down upon as overly feminine. They want to be seen as feminine, but not too much so.

On the other hand, boys gain no social approval by deviating from traditional definitions of masculinity. Any behavior remotely stereotyped as feminine is intensely policed by other boys and some girls. Being stigmatized as "gay" is the primary way masculinity is policed and enforced because it is a potent insult among young males. Being gay and being masculine are seen as contradictory, just as femininity and masculinity traditionally have been. The gay stigma among middle schoolers is really about deviating from gender expectations rather than about homosexuality, although it may draw upon insecurities about sexuality. It is a way of enforcing masculinity. When boys live up to those expectations, they not only establish themselves as masculine, but they also assert their superiority to girls. Boys who hesitate to participate in homophobic or gender policing activities open themselves up to teasing.

Despite the great success in boosting acceptance of gender equality and women's rights, the peer culture of these tween-agers remains incredibly resistant to any changes in defining masculinity for boys. While middle-school girls now are free to sometimes act like boys, as long as they make an effort, at least occasionally, to look feminine, the fear of being called "gay" quite effectively polices boys' gender behavior. Boys' lives seem hardly influenced by any feminist transformation except that they must now compete with girls as well as with each other, at least in the classroom.

For both girls and boys the truly feminine is looked down upon. For boys, this means that to be respected by other boys they must make continual efforts to act in masculine ways. Girls walk a different tightrope. They are strongly pressured to "do gender" with their bodies, although not so much so as to be seen as too girly. But they are free to cross gender borders in the other aspects of their lives.

Boys now have to compete with girls in nearly every realm of life, and they can no longer take for granted that because they are boys they are smarter or superior in any way to the girls they know. And yet their fear of teasing leaves boys more constrained by gender stereotypes than are girls. Perhaps the exaggerated gender difference is the last remnant of male privilege left to this generation of boys.

Boys need a "feminist revolution" of their own.

■ Review Questions

1. For which gender has the experiences of middle school changed more: girls or boys?
2. How do boys police the boundaries of acceptable male behavior?

ENDNOTES

1. Researchers have looked at how multicultural education works (Talbani, 2003), as well as how education and other cultural beliefs reinforce white privilege (Wellman, 1993).
2. Eder, Evans, and Parker (1995) examined the role of gender in the language and socialization of a group of eighth graders.
3. "Doing gender" unlinks biological sex from gender by describing gender not as the traits of a person, but as the embedded social actions that a person takes to express socially accepted gender (West and Zimmerman, 1987).
4. Allison (1991), Cockburn and Clarke (2002), and Krane et al. (2004) discuss female athletes and the challenge of athletics to femininity, while Broad (2001) examines queer athletes. Malcom (2003), Adams, Schmitke, and Franklin (2005), and Enke (2005), on the other hand, discuss the remaking of femininity to include athletics. Adams, Schmitke, and Franklin (2005) find that girls enjoy athleticism and take pride in being tough and competitive.
5. Adams and Bettis (2003), pp. 74–75.
6. Ibid., p. 80.
7. This comes from Adams and Bettis' (2003) study on cheerleading.
8. Bettie (2003).
9. For an more on peer groups and cliques, both Eder, Evans, and Parker (1995) and Adler and Adler (1998) explore adolescent culture. Cockburn and Clarke (2002), Adams and Bettis (2003), and Adams, Schmitke and Franklin (2005) all examine these pressures to be attractive to boys in the context of female athletes. See also Lemish (1998) on modes of femininity and attractiveness.
10. Eder, Evans, and Parker (1995) map the gendered dynamics of teasing. Several researchers examine how this teasing functions to control boys through fear (Kehily and Nayak, 1997; Burn, 2000; Plummer, 2001; Phoenix, Frosh, and Pattman, 2003; Chambers, Tincknell, and Van Loon, 2004), including Pascoe's (2005) "Dude, You're a Fag." Thorne (1993) and Plummer (2001) describe this behavior in elementary school, and Eder, Evans, and Parker (1995), Adler and Adler (1998), and Phoenix, Frosh, and Pattman (2003) discuss it in middle school.
11. See Plummer (2001).
12. See Eder, Evans, and Parker (1995).
13. Pascoe (2003, 2007) and Phoenix, Frosh, and Pattman (2003) have written about masculinity and toughness, while Plummer (2001) and Pascoe (2005, 2007) write about teasing.
14. Froyum (2007).
15. Malcom (2003).
16. This gender-specific cheerleading is very region-specific. In some schools on the West Coat, cheerleading squads are either all-male or mixed sex. As cheerleading has become more athletically demanding, more boys are often included to lift and throw the girls.
17. For more on this, read Kehily and Nayak (1997), Plummer (2001), Pascoe (2003, 2005, 2007) and Phoenix, Frosh, and Pattman (2003).
18. See Deutsch (2007) for a description of the concept of "undoing gender." For an example of "undoing gender," in Gerson's (2002) article, she describes the process of young men an women choosing lives that are distinct from traditional gendered expectations.

CHAPTER 4

Social Class and Family Inequality

The globalization of the world economy has hit blue-collar workers especially hard. Corporations have moved production overseas in order to take advantage of the lower wages paid to workers in the developing world. Computers and other technologies have allowed employers to replace some workers with machines, such as the robots on automobile assembly lines. Consequently, adults without college educations have found it harder to obtain jobs with adequate wages.

These reduced prospects have hurt families in two ways. First, young men who are unemployed, or who are employed but earn low wages, are often reluctant to marry because they don't think that they earn enough to help support a family. Second, the marriages that do exist face more strain because of inadequate incomes. Most generations of Americans have expected to do better economically than their parents' generation. Now, a significant number of working-class families find that those expectations are not being met.

In a 2009 book on the growing instability of American family life, *The Marriage-Go-Round: The State of Marriage and the Family in America Today,* I wrote about the economic and cultural factors influencing young adults as they start families. And I included a chapter, excerpted here, that focuses on the differences between the college-educated and the less-educated. The family lives of the former group look rather traditional: Although they may live with a partner outside of marriage for a time, most of them marry, and nine out of ten wait until after they are married to have children. But among young Americans without college degrees, family formation is different. They will often go ahead and have children within cohabiting unions that have a high likelihood of breaking up. Marriage comes later, if at all. The differences in family life according to education are striking—and growing, as this reading shows.

But social class differences encompass more than income, education, and occupation. These differences may be at once more subtle and more profound. Starting with the work of Melvin Kohn and his colleagues,[1] sociologists have noted that middle-class parents tend to

---

[1] M. L. Kohn, *Class and Conformity: A Study in Values* (Homewood, IL: Dorsey Press, 1969).

raise their children in ways somewhat different from working-class parents. In general, middle-class parents act in ways that encourage autonomy and independence, whereas working-class parents more often encourage conformity and obedience to authority. Not all parents fit this pattern, of course; there is substantial variation within social classes. Moreover, as the twentieth century progressed, parents in all social classes moved toward emphasizing independence.[2]

In the second selection in this chapter, Annette Lareau reports on a study of class differences in how parents act toward their children. Her findings are consistent with the earlier research, but she provides more detail about how the daily lives of children differ across classes. She points to factors such as whether parents heavily structure their children's daily lives, how frequently parents engage them in conversation, and to what extent parents involve them with relatives versus school friends. Lareau claims that middle-class parents tend to follow a particular style she calls "concerted cultivation," whereas working-class and lower-class parents have a style she calls "the accomplishment of natural growth." These styles can influence how children (and parents) interact with teachers, doctors, and other professionals. Although Lareau studied black families and white families, she found that class seemed to matter more than race. In fact, she frames the article around the differences between the upbringing of two 10-year-old black boys, one middle class and the other poor.

---

[2]D. F. Alwin, "From Obedience to Autonomy: Changes in Traits Desired in Children, 1924–1978," *Public Opinion Quarterly* 52 (1988), pp. 33–52.

Blue-Collar Blues/White-Collar Weddings

Andrew J. Cherlin

Social inequality—the differences in standard of living and economic opportunity—is more pronounced in the United States than in other Western countries. The gap between high-income and low-income families is wider. Most other Western governments tax the wealthy more and provide more assistance to low- and moderate-income families. This is a major difference between the United States and other countries, and it matters for family life. Low- and moderate-income families in the United States have less protection against the vagaries of the labor market. And it is among low- and moderate-income Americans that we have seen the greatest increase in the number of people who have multiple partnerships.

We need to look carefully, then, at the economic shock waves that have washed over American workers during the past several decades and at their likely connections to changes in family life. The main story line is as follows: During the past half century, the globalization of production (the movement of jobs overseas) and the automation of production (the use of machines and computers to perform jobs humans used to do) have jointly hit Americans without college educations hard. Their family lives appear to have changed as a result: they are more likely to live with partners without marrying them, to have their partnerships and marriages break up, and to have children outside of marriage. At the other end of the social spectrum, college-educated Americans have, by and large, benefited from globalization and automation, and their family

lives have not changed as much. They show the same trends but in moderation. The result has been a growing social class divide in family patterns. Although other Western nations have also experienced these economic tremors, the effects on families are greater here because low- and moderate-income families have less protection against the winds of economic change.

The forces of globalization and automation can seem obscure, but it is possible to see them plainly at work. For instance, as I was writing a draft of this chapter in Miami, on leave from Johns Hopkins, I saw a huge freighter with "China Shipping Lines" painted on its hull motoring slowly toward the harbor with hundreds of trailer-truck-size containers stacked on its broad-beamed deck. In 2005 the port of Miami imported 155,664 tons of alcoholic beverages, 138,105 tons of clothing and textiles, 126,403 tons of refrigerated fruits and vegetables, 76,021 tons of nonalcoholic beverages, 62,682 tons of lumber and wood, 62,556 tons of furniture and other wood products, 57,459 tons of iron, steel, and other metal products, and 42,304 tons of paper.[1] A half century ago, most of these goods would have been brewed, woven, sewn, grown, harvested, milled, built, or processed in the United States. The factories and farms that used to make these goods employed millions of American workers, most of whom did not have college degrees.

Some of the steel used to be milled at the giant Sparrows Point plant a half hour's drive from my Baltimore home.[2] In the 1950s Bethlehem Steel, the owner of the plant, employed thirty thousand workers. Very few of them had gone to college. Yet with hard work they were able to earn decent wages—not enough to make them rich but enough to buy a home, perhaps with help from a Veterans Administration loan, and to marry, have children, and buy a car and the latest home appliances. They were blue-collar aristocrats, like the hundreds of thousands of workers on the assembly lines at Ford and General Motors who enjoyed comfortable if modest standards of living. The 1950s were a time when a young man could graduate from high school confident that he could find a job. (Young women in the 1950s worked part-time, if at all.) If he was fortunate enough to work at a company such as Bethlehem Steel or GM, he would get health insurance, sick leave, a pension plan, and paid vacations as well. A married couple could raise a family on that. But starting in the 1960s, jobs such as these began to move overseas. Today, fewer than 2,500 people are employed at Sparrows Point. New technologies enabled entrepreneurs in other countries to build smaller, more efficient plants that made dinosaurs of Sparrows Point and the mile-long line of blast furnaces along the Allegheny River in Pittsburgh. In 2004 the United States imported thirty-six million tons of steel but exported only eight million tons. In 2007 Toyota surpassed GM as the largest motor vehicle manufacturer in the world. The blue-collar aristocrats are gone.

Advances in communications and transportation now allow firms to bypass American workers in ways you never would expect. Suppose you order a new battery for your laptop online from an American computer company. Your order may be sent immediately to a computer in a warehouse in China, which will display the part number on its screen and print a shipping label. A shelf clerk will find the right part and box it. Hours later, the day's orders will be driven to an airport, where a jet from a delivery service such as Federal Express will be waiting to fly your battery to the United States. Two days after you placed your order, it will appear at your doorstep with an American return address. You are none the wiser.[3] . . .

In addition, computer-based automation and communication have reduced the number of what economists call routine jobs—those that require some skill but not a college education. Think of bookkeepers, secretaries, call center workers. These are the kinds of jobs that someone with a high school degree could do. Since about 1990 these routine jobs have been disappearing so fast that the wages of Americans who

perform them have been edging closer to the wages of the least-educated workers, who hold manual jobs such as waiters, janitors, and gardeners.[4] Manual jobs, which serve the personal needs of others, can't be automated easily; your basic professional still needs people to take his lunch order, clean his office, and cut his lawn. But manual jobs don't pay well. Put another way, the middle is dropping out of the American labor market. People with college degrees can usually find well-paying professional or managerial jobs (computer programmers, business executives), but what's left for everyone else is a dwindling demand for routine work and a steady demand for low-paying manual work. This is the twenty-first-century economic reality that young adults must contend with as they try to establish their own family lives.

PATHWAYS TO ADULTHOOD

Caught in the disappearing middle of the American economy are people who ended their education after getting their high school degrees, or perhaps took some college courses but never obtained a college degree. The wages of men without college degrees have fallen since they peaked in the early 1970s, and the wages of women without college degrees have failed to grow.[5] In fact, high school-educated young men today may be the first generation in memory to earn less than their fathers did. By 1996, the average thirty-year-old husband with a high school degree earned 20 percent less than a comparable man in 1979.[6]

Although young men are no longer expected to be the sole earners for their families, they still are expected to be the main earners. If they don't have steady jobs with decent pay, they simply aren't attractive marriage partners. A young woman might live with such a man, but she would be reluctant to marry him. In a Toledo study of young adults, most of whom did not have college degrees, about three times as many women as men said that their cohabiting partners needed to do better in the job market before they would consider marrying them. Men felt this pressure. The authors write:

> For example, Henry, a 33-year-old information systems manager, reflects: "Had I been . . . in a financial position where I was able to take care of myself and a family, then it might have moved things along quicker." Jamal, 27 years old, says, "What would make me ready? Knowing that I could provide. . . ." Victor, a 27-year-old male, states that "the male's financially responsible for like, you know, the household, paying the bills."[7]

Increasingly, young adults who feel these financial worries are cohabiting rather than marrying. Young men who are out of school and working, but whose incomes are unstable— maybe they're working part-time or at a series of short-term jobs—are more likely to start a cohabiting relationship than are either men with steady, full-time earnings or men with little or no earnings.[8] Living together seems to be emerging as the lifestyle choice for couples in which the men are doing well enough that they can envision marrying someday but not so well that they feel they can marry now. If the jobs were still there, they might be milling steel at Sparrows Point. . . . An unemployed twenty-nine-year-old man who was living with his girlfriend said, regarding what he needed to marry her, "I don't really know 'cause the love is there . . . trust is there. Everything's there except the money." A roofer said, "We feel when we get financially, you know what I'm saying, stable, then we will be ready." A woman who ended her cohabiting relationship without marrying explained what the issue was: "Money means, um . . . stability. I don't want to struggle; if I'm in a partnership, then there's no more struggling, and income-wise we were still both struggling."[9]

Moreover, because they live in an era when the stigma of childbearing outside of marriage has faded, some of these cohabiting couples are willing to have children together even though they're not willing to marry. Since about 1990,

almost all the growth in the percentage of children born to unmarried women has, in reality, been to women who are in cohabiting relationships. Currently, about one out of six American children are now being born to cohabiting couples.[10] Few observers seem to have noticed this development, probably because it is invisible to government agencies (who treat cohabiting mothers as if they were lone mothers).

Many cohabiting couples, it must be said, are capable of doing a very good job of raising children. In parts of Europe, such as Scandinavia and France, there are many long-term cohabiting parents who maintain families that are little different from lasting marriages. But that's unusual in the United States, where cohabiting relationships are fragile and break up more often than marriages. As a result, children born to parents who are cohabiting face a far higher likelihood that their parents will separate than children born to married parents: more than half of those born to cohabiting parents will see their parents separate by the time they are nine, compared to 25 percent of those born to married parents.[11] Only a minority of cohabiting relationships last long enough to provide a child with a stable home environment until adolescence. Moreover, when a cohabiting relationship breaks up, the former partners tend to form new relationships within a few years, some of which, in turn, do not last very long. Starting in a cohabiting relationship, consequently, increases the chances that young parents will eventually have two or three partnerships.

Among young adults who did not complete high school, one-third who give birth are lone parents. (Another third are cohabiting.) Given the low wages for the jobs available to young people without college educations, fewer of them see the possibility of marriage happening anytime soon. Few among them have faith that if they were to wait to have children, the future would unfold according to the conventional script—that staying in school until high school graduation or taking some college courses would pay off, that good jobs could be found, and that many years into the future they would find suitable spouses. They look at their neighborhoods and social networks and see few signs that following the conventional path of marriage and then childbearing works. Nor do they think that a woman needs to be married to have a child. That's clear from the attitudes of low-income women in Boston, Chicago, and San Antonio whom I and other researchers studied.[12] Seventy-nine percent agreed with the statement "A woman should have children if she wants to, even if she is not married." And 71 percent agreed that "a woman does not need to be married before having a child."

What many of the least educated do instead is follow a different path. With good jobs in short supply, what comes to the fore is their desire to have children. I don't think the poor have a greater absolute desire to have children than the affluent, but relative to the other major rewards adult life holds—meaningful and well-paying jobs, a fulfilling and long-lasting marriage—raising children is the reward they know they can get. So it becomes the reward that they are unwilling to postpone.

In their study of women in low-income neighborhoods in the Philadelphia area, Kathryn Edin and Maria Kefalas wrote:

> Unlike their wealthier sisters, who have the chance to go to college and embark on careers—attractive possibilities that provide strong motivation to put off having children—poor young women grab eagerly at the surest source of accomplishment within their reach: becoming a mother.

It's not the case that all young unmarried women who have children deliberately plan their births. Without doubt, many pregnancies are completely unplanned. But some young women in sexual relationships are not taking any action to prevent pregnancy. Having a child is an outcome they are ambivalent about. Perhaps they don't want it to happen immediately, but they want it to happen soon. Nearly half the mothers in [one] study said their pregnancies were

neither fully planned nor fully unplanned, but rather somewhere in between.[13]

Women in low-income neighborhoods perceive little cost to this strategy. For instance, they don't think having children early will hurt their chances of marrying later and they don't think it's embarrassing.[14] These opinions reflect a cultural sea change since the mid-twentieth century, when having what was called an "illegitimate" child was shameful. Moreover, 44 percent in our study agreed that "it is not important for a woman to get married," a statement that would have seemed ludicrous to most poor women, as well as to affluent women, several decades ago. The set of circumstances many less-educated women see today makes postponing childbearing until marriage seem risky. Marriage is still valued symbolically—it is still a status that one very much wishes to attain someday. But you don't have to wait to have children until you attain it.

Among the college-educated, the picture is different. They are the winners in our globalized and automated economy. . . . Their skills—their ability to do analytic, abstract tasks such as designing new products or coordinating the activities of work groups—are in demand, and their earnings are growing faster than the earnings of people with less education. For them, the conventional life course still seems to provide its promised rewards. Most are able to find spouses first and to have children afterward, often several years after they marry. Their investments in education by and large yield successful careers—sometimes, for women, after a period of withdrawing from the paid workforce to raise young children. Marriage still retains practical advantages for them, in addition to its symbolic value. Marriage offers more protection than cohabitation to a woman who has concentrated on raising children, because if the couple breaks up, the wife can use the divorce laws to ask the court for a fair distribution of assets and income. Also, the higher level of enforceable trust in marriages (the lesser likelihood that either spouse will back out) reduces the risk of making long-term purchases together, such as houses, which require large outlays of cash and recoup their value only after many years of use.

Over the past few decades, the family lives of the college-educated have changed much less than among the people with less education. Consider the percentage of women who become lone mothers at some point during their mid-twenties to mid-thirties. It has doubled since 1965 for women with low to moderate levels of education. But it hardly changed among the well-educated: no change for well-educated white women since 1965 and no change since 1980 for well-educated African American women.[15] What we are seeing is the emergence of two different ways of shooting the rapids of the transition to adulthood—the process of completing one's education, developing a career, having children, and finding a lasting, intimate partnership. Among the college-educated, we see a more orderly, predictable sequence of events, one that has fewer changes of partners. They typically finish college first and then take jobs. They may work for several years, investing in their careers, before they marry; the more education a woman has, the older she tends to be when she marries.[16] They may live with a partner before marrying—nearly half of college-educated women under forty-five have been in a cohabiting relationship. But they don't have their first child until after they marry: nine out of ten college-educated women who give birth are married. It's waiting until they are married to have children that most distinguishes the transition to adulthood for the college-educated.[17]

The sequence employed by the college-educated offers benefits: time to finish an advanced degree and start a career, a second parent to help raise the children, and a greater accumulation of assets before the children arrive. But it requires postponing childbearing into the mid- to late twenties, thirties, or even early forties. It is not an attractive strategy for people who have few assets and who do not see many successful models of marriage around them. The strategy

that many young adults in the bottom third of the educational distribution, and some in the middle third, use is to have children earlier, sometimes in a cohabiting relationship, sometimes as a lone parent. Among high school-educated women, only six out of ten wait until after marriage to have their first child; among high school dropouts, only three or four out of ten wait.[18] This path to adulthood is more disorderly. They may live with a partner while taking courses at a community college or at a technical school; they may have a child while still in school; they may have children with more than one partner; and they may not marry until five, ten, or fifteen years after they start to have children, if they marry at all.

Under current circumstances, then, the college-educated top third of the educational distribution, a group sometimes labeled the "middle class" or "upper middle class," tends to follow the conventional strategy in which you have children after marrying. In contrast, those who haven't completed high school tend to have children as lone parents or in cohabiting unions. Those who stopped their schooling after graduating from high school or who took a few college courses seem to be forging a middle ground, in which childbearing occurs in a mixture of settings. These young adults in the middle, neither poor nor prosperous, are developing family patterns that fit neither the image of the low-income mother living with her own mother and other kin nor the image of the married couple who postpone childbearing until every other step in the transition to adulthood has been completed.

The marriages that do form among the less-educated are precarious. Over the past two or three decades, the divorce rate has fallen for women with college educations while remaining steady or rising for women without college degrees. As a result, large differences now exist in the risk of divorce. According to one estimate, 34 percent of the first marriages of women without high school degrees will end in divorce or separation within five years—a very high breakup rate for just five years of marriage. The breakup rates are still substantial for the marriages of people in the middle: 23 percent for those who ended their education after high school, and 26 percent for those who took some college courses but don't have a degree. Among women with college degrees, on the other hand, just 13 percent will end in divorce or separation within five years. Marriages are much more stable among the college-educated than among the less-educated.[19]

The tensions in the marriages of the non-college-educated reflect, in part, the declining job prospects that husbands face. A woman who had a job as a hotel desk clerk told Lillian B. Rubin six months after her husband lost his job as a welder:

> We did okay for a while, but the longer it lasts, the harder it gets. . . . I tell him maybe he has to get in a different line of work because maybe they don't need so many welders anymore. But he just gets mad and tells me I don't know what I'm talking about.[20]

Her husband later told Rubin:

> I can't go out and get one of those damn flunky jobs like my wife wants me to. I've been working all my life, making a decent living, too, and I got pride in what I do. I try to tell her, but she doesn't listen.

In fact, working-class couples, where the husband had a blue-collar job and both spouses had a high school degree but no college degree, reported the most stressed, least happy marriages of any group in a recent national survey—worse than disadvantaged couples and much worse than middle-class couples. The working-class wives said they had taken jobs because the families needed the money, not to develop careers, and many of them wanted to work fewer hours or not at all.[21] Many thought that the amount of housework and child care they did was unfair compared to how much their husbands did. Husbands, for their part, complained that their wives came home from work irritable and tense and that their jobs interfered with the life of the family. Both wives and husbands were more likely to say that they had problems in their marriage because one of them got angry easily, was critical or moody, or wouldn't talk to the other one. They were also more likely to say that the thought of getting a divorce or separation had crossed their minds or that they had discussed the idea with family members or close friends.

Review Questions

1. What has happened to the routine jobs that make up the middle of the labor market?
2. Whose family lives have changed more during the past few decades, the college educated or the least educated?

ENDNOTES

1. Statistics retrieved December 13, 2005, from http://www.miamidade.gov/portofmiami/port_statistics.asp.
2. Reutter 2001; Connelly 2007. On steel imports and exports, see U.S. Bureau of the Census 2007, Table 997. On the demand for computer specialists, see U.S. Bureau of Labor 2007. On motor vehicle sales, see Bradsher 2007. See also LeMasters 1975.
3. This sequence of events is described in Fallows 2007.
4. Autor et al. 2006.
5. Ellwood and Jencks 2004; Richer et al. 2003.
6. Levy 1998.
7. Smock et al. 2005.
8. Oppenheimer 2003.
9. Smock et al. 2005, p. 687.
10. Official government statistics show only that in the 2000s a little over a third of all children were born to unmarried mothers. But the U.S. government's statistical agencies don't differentiate between unmarried mothers who are cohabiting and those who are truly living without partners.

Other surveys show that by the early 2000s, about half of the unmarried women who gave birth were cohabiting.

11. Kennedy and Bumpass 2007.
12. Cherlin et al. 2008.
13. Edin and Kefalas 2005, p. 46.
14. Women in low-income neighborhoods perceive little cost: Just 20 percent of the women in our three-city study agreed with the statement "Having children when a woman is single hurts her chances

of later getting married," and just 19 percent agreed that "having a child without being married is embarrassing for a woman." Cherlin et al. 2008.
15. Ellwood and Jencks 2004.
16. They may work for several years: Martin 2004.
17. Kennedy and Bumpass 2007.
18. Kennedy and Bumpass 2007.
19. Martin 2006; Raley and Bumpass 2003.
20. Rubin 1994, pp. 121–22.
21. Amato et al. 2007.

READING 4-2

Invisible Inequality

Social Class and Childrearing in Black Families and White Families

Annette Lareau

In recent decades, sociological knowledge about inequality in family life has increased dramatically. Yet, debate persists, especially about the transmission of class advantages to children. Kingston (2000) and others question whether disparate aspects of family life cohere in meaningful patterns. Pointing to a "thin evidentiary base" for claims of social class differences in the interior of family life, Kingston also asserts that "class distinguishes neither distinctive parenting styles nor distinctive involvement of kids" in specific behaviors (p. 134). . . .

[In this reading] I draw on findings from a small, intensive data set collected using ethnographic methods. I map the connections between parents' resources and their children's daily lives. My first goal, then, is to challenge

Annette Lareau, "Invisible Inequality: Social Class and Childrearing in Black Families and White Families," *American Sociological Review,* 2002, Vol. 67 (October). Reprinted with permission from the American Sociological Association and the author.

Kingston's (2000) argument that social class does not distinguish parents' behavior or children's daily lives. I seek to show empirically that social class does indeed create distinctive parenting styles. I demonstrate that parents differ by class in the ways they define their own roles in their children's lives as well as in how they perceive the nature of childhood. The middle-class parents, both white *and* black, tend to conform to a cultural logic of childrearing I call "concerted cultivation." They enroll their children in numerous age-specific organized activities that dominate family life and create enormous labor, particularly for mothers. The parents view these activities as transmitting important life skills to children. Middle-class parents also stress language use and the development of reasoning and employ talking as their preferred form of discipline. This "cultivation" approach results in a wider range of experiences for children but also creates a frenetic pace for parents, a cult of individualism within the family, and an emphasis on children's performance.[1]

The childrearing strategies of white and black working-class and poor parents emphasize the "accomplishment of natural growth."[2] These parents believe that as long as they provide love, food, and safety, their children will grow and thrive. They do not focus on developing their children's special talents. Compared to the middle-class children, working-class and poor children participate in few organized activities and have more free time and deeper, richer ties within their extended families. Working-class and poor parents issue many more directives to their children and, in some households, place more emphasis on physical discipline than do the middle-class parents. These findings extend Kohn and Schooler's (1983) observation of class differences in parents' values, showing that differences also exist in the *behavior* of parents *and* children.

Quantitative studies of children's activities offer valuable empirical evidence but only limited ideas about how to conceptualize the mechanisms through which social advantage is transmitted. Thus, my second goal is to offer "conceptual umbrellas" useful for making comparisons across race and class and for assessing the role of social structural location in shaping daily life.[3]

Last, I trace the connections between the class position of family members—including children—and the uneven outcomes of their experiences outside the home as they interact with professionals in dominant institutions. The pattern of concerted cultivation encourages an *emerging sense of entitlement* in children. All parents and children are not equally assertive, but the pattern of questioning and intervening among the white and black middle-class parents contrasts sharply with the definitions of how to be helpful and effective observed among the white and black working-class and poor adults. The pattern of the accomplishment of natural growth encourages an *emerging sense of constraint*. Adults as well as children in these social classes tend to be deferential and outwardly accepting in their interactions with professionals such as doctors and educators. At the same time, however, compared to their middle-class counterparts, white and black working-class and poor family members are more distrustful of professionals. These are differences with potential long-term consequences. In an historical moment when the dominant society privileges active, informed, assertive clients of health and educational services, the strategies employed by children and parents are not equally effective across classes. In sum, differences in family life lie not only in the advantages parents obtain for their children, but also in the skills they transmit to children for negotiating their own life paths.

METHODOLOGY

Study Participants

This study is based on interviews and observations of children, aged 8 to 10, and their families. The data were collected over time in three research phases. Phase one involved observations in two third-grade classrooms in a public school in the Midwestern community of "Lawrenceville."[4] After conducting observations for two months, I grouped the families into social class (and race) categories based on information provided by educators. I then chose every third name, and sent a letter to the child's home asking the mother and father to participate in separate interviews. Over 90 percent of parents agreed, for a total of 32 children (16 white and 16 African American). A black graduate student and I interviewed all mothers and most fathers (or guardians) of the children. Each interview lasted 90 to 120 minutes, and all took place in 1989–1990.

Phase two took place at two sites in a northeastern metropolitan area. One school, "Lower Richmond," although located in a predominantly white, working-class urban neighborhood, drew about half of its students from a nearby all-black housing project. I observed one third-grade class at Lower Richmond about twice a week for almost six months. The second site, "Swan," was located in a suburban neighborhood about 45 minutes from the city center. It was 90 percent white; most of the remaining 10 percent were middle-class black children.[5] There, I observed twice a week for two months at the end of the third grade; a research assistant then observed weekly for four more months in the fourth grade.[6] At each site, teachers and parents described their school in positive terms.[7] The observations took

TABLE 4.1

**FREQUENCY DISTRIBUTION OF CHILDREN IN THE STUDY
BY SOCIAL CLASS AND RACE**

Social class	White	Black	Total
Middle class[a]	18 (Garrett Tallinger) (Melanie Handlon)	18 (Alexander Williams) (Stacey Marshall)	36
Working class[b]	14 (Billy Yanelli) (Wendy Driver)	12 (Tyrec Taylor) (Jessica Irwin)[c]	26
Poor[d]	12 (Karl Greeley) (Katie Brindle)	14 (Harold McAllister) (Tara Carroll)	26
Total sample	44	44	88

Note: The names in each cell of the table indicate the children selected to take place in the family-observation phase of the study.
[a]Middle-class children are those who live in households in which at least one parent is employed in a position that either entails substantial managerial authority or draws upon highly complex, educationally certified skills (i.e., college-level).
[b]Working-class children are those who live in households in which neither parent is employed in a middle-class position and at least one parent is employed in a position with little or no managerial authority and that does not draw on highly complex, educationally certified skills. This category includes lower-level white-collar workers.
[c]An interracial girl who has a black father and a white mother.
[d]Poor children are those who live in households in which parents receive public assistance and do not participate in the labor force on a regular, continuous basis.

place between September 1992 and January 1994. In the fall of 1993, I drew an interview sample from Lower Richmond and Swan, following the same method of selection used for Lawrenceville. A team of research assistants and I interviewed the parents and guardians of 39 children. Again, the response rate was over 90 percent but because the classrooms did not generate enough black middle-class children and white poor children to fill the analytical categories, interviews were also conducted with 17 families with children aged 8 to 10. (Most of these interviews took place during the summers of 1996 and 1997.)[8] Thus, the total number of children who participated in the study was 88 (32 from the Midwest and 56 from the Northeast).

Family Observations

Phase three, the most intensive research phase of the study, involved home observations of 12 children and their families in the Northeast who had been previously interviewed (see Table 4.1).[9] Some themes, such as language use and families' social connections, surfaced mainly during this phase. Although I entered the field interested in examining the influence of social class on children's daily lives, I incorporated new themes as they "bubbled up" from the field observations. The evidence presented here comes mainly from the family observations, but I also use interview findings from the full sample of 88 children where appropriate.[10]

Nine of the 12 families came from the Northeastern classroom sample. The home observations took place, one family at a time, from December 1993 to August 1994. Three 10-year-olds (a black middle-class boy and girl and a white poor boy) who were not part of the classroom sample were observed in their homes during the summer of 1995.[11]

The research assistants and I took turns visiting the participating families daily, for a total of about 20 visits to each home, often in the space of one month.[12] The observations went beyond the home: Fieldworkers followed children and parents as they participated in school activities, church services and events, organized play, visits to relatives, and medical appointments. Observations typically lasted three hours, but sometimes much longer (e.g., when we observed an out-of-town funeral, a special extended family event, or a long shopping trip). Most cases also involved one overnight visit. We often carried tape recorders and used the audiotapes for reference in writing field notes. Writing field notes usually required 8 to 12 hours for each two- or three-hour home visit. Participating families each were paid $350, usually at the end of the visits.

We worked in teams of three. One fieldworker visited three to four times per week; another visited one to two times per week; and I visited once or twice per week, except for the two families for which I was lead fieldworker. The research teams' composition varied with the race of the family. Two white graduate students and I (a middle-aged white woman) visited the white families; for the black families, the teams included one white graduate student, one black graduate student, and me. All black families with male children were visited by teams that included a black male fieldworker. A white male fieldworker observed the poor family with the white boy; the remaining white fieldworkers were female. Team members met regularly to discuss the families and to review the emerging analytic themes.

Our presence altered family dynamics, especially at first. Over time, however, we saw signs of adjustment (e.g., yelling and cursing increased on the third day and again on the tenth). The children, especially, seemed to enjoy participating in the project. They reported it made them feel "special." They were visibly happy to see the fieldworkers arrive and reluctant to let them leave. The working-class and poor black boys were more comfortable with the black male fieldworkers than with the white female ones, especially at first.[13] Overall, however, family members reported in exit interviews that they had not changed their behavior significantly, or they mentioned very specific alterations (e.g., "the house got cleaner").

A Note on Class

I undertook field observations to develop an intensive, realistic portrait of family life. Although I deliberately focused on only 12 families, I wanted to compare children across gender and race. Adopting the fine-grained differentiations characteristic of current neo-Marxist and neo-Weberian empirical studies was not tenable.[14] Further limitations were imposed by the school populations at the sites I selected. Very few students were children of employers or of self-employed workers. I decided to focus exclusively on those whose parents were employees. Authority in the workplace and "credential barriers" are the criteria most commonly used to differentiate within this heterogeneous group. I assigned the families to a working-class or middle-class category based on detailed information that each of the employed adults provided about the work they did, the nature of the organization that employed them, and their educational credentials. I also included a category traditionally excluded from class groupings: families not involved in the labor market. In the first school I studied, many children were from households supported by public assistance. Omitting them would have restricted the scope of the study arbitrarily.[15]

The three class categories conceal important internal variations. The Williams family (black) and the Tallinger family (white) have very high incomes, both in excess of $175,000; the median income among the middle-class parents was much lower.[16] Income differences among the middle-class families were not associated with differences in childrearing methods. Moreover, no other data in the study showed compelling intraclass divisions. I consider the use of one term—middle class—to be reasonable.

CONCERTED CULTIVATION AND NATURAL GROWTH

The interviews and observations suggested that crucial aspects of family life *cohered.* Within the concerted cultivation and accomplishment of natural growth approaches, three key dimensions may be distinguished: the organization of daily life, the use of language, and social connections. ("Interventions in institutions" and "consequences" are addressed later in this reading.) These dimensions do not capture all important parts of family life, but they do incorporate core aspects of childrearing (Table 4.2). Moreover, our field observations revealed that behaviors and activities related to these dimensions dominated the rhythms of family life. Conceptually, the organization of daily life and the use of language are crucial dimensions. Both must be present for the family to be described as engaging in one childrearing approach rather than the other. Social connections are significant but less conceptually essential.

All three aspects of childrearing were intricately woven into the families' daily routines, but rarely remarked upon. As part of everyday practice, they were invisible to parents and children. Analytically, however, they are useful means for comparing and contrasting ways in which social class differences shape the character of family life. I now examine two families in terms of these three key dimensions. I "control" for race and gender and contrast the lives of two black boys—one from an (upper) middle-class family and one from a family on public assistance. I could have focused on almost any of the other 12 children, but this pair seemed optimal, given the limited number of studies reporting on black

TABLE 4.2

SUMMARY OF DIFFERENCES IN CHILDREARING APPROACHES

Dimension observed	Childrearing approach	
	Concerted cultivation	**Accomplishment of natural growth**
Key elements of each approach	Parent actively fosters and assesses child's talents, opinions, and skills	Parent cares for child and allows child to grow
Organization of daily life	Multiple child leisure activities are orchestrated by adults	Child "hangs out" particularly with kin
Language use	Reasoning/directives Child contestation of adult statements Extended negotiations between parents and child	Directives Rare for child to question or challenge adults General acceptance by child of directives
Social connections	Weak extended family ties Child often in homogeneous age groupings	Strong extended family ties Child often in heterogeneous age groupings
Interventions in institutions	Criticisms and interventions on behalf of child Training of child to intervene on his or her own behalf	Dependence on institutions Sense of powerlessness and frustration Conflict between childrearing practices at home and at school
Consequences	Emerging sense of entitlement on the part of the child	Emerging sense of constraint on the part of the child

middle-class families, as well as the aspect of my argument that suggests that race is less important than class in shaping childrearing patterns.

Developing Alexander Williams

Alexander Williams and his parents live in a predominantly black middle-class neighborhood. Their six-bedroom house is worth about $150,000.[17] Alexander is an only child. Both parents grew up in small towns in the South, and both are from large families. His father, a tall, handsome man, is a very successful trial lawyer who earns about $125,000 annually in a small firm specializing in medical malpractice cases. Two weeks each month, he works very long hours (from about 5:30 A.M. until midnight) preparing for trials. The other two weeks, his workday ends around 6:00 P.M. He rarely travels out of town. Alexander's mother, Christina, is a positive, bubbly woman with freckles and long, black, wavy hair.[18] A high-level manager in a major corporation, she has a corner office, a personal secretary, and responsibilities for other offices across the nation. She tries to limit her travel, but at least once a month she takes an overnight trip.

Alexander is a charming, inquisitive boy with a winsome smile. Ms. Williams is pleased that Alexander seems interested in so many things:

> Alexander is a joy. He's a gift to me. He's very energetic, very curious, loving, caring person, that, um . . . is outgoing and who, uh, really loves to be with people. And who loves to explore, and loves to read and . . . just do a lot of fun things.

The private school Alexander attends[19] has an on-site after-school program. There, he participates in several activities and receives guitar lessons and photography instruction.

Organization of Daily Life   Alexander is busy with activities during the week and on weekends (Table 4.3). His mother describes their Saturday morning routine. The day starts early with a private piano lesson for Alexander downtown, a 20-minute drive from the house:

It's an 8:15 class. But for me, it was a trade-off. I am very adamant about Saturday morning TV. I don't know what it contributes. So . . . it was . . . um . . . either stay at home and fight on a Saturday morning [laughs] or go do something constructive. . . . Now Saturday mornings are pretty booked up. You know, the piano lesson, and then straight to choir for a couple of hours. So, he has a very full schedule.

Ms. Williams's vehement opposition to television is based on her view of what Alexander needs to grow and thrive. She objects to TV's passivity and feels it is her obligation to help her son cultivate his talents.

Sometimes Alexander complains that "my mother signs me up for everything!" Generally, however, he likes his activities. He says they make him feel "special," and without them life would be "boring." His sense of time is thoroughly entwined with his activities: He feels disoriented when his schedule is not full. This unease is clear in the following field-note excerpt. The family is driving home from a Back-to-School night. The next morning, Ms. Williams will leave for a work-related day trip and will not return until late at night. Alexander is grumpy because he has nothing planned for the next day. He wants to have a friend over, but his mother rebuffs him. Whining, he wonders what he will do. His mother, speaking tersely, says:

> You have piano and guitar. You'll have some free time. [Pause] I think you'll survive for one night. [Alexander does not respond but seems mad. It is quiet for the rest of the trip home.]

Alexander's parents believe his activities provide a wide range of benefits important for his development. In discussing Alexander's piano lessons, Mr. Williams notes that as a Suzuki student,[20] Alexander is already able to read music. Speculating about more diffuse benefits of Alexander's involvement with piano, he says:

> I don't see how any kid's adolescence and adulthood could not but be enhanced by an awareness of who Beethoven was. And is that Bach or

TABLE 4.3

PARTICIPATION IN ACTIVITIES OUTSIDE OF SCHOOL: BOYS

Boy's name/race/class	Activities organized by adults	Informal activities
Middle Class		
Garrett Tallinger (white)	Soccer team Traveling soccer team Baseball team Basketball team (summer) Swim team Piano Saxophone (through school)	Plays with siblings in yard Watches television Plays computer games Overnights with friends
Alexander Williams (black)	Soccer team Baseball team Community choir Church choir Sunday school Piano (Suzuki) School plays Guitar (through school)	Restricted television Plays outside occasionally with two other boys Visits friends from school
Working Class		
Billy Yanelli (white)	Baseball team	Watches television Visits relatives Rides bike Plays outside in the street Hangs out with neighborhood kids
Tyrec Taylor (black)	Football team Vacation Bible School Sunday school (off/on)	Watches television Plays outside in the street Rides bikes with neighborhood boys Visit relatives Goes to swimming pool
Poor		
Karl Greeley (white)	Goes to swimming pool Walks dogs with neighbor	Watches television Plays Nintendo Plays with siblings
Harold McAllister (black)	Bible study in neighbor's house (occasionally) Bible camp (1 week)	Visits relatives Plays ball with neighborhood kids Watches television Watches videos

Mozart? I don't know the difference between the two! I don't know Baroque from Classical—but he does. How can that not be a benefit in later life? I'm convinced that this rich experience will make him a better person, a better citizen, a better husband, a better father—certainly a better student.

Ms. Williams sees music as building her son's "confidence" and his "poise." In interviews and casual conversation, she stresses "exposure." She believes it is her responsibility to broaden Alexander's worldview. Childhood activities provide a learning ground for important life skills:

> Sports provide great opportunities to learn how to be competitive. Learn how to accept defeat, you know. Learn how to accept winning, you know, in a gracious way. Also it gives him the opportunity

to learn leadership skills and how to be a team player. . . . Sports really provides a lot of really great opportunities.

Alexander's schedule is constantly shifting; some activities wind down and others start up. Because the schedules of sports practices and games are issued no sooner than the start of the new season, advance planning is rarely possible. Given the sheer number of Alexander's activities, events inevitably overlap. Some activities, though short-lived, are extremely time consuming. Alexander's school play, for example, requires rehearsals three nights the week before the opening. In addition, in choosing activities, the Williamses have an added concern—the group's racial balance. Ms. Williams prefers that Alexander not be the only black child at events. Typically, one or two other black boys are involved, but the groups are predominantly white and the activities take place in predominantly white residential neighborhoods. Alexander is, however, part of his church's youth choir and Sunday School, activities in which all participants are black.

Many activities involve competition. Alex must audition for his solo performance in the school play, for example. Similarly, parents and children alike understand that participation on "A," "B," or "All-Star" sports teams signals different skill levels. Like other middle-class children in the study, Alexander seems to enjoy public performance. According to a field note, after his solo at a musical production in front of over 200 people, he appeared "contained, pleased, aware of the attention he's receiving."

Alexander's commitments do not consume *all* his free time. Still, his life is defined by a series of deadlines and schedules interwoven with a series of activities that are organized and controlled by adults rather than children. Neither he nor his parents see this as troublesome.

Language Use Like other middle-class families, the Williamses often engage in conversation that promotes reasoning and negotiation. An excerpt from a field note (describing an exchange between

Alexander and his mother during a car ride home after summer camp) shows the kind of pointed questions middle-class parents ask children. Ms. Williams is not just eliciting information. She is also giving Alexander the opportunity to develop and practice verbal skills, including how to summarize, clarify, and amplify information:

As she drives, [Ms. Williams] asks Alex, "So, how was your day?"

Alex: "Okay. I had hot dogs today, but they were burned! They were all black!"

Mom: "Oh, great. You shouldn't have eaten any."

Alex: "They weren't *all* black, only half were. The rest were regular."

Mom: "Oh, okay. What was that game you were playing this morning? . . ."

Alex: "It was [called] 'Watcha doin?' "

Mom: "How do you play?"

Alexander explains the game elaborately—fieldworker doesn't quite follow. Mom asks Alex questions throughout his explanation, saying, "Oh, I see," when he answers. She asks him about another game she saw them play; he again explains. . . . She continues to prompt and encourage him with small giggles in the back of her throat as he elaborates.

Expressions of interest in children's activities often lead to negotiations over small, home-based matters. During the same car ride, Ms. Williams tries to adjust the dinner menu to suit Alexander:

Alexander says, "I don't want hot dogs tonight."

Mom: "Oh? Because you had them for lunch."

Alexander nods.

Mom: "Well, I can fix something else and save the hot dogs for tomorrow night."

Alex: "But I don't want any pork chops either."

Mom: "Well, Alexander, we need to eat something. Why didn't you have hamburgers today?"

Alex: "They don't have them any more at the snack bar."

Mom asks Alexander if he's ok, if he wants a snack. Alexander says he's ok. Mom asks if he's sure he doesn't want a bag of chips?

Not all middle-class parents are as attentive to their children's needs as this mother, and none are *always* interested in negotiating. But a general pattern of reasoning and accommodating is common.

Social Connections Mr. and Ms. Williams consider themselves very close to their extended families. Because the Williamses' aging parents live in the South, visiting requires a plane trip. Ms. Williams takes Alexander with her to see his grandparents twice a year. She speaks on the phone with her parents at least once a week and also calls her siblings several times a week. Mr. Williams talks with his mother regularly by phone (he has less contact with his stepfather). With pride, he also mentions his niece, whose Ivy League education he is helping to finance.

Interactions with cousins are not normally a part of Alexander's leisure time. (As I explain below, other middle-class children did not see cousins routinely either, even when they lived nearby.) Nor does he often play with neighborhood children. The huge homes on the Williamses' street are occupied mainly by couples without children. Most of Alexander's playmates come from his classroom or his organized activities. Because most of his school events, church life, and assorted activities are organized by the age (and sometimes gender) of the participants, Alexander interacts almost exclusively with children his own age, usually boys. Adult-organized activities thus define the context of his social life.

Mr. and Ms. Williams are aware that they allocate a sizable portion of time to Alexander's activities. What they stress, however, is the time they *hold back*. They mention activities the family has chosen *not* to take on (such as traveling soccer).

Summary Overall, Alexander's parents engaged in concerted cultivation. They fostered their son's growth through involvement in music, church, athletics, and academics. They talked with him at length, seeking his opinions and encouraging his ideas. Their approach involved considerable direct expenses (e.g., the cost of lessons and equipment) and large indirect expenses (e.g., the cost of taking time off from work, driving to practices, and forgoing adult leisure activities). Although Mr. and Ms. Williams acknowledged the importance of extended family, Alexander spent relatively little time with relatives. His social interactions occurred almost exclusively with children his own age and with adults. Alexander's many activities significantly shaped the organization of daily life in the family. Both parents' leisure time was tailored to their son's commitments. Mr. and Ms. Williams felt that the strategies they cultivated with Alexander would result in his having the best possible chance at a happy and productive life. They couldn't imagine themselves *not* investing large amounts of time and energy in their son's life. But, as I explain in the next section, which focuses on a black boy from a poor family, other parents held a different view.

Supporting the Natural Growth of Harold McAllister

Harold McAllister, a large, stocky boy with a big smile, is from a poor black family. He lives with his mother and his 8-year-old sister, Alexis, in a large apartment. Two cousins often stay overnight. Harold's 16-year-old sister and 18-year-old brother usually live with their grandmother, but sometimes they stay at the McAllisters' home. Ms. McAllister, a high school graduate, relies on public assistance (AFDC). Hank, Harold and Alexis's father, is a mechanic. He and Ms. McAllister have never married. He visits regularly, sometimes weekly, stopping by after work to watch television or nap. Harold (but not Alexis) sometimes travels across town by bus to spend the weekend with Hank.

The McAllisters' apartment is in a public housing project near a busy street. The complex consists of rows of two- and three-story brick units. The buildings, blocky and brown, have small yards enclosed by concrete and wood fences. Large floodlights are mounted on the corners of the buildings, and wide concrete sidewalks cut through the spaces between units. The ground is bare in many places; paper wrappers and glass litter the area.

Inside the apartment, life is humorous and lively, with family members and kin sharing in the daily routines. Ms. McAllister discussed, disdainfully, mothers who are on drugs or who abuse alcohol and do not "look after" their children. Indeed, the previous year Ms. McAllister called Child Protective Services to report her twin sister, a cocaine addict, because she was neglecting her children. Ms. McAllister is actively involved in her twin's daughters' lives. Her two nephews also frequently stay with her. Overall, she sees herself as a capable mother who takes care of her children and her extended family.

Organization of Daily Life   Much of Harold's life and the lives of his family members revolve around home. Project residents often sit outside in lawn chairs or on front stoops, drinking beer, talking, and watching children play. During summer, windows are frequently left open, allowing breezes to waft through the units and providing vantage points from which residents can survey the neighborhood. A large deciduous tree in front of the McAllisters' apartment unit provides welcome shade in the summer's heat.

Harold loves sports. He is particularly fond of basketball, but he also enjoys football, and he follows televised professional sports closely. Most afternoons, he is either inside watching television or outside playing ball. He tosses a football with cousins and boys from the neighboring units and organizes pick-up basketball games. Sometimes he and his friends use a rusty, bare hoop hanging from a telephone pole in the housing project; other times, they string up an old, blue plastic crate as a makeshift hoop. One obstacle to playing sports, however, is a shortage of equipment. Balls are costly to replace, especially given the rate at which they disappear—theft of children's play equipment, including balls and bicycles, is an ongoing problem. During a field observation, Harold asks his mother if she knows where the ball is. She replies with some vehemence, "They stole the blue and yellow ball, and they stole the green ball, and they stole the other ball."

Hunting for balls is a routine part of Harold's leisure time. One June day, with the temperature and humidity in the high 80's, Harold and his cousin Tyrice (and a fieldworker) wander around the housing project for about an hour, trying to find a basketball:

> We head to the other side of the complex. On the way . . . we passed four guys sitting on the step. Their ages were 9 to 13 years. They had a radio blaring. Two were working intently on fixing a flat bike tire. The other two were dribbling a basketball.
>
> Harold: "Yo! What's up, ya'll."
>
> Group: "What's up, Har." "What's up?" "Yo."
>
> They continued to work on the tire and dribble the ball. As we walked down the hill, Harold asked, "Yo, could I use your ball?"
>
> The guy responded, looking up from the tire, "Naw, man. Ya'll might lose it."

Harold, Tyrice, and the fieldworker walk to another part of the complex, heading for a makeshift basketball court where they hope to find a game in progress:

> No such luck. Harold enters an apartment directly in front of the makeshift court. The door was open . . . Harold came back. "No ball. I guess I gotta go back."

The pace of life for Harold and his friends ebbs and flows with the children's interests and family obligations. The day of the basketball search, for example, after spending time listening to music and looking at baseball cards, the children join a water fight Tyrice instigates. It is a lively game, filled with laughter and with efforts to get the adults next door wet (against their wishes). When the game winds down, the kids ask their mother for money, receive it, and then walk to a store to buy chips and soda. They chat with another young boy and then amble back to the apartment, eating as they walk. Another afternoon, almost two weeks later, the children—Harold, two of his cousins, and two children from the neighborhood—and the fieldworker play basketball on a makeshift court in the street (using the fieldworker's ball). As Harold bounces the ball, neighborhood children of all ages wander through the space.

Thus, Harold's life is more free-flowing and more child-directed than is Alexander Williams's. The pace of any given day is not so much planned as emergent, reflecting child-based interests and activities. Parents intervene in specific areas, such as personal grooming, meals, and occasional chores, but they do not continuously direct and monitor their children's leisure activities. Moreover, the leisure activities Harold and other working-class and poor children pursue require them to develop a repertoire of skills for dealing with much older and much younger children as well as with neighbors and relatives.

Language Use Life in the working-class and poor families in the study flows smoothly without extended verbal discussions. The amount of talking varies, but overall, it is considerably less than occurs in the middle-class homes.[21] Ms. McAllister jokes with the children and discusses what is on television. But she does not appear to cultivate conversation by asking the children questions or by drawing them out. Often she is brief and direct in her remarks. For instance, she coordinates the use of the apartment's only bathroom by using one-word directives. She sends the children (there are almost always at least four children home at once) to wash up by pointing to a child, saying one word, "bathroom," and handing him or her a washcloth. Wordlessly, the

designated child gets up and goes to the bathroom to take a shower.

Similarly, although Ms. McAllister will listen to the children's complaints about school, she does not draw them out on these issues or seek to determine details, as Ms. Williams would. For instance, at the start of the new school year, when I ask Harold about his teacher, he tells me she is "mean" and that "she lies." Ms. McAllister, washing dishes, listens to her son, but she does not encourage Harold to support his opinion about his new teacher with more examples, nor does she mention any concerns of her own. Instead, she asks about last year's teacher, "What was the name of that man teacher?" Harold says, "Mr. Lindsey?" She says, "No, the other one." He says, "Mr. Terrene." Ms. McAllister smiles and says, "Yeah. I liked him." Unlike Alexander's mother, she seems content with a brief exchange of information.

Social Connections Children, especially boys, frequently play outside. The number of potential playmates in Harold's world is vastly higher than the number in Alexander's neighborhood. When a fieldworker stops to count heads, she finds 40 children of elementary school age residing in the nearby rows of apartments. With so many children nearby, Harold could choose to play only with others his own age. In fact, though, he often hangs out with older and younger children and with his cousins (who are close to his age).

The McAllister family, like other poor and working-class families, is involved in a web of extended kin. As noted earlier, Harold's older siblings and his two male cousins often spend the night at the McAllister home. Celebrations such as birthdays involve relatives almost exclusively. Party guests are not, as in middle-class families, friends from school or from extracurricular activities. Birthdays are celebrated enthusiastically, with cake and special food to mark the occasion; presents, however, are not offered. Similarly, Christmas at Harold's house featured a tree and special food but no presents. At these and other family events, the older children voluntarily look after the younger ones: Harold plays with his 16-month-old niece, and his cousins carry around the younger babies.

The importance of family ties—and the contingent nature of life in the McAllisters' world—is clear in the response Alexis offers when asked what she would do if she were given a million dollars:

> Oh, boy! I'd buy my brother, my sister, my uncle, my aunt, my nieces and my nephews, and my grandpop, and my grandmom, and my mom, and my dad, and my friends, not my friends, but mostly my best friend—I'd buy them all clothes . . . and sneakers. And I'd buy some food, and I'd get my brothers and my sisters gifts for their birthdays.

Summary   In a setting where everyone, including the children, was acutely aware of the lack of money, the McAllister family made do. Ms. McAllister rightfully saw herself as a very capable mother. She was a strong, positive influence in the lives of the children she looked after. Still, the contrast with Ms. Williams is striking. Ms. McAllister did not seem to think that Harold's opinions needed to be cultivated and developed. She, like most parents in the working-class and poor families, drew strong and clear boundaries between adults and children. Adults gave directions to children. Children were given freedom to play informally unless they were needed for chores. Extended family networks were deemed important and trustworthy.

The Intersection of Race and Class in Family Life

I expected race to powerfully shape children's daily schedules, but this was not evident (also see Conley 1999; Pattillo-McCoy 1999). This is not to say that race is unimportant. Black parents were particularly concerned with monitoring their children's lives outside the home for signs of racial problems.[22] Black middle-class fathers, especially, were likely to stress the importance of their sons understanding "what it means to be a black man in this society" (J. Hochschild

1995). Mr. Williams, in summarizing how he and his wife orient Alexander, said:

> [We try to] teach him that race unfortunately is the most important aspect of our national life. I mean people look at other people and they see a color first. But that isn't going to define who he is. He will do his best. He will succeed, despite racism. And I think he lives his life that way.

Alexander's parents were acutely aware of the potential significance of race in his life. Both were adamant, however, that race should not be used as "an excuse" for not striving to succeed. Mr. Williams put it this way:

> I discuss how race impacts on my life as an attorney, and I discuss how race will impact on his life.

> The one teaching that he takes away from this is that he is never to use discrimination as an excuse for not doing his best.

Thus far, few incidents of overt racism had occurred in Alexander's life, as his mother noted:

> Those situations have been far and few between. . . . I mean, I can count them on my fingers.

Still, Ms. Williams recounted with obvious pain an incident at a birthday party Alexander had attended as a preschooler. The grandparents of the birthday child repeatedly asked, "Who is that boy?" and exclaimed, "He's so dark!" Such experiences fueled the Williamses resolve always to be "cautious":

> We've never been, uh, parents who drop off their kid anywhere. We've always gone with him. And even now, I go in and—to school in the morning—and check [in]. . . . The school environment, we've watched very closely.

Alexander's parents were not equally optimistic about the chances for racial equality in this country. Ms. Williams felt strongly that, especially while Alexander was young, his father should not voice his pessimism. Mr. Williams complained that this meant he had to "watch" what he said to Alexander about race relations. Still, both parents agreed about the need to be vigilant regarding potential racial problems in Alexander's life. Other black parents reported experiencing racial prejudice and expressed a similar commitment to vigilance.

Issues surrounding the prospect of growing up black and male in this society were threaded through Alexander's life in ways that had no equivalent among his middle-class, white male peers. Still, in fourth grade there were no signs of racial experiences having "taken hold" the way that they might as Alexander ages. In terms of the number and kind of activities he participated in, his life was very similar to that of Garrett Tallinger, his white counterpart (see Table 4.3). That both sets of parents were fully committed to a strategy of concentrated cultivation was apparent in the number of adult-organized activities the boys were enrolled in, the hectic pace of family life, and the stress on reasoning in parent-child negotiations. Likewise, the research assistants and I saw no striking differences in the ways in which white parents and black parents in the working-class and poor homes socialized their children.

Others (Fordham and Ogbu 1986) have found that in middle school and high school, adolescent peer groups often draw sharp racial boundaries, a pattern not evident among this study's third- and fourth-grade participants (but sometimes present among their older siblings). Following Tatum (1997:52), I attribute this to the children's relatively young ages (also see "Race in America," *The New York Times,* June 25, 2000, p. 1). In sum, in the broader society, key aspects of daily life were shaped by racial segregation and discrimination. But in terms of enrollment in organized activities, language use, and social connections, the largest differences between the families we observed were across social class, not racial groups. . . .

IMPACT OF CHILDREARING STRATEGIES ON INTERACTIONS WITH INSTITUTIONS

Social scientists sometimes emphasize the importance of reshaping parenting practices to improve children's chances of success. Explicitly and implicitly, the literature exhorts parents to comply with the views of professionals (Bronfenbrenner 1966; Epstein 2001; Heimer and Staffen 1998). Such calls for compliance do not, however, reconcile professionals' judgments regarding the intrinsic value of current childrearing standards with the evidence of the historical record, which shows regular shifts in such standards over time (Aries 1962; Wrigley 1989; Zelizer 1985). Nor are the stratified, and limited, possibilities for success in the broader society examined.

I now follow the families out of their homes and into encounters with representatives of dominant institutions—institutions that are directed by middle-class professionals. Again, I focus on Alexander Williams and Harold McAllister. (Institutional experiences are summarized in Table 4.2.) Across all social classes, parents and children interacted with teachers and school officials, healthcare professionals, and assorted government officials. Although they often addressed similar problems (e.g., learning disabilities, asthma, traffic violations), they typically did not achieve similar resolutions. The pattern of concerted cultivation fostered an *emerging sense of entitlement* in the life of Alexander Williams and other middle-class children. By contrast, the commitment to nurturing children's natural growth fostered an *emerging sense of constraint* in the life of Harold McAllister and other working-class or poor children. (These consequences of childrearing practices are summarized in Table 4.2.)

Both parents and children drew on the resources associated with these two childrearing approaches during their interactions with officials. Middle-class parents and children often customized these interactions; working-class and poor parents were more likely to have a "generic" relationship. When faced with problems, middle-class parents also appeared better equipped to exert influence over other adults compared with working-class and poor parents. Nor did middle-class parents or children display the intimidation or confusion we witnessed among many working-class and poor families when they faced a problem in their children's school experience.

Emerging Signs of Entitlement

Alexander Williams's mother, like many middle-class mothers, explicitly teaches her son to be an informed, assertive client in interactions with professionals. For example, as she drives Alexander to a routine doctor's appointment, she coaches him in the art of communicating effectively in healthcare settings:

> Alexander asks if he needs to get any shots today at the doctor's. Ms. Williams says he'll need to ask the doctor. . . . As we enter Park Lane, Mom says quietly to Alex: "Alexander, you should be thinking of questions you might want to ask the doctor. You can ask him anything you want. Don't be shy. You can ask anything."
>
> Alex thinks for a minute, then: "I have some bumps under my arms from my deodorant."
>
> Mom: "Really? You mean from your new deodorant?"
>
> Alex: "Yes."
>
> Mom: "Well, you should ask the doctor."

Alexander learns that he has the right to speak up (e.g., "don't be shy") and that he should prepare for an encounter with a person in a position of authority by gathering his thoughts in advance.

These class resources are subsequently *activated* in the encounter with the doctor (a jovial white man in his late thirties or early forties). The examination begins this way:

> Doctor: "Okay, as usual, I'd like to go through the routine questions with you. And if you have any questions for me, just fire away." Doctor examines Alex's chart: "Height-wise, as usual, Alexander's in the ninety-fifth percentile."

Although the physician is talking to Ms. Williams, Alexander interrupts him:

> Alex: "I'm in the what?"
>
> Doctor: "It means that you're taller than more than ninety-five out of a hundred young men when they're, uh, ten years old."
>
> Alex: "I'm not ten."

> Doctor: "Well, they graphed you at ten . . . they usually take the closest year to get that graph."
>
> Alex: "Alright."

Alexander's "Alright" reveals that he feels entitled to weigh in with his own judgment.

A few minutes later, the exam is interrupted when the doctor is asked to provide an emergency consultation by telephone. Alexander listens to the doctor's conversation and then uses what he has overheard as the basis for a clear directive:

> Doctor: "The stitches are on the eyelids themselves, the laceration? . . . Um . . . I don't suture eyelids . . . um . . . Absolutely not!. . . Don't even touch them. That was very bad judgment on the camp's part. . . . [Hangs up.] I'm sorry about the interruption."
>
> Alex: "Stay away from my eyelids!"

Alexander's comment, which draws laughter from the adults, reflects this fourth-grader's tremendous ease interacting with a physician.

Later, Ms. Williams and the doctor discuss Alexander's diet. Ms. Williams freely admits that they do not always follow nutritional guidelines. Her honesty is a form of capital because it gives the doctor accurate information on which to base a diagnosis. Feeling no need for deception positions mother and son to receive better care:

> Doctor: "Let's start with appetite. Do you get three meals a day?"
>
> Alex: "Yeah."
>
> Doctor: "And here's the important question: Do you get your fruits and vegetables too?"
>
> Alex: "Yeah."
>
> Mom, high-pitched: "Ooooo. . . ."
>
> Doctor: "I see I have a second opinion." [laughter]
>
> Alex, voice rising: "You give me bananas and all in my lunch every day. And I had cabbage for dinner last night."
>
> Doctor: "Do you get at least one or two fruits, one or two vegetables every day?"

Alex: "Yeah."

Doctor: "Marginally?"

Mom: "Ninety-eight percent of the time he eats pretty well."

Doctor: "OK, I can live with that. . . ."

Class resources are again activated when Alexander's mother reveals she "gave up" on a medication. The doctor pleasantly but clearly instructs her to continue the medication. Again, though, he receives accurate information rather than facing silent resistance or defiance, as occurred in encounters between healthcare professionals and other (primarily working-class and poor) families. The doctor acknowledges Ms. Williams's relative power: He "argues for" continuation rather than directing her to execute a medically necessary action:

Mom: "His allergies have just been, just acted up again. One time this summer and I had to bring him in."

Doctor: "I see a note here from Dr. Svennson that she put him on Vancinace and Benadryl. Did it seem to help him?"

Mom: "Just, not really. So, I used it for about a week and I just gave up." Doctor, sitting forward in his chair: "OK, I'm actually going to argue for not giving up. If he needs it, Vancinace is a very effective drug. But it takes at least a week to start. . . ."

Mom: "Oh. OK. . . ."

Doctor: "I'd rather have him use that than heavy oral medications. You have to give it a few weeks. . . ."

A similar pattern of give-and-take and questioning characterizes Alexander's interaction with the doctor, as the following excerpt illustrates:

Doctor: "The only thing that you really need besides my checking you, um, is to have, um, your eyes checked downstairs."

Alex: "Yes! I love that, I love that!"

Doctor laughs: "Well, now the most important question. Do you have any questions you want to ask me before I do your physical?"

Alex: "Um . . . only one. I've been getting some bumps on my arms, right around here [indicates underarm]."

Doctor: "Underneath?"

Alex: "Yeah."

Doctor: "OK. . . . Do they hurt or itch?"

Alex: "No, they're just there."

Doctor: "OK, I'll take a look at those bumps for you. Um, what about you—um . . ."

Alex: "They're barely any left."

Doctor: "OK, well, I'll take a peek. . . . Any questions or worries on your part?" [Looking at the mother]

Mom: "No. . . . He seems to be coming along very nicely."[23]

Alexander's mother's last comment reflects her view of him as a project, one that is progressing "very nicely." Throughout the visit, she signals her ease and her perception of the exam as an exchange between peers (with Alexander a legitimate participant), rather than a communication from a person in authority to his subordinates. Other middle-class parents seemed similarly comfortable. During Garrett Tallinger's exam, for example, his mother took off her sandals and tucked her legs up under her as she sat in the examination room. She also joked casually with the doctor.

Middle-class parents and children were also very assertive in situations at the public elementary school most of the middle-class children in the study attended. There were numerous conflicts during the year over matters small and large. For example, parents complained to one another and to the teachers about the amount of homework the children were assigned. A black middle-class mother whose daughters had not tested into the school's gifted program negotiated with officials to have the girls' (higher) results from a private testing company accepted instead. The parents of a fourth-grade boy drew the school superintendent into a battle over religious lyrics in a song scheduled to be sung as part of the holiday program. The superintendent consulted the district lawyer and ultimately "counseled" the principal to be more sensitive, and the song was dropped.

Children, too, asserted themselves at school. Examples include requesting that the classroom's blinds be lowered so the sun wasn't in their eyes, badgering the teacher for permission to retake a math test for a higher grade, and demanding to know why no cupcake had been saved when an absence prevented attendance at a classroom party. In these encounters, children were not simply complying with adults' requests or asking for a repeat of an earlier experience. They were displaying an emerging sense of entitlement by urging adults to permit a customized accommodation of institutional processes to suit their preferences.

Of course, some children (and parents) were more forceful than others in their dealings with teachers, and some were more successful than others. Melanie Handlon's mother, for example, took a very "hands-on" approach to her daughter's learning problems, coaching Melanie through her homework day after day. Instead of improved grades, however, the only result was a deteriorating home environment marked by tension and tears.

Emerging Signs of Constraint

The interactions the research assistants and I observed between professionals and working-class and poor parents frequently seemed cautious and constrained. This unease is evident, for example, during a physical Harold McAllister has before going to Bible camp. Harold's mother, normally boisterous and talkative at home, is quiet. Unlike Ms. Williams, she seems wary of supplying the doctor with accurate information:

> Doctor: "Does he eat something each day—either fish, meat, or egg?"

> Mom, response is low and muffled: "Yes."

> Doctor, attempting to make eye contact but mom stares intently at paper: "A yellow vegetable?"

> Mom, still no eye contact, looking at the floor: "Yeah."

> Doctor: "A green vegetable?" Mom, looking at the doctor: "Not all the time." [Fieldworker has not seen any of the children eat a green or yellow vegetable since visits began.]

> Doctor: "No. Fruit or juice?"

> Mom, low voice, little or no eye contact, looks at the doctor's scribbles on the paper he is filling out: "Ummh humn."

> Doctor: "Does he drink milk every day?"

> Mom, abruptly, in considerably louder voice: "Yeah."

> Doctor: "Cereal, bread, rice, potato, anything like that?"

> Mom, shakes her head: "Yes, definitely." [Looks at doctor.]

Ms. McAllister's knowledge of developmental events in Harold's life is uneven. She is not sure when he learned to walk and cannot recall the name of his previous doctor. And when the doctor asks, "When was the last time he had a tetanus shot?" she counters, gruffly, "What's a tetanus shot?"

Unlike Ms. Williams, who urged Alexander to share information with the doctor, Ms. McAllister squelches eight-year-old Alexis's overtures:

> Doctor: "Any birth mark?"

> Mom looks at doctor, shakes her head no.

> Alexis, raising her left arm, says excitedly: "I have a birth mark under my arm!"

> Mom, raising her voice and looking stern: "Will you cool out a minute?" Mom, again answering the doctor's question: "No."

Despite Ms. McAllister's tension and the marked change in her everyday demeanor, Harold's whole exam is not uncomfortable. There are moments of laughter. Moreover, Harold's mother is not consistently shy or passive. Before the visit begins, the doctor comes into the waiting room and calls Harold's and Alexis's names. In response, the McAllisters (and the fieldworker) stand. Ms. McAllister then beckons for her nephew Tyrice (who is about Harold's age) to come along *before* she clears this with the doctor. Later, she sends Tyrice down the hall to observe Harold being weighed; she relies on her nephew's report rather than asking for this information from the healthcare professionals.

Still, neither Harold nor his mother seemed as comfortable as Alexander had been. Alexander was used to extensive conversation at home; with the doctor, he was at ease initiating questions. Harold, who was used to responding to directives at home, primarily answered questions from the doctor, rather than posing his own. Alexander, encouraged by his mother, was assertive and confident with the doctor. Harold was reserved. Absorbing his mother's apparent need to conceal the truth about the range of foods he ate, he appeared cautious, displaying an emerging sense of constraint.

We observed a similar pattern in school interactions. Overall, the working-class and poor adults had much more distance or separation from the school than their middle-class counterparts. Ms. McAllister, for example, could be quite assertive in some settings (e.g., at the start of family observations, she visited the local drug dealer, warning him not to "mess with" the black male fieldworker).[24] But throughout the fourth-grade parent-teacher conference, she kept her winter jacket zipped up, sat hunched over in her chair, and spoke in barely audible tones. She was stunned when the teacher said that Harold did not do homework. Sounding dumbfounded, she said, "He does it at home." The teacher denied it and continued talking. Ms. McAllister made no further comments and did not probe for more information, except about a letter the teacher said he had mailed home and that she had not

received. The conference ended, having yielded Ms. McAllister few insights into Harold's educational experience.[25]

Other working-class and poor parents also appeared baffled, intimidated, and subdued in parent-teacher conferences. Ms. Driver, who was extremely worried about her fourth-grader's inability to read, kept these concerns to herself. She explained to us, "I don't want to jump into anything and find it is the wrong thing." When working-class and poor parents did try to intervene in their children's educational experiences, they often felt ineffectual. Billy Yanelli's mother appeared relaxed and chatty in many of her interactions with other adults. With "the school," however, she was very apprehensive. She distrusted school personnel. She felt bullied and powerless. Hoping to resolve a problem involving her son, she tried to prepare her ideas in advance. Still, as she recounted during an interview, she failed to make school officials see Billy as vulnerable:

> Ms. Yanelli: "I found a note in his school bag one morning and it said, 'I'm going to kill you . . . you're a dead mother-f-er. . . .' So, I started shaking. I was all ready to go over there. [I was] prepared for the counselor. . . . They said the reason they [the other kids] do what they do is because Billy makes them do it. So they had an answer for everything."
>
> Interviewer: "How did you feel about that answer?"
>
> Ms. Yanelli: "I hate the school. I hate it."

Working-class and poor children seemed aware of their parents' frustration and witnessed their powerlessness. Billy Yanelli, for example, asserted in an interview that his mother "hate[d]" school officials.

At times, these parents encouraged their children to resist school officials' authority. The Yanellis told Billy to "beat up" a boy who was bothering him. Wendy Driver's mother advised her to punch a male classmate who pestered her and pulled her ponytail. Ms. Driver's boyfriend added, "Hit him when the teacher isn't looking."

In classroom observations, working-class and poor children could be quite lively and energetic, but we did not observe them try to customize their environments. They tended to react to adults' offers or, at times, to plead with educators to repeat previous experiences, such as reading a particular story, watching a movie, or going to the computer room. Compared to middle-class classroom interactions, the boundaries between adults and children seemed firmer and clearer. Although the children often resisted and tested school rules, they did not seem to be seeking to get educators to accommodate their own *individual* preferences.

Overall, then, the behavior of working-class and poor parents cannot be explained as a manifestation of their temperaments or of overall passivity; parents were quite energetic in intervening in their children's lives in other spheres. Rather, working-class and poor parents generally appeared to depend on the school (Lareau 2000), even as they were dubious of the trustworthiness of the professionals. This suspicion of professionals in dominant institutions is, at least in some instances, a reasonable response.[26] The unequal level of trust, as well as differences in the amount and quality of information divulged, can yield unequal *profits* during an historical moment when professionals applaud assertiveness and reject passivity as an inappropriate parenting strategy (Epstein 2001). Middle-class children and parents often (but not always) accrued advantages or profits from their efforts. Alexander Williams succeeded in having the doctor take his medical concerns seriously. Ms. Marshall's children ended up in the gifted program, even though they did not technically qualify. Middle-class children expect institutions to be responsive to *them* and to accommodate their individual needs. By contrast, when Wendy Driver is told to hit the boy who is pestering her (when the teacher isn't looking) or Billy Yanelli is told to physically defend himself, despite school rules, they are not learning how to make bureaucratic institutions work to their advantage.

Instead, they are being given lessons in frustration and powerlessness.

WHY DOES SOCIAL CLASS MATTER?

Parents' economic resources helped create the observed class differences in childrearing practices. Enrollment fees that middle-class parents dismissed as "negligible" were formidable expenses for less affluent families. Parents also paid for clothing, equipment, hotel stays, fast food meals, summer camps, and fundraisers. In 1994, the Tallingers estimated the cost of Garrett's activities at $4,000 annually, and that figure was not unusually high.[27] Moreover, families needed reliable private transportation and flexible work schedules to get children to and from events. These resources were disproportionately concentrated in middle-class families.

Differences in educational resources also are important. Middle-class parents' superior levels of education gave them larger vocabularies that facilitated concerted cultivation, particularly in institutional interventions. Poor and working-class parents were not familiar with key terms professionals used, such as "tetanus shot." Furthermore, middle-class parents' educational backgrounds gave them confidence when criticizing educational professionals and intervening in school matters. Working-class and poor parents viewed educators as their social superiors.

Kohn and Schooler (1983) showed that parents' occupations, especially the complexity of their work, influence their childrearing beliefs. We found that parents' work mattered, but also saw signs that the experience of adulthood itself influenced conceptions of childhood. Middle-class parents often were preoccupied with the pleasures and challenges of their work lives.[28] They tended to view childhood as a dual opportunity: a chance for play, and for developing talents and skills of value later in life. Mr. Tallinger noted that playing soccer taught Garrett to be "hard nosed" and "competitive," valuable workplace skills. Ms. Williams mentioned the value of Alexander learning to work with others by playing on a sports team. Middle-class parents, aware of the "declining fortunes" of the middle class, worried about their own economic futures and those of their children (Newman 1993). This uncertainty increased their commitment to helping their children develop broad skills to enhance their future possibilities.

Working-class and poor parents' conceptions of adulthood and childhood also appeared to be closely connected to their lived experiences. For the working class, it was the deadening quality of work and the press of economic shortages that defined their experience of adulthood and influenced their vision of childhood. It was dependence on public assistance and severe economic shortages that most shaped poor parents' views. Families in both classes had many worries about basic issues: food shortages, limited access to healthcare, physical safety, unreliable transportation, insufficient clothing. Thinking back over their childhoods, these parents remembered hardship but also recalled times without the anxieties they now faced. Many appeared to want their own youngsters to concentrate on being happy and relaxed, keeping the burdens of life at bay until they were older.

Thus, childrearing strategies are influenced by more than parents' education. It is the interweaving of life experiences and resources, including parents' economic resources, occupational conditions, and educational backgrounds, that appears to be most important in leading middle-class parents to engage in concerted cultivation and working-class and poor parents to engage in the accomplishment of natural growth. Still, the structural location of families did not fully determine their childrearing practices. The agency of actors and the indeterminacy of social life are inevitable.

In addition to economic and social resources, are there other significant factors? If the poor and working-class families' resources were transformed overnight so that they equaled those of the middle-class families, would their cultural

logic of childrearing shift as well? Or are there cultural attitudes and beliefs that are substantially independent of economic and social resources that are influencing parents' practices here? The size and scope of this study preclude a definitive answer. Some poor and working-class parents embraced principles of concerted cultivation: They wished (but could not afford) to enroll their children in organized activities (e.g., piano lessons, voice lessons), they believed listening to children was important, and they were committed to being involved in their children's schooling. Still, even when parents across all of the classes seemed committed to similar principles, their motivations differed. For example, many working-class and poor parents who wanted more activities for their children were seeking a safe haven for them. Their goal was to provide protection from harm rather than to cultivate the child's talents per se.

Some parents explicitly criticized children's schedules that involved many activities. During the parent interviews, we described the real-life activities of two children (using data from the 12 families we were observing). One schedule resembled Alexander Williams's: restricted television, required reading, and many organized activities, including piano lessons (for analytical purposes, we said that, unlike Alexander, this child disliked his piano lessons but was not allowed to quit). Summing up the attitude of the working-class and poor parents who rejected this kind of schedule,[29] one white, poor mother complained:

> I think he wants more. I think he doesn't enjoy doing what he's doing half of the time (light laughter). I think his parents are too strict. And he's not a child.

Even parents who believed this more regimented approach would pay off "job-wise" when the child was an adult still expressed serious reservations: "I think he is a sad kid," or, "He must be dead-dog tired."

Thus, working-class and poor parents varied in their beliefs. Some longed for a schedule of organized activities for their children and others did not; some believed in reasoning with children and playing an active role in schooling and others did not. Fully untangling the effects of material and cultural resources on parents and children's choices is a challenge for future research.[30]

DISCUSSION

The evidence shows that class position influences critical aspects of family life: time use, language use, and kin ties. Not all aspects of family life are affected by social class, and there is variability within class. Still, parents do transmit advantages to their children in patterns that are sufficiently consistent and identifiable to be described as a "cultural logic" of childrearing. The white and black middle-class parents engaged in practices I have termed "concerted cultivation"—they made a deliberate and sustained effort to stimulate children's development and to cultivate their cognitive and social skills. The working-class and poor parents viewed children's development as spontaneously unfolding, as long as they were provided with comfort, food, shelter, and other basic support. This commitment, too, required ongoing effort; sustaining children's natural growth despite formidable life challenges is properly viewed as an accomplishment.

In daily life, the patterns associated with each of these approaches were interwoven and mutually reinforcing. Nine-year-old middle-class children already had developed a clear sense of their own talents and skills, and they differentiated themselves from siblings and friends. They were also learning to think of themselves as special and worthy of having adults devote time and energy to promoting them and their leisure activities. In the process, the boundaries between adults and children sometimes blurred; adults' leisure preferences became subordinate to their children's. The strong emphasis on reasoning in middle-class families had similar, diffuse effects. Children used their formidable reasoning skills to persuade adults to acquiesce to their wishes.

The idea that children's desires should be taken seriously was routinely realized in the middle-class families we interviewed and observed. In many subtle ways, children were taught that they were entitled. Finally, the commitment to cultivating children resulted in family schedules so crowded with activities there was little time left for visiting relatives. Quantitative studies of time use have shed light on important issues, but they do not capture the interactive nature of routine, everyday activities and the varying ways they affect the texture of family life.[31]

In working-class and poor families, parents established limits; within those limits, children were free to fashion their own pastimes. Children's wishes did not guide adults' actions as frequently or as decisively as they did in middle-class homes. Children were viewed as subordinate to adults. Parents tended to issue directives rather than to negotiate. Frequent interactions with relatives rather than acquaintances or strangers created a thicker divide between families and the outside world. Implicitly and explicitly, parents taught their children to keep their distance from people in positions of authority, to be distrustful of institutions, and, at times, to resist officials' authority. Children seemed to absorb the adults' feelings of powerlessness in their institutional relationships. As with the middle class, there were important variations among working-class and poor families, and some critical aspects of family life, such as the use of humor, were immune to social class.

The role of race in children's daily lives was less powerful than I had expected. The middle-class black children's parents were alert to the potential effects of institutional discrimination on their children. Middle-class black parents also took steps to help their children develop a positive racial identity. Still, in terms of how children spend their time, the way parents use language and discipline in the home, the nature of the families' social connections, and the strategies used for intervening in institutions, white and black middle-class parents engaged in very similar, often identical, practices with their children. A similar pattern was observed in white and black working-class homes as well as in white and black poor families. Thus my data indicate that on the childrearing dynamics studied here, compared with social class, race was less important in children's daily lives.[32] As they enter the racially segregated worlds of dating, marriage, and housing markets, and as they encounter more racism in their interpersonal contact with whites (Waters 1999), the relative importance of race in the children's daily lives is likely to increase.

Differences in family dynamics and the logic of childrearing across social classes have long-term consequences. As family members moved out of the home and interacted with representatives of formal institutions, middle-class parents and children were able to negotiate more valuable outcomes than their working-class and poor counterparts. In interactions with agents of dominant institutions, working-class and poor children were learning lessons in constraint while middle-class children were developing a sense of entitlement.

It is a mistake to see either concerted cultivation or the accomplishment of natural growth as an intrinsically desirable approach. As has been amply documented, conceptions of childhood have changed dramatically over time (Wrigley 1989). Drawbacks to middle-class childrearing, including the exhaustion associated with intensive mothering and frenetic family schedules and a sapping of children's naivete that leaves them feeling too sophisticated for simple games and toys (Hays 1996), remain insufficiently highlighted.

Another drawback is that middle-class children are less likely to learn how to fill "empty time" with their own creative play, leading to a dependence on their parents to solve experiences of boredom. Sociologists need to more clearly differentiate between standards that are intrinsically desirable and standards that facilitate success in dominant institutions. A more critical, and historically sensitive, vision is needed (Donzelot 1979). Here Bourdieu's work (1976, 1984, 1986, 1989) is valuable.

Finally, there are methodological issues to consider. Quantitative research has delineated population-wide patterns; ethnographies offer rich descriptive detail but typically focus on a single, small group. Neither approach can provide holistic, but empirically grounded, assessments of daily life. Multi-sited, multi-person research using ethnographic methods also poses formidable methodological challenges (Lareau 2002). Still, families have proven themselves open to being studied in an intimate fashion. Creating penetrating portraits of daily life that will enrich our theoretical models is an important challenge for the future.

■ Review Questions

1. If you grew up in a middle-class family, answer this question: Did your parents practice concerted cultivation? If you grew up in a working-class or poor family, answer this one: Did your parents practice the accomplishment of natural growth?
2. Why might concerted cultivation lead children to have a greater sense of entitlement when dealing with teachers, doctors, or other professionals?

ENDNOTES

1. In a study of mothers' beliefs about childrearing, Hays (1996) found variations in how working-class and middle-class mothers sorted information, but she concluded that a pattern of "intensive mothering" was present across social classes. My study of behavior found class differences but, as I discuss below, in some instances working-class and poor

parents expressed a desire to enroll their children in organized activities.

2. Some significant differences between the study's working-class and poor families (e.g., only the poor children experienced food shortages) are not highlighted here because, on the dimensions discussed in this paper, the biggest differences were between middle-class and nonmiddle-class families. See Lareau (2003) for a more elaborate discussion as well as Lamont (2000) for distinctions working-class families draw between themselves and the poor; see McLanahan and Sandefur (1994) regarding family structure and children's lives.

3. Case studies of nonrandom samples, such as this one, have the limitation that findings cannot be generalized beyond the cases reported. These examples serve to illustrate conceptual points (Burawoy et al. 1991) rather than to describe representative patterns of behavior. A further limitation of this study is that the data were collected and analyzed over an extended period of time (see the "Methodology" section).

4. All names of people and places are pseudonyms. The Lawrenceville school was in a white suburban neighborhood in a university community a few hours from a metropolitan area. The student population was about half white and half black; the (disproportionately poor) black children were bused from other neighborhoods.

5. Over three-quarters of the students at Lower Richmond qualified for free lunch; by contrast, Swan did not have a free lunch program.

6. At both sites, we attended school events and observed many parent-teacher conferences. Also, I interviewed the classroom teachers and adults involved in the children's organized activities. These interview data are not presented here.

7. Both schools had computer labs, art programs, and music programs, but Swan had many more resources and much higher average achievement scores. Graffiti and physical confrontations between students were common only at Lower Richmond. At these two sites and in Lawrenceville, white faculty predominated.

8. I located the black middle-class parents through social networks; the white poor families were located through flyers left at welfare offices and social service programs, and posted on telephone poles. Ten white poor families (only) were paid $25 per interview.

9. Of 19 families asked to participate in the intensive study, 7 declined (a response rate of 63 percent). I tried to balance the observational phase sample by gender, race, and class, and to "mix and match" the children on other characteristics, such as their behavior with peers, their relationships with extended family, and their parents' level of involvement in their education. The aim was to lessen the chance that observed differences in behavior would reflect unknown variables (e.g., church attendance or parents' participation at school). Last, I deliberately included two families (Irwins, Greeleys) who had some "middle-class" traits but who lived in a working-class and poor area, respectively. Including these unusual families seemed conceptually important for disentangling the influences of social class and environment (neighborhood).

10. I analyzed the data for the study as a whole in two ways. I coded themes from the interviews and used Folio Views software to help establish patterns. I also relied on reading the field notes, thinking about similarities and differences across families, searching for disconfirming evidence, and re-reading the field notes.

11. Recruitment to complete the sample was difficult as children needed to be a specific age, race, and class, and to be part of families who were willing to be observed. The white poor boy was recommended by a social service program manager; the black middle-class children were located through extended social networks of mine.

12. We did 12 to 14 observations of the Handlon and Carroll families before settling on the 20-visit pattern. In Alexander Williams's case, the visits occurred over a year. To observe unusual events (e.g., a family reunion), we sometimes went back after formal observations had ended.

13. Families developed preferences, favoring one fieldworker in a team over another. But these preferences were not stable across families, and the field notes did not differ dramatically between fieldworkers. Notes were much more similar than they were different.

14. Wright (1997) uses 12 categories in his neo-Marxist approach. Goldthorpe, a neo-Weberian, operationalizes his class schema at levels of aggregation ranging from 3 to 11 categories (Erikson and Goldthorpe 1993:38–39).

15. Here "poor" refers to the source of income (i.e., government assistance versus labor market) rather than the amount of income. Although lower class is more accurate than poor, it is widely perceived as pejorative. I might have used "underclass," but the literature has defined this term in racialized ways.

16. Dollar figures are from 1994–1995, unless otherwise noted. Income was not used to define class membership, but these data are available from the author.

17. Mr. and Ms. Williams disagreed about the value of their home; the figure here averages what each reported in 1995. Housing prices in their region were lower—and continue to be lower today—than in many other parts of the country. Their property is now worth an estimated $175,000 to $200,000.

18. Alexander's mother goes by Christina Nile at work, but Mrs. Williams at church. Some other mothers' last names also differ from their children's. Here I assign all mothers the same last names as their children.

19. I contacted the Williams family through social networks after I was unable to recruit the black middle-class families who had participated in the classroom observation and interview phase. As a result, I do not have data from classroom observations or parent-teacher conferences for Alexander.

20. The Suzuki method is labor intensive. Students are required to listen to music about one hour per day. Also, both child and parent(s) are expected to practice daily and to attend every lesson together.

21. Hart and Risley (1995) reported a similar difference in speech patterns. In their sample, by about age three, children of professionals had larger vocabularies and spoke more utterances per hour than the *parents* of similarly aged children on welfare.

22. This section focuses primarily on the concerns of black parents. Whites, of course, also benefited from race relations, notably in the scattering of poor white families in working-class neighborhoods rather than being concentrated in dense settings with other poor families (Massey and Denton 1993).

23. Not all professionals accommodated children's participation. Regardless of these adults' overt attitudes, though, we routinely observed that middle-class mothers monitor and intervene in their children's interactions with professionals.

24. Ms. McAllister told me about this visit; we did not observe it. It is striking that she perceived only the black male fieldworker as being at risk.

25. Middle-class parents sometimes appeared slightly anxious during parent-teacher conferences, but overall, they spoke more and asked educators more questions than did working-class and poor parents.

26. The higher levels of institutional reports of child neglect, child abuse, and other family difficulties among poor families may reflect this group's greater vulnerability to institutional intervention (e.g., see L. Gordon 1989).

27. In 2002, a single sport could cost as much as $5,000 annually. Yearly league fees for ice hockey run to $2,700; equipment costs are high as well (Halbfinger 2002).

28. Middle-class adults do not live problem-free lives, but compared with the working class and poor, they have more varied occupational experiences and greater access to jobs with higher economic returns.

29. Many middle-class parents remarked that forcing a child to take piano lessons was wrong. Nevertheless, they continued to stress the importance of "exposure."

30. Similarly, whether concerted cultivation and the accomplishment of natural growth are new historical developments rather than modifications of earlier forms of childrearing cannot be determined from the study's findings. The "institutionalization of children's leisure" seems to be increasing (Corsaro 1997). Hays (1996) argues that families increasingly are "invaded" by the "logic of impersonal, competitive, contractual, commodified, efficient, profit-maximizing, self-interested relations" (p. 11). In addition to evidence of a new increase in children's organized activities (Sandberg and Hofferth 2001), none of the middle-class parents in the study reported having childhood schedules comparable to their children's. Change over time in parents' intervention in education and in

the amount of reasoning in middle-class families also are difficult to determine accurately. Kohn and Schooler's (1983) study suggests little change with regard to reasoning, but other commentators insist there has been a rise in the amount of negotiating between parents and children (Chidekel 2002; Kropp 2001). Such debates can not be resolved without additional careful historical research.

31. The time-use differences we observed were part of the taken-for-granted aspects of daily life; they were generally unnoticed by family members.

For example, the working-class Yanellis considered themselves "really busy" if they had one baseball game on Saturday and an extended family gathering on Sunday. The Tallingers and other middle-class families would have considered this a slow weekend.

32. These findings are compatible with others showing children as aware of race at relatively early ages (Van Ausdale and Feagin 1996). At the two sites, girls often played in racially segregated groups during recess; boys tended to play in racially integrated groups.

CHAPTER 5

Race, Ethnicity, and Families

In 1903, the great African American sociologist W. E. B. DuBois wrote in his book *The Souls of Black Folk* that "the problem of the twentieth century is the problem of the color line—the relation of the darker to the lighter races of men in Asia and Africa, in America, and the islands of the sea." A century later, the "problem" of color still looms large in discussions of American society, including family life.

Recently, the declining rate of marriage among African Americans has attracted much attention, including books with provocative titles such as *Is Marriage for White People?*[1] Perhaps 60 to 70 percent of African Americans will ever marry, at current rates, compared to 80 to 90 percent among whites. In the first reading in this chapter, Shirley A. Hill argues that although African Americans value marriage highly, inequalities having to do with race, class, and gender have combined to make marriage less central to African American family life than is the case

for white Americans. Distinctive patterns of work and of women's independence from men can be traced back to slavery. Transformations in the economy have reduced the demand for the kind of skilled blue-collar labor that African American men could use to support a marriage. These inequalities, Hill argues, explain much of the racial difference in marriage.

Although that black/white distinction is still a central part of American life, there are other "colors" now. The largest of the newer groups is composed of people who speak Spanish and mostly trace their ancestry through Latin America. In the American political discourse, they are increasingly lumped together as "Hispanics," even though there are sharp differences among the major Hispanic groups. Another rapidly growing group is composed of people who are even more diverse than Hispanics: immigrants from the huge expanse of the globe running from South Asia (e.g., India, Pakistan) to Southeast Asia (e.g., Indonesia, Thailand), and on to East Asia (e.g., China, Japan). They do not share a language or common physical features, and yet in the United States they are lumped together in the category "Asian."

---

[1]Banks, Ralph R. (2011). *Is marriage for white people? How the African American marriage decline affects everyone.* New York: Dutton.

With so many immigrants arriving (the current rate of immigration is higher than at any time since the early decades of the twentieth century), the question arises of whether they will marry outside their group. Earlier in American history, intermarriage among major ethnic and racial groups was outlawed in most states. Even as late as 1967, 15 states had laws forbidding marriage between whites and nonwhites. But both the law and American public opinion have changed. In the second selection in this chapter, Zhenchao Qian analyzes trends in intermarriage among blacks, Hispanics, Asians, American Indians, and non-Hispanic whites. He reports that intermarriage is on the rise, although rates for blacks are substantially lower than for other nonwhite groups. In fact, intermarriage is so common among young Asians, Hispanics, and American Indians that one wonders whether these groups will still have their distinctive ethnicities a generation or two from now.

READING 5-1

Why Won't African Americans Get (and Stay) Married? Why Should They?

Shirley A. Hill

AFRICAN AMERICAN MARRIAGES: A CONTEMPORARY PERSPECTIVE

Scholarly inquiry into the demise of marriage has produced a host of studies showing that attitudinal support for marriage among African Americans has remained strong; indeed, blacks often express greater support for traditional ideals about sexuality, marriage, and family than do white Americans. Despite living lives that contradict their expressed ideals, African Americans are as likely as white Americans to idealize marriage (Edin 2000; Harknett and McLanahan 2004) and are less accepting of nonmarital sex, cohabitation, and divorce than whites (Huston and Melz 2004). How, then, does one explain the discrepancy between their support for marriage and their lived experiences? I argue that marriage has traditionally been based on social norms and ideologies that were at odds with the cultural traditions and economic resources of African Americans, and thus has never been as firmly institutionalized among black people. I use an intersectionality framework to show that class, race, and gender inequalities have made and continue to make it difficult for many African Americans to conform to mainstream marital expectations, and that these structural inequalities have fostered their participation in cultural patterns (such as nonmarriage and single motherhood) that contradict their professed ideals. Neither cultural nor structural theorists have adequately dealt with the intersection of these inequalities, and thus have offered at best partial explanations of the marriage decline.

From Shirley A. Hill in Peters & Dush (2009).

The traditional marriage contract is rooted in notions of patriarchy, female subordination, distinct roles for men and women, the protection of property, and the production of legitimate children—all of which were negated for African Americans for centuries by the dictates of slavery. Slavery . . . demanded diversity and flexibility in the family arrangements of black people, depending on factors such as the type of economy, region, size of the plantation, and solvency of the slave owner (Dunaway 2003; Franklin 1997). At best, slavery nearly always undermined the economic basis for male authority in families, fostered female independence, prevented blacks from owning much property, and defined families primarily as mothers and their children. Most evidence suggests that a majority of African Americans married and formed two-parent families after slavery ended. Clearly, however, a significant minority either remained single (Hill 2005, 2006) or lived in informal or cohabiting relationships (Frankel 1999), at least partly because it was difficult for them to reap the benefits and privileges of married life. For example, most former slaves entered the sharecropping system that demanded the labor of men and women, and that criticized black women who tried to exempt themselves from such work as "aspiring to a model of womanhood that was considered inappropriate for them" (Dill 1988). This labor system made it difficult for black men to claim head-of-household status based on economic provisioning or for wives to prioritize caring for their children and homes. Marriage neither exempted women from productive labor nor substantially improved their standards of living, yet those who married sometimes found their husbands eager to assert patriarchal power in their families—a factor blamed for high rates of domestic violence and marital separation among the newly freed slaves (Franklin 1997). Indeed, mainstream gender expectations, economic marginalization, and racism continued to make it difficult for African Americans to create stable marriages.

THE INTERSECTION OF CLASS, GENDER, AND RACIAL INEQUALITY

Intersectionality refers to understanding the "interconnectedness of ideas and the social structures in which they occur, and the intersecting hierarchies of gender, race, economic class, sexuality, and ethnicity" (Collins 1999). In applying this concept to the study of marriage, I focus on how structural factors shape cultural ideas and how multiple forms of inequality affect the challenges of marrying and staying married. For example, class matters a great deal as a factor in whether people will get and stay married: researchers have consistently found that higher income and educational attainment predict marriage and marital stability (Cherlin 2008). The rate of poverty among African Americans remains twice as high as that of white Americans, and much of that poverty is related to joblessness among black men (Wilson 1978). Low-income women, although struggling alone to make ends meet, are unwilling to marry men who cannot contribute much to their economic support (Edin 2000). Moreover, joblessness and poverty help push young African American men from mainstream society, and in their pursuit for manhood and respect many embrace behaviors (e.g., violence, hypersexuality) (Anderson 1999) that do not bode well for marriage and often lead to criminal behavior. Indeed, Western and Beckett (1999) have argued that racially motivated sentencing has made the penal system a major strategy in regulating the labor market, with more than 1.6 million people (disproportionately male and black) incarcerated by the late 1990s.

Economic restructuring has lessened the demand for unskilled labor, but racism in the labor market also undercuts the economic position of African Americans. Data from the Bureau of Labor Statistics reveal that among men twenty-five years of age or older in 2005, black men (7.6 percent) were more than twice as likely as white men (3.5 percent) to be unemployed. Moreover, African American men are discriminated against by employers for numerous reasons (Wilson 1987), including the notion that they simply lack the "soft skills" that are now in demand, such as "skills, abilities and traits that pertain to personality, attitude and behavior rather than formal or technical knowledge" (Moss and Tilly 1996). As Moss and Tilly have noted, employers often describe black men as being unmotivated, defensive, and hostile. Similar stereotypes undermine the ability of black women to find work. They are twice as likely as white women to be unemployed, and employers often stereotype them as unreliable single mothers (Browne and Kennelly 1995).

Neither the end of legalized racial segregation nor the gains made since the civil-rights era have eliminated racism or racial inequality; white Americans still endorse a spate of racist assumptions about African Americans and their families (Bobo, Kluegel, and Smith 1997). Racism and racial exclusion adversely affect the feelings of African Americans about their place in society and their quality of life. Hughes and Thomas, for example, found racial disparities in life quality between black and white Americans, and they argued that racism produces identity problems and a sense of rage and resentment among African Americans. Even when age and social class were considered, "African Americans were less satisfied, less happy, more mistrustful, more anomic, had less happy marriages, and rated their physical health worse than whites" (Hughes and Thomas 1998). This sense of being disrespected and disvalued in the larger society can adversely affect the quality of intimate relationships and the likelihood of marriage.

Persistent class and race inequalities intersect with and shape gender ideologies, making it difficult for African Americans to conform to traditional gender expectations or embrace the evolving ideal of gender-egalitarian marriages. For example, their long tradition of work and socioeconomic gains makes it difficult for many African American women to "marry up," or even marry men whose educational and economic position is comparable to their own. Although African American men earn more than black women, mostly because they hold male-typed jobs and more high-paying professional positions, the gains since the 1950s have been greater for black women. African American women, for example, are more likely than men to hold managerial and professional jobs (albeit in areas such as social work and teaching), more likely to have bachelor and especially graduate degrees, and more likely to feel integrated into the values of the dominant culture. This has created an important status gap between black women and men—and numerous books and movies that suggest the problem could be solved if middle-class black women would accept and marry working- or lower-class black men (Hill 2005). But class matters in forming viable marriages and marrying men of a lower class or status may help explain why black women feel less benefited by marriage than white women (Goodwin 2003). Indeed, the ideology of "marrying up" also affects low-income women, who are concerned about the loss of respectability associated with marrying poor and often jobless men (Edin 2000).

These structural inequalities foster cultural practices and behaviors that militate against marriage and marital success. Economic exclusion and persistent racial inequality, for example, ultimately creates an "oppositional culture that devalues work, schooling, and marriage" (Massey and Denton 1993). The courtship practices of young African American men who lack decent jobs or respect in mainstream society are often characterized by deceit, violence, and a general disrespect for women (Anderson 1990). The skewed gender ratio of men to women favors men and shapes their attitudes toward marriage and women; for example, Harknett and McLanahan found that "when men are in short supply, partner quality and relationship quality tend to be worse, and parents place less emphasis on the two-parent, male breadwinner norm" (Harknett and McLanahan 2004). African American men who marry tend to bring to their relationships more conservative gender

beliefs than white men (Blee and Tickamyer 1995) and, despite being more accepting of employed wives, their marriages are characterized by more work-family conflicts, especially when the wife has a career (Bridges and Orza 1996). Gender traditions also persist in the division of domestic work: African American men spend only about half as much time doing housework as their partners (John and Shelton 1997). Overall, black couples are less satisfied in their marriages than white couples; they report sharing fewer activities and experiencing more conflict and distrust (Harknett and McLanahan 2004).

THE MARRIAGE DECLINE: CAN (SHOULD) IT BE REVERSED?

The strongest arguments for marriage is that married couples have higher levels of health and well-being than singles, that marriage reduces poverty, and that children fare better in two-parent families. For these reasons, the 1996 Personal Responsibility and Work Opportunity Act (PRWOA) declared that marriage "is the foundation of a successful society" and "is an essential institution that promotes the interests of children" (Jayakody and Cabrera 2002). Proponents of marriage contend that married people are happier, healthier, and wealthier than single people (Waite and Gallagher 2000). Still, the extent to which this applies to African American couples is debatable. As indicated earlier, there is a racial gap in marital satisfaction, with married African American couples experiencing more conflict and distrust in their relationships than white couples. Although their lower level of marital satisfaction cannot be explained away by noting class differences between blacks and whites, it is undoubtedly exacerbated by the fact that African Americans are more likely to be in the working and lower classes, where divorce and domestic violence are more common. Staying in unhappy marriages correlates with adverse health outcomes, such as elevated levels of psychological distress and poor health (Hawkins and Booth 2005). There is also evidence that marital unhappiness takes a greater toll on the health of wives than of husbands, with unhappy wives having high levels of depression and substance abuse (Coontz 2005).

From an economic standpoint, black married couple families fare better than single-mother families, although their 2001 median household income ($55,618) was much less than that of white married couple families ($71,155) (Conrad and King 2005). Linda Waite has found that several factors reduce the economic benefits of marriage for African Americans, such as lower wage gap between black men and women, the lower returns black women receive for investing in their husband's earnings, and the expense of raising children, who are more likely to be present in the homes of black couples (Waite 1995). For lower-income couples, where the prospects of unemployment, divorce, and domestic violence are high, the economic benefits of marriage may prove even more meager. D. T. Lichter and colleagues report that poverty rates would still be more than twice as high among African American women if they had the same family background and rates of marriage and unwed childbirth as white women (Lichter, Graefe, and Brown 2003). They also found that among economically disadvantaged black women, marriage is associated with downward educational mobility, and those who marry and divorce have higher rates of poverty than those who never married.

Although the growth in single-mother families has leveled off in recent years, nearly 41 percent of American children live in such families, with African American children (53 percent) more likely to do so than white children (22 percent) (Sigle-Rushton and McLanahan 2004). Children benefit from having the emotional and financial support of their fathers; indeed, many studies have shown that children living with single mothers, regardless of their race or social class, are more likely than those living with two biological parents to experience academic failure, behavioral and psychological

problems, delinquency, and illegal drug use (Ellwood and Jencks 2004; Sigle-Rushton and McLanahan 2004). Still, single-mother families and extended family relationships are more institutionalized among African Americans and may have fewer adverse consequences for black children. A study comparing male adolescents living in white and black single-mother families found that lack of involvement with fathers elevated the risk of problematic behaviors only for white sons—at least partially because they were more likely to live in *divorced* single-mother families and were more likely to have lost a father with whom they had a relationship (Thomas, Farrell, and Barnes 1996). For African Americans, the risks of single-mother families may be more the result of the demise of extended family relationships and higher rates of poverty and extreme poverty; for example, in 2001 the median household income for black single mothers was less than $21,000, compared to $29,650 for white single mothers (Conrad and King 2005).

So, should African Americans get married? There are clearly benefits to be gained from marriage, although most evidence suggests that those benefits are not as great for blacks as for whites. But given the diminishing support single mothers are receiving from the state and their extended families, marriage may become more appealing. Moreover, there is strong ideological support for marriage among African Americans; the majority would like to get married, and they equate marriage with respectability, endorsing more traditional marital, gender, and sexual norms than white Americans. Still, a gap has always existed for African Americans between their endorsement of mainstream family values and their lived experiences. As I have argued, many African Americans have historically lacked the economic and cultural resources to conform to the traditional marriage contract, which was based on male-domination, gendered roles, and property. Today, these institutional aspects of marriage have now given way to marriage as a personal relationship based on gender equality and emotional satisfaction (Amato 2004). Such marital expectations should, at least arguably, make it easier for African Americans to achieve marital success, since the emphasis on economics has declined. Still, these new marital expectations are more likely to be embraced by middle-class couples, and African Americans have primarily been in the working and lower classes, where traditional values are more apparent. For example, as Landry has pointed out, employed wives have always been acceptable among African Americans, but "[it] remained for the upper-middle-class black wives to elevate the *acceptable* to the *desirable* in the early decades of the twentieth century" (Landry 2000).

CONCLUSION

In this chapter, I have argued that multiple forms of social inequality, both historically and currently, have created an important gap between the marital ideals of African Americans and the resources needed to live those ideals. This has made marriage seem less attainable, and thus has fostered cultural alternatives to marriage, such as high rates of single-mother families and nonmarital cohabitation. Mainstream marital traditions, for example, have supported patriarchal marriages headed by men earning the family wage, but exempted African American men from such jobs. These marital traditions have also been based on the primacy of marriage-centered families, but African Americans have often had to rely on extended families networks in order to survive. It has also been traditionally based on a gender division of labor that makes women economic dependents by placing them in the home, yet since slavery African American women have always combined productive and domestic work. Thus, despite high levels of attitudinal support

for marriage among black Americans, dominant marital traditions have been at odds with their experiences. In this sense, marriage has never been fully institutionalized among African Americans.

Multiple social inequalities are responsible for the erosion of marriage among African Americans during the twentieth century, and addressing those inequalities is the key to restoring marriage as a vital institution. For example, workshops have sprung up to teach African American men the value of being involved in their children's lives, but less has been done to bring them into the economic mainstream or enhance their employment skills or educational achievement—both of which are important if they are to participate consistently in family life. Similarly, both politicians and religionists who trumpet the value of marriage and two-parent families have not always acknowledged the gender inequities in those arrangements, which women increasingly refuse to tolerate. Welfare-related marriage-promotion programs have more leverage over poor, young mothers than they do the fathers, and some research suggests that such programs place the responsibility on mothers to "swallow their rage and grievances against men" and bring them into the cultural mainstream of marriage (Huston and Melz 2004). Failing to resolve basic gender issues, though, will not lead to successful marriages. Finally, marriages have changed for all Americans over the past few decades, with more employed wives, more dual-income families, more economic independence, and more couples unwilling to stay in marriages that are emotionally unsatisfying. These changes in marriage have made issues such as gender equity in the home, adequate childcare, and family-friendly practices by employers key factors in the maintenance of families.

■ Review Questions

1. What is holding back more marriages among African Americans?
2. Why might marriage be less beneficial for African Americans than for whites?

Breaking the Last Taboo
Interracial Marriage in America

Zhenchao Qian

Guess Who's Coming to Dinner, a movie about a white couple's reaction when their daughter falls in love with a black man, caused a public stir in 1967. That the African-American character was a successful doctor did little to lower the anxieties of white audiences. Now, almost four decades later, the public hardly reacts at all to interracial relationships. Both Hollywood movies and TV shows, including *Die Another Day, Made in America, ER, The West Wing,* and *Friends,* regularly portray interracial romance.

What has changed? In the same year that Sidney Poitier startled Spencer Tracy and Katherine Hepburn, the Supreme Court ruled, in *Loving v. Virginia,* that laws forbidding people of different races to marry were unconstitutional. The civil rights movement helped remove other blatant legal barriers to the integration of racial minorities and fostered the growth of minority middle classes. As racial minorities advanced, public opinion against interracial marriage declined, and rates of interracial marriage grew rapidly.

Between 1970 and 2000, black-white marriages grew more than fivefold from 65 to 363 thousand, and marriages between whites and members of other races grew almost fivefold from 233 thousand to 1.1 million. Proportionately, interracial marriages remain rare, but their rates increased from less than 1 percent of all marriages in 1970 to nearly 3 percent in 2000. This trend shows that the "social

Zhenchao Qian, "Breaking the Last Taboo: Interracial Marriage in America," *Contexts,* Vol. 4, No. 4, pp. 33–37. © 2005 The American Sociological Association. Used by permission. All rights reserved.

distance" between racial groups has narrowed significantly, although not nearly as much as the social distance between religious groups. Interfaith marriages have become common in recent generations. That marriages across racial boundaries remain much rarer than cross-religion marriages reflects the greater prominence of race in America. While the interracial marriage taboo seems to be gradually breaking down, at least for certain groups, intermarriage in the United States will not soon match the level of intermarriage that European immigrant groups have achieved over the past century.

PUBLIC ATTITUDES

Americans have become generally more accepting of other races in recent decades, probably as a result of receiving more education and meeting more people of other races. Americans increasingly work and go to school with people from many groups. As racial gaps in income narrow, more members of racial minorities can afford to live in neighborhoods that had previously been white. Neighbors have opportunities to reduce stereotypes and establish friendships. Tolerance also grows as generations pass; elderly people with racist attitudes die and are replaced by younger, more tolerant people. The general softening of racial antagonisms has also improved attitudes toward interracial marriage.

In 1958, a national survey asked Americans for the first time about their opinions of interracial marriage. Only 4 percent of whites approved of intermarriage with blacks. Almost 40 years later, in 1997, 67 percent of whites approved of such intermarriages. Blacks have been much more accepting; by 1997, 83 percent approved of intermarriage. Whites' support for interracial marriage—which may to some extent only reflect respondents' sense of what they should tell interviewers—lags far behind their support of interracial schools (96 percent), housing (86 percent), and jobs (97 percent). Many white

Americans apparently remain uneasy about interracial intimacy generally, and most disapprove of interracial relationships in their own families. Still, such relationships are on the increase.

INTERRACIAL DATING

According to a recent survey reported by George Yancey, more than one-half of African-, Hispanic-, and Asian-American adults have dated someone from a different racial group, and even more of those who have lived in integrated neighborhoods or attended integrated schools have done so. Most dates, of course, are casual and do not lead to serious commitments, and this is especially true for interracial dating. Analyzing data from the National Longitudinal Study of Adolescent Health, Kara Joyner and Grace Kao find that 71 percent of white adolescents with white boyfriends or girlfriends have introduced them to their families, but only 57 percent of those with nonwhite friends have done so. Similarly, 63 percent of black adolescents with black boyfriends or girlfriends have introduced them to their families, but only 52 percent of those with nonblack friends have done so. Data from another national survey show similar patterns for young adults aged 18–29 (61 percent versus 51 percent introducing for whites, and 70 percent versus 47 percent for blacks).

While resistance to interracial relationships in principle has generally declined, opposition remains high among the families of those so involved. Interracial couples express concern about potential crises when their families become aware of such relationships. Their parents, especially white parents, worry about what those outside the family might think and fear that their reputations in the community will suffer. Maria Root notes that parents actively discourage interracial romance, often pointing to other peoples' prejudice—not their own—and expressing concern for their child's well-being: "Marriage is hard enough; why make it more difficult?"

The dating and the parental reservations reveal a generation gap: Young men and women today are more open to interracial relationships than their parents are. This gap may be due simply to youthful experimentation; youngsters tend to push boundaries. As people age, they gradually learn to conform. Kara Joyner and Grace Kao find that interracial dating is most common among teenagers but becomes infrequent for people approaching 30. They attribute this shift to the increasing importance of family and friends—and their possible disapproval—as we age. When people are ready to be "serious," they tend to fall in love with people who are just like themselves.

INTERRACIAL COHABITATION AND MARRIAGE

Who pairs up with whom depends partly on the size of the different racial groups in the United States. The larger the group, the more likely members are to find marriageable partners of their own race. The U.S. Census Bureau classifies race into four major categories: whites, African Americans, Asian Americans, and American Indians. Hispanics can belong to any of the four racial groups. Whites form the largest group, about 70 percent of the population, and just 4 percent of married whites aged 20–34 in 2000 had nonwhite spouses. The interracial marriage rates are much higher for American-born racial minorities: 9 percent for African Americans, about 39 percent for Hispanics, 56 percent for American Indians, and 59 percent for Asian Americans (who account for less than 4 percent of the total population). Mathematically, one marriage between an Asian American and a white raises the intermarriage rate for Asian Americans much more than for whites, because whites are so much more numerous. Because of their numbers as well, although just 4 percent of whites are involved in interracial marriages, 92 percent of all interracial marriages include a white partner. About half of the remaining 8 percent are black-Hispanic couples. Racial minorities have more opportunities to meet whites in schools, workplaces, and neighborhoods than to meet members of other minority groups.

Some interracial couples contemplating marriage avoid family complications by just living together. In 2000, 4 percent of married white women had nonwhite husbands, but 9 percent of white women who were cohabiting had nonwhite partners (see Figure 5.1). Similarly, 13 percent of married black men had nonblack spouses, but 24 percent of cohabiting black men lived with nonblack partners. Hispanics and Asian Americans showed the same tendency; only American Indians showed the opposite pattern. Black-white combinations are particularly notable. Black-white pairings accounted for 26 percent of all cohabiting couples but only 14 percent of all interracial marriages. They are more likely to cohabit than other minority-white couples, but they are also less likely to marry. The long history of the ban on interracial marriage in the United States, especially black-white marriage, apparently still affects black-white relationships today.

Given differences in population size, comparing rates of intermarriage across groups can be difficult. Nevertheless, statistical models used by social scientists can account for group size, determine whether members of any group are marrying out more or less often than one would expect given their numbers, and then discover what else affects intermarriage. Results show that the lighter the skin color, the higher the rate of intermarriage with white Americans. Hispanics who label themselves as racially "white" are most likely to marry non-Hispanic whites. Asian Americans and American Indians are next in their levels of marriage with whites. Hispanics who do not consider themselves racially white have low rates of intermarriage with whites. African Americans are least likely of all racial minorities to marry whites. Darker skin in America is associated with discrimination, lower educational attainment, lower income, and segregation. Even among African Americans, those of lighter tone tend to experience less discrimination.

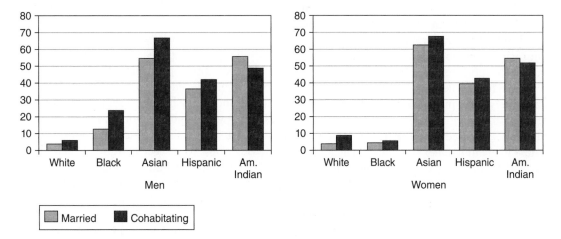

Interracial marriage remains rare among white and black Americans.

FIGURE 5.1

Percentage of Americans in couples married to (dark bars) or cohabiting with (light bars) someone of a different race. (*Source:* 2000 Census.)

RACE AND EDUCATION

Most married couples have similar levels of education, which typically indicates that they are also somewhat similar in social position, background, and values. Most interracial couples also have relatively equal educational attainments. However, when interracial couples do differ in their education, a hierarchy of color is apparent. The darker the skin color of racial minorities, the more likely they are to have married whites "below" them, that is, with less education than themselves. Six of ten African Americans who marry whites with different levels of education marry whites less educated than themselves. Hispanics also tend to marry whites less educated than themselves, but Asian Americans marry whites at about the same educational level.

Highly educated minority members often attend integrated colleges, and their workplaces and neighborhoods are integrated. Although they often develop a strong sense of their group identity in such environments, they also find substantial opportunities for interracial contact, friendship, romance, and marriage. College-educated men and women are more likely to marry interracially than those with less education. The fact that Asian Americans attend college at unusually high rates helps explain their high level of intermarriage with whites. The major exceptions to the interracial influence of higher education are African Americans.

Although middle-class African Americans increasingly live in integrated neighborhoods, they are still much more segregated than other minorities. Well-educated African Americans are less likely to live next to whites than are well educated Hispanics and Asian Americans. One reason is that middle-class black Americans are so numerous that they can form their own middle-class black neighborhoods, while middle-class Hispanic and Asian-American communities are smaller and often fractured by differences in national origin and language. In addition, studies show clearly that whites resist having black neighbors much more than they resist having Hispanic or Asian American neighbors.

Residential and school segregation on top of a long and relentless history of racial discrimination and inequality reduce African Americans' opportunities for interracial contact and marriage. The geographic distance between blacks and whites is in many ways rooted in the historical separation between the two groups. In contrast, the distance of Hispanics and Asian Americans from whites has more to do with their current economic circumstances; as those improve, they come nearer to whites geographically, socially, and matrimonially.

A MAN AND A WOMAN

Black-white couples show a definite pattern: 74 percent involve a black husband and a white wife. Asian American–white couples lean the other way; 58 percent involve an Asian-American wife. Sex balances are roughly even for couples that include a white and a Hispanic (53 percent involve a Hispanic husband) or a white and an American Indian (49 percent involve Indian husbands).

I mentioned before that most black-white couples have similar educations; nonetheless, white women who marry black men "marry up" more often than those who marry white men. This is especially striking because the pool of highly educated white men greatly outnumbers the pool of highly educated black men. More than half of black husbands of white women have at least some college education, but only two-fifths of black husbands of black women do. In that sense, white wives get more than their "share" of well-educated black husbands. This further reduces the chances that black women, especially highly educated black women, will marry, because they often face shortages of marriageable men. African-American women often resent this. Interviewed by Maria Root, one black man in such a relationship reported being accused of "selling out" and "dissing his black sisters."

Half a century ago, Robert Merton proposed a "status exchange" theory to explain the high proportion of marriages between black men and white women. He suggested that men with high economic or professional status who carry the stigma of being black in a racial caste society "trade" their social position for whiteness by marriage. On the other hand, some social scientists argue that racialized sexual images also encourage marriages between white women and black men. Throughout Europe and the West, people have long seen fair skin tone as a desirable feminine characteristic, and African Americans share those perceptions. For example, Mark Hill found that black interviewers participating in a national survey of African Americans rated black women interviewees with lighter skin as more attractive than those with darker skin. But they did not consider male interviewees with light skin any more attractive than darker-skinned men.

Asian Americans show a different pattern; in most of their marriages with whites, the husband is white. Although Asian-American men are typically more educated than white men, in the mixed couples, white husbands usually have more education than their Asian-American wives. As with white wives of black men, the wives have "married up" educationally. Some speculate that Asian-American women tend to marry white men because they perceive Asian-American men to be rigidly traditional on sex roles and white men as more nurturing and expressive. The emphasis in Asian cultures on the male line of descent may pressure Asian-American men to carry on the lineage by marrying "one of their own." But what attracts white men to Asian-American women? Some scholars suggest that it is the widespread image of Asian women as submissive and hyperfeminine (the "Madame Butterfly" icon).

THE FUTURE OF INTERRACIAL MARRIAGE

Rates of interracial marriage in the future will respond to some conflicting forces: the weakening of barriers between groups; increasing numbers of Hispanics and Asians in the nation; and possible rising ethnic consciousness. The continued progress of racial minorities in residential integration and economic achievement promotes contact between members of different races as equals. The color line, however, probably will not disappear. Marriage between African Americans and whites is likely to remain rare. Stubborn economic differences may be part of the reason for the persistence of this barrier, but cultural experiences also play a role. In recent years, the middle-class African-American population has grown, yet the persistence of residential segregation reduces the opportunities for contact between blacks and whites. African Americans also maintain a strong racial identity compared to that of other minorities. In the 1990 census, for example, less than 25 percent of children born to a black-white couple were identified by their parents as white—a much lower percentage than for other biracial children. In the 2000 census, blacks identified themselves or their children as multi-racial much less often than did other racial minorities. The stronger racial identities of African Americans, forged by persistent inequality, discrimination, and residential isolation, along with continued white resistance, will hold down the increase in marriages across the black-white divide.

Increases in the relatively high marriage rates of Hispanics and Asian Americans with whites may slow as new immigrants keep arriving from their homelands. Immigration expands the marriage pools for the native-born, who are more able to find spouses in their own racial or ethnic groups. These pools are expanded further by the way the wider society categorizes Hispanics and Asian Americans. They distinguish among themselves by national origin (Cuban versus Mexican or Thai versus Chinese), but whites tend to lump them into two large groups. Common experiences of being identified as the same, along with anti-Latino and anti-Asian prejudice and discrimination, help create a sense of pan-ethnic identity. This in turn inhibits marriage with whites, fosters solidarity within the larger group, and increases marriage rates between varieties of Hispanics and Asian Americans. Interethnic marriage is frequent among American-born Asians despite small group sizes and limited opportunities for contact. For example, in 1990, 18 percent of Chinese-Americans and 15 percent of Japanese-Americans aged 20–34 married spouses of other Asian ethnic groups (compared to 39 percent and 47 percent who married whites).

Many people view the increasing number of interracial marriages as a sign that racial taboos are crumbling and that the distances between racial groups in American society are shrinking. However, marriages across racial boundaries remain rarer than those that cross religious, educational, or age lines. The puzzle is whether interracial marriages will develop as marriages between people of different nationalities did among European immigrants and their descendants in the early 20th century. Diverse in many ways when they entered the country, these 20th-century European Americans, such as Italians, Poles, and Greeks, reached the economic level of earlier immigrants within a couple generations. Their success blurred ethnic boundaries and increased the rate of interethnic marriage. Many of their descendants now define themselves simply as white despite their diverse national origins. For most white Americans, ethnic identities have become largely symbolic.

Similar trends for interracial marriages are unlikely in the near future. The experiences of European Americans show the importance of equal economic achievement in dissolving barriers, so what happens economically to recent immigrants and African Americans will be important. Even then, the low levels of interracial marriage for middle-class African Americans suggest that this particular color line will persist as a barrier to marriage. And the continuing influx of Asian and Latino immigrants may reinforce those groups' barriers to intermarriage.

RECOMMENDED RESOURCES

Zhenchao Qian. "Breaking the Racial Barriers: Variations in Interracial Marriage between 1980 and 1990." *Demography* 34 (1997): 478–500. An overview of changes in interracial marriage by sex and educational attainment for native-born whites, African Americans, Hispanics, and Asian Americans.

Zhenchao Qian and Daniel T. Lichter. "Measuring Marital Assimilation: Intermarriage among Natives and Immigrants." *Social Science Research* 30 (2001): 289–312. A comparison of interracial marriages between natives and immigrants, showing how immigration may slow down the increases in interracial marriage.

Maria P. P. Root. *Love's Revolution: Interracial Marriage* (Temple University Press, 2001). Presents in-depth interviews with interracial couples.

Howard Schuman, Charlotte Steeh, Lawrence Bobo, and Maria Krysan. *Racial Attitudes in America: Trends and Interpretation* (Harvard University Press, 1997). Using national poll data since 1942, the authors paint a changing picture of racial attitudes for whites and blacks.

George Yancey. "Who Dates Interracially: An Examination of the Characteristics of Those Who Have Dated Interracially." *Journal of Comparative Family Studies* 33 (2002): 179–90. A report on the dating practices of different racial groups.

■ Review Questions ■

1. Why are rates of intermarriage lower for blacks than for nonblack racial-ethnic groups such as Hispanics and Asians?
2. Why may continued immigration slow the growth of intermarriage for Hispanics and Asians?

Part Three

Sexuality, Partnership, and Marriage

CHAPTER 6

Sexualities

Sociology is here to tell you that sexual behavior, our most private activity, and romantic love, our most personal emotion, are heavily influenced by society. That might be obvious in a society where unmarried women's chastity is closely protected and parents choose their children's spouses. It might even be obvious were we to look back at the United States in the 1950s, when many young men and a majority of young women had first sexual intercourse with the person they chose to marry. But the claim is that although social influences are weaker now, sex and love are still structured in large part by society.

But is sexuality *totally* constructed by society? Consider the differing ways women and men experience sexuality. Don't biological differences between women and men play a role? Indeed, best-selling books in the 1990s, such as *Men Are from Mars, Women Are from Venus,*[1] argued that gender differences in sexuality are largely driven by biology. In contrast, most sociologists continue to insist that biological influences are minimal. In the first reading in this chapter, sociologists Pepper Schwartz and Virginia Rutter search

for a middle ground. Although partial to the position that social influences are greater than biological influences, Schwartz and Rutter maintain that *both* mechanisms must be included in a complete explanation of gender differences in sexual behavior and desire. In making their case, they present clear summaries of the opposing theoretical positions in this debate: sociobiology, which emphasizes evolutionary influences on human behavior, and social constructionism, which emphasizes social control.

Until the latter part of the twentieth century, most long-term sexually intimate relationships took the form of marriage. Beginning in the 1970s, cohabitation—living with a partner without marrying—became an increasingly acceptable form of intimate relationship. More recently, we have seen an apparent increase in intimate relationships among couples who are neither married nor living together. No good data on these couples exists in the United States, but government surveys in Canada and the United Kingdom show them to be increasingly common. In the second selection, a Norwegian sociologist writes about these so-called living apart together, or LAT, relationships, which challenge common notions of family life.

---

[1]John Gray, *Men Are from Mars, Women Are from Venus* (New York: HarperCollins, 1992).

READING 6-1

Sexual Desire and Gender

Pepper Schwartz

Virginia Rutter

SOCIOBIOLOGY AND EVOLUTIONARY PSYCHOLOGY

The past few decades of research on sexuality have produced a new school of human behavior—sociobiology and a related discipline, evolutionary psychology—that explains most gender differences as strategies of sexual reproduction. According to evolutionary psychologist David Buss (1995), "Evolutionary psychologists predict that the sexes will differ in precisely those domains in which women and men have faced different sorts of adaptive problems" (p. 164). By "those domains," Buss refers to reproduction, which is the only human function that depends on a biological difference between men and women.

The key assumption of sociobiological/evolutionary theory is that humans have an innate, genetically triggered impulse to pass on their genetic material through successful reproduction: This impulse is called reproductive fitness. The human species, like other species that sociobiologists study, achieves immortality by having children who live to the age of reproductive maturity and produce children themselves. Sociobiologists and evolutionary psychologists seek to demonstrate that almost all male and female behavior, and especially sexuality, is influenced by this one simple but powerful proposition.

Sociobiologists start at the species level. Species are divided into *r* and *K* reproductive categories. Those with *r* strategies obtain immortality

by mass production of eggs and sperm. The *r* species is best illustrated by fish. The female manufactures thousands of eggs, the male squirts millions of sperm over them, and that is the extent of parenting. According to this theory, the male and female fish need not pair up to nurture their offspring. Although thousands of fertilized fish eggs are consumed by predators, only a small proportion of the massive quantity of fertilized eggs must survive for the species to continue. In the *r* species, parents need not stay together for the sake of the kids.

In contrast, humans are a *K*-strategy species, which has a greater investment in each fertilized egg. Human females and most female mammals have very few eggs, especially compared to fish. Moreover, offspring take a long time to mature in the mother's womb and are quite helpless after they are born, with no independent survival ability. Human babies need years of supervision before they are independent. Thus, if a woman wants to pass on her genes (or at least the half her child will inherit from her), she must take good care of her dependent child. The baby is a scarce resource. Even if a woman is pregnant from sexual maturation until menopause, the number of children she can produce is quite limited. This limitation was particularly true thousands of years ago. Before medical advances of the nineteenth and twentieth centuries, women were highly unlikely to live to the age of menopause. Complications from childbirth commonly caused women to die in their 20s or 30s. Where the food supply was scarce, women were less likely to be successful at conceiving, further reducing the possibility of generating offspring.

Sociobiologists and evolutionary psychologists say that men inseminate, women incubate. The human female's reproductive constraints (usually one child at a time, only so many children over a life cycle, and a helpless infant for a long period of time) shape most of women's sexual and emotional approaches to men and mating. According to their theory, women have good reason to be more selective than men about potential mates. They want to find a man who will stick around and continue to provide resources and protection to this child at least until the child has a good chance of survival. Furthermore, because a woman needs to create an incentive for a man to remain with her, females have developed more sophisticated sexual and emotional skills specifically geared toward creating male loyalty and commitment to their mutual offspring.

Sociobiologists and evolutionary psychologists say that differences in reproductive capacity and strategy also shape sexual desire. Buss asserts that reproductive strategies form most of the categories of desire: Older men generally pick younger women because they are more fertile; younger women seek older men who have more status, power, and resources (a cultural practice known as hypergamy) because such men can provide for their children. Furthermore, health and reproductive capacity make youth generally sexier, and even certain shapes of women's bodies (such as an "ideal" hip-to-waist ratio epitomized by an hourglass figure, which correlates with ability to readily reproduce) are widely preferred (Buss 1994)—despite varying standards of beauty across cultures. Likewise, men who have demonstrated their fertility by producing children are more sought after than men who have not (Buss 1994).

According to evolutionary psychologists, men's tastes for recreational sex, unambivalent lust, and a variety of partners are consistent with maximizing their production of children. Men's sexual interest is also more easily aroused because sex involves fewer costs to them than to women, and the ability for rapid ejaculation has a reproductive payoff. On the other hand, women's taste for relationship-based intimacy and greater investment in each sexual act is congruent with women's reproductive strategies.

In a field that tends to emphasize males' "natural" influence over reproductive strategies, evolutionary anthropologist Helen Fisher (1992) offers a feminist twist. Her study of hundreds of

societies shows that divorce, or its informal equivalent, occurs most typically in the third or fourth year of a marriage and then peaks about every four years after that. Fisher hypothesizes that some of the breakups have to do with a woman's attempt to obtain the best genes and best survival chances for her offspring. In both agrarian and hunter-gatherer societies, Fisher explains, women breast-feed their child for three or four years—a practice that is economical and sometimes helps to prevent further pregnancy. At the end of this period, the woman is ready and able to have another child. She reenters the mating marketplace and assesses her options to see if she can improve on her previous mate. If she can get a better guy, she will leave the previous partner and team up with a new one. In Fisher's vision, unlike the traditional sociobiological view (see Table 6.1), different male and female reproductive strategies do not necessarily imply female sexual passivity and preference for life-long monogamy.

Sociobiologists and evolutionary psychologists tell a fascinating story of how male and female reproductive differences might shape sexuality. To accept sociobiological arguments, one must accept the premise that most animal and human behavior is driven by the instinct to reproduce and improve the gene pool. Furthermore, a flaw of sociobiology as a theory is that it does not provide a unique account of sexual behavior with the potential to be tested empirically. Furthermore, other social science explanations for the same phenomena are supported by more immediate, close-range evidence.

Consider hypergamy, the practice of women marrying men slightly older and "higher" on the social status ladder than they are. Sociobiologists would say women marry "up" to ensure the most fit provider for their offspring. But hypergamy makes little sense biologically. Younger men have more years of resources to provide, and they have somewhat more sexual resources. Empirically, however, hypergamy is fact. It is also a fact that men, overall and in nearly every subculture, have

TABLE 6.1

COMPARISON OF TRADITIONAL AND FEMINIST SOCIOBIOLOGICAL EXPLANATIONS OF GENDER DIFFERENCES IN SEXUALITY

Perspective	Gender difference	Explanation
Traditional	Men seek to maximize number of progeny by changing partners as often as possible. Women seek to maximize well-being of progeny by holding on to their partners as long as possible.	Men have biological capacity to inseminate many women in a short period of time; women's biological job is to incubate and nurture young.
Feminist	Men seek to maximize progeny; women seek to maximize well-being of progeny by exchanging partners when improved options are available.	Men and women both seek to maximize number of partners and quality of partners by exchanging when improved options are available.

access to more rewards and status than women do. Furthermore, reams of imagery—in movies, advertising, novels—promote the appeal of older, more resourceful men. Why not, when older, more resourceful men are generating the images? Social practice, in this case, overrides what sociobiologists consider the biological imperative.

THE SOCIAL ORIGINS OF DESIRE

Your own experience should indicate that biology and genetics alone do not shape human sexuality. From the moment you entered the world, cues from the environment were telling you which desires and behaviors were "normal" and which were not. The result is that people who grow up in different circumstances tend to have different sexualities. Who has not had their sexual behavior influenced by their parents' or guardians' explicit or implicit rules? You may break the rules or follow them, but you can't forget them. On a societal level, in Sweden, for example, premarital sex is accepted, and people are expected to be sexually knowledgeable and experienced. Swedes are likely to associate sex with pleasure in this "sex positive" society. In Ireland, however, Catholics are supposed to heed the Church's strict prohibitions against sex outside of marriage, birth control, and the

expression of lust. In Ireland the experience of sexuality is different from the experience of sexuality in Sweden because the rules are different. Certainly, biology in Sweden is no different from biology in Ireland, nor is the physical capacity to experience pleasure different. But in Ireland, nonmarital sex is clandestine and shameful. Perhaps the taboo adds excitement to the experience. In Sweden, nonmarital sex is acceptable. In the absence of social constraint, it may even feel a bit mundane. These culturally specific sexual rules and experiences arise from different norms, the well-known, unwritten rules of society.

Another sign that social influences play a bigger role in shaping sexuality than does biology is the changing notions historically of male and female differences in desire. Throughout history, varied explanations of male and female desire have been popular. At times, woman was portrayed as the stormy temptress and man the reluctant participant, as in the Bible story of Adam and Eve. At other times, women were seen as pure in thought and deed while men were voracious sexual beasts, as the Victorians would have it.

These shifting ideas about gender are the social "clothing" for sexuality. The concept of gender typically relies on a dichotomy of male versus female sexual categories, just as the tradition of women wearing dresses and men wearing pants has in the past made the shape of men and women appear quite different. Consider high heels, an on-again-off-again Western fashion. Shoes have no innate sexual function, but high heels have often been understood to be "sexy" for women, even though (or perhaps because) they render women less physically agile. (Of course, women cope. As Ginger Rogers, the 1940s movie star and dancing partner to Fred Astaire, is said to have quipped, "I did everything Fred did, only backwards and in high heels.") Social norms of femininity have at times rendered high heels fashionable. So feminine are high heels understood to be that a man in high heels, in some sort of visual comedy gag, guarantees a laugh from the audience. Alternatively, high heels are a required emblem of femininity for cross-dressing men.

Such distinctions are an important tool of society; they provide guidance to human beings about how to be a "culturally correct" male or female. Theoretically, society could "clothe" its members with explicit norms of sexuality that de-emphasize difference and emphasize similarity or even multiplicity. Picture unisex hairstyles and men and women both free to wear skirts or pants, norms that prevail from time to time in some subcultures. What is remarkable about dichotomies is that even when distinctions, like male and female norms of fashion, are reduced, new ways to assert an ostensibly essential difference between men and women arise. Societies' rules, like clothes, are changeable. But societies' entrenched taste for constructing differences between men and women persists.

The Social Construction of Sexuality

Social constructionists believe that cues from the environment shape human beings from the moment they enter the world. The sexual customs, values, and expectations of a culture, passed on to the young through teaching and by example, exert a powerful influence over individuals. When Fletcher Christian sailed into Tahiti in Charles Nordhoff's 1932 account, *Mutiny on the*

Bounty, he and the rest of his nineteenth-century English crew were surprised at how sexually available, playful, guilt free, and amorous the Tahitian women were. Free from the Judeo-Christian precepts and straitlaced customs that inhibited English society, the women and girls of Tahiti regarded their sexuality joyfully and without shame. The English men were delighted and, small wonder, refused to leave the island. Such women did not exist in their own society. The women back in England had been socialized within their Victorian culture to be modest, scared of sex, protective of their reputation, and threatened by physical pleasure. As a result, they were unavailable before marriage and did not feel free to indulge in a whole lot of fun after it. The source of the difference was not physiological differences between Tahitian and English women; it was sexual socialization or the upbringing that they received within their differing families and cultures.

If we look back at the Victorian, nineteenth-century England that Nordhoff refers to, we can identify social structures that influenced the norms of women's and men's sexuality. A burgeoning, new, urban middle class created separate spheres in the division of family labor. Instead of sharing home and farm or small business, the tasks of adults in families became specialized: Men went out to earn money, women stayed home to raise children and take care of the home. Although this division of labor was not the norm in all classes and ethnicities in England at the time, the image of middle-class femininity and masculinity became pervasive. The new division of labor increased women's economic dependence on men, which further curbed women's sexual license but not men's. When gender organizes one aspect of life—such as men's and women's positions in the economy—it also organizes other aspects of life, including sex.

In a heterogeneous and individualistic culture like North America, sexual socialization is complex. A society creates an "ideal" sexuality, but different families and subcultures have their own values. For example, even though contemporary society at large may now accept premarital sexuality, a given family may lay down the law: Sex before marriage is against the family's religion and an offense against God's teaching. A teenager who grows up in such a household may suppress feelings of sexual arousal or channel them into outlets that are more acceptable to the family. Or the teenager may react against her or his background, reject parental and community opinion, and search for what she or he perceives to be a more "authentic" self. Variables like birth order or observations of a sibling's social and sexual expression can also influence a person's development.

As important as family and social background are, so are individual differences in response to that background. In the abstract, people raised to celebrate their sexuality must surely have a different approach to enjoying their bodies than those who are taught that their bodies will betray them and are a venal part of human nature. Yet whether or not a person is raised to be at ease with physicality does not always help predict adult sexual behavior. Sexual sybarites and libertines may have grown up in sexually repressive environments, as did pop culture icon and Catholic-raised Madonna. Sometimes individuals whose families promoted sex education and free personal expression are content with minimal sexual expression.

Even with the nearly infinite variety of sexuality that individual experience produces, social circumstances shape sexual patterns. For example, research shows that people who have had more premarital sexual intercourse are likely to have more extramarital intercourse, or sex with someone other than their spouse (Blumstein and Schwartz 1983). Perhaps early experience creates a desire for sexual variety and makes it harder for a person to be monogamous. On the other hand, higher levels of sexual desire may generate both the premarital and extramarital propensities. Or perhaps nonmonogamous, sexually active individuals are "rule breakers" in

other areas also, and resist not only the traditional rules of sex but also other social norms they encounter. Sexual history is useful for predicting sexual future, but it does not provide a complete explanation.

To make explanations more useful, sociologists refer to societal-level explanations as the macro view and to individual-level explanations as the micro view. At the macrolevel, the questions pertain to the patterns among different groups. For example, we may note in our culture that some women wear skirts and all men do not. Why do women and men, generally speaking, differ in this way? Social conflict theory, which examines the way that groups gain and maintain power over resources and other groups, is often used to address macrolevel questions. One might ask: Whose interest does this custom serve and how did it evolve? What does it constrain or encourage? If the custom changes, what social forces have promoted the change? What social forces resist change? Who has power over customs at any given time, and why?

Symbolic interactionism supplements this macrolevel view by looking at the microlevel: How does a particular custom gain its meaning through social interaction? For example, what is really happening when a man opens a door for a woman? Symbolic interactionism proposes that social rules are learned and reinforced through everyday interaction in both small acts, such as a man's paying for a woman's dinner, and larger enactments of male and female roles, such as weddings, manners and advice books, movies, and television. Through such everyday social interaction, norms are confirmed or resisted. When an adult tells a little girl "good girls don't do this," or when boys make fun of her for wanting to be on the football team, or when she observes people scorning or stoning women who venture forth in inappropriate garb (as in countries where women are required to wear a veil), or when she sees women joining a military school getting hazed and harassed, she is learning her society's rules of behavior.

When it comes to sexuality, all these social and behavioral theories hold that biological impulses are subservient to the influence of social systems. Consider high heels again. As anyone who has done so knows, wearing high heels has physical consequences, such as flexed calves while wearing them and aching feet at the end of an evening. But nothing in the physiology of women makes wearing high-heeled shoes necessary, and the propensity to wear high heels is not programmed into women's DNA. A sociobiologist might note that any additional ways a society can invent for women to be sexy accelerate reproductive success. A symbolic interactionist would counter that most rules of sexuality go way beyond what's needed for reproductive success. Footwear has never been shown to be correlated with fertility. Instead, society orchestrates male and female sexuality so that its values are served. A social conflict theorist would go a step further and note that the enactment of gendered fashion norms, individual by individual, serves the political agenda of groups in power (in this case men) at the macrolevel.

An astounding example of gender-based social control of sexuality was the practice of binding the feet of upper-class women in China starting around the tenth century. Each foot was bound so tightly that the last two toes shriveled and fell off. What was left was so deformed that the woman could barely walk and had to be carried. The function was to allow upper-class men to control the mobility of their women. Bound feet, which were thus associated with status and wealth, became erotically charged. Unbound feet were seen as repugnant. By the eighteenth and nineteenth centuries, even poor women participated in this practice. This practice was so associated with sexual acceptability and marriageability that it was difficult to disrupt, even when nineteenth-century missionaries from the West labeled the practice barbaric and unsafe. Only later, in the twentieth century, did foot binding become illegal (Greenhalgh 1977).

Social Control of Sexuality

So powerful are norms as they are transmitted through both social structures and everyday life that it is impossible to imagine the absence of norms that control sexuality. In fact, most images of "liberated" sexuality involve breaking a social norm—say, having sex in public rather than in private. The social norm is always the reference point. Because people are influenced from birth by the social and physical contexts of sexuality, their desires are shaped by those norms. There is no such thing as a truly free sexuality. For the past two centuries in North America, people have sought "true love" through personal choice in dating and mating (D'Emilio and Freedman 1988). Although this form of sexual liberation has generated a small increase in the number of mixed pairs—interracial, interethnic, interfaith pairs—the rule of homogamy, or marrying within one's class, religion, and ethnicity, still constitutes one of the robust social facts of romantic life. Freedom to choose the person one loves turns out not to be as free as one might suppose.

Despite the norm of true love currently accepted in our culture, personal choice and indiscriminate sexuality have often been construed across cultures and across history as socially disruptive. Disruptions to the social order include liaisons between poor and rich; between people of different races, ethnicities, or faiths; and between members of the same sex. Traditional norms of marriage and sexuality have maintained social order by keeping people in familiar and "appropriate" categories. Offenders have been punished by ostracism, curtailed civil rights, or in some societies, death. Conformists are rewarded with social approval and material advantages. Although it hardly seems possible today, mixed-race marriage was against the law in the United States until 1967. Committed same-sex couples continue to be denied legal marriage, income tax breaks, and health insurance benefits; heterosexual couples take these social benefits for granted.

Some social theorists observe that societies control sexuality through construction of a dichotomized or gendered (male-female) sexuality (Foucault 1978). Society's rules about pleasure seeking and procreating are enforced by norms about appropriate male and female behavior. For example, saying that masculinity is enhanced by sexual experimentation while femininity is demeaned by it gives men sexual privilege (and pleasure) and denies it to women. Furthermore, according to Foucault, sexual desire is fueled by the experience of privilege and taboo regarding sexual pleasure. That is, the very rules that control sexual desire shape it and even enhance it. The social world could just as plausibly concentrate on how much alike are the ways that men and women experience sex and emphasize how broadly dispersed sexual conduct is across genders. However, social control turns pleasure into a scarce resource and endows leaders who regulate the pleasure of others with power. . . .

To summarize, social constructionists believe that a society influences sexual behavior through its norms. Some norms are explicit, such as laws against adult sexual activity with minors. Others are implicit, such as norms of fidelity and parental responsibility. In a stable, homogeneous society, it is relatively easy to understand such rules. But in a changing, complex society like the United States, the rules may be in flux or indistinct. Perhaps this ambiguity is what makes some issues of sexuality so controversial today.

AN INTEGRATIVE PERSPECTIVE ON GENDER AND SEXUALITY

Social constructionist explanations of contemporary sexual patterns are typically pitted against the biology of desire and the evolutionary understanding of biological adaptations. Some social constructionists believe there is no inflexible biological reality; everything we regard as either female or male sexuality is culturally imposed. In contrast, essentialists—those who take a biological, sociobiological, or evolutionary point of view—believe people's sexual desires and orientations are innate and hardwired and that social impact is minimal. Gender differences follow from reproductive differences. Men inseminate, women incubate. People are born with sexual drives, attractions, and natures that simply play themselves out at the appropriate developmental age. Even if social constraints conspire to make men and women more similar to each other (as in the 1990s, when the sensitive and nurturing new man is encouraged to get in touch with his so-called feminine, emotional side), people's essential nature is the same: Man is the hunter, warrior, and trailblazer, and woman is the gatherer, nurturer, and reproducer. To an essentialist, social differences, such as the different earning power of men and women, are the consequence of biological difference. In short, essentialists think the innate differences between women and men are the cause of gendered sexuality; social constructionists think the differences between men and women are the result of gendering sexuality through social processes.

Using either the social constructionist or essentialist approach to the exclusion of the other constrains understanding of sexuality. We believe the evidence shows that gender differences are more plausibly an outcome of social processes than the other way around. But a social constructionist view is most powerful when it takes the essentialist view into account. In Table 6.2, we describe this view of gender differences in sexual desire as integrative. Although people tend to think of sex as primarily a biological function—tab B goes into slot A—biology is only one part of the context of desire. Such sociological factors as family relationships and social structure also influence sex. A complex mix of anatomy, hormones, and the brain provides the basic outline for the range of acts and desires possible, but biology is neither where sexuality begins nor where it ends. Social and biological contexts link to define human sexual possibilities.

TABLE 6.2

EXPLANATIONS OF MALE AND FEMALE DIFFERENCES IN SEXUAL DESIRE

Explanations	Causes of desire	Consequences
Essentialist: Desire is biological and evolutionary	Genetically preprogrammed reproductive functions specific to males and females	Male independence in reproduction and female-centered child-rearing practices and passivity are the cause, rather than the result, of gendered social institutions
Social constructionist: Desire is sociological and contextual	Social institutions and social interaction signal and sanction "male" and "female," gendered norms of behavior	Support for or opposition to sex/gender-segregated reproductive and social practices depends on social definitions of men, women, and sexuality
Integrative: Desire is contextual and physical	Bodies, environments, relationships, families, governments shape sexualities	Policies address some biological differences (such as pregnancy and work); emphasize the impact of social forces, interaction, societal programs

The integrative approach follows from a great deal that sexuality researchers have observed. Consider the following example: A research project, conducted over three decades ago, advertised for participants stating that its focus was how physical excitement influences a man's preference for one woman over another (Valins 1966). The researchers connected college men to a monitor that allowed them to hear their heartbeats as they looked at photographs of women models. The men were told that they would be able to hear their heartbeat when it surged in response to each photograph. A greater surge would suggest greater physical attraction. The participants were then shown a photograph of a dark-haired woman, then a blonde, then a redhead. Afterward, each man was asked to choose the picture that he would prefer to take home. In each case, the man chose the photograph of the woman who, as he believed from listening to his own speeding heartbeat, had most aroused him. Or at least the man thought he was choosing the woman who had aroused him most. In reality, the men had been listening to a faked heartbeat that was speeded up at random. The men thus actually chose the women who they believed had aroused them most. In this case, the men's

invented attraction was more powerful than their gut response. Their mind (a powerful sexual organ) told them their body was responding to a specific picture. The participants' physiological experience of arousal was eclipsed by the social context. When social circumstances influence sexual tastes, are those tastes real or sincere? Absolutely. The social world is as much a fact in people's lives as the biological world.

Now let us look at a case where the body's cues were misinterpreted by the mind. An attractive woman researcher stood at the end of a very stable bridge (Dutton and Aron 1974). She approached men after they had walked across the bridge, engaged them in conversation, and then gave the men her telephone number—in case they had further comments, she said. Then the researcher did the same thing with another group of participants, but at the end of an unstable, swinging bridge. People tend to feel a little nervous, excited, or even exhilarated when they make their way across such a bridge. The pulse rises. Adrenaline pumps. Indeed, the anxiety response of walking across the bridge is much like the arousal response caused by meeting a desirable new person. The question was, would that anxiety response confuse men into thinking that they were attracted to the woman at the end of the bridge, more so than the physiologically calm guys who met her on the stable bridge? Yes, a statistically significant, larger number of men from the swinging bridge called the woman. In this case, participants had interpreted an anxiety response as an attraction response, one compelling enough to warrant inviting a stranger on a date. The physical situation transformed the meaning of a casual meeting from anxiety to attraction, again showing the link between biological and social influences. . . .

What do these examples from research illustrate? Sexual desire—in fact, all sexuality—is influenced by the cultural, personal, and situational. But these examples also tell us that people can't escape the biological context of sex and sexuality—nor can they rely on it. Such an integrative approach—the intimate relationship between social context and biological experience—is central to understanding sexuality.

What are the implications of using an integrative approach to sexuality? First, an integrationist will raise questions about biology when social context is emphasized as cause, and will raise questions about social context when biological causes are emphasized. The point is, everything sexual and physical occurs and achieves meaning in a social context.

■ Review Questions

1. Why might women and men have different reproductive strategies?
2. Give an example of the ways in which social institutions seem to influence gender differences in sexuality.

READING 6-2

Living Apart Together

A New Family Form

Irene Levin

Susan and Simon are a couple, and have been so for more than 10 years. The difference between Susan and Simon and many other couples is that they do not share their everyday lives together. They have both been married before and have children from these previous relationships. Susan lives with her children in a neighboring town and

Irene Levin, "Living Apart Together: A New Family Form," *Current Sociology,* March 2004, Vol. 52(2), pp. 223–240. Copyright © 2004. Reproduced with permission of Sage Publications, Inc.

meets Simon every weekend and during holidays. Simon lives alone in the same town as his children, who live with their mother. Simon wants to be close to his children so that he can meet them as often as possible. By living in this current arrangement, Simon can have *both* a couple relationship with Susan *and* a parenting relationship with his children. Susan also likes the current situation because she does not have to choose *between* a partner and her children or make her children move away from their friends in order for her to keep her relationship with Simon.

Susan and Simon are living in a living apart together or LAT relationship—a historically new family form. LAT relationships are a result of changes in our living arrangements. These changes have occurred, little by little, during the past 30 years as a result of changing norms. Previously, it was expected that one would be married in order to live together. Only in marriage was a couple considered to be a "real" couple. Now, however, one can choose to live with one's partner without being married—what we call cohabitation (Trost, 1979; Heimdal and Houseknecht, 2003; Kamp Dush et al., 2003). Today the ritual of marriage is less important and feelings are what matters. Married and cohabiting couples have, however, a lot in common. They live in the same household and in everyday life there is not a lot of difference in their routines. They share "bed and table." The difference is the marriage ritual—cohabiting couples do not have the status of being married. In many aspects of everyday life this does not matter. Their children may not concern themselves about whether or not their parents are married and their routines are often the same in either case. There may be a difference between married and cohabiting couples with regard to differing consequences of relationship breakdown. Generally speaking, economic consequences differ when one of the couple dies, or when the married couple divorces (Hopper, 2001) or the cohabiting couple separates. The exception may be when the cohabiting couple has entered into a special contract.

The question to be considered here is whether two people may be considered to be a couple *without* having a common home. In recent times the answer has become "yes" and a new family form has appeared. To be a couple is no longer dependent upon sharing a common household. It is no longer important for one to be married or to be living in the same household—one can still be a couple, and it is that to which the new term, LAT relationship, refers. Can a LAT relationship be interpreted as a family form? As Levin and Trost (1992) show family can be defined in a range of different terms. The title of this special issue, "Beyond the Conventional Family," suggests that the traditional concept of family and definitions of family norms are increasingly challenged by a range of personal living arrangements. It is argued here that the occurrence of LAT

relationships is closely connected to the occurrence of cohabitation and the changes in norms.

CHANGING NORMS

In the 20th century two major changes occurred in the western world that have affected family situations. One was the emergence of cohabitation (Trost, 1979) and the other was increase in divorce rates (Moxnes, 1990, 2001; Aharons and Rodgers, 1987; Wallerstein and Kelly, 1980). Both of these phenomena occurred before but not to the extent to which they were practiced during this period. Previously, most marriages were dissolved because of the death of one of the spouses. This is shown among other things in the rather high remarriage rate in earlier times. For instance, in England and France during the years 1600–1700, between 25 and 30 percent of all marriages were remarriages (Sogner and Dupâquir, 1981). Nearly all of these remarriages occurred after the death of one of the spouses. As we get closer to the 19th century, the remarriage rate decreased to around 15 percent in Norway (see Sundt, 1975). In the beginning of the 1900s, a new divorce law came into effect (1915) in Norway and remarriages continued to decrease. During the 1900s life expectancy for men and women increased by 25 years. This change in life expectancy must have had many consequences, not the least of which affected marital relations. Previously, when marriages were shorter, death occurred before couples had time to divorce. In our day, divorce has replaced death as one of the main reasons for the dissolution of marriage (Levin, 2001). Today, most marriages dissolve because one of the spouses wants to divorce (Furstenberg and Kiernan, 2001). More often than not, this occurs while children are still living at home.

At the end of the 1960s and the beginning of the 1970s, marriage rates, in most of the western world, started to decrease. In some countries the changes occurred very rapidly, as in Sweden and Denmark, followed by Norway and Finland. In England, this development was somewhat slower than in the Nordic countries, but not as slow as in, for example, Belgium (Trost, 1995). At the same time, the practice of cohabitation began to increase (see Trost, 1979). In the traditional marital system before 1970, four elements were closely connected in time. The prevailing sequence was: the marriage ceremony, moving in together, having sexual intercourse together, having the first child about a year later (Trost, 1993, 1998; Levin and Trost, 2003). The traditional marital system normatively prescribed these four elements, in the given sequence, as the sanctioned practice. With some exceptions, the marriage ceremony and moving in together occurred at the same time, meaning the same day. This seems to have been true for all western societies.

Having sexual intercourse together was only sanctioned after the marriage ceremony. Premarital sex was prohibited for all, but in some countries more than in others, this prohibition was particularly underscored for women. The norm against premarital sex, however, was primarily an ideal norm which did not necessarily translate into a behavioral norm. Norway is a good example of this differentiation: the ideal norm prescribed chastity before marriage but in practice almost all couples had sex before they married. One indicator of this claim is that by the year 1960 one-quarter of all brides in Norway were pregnant at the time of the wedding. The fourth element prescribes that children be born nine to 12 months after the marital ceremony. Preferably and normatively, children should not be born to unwed mothers.

These four elements have lost their normative power and today they are no longer connected to one other. This development is related to the great increase in the rates of cohabitation. It can be argued that cohabitation has become a social institution (Trost, 1979). When cohabitation becomes a social institution of the sort we find in, for example, the Scandinavian countries, there is no normative or expected connection between the four elements that traditionally constituted the marital system. In Sweden, more than half of

all children, and about two-thirds of all first-born children, have unwed mothers. In Norway, the numbers are slightly fewer, but the changes in norms are more or less the same.

Without changes in the normative structure connected to these four elements, LAT relationships would not be as visible or as numerous. The couple would then have probably been defined (by themselves as well as by their own social networks) as "going steady," "engaged to be married" or simply as "lovers." These terms are less definite than a LAT relationship indicates. Prior to normative transformations the couple would not openly stay together overnight. With the changes, they now can do so without any sanctions. Without a general acceptance of cohabitation and its institutionalization which puts it on an equal footing with marriage, LAT relationships would have remained hidden or "invisible" (Levin and Trost, 1999) and they would be much less common than they now are.

The relatively high divorce and separation rates in many western countries might help to make LAT relationships more common and more visible also, especially where cohabitation has become a recognized social institution. Historically, LAT relationships have occurred before but certainly not as commonly as they now do and in the past such relationships were quite hidden from the eyes of others. The higher the divorce and separation rates are, the higher the likelihood not only of remarriages and recohabitations, but also of LAT relationships. Recohabitations always involve a change of home. Either one moves into the other's home or both members of the couple move from separate homes to a common home. In most cases of remarriage the same holds true. But there are instances where married couples remain in separate homes. Some couples who have lived together in a marriage or in a cohabiting relationship cease to live together in a common home without dissolving their relationship; they just form a LAT relationship out of a living together relationship.

Within the context of high rates of divorce today (Moxnes, 1990), many people postdivorce want to start new relationships but they are not ready to risk another divorce. The high rate of divorce and the acceptance of cohabitation as a social institution (Trost, 1995) can account to some extent for the higher incidence of LAT relationships. When Simone de Beauvoir (1908–86) and Jean Paul Sartre (1905–80) established themselves in what we are now calling a LAT relationship, they were seen as being "a little different" from other couples. They were intellectuals and lived, so-called, "Bohemian lives." There are many people today who live in tune with the lifestyle of de Beauvoir and Sartre. They are living in LAT relationships, which have become a new family form in western societies. This is not because the LAT relationship is entirely new, but rather because of the greater visibility and higher frequency of people living in LAT relationships. The greatly elevated numbers make us look upon these couples as representing something new. While journalists both in Norway and in Sweden are now interested in the phenomenon of LAT relationships, there remains little research on the phenomenon.

DEFINING LAT RELATIONSHIPS

The definition of a LAT relationship used here is a couple that does not share a home. Each of the two partners lives in his or her own home in which other people might also live. They define themselves as a couple and they perceive that their close surrounding personal network does so as well. The definition requires three conditions: the couple has to agree that they are a couple; others have to see them as such; and they must live in separate homes. This term refers to homosexual as well as heterosexual couples.

Some consider it unnecessary to give LAT relations a special name. If we go back in time, before cohabitation was common and considered "normal," we had terms such as "going steady"

which designated a premarital form. "Going steady" was usually limited to a certain period of time in which the couple either decided to continue and become a "real" couple and get engaged to be married, or decided to break up the relationship. The "going steady" stage is a part of the LAT relationship and arguably for some the LAT relationship is only a temporary situation which ends up being more like "going steady" ending in relationship dissolution; but for many the LAT relationship is something much more than "going steady," and it lasts over a longer period.

The term "LAT" was first used in the Netherlands, where a Dutch journalist, Michel Berkiel, wrote an article in the *Haagse Post,* in 1978, about a phenomenon he had observed, and in which he lived himself with the person he loved. During one of the morning meetings of the newspaper, while he was writing the article, he asked his colleagues to help him choose a title. Someone suggested that he name the article after a recent movie shown in the Netherlands at that time, titled *Eva and Frank: Living Apart Together.* "Living apart together" seemed too long to him and so he chose to use the acronym LAT or *lat.* Already a word in the Dutch language meaning "stick," this also made its usage easier to accept. The Netherlands is the only country, as far as I know, where the term LAT or *lat* is integrated in everyday speech. In the Scandinavian countries the term *særbo,* in Norwegian, and *särbo,* in Swedish, have now become relatively well-known terms; however, this is more true in Sweden than in Norway.

In France, a different term has been used in a study by Caradec (1996) who uses *cohabitation intermittente* and *cohabitation alternée.* The first term refers to the same phenomenon that is referred to by the phrase LAT relationship— a couple living in separate homes, and looked upon as a couple, by others, and by themselves. The latter term, *cohabitation alternée,* refers to cohabitation where the couple alternates between their two dwellings. Caradec's study claims that nearly 6 percent of the adult population in Paris were living in LAT relationships.

In Germany, Schneider (1996) refers to "partners with different households" or *Partnerschaften mit getrennten Haushalten* in German. Included in his study are only those LAT relationships that have lasted for at least one year. The study is rather special as it contains a majority of "young adults who are in education, mainly studying, or who are in their early period of gainful employment" (Schneider, 1996: 96; my translation). In this study more than 10,000 people, aged 18–61, were interviewed in 1994. He found that 9 percent of the respondents were living in LAT relationships. In the USA, the discussion about LAT relationships is just beginning. There, but also in other places, the term "commuting marriage/cohabitation" is used interchangeably with "dual-households" or "dual-residence living" (see Winfield, 1985). What marks the distinction between commuting marriage/cohabitation and LAT relationships is closely connected to the issue of one's home or domicile. If the two live in *one home* and one (or both of them) has a second apartment where he or she stays when *away from home,* due to their work or studies, these relationships are defined as commuting marital/cohabitational relationships. In order to be a LAT relationship, each partner must have his or her own home, which means that the partners live apart in *two separate residences.*

QUANTITATIVE STUDY

This research on LAT relationships draws upon data collected by both quantitative and qualitative methods. Most of the quantitative data come from Sweden, where we collected data on three different occasions. The first was in August 1993 when SKOP (a Scandinavian opinion research organization) included some of our questions in one of its monthly surveys, with a probability sample of 1021 inhabitants of Sweden, aged 18–74 years. The same questions were asked

in a probability sample of 2121 people, aged 18–74 years, in January/February 1998, again by SKOP.[1] Here the relevant question was (in translation): "Do you live in a marriage-like relationship with someone while maintaining separate homes?" This question followed a previous one about being married or cohabiting. There were also questions concerning how frequently they were together and how far away from one another they lived.

The 1993 Swedish opinion research survey found that 6 percent of those respondents who were neither married nor cohabiting affirmed that they were living in a LAT relationship. The survey suggests that Sweden had about 60,000 couples, or 120,000 persons, living in LAT relationships. The data collected in 1998 found that the relative number of persons living in LAT relationships had increased to 12 percent of those respondents who were neither married nor cohabiting. This suggests that at least 130,000 couples or 260,000 people were living in LAT relationships at that time. Some of these couples are same-sex couples but the majority are heterosexual couples.

In the year 2001, a third data collection was undertaken which showed a slight increase in LAT relationships from the survey results in 1998. Fourteen percent of the respondents that were neither married nor cohabiting said that they were living in a LAT relationship in 2001. This suggests that the numbers had risen to about 300,000 people or about 150,000 couples.[2]

At that time we knew very little about how many LAT relationships there were in Norway. However, in 2002, the Norwegian Bureau of Statistics collected data in order to find out how many LAT relationships there were in Norway. Approximately 1000 people, aged 18–74, were interviewed. Eight percent of those who said that they were neither married nor cohabiting saw themselves as living in LAT relationships. The interview study suggests that about 60,000–70,000 people or 30,000–35,000 couples were living in a LAT relationship in Norway, in 2002.

QUALITATIVE STUDY

In our research we have also interviewed 100 people living in LAT relationships. The interviews were in-depth and structured, but not standardized. The interviews were between one and three hours in length. In order to visualize interviewees' conception of family, a three-step method was used (Levin, 1993). First they were asked: "Who is in your family—could you make a list?" Second, "Could you place your family on this sheet of paper according to closeness and distance to you?" Third, they were interviewed about their relationships to their family members and especially their living arrangements.

In some cases we were able to identify people in a LAT relationship but were unable to interview these couples. These people were given a short semi-standardized questionnaire which they answered and sent back to us.

The sample is a convenience sample, and we found our informants in a variety of ways. Sometimes at lectures or presentations, when we had mentioned LAT relationships, people in the audience approached us. We were interviewed in Norwegian and Swedish magazines and newspaper articles in which we solicited people living in LAT relationships to take part in the research. When people asked us about our research and we mentioned the LAT study, some volunteered to be interviewed and others told us about parents, children or friends in LAT relationships. The age range of our informants in the qualitative study is from 20 to 80 years.

The interviewees may be divided into two subgroups:

1. Those who would like to live together but for one reason or another have decided not to do so.
2. Those who would not live together even if they could, and who want to remain a couple *living apart together.*

I start by describing some patterns we found in the first subgroup.

WE WOULD HAVE LIVED TOGETHER IF IT WERE NOT FOR ONE OR MORE REASONS . . .

Responsibility and Care

One reason why some people choose to live in LAT relationships has to do with their feelings of responsibility for other people. This feeling of responsibility is so strong that they do not want a new relationship to another person to impinge upon their deeply felt duties. In particular, it is the responsibility and care for children still living at home and for older parents that are given as reasons for *not living together* with new partners. If another person moves into his or her apartment or if he or she moves away to another apartment, major changes will occur. When it comes to relationships with older parents, people often did not want to leave them alone as this can be a way of forcing them to move into a home for the aged. These are people who do not believe that their children or their parents have appropriated their own decision-making. Rather, they understand their relationship to the new partner as unrelated to the relationship and responsibility they have for their children or for their parents. Here LAT relationships imply that one simply does not have to move *everyone* into the same living arrangement.

People in this situation look upon the new couple relationship as an *addition to* the relationships they already have and not as being *instead of* those other relationships. The new couple relationship is not allowed to threaten or replace already existing relationships. It is simply easier to give each relationship "its due" by not creating a stepfamily household. By keeping the home as it is, it is easier to keep relationships, with children or aged parents, as they are. Even for a parent who is not the custodian of his or her children, to move to another home can be seen as *cheating* one's own children, to leave the child's parental home for the sake of another adult. The following example illustrates such a situation.

Fred and Freda were first an unmarried LAT and they later got married but kept their LAT relationship until all of the children had moved out of their homes. Fred was 56 years old and Freda was 51 at the time of the interview. They met 10 years before when Fred's three children were living at home with him in his custody. At that time, his children were 14, 16, and 20 years old. Freda had two children. They were 10 and 14 years old, and in her custody. Her ex-husband took care of their children every second weekend and during some holidays. Fred and Freda were decided that they would not move in together until their own children had grown up and left home. Both lived in the same city, 15 minutes apart by public transportation. They met and fell in love and felt that they were a couple very quickly, but it took about a year until they were in a LAT relationship, according to their view at the time of the interview. At the beginning of the relationship, they stayed overnight at each other's home during weekends. They did not tell their children about their true relationship at first, but introduced each other to their children as old and good friends. Neither of them wanted to push the other or to be pushed into relationships with one another's children. After some time, the children on both sides accepted their parent's new relationship.

Two years before the interview took place, Freda and Fred were married. They continued to live in a LAT relationship at the time of the interview. We later learned that they now do live together, after having spent 10 years of their lives in a LAT relationship, both as unmarried and married LATs.

When it comes to caring for elderly parents, LAT relationships can be a solution for those who want to continue to care for their elderly parents and still keep a relationship with a new partner. Often, people in this situation have lived in close contact and proximity to their parents for many years. They might have liked or disliked this arrangement, but they accepted it as a particular feature of their own lives. When the elderly mother or father dies, or becomes severely ill, there are no choices for these people. They dutifully accept the long-term care of their aged or disabled parent.

Taking care of elderly or disabled parents is a strongly felt duty, and a very high priority in the value system and self-understanding of many of those we interviewed that were in this particular situation. If they fail to provide a high level of personal care, they know that they themselves will suffer severely, with feelings of guilt, for not behaving in accordance with their own standards of responsibility and morality. For others in this situation, it is a way of "repaying" the older generation for what it has done for the child in earlier stages of life. Perhaps some respondents had received important help and support with their own children from their parents. All in all, it seems to be preferable for them to remain in their existing surroundings and to continue to care for the elderly parent. It may seem easier, all things considered, to have a LAT relationship, with their partner living in another home. In this way, one can avoid choosing between the aged (and sometimes disabled) parent and the new partner. They can have both.

A strong feeling of responsibility and the duty to care for children and aged parents existed in these people long before they met their new partners. In these examples, the respondents perceive that they are *significant others* for their children and for their parents. If they do not act in accordance with their feelings of responsibility, they know that feelings of guilt will result. The LAT relationship allows them to care for children or aged parents *and* maintain a relationship with a new partner. For these people, the situation is not "either/or" but "both/and." By caring for those others who are so closely related to them they are caring for themselves, too.

They Work or Study in Different Places

In many ways, reconciling the demands created by work or study with a relationship with someone in a different geographic location is tackled by relying upon a similar way of thinking. People in this situation do not want to choose *either* their partner *or* their job. They want both and they decide to keep both. A consequence of this decision requires them to live in separate homes. This might be looked upon as a more temporary condition, in light of their own perceptions, because one's job, at some future date, may be changed. Their couple relationship and their jobs are important to them and they want to maintain both. If either moved to their partner's domicile, career opportunities would diminish. This might not be solely a question of money. Even if the other person could support him or her, the arrangement would not be acceptable. Being economically independent is a value of high importance for these people. This characteristic is sometimes referred to as the tendency towards individualization. A century ago, and even half a century ago, people were seldom able to think in the same terms as these people now do. Individualization is more pronounced today. There is more acceptance for the idea that couples need to find ways to better accommodate one another's needs for self-realization. Formerly, the matter was framed as a way of showing one's love: "If you love me enough, you will relocate." The job and the partner are seen as being in competition, and one has to choose between them. In particular there would have been social expectations pressurizing the woman to relocate. Ordinarily, she was the one who was expected to give up her job and her friends. Today, there is acceptance of the idea that she can keep her job and her friends, as well as her relationship with children, parents, and other relatives, and at the same time have a relationship with a man and maintain separate dwellings.

This situation also includes students who study in different places. We were somewhat surprised when we received answers from students defining themselves as LAT partners. We, in our old-fashioned way, saw them more as "going steady." This is a way of seeing their relationship as less serious and uses the traditional marital system as the guiding model (Trost, 1979). However, these students told us that if it were not for their studies, they would have been living together as a cohabiting couple. Since their studies are preventing them, they define themselves as LAT partners.

Cohabitation, as a socially accepted phenomenon, has changed the definition of the situation for these students, relative to what would have been the case earlier, when cohabitation was generally frowned upon by large groups of people. Our material consists solely of people who define themselves as living in a LAT relationship. This means that we have no access to any data from people who define themselves as "going steady." It would have been interesting to compare those defining themselves in a LAT relationship with those who do not do so, but who do see themselves as "going steady." For students, the LAT relationship is a temporary one. They expect to live together after graduation and find jobs near their common home.

Given the technological realities of our contemporary lives, the world seems to be getting smaller and smaller. Telephones, faxes, emails, airplanes, all function to make it easier and easier to keep in contact with people living far away. Some of our informants report that they live on different continents. One of the respondents in our study told us that she lives in Norway and he in Malaysia. For some periods in their relationship, she has lived with him in Malaysia, and he with her in Oslo. They define their two homes as theirs in common, but pay the expenses for them separately.

These couples look upon their lives as a process that changes all the time. Their decisions are only made *for the time being*. When their working situation changes, they may also change their living arrangements. At the same time, they are aware that moving to their partner's home might very well mean losing a lot of the friendships and the close quality of their own social network. Moving away will probably lessen one's contacts with children and grandchildren.

The next subgroup we consider is very different from the first one. Whereas people in the first subgroup do not really want to be in a LAT relationship, for the people in this subgroup the LAT relationship is the *preferred* living arrangement.

THOSE WHO WOULD NOT WISH TO LIVE TOGETHER EVEN IF THEY COULD DO SO, AND STILL WANT TO REMAIN AS A COUPLE

They Don't Want to Repeat the Same Mistake Twice

People in this situation often choose this way of living in order to avoid creating the same conditions that led to the break-up of a former marriage or cohabitation. For many years, they had all experienced living together with another person in a couple relationship—a living situation that ended in divorce or separation. In order to try being in a new couple relationship they feel it is important for them to structure the situation so that another break-up will not occur. They believe that living together, in itself, will change the way each of them relates to the other and that those changes could threaten the relationship's survival. Choosing to live apart is a strategy used in order to avoid another painful separation.

The following example illustrates this approach. A woman had been married for 23 years and had three children from that marriage. When her husband asked her for a divorce, because he had started a relationship with his secretary, her whole world fell apart. But somehow, she managed to pull herself together. She bought an apartment and found meaning in her life as a mother, as a grandmother, and as a professional woman. Time passed, and she began to like her new situation. She enjoyed the freedom of only being responsible for herself, but did not use this freedom to meet new men. She simply did what she wanted to do whenever she wanted to do so, and she enjoyed the realization that no one expected her to "boil the potatoes" each and every day. She liked being able to join her colleagues for a glass of beer, after work, without inconveniencing anybody else. Eventually, she met a man with whom she fell in love. He was living half an hour's car drive away, and he wanted them to live together like ordinary couples do, in the same home. However, she was worried about making the same mistake twice. Her divorce had been too much of a shock for her, and she would do anything to avoid repeating that experience. She refused his offer to live together, but her refusal was not a sign of her lack of affection and love. On the contrary, she says that she loves him very much, but she does not want to tell him *just how much* she loves him. She says that she would rather live alone during the week and meet him on weekends and spend holidays together. She does not dare to live with him "full-time." The risk is connected to her understanding of her marriage and of its break-up and divorce.

She believes that the break-up of her marriage resulted from the fact that she became less interesting as a woman. She is afraid that she will do the same things that eventually made her boring to her husband. She believes that she knows herself very well, and she is certain that she would begin to perform all the traditional housewife activities. She would prepare food for him when he came home from work, and she would become the person responsible for all their home comforts. This is the behavior she would expect from herself and they are related to her own self-esteem and to her identity as a woman. Since she loves him very much, she does not want to risk the good relationship they share, just to live under the same roof, with all of the everyday duties which he (or she) might define as humdrum and boring. She simply does not want to experience another break-up. She has decided to live in a LAT relationship in order to maintain a good couple relationship and to learn the lesson of her past experiences. Her answer to the question "Do you think that you might move in together one day?" is that they probably will do so when she retires, "if he still wants me."

Retired Couples

For retired people, the situation is somewhat different even though the result is the same. These people too do not want to live together even though they are a couple and love one another. Since one or both are not working any more, there is the possibility of moving in together; but deciding to move in together would create difficult practical decisions and necessitate some sacrifices. For instance, who would make the move? Whose furniture would be redundant? Since both might have lived in a one-person home for many years, a lot of the *things* they own are connected to memories of important happenings from their previous lives. The things are *cherished* as symbols of shared experiences. They are reminders of people, and are not just *dead things* as some people may seem to believe—and as such, they are important to them for their own well-being.

Another reason for not wanting to trade two homes for one is their relationship to children and grandchildren. It may be easier to maintain those relationships if they keep their own homes, rather than living together with a partner in one home. One woman told us that she lives 30 km away from her partner and that she sees him every weekend and every Wednesday, and that they go on holiday together. Moving in together is not discussed as a serious possibility because she gets what she wants from their relationship *as it is.* Why would (or should) she change it? When he is ill, she goes over to his home in order to help him. However, he does not do the same when she is ill. When that happens, she gets help from neighbors and from her daughter-in-law. She likes the situation as it is and it has suited her for 18 years. Early on in their relationship they talked of moving in together but it is not a question they discuss any more. They are quite satisfied with their relationship.

She has been hurt by her partner's criticism of her relationship with her disabled son who lives away. When he comes home her partner feels that she favors him. This criticism was unacceptable for the woman and she gave her partner

an ultimatum. Now things have cooled down again and the relationship is back to normal. She is very happy with matters as they stand. One of the things that she most enjoys is their Sunday dinners. She drives them to a neighboring town and he pays for their meal in a nice restaurant. He is also very generous when it comes to giving her gifts and that is something she greatly appreciates.

From Marriage or Cohabitation to a LAT Relationship

Most of the LAT relationship patterns we found consist of people who begin their LAT relationship without first deciding whether or not their relationship was headed for cohabitation or marriage. For some of our respondents the situation has been the other way around. They started as a married or cohabiting couple and the LAT relationship was a solution to difficulties they experienced in those relationships. They lived together for several years but found that they got on each other's nerves in the course of everyday life together. At the same time, they love each other and feel bound to one another. For that reason, they do not want a divorce or a final end to their relationship. It is not what they want, nor is it what their children want. As a solution, one of the partners moves to a nearby apartment and in so doing an alternative way of living, an arrangement that might better fit their lifestyles, for the time being, is undertaken.

An example of this situation is Paul and Paula who met about 20 years ago. They soon became a couple and moved in together. A few years later, they had their first child, and a few years after that their second one. For several years their relationship had been deteriorating and it had become boring. They were finding one another irritating. They still loved one another, but a year before our interview, they decided to separate. They sold their house and bought two apartments just a few minutes' walk from one another. Their children stay with their mother, but they both spend a lot of time with their father, who also spends a lot of time in his ex-cohabitant's apartment, which is larger than his own. This is their way of saving their couple relationship, which in both their opinions would have ended in a breakup without the LAT relationship.

They are clearly still *significant others* to one another and they both want to maintain their relationship but everyday life together simply became too trying. By having two separate homes they hope to be able to maintain the emotions necessary for them to be a loving couple, for each other, and to be good parents to their children. Here the LAT relationship is an alternative to ending their couple relationship. For some people, this alternative might be a peaceful way to a slow divorce without any abrupt changes for themselves or their children.

EXPLAINING LATS

This article has presented a range of situations where the LAT relationship has been established by couples in ways which differ from marriage or cohabitation. Couples often choose a LAT relationship as their living arrangement in order to avoid choosing between (the felt responsibility to care for) an elderly parent, or their own children, and the new partner, which sharing a home would present. An alternative arrangement is partly made possible by LAT relationships because the pressure upon couples "to settle down together" in a common dwelling has decreased. More and more people are accepting the "both/and" solution that LAT relationships provide. As Lewis and Meredith (1989) remark, some adult children live together with a parent, not only because of their sense of duty to care for the parent, but also because they enjoy spending time together with the parent.

A question frequently asked is whether or not LAT relationships occur in all classes within society. Is it a decision that only the financially well-off can make? Our findings show that one can find LAT relationships among all sorts of people. This does not imply that being financially well-off does not make the living arrangements easier to manage. Certainly long-distance LAT relationships require the couple to spend more money on telephone calls and travel, and one home is cheaper to maintain than two. There is no argument with these matters of fact. In most cases, however, in our research, where LAT relationships are found to exist, the couple already each have their own home and are used to paying for their own home expenses.

Why is it that the number of LAT relationships has been increasing? Why have we not noticed or registered LAT relationships before? There may be more than one answer to these questions. One factor is the mortality rate. The lower the mortality rate, the greater the likelihood for a person not only to live longer, but also to experience divorce, the death of a spouse and separation from a non-marital cohabitant, and thus, the greater the likelihood, *ceteris paribus,* for the person to enter into a LAT relationship, or some other new relationship, for that matter. When mortality rates were higher, a greater number of marriages were dissolved by the death of one of the spouses. The need for divorce lessens, therefore, when mortality rates are high.

The closer society got to the 20th century, the greater the decline in remarriages, the greater the rise in the divorce rates, and the greater the fall in mortality rates. The remarriage rate near the middle of the 19th century was about 20 percent, in Norway, but by 1885, it had decreased to about 15 percent (see Sundt, 1975). The remarriage rate continued to decrease during the 20th century, and the lowest rate was reached just before the outbreak of the Second World War, when the remarriage rate was approximately 8 percent (Levin, 1994). During the same period of time, divorce increased and new laws regulating divorce in Norway in 1915 and in Sweden in 1916 came into effect. These laws accepted fault and no-fault grounds for divorce and subsequently the divorce rate continued to increase.

A second factor that has contributed to the increase in LAT relationships has to do with changes in the labor market. A higher degree of specialization is required, these days, and that means a demand for higher levels of education for most job applicants. Fewer people can simply decide to relocate and assume that they will be able to find a good job. This is true for both men and women. Working women are less able to follow their husbands and find a job when they relocate. The relatively short history of the full-time housewife is almost over, in many countries, and in some others, this role has already become a thing of the past. In order to really understand the new structure of relationships between women and men, including LAT relationships, one has to look into the many processes promoting gender equality and equity in contemporary society.

A third factor has to do with the frequency of travel and with the availability and use of IT communication. People on holiday, or travelling because of their job, meet people living in other places. Some of these meetings result in couples falling in love. Many of these relationships will last, and if one or both cannot or does not want to relocate, they might form a long-distance LAT relationship. Travel for leisure or for work will probably increase, even though advances in IT communication continue apace. Couples are being generated on the Internet. Some of those *virtual* relationships may develop into long-distance LAT relationships. We will probably see an important increase in LAT relationships in the near future, and the growth will include married and unmarried couples choosing to live in a LAT relationship.

Traditionally, informal social norms prescribed that a couple should live in the same home. Sharing a domicile was the taken-for-granted pattern for couples. In cases where the two could not live together, living arrangements were considered to be merely temporary. With the high divorce rate, the increasing numbers of women who are gainfully employed, and the

considerable victories that have been won, by women, in the battle for equity, society and its norms have changed. The move towards greater gender equality and equity has had consequences for intimacy and for couple relationships (see Giddens, 1994). Few men, but many women, see advantages in LAT relationships. Therefore the woman is usually the active one in suggesting to move apart.

To summarize, only a few decades ago, marriage was the sole socially approved institution for couples planning to live together. Cohabitation was frowned upon and seen as a deviant phenomenon. There has been a remarkable change in the acceptance of cohabitation. These days, it is more often seen as being a viable option, and it has become an accepted social institution, in its own right, alongside marriage. Without this acceptance of cohabitation, LAT relationships would not have emerged. One might say that cohabitation, as a socially accepted institution, was a prerequisite for the establishment of LAT relationships. The recognition of LAT relationships as a new social phenomenon, in several western societies, and the documented rise in its frequency, as well as the general increasing awareness of the term "LAT relationship," are factors at work today that may some day establish the LAT relationship as a generally recognized and accepted social institution in many more countries.

There are many reasons for predicting that LAT relationships will be more common in the near future. The labor market will probably not return to the relatively simple structure it had only a few decades ago. Specialization will probably continue to increase, affecting even more job-holders. Holiday and work-related travel probably will not decrease, even if IT communication becomes even more important. In fact, IT communication might be used more frequently as a way for people to meet new partners. Same-gender couples may increasingly "come out of the closet" and cohabit or form LAT relationships. Divorce and separation rates will probably not decrease, and new partnerships will be formed in increasing numbers. The LAT relationship may become a more common way for dealing with a difficult marriage or non-marital cohabitation. The mortality rate will probably continue to decrease in most countries, and that means that people will live longer, and probably be healthier, and thus more prone to find new partners.

ENDNOTES

The research reported on in this article was carried out with Professor Jan Trost, Uppsala University, Sweden.

1. This second survey was financed by SKOP and by the Magnus Bergwall Foundation.
2. If the percentages in England were the same as in Sweden, there would be, approximately, 750,000 couples living in LAT relationships.

■ Review Questions

1. Are LAT relationships "families"?
2. Why might couples choose not to live together?

CHAPTER 7

Cohabitation and Marriage

A majority of marriages now begin with a period of cohabitation—the couple first lives together without marrying. Prior to about 1970, cohabitation was frowned upon and was very rare except among the poor. Today, it is widely accepted. This new relationship stage has greatly changed the ways couples think about marriage. A half century ago, women and men married soon after high school or college and expected to cope with tight budgets for a while until they achieved financial stability. But today, many young couples are postponing marriage until after they have achieved financial stability. Marriage was the start of young adulthood in the mid-twentieth century; today it is often the end of it. The interviews with cohabiting couples that Pamela J. Smock, Wendy D. Manning, and Meredith Porter describe in the first reading in this chapter illustrate this change.

While presenting excerpts from these interviews, the authors also write about the process of sociological research. They contrast "quantitative" and "qualitative" studies. The former are the statistical studies of survey or government data that dominate much of social scientific research. Reading 1-1, "The Family in Trouble:

Since When? For Whom?" is an example of a quantitative study. Qualitative studies consist of analyses of what people say or do in real life or what they have written in diaries or letters. Many qualitative studies involve detailed, first-person observations of a small sample of individuals or families over a long time period, a method that is called "ethnography" by anthropologists. The Smock et al. reading does not have the intensive, long-term observations of an ethnography, but it is qualitative because the authors rely on the words that people said to them in discussion groups (i.e., person x said to us . . .) rather than on statistical summaries (i.e., 75 percent of the sample said "yes"). Although sociologists sometimes define themselves as either quantitative or qualitative researchers, the two methods can be used to complement each other. Smock et al. have done statistical research in the past. They chose to conduct a qualitative study because it could help them understand the meanings of the patterns they were seeing in their statistical data. By alternating between quantitative and qualitative studies, the authors hope to combine a broad statistical portrait of cohabitors with an in-depth understanding of what they are thinking.

Kathryn Edin and Maria Kefalas conducted an ethnographic study to answer the question of why women in low-income families have been postponing marriage but not postponing having children—with the result that the percentage of children born outside of marriage has risen dramatically among low-income women. This phenomenon has been puzzling social scientists and policy makers. In order to understand it better, Edin and Kefalas studied women and men in eight low-income neighborhoods in the Philadelphia area for over two years. The authors wanted to learn more about the nature of intimate relationships in low-income communities and about low-income women's attitudes and values about childbearing and marriage. They published their findings in a 2005 book, *Promises I Can Keep: Why Poor Women Put Motherhood before Marriage.* The second reading in this chapter is an article they wrote for the magazine *Contexts* summarizing what they found.

READING 7-1

"Everything's There Except Money"
How Money Shapes Decisions to Marry among Cohabitors

Pamela J. Smock

Wendy D. Manning

Meredith Porter

The last few decades have ushered in significant changes in family patterns (Casper & Bianchi, 2002; Thornton, Fricke, Axinn, & Alwin, 2001; Thornton & Young-Demarco, 2001). After a brief period characterized by early marriage and low levels of divorce after World War II, recent decades have been marked by lower levels of childbearing, higher divorce rates, increases in the average age at marriage, rising nonmarital childbearing, and rising levels of cohabitation. Although most Americans still marry at some point and the vast majority express strong desires to marry, unmarried cohabitation has dramatically transformed the marriage process. Today, the majority of marriages and remarriages begin as cohabiting relationships. Most young men and women have cohabited or will cohabit, cohabitation has increased in all age groups, and cohabitation is increasingly a context for childbearing and childrearing (Bumpass & Lu, 2000; Casper & Bianchi; Manning, 2002).

Given that cohabitation is now the modal path to marriage, an important issue is whether and under what circumstances cohabitation leads to marriage. A long line of research in the social sciences has drawn on data from surveys to examine the economic determinants of marriage. More recently, studies have emerged examining similar

Pamela J. Smock, Wendy D. Manning, and Meredith Porter, "'Everything's There Except Money': How Money Shapes Decisions to Marry among Cohabitors," *Journal of Marriage and Family* 67 (August 2005): 680–696. Reprinted by permission.

issues for cohabiting unions (e.g., Clarkberg, 1999; Oppenheimer, 2003; Sassler & McNally, 2003). . . .

CURRENT INVESTIGATION

Our study builds on prior work by exploring how cohabiting men and women link economic circumstances and the marriage decision-making process. One motivation for this work is that it is difficult with quantitative research alone to understand why education, income, or employment measures are positively and significantly correlated with marriage. Our general aim is to triangulate existing quantitative studies with new qualitative data to explore what positive economic circumstances mean to cohabiting men and women and how those meanings shape marriage decisions. As Lin (1998) argues, analyses based on quantitative data can often provide us with the *what*—that two or more variables are related and that there may be a credible causal story—but they cannot necessarily provide us with the *how* and the *why*.

We thus draw on data from 115 in-depth interviews with men and women who are now, or were recently, cohabiting to explore whether and how financial issues are involved in cohabitors' thoughts and feelings about marriage. Our approach is informed by the social psychological paradigm of symbolic interactionism, which posits that individual behavior is based not only on what is, but also on individuals' interpretations of what is. This perspective assumes that individuals categorize and construct their social world, subjectively define situations, and use these interpretations to adapt their behavior (Mead, 1934; Stryker, 1972). Most broadly, the symbolic interactionist paradigm holds that identifying subjective meanings and interpretations is essential for understanding individual behavior.

Our study adds to extant knowledge in two additional ways. First, we focus on working- and lower middle-class individuals. The few qualitative studies on our general topic tend to focus on the disadvantaged, particularly low-income mothers. We purposefully set out to study young men and women who have not made it solidly into the middle class, but, for the most part, are not officially poor or involved in the welfare system. A quantitative study spanning the years from 1960 to 2000 underscores the importance of this endeavor. Ellwood and Jencks (2001) show that the increase in single parenthood over the past 40 years has been concentrated in the middle and lower thirds of the educational distribution, and not just the lower third.

Second, we interview both parents and nonparents and restrict our focus to cohabiting (or recently cohabiting) young adults rather than including those in an array of relationship statuses. Our exclusive focus on cohabitors is important because the modal path to marriage is through cohabitation. Including those who are childless is useful because it reflects the actual composition of cohabiting couples today; approximately 60% of cohabiting unions do not include children (Fields & Casper, 2001).

METHOD

Our analysis is based on semistructured in-depth interviews with 115 young adults who were currently cohabiting or had recently cohabited. For the latter group, the median time since the end of the cohabitation in either dissolution or marriage (see below) was one and a half years, with the majority having ended the cohabitation within the last 3 years. Our interview strategy drew on the idea of the relationship as "career" by asking how and why cohabiting relationships began, perceptions of the future of the relationship at the beginning of the cohabitation, numerous aspects of the relationship itself, views on prerequisites for marriage, perceptions of how being married would differ from cohabiting, perceptions of how cohabitation differs from dating, and how and why the cohabiting relationship ended (if relevant).

At the time of interview, 47% of our sample were cohabiting, 26% were married (after having cohabited with their spouse or someone else), 26% were currently single after having recently cohabited, and one respondent was divorced after having cohabited and then married. The respondents were interviewed in 2002, largely between April and October, and were 18–36 years old, with a median age of 26, at the time of interview. Additionally, our sample is diverse such that we have at least 15 interviews with each gender and race/ethnic group (White, Black, Latino, or Latina).

The respondents all live in the vicinity of Toledo, Ohio, which has a sociodemographic distribution quite similar to that of the entire nation. For example, 2000 Census data indicate that the populations of the Metropolitan Statistical Area of Toledo and the nation are similar in terms of race (13% in Toledo and 12% in the United States are Black), education (80% in Toledo and 84% in the United States are high school graduates), median income ($50,046 in Toledo and $50,287 in the United States), and marital status (74% in Toledo and 76% in the United States are married couple families).

We recruited our sample by means of personal contacts, as well as encounters with potential respondents in various parts of the community (e.g., local coin laundry, grocery stores, restaurants, the neighborhood, parties). This was a time-consuming effort in that the key requirement was to interview a racially and ethnically diverse sample of men and women who were currently cohabiting or recently cohabiting. In addition, to meet the demographic specifications of the sample, some respondents were referred by community organizations or agencies or were recruited in areas in which the pool of prospective participants had a greater probability of being a specific race or ethnicity. Note, though, that respondents were not necessarily clients of the agencies but often employees of them; thus, we remained cognizant of seeking interviews largely with working- and lower middle-class men and women. Some interviews were conducted immediately following an introduction but most were

TABLE 7.1

DISTRIBUTION OF SAMPLE (%) ACCORDING TO RACE, GENDER, EDUCATION, INCOME, AND EMPLOYMENT STATUS

%	White male 19.1	White female 25.2	Black male 13.9	Black female 14.8	Latino 13.0	Latina 13.9	Total 100.0
Educational attainment							
Less than high school	4.5	3.4	18.8	0	33.3	25	12.2
High school or GED	22.7	10.3	31.3	41.2	40.0	18.8	25.2
Technical or some college	50.0	48.3	43.8	41.2	20.0	56.3	44.3
College graduate	22.7	37.9	6.3	17.6	6.7	0.0	18.3
Personal income							
Less than $20,000	22.2	50	56.3	64.7	69.2	92.9	57.3
$20,000–$40,000	50.0	50.0	31.3	35.3	30.8	7.1	35.4
More than $40,000	27.8	0.0	12.5	0.0	0.0	0.0	7.3
Employment status							
Employed	95.5	93.1	81.3	88.2	53.3	62.5	81.7
Not employed	4.5	6.9	18.7	11.8	46.6	37.5	18.2
N	22	29	16	17	15	16	115

scheduled for a later time. Additionally, the sample was partially a snowball sample, with approximately 30% of the respondents referred from the pool of participating respondents.

The interviews were semistructured and lasted, on average, 2 hours, with the mean length of a transcribed interview being 39 pages. Although semistructured interviews provide some organization, they also allow the interviewer to probe with follow-up questions and pursue additional lines of inquiry. Generally, in-depth interviews are an excellent method for exploring perceptions, behavioral patterns, and their cognitive justifications, ultimately helping to illuminate the causal processes that quantitative social science seeks to uncover (Weiss, 1994). We used one interviewer for all interviews: She is a member of the community who is experienced in interviewing racially and economically diverse populations in the area, and our reading of the transcripts suggests that she achieved outstanding rapport with the vast majority of respondents.

Table 7.1 shows the distribution of our sample according to education, personal income, and employment status. Our sample can be characterized as largely working class and lower middle

class (i.e., high school graduates and those with some college or technical school training). The educational breakdown of our sample is as follows: less than high school (12.2%), high school (25%), some college (44.3%), college graduate or more (18.3%). The majority of our respondents are currently employed (82%), although a few are enrolled in school full time, and some are both employed and enrolled in school part time. Yearly individual incomes range from about $10,000 per year to $55,000 per year, with the majority (57%) earning less than $20,000 per year and only 7% earning more than $40,000. Couple incomes range from approximately $15,000 to $60,000, with most reporting combined incomes in the $20,000 to $40,000 range (not in table). Income varies significantly by race/ethnicity and gender. White men and women are the most highly educated; White men are most likely to earn at least $40,000 per year; and over half of all Latinos and Blacks earn less than $20,000 per year. Also noteworthy is that Latinos and Latinas are least likely to be currently employed. Finally, a range of parenthood statuses is represented in our data: 45% are childless, 23% have a biological child with their partner, 6% have a biological child from a prior relationship, 10% have a stepchild(ren), with the remainder having some combination of stepchildren and biological children from a prior relationship (not in table).

Our coding proceeded whereby categories were derived as they emerged from the data. We used a computer program called Atlas/ti to aid in our data management and analyses. The program assists with coding and analysis of qualitative data (Weitzman, 1999), and provides tools to manage, store, extract, compare, explore, and reassemble meaningful pieces of data flexibly and systematically. The development of our coding scheme was an intensive, iterative analytic task. Essentially, coding applies a meaning or interpretation to a segment of data—in our case, textual data from the interviews. It consists of creating categories and marking segments of the data with these codes. A single paragraph or sentence may have one code or several and these may be overlapping with other text segments.

The authors each read a subset of transcripts, coding them independently. We then examined *intercoder reliability* by using a merge function in the program to juxtapose codes, review similarity of code lists, compare the number of codes derived, and assess consistency between coders in segments of text coded (i.e., where segments begin and end). Although we had few interpretive disagreements, we used the merge function as a tool to explore and discuss the meaning of minor discrepancies in our interpretations and, eventually, to generate a coding scheme capturing our consensus on the issues.

Our analyses involved first searching for instances in the interviews in which the issue of money was raised by the respondent either in response to a question about "what would need to be in place for marriage" or at other points in the interview when respondents raised the issue themselves. We then analyzed the context in which finances were raised—that is, whether and how respondents themselves made the connection between economic factors and marriage. We organize our results around several emergent themes regarding aspects of finances, providing representative quotations to illustrate these themes. Note that the interviewer did not probe to specifically seek *economic* prerequisites for marriage. Thus, the findings we report here may be conservative estimates of the salience of economics in marital decision making among cohabitors.

RESULTS

We asked cohabitors about their views on marriage prerequisites, or what kinds of things needed to be "in place" to decide to marry; we also take account of instances in which these issues were raised or elaborated by the respondent at other points in the interview. To obtain a broad view of this issue, Table 7.2 categorizes individuals into four groups: mentioned only economic issues, mentioned only relationship/individual qualities, mentioned both types of issues, and gave no response. Economic aspects include money, jobs, assets (e.g., houses, savings), or education. Relationship/individual factors include concerns such as needing more time in the relationship, quality of the relationship, age/maturity, and substance abuse or violence.

As shown in Table 7.2, most respondents perceive both relationship and economic factors as important for marriage. Approximately 23% named only economic criteria or only relationship criteria; nearly 50% named both. Thus, overall, 72% of the sample identified at least one economic factor as a prerequisite for the relationship to result in marriage. Table 7.2 also suggests that the prominence of economic concerns may vary by race, with Blacks more likely to cite economic factors than Latinos or Whites (82% vs. 67% and 71% among Whites and Latinos, respectively).

In the remainder of the paper we explore the specific aspects of economics that cohabitors believe important for marriage. Five central themes emerged from the data: (a) having enough money, (b) the ability to pay for a "real" wedding,

TABLE 7.2

DISTRIBUTION OF SAMPLE (%) BY PERCEIVED PREREQUISITES FOR MARRIAGE

Total sample	N 115	Only economic 22.6	Only relationship 23.5	Relationship and economic 49.6	No mention of either 4.3
Gender					
Male	53	20.8	24.5	47.2	7.5
Female	62	24.2	22.6	51.6	1.6
Race/ethnicity					
White	51	25.5	29.4	41.2	3.9
Black	33	18.2	18.2	63.6	0.0
Latinos/Latinas	31	22.6	19.4	48.4	9.7

(c) achieving a set of financial goals before marriage, (d) the male partner's capacity to be an economic provider, and (e) lack of money as a source of stress and relationship conflict.

Money as Capstone in the Cohabitation-Marriage Sequence: "Everything's There Except Money"

About one third of those citing any economic factor mentioned money needed to be in place for them to marry (or have married) their cohabiting partner. Leroy, who is 29 years old and recently unemployed, says, "I don't really know 'cause the love is there uh . . . trust is there. Everything's there except money." Similarly, 25-year-old Ofilia says, "Money, it's just money. Nothing else." And Joseph, 31 years old, says, "Basically everything was in place, just basically it gets back to the money." Patricio, a 20-year-old unemployed young man who dropped out of high school, puts it perhaps most straightforwardly: "If I ever got rich I would marry Melissa." Calvin, who is 24 and also unemployed, says, "I want to be financially okay when I, when I've decided to take that step."

Other respondents are somewhat more specific. The idea of marriage appears to be associated with having attained a certain "comfortable" financial status. Holly, a 36-year-old store supervisor whose cohabiting relationship dissolved without marriage, describes how getting married

should signify that one is no longer struggling economically:

I: Ok. How then, like what would have had to been in place for you to have gotten married?

R: Money.

I: Ok. Tell me a little bit about what that means.

R: Money means um . . . stability. I don't want to struggle, if I'm in a partnership, then there's no more struggling, and income-wise we were still both struggling.

The implication is that one does not marry if one is struggling financially; marriage both connotes and requires a certain level of economic stability. Holly's comment about financial stability was echoed in some other cohabitors' concerns. Donald, a roofer, tries to describe what he means: "We feel when we get financially, you know what I'm saying, stable, then we will be ready."

Andy, a 26-year-old computer technician whose relationship recently ended, also talks about wanting to be financially comfortable, but expresses it in negative terms, mainly focusing on debt: "I'm still at a financially unstable point because of like school loans. And I don't want to impose that upon anybody else. Like that's one of my major things before I get married, I want to be paid up. . . ."

Thus, empathizing with what he thinks a future partner might feel, Andy will not marry unless he is basically debt free. This concern was echoed by several others as they thought about what needed to be in place to marry: Getting "bills paid down," "caught up on some bills," and dealing with student loans, all inhibited the sense of being ready to marry.

Heidi, an assistant manager at a shoe store, lives with her boyfriend and her boyfriend's parents. She implies that marriage, but not cohabitation, requires economic and residential independence, which boils down to having enough money:

> Right now, we wouldn't be able to afford, you know, to be out on our own. . . . To have to pay rent . . . to pay bills . . . I mean, I realize that you're going to have rent and I realize that you're going to have you know, utilities and groceries and furnishings and stuff like that. I don't think he realizes that half the time, and he's like, "Hmmm, so let's go!" I think that we need to have more income coming in so we can be able to do that.

Money and the Symbolic Meaning of the Wedding Ceremony: A Real Wedding

For some cohabitors, the issue of enough money is tied directly to the ability to afford a wedding. Overall, one fifth of those mentioning any economic issue as important for marriage mentioned weddings, or more precisely, the cost of weddings, as an impediment to getting married. This is especially noteworthy because the interviewer never raised the issue of weddings, and it emerged without prompting.

Respondents often cite saving to have a real wedding as a prerequisite to marriage. Abram, a 27 year old, said he knew right away that he wanted to marry his girlfriend, but "we never saved up enough money to have the wedding we wanted." (He also mentioned the cost of a honeymoon as part of what he considers a proper wedding.) Another respondent, Vicente, currently cohabiting with his fiancée, posited that the purpose of cohabitation is actually to pay for a wedding: "I mean cohabitation, I think it's alright I mean. You see someone you love and if

you want to have a big wedding, you can't afford it, you go live with them until you can afford it."

Other respondents said they simply could not afford a wedding, even if they had plans to marry. Petra, who works as an administrative assistant, reported that her boyfriend tells her he "wants to marry me and that he wants a big wedding and, you know, he wants the whole nine yards, but right now we can't really afford it." And, for Ofilia, having a wedding competes monetarily with raising children; she and her boyfriend do not have enough money to do both:

> . . . he gave me a ring, he asked me to marry him a long time ago. We talked about getting married, it's just we don't have anyone to pay for the wedding and I don't want to go downtown. So, it's on us . . . and when we came down to the decision of do we want kids or do we want the marriage and for now we wanted the kids. . . .

Typically, respondents who talked about weddings aim to have sufficient financial resources for a relatively large wedding. But for others the impediment is just being able to afford an engagement ring or a modest wedding. Geraldine, a 28-year-old law clerk, reported that her partner was "trying to sell his trumpet" to pay for her ring. Indeed, even very modest weddings may pose a serious obstacle to marriage for working- and middle-class young adults. Ben, a 30-year-old railroad conductor, said he did not know how he would come up with $5,000 for a wedding, exclaiming "Weddings are expensive!"

Several men and women made a distinction between a "church" wedding and a "downtown" (or "courthouse" or "justice of the peace") wedding; this distinction was quite salient to them. When asked whether she and her partner considered marriage, Terri, a beautician, says:

> I did, I did a lot. He just said he wasn't ready or we don't have the money, you know wait until we get our finances straight. Well, you never can get your finances straight, it don't matter how long and I don't want a big wedding, I already told him that, I want to go downtown and that's it, it's not going to cost that much but for some odd reason he just,

I don't think he ever wants to get married to be truthful.

Here, note that Terri believes that her partner's persistent desire to wait until their finances are "straight"—despite her willingness to compromise on a downtown weddings—amounts to a strategy to avoid marriage.

Heidi, too, decides that although she yearns for a church wedding, a downtown wedding would be acceptable:

> I've always wanted a church wedding. You know . . . I want to walk down the aisle with my Dad, and you know, I want to dance with my Grandpa (laughs). . . . But if it came down to the point where Eric was just like, I really don't want to have a church wedding, let's just go downtown, I, I love him so much, I want to be with him so much, that I probably would do it.

Among other cohabitors, especially some women, the resistance to "going downtown" was formidable. Annie, a 22-year-old home health care aid, explains that she's just waiting for her boyfriend to change his mind because "until he does, we just won't get married. I'm not going downtown. . . . I say, you don't want a big wedding, we're not going to get married." Gloria, a 25-year-old woman who works for a telephone company says, "We're gonna do it right. So, we wouldn't rush a wedding like—let's just go get married 'justice of peace.'. . . We want to have a big wedding. We want to have, you know, both of our families enjoy it." Here, one can see that perceptions of prerequisites for marriage also involve relations to others such as family members. Asked whether he is considering marriage, Leroy answered:

> R: Well, it crossed my mind. Um . . . I always said I just couldn't afford it. If I could afford it I probably would be married by now. . . .You can't get married for free.
>
> I: Ok. But you could go down to the justice of the peace, you could have a simple church wedding, you could, I mean. . . .
>
> R: But that's the poor people way.

Despite the fact that Leroy is nearly poor—having recently lost a job paying him about $15,000 per year—it is vital to him to have a real wedding rather than a "poor people" wedding. Leroy goes on to explain his reactions to his cousin's recent wedding. Although it was in a church, it was small, simple, and inexpensive. There were no bridesmaids, groomsmen, or flower girls, leading Leroy to say that "it just didn't seem like a wedding" and it was more like a "get together." Kerry, a homemaker, appears to agree. She reports that her sister-in-law told her, "Oh, don't go downtown, you should have a wedding!"—implying that marriage by a justice of the peace is not considered a "real wedding." Other cohabitors also spoke of "just" going downtown, with the implication that this is a minimal, lesser sort of wedding.

James, a 36-year-old carpenter, describes how he and his girlfriend are trying to save up for a house, so he suggested that they go downtown to marry and then have a real wedding in a couple of years when they could afford it:

> And her thing was "No, I don't want to do that. I want to go back home, I want to have this big ceremony with my mother by my side." My thing was "We just can't afford it, your mother doesn't have any money. It's not like she's going to pay for anything. I'm going to pay for this and we can't afford it. You know. So, no we can't do it." Then her thing was "Well, no I'm not going down to the court house and getting married." You know, and that was about the extent of our conversation.

Wesley, a 22 year old who works as a supervisor at a manufacturing plant, was quite specific about the need for a little "financial time" because of his girlfriend's desire for a "big 30, 40 thousand thing and I'm not quite ready for that . . . we need to get some more of my student loans paid off and stuff like that before I can even do that."

It is noteworthy that in all cases the young couples appear to have sole responsibility to pay for the wedding; parents or other relatives are not mentioned as potential resources. These young adults, unlike their more privileged, upper middle class counterparts, are unable to rely on family members to absorb the cost, or even some of the cost, of a wedding. This is not surprising, given their modest backgrounds, including that over 60% did not grow up with their two biological married parents (not in table).

Money as Part of the Respectability Package: "After X, Y, and Z, We'll Get Married"

A theme that emerged in the interviews is the importance of accomplishing a *set* of financially related goals before marriage. Respondents who mention any one economic factor as a prerequisite for marriage tend to mention more than one. These responses were generally stated as "when we have x, y, and z, we'll get married."

LaTonya, a 24-year-old customer service supervisor, says of her partner: "So he thinks that he needs to graduate and be making more money and, you know, buy me a house and a really big ring and all that kind of thing before we get married." Russell, 19 years old and unemployed, says, "For us to get married we'd have to have a lot. Like we'd have to both have good jobs, money, and a place to stay. And all of that." Fred, a 22-year-old UPS worker, states: "If I had the money, I would, I'd get married, but all that wedding and stuff and I want to get my own place before—I want to settle down before I get married." For Fred, financial resources for a wedding and a home are required before marriage. Malcolm, a 25-year-old waiter, wants a car and a good career prior to marriage: "I don't have a car. . . . I want a nice dependable car, I want a good job as far as career-wise. . . . I want to either be back at school or take a path to going back to school or being in school and being successful and on my way to graduating." Ellen, a graduate student and part-time Medicaid eligibility worker, says, "I think, have enough money set aside, and maybe even living in our own apartment or a house maybe?"

Candace, 25 years old and currently on worker's compensation, provides a more elaborate response. She talks about how she and her partner are interested in marrying, but there are some things they want first:

> Um, we have certain things that we want to do before we get married. We both want very good jobs, and we both want a house, we both want reliable transportation. I'm about to start taking cake decorating classes, and so I can have me some good income, and he—he's trying his best you know? He's been looking out for jobs everywhere, and we—we're trying. We just want to have—we gotta have everything we need before we say "Let's get married."

Although Candace and her partner have discussed these issues at some length and generally agree on their goals, lack of money still intervenes. Candace has passed the General Educational Development (GED) tests and she is not quite sure how many years of schooling her partner has. Their relatively low levels of schooling and unemployed status suggest that they may have enormous difficulty achieving their goals of well-paying jobs in order to marry.

As suggested by several of the above quotations, home ownership is often part of the desired package. Approximately 22% of those mentioning at least one economic factor say that owning their own home is an important prerequisite for marriage.

The case of Peter, 28 years old and in sales, who did end up marrying his partner, is illustrative. Reflecting on the timing of the marriage, he says, "Probably the biggest thing of all . . . was a . . . just a financial stability before we would jump into something like that. I didn't want to get married and go living in an apartment or townhouse. I wanted to save on up to, you know, buy a home, start a family." These results are consistent with a quantitative analysis showing that housing opportunities influence young adults' living arrangements. Hughes (2003) finds that people are more likely to be married when potential earnings are high and housing costs are low.

Sandra, 19 years old, voices a similar concern. She and her partner live half of the time at her parents' house and half at his parents' house. She explained that they are not yet ready for marriage because they lack the resources to set up an independent household, which to her is necessary for marriage:

> I feel like we don't have the resources, I mean he lives here, and my mom always says you know, "if you want to get married, you can live here and it wouldn't matter," 'cause, but I, I wouldn't feel right. I feel like if you get married, you need to go out on your own, and start your own life, and I'm not ready for that right now. And neither is he.

Another factor sometimes mentioned in the set of economic prerequisites for marriage is finishing school. This is consistent with both quantitative (e.g., Manning & Smock, 1995; Thornton, Axinn, & Teachman, 1995) and qualitative research (Sassler, 2004), suggesting that school enrollment inhibits marriage among cohabitors.

Finishing school is not necessarily viewed as an end in itself but as part of a package, tied to attaining economic stability. As Geraldine, a teacher who ended up marrying her partner, says, "I wanted to be graduated from college. . . . I wanted to have a job." Gloria, who also married her partner, has a similar view about the timing of her marriage: "See, I had the degree and I was ready to move to this next step which would be my mate . . . because I've done the schooling and I've secured the job with the security, financial security."

Money and Gendered Expectations: "The Guy Takes Care of the Woman and His Kids"

Another theme that emerged in our interviews is a perception on the part of some cohabitors that men's economic situations are relatively more important than women's for marriage. This came across in two ways. First, it was more common for women than for men to be concerned about their *partner's* jobs. About three times as many women than men reported that they wanted a change in some aspect of their partner's employment (e.g., get a job or get a better paying job) in order to marry. Additionally, whereas women might mention wanting to finish their degrees and get their career on track before marriage, both men and women made far more references to men's jobs and men's income stability. This is of particular interest, given that cohabitors express more gender-egalitarian views than those who do not cohabit (e.g., Clarkberg, Stolzenberg, & Waite, 1995).

Second, a significant minority of our respondents directly expressed the expectation that men should be able to "provide for" or "support" a family. Such views were expressed by one third of those mentioning at least one economic factor ($n = 26$) and about equally by women and men.

For example, Henry, a 33-year-old information systems manager, reflects: "Had I been . . . in a financial position where I was able to take care of myself and a family, then it might have moved things along quicker." Jamal, 27 years old, says, "What would make me ready? Knowing that I could provide. . . ." Victor, a 27-year-old male, states that "the male's financially responsible for like, you know, the household, paying the bills."

The following interchange with Hector, a 20-year-old student, clearly reveals gendered expectations. Here he is describing why he and his former cohabiting partner did not marry:

> R: . . . if I do get married I need myself to be able to support [her] as well as me and everybody else that gets brought into this family. That's what I, that's what you know, ideally what I was brought up to be. The guy takes care of the woman and his kids. . . .
>
> I: Is that machismo?
>
> R: Not machismo. That's just how I was brought up. I mean I . . . I could be wrong. I'm probably wrong to most people now because women are taking care of themselves, which is fine.
>
> I: You're more of a traditionalist.
>
> R: Yeah.

I: So you wanted to be able to support her financially?

R: Right.

Sometimes the belief that men are more responsible for the finances in a marriage comes out in subtler ways. Lester, an 18-year-old house painter, says that in order to marry his partner, "I would have to be able to take care of myself before I'd be able to take care of a family." This implies his expectation that it would be his responsibility to take care of a family. Perhaps less realistically, Donald, who is 30 years old and currently cohabiting, muses that he would marry his partner "if I was to hit the lottery and could take her somewhere and we wouldn't have to worry about no problems for the rest of our life."

Women also sometimes express views that men have more responsibility for providing in marriage than women. Kerry, a 25-year-old married homemaker, reflects on what had to be in place for her to marry her partner: "I don't know if he was really thinking about what marriage meant. You know, he was gonna have to take care of us, and have a family now, and be a provider. He was just being kind of immature still. . . ." Kerry also says that they were "trying to get him into a career that, you know, was gonna make enough money for us. . . . And then worry about getting married. . . ." Gloria puts it this way:

> I'm just saying that I feel like, ok, I do want my man to make more money than me, I believe he needs to be the breadwinner and I also feel like, as a wife . . . those are my responsibilities to keep the house clean and all this. . . .

(Gloria went on to say that the minute she would start helping her husband to earn money, then household chores ought to be split.) Candace explains her hesitancy to marry her partner because she needs to know whether "he can take care of us"—Candace has four children—if anything happens to her to prevent her from working.

A case in which we did hear a woman talking about needing to be able to support a family herself was Geraldine's. When describing how she wanted to finish school and start a job before marriage she explained, "If anything happened, or if he died or something, or we did end up getting divorced somewhere down the line, I wouldn't be destitute." Thus, her concern with economic independence, seemingly a prerequisite for marriage, was more a precaution in case of her partner's death or a divorce.

Money and Relationship Quality: "Whenever We'd Get in Fights, It'd Be About Money"

Although not typically referenced in the quantitative literature on the economic determinants of marriage or cohabitation, there is a body of research linking forms of economic distress to marital quality and stability (e.g., Clark-Nicolas & Gray-Little, 1991; Conger et al., 1990; Fox & Chancey, 1998; Johnson & Booth, 1990). Studies suggest that perceived economic hardship has negative effects on relationship quality and is positively related to thoughts of divorce, that employment uncertainty and low income are associated with psychological distress among husbands and wives, and that husbands' job insecurity has a significant positive effect on wives' reports of marital conflict and thoughts of divorce. One study of farm families, for example, suggests that economic hardship is related to thoughts of divorce, with depression accounting for about half of this effect (Johnson & Booth). Another finds that perceived economic adequacy—as measured by adequacy of income for food, clothing, medical care, leisure, and monetary surplus left at month's end—is a significant predictor of marital satisfaction (Clark-Nicolas & Gray-Little).

Our interviews with cohabitors are consistent with these findings, suggesting that financial constraints are sometimes perceived as a source of relationship conflict affecting relationship quality and the sense of a stable future. Over one quarter of the total sample ($n = 31$) told us that money was a problem area when asked about conflict in their relationships. Larry, for example, reports that he had no hopes for the future with his partner at the beginning of their relationship because they argued about "how we're going to pay for these bills. . . ." Aileen, a 32-year-old computer technician, says about her partner:

> [He] doesn't work enough, sometimes. He like, you know, he won't go to work for four days, so his paycheck will be half of what it should be. And then he'll want to pay his bills, before he gives, gives me the money that I, I need. And that pisses me off.

Vicente, when asked about the stability of his relationship, says that "just finances, pretty much, is about the only instability in the relationship." And when asked about the main source of conflict in her relationship, Rose, a married, 27-year-old medical worker, had this to say:

> R: Money.
>
> I: Money. Okay. Does that mean like choices in what each other spends it on?
>
> R: Oh no. Just 'cause we don't have enough . . . to pay all the bills at one time.

The severity of the problem varies of course with economic resources. Thus, although some cohabitors may feel money is a source of tension, they are able to resolve ensuing conflicts. As described by Ellen, a graduate student: "Sometimes when it's dwindling down before we're gonna get paid, and it's like not really a conflict, it's just like, 'What are we gonna do?' And then, like the last fight we had, we fought about money a little bit, we kind of just didn't talk for 10 minutes, then we just started talking about it . . . and we worked it out."

Notably, in the event that financial circumstances improve and stabilize, relationship quality can be positively affected. Ben, now married to his partner, reports that "I think things stabilized quite a bit too with when I started working for the railroad. It stabilized us a lot more. We were making better money . . . it wasn't an up and down, it was a constant." In his prior job, "it was a lot of stress. It was a lot of 'Okay, am I gonna be able to make my bills this month?'" Recalling this earlier time, Ben says:

> It's hard when you don't have money and you can't get what you want to get and you . . . might not be able to get all the groceries that you want to get, you might not be able to put gas in your car to go somewhere. . . . So, I think it's helped us a lot being able to do what we want, when we want, and get the things that we need.

CONCLUSION

Drawing on in-depth interviews with 115 young adults, we find that cohabitors believe that economic circumstances matter for marriage in several different ways. First, having "enough" money is a common consideration, alongside the view that marriage signifies that one is no longer struggling economically. Second, we find that lack of money is associated with relationship conflict, suggesting a significant indirect pathway by which financial difficulties inhibit marriage. Third, although our sample is largely nonpoor, having sufficient money or savings to afford a real wedding is also a concern. Going downtown to the courthouse is not deemed a real wedding, and some cohabitors say they will delay marriage until they can afford a church wedding and reception. Noteworthy is that these young couples, generally from modest backgrounds, anticipate paying for their weddings themselves, without help from parents. Fourth, it is often not attaining a single financial goal, but several as a package, that is perceived as necessary for marriage. Cohabitors' thoughts on this issue often took the form of "after x, y, and z, we'll get married." Most commonly, this economic package includes home ownership, getting out of debt, and financial stability (not living from paycheck to paycheck).

Finally, we find that some cohabitors, both men and women, tend to think that the decision to marry hinges on the male partner's ability to fulfill the breadwinner role—despite the prevailing view that cohabitors are less invested in traditional normative practices than those who do not cohabit. Our study illustrates that some cohabitors are making a direct and conscious connection between willingness to marry and the male partner's ability to provide. This finding is consistent with quantitative studies that have found that men's economic situations may matter more for marriage than women's (e.g., Oppenheimer, 2003; Smock & Manning, 1997; Xie et al., 2003). Landale and Forste (1991, p. 603) speculate that cohabitation is an adaptive family strategy that allows for union formation in the face of economic uncertainty because it makes few unambiguous demands on the man as breadwinner.

Interestingly, the notion of marriage as preferably occurring after economic stability has been achieved contrasts sharply with the experiences of the working-class married couples studied some three decades ago by Rubin (1976). Rubin describes how financial difficulties pervaded the early years of marriage in her sample. Our results suggest that, today, those years of economic struggle often occur during cohabitation rather than marriage.

Why have perceptions about economic readiness to marry altered since Rubin's study? This question is intricately tied to the issue of the retreat from marriage in general over the past 30 years, a topic that numerous social scientists have pondered; a recent issue of this journal (November, 2004) is, in fact, devoted to the topic. As emphasized by Cherlin (2004), although marriage remains quite desirable, as all surveys show, its practical importance has decreased. At the same time, Cherlin argues that marriage has become the most prestigious family form and indicator of achievement, with even the wedding symbolic of such achievement (see, also, Furstenberg, 1995). We agree with this assessment and underscore that the increasing acceptability and prevalence of living together unmarried, as well as having children outside of marriage, have raised the bar as far as marriage is concerned. As long as a living arrangement is available that has become normative and offers many of the same benefits as marriage (i.e., companionship, financial economies of scale, sexual access, and even

procreation), there is no reason why marriage should occur unless expectations, economic and otherwise, are met.

Our research has several limitations. First, our interviews were geared to attaining a wide array of information so that the focus on the prerequisites for marriage comprised only a relatively small part of the interview. Had this issue been our main focus, we would have had more and richer data, allowing us to further explore issues such as those raised by Terri (who suspects her partner of using financial concerns as a tactic to avoid marriage). Second, our findings are based on a nonrepresentative sample of cohabitors who were living in the Toledo, Ohio, area. Given this, and the qualitative nature of our study, the results cannot be generalized to a larger population. A third limitation is that we rely on data from respondents at one point in time. We plan follow-up interviews with respondents who were cohabiting at the time of the interview to gain a better understanding of the dynamics of cohabiting relationships.

Nonetheless, our findings make several contributions to extant knowledge. First, our data suggest that the associations between money and marriage . . . are more than correlations. Cohabitors consciously draw on perceptions of their economic position in thinking about whether and when to marry. In this way, our data triangulate already existing quantitative data, making a stronger case for a causal relationship between marriage and economic opportunity as well as eliciting particular aspects of economics salient to young adults that are generally unmeasured in the data used by [previous] studies. . . . Our study also identifies relationship *processes* such as stresses and conflict over money that likely partially account for the quantitative association between good economic circumstances and marriage.

Second, qualitative work to date on the economic barriers to marriage has focused on disadvantaged, unmarried parents, primarily mothers (e.g., Edin, 2000; Gibson et al., 2003). By widening the socioeconomic spectrum to include the working and lower middle classes, our study enlarges the discourse on marriage and its retreat. Our work underscores the ubiquity of financial problems confronting those in our society who are not privileged economically, who may be just a step or two away from poverty, and the linkage between financial struggles and the retreat from marriage (Ellwood & Jencks, 2001; Lichter, Graefe, & Brown, 2003; Oppenheimer, 2003; Smock, 2004).

Third, our study has two implications for how social scientists study marriage. First, our findings can inform the development of new measures . . . to investigate why economic circumstances influence marriage decisions. We would suggest, as one example, that gauging perceptions of financial difficulties (e.g., perceived economic adequacy) could enhance our understanding of relationship quality, stability, and the transition to marriage (see Clark-Nicolas & Gray-Little, 1991).

Finally, family demographers Bumpass and Sweet (2001) have argued that, to be motivated to marry, cohabitors must feel that marriage will change their lives. This reasoning is consistent with the arguments of some scholars that marriage itself causes changes that lead to higher incomes and other positive outcomes (Waite, 1995, 2000). Our findings suggest a slightly different take on these matters, at least in terms of economic factors. We find that cohabitors feel that marriage ought to occur once something has *already* changed. In the end, our results suggest that a feeling of readiness to marry hinges not on the hope of a comfortable financial future but on the sense that it has already been attained.

■ Review Questions

1. Why do many cohabitors reject the idea of a "downtown" (i.e., civil marriage at a courthouse) marriage even though it is much less expensive?
2. What do the authors mean when they write, "We find that cohabitors feel that marriage ought to occur once something has *already* changed"?

READING 7-2

Unmarried with Children

Kathryn Edin

Maria Kefalas

Jen Burke, a white tenth-grade dropout who is 17 years old, lives with her stepmother, her sister, and her 16-month-old son in a cramped but tidy row home in Philadelphia's beleaguered Kensington neighborhood. She is broke, on welfare, and struggling to complete her GED. Wouldn't she and her son have been better off if she had finished high school, found a job, and married her son's father first?

In 1950, when Jen's grandmother came of age, only 1 in 20 American children was born to an unmarried mother. Today, that rate is 1 in 3—and they are usually born to those least likely to be able to support a child on their own. In our book, *Promises I Can Keep: Why Poor Women Put Motherhood before Marriage,* we discuss the lives of 162 white, African American, and Puerto Rican low-income single mothers living in eight destitute neighborhoods across Philadelphia and

Kathryn Edin and Maria Kefalas, "Unmarried with Children," *Contexts,* Vol. 4, No. 2, pp. 16–22. © 2005 The American Sociological Association. Used by permission. All rights reserved.

its poorest industrial suburb, Camden. We spent five years chatting over kitchen tables and on front stoops, giving mothers like Jen the opportunity to speak to the question so many affluent Americans ask about them: Why do they have children while still young and unmarried when they will face such an uphill struggle to support them?

ROMANCE AT LIGHTNING SPEED

Jen started having sex with her 20-year-old boyfriend Rick just before her 15th birthday. A month and a half later, she was pregnant. "I didn't want to get pregnant," she claims. "*He* wanted me to get pregnant." "As soon as he met me, he wanted to have a kid with me," she explains. Though Jen's college-bound suburban peers would be appalled by such a declaration, on the streets of Jen's neighborhood, it is something of a badge of honor. "All those other girls he was with, he didn't want to have a baby with any of them," Jen boasts. "I asked him, 'Why did you choose me to have a kid when you could have a kid with any one of them?' He was like, 'I want to have a kid with *you*.'" Looking back, Jen says she now believes that the reason "he wanted me to have a kid that early is so that I didn't leave him."

In inner-city neighborhoods like Kensington, where child-bearing within marriage has become rare, romantic relationships like Jen and Rick's proceed at lightning speed. A young man's avowal, "I want to have a baby by you," is often part of the courtship ritual from the beginning. This is more than idle talk, as their first child is typically conceived within a year from the time a couple begins "kicking it." Yet while poor couples' pillow talk often revolves around dreams of shared children, the news of a pregnancy—the first indelible sign of the huge changes to come—puts these still-new relationships into overdrive. Suddenly, the would-be mother begins to scrutinize her mate as never before, wondering whether he can "get himself together"—find a job, settle down, and become a family man—in time. Jen began pestering Rick to get a

real job instead of picking up day-labor jobs at nearby construction sites. She also wanted him to stop hanging out with his ne'er-do-well friends, who had been getting him into serious trouble for more than a decade. Most of all, she wanted Rick to shed what she calls his "kiddie mentality"—his habit of spending money on alcohol and drugs rather than recognizing his growing financial obligations at home.

Rick did not try to deny paternity, as many would-be fathers do. Nor did he abandon or mistreat Jen, at least intentionally. But Rick, who had been in and out of juvenile detention since he was 8 years old for everything from stealing cars to selling drugs, proved unable to stay away from his unsavory friends. At the beginning of her seventh month of pregnancy, an escapade that began as a drunken lark landed Rick in jail on a car-jacking charge. Jen moved back home with her stepmother, applied for welfare, and spent the last two-and-a-half months of her pregnancy without Rick.

Rick sent penitent letters from jail. "I thought he changed by the letters he wrote me. I thought he changed a lot," she says. "He used to tell me that he loved me when he was in jail. . . . It was always gonna be me and him and the baby when he got out." Thus, when Rick's alleged victim failed to appear to testify and he was released just days before Colin's birth, the couple's reunion was a happy one. Often, the magic moment of childbirth calms the troubled waters of such relationships. New parents typically make amends and resolve to stay together for the sake of their child. When surveyed just after a child's birth, eight in ten unmarried parents say they are still together, and most plan to stay together and raise the child.

Promoting marriage among the poor has become the new war on poverty, Bush style. And it is true that the correlation between marital status and child poverty is strong. But poor single mothers already believe in marriage. Jen insists that she will walk down the aisle one day, though she admits it might not be with Rick. And demographers still project that more than seven in ten women who had a child outside of marriage will eventually wed someone. First, though, Jen wants to get a good job, finish school, and get her son out of Kensington.

Most poor, unmarried mothers and fathers readily admit that bearing children while poor and unmarried is not the ideal way to do things. Jen believes the best time to become a mother is "after you're out of school and you got a job, at least, when you're like 21. . . . When you're ready to have kids, you should have everything ready, have your house, have a job, so when that baby comes, the baby can have its own room." Yet given their already limited economic prospects, the poor have little motivation to time their births as precisely as their middle-class counterparts do. The dreams of young people like Jen and Rick center on children at a time of life when their more affluent peers plan for college and careers. Poor girls coming of age in the inner city value children highly, anticipate them eagerly, and believe strongly that they are up to the job of mothering—even in difficult circumstances. Jen, for example, tells us, "People outside the neighborhood, they're like, 'You're 15! You're pregnant?' I'm like, it's not none of their business. I'm gonna be able to take care of my kid. They have nothing to worry about." Jen says she has concluded that "some people . . . are better at having kids at a younger age. . . . I think it's better for some people to have kids younger."

WHEN I BECAME A MOM

When we asked mothers like Jen what their lives would be like if they had not had children, we expected them to express regret over forgone opportunities for school and careers. Instead, most believe their children "saved" them. They describe their lives as spinning out of control before becoming pregnant—struggles with parents and peers, "wild," risky behavior, depression, and school failure. Jen speaks to this poignantly. "I was just real bad. I hung with a real bad crowd.

I was doing pills. I was really depressed. . . . I was drinking. That was before I was pregnant." "I think," she reflects, "if I never had a baby or anything, . . . I would still be doing the things I was doing. I would probably still be doing drugs. I'd probably still be drinking." Jen admits that when she first became pregnant, she was angry that she "couldn't be out no more. Couldn't be out with my friends. Couldn't do nothing." Now, though, she says, "I'm glad I have a son . . . because I would still be doing all that stuff."

Children offer poor youth like Jen a compelling sense of purpose. Jen paints a before-and-after picture of her life that was common among the mothers we interviewed. "Before, I didn't have nobody to take care of. I didn't have nothing left to go home for. . . . Now I have my son to take care of. I have him to go home for. . . . I don't have to go buy weed or drugs with my money. I could buy my son stuff with my money! . . . I have something to look up to now." Children also are a crucial source of relational intimacy, a self-made community of care. After a nasty fight with Rick, Jen recalls, "I was crying. My son came in the room. He was hugging me. He's 16 months and he was hugging me with his little arms. He was really cute and happy, so I got happy. That's one of the good things. When you're sad, the baby's always gonna be there for you no matter what." Lately she has been thinking a lot about what her life was like back then, before the baby. "I thought about the stuff before I became a mom, what my life was like back then. I used to see pictures of me, and I would hide in every picture. This baby did so much for me. My son did a lot for me. He helped me a lot. I'm thankful that I had my baby."

Around the time of the birth, most unmarried parents claim they plan to get married eventually. Rick did not propose marriage when Jen's first child was born, but when she conceived a second time, at 17, Rick informed his dad, "It's time for me to get married. It's time for me to straighten up. This is the one I wanna be with. I had a baby with her, I'm gonna have another baby with her."

Yet despite their intentions, few of these couples actually marry. Indeed, most break up well before their child enters preschool.

I'D LIKE TO GET MARRIED, BUT . . .

The sharp decline in marriage in impoverished urban areas has led some to charge that the poor have abandoned the marriage norm. Yet we found few who had given up on the idea of marriage. But like their elite counterparts, disadvantaged women set a high financial bar for marriage. For the poor, marriage has become an elusive goal—one they feel ought to be reserved for those who can support a "white picket fence" lifestyle: a mortgage on a modest row home, a car and some furniture, some savings in the bank, and enough money left over to pay for a "decent" wedding. Jen's views on marriage provide a perfect case in point. "If I was gonna get married, I would want to be married like my Aunt Nancy and my Uncle Pat. They live in the mountains. She has a job. My Uncle Pat is a state trooper; he has lots of money. They live in the [Poconos]. It's real nice out there. Her kids go to Catholic school. . . . That's the kind of life I would want to have. If I get married, I would have a life like [theirs]." She adds, "And I would wanna have a big wedding, a real nice wedding."

Unlike the women of their mothers' and grandmothers' generations, young women like Jen are not merely content to rely on a man's earnings. Instead, they insist on being economically "set" in their own right before taking marriage vows. This is partly because they want a partnership of equals, and they believe money buys say-so in a relationship. Jen explains, "I'm not gonna just get into marrying him and not have my own house! Not have a job! I still wanna do a lot of things before I get married. He [already] tells me I can't do nothing. I can't go out. What's gonna happen when I marry him? He's gonna say he owns me!"

Economic independence is also insurance against a marriage gone bad. Jen explains, "I want to have everything ready, in case something

goes wrong. . . . If we got a divorce, that would be my house. I bought that house, he can't kick me out or he can't take my kids from me." "That's what I want in case that ever happens. I know a lot of people that happened to. I don't want it to happen to me." These statements reveal that despite her desire to marry, Rick's role in the family's future is provisional at best. "We get along, but we fight a lot. If he's there, he's there, but if he's not, that's why I want a job . . . a job with computers . . . so I could afford my kids, could afford the house. . . . I don't want to be living off him. I want my kids to be living off me."

Why is Jen, who describes Rick as "the love of my life," so insistent on planning an exit strategy before she is willing to take the vows she firmly believes ought to last "forever"? If love is so sure, why does mistrust seem so palpable and strong? In relationships among poor couples like Jen and Rick, mistrust is often spawned by chronic violence and infidelity, drug and alcohol abuse, criminal activity, and the threat of imprisonment. In these tarnished corners of urban America, the stigma of a failed marriage is far worse than an out-of-wedlock birth. New mothers like Jen feel they must test the relationship over three, four, even five years' time. This is the only way, they believe, to insure that their marriages will last.

Trust has been an enormous issue in Jen's relationship with Rick. "My son was born December 23rd, and [Rick] started cheating on me again . . . in March. He started cheating on me with some girl—Amanda. . . . Then it was another girl, another girl, another girl after. I didn't wanna believe it. My friends would come up to me and be like, 'Oh yeah, your boyfriend's cheating on you with this person.' I wouldn't believe it. . . . I would see him with them. He used to have hickies. He used to make up some excuse that he was drunk—that was always his excuse for everything." Things finally came to a head when Rick got another girl pregnant. "For a while, I forgave him for everything. Now, I don't forgive him for nothing." Now we begin to understand the source of Jen's hesitancy. "He wants me to marry him, [but] I'm not really sure. . . . If I can't trust him, I can't marry him, 'cause we would get a divorce. If you're gonna get married, you're supposed to be faithful!" she insists. To Jen and her peers, the worst thing that could happen is "to get married just to get divorced."

Given the economic challenges and often perilously low quality of the romantic relationships among unmarried parents, poor women may be right to be cautious about marriage. Five years after we first spoke with her, we met with Jen again. We learned that Jen's second pregnancy ended in a miscarriage. We also learned that Rick was out of the picture—apparently for good. "You know that bar [down the street]? It happened in that bar. . . . They were in the bar, and this guy was like badmouthing [Rick's friend] Mikey, talking stuff to him or whatever. So Rick had to go get involved in it and start with this guy. . . . Then he goes outside and fights the guy [and] the guy dies of head trauma. They were all on drugs, they were all drinking, and things just got out of control, and that's what happened. He got fourteen to thirty years."

THESE ARE CARDS I DEALT MYSELF

Jen stuck with Rick for the first two and a half years of his prison sentence, but when another girl's name replaced her own on the visitors' list, Jen decided she was finished with him once and for all. Readers might be asking what Jen ever saw in a man like Rick. But Jen and Rick operate in a partner market where the better-off men go to the better-off women. The only way for someone like Jen to forge a satisfying relationship with a man is to find a diamond in the rough or improve her own economic position so that she can realistically compete for more upwardly mobile partners, which is what Jen is trying to do now. "There's this kid, Donny, he works at my job. He works on C shift. He's a supervisor! He's funny, three years older, and he's not a geek or

anything, but he's not a real preppy good boy either. But he's not [a player like Rick] and them. He has a job, you know, so that's good. He doesn't do drugs or anything. And he asked my dad if he could take me out!"

These days, there is a new air of determination, even pride, about Jen. The aimless high school dropout pulls ten-hour shifts entering data at a warehouse distribution center Monday through Thursday. She has held the job for three years, and her aptitude and hard work have earned her a series of raises. Her current salary is higher than anyone in her household commands—$10.25 per hour, and she now gets two weeks of paid vacation, four personal days, 60 hours of sick time, and medical benefits. She has saved up the necessary $400 in tuition for a high school completion program that offers evening and weekend classes. Now all that stands between her and a diploma is a passing grade in mathematics, her least favorite subject. "My plan is to start college in January. [This month] I take my math test . . . so I can get my diploma," she confides.

Jen clearly sees how her life has improved since Rick's dramatic exit from the scene. "That's when I really started [to get better] because I didn't have to worry about what *he* was doing, didn't have to worry about him cheating on me, all this stuff. [It was] then I realized that I had to do what I had to do to take care of my son. . . . When he was there, I think that my whole life revolved around him, you know, so I always messed up somehow because I was so busy worrying about what *he* was doing. Like I would leave the [GED] programs I was in just to go home and see what he was doing. My mind was never concentrating." Now, she says, "a lot of people in my family look up to me now, because all my sisters dropped out from school, you know, nobody went back to school. I went back to school, you know? . . . I went back to school, and I plan to go to college, and a lot of people look up to me for that, you know? So that makes me happy . . . because five years ago nobody looked up to me. I was just like everybody else."

Yet the journey has not been easy. "Being a young mom, being 15, it's hard, hard, hard, you know." She says, "I have no life. . . . I work from 6:30 in the morning until 5:00 at night. I leave here at 5:30 in the morning. I don't get home until about 6:00 at night." Yet she measures her worth as a mother by the fact that she has managed to provide for her son largely on her own. "I don't depend on nobody. I might live with my dad and them, but I don't depend on them, you know." She continues, "There [used to] be days when I'd be so stressed out, like, 'I can't do this!' And I would just cry and cry and cry. . . . Then I look at Colin, and he'll be sleeping, and I'll just look at him and think I don't have no [reason to feel sorry for myself]. The cards I have I've dealt myself so I have to deal with it now. I'm older. I can't change anything. He's my responsibility— he's nobody else's but mine—so I have to deal with that."

Becoming a mother transformed Jen's point of view on just about everything. She says, "I thought hanging on the corner drinking, getting high—I thought that was a good life, and I thought I could live that way for eternity, like sitting out with my friends. But it's not as fun once you have your own kid. . . . I think it changes [you]. I think, 'Would I want Colin to do that? Would I want my son to be like that . . . ?' It was fun to me but it's not fun anymore. Half the people I hung with are either . . . Some have died from drug overdoses, some are in jail, and some people are just out there living the same life that they always lived, and they don't look really good. They look really bad." In the end, Jen believes, Colin's birth has brought far more good into her life than bad. "I know I could have waited [to have a child], but in a way I think Colin's the best thing that could have happened to me. . . . So I think I had my son for a purpose because I think Colin changed my life. He *saved* my life, really. My whole life revolves around Colin!"

PROMISES I CAN KEEP

There are unique themes in Jen's story—most fathers are only one or two, not five years older than the mothers of their children, and few fathers have as many glaring problems as Rick— but we heard most of these themes repeatedly in the stories of the 161 other poor, single mothers we came to know. Notably, poor women do not reject marriage; they revere it. Indeed, it is the conviction that marriage is forever that makes them think that divorce is worse than having a baby outside of marriage. Their children, far from being liabilities, provide crucial social-psychological resources—a strong sense of purpose and a profound source of intimacy. Jen and the other mothers we came to know are coming of age in an America that is profoundly unequal— where the gap between rich and poor continues to grow. This economic reality has convinced them that they have little to lose and, perhaps, something to gain by a seemingly "ill-timed" birth.

The lesson one draws from stories like Jen's is quite simple: Until poor young women have more access to jobs that lead to financial independence—until there is reason to hope for the rewarding life pathways that their privileged peers pursue—the poor will continue to have children far sooner than most Americans think they should, while still deferring marriage. Marital standards have risen for all Americans, and the poor want the same things that everyone now wants out of marriage. The poor want to marry too, but they insist on marrying well. This, in their view, is the only way to avoid an almost certain divorce. Like Jen, they are simply not willing to make promises they are not sure they can keep.

RECOMMENDED RESOURCES

Kathryn Edin and Maria Kefalas. *Promises I Can Keep: Why Poor Women Put Motherhood before Marriage* (University of California Press, 2005). An account of how low-income women make sense of their choices about marriage and motherhood.

Christina Gibson, Kathryn Edin, and Sara McLanahan. "High Hopes but Even Higher Expectations: The Retreat from Marriage among Low-Income Couples," *Journal of Marriage and Family* 67 (December 2005), pp. 1301–1312. The authors examine the rising expectations for marriage among unmarried parents.

Sharon Hays. *Flat Broke with Children: Women in the Age of Welfare Reform* (Oxford University Press, 2003). How welfare reform has affected the lives of poor moms.

Annette Lareau. *Unequal Childhoods: Class, Race, and Family Life* (University of California Press, 2003). A fascinating discussion of different child-rearing strategies among low-income, working-class, and middle-class parents.

Timothy J. Nelson, Susan Clampet-Lundquist, and Kathryn Edin. "Fragile Fatherhood: How Low-Income, Non-Custodial Fathers in Philadelphia Talk about Their Families." In *The Handbook of Father Involvement: Multidisciplinary Perspectives,* ed. Catherine Tamis-LeMonda and Natasha Cabrera (Lawrence Erlbaum Associates, 2002). What poor, single men think about fatherhood.

■ Review Questions

1. Have low-income women rejected marriage?
2. Are their standards for marriage too high?

CHAPTER 8

Work and Families

The movement of mothers into the paid workforce is one of the most significant changes in family life over the past half century. Because most mothers are employed outside the home, they cannot do as much housework and child-rearing as they used to. Men are doing more work in the home but not enough to fully compensate. Many parents are now paying childcare providers or cleaning services to perform tasks mothers used to do for free. It is now clear how valuable was the unpaid labor mothers did in the home and how expensive it is to replace.

The families most in need of replacing household labor are the growing numbers of two-earner couples and single parents. Neither has the luxury of having a partner caring for their homes and children full-time. The time squeeze is greatest among couples in which both partners have demanding professional or technical jobs and are also raising children. They sometimes complain of overwork. But as Kathleen Gerson and Jerry A. Jacobs show in the first selection in this chapter, the problem for other Americans is underwork. Many people without college educations have had

difficulty finding the full-time work they desire. So, while the members of some American families are concerned about having too much work, others are concerned about having not enough.

Should we expand government programs to ease the time crunch for parents who are employed and are also raising children? They do receive some support already. The mostly middle-class parents who pay for child care services can deduct a portion of their expenses from their incomes when they calculate taxes. Child care subsidies for low-income parents doubled between the 1990s and the 2000s in response to new rules for welfare recipients that require them to work. Still, working parents in the United States receive less support from government than do working parents in most other wealthy countries. For instance, American parents are allowed to take up to 12 weeks of leave from their jobs to care for a newborn child. But the leave is unpaid, which means that most low-income workers can't afford to take it. In most other countries, parents can take a longer leave and receive partial pay. Some countries such as

France have national preschool programs for all 3- and 4-year-olds. Due to the large increase over the past half-century in the percentage of mothers who work outside the home, the demand for greater assistance to working parents has risen.

Joan Williams, in the second reading in this chapter, argues that we now have an "odd disconnect" in American politics between the kinds of policies and programs and the kinds of families that exist today. Our policies and programs were basically established in an era when most married mothers did not work outside the home and there were fewer unmarried mothers; these policies supported the breadwinner–homemaker marriages that were prevalent in the mid-twentieth century. Policies have changed somewhat, but

the "disconnect" is still visible—at least in comparison to most other wealthy countries. Williams goes further to argue that the United States has a "family-hostile public policy." Not everyone would agree with that assertion. What she means, essentially, is that public policy is "hostile"—that is, nonsupportive—to dual-earner couples who are raising children and to working single parents. It is not hostile toward married couples where the wife stays home, a decreasing but still significant share of all couples who are raising young children. And it does provide some assistance to working parents. Nevertheless, her general point is worth considering, and she explains how the work-family balance issues differ for parents of higher, medium, and lower social class.

READING 8-1

The Work-Home Crunch

Kathleen Gerson

Jerry A. Jacobs

More than a decade has passed since the release of *The Overworked American,* a prominent 1991 book about the decline in Americans' leisure time, and the work pace in the United States only seems to have increased. From sleep-deprived parents to professionals who believe they must put in long hours to succeed at the office, the demands of work are colliding with family responsibilities and placing a tremendous time squeeze on many Americans.

Yet beyond the apparent growth in the time that many Americans spend on the job lies a more complex story. While many Americans are working more than ever, many others are working less. What is more, finding a balance between work and other obligations seems increasingly elusive to many workers—whether or not they are actually putting in more time at work than workers in earlier generations. The increase in harried workers and hurried families is a problem that demands solutions. But before we can resolve this increasingly difficult time squeeze we must first understand its root causes.

AVERAGE WORKING TIME AND BEYOND

"There aren't enough hours in the day" is an increasingly resonant refrain. To most observers, including many experts, the main culprit appears to be overwork—our jobs just take up too much of our time. Yet it is not clear that the average American is spending more time on the job. Although it may come as a surprise to

those who feel overstressed, the average work week—that is, hours spent working for pay by the average employee—has hardly changed over the past 30 years. Census Bureau interviews show, for example, that the average male worked 43.5 hours a week in 1970 and 43.1 hours a week in 2000, while the average female worked 37.1 hours in 1970 and 37.0 hours in 2000.

Why, then, do more and more Americans feel so pressed for time? The answer is that averages can be misleading. Looking only at the average experience of American workers misses key parts of the story. From the perspective of individual workers, it turns out some Americans are working more than ever, while others are finding it harder to get as much work as they need or would like. To complicate matters further, American families are now more diverse than they were in the middle of the 20th century, when male-breadwinner households predominated. Many more Americans now live in dual-earner or single-parent families where all the adults work.

These two trends—the growing split of the labor force and the transformation of family life—lie at the heart of the new time dilemmas facing an increasing number of Americans. But they have not affected all workers and all families in the same way. Instead, these changes have divided Americans into those who feel squeezed between their work and the rest of their life, and those who have more time away from work than they need or would like. No one trend fits both groups.

So, who are the time-squeezed, and how do they differ from those with fewer time pressures but who may also have less work than they may want or need? To distinguish and describe the two sets of Americans, we need to look at the experiences of both individual workers and whole families. A focus on workers shows that they are increasingly divided between those who put in very long work weeks and who are concentrated in the better-paying jobs, and those who put in comparatively short work weeks, who are more likely to have fewer educational

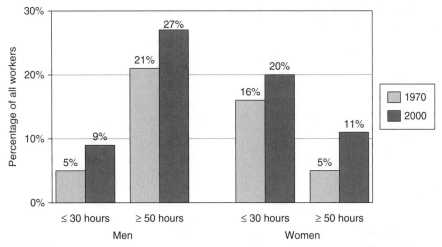

FIGURE 8.1

The percentage of men and women who put in 30 or fewer hours and who put in 50 or more hours a week in 1970 and 2000. (*Source:* March Current Population Surveys; nonfarm wage and salary workers.)

credentials and are more likely to be concentrated in the lower-paying jobs.

But the experiences of individuals does not tell the whole story. When we shift our focus to the family, it becomes clear that time squeezes are linked to the total working hours of family members in households. For this reason, two-job families and single parents face heightened challenges. Moreover, women continue to assume the lion's share of home and childcare responsibilities and are thus especially likely to be squeezed for time. Changes in jobs and changes in families are putting overworked Americans and underemployed Americans on distinct paths, are separating the two-earner and single-parent households from the more traditional households, and are creating different futures for parents (especially mothers) than for workers without children at home.

A GROWING DIVIDE IN INDIVIDUAL WORKING TIME

In 1970, almost half of all employed men and women reported working 40 hours a week. By 2000, just 2 in 5 worked these "average" hours.

Instead, workers are now far more likely to put in either very long or fairly short work weeks. The share of working men putting in 50 hours or more rose from 21 percent in 1970 to almost 27 percent in 2000, while the share of working women putting in these long work weeks rose from 5 to 11 percent.

At the other end of the spectrum, more workers are also putting in shorter weeks. In 1970, for example, 5 percent of men were employed for 30 or fewer hours a week, while 9 percent worked these shortened weeks in 2000. The share of employed women spending 30 or fewer hours on the job also climbed from 16 percent to 20 percent (see Figure 8.1). In total, 13 million Americans in 2000 worked either shorter or longer work weeks than they would have if the 1970s pattern had continued.

These changes in working time are not evenly distributed across occupations. Instead, they are strongly related to the kinds of jobs people hold. Managers and professionals, as one might expect, tend to put in the longest work weeks. More than 1 in 3 men in this category now work 50 hours or more per week, compared to only 1 in 5 for men in other occupations. For women, 1 in 6 professionals and managers work these long weeks, compared to fewer than 1 in 14 for women in all other occupations. And because jobs are closely linked to education, the gap in working time between the college educated and those with fewer educational credentials has also grown since 1970.

Thus, time at work is growing most among those Americans who are most likely to read articles and buy books about overwork in America. They may not be typical, but they are indeed working more than their peers in earlier generations. If leisure time once signaled an elite lifestyle, that no longer appears to be the case. Working relatively few hours is now more likely to be concentrated among those with less education and less elite jobs.

Workers do not necessarily prefer these new schedules. On the contrary, when workers are asked about their ideal amount of time at work, a very different picture emerges. For example, in a 1997 survey of workers conducted by the Families and Work Institute, 60 percent of both men and women responded that they would like to work less while 19 percent of men and women said that they would like to work more. Most workers—both women and men—aspire to work between 30 and 40 hours per week. Men generally express a desire to work about 38 hours a week while women would like to work about 32 hours. The small difference in the ideal working time of men and women is less significant than the shared preferences among them. However, whether their jobs require very long or comparatively short work weeks, this shared ideal does stand in sharp contrast to their job realities. As some workers are pressured to put in more time at work and others less, finding the right balance between work and the rest of life has become increasingly elusive.

OVERWORKED INDIVIDUALS OR OVERWORKED FAMILIES?

Fundamental shifts in family life exacerbate this growing division between the over- and under-worked. While most analyses of working time focus on individual workers, time squeezes are typically experienced by families, not isolated individuals. A 60-hour work week for a father means something different depending on whether the mother stays at home or also works a 60-hour week. Even a 40-hour work week can seem too long if both members of a married couple are juggling job demands with family responsibilities. And when a family depends on a single parent, the conflicts between home and work can be even greater. Even if the length of the work week had not changed at all, the rise of families that depend on either two incomes or one parent would suffice to explain why Americans feel so pressed for time.

To understand how families experience time squeezes, we need to look at the combined working time of all family members. For example, how do married couples with two earners compare with those anchored by a sole, typically male, breadwinner? For all married couples, the work week has indeed increased from an average of about 53 hours in 1970 to 63 hours in 2000. Given that the average work week for individuals did not change, it may seem strange that the couples' family total grew so markedly. The explanation for this apparent paradox is both straightforward and crucial: married women are now far more likely to work. In 1970, half of all married-couple families had only male breadwinners. By 2000, this group had shrunk to one-quarter (see Figure 8.2). In 1970, one-third of all married-couple families had two wage-earners, but three-fifths did in 2000. In fact, two-earner families are more common today than male-breadwinner families were 30 years ago.

Each type of family is also working a little more each week, but this change is relatively modest and certainly not large enough to account for the larger shift in total household working time. Two-earner families put in close to 82 working hours in 2000 compared with 78 hours in 1970. Male-breadwinner couples worked 44 hours on average in 1970 and 45 hours in 2000.

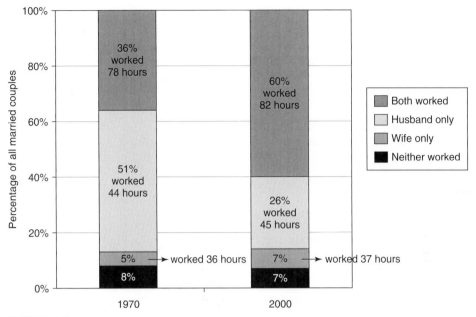

FIGURE 8.2

Total hours of work per week for married couples, 1970 and 2000. (*Source:* March Current Population Surveys; nonfarm married couples aged 18–64.)

The vast majority of the change in working time over the past 30 years can thus be traced to changes in the kinds of families we live in rather than to changes in how much we work. Two-earner couples work about as much today as they did 30 years ago, but there are many more of them because more wives are working.

Single parents, who are overwhelmingly mothers, are another group who are truly caught in a time squeeze. They need to work as much as possible to support their family, and they are less likely to be able to count on a partner's help in meeting their children's daily needs. Although these households are not displayed in Figure 8.2, Census Bureau data show that women headed one-fifth of all families in 2000, twice the share of female-headed households in 1970. Even though their average work week remained unchanged at 39 hours, the lack of child care and other support services leaves them facing time squeezes at least as sharp. Single fathers remain a much smaller group, but their ranks have also

grown rapidly. Single dads work almost as much as single moms—37 hours per week in 2000. Even though this represents a drop of two hours since 1970, single fathers face time dilemmas as great as those facing single mothers. Being a single parent has always posed daunting challenges, and now there are more mothers and fathers than ever in this situation.

At the heart of these shifts is American families' growing reliance on a woman's earnings—whether or not they depend on a man's earnings as well. Women's strengthened commitment to paid employment has provided more economic resources to families and given couples more options for sharing the tasks of breadwinning and caretaking. Yet this revolution in women's work has not been complemented by an equal growth in the amount of time men spend away from the job or in the availability of organized child care. This limited change at the workplace and in men's lives has intensified the time pressures facing women.

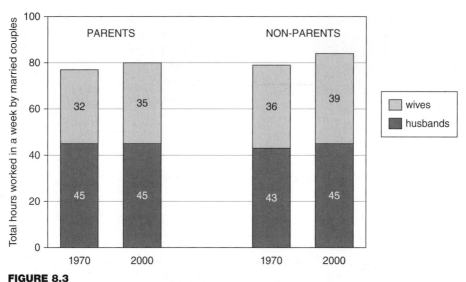

FIGURE 8.3

Average hours of work per week of couples (parents and non-parents). (*Source:* March Current Population Surveys; nonfarm married couples aged 18–64.)

DUAL-EARNER PARENTS AND WORKING TIME

The expansion of working time is especially important for families with children, where work and family demands are most likely to conflict. Indeed, there is a persisting concern that in their desire for paid work, families with two earners are shortchanging their children in time and attention. A closer looks reveals that even though parents face increased time pressure, they cope with these dilemmas by cutting back on their combined joint working time when they have children at home. For example, U.S. Census data show that parents in two-income families worked 3.3 fewer hours per week than spouses in two-income families without children, a slightly wider difference than the 2.6 hours separating them in 1970. Working hours also decline as the number of children increase. Couples with one child under 18 jointly averaged 81 hours per week in 2000, while couples with three or more children averaged 78 hours. Rather than forsaking their children, employed parents are taking

steps to adjust their work schedules to make more time for the rest of life.

However, it is mothers, not fathers, who are cutting back. Fathers actually work more hours when they have children at home, and their working hours increase with the number of children. Thus, the drop in joint working time among couples with children reflects less working time among mothers. Figure 8.3 shows that in 2000, mothers worked almost 4 fewer hours per week than married women without children. This gap is not substantially different than in 1970.

This pattern of mothers reducing their hours while fathers increase them creates a larger gender gap in work participation among couples with children compared to the gender gap for childless couples. However, these differences are much smaller than the once predominant pattern in which many women stopped working for pay altogether when they bore children. While the transition to raising children continues to have different consequences for women and men, the size of this difference is diminishing.

It is also important to remember that the rise in working time among couples is not concentrated among those with children at home. Though Americans continue to worry about the consequences for children when both parents go to work, the move toward more work involvement does not reflect neglect on the part of either mothers or fathers. On the contrary, employed mothers continue to spend less time at the workplace than their childless peers, while employed fathers today do not spend substantially more time at work than men who are not fathers.

SOLVING THE TIME PRESSURE PUZZLE

Even though changes in the average working time of American workers are modest, many American families have good reason to feel overworked and time-deprived. The last several decades have witnessed the emergence of a group of workers who face very long work weeks and live in families that depend on either two incomes or one parent. And while parents are putting in less time at work than their peers without children at home, they shoulder domestic responsibilities that leave them facing clashes between work demands and family needs.

The future of family well-being and gender equality will depend on developing policies to help workers resolve the time pressures created by the widespread and deeply rooted social changes discussed above. The first step toward developing effective policy responses requires accepting the social transformations that sent women into the workplace and left Americans wishing for a balance between work and family that is difficult to achieve. Unfortunately, these changes in the lives of women and men continue to evoke ambivalence.

For example, mothers continue to face strong pressures to devote intensive time and attention to child rearing. Indeed, generally they want to, despite the rising economic and social pressure to hold a paid job as well. Even though most contemporary mothers are counted on to help support their families financially, the United States has yet to develop the childcare services and flexible jobs that can help workers meet their families' needs. Whether or not mothers work outside the home, they face conflicting expectations that are difficult to meet. These social contradictions can be seen in the political push to require poor, single mothers to work at a paid job while middle-class mothers continue to be chastised for spending too much time on their jobs and away from home.

To a lesser but still important extent, fathers also face intensifying and competing pressures. Despite American families' increasing reliance on women's earnings, men face significant barriers to family involvement. Resistance from employers and co-workers continues to greet individual fathers who would like to spend less time at work to care for their children. For all the concern and attention focused on employed mothers, social policies that would help bring men more fully into the work of parenting get limited notice or support. New time squeezes can thus be better understood by comparing the large changes in women's lives with the relative lack of changes in the situation for men. The family time bind is an unbalanced one.

Even as family time has become squeezed, workers are also contending with changes in the options and expectations they face at work. Competitive workplaces appear to be creating rising pressures for some workers, especially professionals and managers, to devote an excessive amount of time to their jobs, while not offering enough work to others. In contrast to these bifurcating options, American workers increasingly express a desire to balance the important work of earning a living and caring for a new generation.

Finding solutions to these new time dilemmas will depend on developing large scale policies that recognize and address the new needs of 21st century workers and their families. As we suggest in our book, *The Time Divide,* these policies need to address the basic organization of American work and community institutions. This includes revising regulations on hours of work and providing benefit protections to more workers, moving toward the norm of a shorter work week, creating more family-supportive workplaces that offer both job flexibility and protections for employed parents, and developing a wider array of high-quality, affordable childcare options.

Extending protections, such as proportional benefits and overtime pay, to workers in a wider range of jobs and occupations would reduce the built-in incentives employers have to extract as much work as possible from professionals and managers while offering less work to other employees. If professionals and managers were given overtime pay for overtime work, which wage workers are now guaranteed under the Fair Labor Standards Act, the pressures on these employees to put in endless workdays might lessen. . . . Similarly, if part-time workers were offered fringe benefits proportional to the hours they work (such as partial pensions), there would be fewer reasons for employers to create jobs with work weeks so short that they do not provide the economic security all families need.

Reducing the average work week to 35 hours would also reduce the pressures on workers and help them find a better work-family balance. While this goal may seem utopian, it is important to remember that the 40-hour standard also seemed unimaginably idealistic before it was adopted in the early 20th century. Other countries, most notably France, have adopted this standard without sacrificing economic well-being. A shorter work week still would allow for variation in work styles and commitments, but it would also create a new cultural standard that better reflects the needs and aspirations of most contemporary workers. It would also help single parents meet their dual obligations and allow couples to fashion greater equality in their work and caretaking responsibilities.

Time at work is clearly important, but it is not the whole story. The organization of the workplace and the structure of jobs also matters, especially for those whose jobs and occupations require intensive time at work. Among those putting in very long work weeks, we find that having job flexibility and autonomy helps ease the perceived strains and conflicts. The work environment, especially in the form of support from supervisors and co-workers, also makes a difference. In addition, we find that workers with access to such family-friendly options as flexible work schedules are likely to use them, while workers without such benefits would like to have them.

Flexibility and autonomy are only useful if workers feel able to use them. Women and men both express concern that making use of "family-friendly" policies, such as extended parental leaves or nonstandard working hours, may endanger their future work prospects. Social policies need to protect the rights of workers to be involved parents without incurring excessive penalties at the workplace. Most Americans spend a portion of their work lives simultaneously immersed in work for pay and in parenting. Providing greater flexibility at the workplace will help workers develop both short- and longer-term strategies for integrating work and family life. However, even basic changes in the organization of work will not suffice to meet the needs of 21st-century families. We also need to join the ranks of virtually all other industrialized nations by creating widely available, high-quality and affordable child care. In a world where mothers and fathers are at the workplace to stay, we need an expanded network of support to care for the next generation of workers.

These changes will not be easy to achieve. But in one form or another, they have been effectively adopted in other societies throughout the modern world. While no one policy is a cure-all, taken together they offer a comprehensive approach for creating genuine resolutions to the time pressures that confront growing numbers of American workers and their families. Ultimately, these new time dilemmas cannot be resolved by chastising workers (and, most often, mothers) for working too much. Rather, the time has come to create more flexible, family-supportive, and gender-equal workplaces and communities that complement the 21st-century forms of work and family life.

RECOMMENDED RESOURCES

Bond, James T. *Highlights of the National Study of the Changing Workforce.* New York: Families and Work Institute, 2003. Bond reports findings from a major national survey of contemporary American workers, workplace conditions, and work-family conflict.

Gornick, Janet, and Marcia Meyers. *Families that Work: Policies for Reconciling Parenthood and Employment.* New York: Russell Sage Foundation, 2003. This important study compares family-supportive policies in Europe and the United States.

Hays, Sharon. *The Cultural Contradictions of Motherhood.* New Haven, CT: Yale University Press, 1997. Hays examines how American mothers continue to face pressure to practice intensive parenting even as they increase their commitment to paid work.

Heymann, Jody. *The Widening Gap: Why America's Working Families Are in Jeopardy and What Can Be Done about It.* New York: Basic Books, 2000. Drawing from a wide range of data, this study makes a compelling case for more flexible work structures.

Hochschild, Arlie. *The Time Bind: When Home Becomes Work and Work Becomes Home.* New York: Metropolitan Books, 1997. This is a rich study of how employees in one company try to reconcile the tensions between spending time at work and caring for their families.

Jacobs, Jerry A., and Kathleen Gerson. *The Time Divide: Work, Family, and Gender Inequality.* Cambridge, MA: Harvard University Press, 2004. An overview of trends in working time, our book shows why and how time pressures have emerged in America over the past three decades, how they are linked to gender inequality and family change, and what we can do to alleviate them.

Robinson, John P., and Geoffrey Godbey. *Time for Life. The Surprising Ways Americans Use Their Time.* University Park: Pennsylvania State University Press, 1999. Drawing on time diaries, Robinson and Godbey conclude that Americans' leisure time has increased.

Schor, Juliet. *The Overworked American: The Unexpected Decline of Leisure.* New York: Basic Books, 1991. This early and original analysis of how Americans are overworked sparked a national discussion on and concern for the problem.

■ Review Questions

1. How does a person's education affect how many hours per week she or he is likely to work outside the home?

2. How have changes in the kinds of families Americans live in affected what the authors call the "work-home crunch"?

The Odd Disconnect
Our Family-Hostile Public Policy

Joan C. Williams

Imagine two families, one in the United States and one in Sweden, both of which experience the birth of a child.[1] In the first family, a working couple in Sweden has a newborn son in January. Both parents stay home during the first two weeks of the child's life, because, since the 1970s, fathers have been granted ten days of paid leave after childbirth (Crittenden 2001). After that, the mother continues her paid leave and the father returns to work at 80 percent of his former schedule, taking advantage of the government's policy that both parents can return to work on a reduced schedule until their youngest child is eight years old (ibid.). In August, the father takes a full month off at 80 percent of his pay—Sweden has guaranteed fathers an extra month off at 80 percent pay during the first year of their children's lives since 1984 (ibid.). Swedish law also provides that new parents have fifteen months of paid leave to share as they choose (in addition to the "daddy days" described above) (Clearinghouse on International Developments in Child, Youth, and Family Politics at Columbia University [Clearinghouse] 2002; Crittenden 2001; European Union Online n.d.). The following January, the parents switch roles: The mother returns to work at 80 percent of her former schedule, while the father stays home to care for the child for six more months. The parents decide not to use the additional leave available to them: three months at a flat rate and three months unpaid leave (Clearinghouse 2002). Beginning in June, when the child turns one and a half, both parents stagger their schedules so each gets some one-on-one time with their son; for the remaining time they enroll their son in a government-subsidized childcare center. Although Sweden has not yet reached its goal of making quality childcare

available to every child, it does ensure that lower-income families receive financial assistance for childcare (Crittenden 2001; Skolverket n.d.).

In the second family, a working couple in the United States has a daughter. The father takes no leave, since he has no right to paid leave and they cannot afford to lose any of his salary. They are fortunate: the mother's employer is covered by the Family and Medical Leave Act, and, meeting the act's requirements, they can afford to be without her salary for her twelve weeks of unpaid leave. During her pregnancy, the mother continues to hunt for quality childcare at an affordable price, with little success. Finally, shortly before the mother's leave is up, they find a suitable daycare that takes infants and has an opening. It is not convenient to their home or either parent's workplace, and knowing that over half of all infant care in the United States is fair to poor in quality (Gornick and Meyers 2003) makes them nervous. The mother returns to work, which given her hour-long daily commute, means she is away for fifty hours a week. Since she does the daycare drop-off and pick-up, the father has very little time with the child. Every time the mother asks for time off to take her daughter to the pediatrician, she feels the backlash: her employer sees her as less committed, and her co-workers feel that she is not pulling her own weight.

After a year of this, feeling that her career is not advancing as she had hoped and worried about the scarcity of time with her child, the mother decides to work part-time. She finds that she is given mommy-track work: the stigma increases, her hourly pay decreases, and she loses most of her benefits and any chance for promotion (Glass 2004). Like many parents, she cannot find part-time childcare; accordingly, she continues to pay for expensive full-time care while working only part-time.

After another year, this mother joins the one in four U.S. mothers who are out of the labor force. She and her husband have decided that, given her low salary, lack of career prospects, and high childcare costs, she does not earn enough to justify having her child "raised by strangers." Once her salary is gone, her husband feels under increased pressure to work longer hours, and becomes one of the one-third of fathers who works forty-nine or more hours a week (Williams 2000). Eight years later, after the birth of a second child, both children are in school all day, and the mother attempts to return to work despite her now-stale job skills.

While the families sketched here are fictional, many real families face similar situations. This chapter is written from the perspective of a theorist pondering the landscape from the height of ten thousand feet, using data developed by the Center for WorkLife Law. It begins by highlighting how work-family conflict—which places families at all income levels in impossible situations—differs in different class contexts. This discussion is vital to forging a legislative coalition to address work-family conflict in the United States. The chapter then considers the role of the press in creating an environment in which the high levels of work-family conflict are discussed chiefly in terms of professional women's personal choice to "opt out." Next, the chapter examines why it may be more challenging to build a coalition for successful work-family policy in the United States than in other countries. It concludes by discussing how, true to habit, the United States is once again engaging in public policy through the courts, with a recent spike in cases involving family responsibilities discrimination.

WORK-FAMILY CONFLICT ACROSS CLASS LINES: THE ODD DISCONNECT IN AMERICAN POLITICS

Work-family conflict is felt by all American families, yet how families experience it differs by their class context: whether they belong to the professional-managerial class, form part of the "missing middle," or are among those earning the lowest wages. Understanding these differences is an essential precursor to public policy efforts designed to reduce work-family conflict.

Professional-Managerial Class (PMC) Families

Claudia Goldin (2004) examined five cohorts of college graduate women, and concluded that few successfully combined family with careers, even defining "career" very modestly. Only 13 to 18 percent of baby boomers attained both their career and family goals, as did only 21 to 28 percent of Gen-Xers (those graduating from college between 1980 and 1990; Goldin 2004). A key problem faced by professional-managerial class (PMC) families is the 24/7 schedule that defines commitment among high-level professionals. More than one-third of PMC men (37.2%) work fifty or more hours a week (Jacobs and Gerson 2004, 37). Twice as many men (40%) as women (20%) with college degrees work such hours (ibid., 35).

The gender effect of long hours is greatly exacerbated by motherhood. Nationwide, 95 percent of mothers aged twenty-five to forty-four work less than fifty hours per week, year-round (U.S. Census Bureau 2006a), which is less than "full-time" in most high-level jobs in business, academia, and the professions. "The best jobs have become more demanding over time. Long hours on the job are expected in many professional and managerial settings, far in excess of the forty-hour workweek that was established as the national standard more than sixty years ago" (Jacobs and Winslow 2004, 106). Given that college-educated women tend to be married to college-educated men who are often working long hours, the demand for part-time work among PMC women is intense. A survey of highly educated women found, of those in business, 89 percent wanted access to reduced-hour jobs (Hewlett et al. 2005, 62). In a national survey of five hundred dual-career families, 65 percent of women working full-time said they would prefer to work part-time (Grossman 2001).

If women feel this way, why do they not work part-time? The penalties associated with part-time work are very harsh. Women working part-time in the United States earn 21 percent less per hour than full-timers, a part-time penalty that is seven times higher than in Sweden and over twice as high as in the United Kingdom (Gornick and Meyers 2003, 63, figure 3.4). "Ultimately, choosing a part-time job is almost always synonymous with choosing a lower-paying job" (Wenger 2001, 2). Not only do workers have to take "scut work at low pay to get a part-time schedule" (Lewis 2005), they also often sacrifice benefits such as pensions and health insurance. What the United States lacks is thirty- to forty-hour-a-week jobs accompanied by benefits (Gorrick and Meyers 2003, 152).

The ideal worker in high-level jobs not only works long workweeks but also works for forty years straight, taking no time off for childbearing, childrearing, or eldercare. High-level managers and professionals "are expected to make work the central focus of their lives" (Blair-Loy and Wharton 2004, 151), a norm of "work devotion" that does not mesh with the social roles of women. Eighty-one percent (81%) of American women become mothers by age 44 (Dye 2008, 2), who typically need time off for childbearing. American mothers also do a disproportionate share of family work: 75 percent of routine housework such as laundry and cleaning, and 61 percent of the childcare (Gornick and Meyers 2003, 71). Women also provide three-fourths of the care for elderly parents (Wachovia n.d.).

The norm of work devotion is a particularly poor fit for American women, who are expected to show their devotion to family in ways that strike many people in other countries, primarily European ones, as excessive and bizarre. Sociologists have documented the "ideology of intensive mothering" that now pervades families in the professional-managerial class (Hays 1996; Lareau 2002). Judith Warner (2005) both documents and critiques this new model of motherhood from the perspective of her experience of almost six years in France. In France, Warner writes, "work was considered a normal part, even a desirable part, of a modern mother's life. It was considered something that broadened her horizons and enhanced her self-esteem—healthy and good things for herself and her children. Taking time for herself was equally considered to be a mother's right—indeed, a mother's responsibility—as was taking time for romance and a social life" (10).

Upon her return to the United States, Warner "was surprised to see laudatory stories [in the local press] of 'dedicated' mothers who spent their evenings and weekends driving to and from soccer, attending Girl Scout cookie meetings, uber-momming, generally, twenty-four hours a day. I had never once, in almost six years, met a woman in France living her life at this level of stress" (13).

As I have noted elsewhere, this is quite a new phenomenon:

> A sharp shift occurred between the generations of my mother (b. 1918) and mother-in-law (b. 1923) and my own (b. 1952). Both my mothers—one affluent, one working-class—think my generation is truly odd because we focus so much attention on our children. If one rereads the Mrs. Piggle-Wiggle books, published in the late 1940s and early 1950s, one finds their attitude fleshed out. These charming children's books tell the story of Mrs. Piggle-Wiggle, an expert at curing children of misbehavior. In the books, mothers focus on getting invited to Mrs. Workbasket's Earnest Workers Club and having the boss to dinner in order to help their husband's careers; serving meals to husbands who are cross if they are late; appeasing husbands to avoid having them spank some sense into the children. No mother is ever shown playing with her children. Nor do children expect to be entertained. They do an endless stream of errands and chores for the adults and they entertain themselves. . . . The notion that mothers' role was to "entertain" children (as they would describe it) would have seemed as bizarre as the contemporary notion of "floor time." (Williams 2000, 36)

"Floor time," suggested by Dr. Stanley Greenspan, a renowned child psychiatrist who teaches at George Washington Medical School, epitomizes the ideology of intensive motherings:

> Spend at least thirty minutes a day focusing exclusively on your child, and let her take the lead.

Tune in to her interests and feelings, and march to her drummer. If she wants you to get down on all fours and bark like a dog, do it. Participate in the action, but don't control it—she's the director, and you're the assistant director. . . . Floor time, writes Greenspan, "creates the whole basis for security, trust, and self-worth that a child will need from here on." (Cited in Williams 2000, 36)

Greenspan admits that floor time played no part of his own childhood. "In fact, Greenspan's mother used to tell him that he was such an easy, independent baby that she would leave him outside the house in a crib while she was inside doing chores" (Williams 2000, 37).

Work-family conflict of PMC families stems chiefly from the expectation that committed workers will devote fifty-plus hours per week to their jobs for forty years straight, in a society with both harsh penalties for part-time work and hyped-up ideals of motherhood.

The Missing Middle

In talking about families in the middle, one immediately runs into terminological problems. Families whom PMC academics call "working class" often refer to themselves as "middle class." As is the academic tradition, this chapter refers to these families as "working class," but also (following Theda Skocpol) as the "missing middle" (Skocpol and Leone 2001). Missing middle families are a vital, but often forgotten, element of any social change coalition.

Missing middle workers have been much less studied than managers and professionals. Indeed, the erasure of class in the United States has also meant that they are studied less than low-income families. The Center for WorkLife Law's report, *One Sick Child Away from Being Fired: When Opting Out Is Not an Option* (Williams 2006), uses the Center's database of union arbitrations to explore work-family conflict in these families. One striking difference that emerges immediately between these and more affluent families is many working-class employees' lack of flexibility (Heymann 2000, 116; Williams 2006).

Whereas PMC families typically can take off time at will to go to a school play, attend a parent-teacher conference, or take a child to the doctor, many working-class employees cannot. Indeed, nearly three-quarters of working adults in the United States say they have no control over their work schedules (American Federation of Labor-Congress of Industrial Unions [AFL-CIO] n.d.). Higher-income workers are much more likely to exercise control than are those with lower incomes: two-thirds of working parents earning $71,000 or more have access to flexible scheduling, as compared to less than one-third of those earning less than $28,000 (ibid.). Only 30 percent of Americans with incomes in the top quartile—but over half (54%) of those in the bottom quartile—cannot choose when they begin and end their workdays (Heymann 2000, 116).

In addition to their lack of flexibility, many American workers have a striking lack of leave. More than a third of all working parents in the United States lack *both* sick leave *and* vacation time (Kornbluh 2003), and, of course, many more have sick leave but no vacation time, or vice versa. The result is that many workers are one sick child away from being fired. Examples from union arbitrations are eye-opening. A single mother who worked as a packer was fired when she left work in response to a call from her brother, telling her that her four-year-old had fallen in a playground accident, resulting in a head injury (*Knauf Fiber Glass* 1983). A bus driver was fired when she arrived three minutes late because her severely asthmatic son had suffered an asthma attack (*Chicago Transit Authority* 1999). A single mother was fired for tardiness stemming from the fact that her son had Crohn's disease, which required her to unhook him from his IV, bandage him, administer medication, and get him to school, then take two buses to bring her baby to childcare, before taking a third bus to reach her job (*Chicago Transit Authority* 1997). She often worked through lunch to make up the time she missed when she was late, but she was fired nevertheless (ibid.).

Illness is not the only exigency that causes conflicts between work and family for divorced parents, single moms, and tag-team couples (those who work opposite shifts to cover their childcare needs). A mother in the midst of a divorce was fired from her job at a factory that produced night vision goggles when she refused a shift change that (she felt) would cause her to lose custody of her children (*ITT Industries, NightVision Roanoke Plant* 2003). A material handler, who was a divorced father of an asthmatic son, was fired when he needed to stay home with his sick child (*Interlake Material Handling Div., Interlake Conveyors Inc.* 2000). A single mother working as a Social Security Administration contact representative was treated as absent without leave (AWOL) when she refused to report for work because her regular babysitter had car trouble and her back-up babysitter was in the hospital with her own husband, who had suffered a heart attack (*Social Security Administration, Westminster Teleservice Ctr.* 1990). A tag-team father, a factory worker, was fired when his regular babysitter was sick; he had taken the day off instead of his wife, because her employer's absenteeism policy was stricter than his employer's (*U.S. Steel Corp.* 1990). These real-life illustrations show a face of work-family conflict that is virtually unknown. The press rarely, if ever, writes about it (Marcus 2006), and even the unions that represent such workers are often unaware of the prevalence of these types of problems.

Another equally unknown problem is mandatory overtime. Although it is difficult to quantify the prevalence of mandatory overtime in the United States, in one recent study over one-quarter (28%) of full-time workers surveyed faced mandatory overtime requirements, and over one in five (21%) actually worked overtime hours because it was mandated by their employers (Golden and Wiens-Tuers 2005). Whether required or not, Americans are working increasingly longer hours, with nearly one-third of U.S. workers regularly putting in more than forty hours per week, and one-fifth over fifty hours per week (Golden and Jorgensen 2002).

Often, the assumption is that overtime is desirable, on the grounds that union members earn time-and-a-half for each overtime hour worked, as non-exempt workers under the Fair Labor Standards Act (1938). However, the Center for WorkLife Law's arbitration database shows that many workers often face discipline or discharge due to work-family conflicts stemming from the requirement to work overtime. American workers work among the longest hours in the world, even longer than workers in Japan (International Labour Organization 2003; Jacobs and Gerson 2004, 126–27). Mandatory overtime requirements place many tag-team families in the situation of having to choose between the job of the mother and the job of the father. To quote the general counsel of the American Transit Union:

> Our members were being fired because they refused to stay for mandatory drug and alcohol tests, which last up to three hours. They had no problem taking the tests; the problem was that they were triggered at or near the end of their shifts. And with little or no advance notice, they could not stay even as paid overtime, because they had to get home to take care of their kids. (Cited in Williams 2006, 15)

Single mothers face equally harsh "choices." For example, a single mother who worked as a telephone installer was fired when she left work in defiance of a new company policy requiring that installers respond to every customer who called before 3 p.m. The policy made it impossible for workers to know when they would get off work. The installer was fired for insubordination when she refused to work overtime for fear of losing her childcare (*GTE California, Inc.* 1992).

Unlike professionals, whose work often can be done anywhere or during flexible hours, union workers often have jobs in factories, hospitals, or emergency services, such as the police or the fire service. For these on-site jobs in which specific hours must be covered, the professional model of individually negotiated flexible work arrangements is not particularly suitable. Job shares, however, may be: although factory workers typically work a standard eight- or ten-hour day, not everyone should be required to work all five days—one person working three days a week could share a job with another working the remaining two days (Appelbaum et al. 2001).

The ability to use personal time in two-hour increments is also an important consideration, to enable a worker to take unpaid time off for parent-teacher conferences or to take an ailing elder to a doctor's appointment. State laws also are relevant here—for example, California statutes allow workers forty hours a year of unpaid leave to participate in activities at their children's school (California Labor Code §§ 230.7, 230.8); allow workers to use up to half of their accrued annual sick leave to care for a sick child, parent, spouse, or domestic partner (Cal. Labor Code § 233); and, in certain circumstances, allow employees to take time off on one day and make it up on another day, without requiring overtime pay (Cal. Labor Code § 513).

Low-Wage Workers

Low-wage workers face particularly harsh work-family conflicts, which thankfully have been better documented than those of the missing middle. Low-wage workers are much more likely than are others to be single mothers: women who have spent at least five years as a single mother have half the income of women who have never been a single parent (Rose and Hartmann 2004). These women are also much more likely than other workers to depend on family members or friends for childcare, given the lack of government subsidies for all but a small percentage of those in need, the high cost of childcare, and the low minimum wage they typically are paid (Albelda and Cosenza 2000; Heymann 2000). Such informal childcare arrangements are more likely to break down than the kind of formal childcare most PMC families can afford (Heymann 2000). In addition, many low-wage single mothers have little choice but to leave their children home alone in dangerous neighborhoods, often at shockingly young ages. As a result, low-income parents are more likely than others to have to interrupt work because of problems with childcare (ibid.).

Low-wage workers also are far more likely than others to be providing more than thirty hours a week of unpaid assistance to parents or in-laws (ibid., 118). Additionally, the lack of sufficient public transportation in many U.S. cities leaves many parents to take slow, cumbersome, and undependable public transportation, such as the single mother, discussed above, who lost her job because she was late to work: she had to take three buses to deliver her kids to school and to childcare and to reach her job (*Chicago Transit Authority* 1997). Furthermore, low-income families are more likely than other U.S. families to be dealing with issues of ill health and lack of health insurance, where access to medical care, if available, is received only by waiting long and unpredictable periods of time (Heymann 2000). Finally, low-wage workers are more likely than other workers to lack paid sick and/or vacation leave and to face inflexible schedules at work (ibid., 115–16). Mothers with a high school education or less are more likely than other mothers to work rotating schedules or "unsocial hours" (the European term for evening and weekend work), and single mothers within this group are the most likely to do so (Presser 2003, 202–3).

Arbitrations dramatize the kinds of brutal conflicts that low-wage employees often face (Williams 2006). In *Tenneco Packaging Burlington Container Plant* (1999), the arbitrator reinstated with full back pay the grievant, a single parent of a mentally handicapped son, who was terminated after twenty-seven years for failing to report to work when her son's caregiver could not work. In *State of New York, Rochester Psychiatric Center* (1986), a healthcare center fired a mental health aide who had worked for her employer for nine years. She had a history of attendance problems, almost all of which stemmed from her status as a single parent. The arbitrator overturned her discharge, stating that the situation was "shocking to one's sense of fairness."

The Odd Disconnect

Fully 95 percent of American women and 90 percent of American men say they wish they had more time to devote to family (Gornick and

Meyers 2003, 53). In Europe the national debate tends to be not whether to implement policies to help reconcile work and family, but how best to do so (Kamerman 2005). In the United States, in contrast, work-family issues have been barely a blip on the radar screen of American politics. Why has the widespread experience of work-family conflict failed to spur action in the United States to date?

This description of work-family conflict in different social locations can help answer the question of why, given the acute levels of work-family conflict, this issue has not gained political purchase. One clue emerged in a Capitol Hill conversation. A staffer for a member of Congress who represents an urban area was puzzling over how to connect with the voters on work-family issues. The staff had developed a work-family bill, and the congressional district was an urban area, full of professional women who clearly cared about work-family issues. Yet there remained a strange disconnect, an inability to engage and inspire these voters. The problem, it seems, was that the bill in question focused on short-term leaves and subsidized childcare, neither of which is of much help to PMC women—most of whom already have short-term leave, and none of whom would be eligible for subsidized childcare.

One policy alternative with the potential to help women—and men—in all three groups (PMC, working class, and low-income) is part-time equity: proportional pay, benefits, training, and advancement for part-time work. Part-time equity would help PMC workers because they could opt for thirty-five- to forty-hour workweeks, in return for proportional pay and advancement, thereby avoiding the outlandish hours often required of fast-track professionals. It would help working-class single mothers and tag-team families struggling with long hours of mandatory overtime and also help low-income workers by discouraging employers from keeping them in part-time work as a way of depressing wages and eliminating benefits.

Part-time equity presents significant and, for now, somewhat insuperable challenges in terms of coalition building. Yet it will be important to begin to create the kind of cross-class academic literature that will provide the basis for assessing the potential of various policy alternatives. The challenge is in designing policy initiatives that yoke three forces: (a) the political power of professional women; (b) support from a union movement apprized of the important role work-family conflict in the lives of its members; and (c) the moral clout and political capital of poverty advocates. Although this approach is not the only answer, it does help formulate the right question.

ENDNOTE

1. Scenarios adapted from those originally published in "The Public Policy of Motherhood," by Joan C. Williams and Holly Cohen Cooper, *Journal of Social Issues* 60 (2004): 849–65.

■ Review Questions ■

1. How is the work-family conflict faced by professional and managerial workers different from the work-family conflict faced by the "missing middle" and low-wage workers?
2. Why, according to the author, hasn't more been done politically to ease work-family conflict?

Part Four

Links across the Generations

CHAPTER 9

Children and Parents

Being a good parent is challenging enough when everyone lives in the same home, when the family remains together over time, and when there's enough money to maintain a decent standard of living. Unfortunately, not all children grow up in families such as these. In fact, the proportion of children whose families have all of these characteristics has been declining. As is well known, divorce has increased since the mid-twentieth century, although it has recently declined for the college educated. Less well known is that a growing proportion of children, perhaps one out of six, are now being born to parents who are cohabiting but are not married. In fact, demographers think that almost the entire increase in childbearing outside of marriage in the 1990s and 2000s was due to births to cohabiting couples, rather than to mothers who were living without partners. In principle, these cohabiting parents could provide stable environments for children. That's what occurs in European countries such as France and Sweden, where decades-long cohabiting unions function as substitutes for marriage. But in the United States, cohabiting unions tend to be brief: most couples either break up or marry within a few years.

The great growth in cohabiting parents has occurred among low- and moderate-income individuals who have no more than a high school degree. Sara McLanahan, in the first reading in this chapter, refers to these young, dating, or cohabiting parents as "fragile families" because of their tenuous ties to each other and their high likelihood of breaking up. She presents findings from a study in which the researchers interviewed unmarried mothers, and if possible the fathers, in urban hospitals immediately after the birth of their children. The researchers were surprised to learn that about half of the mothers were living with the fathers at the time of the birth. The researchers followed the mothers and fathers, reinterviewing them one, two, and five years later. The reading describes them and tells what happened to their relationships—how many married, how many remained as cohabiting partners, and how many grew apart. It provides a window on an increasingly common way in which American children of low- and moderate-income parents are being raised.

Another reason parents and children may not live together is sheer distance—sometimes thousands of miles of distance—between them. As the world economy has evolved, it has become more common for women in poorer countries—many of them mothers of young children—to leave their children in the care of grandmothers or other relatives, to migrate to wealthier countries in order to seek work, and then to send money back home. There is a growing demand in countries such as the United States for workers to do jobs such as being a nanny for a dual-earner married couple. Advances in communication such as e-mail, text messages, and video services have made it easier for migrants to keep in touch with family members. As a result, we have seen an increase in the number of families that are split between two countries and that maintain continual contact between members in the sending and receiving countries—a phenomenon researchers are calling *transnational families*.

Being a member of a transnational family can produce contradictory emotions. Mothers are proud of the money they send home, which can pay for school clothes or a new room in a grandmother's house; but they miss being with their children. For their part, children know their parents are making sacrifices for their benefit, but they may not like the separation. As they become teenagers, they may become too difficult for aging grandmothers to handle. In the second reading, Joanna Dreby tells the four-year saga of the attempts of a Mexican couple who are living and working in New Jersey to have their son, Germán, join them. The reading begins with a description of Dreby's first meeting in New Jersey with Ofelia, the mother of Germán. Her struggles illustrate the dilemmas transnational families face.

Fragile Families and the Reproduction of Poverty

Sara McLanahan

In his report on the Negro family, Daniel Patrick Moynihan (1965) noted that nonmarital childbearing was increasing among African Americans and that the root causes of the increase were the legacy of slavery, urbanization, and persistent male unemployment. He further argued that these forces had led to a self-reinforcing "tangle of pathology," consisting of nonmarital childbearing, high male unemployment, and welfare dependence, which was undermining the progress of African Americans and contributing to the perpetuation of poverty. In the final paragraph of the report, Moynihan stated,

> The policy of the United States is to bring the Negro American to full and equal sharing in the responsibilities and rewards of citizenship. To this end, the programs of the federal government bearing on this objective shall be designed to have the effect, directly or indirectly, of enhancing the stability and resources of the Negro American family. (Moynihan 1965, 48)

Although initially praised by the black leadership for focusing national attention on a serious problem, the Moynihan Report soon become the target of harsh and widespread criticism from liberals (and eventually from black leaders) for using words like *pathology* to describe the black family and for attributing the disadvantages of African Americans to family structure rather than structural factors such as racial discrimination and poverty (Rainwater and Yancey 1967). In contrast, social conservatives praised

Sara McLanahan, "Fragile Families and the Reproduction of Poverty," *The ANNALS of the American Academy of Political and Social Science,* Vol. 621 (1), January: 111–131. © 2009. Reprinted by permission of Sage Publications, Inc.

the report and used it to support a "culture-of-poverty" argument that emphasized values and behaviors rather than poverty as the root cause of intergenerational poverty (Ryan 1976).

In the aftermath of the Moynihan controversy, liberal researchers avoided the topic of family structure, or they wrote only about the positive aspects of the black family (Stack 1974), until the 1980s when William Julius Wilson reopened the debate. In his book *The Truly Disadvantaged,* Wilson (1987) refocused attention on the instability of the African American family and its role in undermining the life chances of black children. Like Moynihan, Wilson distinguished between a black middle class, which he saw as advancing in terms of socioeconomic status, and a black lower class, which he saw as losing ground. Unlike Moynihan, however, Wilson argued explicitly that the best way to strengthen families was to increase men's employment and earnings.

Since the publication of the Moynihan Report, the proportion of African American children born outside marriage has grown dramatically, from 24 percent in 1965 to 69 percent in 2000 (see Figure 9.1). Nonmarital childbearing has also increased among other racial and ethnic groups, however. The proportion of white children born to unmarried parents has grown from 6 percent in 1965 to 24 percent today, and the proportion of Hispanic children has grown from 37 percent in 1990 to 42 percent in 2000.[1] Yet, after four decades of discussion, the debate over the role of family structure in the reproduction of poverty continues, with the basic positions showing very little change. At one extreme are analysts who argue that nonmarital childbearing is a consequence but not a cause of poverty (Coontz and Folbre 2002); at the other extreme are those who argue it is a cause but not a consequence (Murray 1984; J. Wilson 2002); and in between are those who, like Moynihan and William Julius Wilson, view it as both a cause and a consequence (Massey 2007; Western 2007).[2]

Despite the importance of the topic and the intensity of the debate, empirical data pertaining

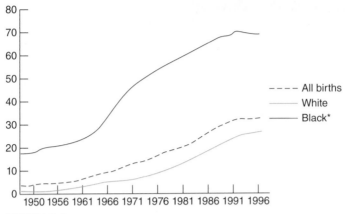

FIGURE 9.1
Trends in non marital childbearing: 1950–2000.
Note: *Births before 1969 classified as nonwhite.

to unmarried parents and their children has been limited until recently. Although we know something about the characteristics of the women who give birth outside marriage, we know much less about the fathers of these children; and although we know something about the role of economic factors in predicting nonmarital childbearing, we have very little data on the role of values and social skills. Finally, although a large body of research exists on the consequences of father absence and single motherhood for parents and children, most of this research is based on divorced families, which are likely to differ in important ways from families formed by unmarried parents (McLanahan and Sandefur 1994).

THE FRAGILE FAMILIES STUDY

To learn more about unmarried parents and their children and to address some of the unanswered questions first raised during the debate over the Moynihan Report, my colleagues and I began work (in 1998) on the Fragile Families and Child Wellbeing Study, a longitudinal survey of about five thousand births, including more than thirty-six hundred births to unmarried parents.[3] The study design called for sampling new parents shortly after the birth of their

child, and then reinterviewing both mothers and fathers when the focal child was one, three, and five years old. Child outcomes were assessed at years three and five. To maximize our chances of interviewing fathers as well as mothers, we started at the hospital and sampled new births. In cases where fathers could not be contacted at the hospital, we interviewed them by phone or in person as soon after the birth as possible. Births were sampled in seventy-five hospitals in twenty large cities throughout the United States, and when weighted, the data are representative of births in U.S. cities with populations of two hundred thousand or more people (Reichman et al. 2001). The study was designed to address the following questions:

- What are the capabilities of unmarried parents when their child is born, especially fathers?
- What is the nature of relationships in fragile families at birth? How do relationships change over time?
- How do parents and children fare in fragile families?[4]

The answers to these questions are important for resolving the debate over the Moynihan Report. For example, the answer to the first question can tell us the extent to which nonmarital childbearing is selective of people with different human capital and social skills and whether these differences are large enough to account for differences in children's outcomes later on. If poverty and low education are the root causes of nonmarital childbearing, as some people suggest, we would expect to find substantial differences in the human capital and social skills of married and unmarried parents at the time of their child's birth. If poverty is not a cause, we would expect differences to be small.

The answer to the second question can tell us something about whether families formed by unmarried parents are different from families formed by married parents in terms of parental values and commitment. In addition, by following parents over time, we can compare the stability of marital and nonmarital relationships and identify the factors that predict stability. If nonmarital unions are less stable than marital unions and if relationship stability is strongly associated with differences in human capital at birth, this finding would support the argument that poverty and economic insecurity cause family instability; alternatively, if instability is associated with differences in commitment and social-emotional skills, this finding would support the argument that the latter are contributing to family instability.

Finally, the answer to the third question can tell us something about whether a nonmarital birth leads to differences in parental resources and ultimately to poor child outcomes. If parental resources and child outcomes are no different in married- and unmarried-parent families, once socioeconomic status at birth is taken into account, this finding would lend support to the argument that nonmarital childbearing is a marker but not a cause of future poverty. Alternatively, if family structure is associated with poorer parenting, even after controlling for socioeconomic status at birth, or if changes in family structure are associated with changes in parental resources, these findings would lend support to the argument that family structure

is a mechanism in the reproduction of poverty. Here, I describe what we have learned about these questions during the first five years of the Fragile Families Study, and then move on to discuss how the findings inform our understanding of the processes underlying intergenerational mobility.

WHAT ARE UNMARRIED PARENTS' CAPABILITIES?

When we began our study in the late 1990s, quite a bit was known about the demographic characteristics of unwed mothers (age, education, parity), thanks to several national surveys that routinely collect information on women's marital and fertility histories. Much less was known about unmarried fathers, however. One reason for the lack of data on fathers was that these men are often omitted from national and local surveys either because they are not identified by standard survey techniques or because they do not report their paternity status (Rendall et al. 1999; Garfinkel, McLanahan, and Hanson 1998). The so-called missing fathers problem is especially serious among low-income men, and a major objective of the Fragile Families and Child Wellbeing Study was to obtain an accurate description of the capabilities of the men who father children outside marriage as well as the values and social skills of unmarried mothers.

Table 9.1 presents data on the characteristics of new parents at the time of their child's birth. The table distinguishes between unmarried parents who are cohabiting and living apart because we expect these two types of unmarried couples to differ from one another. To date, we have not identified large racial or ethnic differences in our sample, and thus the information reported in the table is based on all parents. Where important differences exist, they will be noted in the text.

A brief comparison of the columns in Table 9.1 indicates that married and unmarried parents come from very different worlds. As compared with their married counterparts,

TABLE 9.1

CAPABILITIES OF PARENTS AT BIRTH: SOCIOECONOMIC (IN PERCENTAGES)

	Mothers			Fathers		
	Married	Cohabitating	Single	Married	Cohabitating	Single
Age (mean)	29.6	24.3	22.5	32.0	27.6	25.0
Teen parent	4.2	17.5	33.9	0	9.1	22.2
Child with other partner	13.6	39.5	32.8	16.4	38.5	38.9
Race						
White, non-Hispanic	50.9	22.5	14.9	51.1	16.9	8.8
Black, non-Hispanic	11.6	29.4	49.9	13.0	34.4	59.2
Hispanic	27.0	44.0	31.6	27.7	46.8	26.7
Other	10.6	4.1	3.6	8.2	2.0	5.3
Education						
Less than high school	18.0	41.5	48.0	21.5	40.7	44.3
High school	24.7	39.6	36.1	20.1	39.6	35.5
Some college	21.0	17.5	14.4	25.9	15.9	16.2
College	36.3	1.4	1.4	32.6	3.7	4.0
Weeks worked (mean)	46.2	42.2	42.7	47.5	45.1	40.7
Earnings ($) (mean)	28,507.0	11,446.0	10,792.0	40,125.0	21,166.0	16,393.0
Poverty status	12.3	33.7	52.9	11.4	33.4	53.4

unmarried parents are disproportionately African American and Hispanic, they are younger and more likely to be teen parents, and they are more likely to have children by other partners. Cohabiting parents are somewhat better off than noncohabiting parents, but the gap with married parents is large for both groups. The high prevalence of "multipartnered fertility"—defined as having children with different partners—is one of several important new findings to have emerged from the study. Whereas between 14 and 16 percent of married parents report having had a child with another partner, between 35 and 40 percent of unmarried parents report having done so (Carlson and Furstenberg 2006, 2007).

Perhaps the most striking difference between married and unmarried parents is the gap in education. Whereas a majority of married parents has attended at least some college, a large minority of unmarried parents has not even completed high school, and although both groups of parents report working a similar number of weeks in the past year, unmarried parents report much lower

earnings and much higher poverty rates. The large marital status gap in human capital and earnings underscores the fact that many unmarried parents are poor *prior* to having a child. To make sure that the differences we observe were not due to differences in the stage of the family life cycle, we redid the analyses for parents having a first birth. Limiting the sample in this way does not alter the disparities reported in Table 9.1.

Table 9.2 presents data on the mental health and health behaviors of married, cohabiting, and noncoresident parents. We view these measures as good indicators of parents' social-emotional skills and ability to form stable relationships. According to Table 9.2, unmarried parents—both cohabiting and noncoresident—are more likely to suffer from depression than married parents and somewhat more likely to report more problems with alcohol (DeKlyen et al. 2006). Unmarried fathers are twice as likely as married fathers to have problems with drug use, three times as likely to be violent, and nearly seven times as likely to have been incarcerated in the

TABLE 9.2

CAPABILITIES OF PARENTS AT BIRTH: HEALTH (IN PERCENTAGES)

	Mothers			Fathers		
	Married	Cohabitating	Single	Married	Cohabitating	Single
Depression	11.9	15.5	17.8	6.8	9.5	14.8
Heavy drinking	3.9	7.6	7.4	24.0	29.9	23.1
Illegal drug use	0.7	2.0	3.3	3.1	9.1	10.4
Partner violence	—	—	—	2.6	8.0	9.6
Father incarcerated	—	—	—	9.4	36.8	46.2

past. Again, although cohabiting fathers look better than noncoresident fathers on some indicators, the major gap is between married and unmarried fathers.

Drug use and violence are likely to be underreported in these data. However, there is no reason to expect that underreporting differs by marital status, which means that our estimates of the gap between married and unmarried parents is likely to be accurate. The high level of incarceration among unmarried fathers is particularly striking and underscores the fact that the changes in penal policy that occurred after 1980 have played an important role in the lives of these parents (Geller, Garfinkel, and Western 2006; Swisher and Waller forthcoming).

In sum, we found important race/ethnic differences in three domains: multipartnered fertility, drug/alcohol problems, and fathers' incarceration. In each domain, the marital status gap was smaller among blacks than among whites and Hispanics, primarily because the behaviors were more common among married blacks.

WHAT IS THE NATURE OF RELATIONSHIPS IN FRAGILE FAMILIES?

One of the most important questions in the ongoing debate over the role of nonmarital childbearing in the reproduction of poverty is whether the relationship between unmarried parents is committed or casual. When we began our study, much of the existing research on unwed parents' relationships was based on ethnographic studies, which present a rather mixed picture (Waller 2002). Some researchers have reported that unmarried fathers are committed to their families but face serious barriers to forming a stable family because of limited resources (Sullivan 1989); others have argued that nonmarital childbearing is the by-product of a "mating game" in which young (uncommitted) men take advantage of young women's fantasies of marriage and motherhood to gain sexual favors (Anderson 1989), and still others describe a world composed of "good daddies" and "bad daddies" (Furstenberg, Sherwood, and Sullivan 1992).

Thus, a major objective of the Fragile Families Study was to learn more about the nature of parental relationships at birth, including how parents viewed marriage, whether they expected to marry, and whether their relationships were of sufficient quality to sustain a long-term commitment. We also sought to learn more about parents' attitudes toward marriage and the extent to which gender conflict and mistrust were serious problems as some qualitative studies have suggested. By following parents over time, we hoped to gain information about the prevalence of stable relationships as well as the factors affecting stability. We also hoped to learn about new partnerships and new children and the extent to which these new unions represent a gain or a loss for children.

Finally, we were interested in whether unmarried fathers were involved in the lives of their children. Research on divorced fathers had shown that father involvement declines rather dramatically during the years following a divorce (Seltzer 1991), but whether this pattern extended to unmarried fathers was an open question. On one hand, we might expect unmarried fathers to be more involved with their children than divorced fathers, given that many of these men are still romantically involved with the child's mother. On the other hand, we might expect them to be less involved given that the rights and obligations of unmarried fathers are less institutionalized (Nock 1998).

Relationships at Birth

Figure 9.2 provides information on the nature of unmarried parents' relationships at the time of the child's birth. As shown in the figure, more than half of parents are cohabiting and another 32 percent are romantically involved. Fewer than 10 percent of mothers say they have "no contact" with the father. Overall levels of romantic involvement are similar for whites, blacks, and Hispanics, although blacks are less likely to be cohabiting at birth.

According to Table 9.3 most unmarried parents hold positive attitudes toward marriage, although not as positive as those of married

parents (Waller and McLanahan 2005). Half of the cohabiting mothers "strongly agree" with the statement "it is better for children if their parents are married," and 90 percent say their chances of marriage are "fifty-fifty or better." Noncohabiting parents also hold positive views toward marriage, although they rate their chances of marriage much lower. Finally, most parents describe their relationships as being "very supportive" and "low conflict" (scales range from 1 to 3, with 3 being high), with cohabiting parents being closer to married parents than to noncoresident parents. Unmarried fathers are slightly more positive and more optimistic about their relationships than unmarried mothers (not shown in table).

We found only two areas in which unmarried parents' attitudes might be described as less than positive toward marriage: first, unmarried mothers are much more likely than married parents to strongly agree with the statement that "a single mother can raise a child alone," and second, unmarried mothers are much more likely to agree with the statement "men cannot be trusted to be faithful." Cohabiting parents are closer to married parents in their beliefs about single mothers and in between married and single parents in gender distrust.

In general, black mothers are more positive about marriage than white mothers, and the gap between married and unmarried parents is also smaller. Black mothers are also less likely than white mothers to believe that their chances of marriage are good. These findings are consistent with the argument that the increase in single motherhood has feedback effects on marriage, not by undermining positive attitudes toward marriage but rather by altering expectations and making single motherhood a more acceptable alternative. Hispanic mothers are the most likely to report distrust.

Relationships at Five Years

Despite their high hopes for a future together, only a small proportion of unmarried parents (22 percent) ever follow through on their plans,

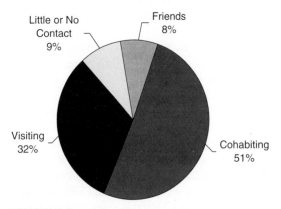

FIGURE 9.2
Unmarried parents' relationships status at birth.

TABLE 9.3

MARRIAGE ATTITUDES AND EXPECTATIONS AT BIRTH (IN PERCENTAGES)

	All Mothers			White Mothers		
	Married	Cohabitating	Single	Married	Cohabitating	Single
Premarriage attitudes	72.6	49.3	49.3	67.7	40.3	27.2
Approval of single mom	57.6	80.7	85.4	46.8	75.2	74.7
Gender distrust	10.4	19.8	33.7	3.3	11.1	20.1
Supportiveness (mean)	2.7	2.7	2.4	2.7	2.7	2.3
Conflict (mean)	1.3	1.4	1.5	1.3	1.4	1.4
Chances of marriage						
Almost certain	—	51.6	13.7	—	72.9	49.8
Good	—	26.0	17.1	—	17.1	17.9
Fifty/fifty	—	14.5	19.7	—	7.9	8.3
Not so good	—	4.0	12.5	—	1.4	5.7
No chance	—	3.9	37.1	—	0.8	18.3

	Black Mothers			Hispanic Mothers		
	Married	Cohabitating	Single	Married	Cohabitating	Single
Premarriage attitudes	81.2	58.9	53.9	74.4	49.1	52.7
Approval of single mom	72.5	83.2	89.1	74.6	80.5	88.2
Gender distrust	7.1	16.4	30.2	25.7	28.3	45.9
Supportiveness (mean)	2.7	2.7	2.4	2.6	2.7	2.4
Conflict (mean)	1.4	1.5	1.5	1.3	1.4	1.4
Chances of marriage						
Almost certain	—	45.5	15.0	—	40.9	11.8
Good	—	30.7	18.1	—	28.9	13.6
Fifty/fifty	—	15.0	22.8	—	6.5	12.6
Not so good	—	3.2	12.9	—	6.5	12.6
No chance	—	5.6	31.3	—	4.4	43.4

and even fewer (16 percent) are still married by the time of the five-year interview. Counting both cohabiting and married parents, about one-third of unmarried parents were living together five years after the birth of their child. Most of these parents were cohabiting at birth, although some were romantically involved and living apart and a few reported no romantic relationship at birth.

White and Hispanic mothers are more likely than African American mothers to marry the fathers of their children. Indeed, union dissolution overall is higher among blacks than among the other groups, in part because fewer parents are cohabiting at birth and in part because breakup rates are higher among black couples

irrespective of status. Much of the postbirth marriage gap between blacks and whites can be accounted for by a shortage of "marriageable men," defined as the ratio of employed men to all women in a city (Harknett and McLanahan 2004). Black mothers are almost as likely to marry as white mothers when marriage market conditions are similar.

To learn more about their motivations for marriage, we conducted in-depth interviews with a subgroup of parents who participated in the core survey. When asked why they were not married, parents often said that they were waiting until they had achieved a certain standard of living that they viewed as necessary for a successful marriage (Gibson-Davis, Edin, and

McLanahan 2005). One young Hispanic father in his twenties put it this way:

> I want to be secure. . . . I don't want to get married and be like we have no money or nothing. . . . I want to get my little house in Long Island, you know, white-picket fence, and two-car garage, me hitting the garbage cans when I pull up in the driveway. (McLanahan 2004, 619)

Mothers also emphasized the importance of sexual fidelity as a condition for marriage. Both rationales are supported by the quantitative analyses. Fathers' income increases the chances of marriage, and mothers' distrust reduces the chances (Carlson, McLanahan, and England 2004). Furthermore, fathers (but not mothers) who have had a child by another partner are less likely to marry postbirth. The fact that fathers' multipartnered fertility is more likely to undermine union stability than mothers' suggests that multipartnered fertility creates tension between the parents by causing a drain on fathers' resources (time and money) and by creating conflict between the couple. In the qualitative interviews, mothers often express jealousy over the time fathers spend with a child who lives in another household, including jealousy about the time he spends with the child's mother. This source of conflict is referred to as the "baby mama drama" (Monte 2007).

New Partnerships

Many unmarried parents have formed new partnerships by the time their child is age five. About half of mothers who have ended their relationships with the biological father have a new partner (about 30 percent of all mothers), and two-thirds of these are living with a new partner. Whereas we might have expected mothers' new partners to be of lower quality than the original biological fathers—previous research suggests that having a child outside marriage reduces a woman's chances of marriage (Bennett, Bloom, and Miller 2005)—in fact these men are of higher quality (Bzostek, Carlson, and McLanahan 2006). New

partners are much more likely to have a high school degree, more likely to be employed, less likely to have problems with drugs or alcohol, less likely to engage in domestic violence, and less likely to have been incarcerated than original biological fathers. Some of this improvement is due to aging and greater maturity, and some is due to mothers being more selective in choosing new partners.

The high prevalence of new partnerships underscores an important feature of fragile families—*high partnership instability.* We estimate that by the time of the child's third birthday, two-thirds of unmarried mothers have experienced at least one partnership change, more than a third have experienced at least two changes, and nearly 20 percent have experienced three or more changes. In contrast, only 13 percent of married mothers have experienced a partnership change by the time their child is three, and only 6 percent will have experienced two or more changes (Osborne and McLanahan 2007).

Interestingly, the difference in partnership stability between married and unmarried mothers is not due to the fact that married mothers have fewer partnerships overall. Indeed, married mothers report having had more partners than unmarried mothers at the time of their child's birth. What is different, however, is that married mothers have not had children with their prior partners, whereas unmarried mothers have. Despite the fact that many mothers are able to improve their living conditions by partnering with a new man, the search process itself can be stressful for both the mother and the child. Thus, the gains associated with improving the quality of mothers' partners may be offset by the losses associated with greater instability.

Biological Fathers Commitment

Most unmarried fathers are generally highly involved at birth (see Table 9.4), with cohabiting fathers showing much higher levels of involvement than noncoresident fathers. According to mothers' reports, more than 90 percent of

TABLE 9.4

UNMARRIED FATHERS' INVOLVEMENT AT BIRTH (IN PERCENTAGES)

	Cohabitating	Single
Gave money/bought things for child	95.3	64.1
Helped in another way	97.7	56.1
Visited baby's mother in the hospital	96.5	54.9
Child will take fathers surname	93.1	63.9
Father's name is on birth certificate	96.0	71.0
Mother says father wants to be involved	99.5	89.3
Mother wants father to be involved	99.5	87.6

cohabiting fathers provided financial support and other types of help during the pregnancy, and 95 percent visited the mother at the hospital. Most important, nearly 100 percent of these men told the mothers that they wanted to help raise the child, and nearly 100 percent of mothers said they wanted the father to be involved (Johnson 2001). The proportions are lower for noncoresident fathers, with more than half providing some type of support during the pregnancy, and much higher levels reporting that they wanted to be involved.

Despite their best intentions, just a little more than a third of fathers are living with their children five years later, and there is substantial variation in the involvement of nonresident fathers: a third have no contact and 43 percent have monthly contact with their child. Among the latter, the average number of days a father sees his child is twelve per month (Carlson, McLanahan, and Brooks-Gunn forthcoming). Not surprisingly, the quality of the parents' relationship is a strong predictor of fathers' involvement (Waller and Swisher 2006). When the mother trusts the father and the parents are able to communicate about the child's needs, the father is more likely to visit and engage in activities with the child. Although one might argue that causality is operating in the opposite direction—father involvement is leading to better cooperation—analyses indicate that most of the effect is going from cooperation to involvement (Carlson, McLanahan, and Brooks-Gunn forthcoming). Other factors that predict father involvement include whether a father has

a child by another partner, whether he was born outside the United States, and whether he was ever incarcerated, all of which reduce parental cooperation and father involvement.

Just over half of nonresident fathers provide some kind of financial support to their child, and just under half provide in-kind support (Nepomnyaschy and Garfinkel 2006). Informal support is somewhat more common than formal child support at year five, although the proportion of mothers receiving formal support increases over time. Interestingly, stronger child support enforcement does not appear to increase the amount of money the father contributes, at least not during the first five years after birth. Rather, strong enforcement simply replaces informal payments with formal payments. When a mother receives welfare, formal child support payments are taken by the state to offset welfare costs, which means that the mother has less income overall.

HOW DO PARENTS AND CHILDREN FARE?

Marriage is expected to increase parents' resources (financial, health, and social), which, in turn, is expected to improve children's home environments and future life chances. In theory, marriage increases family income by creating economies of scale and by encouraging parents to work harder and more efficiently (for example, through specialization—see Becker 1981).

Marriage also increases parents' mental health by promoting social integration and emotional support (Gove, Hughes, and Style 1983). Finally, marriage increases access to social support by increasing neighborhood quality and residential stability and by expanding family networks and reinforcing family commitments (Coleman 1988). Each of these resources is important for the quality of the child's home environment.

The theoretical arguments for the benefits of marriage are supported by a large body of empirical research, including research on parents' economic and social resources as well as research on outcomes for children and young adults (Waite 1995). Most of this research, however, is based on samples of adults (parents) who were married at birth and subsequently divorced. Thus, many questions remain about whether the benefits of marriage and the costs of union dissolution are as great for children born to unmarried parents. More important, perhaps, research on the benefits of marriage and the costs of divorce is frequently criticized for making causal inferences from evidence of correlations.

Part of our rationale for following a cohort of new parents and their children was to determine whether the correlations between family structure and child outcomes found in previous studies were due to the number of parents in the household, the marital status of the parents, and/or the stability of the household. Specifically, we wanted to know whether the benefits of marriage extended to children raised in stable cohabiting parent families and whether the benefits of stability extended to households headed by a single mother.

A second motivation was to address the issue of causality by collecting better data on the specific mechanisms that are expected to mediate (or account for) the association between family structure and child outcomes. By starting with the birth of the child and by collecting data on a wide range of parental and relationship characteristics at the time of the birth, we hoped to be able to rule out some of the alternative arguments for why divorce and marital instability might be

correlated with poor outcomes in children. For example, many analysts argue that divorce is a proxy for high conflict between parents. Thus, we measured this construct at birth so that we could include it in our analyses. We also measured prior relationship instability, alcohol and drug abuse, antisocial behavior, and incarceration history.

Finally, by identifying and measuring the key theoretical pathways linking family structure with child outcomes, we sought to test specific hypotheses about the causal processes underlying the correlation between family structure and outcomes, including hypotheses about the effects of nonmarital childbearing on family income, parental health, social support, and parenting quality. While observational data can never provide conclusive evidence of causal effects, a more detailed description of the mechanisms that link family structure with particular outcomes is better than a simple correlation.

Fathers' Earnings and Health Trajectories

. . . Fathers who are stably married report the highest earnings of all groups in the year prior to the birth.[6] [Next] are married fathers who subsequently divorce, and next in line are unmarried fathers, followed by fathers who marry after the birth, fathers who are stably cohabiting, and fathers who never cohabit (stably single). [A]ll fathers experience earnings growth over time, but fathers who divorce experience less of an increase than fathers who remain married, a finding consistent with previous research. Note also that fathers who marry after their child's birth experience a greater gain in earnings than unmarried fathers who remain single (Garfinkel et al. 2008).

In separate analyses, we found that much of the relatively lower earnings growth of fathers who are stably single is due to the fact that these men have more mental health problems and are more likely to have been incarcerated than other fathers. When these factors are taken into account, the difference in earnings growth between those who marry and stably married fathers and stable single fathers is cut in half. The lower earnings growth of single fathers is consistent with the argument that marriage increases fathers' earnings. It is also consistent with the argument that women are less likely to marry men whom they view as having poor earnings trajectories.

The pattern for fathers' mental health is somewhat different. Married fathers and fathers who subsequently marry report the fewest mental health problems at birth; fathers who subsequently divorce report the most mental health problems. Cohabiting and single fathers fall in between (Meadows 2007). All fathers experience increases in mental health problems over time, but there is no evidence of growing disparities. These results do not support the argument that marriage after birth helps close the gap in mental health between married and unmarried fathers.

Mothers' Economic Status and Health

As was true for fathers, married mothers are in a much better economic condition than other mothers at the time their child is born. Single mothers who never marry report the lowest incomes. Most mothers experience improvements in economic status over time; divorced mothers are an exception. However, some groups of mothers experience smaller gains than others. Mothers who are stably single experience growing gaps with married mothers. Otherwise, unmarried mothers, including those who marry or move in with the father, experience income gains similar to those of stably married mothers. Regarding mental health, married mothers in stable unions report the fewest mental health problems at birth, whereas mothers who eventually divorce (or separate) report the most problems (Meadows, McLanahan, and Brooks-Gunn 2007). Mental health problems increase among all women after birth regardless of relationship status. In other analyses (not shown in the figure), we find that all partnership changes (entrances as well as exits) have short-term negative effects on mothers' mental health. The only exception is mothers who marry the fathers of their child before the child's first birthday; these

mothers experience no short-term increase in mental health problems.

Social Support

Social support, defined as instrumental and emotional assistance from family or friends, is an important family resource, especially for new parents and single mothers (Cowan and Cowan 1992; Eggebeen 1992). Social support serves as a form of insurance against poverty and economic hardship and is expected to improve the quality of the child's home environment by reducing parental stress. The Fragile Families and Child Wellbeing Study asked parents whether they knew someone who would lend them money, provide them with a place to live, and/or provide child care in case of an emergency. Using these measures, researchers find that unmarried mothers have less access to social support in the form of housing and cash assistance than married mothers. The disparity in support is due to several factors: First, access to support is higher in neighborhoods with higher median incomes (Turney and Harknett 2007), and unmarried parents are less likely than married parents to live in such neighborhoods. Second, access to support is positively associated with residential stability, and unmarried parents are less likely than married parents to have stable housing ("The Frequency and Correlates of Mothers' Residential Mobility" 2007). Indeed, unmarried parents are twice as likely as married parents to move during the five years following their child's birth and three times as likely to move three or more times.[7] Finally, mothers who have children by different partners report having less access to support, especially financial support (Harknett and Knab 2007).

Parenting Quality

Nonmarital childbearing reduces the quality of parenting by contributing to partnership instability and multipartnered fertility. Just as partnership changes reduce mothers' income and increase mental health problems, we find that most types of instability (marriage to the biological father is an exception) increase maternal stress (Cooper et al. 2007). The negative effects of instability persist even after controlling for pre-disruption characteristics and parental resources. Importantly, the negative effects of partnership instability appear to be limited to mothers with a high school degree or less. Mothers with some college education do not report increases in maternal stress unless they experience multiple transitions.

Multipartnered fertility also undermines the quantity and quality of parenting by reducing parents' ability to get along and to cooperate in raising their child. Mothers report less support from the nonresident father and lower overall relationship quality when either parent has a child by another partner. Mothers also report less shared parenting and less cooperation in raising their child when the father has a child with another partner (Carlson and Furstenberg 2007).

Child Well Being

Insofar as families formed outside marriage are quite diverse—ranging from stable cohabiting parent families to highly unstable families—distinguishing among these different types of households is likely to be important. Although we have only recently begun to examine how being born to unmarried parents affects child outcomes, the evidence garnered thus far suggests that both instability and material hardship have negative effects. Children who live with stably single mothers and children who live with mothers who experience multiple partnership changes show higher levels of aggression and anxiety/depression than children who live with stably married parents (Osborne and McLanahan 2007). In contrast, children who live with parents who are stably cohabiting do not differ from children raised by married parents. Half of the negative association between children's family context and behavioral problems can be accounted for by the fact that single mothers and mothers in unstable partnerships report higher levels of maternal stress and are more likely to exhibit poor parenting.

DOES NONMARITAL CHILDBEARING HELP REPRODUCE POVERTY?

For nonmarital childbearing to be a mechanism in the reproduction of poverty, it must be both a consequence and a cause of poverty. With respect to the first question, the findings from the Fragile Families and Child Wellbeing Study are consistent with the argument that unmarried mothers come from disadvantaged backgrounds and that low education reduces a mother's chances of forming a stable union after a nonmarital birth. Although attitudes toward marriage and single motherhood also affect union stability, these differences do not negate the fact that factors associated with poverty play an important role in family formation.

With respect to the second condition, the evidence is also consistent with the argument that nonmarital childbearing reduces children's life chances by lowering parental resources and the quality of parenting. Unmarried mothers experience less income growth, more mental health problems, and more maternal stress than married mothers. They also receive less help from the fathers of their children, and they have less access to much-needed social support from family and friends. Each of these factors increases the risk of poor parenting.

Finally, these data highlight the importance of two causal mechanisms in the link between family structure and child outcomes: *partnership instability* and *multipartnered fertility*. Both conditions, which are inevitable consequences of a process in which women have children while they continue to search for a permanent partner, create considerable stress for mothers and children and reduce a mother's prospects of forming a stable union by contributing to jealousy and distrust between parents. Moreover, multipartnered fertility increases the costs of children to fathers and thus reduces their willingness to pay child support (Willis 2000). Finally, by spreading fathers' contributions across multiple households, partnership instability and multipartnered fertility undermine the importance of individual fathers' contributions of time and money to the family economy, which is likely to affect the future marriage expectations of both sons and daughters. In sum, the processes described above have important feedback effects on family formation, which retard upward mobility for children born to disadvantaged parents.

WHAT IS THE SOLUTION?

In his report on the family, Moynihan argued that government policy should be directed toward enhancing the stability and resources of the African American family. Twenty years later, William Julius Wilson (1987) argued that government could strengthen the family by increasing employment opportunities and wages of low-skilled men. For many years, neither message was heeded. Cash and in-kind benefits for poor families were highly income-tested and thus not available to most two-parent families, which created large disincentives for marriage among low-income parents. Moreover, the plight of poor unmarried fathers was virtually ignored except insofar as they were the target of child support enforcement.

Conditions changed in the early 1990s, however, beginning with the rapid expansion of the Earned Income Tax Credit, which represented a substantial earnings subsidy for many two-parent families, and followed up by welfare reform legislation in 1996, which made it harder for a single woman to raise a child alone. Most recently, the federal government has begun funding programs designed to promote marriage by enhancing parents' relationship skills and ability to manage disputes. While some portion of unmarried (and married) couples are likely to benefit from this new initiative, many will need additional help to form stable families, including mental health services, employment services, and help with reentry into their communities after incarceration (Garfinkel and McLanahan 2003).

Most important, none of these programs are likely to have a large effect as long as mothers continue to have children before they find a long-term partner. Although wage subsidies and relationship counseling may ameliorate some of the problems associated with nonmarital childbearing, they are likely to be limited in what they can accomplish. Thus, to break the intergenerational cycle of poverty, we will need to find a way to persuade young women from disadvantaged backgrounds that delaying fertility while they search for a suitable partner will have a payoff that is large enough to offset the loss of time spent as a mother or the possibility of forgoing motherhood entirely.

ENDNOTES

1. Trends—National Center for Health Statistics, http://www.cdc.gov/nchs/data/nvsr/nvsr55/nvsr55_01.pdf.
2. What is new about the current debate is the argument that nonmarital childbearing is *not* a problem but just an alternative family form (Stacey 1998; Coontz 1997). This position is based on the fact that nonmarital childbearing is growing in all Western industrialized countries and that in many countries (e.g., Sweden and France) a large proportion of nonmarital births are to parents in stable cohabiting relationships (Chase-Lansdale, Kiernan, and Friedman 2004).
3. The Fragile Families Study is supported by grants from NICHD and a consortium of private foundations. See http://www.fragilefamilies.princeton.edu/.
4. A fourth question was, "How do policies affect family formation and child well-being?"
5. Thanks to Kevin Bradway and Kate Bartkus for producing these numbers.
6. Sarah Meadows supplied the data.
7. Rebecca Casciano provided these numbers.

■ Review Questions

1. How do the characteristics of unmarried parents and married parents compare?
2. What are the consequences of multipartnered fertility?

Migrant Time versus Child Time

Joanna Dreby

November 2003. I had arranged to meet Ofelia at her home at six o'clock on a November evening. I had known one of Ofelia's brothers and her husband, Ricardo, for years. Among other things, they had both been students in one of my ESL classes. I had never met Ofelia, however, and did not know that she and Ricardo had a son in the coastal town of Las Cruces, Mexico, until I started interviews for this project. On this particular evening, I arrived at Ofelia's house to find that she was out shopping. I sat in the narrow living room making small talk with Ofelia's brother over the cartoons blasting from the TV as a number of family members came and went from the room. Later I learned they were all relatives who shared the small home and that Ricardo had been upstairs the whole time. Throughout this project, most of my contact with his family has occurred through Ofelia and her kin.

After a bit, Ofelia's brother left for his class at the local community college. His wife, Chavela, politely waited with me and told me about what it was like to live in Las Cruces. Chavela was from the northern state of Jalisco but had moved in with Ofelia's mother when she married Ofelia's brother. "I grew up in the city. We weren't rich, but we weren't poor either. There was always enough to eat, and all I had to do as a child was worry about getting up, going to school, and doing my homework. . . . [Ofelia's] family is of a much more humble background. When I first got married, they all said it wouldn't last. But when

Joanna Dreby, "Migrant Time versus Child Time," pp. 38–54 from J. Dreby, *Divided by Borders: Mexican Migrants and Their Children.* Berkeley: University of California Press. 2010. Reprinted by permission.

I went to live in his town, I got along very well with his mother. She is a really patient person. I learned how to cook, make tortillas, and do other things around the house. It was hard, but I learned. And I learned that my husband's family is much more united than my own."

Chavela's description was cut short when Ofelia arrived, lugging Wal-Mart shopping bags. She giggled nervously upon finding me in the living room, excusing herself by saying she had thought the interview was to have been an hour earlier. When I had not appeared, she had gone out to pick up some diapers for her three-year-old daughter. As if in proof, a chubby toddler with messy pigtails trailed in behind her. Ofelia went upstairs to leave her bags. Within minutes of her return, everyone cleared the room to give us privacy.

Ofelia smiled and giggled again. "I have been asking everyone what they think you will ask me about." The laughter seemed a sign of her anxiety about being interviewed. It resurfaced every time we broached an emotionally charged topic. I tried to reassure her and asked simply that she tell me a little bit about how she had come to the United States and about her son who lives in Mexico.

"I came like everyone else," she said, "because there is no work in Mexico. The economic situation is very bad, and I wanted my family to get ahead." She explained that her husband was the first to leave. He worked in Los Angeles for about a year, and Ofelia stayed with her own mother and newborn son in Las Cruces. This was a hard time for Ofelia. "It was really difficult not knowing where he was, since it was the first time we had ever been apart. In Mexico, when the women are washing clothes, they say, 'Watch out, you could be using your husband to wash your clothes.'" She laughed. "You see, since we don't know anything about them when they leave, we joke that they come back as [laundry] soap."

Within a year, Ricardo asked Ofelia to join him. Ofelia was eager to migrate to New Jersey to see the place where her father and brothers had worked for a number of years when she was a teenager. "You see, my father left when I was thirteen. He was in the United States for nine years before he went back. While he was away [and after I married], it was my husband who was really the man of the house there in Mexico, helping out with the work. But just my luck, once I came to the United States, my father returned to Mexico. We crossed paths. I am the only one who doesn't know him. It has been fifteen years now. Oh, how I want to see my father."

According to Ofelia, Ricardo had wanted her to migrate with their only child, Germán. But Ofelia was concerned about where she would live when she got to the United States and who would take care of the two-year-old boy. At the urging of her mother, she left Germán behind and planned to send for him once she settled in the United States.

After Ofelia's arrival in California, the couple moved to central New Jersey to live with Ofelia's siblings. She started working at a factory; it was the first job she had ever had outside her home. "I felt really bad at first, it was like . . ." Ofelia struggled to find the words and instead laughed drily. "But then at the factory where I worked I found out that so many women had their children in Mexico, and then I didn't quite feel so bad, although I still really missed him, especially at the beginning."

"Do you like working?" I asked.

Ofelia answered: "No. If I could, I wouldn't work. I never worked in Mexico except in the house helping my mother out with things. But, you know, when you get older and get married, you need to do things for yourself, for your own family. So, that is why I came to work in the United States."

"Do you think you will miss working if you ever go back to Mexico?"

Again, Ofelia said that the work is not important to her. "It is not the work that people miss back there. It is that [in Mexico] no one pays you to sit around eating all day long. That is what everyone misses when they go back to Mexico, getting a check at the end of the week."

"Every day, everything in Mexico is more and more expensive," she continued. Recently, one of her brothers had returned from visiting Mexico and had told Ofelia that a pair of pants costs between 250 and 300 pesos (roughly twenty-five to thirty U.S. dollars). She was shocked. For this reason, Ofelia explained, she feels satisfied that her earnings in the United States are helping provide for her son's needs. "I know my son is missing the love of a mother. But I also know that he eats well, that he doesn't suffer from hunger, that he has clothes, and that he can study. I know that he is okay."

At the time of the interview, Ofelia had not seen nine-year-old Germán in more than seven years. "I don't have any recent pictures," she explained, "but when I first left, my mother sent me pictures all the time. I watched my son grow up through photographs."

Ofelia said she calls home about once a week. Her son is the only grandchild living with her mother and father, and although she wants to bring him to the United States, she is making no progress toward this goal. She said that Germán did not want to migrate and added that she was reluctant to take him away from her parents. "When I call him, he asks me to come home. But he says he doesn't want to come here, because he doesn't want to leave his mama in Mexico. You see, he calls my mother 'Mama.' But he does – know that I am his mother, because he says so. He says, 'I know you are my mother, but I don't want to leave my mother here.' And I don't want to force him to do something he doesn't want to do, even though I know there are more opportunities here in the United States than in Mexico."

When I interviewed Ofelia, she had recently lost her job at the factory because of a downturn in production. Even though a trip to Mexico would mean a risky border crossing on her return, Ofelia explained that if she did not find another job soon, she wanted to go home for the holidays. If not in December, she would travel back home in May. "Ricardo doesn't want to go home at all, but I do. I cannot wait to go back.

But I would just stay for three months or so. This way I would have time to warm up to my son again so I can bring him back with me."

LIFE WITH GRANDMA AND GRANDPA

October 2004. Ofelia did not go back that year or the next. I first met Germán and his grandparents in 2004, when I visited their family home in Oaxaca. I had vague directions from Ofelia's brother, who had told me I should look for the house across from the basketball court. We first drove by the ice-cream shop and arcade, where a skinny, shirtless boy was hanging out with four older men, and then doubled back after realizing that we had been in the right place and that the young boy must have been Germán. His grandmother, whom I had talked to the day before to confirm my visit, was not there, Germán told us brusquely.

Germán's grandfather, also shirtless and in grubby pants, lay on a *petate* (a woven straw mat) on the dusty floor of the arcade. He instructed Germán to bring us chairs. Once seated, I was uncomfortable, feeling evaluated by these men and unsure what to say. Germán's wary eyes monitored me closely as well. I struggled through the awkward silences in conversation with Germán's grandfather, Don Francisco, who had worked in New Jersey for a number of years.

It was not until my second visit that I fully appreciated Don Francisco's gold-tooth smile when we spoke more comfortably. He described himself as a homebody, explaining that he had spent most of his eight years in the United States either working at an industrial factory job or holed up in his room watching TV. Don Francisco also explained that he was the first in the family to leave for *el norte.* He had been quite successful working abroad. The family used the money he sent home to move from a house in a nearby *rancho* to one he built in the town of Las Cruces. He and his wife were also later able to purchase the store where they currently live. They owned a number of cattle and

also a palm tree grove. "I like life in the United States better than here, because here it is so hot. And there, things are more orderly, and they are cleaner," Don Francisco told me. He came back only because his sons migrated, and once they were no longer in Las Cruces to work his land, it began losing value.

Doña María was more outgoing than the reserved Don Francisco. On subsequent visits she admitted that it had been hard living with Don Francisco again after he came back from the United States. "I didn't get used to it, and I'm still not," she said, laughing. Doña María, a woman filled with an often-contagious exuberance and energy, was well respected in town. She introduced me to the directors at the local schools, all of whom she knew personally, facilitating my research in the schools. On my visit during the town *feria,* a number of indigenous women in town who did not speak Spanish were selling their wares. They all frequented Doña María's shop, because she was one of the few who readily allowed them access to the bathroom and to water.

On that first visit, I learned little directly from Germán, who was then ten years old. He did, however, scoff when I jokingly mentioned expecting to see him in New Jersey in a few years, which suggested he did not expect to join his parents there. He also seemed suspicious of me. On the last day of our visit, when we went to the beach, I mentioned to Doña María that Germán looked more like his father than his mother. Germán looked up from his soda at me warily. "So you really know my dad in the United States?"

"Yeah," I answered. "He was once in my English class and played soccer with some of my friends there."

"And what is his name?" Germán challenged me. He looked rather surprised when I successfully answered "Ricardo."

March 2005. Five months later when I visited, I learned more directly from Germán, who was still playing it cool but was noticeably excited when we arrived. On this visit he warmed up to us considerably, playing affectionately with my son, Temo, and talking more openly with me. He agreed to an interview. When I asked Germán if he remembered living with his parents, he answered, "No, because I was two when they left me."

"Do you remember anything about them?"

"Just from pictures."

"Why do you think they left?" I asked.

"To go where the money is," Germán explained.

Germán said he spoke with his parents often, usually once a week, and that he liked talking with them on the phone. "I mostly [talk] with my mom, not so much with my dad because he works."

"How do you feel when you hang up the phone?"

"Sad . . . because they are on the other side."

Germán told me he wanted his parents to come back to Mexico. When I asked, "Would you like to go over there to be with them?" he answered decidedly, "No, I don't want to go."

"Why not?" I wondered.

"Because it is cold."

"What's that about? When it's cold, you wear gloves, a hat . . ."

"It's just that I am used to living here," Germán explained.

"So you prefer that they come back?"

"Yes."

"And you don't want to go there?"

"Nah, I am all right here with my grandma."

I asked Germán about his sister; other children had complained about their U.S.-born siblings. Germán denied feeling jealous, said he loves his sister, and even talks with her on the phone. He could not tell me how old she was, however, and called in to his grandmother for an answer. I asked him, "Do you feel closer to your mother or your father?"

"Both the same."

"Do you feel like you need your parents, or are you okay the way you are?"

Germán did not hesitate in answering, "I feel like I need them."

"Why?"

"Yes, I need them because they are my parents."

Doña María told me later that Germán did feel uncomfortable about his U.S.-born sister and that this was one reason he did not let his parents send for him and insisted that they come back to Mexico if they wanted to see him. "Once he said to me, Gram, I think my parents love Stacy more than they love me." Doña María confirmed repeatedly on both my visits that Germán did not want to join his parents in the United States. "[Germán] talks to his mother about once a week. You know, they want to take him there. His father says they are ready to send for him. But he doesn't want to go."

I was not sure if Doña María was holding on to Germán. After all, Germán seemed highly affectionate with his grandmother, especially given his rather independent manner. Moreover, Germán seemed to enjoy being the only child in his grandparents' home. Clinging to Germán, however, did not seem to be Doña María's style. Doña María had many friends in town and a clear identity independent of caring for her grandson. She often chatted and joked with those who passed her store and was frequently out doing errands. On a day-to-day basis, she often acted indifferent to Germán, going about her daily routine with little oversight of Germán's activities. For example, during the town *feria*, Doña María was not concerned that the ten-year-old went to the rodeo with some friends. And on the evening of the dance, Germán meticulously ironed his own pants and shirt to get ready to go out on the town. Doña María's hands-off style did not seem to match Ofelia's concerns that her mother would feel lonely and abandoned if Germán left for the states. Wondering about this, I asked Doña María how long she thought the current arrangement would continue. "Of course I will be sad for him to go," she answered. "But I cannot stop it, because they are his parents, and they should be with the boy. I know it is not the same to be [raised] by grandparents as to be with your parents. I am always conscious of this." . . .

THE LONG ROAD TO REUNIFICATION

April 2006. As had been the case since I first met with Ofelia in the fall of 2003, talk of Germán's reunification with his parents continued. Once, when I called Doña María a few months after returning from my visit, Germán answered and chatted away about the party his family threw for his First Communion. "It was a big party. There was a D.J.," he reported eagerly. "My dad said that he would either put [money up] for a D.J. or a cow [to provide the meat for the party], but then my dad put [money] for the D.J. and my grandfather put the cow so I had both." After a bit, Germán asked, "So when are you going to come again so we can go to the beach?"

"I don't know," I explained. "Probably not for a little bit. When are you coming here? I bet you'll come here before I go there."

I was surprised when Germán answered decisively, "April 30th."

"Really?" I asked.

"Yeah, my dad says he is going to send for me. I am going to go with my cousin Trini. Antonio [Chavela's young son and Germán's cousin] is going to go back also."

"Wow."

"But I don't want to go," Germán added, although the excitement in his voice seemed to belie his reluctance.

After we spoke for a bit, Doña María came on the line. We exchanged news, again of the party and also reports on who in the family had been ill. I then added, "So are they really going to send for Germán?"

"His father says that he is going to come back for Germán and take him to the United States. But I don't know. I tell them to wait until he finishes school. You see, now he is in fifth grade, and he just has one more year left to graduate, so I think they should wait until he is done with school."

"Oh. Well, Germán said he is going to come in April," I explained.

Doña María simply laughed and changed the subject.

April came and went. Germán remained with his grandparents. Germán's cousin Trini, a single mother, did migrate to New Jersey and left her three children, then ages four, six, and seven, with Doña María. Although talk of Germán's migration still hung in the air, the next year he went on to the sixth grade in Las Cruces.

May 2007. Exactly one year later, I visited Ofelia, who spoke of her plans to return for Germán over the summer. Although this was only one of many conversations I had had with her about Germán's migration, this time it seemed that a number of factors had converged to make the reunification more likely.

First, Germán would now graduate from the sixth grade, which was the benchmark his grandmother had set for his migration. Second, according to Ofelia, Doña María was overwhelmed with the care of Trini's three children. Trini, now pregnant and living with a new boyfriend in the United States, was not sending enough money to provide for the children properly. Ofelia was providing most of the economic support for their care and had hired a girl locally to help her mother, much to Ricardo's chagrin. "My mother is getting too old to look after these kids; they are all young, not like Germán. And when I left Germán, she wanted me to. That was one of the reasons I left him, to give her company. But these three, they need a lot of work. My mother is getting too tired to look after them."

Not only did the changed circumstances in Las Cruces make Germán's migration seem likely, but Ofelia and Ricardo's economic situation seemed to have improved markedly since I had last seen them. They now rented a three-bedroom apartment on the outskirts of the city, which they shared with just one young woman. The living room was furnished with a new white sofa and love seat (covered in plastic to protect against spills), a large TV, and a bookshelf displaying pictures of the family. I looked over the framed pictures of Germán as a little boy, and Ofelia pointed out the pictures of her, Ricardo, and their daughter, Stacy, from their vacation the summer before. Ofelia had a new job with benefits, including a yearly two-week vacation, which they used for the first time to go away to Virginia Beach. Both Ofelia and Ricardo owned vans they drove to work, providing rides for coworkers at the going rate of twenty-five dollars per week per person, which augmented the family income. When I asked if they planned to have more children, Ofelia gave a decisive no. "When they are little, it is so hard economically. I didn't work for two years to stay with Stacy, and we only had Ricardo's [income]. But now she is in school, and I can work too. We are much better off. No, it is too hard when they are little. Two are enough for me."

Aside from the improvements in Ofelia and Ricardo's economic situation, Ofelia explained that she now had a concrete plan for bringing Germán back with her to the United States. She had finally caught up with the woman who had helped the family cross the first time. The expense would be great, two thousand dollars more than it would have cost ten years earlier, but she and Ricardo felt it was worth it. Over the summer they hoped to take Stacy back to Mexico, so she could meet her grandparents for the first time. If all went according to plan, the family would be living together in New Jersey by September.

As I was leaving Ofelia's house that afternoon, I admired a wall hanging I had overlooked earlier. It was a painted family portrait, depicting Ofelia and Ricardo at the center and Stacy just below them. Never forgotten, Germán was in the portrait as well. Ofelia explained that they had had a photograph sent so the artist could add him to the painting. Although recognizable, it showed Germán as he must have looked years before I had met him. The two siblings looked at most a year apart in age, while there is actually seven years between them. The wall-hanging captured the time disparities that governed the family's memories and realities: American-born Stacy had an up-to-date portrait, as did the parents who stood with her, while Germán was incorporated into the family as he had been years before.

PARALYSIS

What accounts for the dynamic between Germán and Ofelia, which led to indefinite postponement of their reunion? It is possible that caregivers in Mexico, in this case Doña María, resist family reunification so they can continue to garner economic support from parents' migration. Grandparents do rely on the remittances of their migrant children and develop close emotional bonds with their grandchildren while parents are away. Yet caregivers are not responsible for preventing the reunification of parents and children. Caregivers, in fact, respect the priority of parent-child bonds: They often reinforce these ties, and the obligations they entail, as did Doña María when she told me in front of Germán that she had to go to his Communion class because his mother was not there to go. If the prolonged separation of mother and child did not result from the grandparents' wishes, why did it occur?

Ofelia and Germán's standoff arose in part from differences in how family members perceived each other over the passage of time. For Ofelia, Germán remained a young boy bonded with his grandmother, even while her own life changed radically with the birth of another child and the work required of her and her husband to create an economic foothold in New Jersey. For the grandmother, another year or two in her care were worth it if Germán could reach a more natural stopping point at his local school. And for Germán himself, time brought big changes in both his feelings and his understanding of his situation.

From Germán's perspective, and that of other children like him, migrant parents are a presence even when physically absent. Germán felt that his parents were important to him, and he knew that they should provide and care for him. He felt resentful that they left him and now gave more attention to his U.S.-born sister. At the same time, Germán understood that they had migrated out of economic necessity and, in part, to support him. He liked living with his grandparents and in Las Cruces; in fact, that was the only life he knew. In essence, he did not want his life to change drastically, except that he would like his parents to return to show they care. With each passing year, the ways Germán communicated these mixed emotions to the adults in his life changed. Germán's jeers at my suggestions that I would soon see him in New Jersey gave way, within a little more than a year, to his boasts that he would soon be in the United States, even if against his will. More recently, Germán left school in Mexico and more wholeheartedly accepted the idea of coming north. As for children anywhere, each year brought developmental and emotional changes, and those changes affected his interpretation of his parents' sacrifice.

But for parents, the gains won each year as a migrant come painfully slowly. Stability in housing and employment may take years to achieve. Migrants invest huge amounts of energy and resources to carve out successful lives in U.S. cities. These investments made it hard for Ofelia and Ricardo to return for Germán, as he wanted them to do. They had to weigh the cost and the risk of doing so. They had to consider that Ofelia's family in Mexico depended on remittances from the United States and that their standard of living would fall if Ofelia went back. Moreover, Ofelia had a strong link to New Jersey through her U.S.-born daughter. If she returned to Las Cruces and had trouble crossing the border on her return, who would look after Stacy during her absence? What would happen if she could not return? Ofelia reasoned that she might convince Germán to join them if she could spend some time with him, but the danger of the border crossing made a short return visit a great risk. It would also be extremely costly and would require economic stability that Ofelia and Ricardo were unable to achieve until Stacy started kindergarten and they both were working full time and did not have to pay for child care. Like Germán, Ofelia felt conflicted in deciding

on her best course of action. As a migrant father explained to me, "Sometimes, Joanna, you simply cannot have everything you want at once."

Over time, parents become more engrossed—and invested—in their lives in the United States and even more conscious of the rising price of having left their children. Trapped by the lifestyle they adopt in the United States, scheduled almost entirely around the workweek, parents worry about their relationships with their children. Being absorbed by work at the expense of the family is not a novel concept. Working parents in the United States may have similar reactions of being in a "time bind."[1] Yet the physical distance considerably increases the dissonance between the pace of parents' lives at work and the pace of the lives of their children at home.[2] One migrant father's comment summarizes the effects of migrant parents' unique time bind on relationships with children whom they do not get to see at the end of each day:

> For a time, the phone works wonders. It is like your weapon, your love, your everything, because you talk, you listen; it's everything. But after a time, you lose that passion of talking. You lose that dream of waiting for Sunday to call your kids and talk to them. Why? Because you realize that it starts becoming ordinary. . . . Instead of seeing it as [a means of] affection, love for your children and to your family in Mexico, it becomes ordinary, like a line you have to follow. And you just don't feel the same anymore. . . .
>
> The distance makes you forget, it makes you lose something, it makes you . . . How can I explain? It makes it so that the affection, that which was love, becomes almost ordinary. It becomes commercial. Why? Because you only think about working, sending money, and that they [the kids] are okay over there. . . .[It is routine] because you cannot enjoy what you sent and take your child out to eat, take him on an outing, or buy him some clothes. All of this makes it so that you forget what the love of your child is like.

Conflicting emotions that result from the passage of time at different paces in different places often prolong periods of separation. Ironically, it is also the passage of time that can resolve standoffs between parents and children, like the one between Ofelia and Germán. Because parents and children have few opportunities for interaction, they do not have the ability to negotiate small solutions to their difficulties. They must wait for a combination of factors to converge, including economic stability, opportunity, and the willingness of children to migrate, in order to plan a reunification. In some cases, parents and children are reunited within a few years. In other cases, as for Ofelia and Germán, reunification is delayed for most or all of a child's childhood.

ENDNOTES

1. Hochschild 1997.
2. Scholars assert that the dissonance between work time and family time causes tensions in families and that those with few resources experience different time pressures than do those with more resources (Hochschild 1997 and Roy, Tubbs, and Burton 2004). Research also suggests that children and adults have different perceptions of family time owing to their relative position in the family (Daly 2001 and Thorpe and Daly 1999). Parents and children divided by borders experience dissonance to a greater degree than any of these families because of the very few resources available to them, the socioeconomic differences between the geographic locations in which parents and children live, and the effects that physical distance may have on relationships.

■ Review Questions

1. Why had Ofelia stayed in the United States during most of her son Germán's childhood?
2. Why did Germán have mixed feelings about reuniting with his parents in the United States?

CHAPTER 10

Older People and Their Families

Many observers of the changing lives of children have concluded that the family is in crisis. The litany is familiar: more divorce, more stepfamilies, more childbearing outside of marriage, more day care, more sex and violence in the media, and so forth. Even commentators who disagree with this position feel compelled to explain why divorce, day care, and so on don't have the negative effects that one might expect. In other words, when you look at the family from the vantage point of its youngest members, the changes that occurred during the last half of the twentieth century seem problematic.

But when you look at families from the vantage point of their oldest members, the picture is quite different. The changes that occurred in the lives of older people in the last half of the twentieth century were generally positive: longer life expectancy, higher incomes, and greater independence. The better health and greater affluence of older people has allowed them to lead independent lives while still retaining frequent contact with their children and grandchildren—a style of life both older people and their children, for the most part, preferred.

Yet when a family crisis arises, older people are often willing and able to help. In fact, gerontologist Vern L. Bengtson argues that the great social changes in American families over the past several decades have increased the importance of multigenerational bonds in family life—a trend he thinks will continue in the early twenty-first century. Longer lives and better health for older people, he notes, mean more shared years of life for grandparents, parents, and children. The increases in divorce and in childbearing outside marriage have lessened the importance of the nuclear family, he maintains, and have made parents more reliant on their own aging parents.

Not everyone agrees with Bengtson—his scenario may be a bit too rosy. But it is an interesting and provocative argument. In the first reading in this chapter, Bengtson presents his case.

One place where multigenerational bonds would be expected to dominate family life is the inner city, where marriage has declined among low-income minority populations. Because of divorce and childbearing outside marriage, there are relatively few nuclear families. Instead, many middle-aged grandmothers are deeply involved in their young grandchildren's lives. But what happens to these grandmothers later in life when they are old and need care and companionship? What happens to self-reliant women when their health begins to fail? And who will care for older men who, in many cases, have lived apart from their children for decades?

Katherine S. Newman sought answers to these questions by returning to some of the same inner-city neighborhoods—and some of the same people—she had observed in her earlier book *No Shame in My Game.* In her more recent book, *A Different Shade of Gray,* excerpted here, she writes about the family lives of inner-city adults in late midlife and old age.

READING 10-1

Beyond the Nuclear Family

The Increasing Importance of Multigenerational Bonds

Vern L. Bengtson

During the past decade, sociologists have been engaged in an often heated debate about family change and family influences in contemporary society. This debate in many ways reflects the legacy of Ernest W. Burgess (1886–1965), the pioneer of American family sociology. It can be framed in terms of four general hypotheses, each of which calls attention to significant transitions in the structure and functions of families over the 20th century.

The first and earliest hypothesis concerns the *emergence of the "modern" nuclear family form* following the Industrial Revolution. This transition (suggested by Burgess in 1916 and elaborated by Ogburn, 1932, and Parsons, 1944) proposed that the modal structure of families had changed from extended to nuclear, and its primary functions had changed from social-institutional to emotional-supportive. The second hypothesis concerns the *decline of the modern nuclear family* as a social institution, a decline said to be attributable to the fact that its structure has been truncated (because of high divorce rates) and its functions further reduced (Popenoe, 1993). A third hypothesis can be termed the *increasing heterogeneity of family forms,* relations that extend beyond biological or conjugal relationship boundaries. Growing from the work of feminist scholars (Coontz, 1991; Skolnick, 1991; Stacey, 1990), and research on racial and ethnic minority families

(Burton, 1995; Collins, 1990; Stack, 1974), this perspective suggests that family structures and relationships should be redefined to include both "assigned" and "created" kinship systems (Cherlin, 1999). I suggest a fourth hypothesis for consideration: the *increasing importance of multigenerational bonds.* I propose that relations across more than two generations are becoming increasingly important to individuals and families in American society; that they are increasingly diverse in structure and functions; and that in the early 21st century, these multigenerational bonds will not only enhance but in some cases replace nuclear family functions, which have been so much the focus of sociologists during the 20th century.

In this reading, I first summarize the "Burgess legacy" in American family sociology and relate it to the four hypotheses summarized above. Then I suggest some foundations for my hypotheses concerning the increasing importance and diversity of multigenerational relationships, starting from a discussion of macrosocial trends (population aging and intergenerational family demography) and moving to micro-social dimensions (solidarity and types of cross-generational relationships). I conclude with some suggestions about future research that will be needed to examine further the role of multigenerational bonds in 21st century society.

THE BURGESS LEGACY: AS FAMILIES HAVE CHANGED, HAVE THEY DECLINED IN IMPORTANCE? . . .

The Emergence of the "Modern" Nuclear Family Form

Burgess' groundbreaking analyses of the American family started from a consideration of macrosocial trends brought about by the Industrial Revolution and continued with his exploration of the microsocial dynamics within families. One of his earliest concerns was the family as an aspect of social organization in the context of social evolution. His first book (Burgess, 1916) would today

Vern L. Bengtson, "Beyond the Nuclear Family: The Increasing Importance of Multigenerational Bonds,"*Journal of Marriage and Family* 63 (February 2001), pp. 1–16. Reprinted by permission.

be regarded as a polemic in support of the traditional extended family and its functions because he argued that this family form was necessary for the socialization of children if social evolution were to continue. Within the next decade, however, he shifted his perspective. From the structural "functions" of families applied to the modernizing societies of the early 20th century, he turned to an emphasis on family members' "interactions."

Burgess' hypothesis was that families had changed. He broke from late-19th-century views of the extended family structure as the bedrock of social organization and progress to say, "The family in historical times has been, and at present is, in transition from an institution to a companionship" (Burgess, 1926, p. 104). He focused on the nuclear family and its changing functions as the consequence of industrialization and modernization, arguments echoed later by Ogburn (1932), Davis (1941), and Parsons (1944). His thesis was that urbanization, increased individualism and secularism, and the emancipation of women had transformed the family from a social institution based on law and custom to one based on companionship and love.

Burgess advanced his position very quietly in a number of scholarly journal publications. These appeared to have escaped notice by the popular press at that time, quite unlike today's debates about the family. He argued that the family had become more specialized in its functions and that structural and objective aspects of family life had been supplanted by more emotional and subjective functions. This he termed the "companionship" basis of marriage, which he suggested had become the underlying basis of the "modern" family form.

But Burgess went further. He proposed that the most appropriate way to conceptualize and study the family was as "a unity of interacting personalities" (Burgess, 1926). By this he meant three things: First, "the family" is essentially a *process,* an interactional system influenced by each of its members; it is not merely a *structure,* or a household. Second, the behaviors of one family member—a troubled child, a detached father—could not be understood except in *relationship* to other family members, their ongoing patterns of interactions, and personalities developing and changing through such interactions. This conceptualization provided the intellectual basis for the first marriage and family counseling programs in the United States. Third, the central *functions* of families had changed from being primarily structural units of social organization to being relationships supporting individuals' needs. Marriage was transformed from a primarily economic union to one based on sentiment and companionship.

Thus, Burgess represented a bridge between 19th-century conceptions of the family as a unit in social evolution to 20th-century ideas of families as supporting individuals' needs. His work also provided a bridge in sociological theory, from structural-functionalism to symbolic interactionism and phenomenology. But in all this, Burgess' focus was on the nuclear family, a White, middle-class, two-generation family; and the family forms emerging in the 21st century will, as I argue below, look much different than the family that Burgess observed.

The Decline of the Modern Nuclear Family Form

The "decline of the family" in American society is a theme that has become the focus of increasingly heated debates by politicians, pundits, and family sociologists during the last decade. David Popenoe (1993), the most articulate proponent of this position, has argued that there has been a striking decline in the family's structure and functions in American society, particularly since 1960. Moreover, his hypothesis is that recent family decline is "more serious" than any decline in the past, because "what is breaking up is the nuclear family, the fundamental unit stripped of relations and left with two essential functions that cannot be performed better elsewhere: child-rearing and the provision to its members of affection and companionship" (Popenoe, p. 527).

Supporters of the family decline hypothesis have focused on the negative consequences of changing family structure, resulting from divorce and single parenting, on the psychological, social, and economic well-being of children. Furthermore, they suggest that social norms legitimating the pursuit of individual over collective goals and the availability of alternate social groups for the satisfaction of basic human needs have substantially weakened the social institution of the family as an agent of socialization and as a source of nurturance for family members (Popenoe).

There is much to support Popenoe's hypothesis. There has been a significant change in nuclear family structure over the past 50 years, starting with the growing divorce rate in the 1960s, which escalated to over half of first marriages in the 1980s (Amato & Booth, 1997; Bumpass, Sweet, & Martin, 1990). There also has been an increase in single-parent families, accompanied by an increase in poverty for the children living in mother-headed families (McLanahan, 1994). The absence of fathers in many families today has created problems for the economic and emotional well-being of children (Popenoe, 1996).

At the same time, the "family decline" hypothesis is limited, and to some critics flawed, by its preoccupation with the family as a coresident household and the nuclear family as its primary representation. Popenoe defined the family as "a relatively small domestic group of kin (or people in a kinlike relationship) consisting of at least one adult and one dependent person" (Popenoe, 1993, p. 529). Although this might be sufficient as a demographic definition of a "family household," it does not include important aspects of family functions that extend beyond boundaries of coresidence. There is nothing in Popenoe's hypothesis to reflect the function of multigenerational influences on children—the role of grandparents in socializing or supporting grandchildren, particularly after the divorce of middle-generation parents (Johnson & Barer, 1987; Minkler & Rowe, 1993). Nor is there any mention of what Riley and Riley (1993) have called the "latent matrix of kin

connections," a web of "continually shifting linkages that provide the potential for activating and intensifying close kin relationships" in times of need by family members (Riley & Riley, p. 169). And there is no consideration of the longer years of shared lives between generations, now extending into many decades, and their consequences for the emotional and economic support for family members across several generations (Bengtson & Allen, 1993; Silverstein & Litwak, 1993).

The Increasing Heterogeneity of Family Forms

A third hypothesis has been generated by feminist scholars (Coontz, 1991; Osmond & Thorne, 1993; Skolnick, 1991; Stacey, 1993, 1996; Thorne & Yalom, 1992) and researchers studying minority families (Burton, 1995; Collins, 1990; Stack, 1974). This hypothesis can be summarized as follows: Families are changing in both forms and meanings, expanding beyond the nuclear family structure to involve a variety of kin and nonkin relationships. Diverse family forms are emerging, or at least being recognized for the first time, including the matriarchal structure of many African American families. Stacey (1996) argued that the traditional nuclear family is increasingly ill-suited for a postindustrial, postmodern society. Women's economic and social emancipation over the past century has become incongruent with the nuclear "male breadwinner" family form and its traditional allocation of power, resources, and labor. We have also seen a normalization of divorce and of stepparenting in recent years. Many American families today are what Ahrons (1994) has described as "binuclear." Following divorce and remarriage of the original marital partners and parents, a stable, child-supportive family context may emerge. Finally, because some four million children in the United States are being raised by lesbian or gay parents (Stacey & Biblarz, 2001), these and other alternative family forms "are here . . . and let's get used to it!" (Stacey, 1996, p. 105).

In responding to Popenoe, Stacey (1996) argued that the family is indeed in decline—if what we mean by "family" is the nuclear form of dad, mom, and their biological or adopted kids. This form of the family rose and fell with modern industrial society. In the last few decades, with the shift to a postindustrial domestic economy within a globalized capitalist system and with the advent of new reproductive technologies, the modern family system has been replaced by what Stacey has called "the postmodern family condition," a pluralistic, fluid, and contested domain in which diverse family patterns, values, and practices contend for legitimacy and resources. Stacey suggested that family diversity and fluidity are now "normal," and the postmodern family condition opens the possibility of egalitarian, democratic forms of intimacy, as well as potentially threatening levels of insecurity.

The Increasing Importance of Multigenerational Bonds

I want to suggest a fourth hypothesis about family transitions during the 20th century that builds on those of Burgess, Popenoe, Stack, and Stacey but reflects the recent demographic development of much greater longevity. It is this: *Relations across more than two generations are becoming increasingly important to individuals and families in American society.* Considering the dramatic increase in life expectancy over the past half century, this is not a particularly radical departure from conventional wisdom. But I suggest a corollary to this hypothesis, which I hope will lead to spirited debate: *For many Americans, multigenerational bonds are becoming more important than nuclear family ties for well-being and support over the course of their lives.*

I will attempt to provide a foundation for this hypothesis in the remainder of this article. First, I argue that changes in intergenerational demography (changing societal and family age structures, creating longer years of "shared lives") have resulted in increased opportunities—and needs—for interaction, support, and mutual influence across more than just two generations. Second, I will note the strength of intergenerational

solidarity over time and the diversity of cross-generational types. Third, because the increase in marital instability and divorce over the last several decades has weakened the ability of nuclear families to provide the socialization, nurturance, and support needed by family members, I argue that kin across several generations will increasingly be called upon to provide these essential family functions in 21st-century society.

THE MACROSOCIOLOGY OF INTERGENERATIONAL RELATIONSHIPS

The demographic structure of American families has changed significantly in recent years. We hear most about two trends: The increase in divorce rates since the 1960s, with one out of two first marriages ending in divorce (Cherlin, 1992); and the increasing number of children living in single-parent households, often accompanied by poverty (McLanahan & Sandefur, 1994; Walker & McGraw, 2000). But there is a third trend that has received much less attention: The increased longevity of family members and the potential resource this represents for the well-being of younger generations in the family.

Multigenerational Family Demography: From Pyramids to Beanpoles

First consider how much the age structure of the U.S. population has changed over the past 100 years. Treas (1995b) provided a valuable overview of these changes and their consequences for families. In 1900, the shape of the American population structure by age was that of a pyramid, with a large base (represented by children under age 5) progressively tapering into a narrow group of those aged 65 and older. This pyramid characterized the shape of the population structure by age in most human societies on record, from the dawn of civilization through the early Industrial Revolution and into the early 20th century (Laslett, 1976; Myers, 1990). But by 1990, the age pyramid for American society had come to look more like an irregular triangle.

By 2030, it will look more like a rectangle, with strikingly similar numbers in each age category starting from children and adolescents through those above the age of 60. The story here is that because of increases in longevity and decreases in fertility, the population age structure of the United States, like most industrialized societies, has changed from a pyramid to a rectangle in just over a century of human historical experience.

Second, consider the implications of these macrosocietal changes in age distribution for the generational structure of families in American society. At the same time, there have been increases in life expectancy over the 20th century, decreases in fertility have occurred, and the population birthrate has decreased from 4.1 in 1900 to 1.9 in 1990 (Cherlin, 1999). This means that the age structure of most American families has changed from a pyramid to what might be described as a "beanpole" (Bengtson, Rosenthal, & Burton, 1990), a family structure in which the shape is long and thin, with more family generations alive but with fewer members in each generation. Whether the "beanpole" structure adequately describes a majority of families today has been debated (Farkas & Hogan, 1995; Treas, 1995a). Nevertheless, the changes in demographic distribution by age since 1900 are remarkable, and the progression "from pyramids to beanpoles" has important implications for family functions and relationships into the 21st century.

The Changing "Kin Supply" Structure across Generations What might be lost in a review of macrosocial demographic trends are the consequences for individual family members and their chances of receiving family support. For example, the "family decline" hypothesis of Popenoe (1993) suggests that U.S. children are at greater risk today because of the breakdown of the nuclear family structure and the too-frequent disappearance of fathers. The decrease in mortality rates over the last century suggests a more optimistic story, however: The increasing availability of extended intergenerational kin

(grandparents, great-grandparents, uncles, and aunts) has become a resource for children as they grow up and move into young adulthood.

Peter Uhlenberg (1996) examined the profound effects that mortality changes over the 20th century have had on the "supply" of kin available for support of family members in American society. He noted that for children born in 1900, the chances of being an orphan (both parents dying before the child reached age 18) were 18%. But for children born in 2000, 68% will have four *grand*parents still living by the time they reach 18. Further along the life course, by the time these children are themselves facing the responsibilities of rearing children, the effects of mortality declines on the availability of older kin for support are even more substantial. For those born in 1900, by age 30 only 21% had *any* grandparent still living. For those born in 2000, by age 30, 76% will still have at least one grandparent alive. Today it is more likely that 20-year-olds will have a grandmother still living (91%) than 20-year-olds alive in 1900 had a mother still living (83%; Uhlenberg).

Another perspective on this issue is provided by Wachter (1997) in computer simulations about availability of kin for 21st-century family members. He examined implications of longevity, fertility, and divorce for the future. He noted that although low fertility rates in the late 20th century will lead to a shortage of kin for those reaching retirement around 2030, the effects of divorce, remarriage, and family blending are expanding the numbers and types of stepkin, "endowing the elderly of the future with kin networks that are at once problematic, rich, and varied" (Wachter). The implication is that stepkin are increasing the kin supply across generations, becoming potential sources of nurture and support for family members in need, and that this may compensate, in part, for lower fertility rates (Amato & Booth, 1997).

Longer Years of "Shared Lives" across Generations Other implications of these demographic changes over the 20th century should be noted. First, we now have more years of "cosurvivorship between generations" than ever before in human history (Bengtson, 1996; Goldscheider, 1990). This means that more and more aging parents and grandparents are available to provide for family continuity and stability across time (Silverstein, Giarrusso, & Bengtson, 1998). This also means a remarkable increase in multigenerational kin representing a "latent network" (Riley & Riley, 1993) who can be activated to provide support and well-being for younger family members. The increased longevity of parents, grandparents, great-grandparents, and other older family members in recent decades represents a resource of kin available for help and support that can be, and frequently is, activated in times of need (King, 1994; Silverstein, Parrott, & Bengtson, 1995). These older kin will also be in better health (Hayward & Heron, 1999).

At the same time, there are potentially negative consequences of the "longer years of shared lives" across generations. One involves protracted years of caregiving for dependent elders (Bengtson, Rosenthal, & Burton, 1995). A second involves protracted conflict—what an 84-year-old mother in the Longitudinal Study of Generations termed a "life-long lousy parent-child relationship." Family researchers have not adequately addressed intergenerational conflicts throughout the adult years (Clarke, Preston, Raskin, & Bengtson, 1999). Because of longer years of shared lives, intergenerational relationships—in terms of help given or received, solidarity or conflict or both—will be of increasing importance for family life in the future.

Finally, to the story of multigenerational family demography and its changes over the 21st century must be added a recognition of "alternative family forms," reflected in gay and lesbian couples raising children (Kurdek & Schmidt, 1987), never-married singles and couples raising children (Smock & Manning, 1997), and other nonbiological but socially significant family forms. We know little about the intergenerational relationships of these variations beyond the White, middle-class, two-generation household

in America today. What they represent in "latent kin support networks" or "cosurvivorship across generations" must be a focus of future research.

When Parenting Goes across Several Generations

A function not addressed by Burgess was the importance of grandparents to family members' well-being, an understandable oversight given the historical period when he was writing, when the expected life span of individuals was almost 3 decades shorter than today. Popenoe (1993) also did not discuss the importance of grandparents in the potential support they represent for younger generation members.

Grandparents provide many unacknowledged functions in contemporary families (Szinovacz, 1998). They are important role models in the socialization of grandchildren (Elder, Rudkin, & Conger, 1994; King & Elder, 1997). They provide economic resources to younger generation family members (Bengtson & Harootyan, 1994). They contribute to cross-generational solidarity and family continuity over time (King, 1994; Silverstein et al., 1998). They also represent a bedrock of stability for teenage moms raising infants (Burton & Bengtson, 1985).

Perhaps most dramatic is the case in which grandparents (or great-grandparents) are raising grandchildren (or great-grandchildren). Over four million children under age 18 are living in a grandparent's household. Frequently this is because these childrens' parents are incapacitated (by imprisonment, drug addiction, violence, or psychiatric disorders) or unable to care for their offspring without assistance (Minkler & Rowe, 1993). Research by Harris (2000) indicates that about 20,000 children in Los Angeles County alone are now the responsibility of grandparents or great-grandparents because of recent court decisions concerning the parents' lack of competence. In Harris' study, one grandmother had been assigned by the court as guardian to 13 of her grandchildren, born to two of her daughters, each of whom had been repeatedly imprisoned on crack cocaine charges (Harris & Pedersen, 1997). Similar instances are related by Minkler and Rowe in their study of crack-addicted parents in the San Francisco area.

When Parents Divorce and Remarry, Divorce and Remarry

The rising divorce rate over the last half of the 20th century has generated much concern about the fate of children (McLanahan & Sandefur, 1994). The probability that a marriage would end in divorce doubled between the 1960s and the 1970s, and half of all marriages since the late 1970s ended in divorce (Cherlin, 1992). About 40% of American children growing up in the 1980s and 1990s experienced the breakup of their parents' marriages (Bengtson, Rosenthal, & Burton, 1995; Furstenberg & Cherlin, 1991), and a majority of these also experienced their parents' remarriage and the challenges of a "blended family."

In the context of marital instability, the breakup of nuclear families, and the remarriage of parents, it is clear that grandparents and step-grandparents are becoming increasingly important family connections (Johnson & Barer, 1987). Two-fifths of divorced mothers move during the first year of the divorce (McLanahan, 1983), and most of these move in with their parents while they make the transition to single parenting (Goldscheider & Goldscheider, 1993).

When Help Flows across Generations, It Flows Mostly Downward

An unfortunate stereotype of the older generation today is of "greedy geezers" who are spending their children's inheritance on their own retirement pleasures (Bengtson, 1993). This myth is not in accord with the facts. Intergenerational patterns of help and assistance flow mostly from the older generations to younger generations in the family. For example, McGarry and Schoeni (1995) have shown that almost one-third of U.S. parents gave a gift of $500 or more to at least one of their adult children during the past year;

however, only 9% of adult children report providing $500 to their aging parents. Similar results are reported by Bengtson and Harootyan (1994) and Soldo and Hill (1993).

Silverstein et al. (1995) noted that intergenerational support patterns ebb and flow over time. Multigenerational families represent "latent kin networks" of support (Riley & Riley, 1993) that often are enacted only in times of crisis. This is similar to Hagestad's (1996) notion of elders as the "Family National Guard": Although remaining silent and unobserved for the most part, grandparents (and great-grandparents) muster up and march out when an emergency arises regarding younger generation members' well-being.

THE MICROSOCIOLOGY OF INTERGENERATIONAL RELATIONSHIPS

Although there have been important changes in the demography of intergenerational relationships since the 19th century, population statistics about family and household structure tell only one part of the story. At the behavioral level, these changes have more immediate consequences in the ways family members organize their lives and pursue their goals in the context of increasing years of intergenerational "shared lives." How to conceptualize and measure these intergenerational interactions has become increasingly important since Burgess (1926) put forth his definition of the family as "a unity of interacting personalities."

The Solidarity Model: Dimensions of Intergenerational Relationships

In discussing these social-psychological approaches to intergenerational relations, I should first identify the study from which my colleagues and I have examined them, the Longitudinal Study of Generations (LSOG). This study began as a cross-sectional survey of more than 2,044 three-generational family members, sampled from more than 840,000 members of the primary HMO serving Southern California at that time (see Bengtson,

1975 and 1996, for details of the sampling procedures). It has continued as a longitudinal study with data collected at 3-year intervals, adding the great-grandchild generation in 1991.

A concern in the LSOG since it began 3 decades ago has been the conceptualization and measurement of intergenerational relationships. We use the theoretical construct of *intergenerational solidarity* as a means to characterize the behavioral and emotional dimensions of interaction, cohesion, sentiment, and support between parents and children, grandparents and grandchildren, over the course of long-term relationships. We define six conceptual dimensions of intergenerational solidarity (Bengtson & Mangen, 1988; Bengtson & Schrader, 1982; Roberts, Richards, & Bengtson, 1991).

1. Affectual solidarity: the sentiments and evaluations family members express about their relationship with other members (How close do you feel to your father or mother? How well do you get along with your child or grandchild? How much affection do you feel from them?)
2. Associational solidarity: the type and frequency of contact between intergenerational family members
3. Consensual solidarity: agreement in opinions, values, and orientations between generations
4. Functional solidarity (assistance): the giving and receiving of support across generations, including exchange of both instrumental assets and services as well as emotional support
5. Normative solidarity: expectations regarding filial obligations and parental obligations, as well as norms about the importance of familistic values
6. Structural solidarity: the "opportunity structure" for cross-generational interaction reflecting geographic proximity between family members

The theoretical rationale for these six dimensions and the adequacy (or limitations) of their measurement in survey research have been described at length in a volume by Mangen, Bengtson, and Landry (1988) and in subsequent articles (Roberts & Bengtson, 1990; Roberts et al., 1991; Silverstein et al., 1995). The solidarity paradigm has proven useful in research by other investigators (Amato & Booth, 1997; Lee, Netzer, & Coward, 1994; Marshall, Matthews, & Rosenthal, 1993; Rossi & Rossi, 1990). It can be seen as exemplifying an operational definition of the life course theoretical perspective (Bengtson & Allen, 1993; Elder, Rudkin, & Conger, 1994).

The Strength of Intergenerational Relationships Over Time

Using longitudinal data from the LSOG, we have been able to chart the course of intergenerational solidarity dimensions over time. Our design allows consideration of the development and aging of each of the three and now four generations in our sample, as well as the sociohistorical context of family life as it has changed over the years of the study (Bengtson et al., 2002).

One consistent result concerns the high levels of affectual solidarity (reflecting the emotional bonds between generations) that have been found over six times of measurement, from 1971 to 1997 (Bengtson et al., 2000). Three things should be noted. We find that the average solidarity scores between grandparents and parents, parents and youth, grandparents and grandchildren are high, considerably above the expected midpoint of the scale. Second, these scores are remarkably stable over the 26 years of measurement; there are no statistically significant differences by time of measurement, and the scores are correlated over time between .5 and .8. Third, there is a "generational bias" in these reports: Parents consistently report higher affect than their children do over time, as do grandparents compared with grandchildren. This supports the "intergenerational stake" hypothesis first proposed 30 years ago (Bengston & Kuypers, 1971; Giarrusso, Stallings, & Bengtson, 1995). The older generation has a greater psychosocial investment, or "stake," in their joint relationship than does their younger generation, and this influences their perceptions and evaluations of their common intergenerational relationships.

These results indicate the high level of emotional bonding across generations and the considerable stability of parent-child affectual relationships over long periods of time.

At the same time, it should be noted that not all intergenerational relationships display such high levels of emotional closeness. We find that about one in five relationships are characterized by either significant conflict (Clarke et al., 1999) or detachment. . . .

The Effects of Changing Family Forms on Intergenerational Influence

Situating multigenerational families in sociohistorical context allows us to broaden our inquiry about their importance and functionality. How have intergenerational influences changed over recent historical time? Are families still important in shaping the developmental outcomes of its youth? What have been the effects of changing family structures and roles, the consequences of divorce and maternal employment, on intergenerational influences? We used the 30-year LSOG to explore these issues.

An important feature of the LSOG is that enough time has elapsed since its start in 1971 that the ages at which members of different generations were assessed have begun to overlap. This provides what we call a generation-sequential design. A limitation of existing data sets has been that researchers could not track changes across generations within specific families over decades of time, nor draw conclusions about the relationship between historical change in family structures and intergenerational influence and socialization outcomes. The LSOG is unique because of its accumulation of parallel longitudinal assessments for multiple generations within the same families in different historical periods.

Within a life course framework that focuses on the interplay of macroeconomic and microrelational processes, Bengtson, Biblarz, and Roberts (2002) examined the development and cultivation of youth's achievement orientations: Their educational and occupation career aspirations, their

values, and their self-esteem. Achievement orientations are viewed as personal attributes that may be passed down, or "transmitted," from generation to generation in families, promoting continuity over multiple generational lines across many decades of history. We also know that parent-child affectual bonds can mediate this process. It is therefore useful to study these intergenerational transmission processes. In so doing, we can empirically examine the hypotheses concerning family decline or intergenerational family importance and diversity.

Our analysis (Bengtson et al., 2002) contrasted the achievement orientations of Generation X youth (18- to 22-year-olds) today with their baby-boomer parents when they were about the same age in 1971. We know that Generation Xers have grown up in families that were quite different in structure than their parents' families were. How has this affected their achievement orientations: their aspirations, values, and self-esteem?

Figure 10.1 illustrates just how different the family context of these two successive generations has been. Generation Xers were much more likely than their baby-boomer parents to have grown up in a family with less than two siblings, with a father and mother who were college graduates, with a mother who was working full time, and, above all, in a divorced household (40% for Generation Xers, 20% for their baby boomer parents). Given these differences, how do the two generations compare in terms of family solidarity and achievement orientations?

Our analysis suggests that today's Generation Xers are surprisingly similar to what their baby-boomer parents were on these measures at the same age, almost 30 years ago. This suggests that despite changes in family structure and socioeconomic context, intergenerational influences on youths' achievement orientations remain strong. Generation Xers whose parents divorced were slightly less advantaged in terms of achievement orientations than Generation Xers who came from nondivorced families but were nevertheless higher on these outcome measures than were their baby-boomer parents at

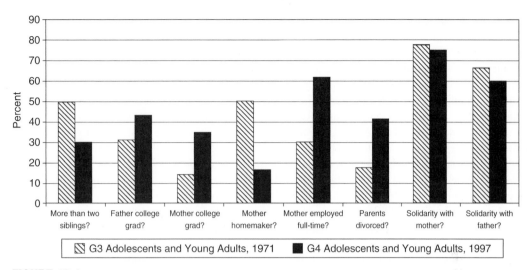

FIGURE 10.1

Historical changes in family structure and parental attributes: "Generation X" compared with their baby-boomer parents at the same age. (*Source:* Vern L. Bengtson, "Beyond the Nuclear Family: The Increasing Importance of Multigenerational Bonds," *Journal of Marriage and Family* 63 (February 2001), pp. 1–16. Reprinted with permission.)

the same age, regardless of family structure. We also found that maternal employment has not negatively affected the aspirations, values, and self-esteem of youth across these two generations, despite the dramatic increase in women's labor force participation over the past 3 decades. Finally, we found that Generation Xer women have considerably higher educational and occupational aspirations in 1997 than did their baby-boomer mothers almost 30 years before. In fact, Generation X young women's aspirations were higher than Generation X young men's.

These findings challenge the hypothesis that families are declining in function and influence and that "alternative" family structures spell the downfall of American youth. Multigenerational families continue to perform their functions in the face of recent social change and varied family forms. . . .

MULTIGENERATIONAL FAMILY BONDS: MORE IMPORTANT THAN EVER BEFORE?

My hypothesis is that multigenerational family bonds are important, more so than family

research has acknowledged to date. I have argued that demographic changes over the 20th century ("from pyramids to beanpoles" and "longer years of shared lives") have important implications for families in the 21st century, particularly with regard to the "latent network" of family support across generations. I have suggested that multigenerational relationships are increasingly diverse in structure and functions within American society. I propose that because the increase in marital instability and divorce has weakened so many nuclear families, these multigenerational bonds will not only enhance but in some cases replace some of the nuclear family functions that have been the focus of so much recent debate.

To test this hypothesis concerning the increasing importance of multigenerational bonds will require research such as the following: First, we will need to examine longitudinal data to trace the salience over time of the multigenerational model. My argument (following Riley & Riley, 1993) is that multigenerational relations represent a "latent kin network" that may be inactive and unacknowledged for long periods of time, until a family crisis occurs. Such is the case when grandparents are called to help in the raising of grandchildren; when family elders become incapacitated and adult children and other kin provide caregiving support. Fortunately, by now we have several large ongoing longitudinal studies (such as the National Survey of Families and Households, Health and Retirement Survey, Analysis of Household Economics and Demography, etc.) that can be used to examine the activation of latent kin networks over time.

[Second, w]e will need trend data so as to examine whether multigenerational families are indeed interacting more and fulfilling more functions for members in the 21st century than in the past. We need to explore how trends in longevity, elder health, the beanpole intergenerational structure, and the aging of baby boomers are affecting intergenerational solidarity and support.

Third, we need more data on the ethnic and racial diversity of American family forms. We need to examine multigenerational influences across and within special populations, such as minority families and first- and second-generation immigrants. For example, considerable evidence shows that for many African Americans, extended kin relationships are more salient than they are for White families (Burton, 1995). As has been observed so many times in our recent history, minority patterns can signal changes on the horizon for White majority families.

We also need data reflecting the increasing diversity of American family forms beyond biological and conjugal relationships. We need to examine the multigenerational relationships of gay and lesbian families and of never-married parents.

We need cross-national data to examine how multigenerational relations are changing and the implications of these changes. For example, in the face of rapid industrialization and population aging, we are seeing changes in the meaning and expression of "filial piety" in Asian societies. In Korea and Japan, for example, multigenerational household sharing is becoming less prevalent (Bengtson & Putney, 2000). What does this imply in terms of Confucian norms about caring for one's parents? We need also to examine the

changing mix between state and family provisions for the elderly. Paradoxically, it appears that Eastern societies are becoming more dependent on state provisions for the elderly, whereas Western societies are facing declining governmental resources and placing more responsibilities on families (Bengtson & Putney).

Finally, we need to focus on policy implications of the growing importance of multigenerational bonds. What can be done to strengthen multigenerational family supports? Grandparent visitation rights have been challenged recently in the U.S. Supreme Court; what does this mean in light of other court decisions to place more responsibility on grandparents as court-mandated guardians of grandchildren?

CONCLUSION: BEYOND THE NUCLEAR FAMILY

Are families declining in importance within American society? Eight decades ago, Ernest W. Burgess addressed this question from the standpoint of family transformations across the 19th and 20th centuries. His hypothesis was that families and their functions had changed from a social institution based on law and custom to a set of relationships based on emotional affect and companionship (Burgess, 1926). But this did not mean a loss of social importance. He suggested that the modern family should be considered as "a unity of interacting personalities" (Burgess) and that future research should focus on the interactional dynamics within families. In all this, Burgess' focus, and that of those who followed him (Ogburn, 1932; Parsons, 1944), was on the nuclear family form.

Eight decades later, this question—are families declining in importance?—has resurfaced. Some family experts have hypothesized that families have lost most of their social functions along with their diminished structures because of high divorce rates and the growing absence of fathers in the lives of many children (Popenoe, 1993). A contrasting hypothesis is that families are becoming more diverse in structure and forms (Skolnick, 1991; Stacey, 1996).

In this article, I have suggested another hypothesis, one that goes beyond our previous preoccupation with the nuclear or two-generation family structure. This concerns the increasing importance of multigenerational bonds and the multigenerational extension of family functions. I want to be clear about this hypothesis because it differs from contemporary wisdom about the most pressing problems of American families today and because I hope it will generate much debate. I have proposed that (a) multigenerational relationships (those involving three or more generations) are becoming increasingly important to individuals and families in American society; (b) these multigenerational relationships are increasingly diverse in structure and functions; and (c) for many Americans, multigenerational bonds are becoming more important than nuclear family ties for well-being and support over the course of their lives.

Burgess was right, many decades ago: The American family is in transition. But it is not only in transition "from institution to companionship," as he argued. Over the century, there have been significant changes in the family's structure and functions. Prominent among them has been the extension of family bonds, of affection and affirmation, of help and support, across several generations, whether these be biological ties or the creation of kinlike relationship. But as families have changed, they have not necessarily declined in importance. The increasing prevalence and importance of multigenerational bonds represent a valuable new resource for families in the 21st century.

■ Review Questions

1. What are the reasons, in Bengtson's opinion, multigenerational ties are becoming more important to many Americans than nuclear family ties?
2. What are the characteristics of the "beanpole family"? What are its strengths and limitations?

READING 10-2

Men and Women
Together and Apart in the Later Years

Katherine S. Newman

"King, you don't understand. I don't want everything. That's not why I'm living . . . to want things. I done lived thirty-five years without things. I got enough for me. I just want to wake up in the bed beside you in the morning. . . . Your job is to be around so this baby can know you its daddy. Do that. For once, somebody do that. Be that. That's how you be a man, anything else I don't want."

—Tonya, speaking to her husband, King,
in August Wilson's play *King Hedley II*[1]

In the backyard of a run-down tenement in the Hill District, August Wilson's fictional Pittsburgh neighborhood, two African-American couples are wrestling with the history of their relationships. Elmore wants to reclaim his relationship with Ruby, now in her sixties, after a long absence. King (Ruby's grown son) wants to please Tonya, his thirty-five-year-old wife who is pregnant with his child, though she loudly proclaims that she does not want to bring a baby into a world—or a marriage—like this. King and Elmore have both been in and out of jail as a consequence of hot-headed murders, outbursts against men who wronged them in the past. Tonya and Ruby are fed up with the excuses, the absences, and the disappointments. They have learned the hard way how to live without men.

Ruby makes it clear that Elmore needs to make up for lost time if he wants to win her affection. She wants new dresses, some jewelry, and twenty dollars for some food, right now. Then she'll think about marrying Elmore. Tonya wants nothing of the kind from King. She knows he will do something crazy in order to "be a real man," something that will land him in jail. She cautions him, pleads with him, begs him not to sacrifice their lives together for the sake of "things." "I don't need things," she tells him. "I saw what they cost. I can live without them and be happy." Most of all, Tonya does not want to hear that King is stealing on her account. Her first husband followed that pathway to the penitentiary. Her teenage daughter, Natasha, hardly knows her father because he has been in jail for half her life. Like King, Ruby's first husband robbed in order to provide for his family, but this brought them nothing but grief. She wants King to abandon that destructive path.

> [Natasha's] daddy been in jail for half her life. She wouldn't know him if she saw him. For what? The same stuff you be talking. How he gonna get his. He don't want it all. He just want his little bit. What he got now. He ain't got nothing . . . Natasha don't even know what a daddy is. I don't want that for my children.

It is not the fate of black women, Wilson's plays tell us, to hold their men for long. Whatever happiness they can cobble together is sure to be temporary, cut short by the ambitions of men who have few options for making something of themselves. Hemmed in by racism, by disappearing jobs, by the erosion of the old black middle class and the ascendance of new generations who reject their values, these fictional men are waging a losing battle to find themselves in the world. As King explains to Tonya, he has to claim a place in a world that defines manhood in material ways.

> I ain't gonna stop living. The world ain't gonna change and all of a sudden get better because I be somebody's daddy. I can't go and get no job just because I'm gonna be somebody's daddy . . . I'm just trying to do my get. Get you the things you want.

Tonya and King are more eloquent than ordinary people, but this is all that separates Wilson's characters from very real New Yorkers. Surprisingly, though, we see very little in social science about how men and women in poor, minority communities think about their relations with each other in later life.

Virtually all of the research literature focuses instead on "disrupted" patterns of family formation, and with some reason. The sharp increase in single-parent households, always at greater risk for poverty, attracts the attention of anyone concerned with the fate of adults and the children they raise.[2] Yet the consequences of single parenthood do not end when the children are grown. What happens to the men who father children and then "disappear"? Where do they go when they hit their fifties? What are their lives like when they are no longer young enough to live a high life? To what extent, if at all, do they maintain ties to the women they have loved, to the children they helped bring into the world? If these men come looking for their families, asking to be let into their lives, will they be welcomed? Or are they shown the door, cut off from their children and the women they have known because it is less risky to leave the past behind than to open up to future disappointment?

And what of the women, who have soldiered on, raising children by themselves, often on the most meager of incomes? How does the experience of single parenthood affect the way their lives unfold when they hit their sixties? Popular culture provides us with images of what ought to happen to men and women in old age: gray-haired couples living out their lives together, mutually supportive as physical decline inevitably intrudes. Does this happen in the inner city?

The scholarship that has been done would incline most experts to answer, "No." Once lovers break up—early on in the relational "careers" of young adults—they are finished, period. My research suggests this is not always so. Men and women *do* try to reconnect on the other side of the age spectrum. They engage in a complicated dance of longing and bad blood, of water that has passed under the bridge long ago, and fears of what the future might bring if a relationship falls apart again. That leeriness operates on aging adults and the adult children whom they have raised, who also have something at stake in reconnecting to fathers lost to them in their youth. It's a risky business, but one that unfolds often enough to make the question of relationships between men and women part of life in late middle age.

It doesn't happen to everyone, of course. Many poor women and men of color grow old by themselves. Widowhood arrives early. A rocky history of never-married parenthood, or serial divorce, leaves a void that is never filled. Old age may pass in the company of adult children and grandchildren, or with good friends who have stuck together through many years of difficult times. But the bond between husband and wife may not be part of the picture, even when a man has come knocking.

Some men establish new relationships in their later years, especially with younger women. Men are in short supply and can often rely on this scarcity to start over again rather than entangle themselves with former lovers or ex-wives. A goodly number, too, pass into their senior years without any romantic attachments, hanging on the fringes of their sisters' households or daughters' families. . . .

THICK SKINS AND HARD SHELLS

The distinguished sociologist of race, Orlando Patterson,[3] has issued a challenge to romantic— or, at least, benign—portraits of African-American families. Conventional wisdom, he argues, posits either that black families have remained strong even in the face of overwhelming numbers of never-married mothers and high divorce rates or that there is nothing race-specific about these patterns. Scholars rushing to the defense of black single mothers have argued with great conviction that there is nothing pathological or debilitating about these families.[4] Or, if there is something broken about broken families, it is a consequence of poverty and the economic marginalization of black men rather than of poisonous gender relations.

Nonsense, answers Patterson. Slavery hammered the self-respect of black men and undermined the stability of African-American families. Poverty creates pressures of its own, but the black working and middle classes look only marginally better where marriage is concerned. Survey evidence presented in Patterson's work offers a blistering portrait of distrust between men and women in the black community. Women seem to believe men are generally no good: irresponsible, self-absorbed, looking out for number one. Men spit back that women are domineering, calculating, and manipulative. It's a catastrophe, Patterson tells us, and one that has lasting consequences, particularly for the more than 50 percent of black children growing up in single-parent households today.[5]

By many measures, marriage is in rocky condition in the United States, and not just among minority families. The divorce rate doubled in the 1960s and '70s, owing in part to the expansion in women's labor-force participation and the more generous provision of welfare benefits, both of which freed women from financial dependence upon men and from relationships they deemed destructive. A million children experience a parental divorce every year.[6] Yet Patterson suggests that more is at stake in the case of African Americans than these secular, cross-race trends. The preexisting tensions that he argues hold sway over men and women in the black community are so bad that they don't even get to the point of divorce; they don't marry in the first place.

Patterson makes important points based on survey research, but as with all work of this kind there is more to this than meets the statistical eye. First, as I noted earlier, this "never married" designation is a multifaceted category. Many of the people in it are what we might call "behaviorally married," even when they lack the paperwork. Others are closer to the object of Patterson's scorn: the one-night-stand relationship, resulting in a child, which can never progress because it is steeped in bad blood. And like the 50 percent of marriages that dissolve into divorce, some of these never-marrieds begin at one end of this continuum—acting in consort as full partners—only to dissolve into something that looks a lot like divorce, often of the bitter variety. We are poorly positioned to examine these patterns given the current resources of survey research. They cannot accurately capture the nuances. This is unfortunate because much of the Western world is in the midst of a fundamental change in patterns of marriage that we do not yet understand. We won't make much progress if we cannot figure out how to describe the "semi-marriages" that characterize cohabitation with children that is so evident in, for instance, inner-city New York.

These patterns are mainly of interest to those concerned with family formation. They matter a great deal, however, throughout the life course and come home to roost when men and women reach their mature years. Brief encounters, even those that bring children into the world, rarely resurface when former partners reach their elder years. Men don't try to reconnect and women usually have no idea what has become of them. Relationships of greater duration often take a different path. Cohabiting mothers . . . both permit and encourage ongoing contact between dads and kids. These are the cohabitations that are more likely to reemerge in middle age or the elder years, albeit with many of the reservations and worries that August Wilson's fictional women express. But for every [man], who remained in contact with his kids, there is another man who makes the effort only to face a slamming door. They are rebuffed by their former partners, who are bitter about being abandoned or convinced the fathers will be a bad influence in their kids' lives.

Ironically, older women often realize too late that cutting their ex-partners out has hurt their (now adult) children. When they see the pattern recur in the next generation, they often try to make up for lost time. They encourage their cohabiting daughters who suffer a breakup to let their grandkids maintain some kind of relationship with the errant fathers. This is delicate ground, for the adult daughters are often looking to their mothers to take sides, to validate their own damaged feelings by ratifying the daughter's decision to sever her ties with her partner. Yet from the vantage point of their own mature lives, these grandmothers often risk the ire of their daughters and tell them to let the children keep in touch with their fathers. Such grandmothers are trying to repair, at a distance, wounds that opened up in the course of their own adult lives.

Cheryl Naylor's experience illustrates the ways in which relationships that come and go in the space of early adulthood come back to have an impact on a woman's mature years. Elegantly thin, Cheryl is now nearly sixty years old, her features worn by time. A chain-smoking fan of Kool 100s, she is most at ease stretched out on the long, black leather sectional couch that sits in the living room of her two-bedroom apartment. The housing project where she lives is one of the better-known public developments in central Harlem and she has been a resident for nearly twenty years now. The walls are festooned with baby pictures and posters of rap groups she likes.

Cheryl met her first serious boyfriend in the neighborhood where she grew up. She was eighteen when she first noticed him, sitting on the stoop of the apartment building next door.

> He was nice looking all right. He had just came from the South, I think. He was likin' one of my girlfriends, but she didn't like him and me and her used to be together all the time. And he asked her who I was and it just started like that. So I met his mother and his brothers. By being right across the streets I used to always go up to his mother's house.

They started hanging out on the sidewalk outside the apartment building, leaning against the cars on the curb, and graduated to going out to the movies together. Cheryl's mother was wary of Lucas; she didn't think he was right for her daughter, and she took to looking out the window, watching over them, telegraphing her disapproval.

> She just kept saying he wasn't no good. You know how them mothers was back then. He wasn't no good; he wasn't no future for me and stuff like that. I don't know what made her say that because she never really saw that much of him. I guess she heard what the neighbors were saying about him.

Mama's dour gaze did not dissuade Cheryl from pursuing her relationship with Lucas, but it did convince her that she had to keep at least one big secret: she was pregnant. Even as a teenager Cheryl was tall and slender; her figure helped her to conceal the baby. She was nearly eight months along when her mother finally discovered the truth.

> I worked in a hospital at the time and didn't used to get home until about 1:00 A.M. Lucas called me at about 3:00 A.M. one day and [my mother] picked up the other extension. I answered the phone, but she could tell [something was up] because he kept saying, "Did you tell your mother yet? You told her?" I said, "No, I ain't gonna tell her." And she said to me, "Who's that, that black snake!"

Things went from bad to worse thereafter. Cheryl went crying to her brothers, asking them to intervene. Then Lucas's mother came calling to try to reason with Cheryl's mother. She wanted to see a marriage take place, but Cheryl was somewhat reluctant herself and Lucas seemed resistant. The truth of that interchange is buried in the past. Whatever the intentions and desires were, no wedding took place. Instead, Cheryl carried the pregnancy to term for the "whole, miserable nine months." They stayed together as girlfriend and boyfriend from the distance of separate houses for a time, but they never did try to form a family. Eventually their relationship unraveled, mainly because Cheryl was disappointed in the meagerness of Lucas's own contributions toward their daughter's care.

Nonetheless, Lucas "recognized" his daughter, meaning he made it public that he was the father and extended the helping hands of his own mother toward her granddaughter.

> His mother, every week, used to send cases of Carnation milk and baby food and stuff like that. And I told her that I appreciated it, even though I was working. I said, he's not gonna never do anything, and I took him to court and everything. But he always somehow bailed out of it or something for child support. I never got child support from him.

Cheryl appreciated the way Lucas's mother "did the right thing." But she was annoyed that Lucas himself had been let off the hook. Lucas's own contributions were limited to occasional donations of cash over the two or three years that followed Yvonne's birth. Sensing that this was the most she was ever going to see out of him led Cheryl to reject the idea of marrying him in the first place.[7]

Eventually, Lucas took up with Robin (a friend of Cheryl's) and they had four or five children together. Because Cheryl and Robin were friends, they didn't fight over Lucas. In fact, Robin admonished Lucas about the importance of taking care of baby Yvonne. Robin and Lucas managed to make a go of things. They still live together in a big house in Queens where Robin has established a real estate business. They have grandchildren whom Cheryl knows. "They really doing all right. They come over here every now and then. Robin calls me; we talk on the phone and it's just like it was way back there in the sixties and seventies."

Cheryl is more comfortable maintaining her friendship with Robin than any semblance of her former relationship with Lucas. Even so, over the years he has been an occasional figure in his daughter Yvonne's life. "He'll come and see her every now and then. You know, he'd give her money to give me or something like that, but really he never was into her life [in a big way]."

Cheryl's experience with Lucas was the norm as she remembers it. A few of her more fortunate friends married Prince Charming and rode out of Harlem. But this was the exceptional case, not the rule. Most of the time, boys would get together with girls until the babies started coming and would disappear thereafter.

> Some of my friends was all right. They went off and got married. And they lived happily ever after. The other ones was in predicaments like I was. They had babies and the guys stepped off; they never saw them anymore and they had to fend for theirselves. They had to get up and start going to work for theirselves to take care of their children.

This pattern stands in contrast to Cheryl's own childhood and the experience of her own parents. Her mother and father both grew up in intact families and Cheryl was, by her own admission, much closer to her dad than her mom as she grew up. It was not a matter of long-standing custom that men were rotten deserters. In Cheryl's own generation, though, expectations for a happy marriage, or even a long-lasting partnership, receded sharply, to be replaced by low aspirations for intimacy. After Lucas, who was a disappointment, Cheryl has experienced mostly short stints when she felt she mattered to her man. The father of her second child did not work out any better than Lucas.

> He was never here; he was always back and forth, in and out, in and out. Him and his mother had a terrible relationship. He always hated his mother and used to tell me [so]. I said, you not gonna have a good life, you hate your mother.

Cheryl moved in with her own mother and went out to work to support herself and her two children. She would hear periodically about her ex-partner's "career" in jail and the other relationships he started (and finished), but she didn't give him a lot of thought.

The third—and last—of Cheryl's men turned out to be a more durable presence in her life, but for that reason an even more profound disappointment. By this time she was in her mid-thirties. She was working as a waitress in a bar and met Rodney on the job. It was, perhaps, not the most propitious of circumstances for beginning a new relationship, but Cheryl was looking for someone to love, and Rodney seemed to be in search of a new home, and a stepmother for his own children. She fell into the role, almost without thinking. Rodney would call her up and ask her to come over to his mother's house and she took him up on the invitation. She braved the hostility of Rodney's then-girlfriend, the mother of his children, and gradually established a relationship with him, and perhaps even more so with his children.

Rodney moved in slowly, but eventually he became a fixture in Cheryl's life. More than anything, though, Cheryl grew attached to his children. They were the magnet that drew her into the relationship.

> His kids started coming. That's just how it was. But I love kids and I just fell in love with his kids. His daughter had that thick hair with the wave in it that comes down her back. I'd love them kids; I still love them.

Rodney and Cheryl were together for nearly a decade. The early years were wonderful, despite the tensions with his ex-lover. Cheryl felt she had found a man who not only loved her, but who would help her care for Yvonne and her younger daughter, Janet. She set limits on his authority over them and he adhered to them, while doing the same for his kids.

> The first three years was beautiful. . . . He had good rapport with my kids. I told him, "You're not their father, but they're goin' to have to respect you. Don't hit my kids. You can chastise them but don't put your hands on them." And they loved Rodney to death. They called him Daddy and everything. We went to dinner all the time. Every weekend he would take us up to Sammy's [a well-known restaurant]. One week he would just take me, the next week he would take Yvonne and Janet and some of the kids from our building. We went to amusement parks. You know it was just really good.

As Cheryl looks back, this was just about the happiest part of her life. Her kids had a dad; his kids had a more responsible mom in Cheryl than they did in their own mother; Rodney and Cheryl had each other. But it didn't last. Simultaneously, Yvonne went off the rails and Rodney's daughter Quanda sank into total rebellion. Yvonne started running away from home, indulging in drugs, and storming through the apartment in defiance when Cheryl tried to discipline her. Quanda was worse, as Cheryl discovered by prying into her diary.

Cheryl turned to Rodney, warning him that Quanda could not continue her weekend visits if she was going to dabble in drugs and sex. No change. Quanda continued to indulge, particularly since she met no resistance from her own mother who was, by this time, a crack cocaine user and a heavy drinker. The mother neglected Quanda and her siblings, who would turn to Cheryl, calling to complain that there was no food in the house. Cheryl did what she could from a distance and earned the enduring love of Rodney's sons, and the equally permanent enmity of Quanda. Telling them they should respect their mother, no matter how badly she behaved, Cheryl stood up for what she thought was a better model of child rearing. To be truthful, the model wasn't working very well with her own daughter Yvonne.

Coincident with these traumas, Rodney began to insist that Cheryl stay close to home. Cheryl's cousin had offered her a job working as a teacher's aide in a Muslim school in Queens. The job required that she travel from Harlem to Jamaica Bay, but she enjoyed it since it was a step up from working in the bar where she had met Rodney. Cheryl couldn't understand why Rodney was losing his temper over her whereabouts, because she was always home by six o'clock to cook dinner. He issued an ultimatum: "It's me or the job." She turned him down.

Rodney's insistence was particularly irritating because he was becoming a less dependable figure himself. He would disappear for a day or two without explanation. Rodney ditched the construction job he had held down for most of their years together. Cheryl wasn't sure where the money was coming from, but she began to hear

from other women in his life who wanted some. They would call, ask for Rodney, and hang up when Cheryl said he wasn't there. The calls grew a bit bolder: women demanding Rodney pay their rent, or buy Pampers for their children. One showed up on Cheryl's doorstep holding a baby she claimed, loud enough for all the neighbors to hear, was Rodney's child. That was the end for Cheryl. She issued an ultimatum of her own: get out. Cheryl gave Rodney thirty days to pack up and leave. The next week, his belongings disappeared from her house and that was that.

The disappointment she felt was powerful enough to convince Cheryl that there really are no good men in this world. Women should be suspicious of men's intentions, she says, and ready to treat them instrumentally. She does not want any man in her house or her life.

> When that box [of Rodney's belongings] was gone and all his stuff was outta my house, I knew that he was gone. And that was that. He just left. And after that I said I wouldn't even let [repair] men come into my house. I used to just hate men. To this day, I don't want any of them in my life. I'm getting over it now, gradually. The first year, it was hard. I'm not gonna lie to you. . . . Now I don't want nobody to come back in my house and put no shoes under my bed.

Cheryl "got over" Rodney, and now after many years on her own she wants nothing to do with men at all. She has become the kind of woman Orlando Patterson bemoans when he writes about poisonous relations between black men and women. Yet she did not start out from that position. For many years she believed that love was possible and she acted on that assumption through several relationships. Belatedly, and bitterly, she has concluded she was wrong about all that.

Cheryl knows that her youngest daughter Janet has inherited some of this ill will. Much as Cheryl bears these internal scars, she did not wish them on her daughters. Hence she has tried to make amends by encouraging Janet to keep her own ex-partner in touch with the son they share. Janet was resistant, having also learned through her own bad experience that men are not to be trusted and that women have to make do on their own. It fell to Cheryl to try to maintain the links between her grandson and his father.

> Janet told me that she was glad her father wasn't in my life because it made me a stronger woman. And her son's father is the same way. My daughter has been taking care of her own son for sixteen years on her own. You know, she don't ask [that man] for anything. But when [the father] Tom comes around my house, her son sees his father. Like Janet said, there will never be no real relationship there because he don't even know how to converse with this kid because he's never around him. But they sit outside, they play basketball.
>
> Janet said, "Ma, take [my son] upstairs when [he comes around]." And I said, "No, Janet. He don't see his father, so let him stay out there and play." They stayed outside until like two or three o'clock in the morning. I looked out the window and there they was out there playing [basketball]. I said, "Tom, don't you think it's time for that boy to come upstairs?" And he said, "Okay Miss Cheryl, I'm gonna bring him up." And he sent him up. And the boy looked so happy that day because he really loved his father. He knows his father.

Tom is not the perfect father or son-in-law. Yet his son knows him and his lineage. He doesn't have a dad he can rely on for steady advice or support, but he does not suffer the confusion of not having a clue about where he comes from. As Cheryl explains, he has a set of kinship coordinates, a sense of location.

> He knows his father. He know his grandmother. He [knew] his [other] grandmother before she passed away and his aunts and uncles. Whenever they come and get him, or ask Janet [if] he can go, she always let him go.

Getting Janet to this point, moving her beyond bitterness, has not been easy either. Cheryl has had to pull her over that hurdle.

> Years ago, Janet would say, "Ma, if Tom ever died, my son is not going to his funeral." And I sat her down and said, "Janet, you can't do that; it's

not right. He'll never forgive you for doing that. He know now, he's sixteen. He understand. He know that his father never did anything for him. But when [Tom] do come around, he try to be with him. So you can't do that. If he pass away today or tomorrow, that still his son. You can't deny that. Maybe he wasn't nothing, but that's still his son and that's still his father. And that wouldn't be right. I might not be here to see it, but you will regret what you did because he would tell you about it in years to come."

Bringing Janet around to this way of thinking took some courage because Cheryl could easily have been defined as a hypocrite, unwilling to admit the mistakes she made in raising her own two daughters. As it happens, she does recognize the error of her ways and regrets much of the pathway she herself took as a mother. She blames herself for the tension between her two daughters, the jealousy that pitted them against each other and hurled Yvonne into such a state of fury that she lashed out physically at Janet and then turned around and hurt herself. She blames herself for the drug habit Yvonne developed, which landed her on Rikers Island and bequeathed to the next generation a twisted life of acting out, flunking out, and striking out in retaliation for neglect and abuse.

The only real pride Cheryl takes in surveying her family is vested in Janet. The younger daughter has made her own mistakes and fallen off the deep end more than once. But Cheryl worked hard to rescue this one and turn her around. Today she has a regular job as a beautician and earns a decent living. She has raised her son, without his father but with enough of a backbone to keep him out of trouble. Janet has become a new woman and a solace to Cheryl, the mainstay of the family. She is the person Cheryl knows will keep her company in her own old age.

Thousands of African-American women in inner-city neighborhoods have known this kind of disappointment in their lives. They are reaching their late fifties, as has Cheryl, with a rocky history of broken marriages or no marriages at all, with sons and daughters who go on to repeat their experience. They have learned to fend for themselves as the sole workers in the household, to lean on their mothers to help them raise their children, and to return the favor to succeeding generations when they become grandmothers themselves. Emotional satisfaction endures less in the bond that ties men to women than in the vertical link that binds mothers to children. The company they keep is only episodically punctuated by lovers or husbands, brothers and fathers. Mostly, it is a community of women.

From the perspective of the middle class, including its African-American members, this is a poor substitute for a real family, which is supposed to have, at its core, a couple. From an economic perspective, there can be no doubt that families like Cheryl's are disadvantaged in almost every respect. They are poorer, the children who grow up in them often have problems in school or get in trouble with the law. Girls, like Yvonne and Janet, are "at risk" for repeating their mothers' experience. All of this is true. Yet there is another truth that bears observation as well: there is strength in these women and they are, in many respects, better off than the men whom they have cast off or who have let them go. They *do* have family to lean on. There are constants in their lives, alongside the hardship. Cheryl does have Janet and together they have Janet's son.

When Cheryl was thirty, she felt bad about the men in her life. She was reconciled to a cordial, though distant, relation to Lucas, but felt burned and resentful toward Rodney. Now that she is nearly sixty, she has come out on the other side of this stress. Yes, she wishes it might have turned out more like the storybook weddings she dreamed about as a young girl. But no, she is not living out her life as a sob sister. On the other side of middle age, that couple-centered existence doesn't matter as much to her. So many of the women she knows never had it either. They are the norm in her inner-city neighborhood, not the exception. Hence what matters to her most is not the lack of marriage but the presence of her

daughter and her grandson. She knows that Janet will be there for her over the long haul and feels blessed that she has someone to rely on. The people she feels sorry for are the ones who don't have such a daughter, who only have kids like Yvonne out on Rikers Island. Everyone needs to have at least one person they can count on and that much Cheryl has for sure.

FROM THE MEN'S SIDE

Sociologists focus their attention on poor families primarily from the viewpoint of women and children. Men are present in scholarly writings only peripherally, often because they have absented themselves from the families they helped to create. But they don't just disappear. How do *they* think about the trajectories of their relations with the womenfolk? Virtually everything we know about this subject from the man's angle is really about boys, or rather adolescents. Elijah Anderson's provocative essays[8] provide key insights into the competitive psychology of young men, intent mainly on proving their mettle to their fellow males using the currency of female attention. As he tells it, the boys are not interested in what one might call a relationship. They are interested in "getting one over" on the girls, on getting the sexual goods from as many admiring girls as possible for use in bragging rights.

Journalists and social scientists have seized on this kind of instrumental behavior as a prime mover in the story of broken families. The disinterest that men show in "settling down" or being "responsible fathers" leads directly to female-headed households, increased risk of family poverty, the absence of role models for children (especially male children), and a growing suspicion among women that men are just no good.[9] To be fair, women often come to the conclusion that two can play this game and, like Cheryl, decide they are the ones who want out of binding commitments. In the main, though, it is men who are seen (both by women and by themselves) as free agents. But for how long? Is this a pattern of disconnection that lasts throughout the life cycle? What happens when men begin to feel their age?

Some men we interviewed who have now reached sixty-five look back on their wilder days as something of a burden. Living up to an image of virility, performing in bed or on the streets, often to impress other men, left them exhausted, and not particularly satisfied or proud of themselves. They don't claim to be looking for sympathy, nor would they deny that their high-living days weren't fun at times, but they also note (quietly and not for public consumption) that there were times when they just wanted to go home, relax, and forget about posturing for anyone else's sake.

Geoffrey Powers certainly sees his life in this light. Now in his late forties, Geoffrey comes from a South Carolina farm family. He moved to New York to join his older brother, the first of his seven siblings to move north in the 1970s. They had heard there were good jobs in New York and the opportunities for young, black men in the rural South were not very appetizing. Geoffrey did not get much of an education. The GED he acquired after dropping out of high school was not nearly as important as the carpentry he learned in the Job Corps. With these blue-collar skills in his back pocket, Geoffrey made a solid living in the building trades. These days he works as a shipping manager for a firm in Queens, where he hopes to stay until he turns seventy. Geoffrey has come a long way and he knows it. He grew up in a house with no inside toilet and not enough food on the table. Today he can look forward to retiring on his pension in the rent-controlled apartment he now lives in.

In his youth, Geoffrey did his share of "acting foolish," running around on the streets and getting into trouble. Job Corps training came his way because he was regarded as "at risk" and it did the trick in terms of providing him with skills. But Geoffrey had a field day in New York. He partied, drank more than he should have, had lots of girlfriends. He finally found a girl he really treasured and they had a child together, even as he was living at home with his older sister.

My biggest problem was, well, I had no real job at the time. And I didn't know nothing about really raising no kids. I didn't know how to keep money to take care of my kid.

This saga sounds quite familiar by now, except that in Geoffrey's case he finally did settle down and marry (a different woman). He had a second family with his new wife and they now have two adolescent children, a girl and a boy. They are not problem-free kids and Geoffrey often finds it a challenge to separate them from the untoward influences of the poor neighborhood where they live. He lectures his son about drugs and his daughter about boys and is never entirely sure that either sermon has hit its mark. They are latchkey kids because Geoffrey is a working man and so is his wife.

Yet there is a lot of pleasure in such a stolid, settled life, with basic rhythms that change very little from day to day. Among them is the knowledge that he no longer has to walk on the wild side. Indeed, Geoffrey takes satisfaction from raising his second set of teenagers with more care than those he had when he was not much more than a teenager himself.

I'm proud of my family, proud of my kids. I'm proud of being able to get up and go to work every day. I'm proud of just being still alive! My family, though, that's the best part, the proudest part of my life. I really ain't got too much in my life but my family. Failure is when you sitting in the street being a wino. You ain't got no job, you don't have a place to live. That's a big failure. But me? I mean, I got an apartment, I go to work every day. That's a blessing in disguise.

Most of all, Geoffrey is glad that he lived long enough to outgrow the pathways that he followed when he was a young man without much sense of obligation toward anyone else. Those wild days might have been fun for a while, but they got to be wearing.

I don't hang on the street like I used to, you know. I don't run around. When I come home from work, I [am] tired. I go to bed. There's a big change in me. I used to be on the street all night long. Can't do that no more. I'm at the middle age time when you just come from work, go home and take a bath, eat your supper and get to bed. 'Cause I have to work every day now.

These days he can let all of the pressures of that macho stereotype flow off his back. Geoffrey's focus is on planting his feet in one place and making sure his family is secure.

When you get to be forty . . . that's the time you're supposed to be done, situated, ready to just . . . watch your kids grow up and be helping your kids out. You go to work and sit back and relax and pay the bills. And take care of your family. Life changes for the better. No more hotdogging. No more running around. I think it's time to settle down and just look after family.

On occasion Geoffrey regrets that it took him so long to come around to this settled version of himself. He left a lot of trouble in his wake before he figured out that the old street-gang lifestyle wasn't for him. There is that lost daughter and a lost common-law wife and no amount of excuses can really make up for those errors of judgment. Like the other men we interviewed, Geoffrey has come to a belated recognition of the collateral damage done when he was "young and foolish." By the time it registered in the life of his first child and her mother, it was really too late for Geoffrey to remedy the past. What he could do was to try again and that is exactly what he did.

Middle-aged men in the inner city who have not managed to stabilize as well as Geoffrey also seek some kind of home life in their later years. More often than not, they look to settle down at last with a new and untainted woman or someone they've known as an acquaintance for a long time but were not romantically involved with in the past. Their "new" partners are beyond the childbearing phase, though they may be responsible for someone else's kids off and on. Like an old married couple, they mainly attend to each other. Old men try to find some peace and comfort in the arms of the one kind of woman they may not have had for a long time: a wife.

Clark is a case in point. A brown-skinned, muscular man whose body has seen better days, Clark is now fifty-seven years old. He lives in a one-room studio apartment in a housing development in Harlem that was once a middle-class enclave but is now inhabited mainly by the working poor. The whole apartment is about 300 square feet, with a kitchen in one corner and a computer in another. A nice-looking man, whose 5 foot 9 inch frame is overburdened by muscle that has gone to seed, Clark has had a rocky road since adolescence. Like many other men he knows, Clark comes from stable, working stock. But his own life has not been so stable, and his downward drift crisscrossed the lives of several women.

Clark was born in Brooklyn, one of six children. Both of his parents were from South Carolina and came up to New York as teenagers, in the river of African Americans that flowed out of the Deep South during the Great Migration.[10] They met as teenagers in the Bronx and married in their early twenties. Clark's mother was an educated woman who found a job as an elementary schoolteacher, and his father worked as an auto mechanic. Together they made a good living, but with so many children to provide for the household was always a bit chaotic. Misbehavior brought forth spanking from their father. Mother took a different tack: she would "brow beat" the kids, urging them to buckle down, get an education, work hard. With hindsight, Clark says, he recognizes she was right. In his youth, though, he wanted to have his own way. He saw his mom as old-fashioned, out of touch, with "ideas that were for her time," while he wanted to "pursue what [he] wanted to pursue." Clark humored his mother by heading off to school, and then pleasured himself by cutting classes. Ultimately, he skipped school, playing hooky.

Clark's parents drifted apart emotionally in their later years. They remained under the same roof until the day his dad died, but the tight bond between them loosened and Clark knew it. "When I was younger," he says casting his mind back to childhood, "everything was hunkydory." Clark could just see that his parents did not seem to share very much with each other after a time. "The relationship was strained," he says. "They didn't speak as much and my father spent a lot of time out of the house. . . . They just grew apart."

Clark's interest in the opposite sex kindled at thirteen or fourteen, but wasn't serious until he was sixteen. That was the year he met Sandra. Sandra and Clark lived in the same neighborhood and passed each other on the way to school. But Clark wasn't the only guy in the picture. "All of the guys wanted to be with her," he says smiling broadly. She was "hotsy totsy," he remembers, but she was also widely known as a "good girl," who was respected for her virtues.

> You know how guys are, right? They will stand around and brag [about girls] even when they have no basis in fact to do so. And you never heard [Sandra's] name come up in those kind of conversations. She always carried herself well. She was somebody you could take home to your mother.

And he did. Clark's mother, the schoolteacher, liked Sandra a lot. Clark was in a slight state of shock since he didn't expect to gain approval for any of his relationships. "It was scary," he says with a laugh. "Scary when your mother likes someone . . ."

Her churchgoing family, especially her father, a deacon, ensured Sandra's standing. Accorded much respect in the neighborhood, Sandra's kin took it for granted that she would only go out with a "good boy," and Clark—son of a schoolteacher and a steadily employed father—fit the bill. No fool he, Clark joined the church choir, even though "you know, I can't sing at all." With this fiction, he "got past her father," and they started dating under the watchful, and approving, eyes of both sets of parents. They went to movies, dinner, and long walks on the promenade facing the magnificent harbor alongside Brooklyn Heights. Clark and Sandra were an item for nearly three years, although they saw other people as well (or at least Clark did). But he knew his mother did not approve of anyone other than Sandra.

> My mother was a mental disciplinarian. [I would see girls in between] and you would know immediately, immediately how my mother felt about it. She didn't have to say a word. She could be standing at the refrigerator with her back turned. If I brought somebody into the house that she didn't like, a young lady, especially while I was Sandra's [steady], she didn't say anything. And you know what, the girl could feel [the chill]. My mother might not say a word. You might not even see the expression. It's just like the whole house got cold.

Though not one to keep his mother happy, Clark tended to stick with Sandra. And she returned the affection, giving him the one gift that really signaled how much she loved him: her virginity.

Given this praiseworthy young lady, he might have felt on the top of the world were it not for the troublesome influence of his peers. Boys in Clark's neighborhood were impressed that he "got Sandra," but having one steady girlfriend was not exactly their idea of success. Just in case something happened with "your main girl," you should always have some action on the side. The point, as Elijah Anderson would say, was to compete.

> It's not even cheating, really. It is, but we're talking at the time as a young guy. You're gonna try to, as many young boys do, try to meet as many women as you possibly can. Whether or not anything happens between you and the young lady [as a consequence] is kind of irrelevant. The thing is to meet as many as you can. That was the attitude at the time.

What the boys were interested in was not the occasional churchgoing, good girl so much as the number of conquests they could brag about to one another. Hanging out on the stoop of their Brooklyn flats, Clark and his buddies gathered in groups to take in the perpetual show of women "on parade." They compared notes on a girl's body, her walk, the way her clothes fit. "Typical, ridiculous stuff," he laughs, the stuff of short relationships and temporary commitments. "We didn't want to hear about marriage at that age. Marriage? Please!"

Truth be told, Clark was happy enough to bask in Sandra's attention. But all around him he saw a different model of men and women together. Even his father, loyal spouse that he was, was constantly the subject of sidelong glances and inappropriate attention from other women. "Women used to speak to my father," Clark remembers, "and it was probably a source of tension between him and my mother." As far as Clark knows, his dad never acted on impulse and declined to pursue whatever it was that was "on offer." His attractiveness, Clark thought, might have been a "weapon against my mother, because she could be quite intimidating mentally." Smart, professional, and respected, Clark's mother cut a higher-class figure than her auto mechanic husband, at a time when it was not "done" for wives to be superior in status.[11]

When Clark ventured out into the territory of boy/girl relations, he was operating with contradictory "instructions." He had his parents to look to, a long-married couple, but one where temptations from the outside were visible even to the children. And he had his friends, none of whom were lucky enough to find a girl of Sandra's caliber and who substituted a numbers game for relationships of any great meaning. For them, masculinity was a matter of conquest, and a deliberate eschewing of the kind of "go steady" commitment that Sandra expected.

Competing models finally got the better of Clark, and not just with respect to Sandra. He started to lose face because he was acting too much like the good boy her deacon father admired and too little like the badass his friends put some store in. So Clark started cutting school more often. He dabbled in the drug trade for a bit of fast cash. Clark started going out with other girls in a secretive, evasive fashion. Worst of all, he was hard-hearted in the face of Sandra's extreme disappointment and played the big man, the tough guy. He became the one that was "hard to get" and impossible to keep.

We just grew apart. Yeah, she didn't like the direction some parts of my life was going in. I wanted

to do what I wanted to do. And you know, at that age, there's a lot of ego involved. So it was like, "You can't get with my program." We eventually just drifted apart.

It didn't take long for Clark to find another lady and this one was different than Sandra. Tricia was easygoing, independent, and didn't hang on Clark. She had long legs and tight shorts—all the requirements. Clark had felt a bit burdened by Sandra's middle-class expectations about high school, church, and loyalty. Tricia was different.

She didn't try to pressure [me] on a lot of stuff. She had an attitude like . . . she was always secure in herself. You know, you do your thing and I'll do my thing. A lot of women want you to account for every second of your time. Tricia wasn't like that. She was secure enough I guess by herself to let [me] go off without pressing [me] about where I was gonna go. And trust in you and herself enough to know that [I was] gonna come back.

Other girls—Sandra included—were possessive, annoyed by the flirtatious behavior of other young girls with boys who were spoken for. Clark found the flings fun and the jealousy of girlfriends a drag. Tricia never pulled that chain; so as far as Clark was concerned she was the perfect girl, and they became an item.

Indeed, they saw each other fairly steadily for about three years. Out of the blue one day, or so Clark remembers, Tricia went into the bathroom and came out leaking water. She had a full-term baby on the way.

Up until my daughter was born, the day she was born, neither one of us thought about kids. I didn't even know [Tricia] was pregnant. . . . [Tricia] didn't grow at all. She had no stomach . . . her face was a little fat and her butt got big. The day her water broke, we were going crazy. We took her to the hospital and she had the baby, who was about four or five pounds. . . . She was underweight. But, no, we never planned on anything.

Clark moved in with Tricia and her parents after Sonya was born. Despite their reservations about Clark, Tricia's parents seem to have accepted his role in their grandchild's life. Even though she was not the result of careful planning, Sonya was loved, "a happy addition to the family," he says with satisfaction. Tricia looked after the baby for a time and then went to work in a hospital, leaving her mother on child-care duty. Clark got a job in shipping and receiving and began making his "little money" contributions to the coffers of the extended household. He took Sonya out for walks, and while he admits he wasn't one for the diapers, as he looks back on her infancy he sees himself as a dutiful and attentive father, within limits. Tricia and her mother were the full-time caregivers for Sonya. What he did was play a part that was, from his perspective, far more involved than many other men who had children in his peer group. At twenty-two, he was helping to support his daughter and living with her mother. He was not an absentee dad.

Clark and Tricia talked about getting married off and on, but seem to have felt little urgency about the prospect. More important to Tricia was just the fact that Clark was still there and still hers. They were managing financially, with the pooled resources of the several generations in Tricia's household, and Clark's steady job was part of the equation. But whatever they learned from the accidental birth of Sonya didn't stick because, within a year or so, another baby girl was on the way. Now the pressures on Clark to form an independent household began to grow. To make matters worse, both Clark and Tricia boosted their drug use from an occasional indulgence to a more serious habit. Money started to become a big problem.

> I used drugs casually before we met. But during the time I was with her, that's when I started indulging heavily. Heavily. I got in with a group of guys who were also making money and it looked good, wearing glamorous clothes. Always had a bunch of money in their pockets. But with all of that stuff came a whole lot of other stuff. I was out there [selling]. The lifestyle, everything. I went for it.

Space was very tight in Tricia's parents' house and her parents were distraught about the erratic behavior that Clark began to display. Tricia

was working, drugs notwithstanding, but Clark started disappearing without warning, flashing leather jackets they knew he couldn't afford on his clerk's income. They didn't get mad, they just got worried, and tried repeatedly to talk sense into Clark. He couldn't hear them.

> I was like a son to them. They tried to talk to me as you would to a son, but my mind was in the streets. My own mother was going crazy too. I had a lot of opportunities that I passed by, that I blew through stupidity, not staying in focus and know what my goals were supposed to be.
>
> My mother says I'm scared of success. She said, "Every time you get close to something, you find a way to blow it."

Her views were pretty far from Clark's mind at the time, though. He was fixed on "the streets" and Tricia was focused on moving out on their own. With two baby girls and the uncomfortable, prying eyes of his "in-laws" watching them, the couple was desperate for a little privacy.

> She really wanted to get out of [her parents' house]. We wanted to get out of there. We wanted to get our own place, naturally. And I felt like I wasn't making enough money. I guess you never make enough money. And whatever little money we made, we spent on drugs, too. So there's never enough money in that situation.

They didn't move out. Clark blew the chance by diving headlong into the drug trade until he attracted the attention of the police.[12] In some respects, he was relieved. Clark was not exactly the king of the mountain. He was trying to make it in a business for which he was temperamentally unsuited. "I am not a killer-type guy, you know. I am not ruthless." Ruthless is what you have to be to become a successful drug dealer. In retrospect, he realizes he was terrified of the trade. "They committed heinous crimes and hurt people." "Thank God there are prisons" for people like that because, as Clark sees it, "I would never want to see those guys on the street or to be near my daughters." He did not have the fortitude to follow in their footsteps.

Busted under Rockefeller's draconian drug laws, he started cycling in and out of jail. After eight years of life with Tricia, he found himself doing some serious time, leaving his "wife" at wit's end. They broke up in 1989, during Clark's third stint in jail. With a lot of time on his hands, and the benefit of hindsight, he knows now that she didn't have much choice but to break it off. She had just had enough of him, and probably of her own drug troubles. Tricia had two kids to take care of and parents to whom she needed to prove she could be trusted. Clark had to go.

> She told me that she would always love me, but that she was not making jail a part of her life. That threw me for a loop 'cause it wasn't like I didn't love her. But she cut me off. I was still in love with her and tried to hold her. But if a woman's fed up, don't you try to hold on. That was one of the lessons she taught me. That took a lot of my self-esteem. 'Cause she had to be brutal with me to get me to understand that it was really over. I used to call the house. . . . She used to hang up on me. You can't keep a person there who doesn't want to be there.

It took many years for him to work his way toward some kind of reconciliation with Tricia. They were never together again as a couple, but they found some kind of peace between them that enabled Clark to reconnect with his daughters in middle age.

> I wasn't there for them as a father. They never had the opportunity to be around me and I didn't have the chance to be around them as much as I would have like to, or as much as they would have liked me to.

To Tricia's everlasting credit, she did not prevent Clark from connecting with his daughters even when he was in jail. She made sure they sent him cards and kept in touch with him no matter where he was and no matter how recalcitrant he became.

> I stayed in touch off and on. Guilt kills, though. When you're wrong and you know it, you sit up in the cell sometimes and think. . . . I won't even bother them. I would stop writing to them.

> I stopped writing to everybody for years. I just wouldn't even call home. The correctional officials would tell me to call home and I wouldn't.

Reverting to his father's "strong, silent" mode of noncommunication, Clark closed himself off from everyone in his family and cut his links to his children before they had much of a chance to develop in the first place. Yet Tricia persisted in trying to keep a line open.

> I'm grateful to Tricia for that. She never tried to keep my daughters from me. She never talked bad about me. And I will always respect her for that because she could have. She never talked bad about me. None of that. My mother, other people told me, "[Tricia] never [badmouthed] you."

Clark's family was brought into the circle and kept close so that the girls would know their kin on his side.

> She let the children know my mother, my sisters. You understand? She knew that the loss of her relationship with me affected her [ability to] integrate the children with all aspects of the family.

When Clark got out of jail, Tricia cultivated his affection, not for herself but for her kids. Eventually he came out of his shell and shed some of the shame he'd built up in prison.

He found some joy in reconnecting to the kids, though he never tried to push the father/ daughter relationship very far. Instead, Clark kindled a quiet kind of friendship with his children and through it hoped to make up for some lost time. Perhaps his take is self-serving, but today he believes they understand—in ways they could not have known in their childhood— that he made big mistakes in his life. The crater that opened up where a father was supposed to be developed not because he didn't care about them, but because he cared more about himself.

> They understand that I love them. Yeah, [they think], my father did some stupid things. He's been in prison. He's done it on more than one occasion, but he loves me. And now they're able to understand that. They understand it's not nothing that I

specifically did to them, you know. Daddy didn't leave you because Daddy didn't want to be with you. You understand. Daddy left because he was an asshole. Okay.

Clark expects no sympathy or understanding for this destructive drift. He just feels better knowing that his kids realize it was indeed his self-absorbed mistakes and not any disregard for them that left a big zero where a father should have been standing. That recognition cleared the way for him to reconnect with his daughters as a friend. "I call them up, 'Watcha doin'?' You know, I'm knowing my daughters now. We are rebuilding our relationship now. They are pretty cool about it."

Clark might not have been able to reconstruct his family life years later if it had not been for Ramona, the woman he ultimately married. She gave him new hope and some of the emotional reserves that he needed to put his life back together after his jail term. Clark and Ramona met in Phoenix House, the drug-rehab program where he got a job as a staff counselor. Clark's job involved designing and monitoring treatment programs for as many as ten and twenty people at a time, running encounter groups where all kinds of hostilities and fears are aired, and young drug addicts are "busted down," their egos battered into submission. Only then will they accept their responsibility for treatment, or so the Phoenix House philosophy goes. Clark was seen as a successful graduate of the program, a veteran of more than a year's worth of tough love.

When Clark arrived in the Bronx facility to collect a group of new drug-treatment "clients," he found Ramona standing on the steps, looking quite fetching. "I swear to God," Clark says with a slightly sheepish grin, "this might sound corny, but when I looked at her I knew she was gonna be mine." He didn't say a word to Ramona, but his heart skipped a beat or two and he scurried around looking for her records. Clark managed to get Ramona assigned to Phoenix House where he knew he'd get a chance to get a bit closer. They spent weeks circling each other. Ramona

was suspicious of his attention and Clark, well, he was too cool to let on about his intentions. They sparred over her treatment, with Clark taking advantage of the authority his counseling position afforded.

> She was leaning against the wall when she came in, and in Phoenix House you are not supposed to lean against the wall. No. You stand up straight. You're not supposed to have your hand in your pocket or nothing like that. Right? So I'm a counselor, so I give out "haircuts" on the floor. A haircut is when you verbally chastise somebody. So Ramona is leaning on the wall. "Get up off my wall!" I let her have it. She was just coming out of induction [intake] and knows the basics, but she don't know [exactly] where this guy's coming from.

Clark started visiting her "encounters," group counseling sessions designed to get the anger out. He would "let her have it" some more and then walk out. Eventually, for reasons known perhaps only to Ramona, they started having more civilized conversations. They fell for each other to the point where all Clark wanted was to get Ramona out of Phoenix House and into his house. She obliged by dropping out of the program and joining him at home.

They lived together for the next eleven years or so and then finally tied the knot. Their wedding day was one of the high points of his life, Clark says. They have been together now for sixteen years, though their lives have hardly been trouble free. Clark's drug problems always linger in the background and threaten to erupt, despite the fact that he was once a poster boy for Phoenix House, praised for having overcome his habit, his prison record, and his bad attitude. He has been in and out of jail during his years with Ramona, most recently for posing as a janitor and stealing laptop computers and pocketbooks from midtown offices. Ramona sticks by him and is always waiting for him upon his return, but it has not been an easy ride. She faces a lot of criticism from her family for putting up with Clark. They are right, lord knows, that he has serious problems. He doesn't blame them for being worried.

"They want to see her happy," he says, "but with someone who is doing something with his life." Unfortunately, and with cause, "they don't see it coming from me."

> I don't want to be responsible for anybody's happiness in that way because I have a history of letting people down. I build people up to the point where they depend on me for a lot of things. I deliver up to a certain point and then I just . . . [blow it]. I carry a lot of guilt because I have disappointed a lot of people . . . a lot of people, and myself as well. I have seen people cry over me. I don't like to disappoint people. So don't make me responsible for your happiness. I like a woman who have lives other than me . . . who have their own job, own career and their own interests other than me.

The last time we interviewed Clark, he had been on release for a month and swore that this time it would be different. For better or for worse, though, Ramona and Clark remain a couple. It is more than he deserves, as Clark is all too quick to point out.

Entering middle age with a rocky biography and limited prospects for an economically feasible "retirement," Clark is almost entirely dependent upon his wife's fortunes. He has no money, no job, and no serious prospects for one. What he has is Ramona. To a more limited extent, he also has his daughters, thanks to Tricia's desire to keep their father in the picture. Most men with prison records of this kind are not so fortunate; they lose everyone.[13] It is hard to know the degree to which necessity has been the mother of invention in Clark's case.[14]

If we want to know what growing old is going to mean for Clark and Ramona, we can see at this point that it is probably going to be shared. At least if the past sixteen years is any guide, Clark will most likely remain "coupled," while Cheryl will not. Older men, even those with very complicated pasts, are "in demand" in communities where so many men have disappeared from women's lives.

Pulling the lens backward from the details of these individual lives, it seems clear that the story of men and women in the inner city remains complex throughout middle age and the elder years. For some, like Reynaldo's parents, it is a story that looks to a census taker like a marriage that dissolved into divorce, even though the divorce was "in name only," to protect welfare benefits. Those on the inside know that this is a long-"married" couple that can now dandle a couple of grandchildren on their knees. . . .

Clark, too, has found a family in Ramona, and has tentatively reached out to the children he left behind through his many bouts in jail and the end of his relationship with their mother. Though he hates to admit it, his relationship with Ramona is really "her call," since she is the one with steady employment and he is, for all intents and purposes, dependent upon her. That is rarely a recipe for stability and his history does not suggest much stability in his future. Yet he would retort that he and Ramona have been together for sixteen years now and if that is not evidence of staying power, what is?

It is a long run that women like Cheryl have not really known in their lives, sometimes by choice and other times by default. They are without much male company nowadays and have not been active in the romance department for some time. Still, they are hardly alone in any other sense. For years now they have had their children and now their grandchildren for company. It is not always quite what they wanted. At times they would have been just as happy to be alone, or at least free from obligation, especially from their teenage grandchildren, who are often a source of trouble in their lives. Yet each of them has one special child who has managed to hang in there and made their elder years more worthwhile, and certainly not bereft of company.

During the 1970s, minority families—particularly "the black family"—came under heavy attack as deviant, destructive, and the source of our poverty problem. Liberal social scientists rushed to the rescue, pointing to the resilience of single-parent households, the creative use of social networks and private safety nets to shore up a poverty-stricken community, the essential dignity of mothers and the struggling, and morally culpable, absent fathers. From the vantage point of a new century, it seems only fair to note that the resilience and heroic effort is real enough. *A Different Shade of Gray* is filled with stories of women (and sometimes men) who have shouldered burdens that would break most people. They are the only safety net under their children, the main caretakers who look after the elderly, and even the final safe haven for men who may have been an irregular presence for twenty years. Their steadfastness in the face of adversity is to be admired.

At the same time, the costs of problematic family life are enormous and should not be cast aside in a rush to avoid "blaming the victim." The emotional toll that failed relationships take, particularly on women, can be devastating to self-esteem and foster a hard shell as they try to shield themselves from future disappointments. Children are damaged by the loss of their fathers, and even if they reconnect when they are all grown up, they are less trusting and more likely to repeat the family breakdown in their own lives. Finally, the financial costs, to which we return in the conclusion, are enormous. Without two incomes to support a household, it is increasingly difficult to escape the clutches of poverty; if they had had more

money in the bank, they would probably have departed along with the millions of others who took to the highways and headed for the suburbs. Lacking income, they were stuck in deteriorating neighborhoods, unable to amass the equity in housing, the savings in bank accounts, or the social security that comes to married people. As inequality has grown in the United States since the mid-1970s, single parents have fallen further and further behind married couples in financial terms. The consequences for their children, in school performance, in health outcomes, and in risks of poverty, are severe and lasting.

August Wilson's fictional character Tonya knew all this without cracking the cover of a sociology textbook. That's why she wanted King to stay with her, whatever the cost to his manhood. "Be there," she said. But by the end of *King Hedley II,* Tonya's worst nightmare comes to pass: King dies, killed accidentally by his own mother. It is a sorrowful and sobering tale without even a semblance of a happy ending. We come away respecting the sacrifices Tonya and Ruby have made to raise their kids, acknowledging the noble aims King and Elmore have for wanting to make something of themselves. We know as well that those many years of separation and disappointment have taken a huge toll on everyone onstage—and in the real world, too.

■ Review Questions

1. What led Cheryl to urge her daughter Janet to keep the father of Janet's children in the children's lives?
2. Why are older men in African American communities more isolated from kin than are older women?

ENDNOTES

1. All quotations taken from August Wilson, *King Hedley II: A Play in Two Acts* (1999). Performed May 24, 2000, by Huntington Theatre Company, Boston.
2. See Andrew J. Cherlin, ed., *The Changing American Family and Public Policy* (Washington, D.C.: Urban Institute Press, 1988); Frank F. Furstenberg, Jr., and Andrew J. Cherlin, *Divided Families: What Happens to Children When Parents Part* (Cambridge, MA: Harvard University Press, 1991); Andrew J. Cherlin, *Marriage, Divorce, Remarriage* (revised and enlarged edition) (Cambridge, MA: Harvard University Press, 1992); Irwin Garfinkel, Sara S.

McLanahan, Philip Robins, eds., *Child Support and Child Well-Being* (Washington, D.C.: Urban Institute Press 1994); Sara McLanahan, Irwin Garfinkel, and Dorothy Watson, *Family Structure, Poverty, and the Underclass* (Madison: University of Wisconsin-Madison, Institute for Research on Poverty, 1987); Sara McLanahan and Gary Sandefur, *Growing Up with a Single Parent: What Hurts, What Helps* (Cambridge, MA: Harvard University Press, 1994); Sara McLanahan and Karen Booth, *Mother-Only Families: Problems, Reproduction, and Politics* (Madison: University of Wisconsin-Madison, Institute for Research on Poverty, 1988); Irwin Garfinkel and Sara S. McLanahan, *Single Mothers and Their Children: A New American Dilemma* (Washington, D.C.: Urban Institute Press, 1986).

3. Orlando Patterson, *Rituals of Blood: Consequences of Slavery in Two American Centuries* (New York: Civitas/CounterPoint, 1998), writes: "Afro-Americans are the most unpartnered and isolated group of people in America and quite possibly in the world. Unlike any other group of Americans, most of them will go through most of their adult lives without any deep and sustained attachment to a non-kin companion" (p. 4). Patterson argues that gender relations in the black world are as bitter and dysfunctional as they could be. Patterson cites a study conducted at Temple University in which working- and lower-class blacks were asked if there was distrust and even hatred between black men and black women. Sixty-six percent of men and 74 percent of women answered affirmatively (p. 5). Patterson traces much of the problem to the legacy of slavery. He argues that while other groups in the United States have faced similar economic and social problems, such as "rural and urban poverty, ethnic persecution, and economic discrimination," only blacks exhibit such strained gender relations and the high rate of paternal abandonment (p. 159). What sets Afro-Americans apart is the historical fact of slavery and no explanation of Afro-American families is complete without a discussion of the slave system. The slavery system conducted an "[assault] on the roles of father and husband" and produced a hostile environment for "pregnancy, women, childbirth, infancy, and childrearing" (p. 159).

4. See Robert William Fogel and Stanley Engerman, *Time on the Cross: The Economics of American Negro Slavery* (Boston: Little, Brown, 1974); Eugene Genovese, *Roll, Jordan Roll* (New York: Pantheon Books, 1974); Herbert G. Gutman, *The Black Family in Slavery and Freedom, 1750–1925* (New York: Pantheon, 1976); Paul J. Lammermier, "The Urban Black Family in the Nineteenth Century: A Study of Black Family Structure in the Ohio Valley, 1850–1880," *Journal of Marriage and the Family* 35 (August 1973), pp. 440–56; Charles Vert Willie, *Black and White Families: A Study in Complementarity* (New York: General Hall, 1985).

5. This pattern refers to children in any single-parent family. Patterson, *Rituals of Blood,* writes: "Sixty percent of Afro-American children are now being brought up without the emotional or material support of a father" (p. 4).

6. Andrew J. Cherlin, "Generation Ex-: Review of the Unexpected Legacy of Divorce: A 25-Year Study by Judith S. Wallerstein, Julia Lewis and Sandra Blakeslee: Hyperion Press," *The Nation,* December 11, 2000, pp. 62–64. Divorce rates have skyrocketed over the past century. About half of all marriages contracted in 1967 will end in divorce. Of the marriages contracted a hundred years earlier, only about 5 percent ended in divorce. Steven Ruggles, "The Rise of Divorce and Separation in the United States, 1880–1990," *Demography* 34 (2) (November 1997), pp. 455–66. See also Cherlin, *Marriage, Divorce, Remarriage;* Teresa Castro Martin and Larry L. Bumpass, "Recent Trends in Marital Disruption," *Demography* 26 (1) (February 1989), pp. 37–51; David Lester, "Trends in Divorce and Marriage around the World," *Journal of Divorce and Remarriage* 25 (1–2), pp. 169–71.

7. Kathryn Edin, "What Do Low-Income Single Mothers Say about Marriage?" *Social Problems* 47 (1) (February 2000), pp. 112–33, provides a discussion of women's reluctance to marry. She interviews 292 low-income single mothers and finds that several factors contribute to the women's reluctance to marry. The economic position of potential husbands is very important. Most of the women believe that the man should earn considerably more than minimum wage before he becomes marriage material. The women assess a man's economic position by looking at the regularity of his earnings, the effort expended to keep his job, and the sources of his income. Irregular earnings, illegal

sources of income, and little effort in maintaining or looking for work all disqualify potential mates as spouses. Other studies substantiate Edin's findings. See Pamela J. Smock and Wendy D. Manning, "Cohabiting Partners' Economic Circumstances and Marriage," *Demography* 34 (3) (August 1997), pp. 331–41, and Wendy D. Manning and Pamela J. Smock, "Why Marry? Race and the Transition to Marriage among Cohabitors," *Demography* 32 (4) (November 1995), pp. 509–20. Kathryn Edin also finds that women are reluctant to marry for non-monetary reasons. The respondents believe that a woman's social standing is tied to that of her husband. Thus, only a man who can bring a woman "respectability" is viewed as a good match. If the man is not able to maintain a job, then his class standing disqualifies him from consideration. Issues of control also enter into marriage decisions. Many women are unwilling to enter into marriage if they believe they will have to fulfill a subservient role. Finally, many women avoid marriage because of their distrust of men in general and because of their fear of domestic violence.

8. Elijah Anderson, *Streetwise,* suggests that "sexual relations, exploitative and otherwise" are as common among middle-class teenagers as they are among the lower-class adolescent respondents. In contrast to the middle-class youths, however, the young men see "no future to derail" by having a child (p. 113). Thus sex, and the offspring as the result, becomes a source of status for the boys. Anderson finds that the young fathers who maintain strong links to their peer group, often "congregate on street corners, boasting about their sexual exploits and deriding conventional family life" (p. 112). This boasting is important because it provides proof of the man's sexual prowess. Finding willing female partners requires men to have a good game: gaining a girl's confidence and favor enough for her to sleep with him. Seducing many different women garners the boy more respect from his friends while continued rejection by women earns him strong ridicule. See also Anderson, *Code of the Street,* pp. 142–78; and Anderson, "Sex Codes and the Family Life among Poor Inner-City Youths," pp. 59–78.

9. Timothy Nelson, Kathryn Edin, and Susan Clampet-Lundquist, "'Doin' the Best I Can': How Low-Income Non-Custodial Fathers in Philadelphia Talk about Their Families," unpublished manuscript (May 16, 2000), find in their sample of low-income, noncustodial fathers that few of them provide consistent financial support to all of their offspring. Many of the men are highly involved when the children are initially born yet this involvement tends to drop off sharply as the children get older. This is particularly true if the relationship between the man and the child's mother is not amicable. Despite this fact, Nelson et al. find that fatherhood has strong symbolic meaning for the men. Indeed, the authors assert that "low-income non-custodial fathers generally ascribe tremendous importance to their children and firmly believe that their lives would be infinitely less meaningful without [them]" (p. 2). Many of the men in the study describe their lives in "before and after": before having children and after having them. Contrary to what the researchers expected, most of the men said that becoming fathers changed their lives for the better. Many of the men describe fatherhood as their salvation: having children had prompted them to change their ways or at least cut back on dangerous behavior. Many also describe the "irrevocable nature of one's status as a father" (p. 22). Unlike other relationships, this bond could not be broken. The authors suggest that fatherhood holds such a cherished position in these men's lives for several reasons. First, children provide the only opportunity for the men to experience social advancement. Secondly, children provide a means of achieving "immortality" (p. 23). Having children leaves some evidence that you were "on the planet" (p. 24). See also Kathryn Edin, Timothy Nelson, and Rechelle Paranal, "Fatherhood and Incarceration as Potential Turning Points in the Criminal Careers of Unskilled Men," unpublished manuscript (May 5, 2001).

10. The Great Migration began between World War I and World War II and gathered steam as the factories pumped out munitions for the war effort. Altogether, some 5 million African Americans decamped from the rural South and journeyed first to the southern cities and then to the northern cities where booming factories were short of labor. See Nicholas Lemann, *The Promised Land: The Great Black Migration and How It Changed America* (New York: Knopf, 1991).

11. Research has shown that people of similar socioeconomic status usually marry one another. This is commonly measured using education: the spouses

have equivalent levels of education. However, persons with dissimilar amounts of education do get married. During the 1990s, when marriage (or cohabitation) occurred between people of dissimilar educational attainment, it was more likely for the woman to be better educated than the man. Zhenchao Qian, "Changes in Assortative Mating: The Impact of Age and Education, 1970–1990," *Demography* 35 (3) (August 1998), pp. 279–92. Moreover, these dissimilar unions were more likely to take place between people of lower educational attainment. Robert Mare, "Five Decades of Educational Assortative Mating," *American Sociological Review* 56 (February 1991), pp. 15–32. See also Matthijs Kalmijn, "Assortative Mating by Cultural and Economic Occupational Status," *American Journal of Sociology* 100 (2) (September 1994), pp. 422–52; Matthijs Kalmijn, "Status Homogamy in the United States," *American Journal of Sociology* 97 (2) (September 1991), pp. 496–523; and Robert Mare, "Five Decades of Educational Assortative Mating," *American Sociological Review* 56 (February 1991), pp. 15–32.

12. See Bruce Western and Katherine Beckett, "How Unregulated Is the US Labor Market?: The Penal System as a Labor Market Institution," *American Journal of Sociology* 104 (4) (January 1999), pp. 1030–60. The number of people incarcerated in the United States has risen dramatically since 1980. In 1980, 500,000 people were in prison. By 1996 the number of people had risen to more than 1.6 million (pp. 1034–1035). Moreover, an increasing percentage of inmates are black. Afro-Americans accounted for 22 percent of the prison population in 1930. Sixty-two years later blacks comprised more than half of the country's inmates (p. 1035). Prison time has become part of many black men's lives: one out of every three black male youth "was under some form of state supervision" and about 7 percent of black male adults were serving time in 1995 (p. 1035). This situation is not found with whites. While the incarceration rate (incarceration per 100,000) for blacks in 1992–93 was 1,947, the rate was only 306 for whites (p. 1036, Table 2). The United States has a much larger prison population than other industrialized countries. Western and Beckett argue that this is not a product of higher crime

rates in the United States. Instead, they suggest that incarceration rates have risen because of "more aggressive prosecutorial practices, tougher sentencing standards, and intensified criminalization of drug-related activity" (p. 1037). The United States imprisons more drug and property offenders than other industrialized countries. In 1994, for instance, about 30 percent of state prison inmates were convicted of nonviolent drug offenses. In contrast, nonviolent offenders made up only 6 percent of the state prison population in 1979 (p. 1037). See also Bruce Western, Jeffrey R. Kling, and David F. Weiman, "The Labor Market: Consequences of Incarceration," *Crime and Delinquency* 47 (3) (July 2001), pp. 410–27.

13. Edin, Nelson, and Paranal, "Fatherhood and Incarceration as Potential Turning Points in the Criminal Careers of Unskilled Men," conducted a study between 1995 and 2001 of 300 low-income noncustodial fathers living in Philadelphia and Charleston. The researchers find that many men who are incarcerated attempt to reconnect with their families after they are released. However, this process can be quite difficult and in many cases incarceration severely damages relationships that were fragile to begin with. Nearly all of those respondents who had a romantic relationship before going to prison saw their relationship crumble due to incarceration. Their girlfriends either broke it off and/or began a relationship with someone else. After the men were released, their former partners often refused to reestablish the connection. This refusal to let the men back in their lives also caused problems in the relationship between the father and the child. "[Mothers] are generally the conduit through which communication with children flows"; thus the men had a more difficult time remaining in their children's lives (p. 8). The researchers even found some cases in which fathers attempted to reconnect with their girlfriends/wives and children but were unable to because they could not find them. The women had moved away without notifying the father (p. 22). U.S. law can also make it more difficult for fathers to reunite with their children. The 1997 ASFA adds more criteria to a previous law, which enables the state to terminate the parents' rights if the child has been in foster care for fifteen or more months out of the last

twenty-two months. John Hagen and Juleigh Petty Coleman, "Returning Captives of the American War on Drugs: Issues of Community and Family Reentry," *Crime and Delinquency* 47 (3) (July 2001), pp. 352–67. See also C. F. Hairston, "The Forgotten Parent: Understanding the Forces that Influence Incarcerated Fathers' Relationships with their Children," *Child Welfare* 77 (5), pp. 617–39; Sara McLanahan and Bruce Western, "Fathers Behind Bars," *Contemporary Perspectives in Family Research* 2 (1996), pp. 309–24; Robert J. Sampson and John H. Laub, "Crime and Deviance over the Life Course: The Salience of Adult Social Bonds," *American Sociological Review* 55 (1990), pp. 609–27.

14. Economic necessity, and the need for caretaking services, keeps many a middle-class couple together too. Data collected since 1860 show a general rise in divorce rates over the past 150 years. However, the divorce rate has fluctuated with economic expansion and depression. Cherlin, *Marriage, Divorce, Remarriage,* finds that the annual divorce rate increased after every major war. In contrast, it decreased during the Great Depression. There is no reason to believe this is the case because somehow people get along so much better under conditions of economic stress. More likely, men and women who would be even more vulnerable apart stick together out of necessity. Indeed, Cherlin argues this very point: because jobs and housing were scarce, many couples chose to stay together (or at least to postpone their divorce). Cherlin, *Marriage, Divorce, Remarriage,* pp. 21, 23. By the same token, it has been suggested that welfare freed up poor women from a degree of dependence and that divorce rates rose in response to their freedom. That freedom can evaporate, as it has in Clark's case, when there are no good options for economic independence. Indeed, he has to hope that he and Ramona stick with their relationship, because without it he would be in deep, deep trouble.

Part Five

Conflict, Disruption, and Reconstitution

CHAPTER 11

Domestic Violence

The problem of violence against women in families and in other intimate settings is not new. Yet only within the past few decades has much attention been paid to it, thanks mostly to the feminist movement. Government responses were initially modest. The U.S. Congress did not pass the Violence Against Women Act until the summer of 1994, when the conviction of former football star O. J. Simpson for the murder of his wife, Nicole, focused the public's attention on battered women. Since then, however, there has been much public and scholarly attention to the topic.

Physical abuse by a spouse or romantic partner is sometimes not just an isolated act but, rather, part of a broader attempt by the man to control the woman. In fact, Michael P. Johnson, in the first selection, argues that we should distinguish between two kinds of domestic violence. The first, and most common, kind occurs in couples who have an occasional dispute that leads to some moderately violent act, such as slapping or hitting, by both men and women. Most surveys that ask about abuse, Johnson says, capture responses about this "situational" kind of violence. Less common but more damaging, he argues, is a pattern of severe, repeated violence on the part of men who seek to control their partner's behavior. The helping professionals who run shelters for battered women see the victims of these "intimate terrorists," as Johnson calls them.

How should law enforcement respond to domestic violence? Before the 1980s, when the police were called by a victim of intimate partner violence, who was almost always a woman, they rarely arrested the alleged assailant, almost always a boyfriend or husband. But starting in the 1980s, police departments, under pressure from advocates for battered women, began arresting the violent man more often in domestic violence calls. In an influential experiment in Minnesota, police officers were randomly assigned to arrest the batterer rather than merely offering mediation or telling the man to leave the location. If they were assigned to arrest a batterer, they did so whether or not the victim requested it. Supporters of mandatory arrest laws argued that some victims did not request an arrest or press charges because they were afraid of retaliation by the man or did not want him to go to jail. The mandatory arrest policy took the matter out of the victims' hands.

The results of the experiment suggested that men who were arrested were less likely to commit future violence. In response, many states and localities enacted laws that required the police to arrest an assailant if probable cause existed that he (or, more rarely, she) had been violent. But the mandatory arrest policy has been controversial. Subsequent studies have shown that it is not always better to arrest the perpetrator; rather,

it depends on the situation. As a result, some advocates and observers are backing off from supporting mandatory arrests. But what kind of guidance does one then provide to the police and the courts? In the second reading, Amy Leisenring reviews and comments on this issue. In doing so, she returns to the distinctions between different kinds of domestic violence that Johnson makes in the first reading.

READING 11-1

Control and Violence in Intimate Relationships

Michael P. Johnson

One woman we interviewed told us that she was first beaten on her honeymoon and when she cried and protested, her husband replied, "I married you so I own you."[1]

In order to understand the nature of an individual's use of violence in an intimate relationship, you have to understand its role in the general control dynamics of that relationship. Some people use violence as one of many tactics in a general strategy aimed at taking complete control over their partner, as in the case of the newlywed husband quoted above. Others may become violent in order to resist their partner's attempts to control them. For still others, their violent behavior may have little to do with control. In this chapter I will distinguish among four types of intimate partner violence that are defined by the extent to which the perpetrator and his or her partner use violence in order to attempt to control the relationship. The four types constitute a typology of *individual* violence that is rooted in information about the couple and defined by the control context within which the violence is embedded (Table 11.1).

In *intimate terrorism,* the perpetrator uses violence in the service of general control over his or her partner; the partner does not. In *violent resistance,* the partner is violent and controlling—an intimate terrorist—and the resister's violence arises in reaction to that attempt to exert general control.[2] In *mutual violent control,* both members of the couple use violence in attempts to gain general control over their partner. Thus, three of the four types of intimate partner violence are

Michael P. Johnson, *A Typology of Domestic Violence* (Boston: Northeastern University Press, 2008). Chapter 1, pp. 5–24, "Control and Violence in Intimate Relationships." © University Press of New England, Lebanon, NH. Reprinted with permission.

TABLE 11.1

TYPES OF DOMESTIC VIOLENCE

Intimate Terrorism
The individual is violent and controlling.
The partner is not.

Violent Resistance
It is the partner who is violent and controlling.
The individual is violent, but not controlling.

Situational Couple Violence
Although the individual is violent,
neither partner is both violent and controlling.

Mutual Violent Resistance
Both individual and partner are violent and controlling.

organized around attempts to exert or thwart general control. In the fourth type of intimate partner violence, *situational couple violence,* the perpetrator is violent (and his or her partner may be as well); however, neither of them uses violence to attempt to exert general control.

The control that forms the basis of this typology of intimate partner violence and is the defining feature of intimate terrorism, is more than the specific, short-term control that is often the goal of violence in other contexts. The mugger wants to control you only briefly in order to take your valuables and move on, hopefully never to see you again. In contrast, the control sought in intimate terrorism is general and long term. Although each particular act of intimate violence may appear to have any number of short-term, specific goals, it is embedded in a larger pattern of power and control that permeates the relationship. This is the violence employed by the newlywed batterer quoted above, who sees his behavior as the embodiment of his "ownership" of his partner.

The core idea of this book is that this "intimate terrorism"—violence deployed in the service of general control over one's partner—is quite a different phenomenon than violence that is not motivated by an interest in exerting general control over one's partner. I would argue, also, that intimate terrorism is what most of us *mean* by "domestic violence." This is the violence that

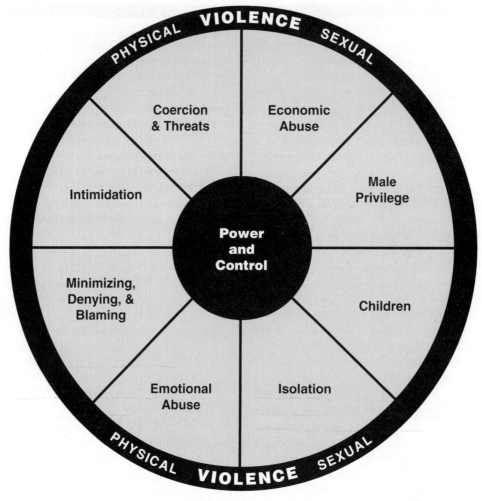

FIGURE 11.1
The Power and Control Wheel. (*Source:* Domestic Violence/Intimate Terrorism adapted from Ellen Pence and Michael Paymar, *Education Groups for Men Who Batter: The Duluth Model* [New York: Springer, 1993].)

has received massive media attention, and that has been the focus of thirty years of feminist activism and research in the United States.

INTIMATE TERRORISM AND OTHER TYPES OF PARTNER VIOLENCE

Intimate Terrorism

Our discussion of the four types of partner violence begins with intimate terrorism because it involves the general exercise of coercive control that is the heart of the distinctions posed here. Figure 11.1 is a widely used graphical representation of partner violence deployed in the service of general control. This diagram and the understanding of domestic violence that lies behind it were developed over a period of years from the testimony of battered women in the Duluth, Minnesota, area, testimony that convinced the staff of the Duluth Domestic Abuse Intervention

Project that the most important characteristic of the violence that they encountered was that it was embedded in a general pattern of power and control.[3] A *pattern* of power and control cannot, of course, be identified by looking at violence in isolation or by looking at one incident. It can only be recognized from information about the use of multiple control tactics over time, allowing one to find out whether a perpetrator uses more than one of these tactics to control his or her partner, indicating an attempt to exercise general control.

Let's work our way around the "spokes" of the diagram, clockwise, beginning with economic abuse at one o'clock. It is not unusual for an intimate terrorist to deprive his partner of control over economic resources.[4] He controls all the money. She is allowed no bank account and no credit cards. If she works for wages, she has to turn over her paychecks to him. He keeps all the cash and she has to ask him for money when she needs to buy groceries or clothes for herself or the children. He may require a precise accounting of every penny, demanding to see the grocery bill and making sure she returns every bit of the change. This economic abuse may be justified through the next form of control, male privilege: "I am the man of the house, the head of the household, the king in my castle." Of course, this use of male privilege can cover everything. As the man of the house, his word is law. He doesn't have to explain. She doesn't disagree with him. She is to do his bidding without question. And she doesn't talk back. All of this holds even more rigidly in public, where he is not to be humiliated by smart-talk from "his woman."

How does he use the children to support his control? First of all, they, too, know he is the boss. He makes it clear that he controls not only them, but their mother as well. He may use them to back him up, to make her humiliation more complete by forcing them into the room to assist him as he confronts her, asking them if he isn't right, and making them support his control of her. He may even have convinced them that he *should* be in charge, that he does know

what is best (father knows best), and that she is incompetent or stupid or immoral. In addition, he may use her attachment to the children as a means of control, by threatening to take them away from her or hurt them if she isn't a "good wife and mother." Of course, being a good wife and mother means doing as he says.

Then there's isolation. Keep her away from everyone else. Make *himself* her only source of information, of support, of money, of everything. In a rural setting he might be able to literally isolate her, moving to a house trailer in the woods, with one car that he controls, no phone, keeping her there alone. In an urban setting, or if he needs her to go out to work, he can isolate her, though less literally, by driving away her friends and relatives and intimidating the people at work, so that she has no one to talk to about what's happening to her. When she's completely isolated, and what he tells her about herself is all she ever hears about herself, he can tell her over and over again that she's worthless, humiliate her, demean her, emotionally abuse her. She's ugly, stupid, a slut, a lousy wife, an incompetent mother. She only manages to survive because he takes care of her. She'd be helpless without him. And who else is there to tell her otherwise? Maybe he can convince her that she can't live without him.

Related to this emotional abuse is minimizing or denying his own abuse, and blaming her for what is going on in the relationship. It's her crazy behavior or incompetence or sexual misconduct that requires him to control her the way he does, in her own best interests. How could she see him as abusive? He's never really hurt her. On the contrary, she's the abusive partner. She's so out of touch with reality that maybe she should get some help.

If she resists, intimidate her. Show her what might happen if she doesn't behave. Scream at her. Swear at her. Let her see his rage. Smash things. Or maybe a little cold viciousness will make his point. Kick her cat. Hang her dog. That ought to make her think twice before she decides not to do as he says. Or threaten her. Threaten to hit her, or beat her, or pull her hair out, or burn her. Or tell her he'll kill her, maybe the kids, too.

Put all these means of control together, or even a few of them, and the abuser builds what Catherine Kirkwood calls a "web" of abuse.[5] He entraps and enslaves his partner. If she manages to thwart one means of control, there are others at his disposal. Wherever she turns, there is another way he can control her. Sometimes she is ensnared by multiple strands. She can't seem to escape—she is trapped. But with the addition of violence, there is more than entrapment. There is terror.

For this reason the diagram does not include the violence as just another means of control, another spoke in the wheel. The violence is depicted, rather, as the rim of the wheel, holding all the spokes together. When violence is added to such a pattern of power and control, the abuse becomes much more than the sum of its parts. The ostensibly nonviolent tactics that accompany that violence take on a new, powerful, and frightening meaning, controlling the victim not only through their own specific constraints, but also through their association with the general knowledge that her partner will do anything to maintain control of the relationship, even attack her physically. Most obviously, the threats and intimidation are something more than idle threats if he has beaten her before. But beyond that, his "request" to see the grocery receipts becomes a "warning" if he has put her into the hospital this year. His calling her a stupid slut may feel like the beginning of a vicious physical attack. As battered women often report, "All he had to do was look at me that way, and I'd jump." What is for most of us the safest place in our world, home, is for her a place of constant fear.

Violent Resistance

What is a woman to do when she finds herself terrorized in her own home?[6] At some point, most women in such relationships do fight back physically. For some, this is an instinctive reaction to being attacked, and it happens at the first

blow—almost without thought. For others, it doesn't happen until it seems he is going to continue to assault her if she doesn't do something to stop him. For most women in heterosexual relationships, the size difference ensures that violent resistance won't help, and may make things worse, so they turn to other means of coping. For a few, eventually it seems that the only way out is to kill him.

The critical defining pattern of violent resistance is that the resister is violent but *not* controlling and is faced with a partner who is *both* violent and controlling; i.e., he is an intimate terrorist. Violence in the face of intimate terrorism may arise from any of a variety of motives. She may (at least at first) believe that she can defend herself, that her violent resistance will keep him from attacking her further. That may mean that she thinks she can stop him right now, in the midst of an attack, or it may mean that she thinks that if she fights back often enough he will eventually decide to stop attacking her physically. Even if she doesn't think she can stop him, she may feel that he shouldn't be allowed to attack her without getting hurt some himself. This desire to hurt him in return even if it won't stop him can be a form of communication ("What you're doing isn't right and I'm going to fight back as hard as I can"), or it may be a form of retaliation or payback, along the lines of "He's not going to do that without paying some price for it." In a few cases, she may be after serious retaliation, attacking him when he is least expecting it and doing her best to do serious damage, even killing him. But there is another, more frequent motive for such premeditated attacks—escape. Sometimes, after years of abuse and entrapment, a victim of intimate terrorism may feel that the only way she can escape from this horror is to kill her tormenter. Such cases have been the focus of some media attention, as in movies such as *The Burning Bed, Sleeping with the Enemy,* and *Enough.* More importantly, the "battered woman defense" has achieved some credibility in the courts;[7] governors and parole boards have been considering clemency, pardons, or parole in cases in which the motive for the murder of an abusive partner was clearly to escape from a seemingly hopeless situation.[8]

Situational Couple Violence

Probably the most common type of partner violence does not involve any attempt on the part of either partner to gain general control over the relationship. The violence is situationally provoked, as the tensions or emotions of a particular encounter lead someone to react with violence. Intimate relationships inevitably involve conflicts, and in some relationships one or more of those conflicts may escalate to violence. The violence may be minor and singular, with one argument at some point in the relationship escalating to the level that someone pushes or slaps the other, is immediately remorseful, apologizes, and never does it again. Or it could be a chronic problem, with one or both partners frequently resorting to violence, minor or severe. I don't want to minimize the danger of such violence. Situationally provoked violence can be life-threatening.

The motives for such violence vary. A physical reaction might feel like the only way one's extreme anger or frustration can be expressed. It may well be intended to do serious injury as an expression of anger. It may primarily be an attempt to get the attention of a partner who doesn't seem to be listening. Or there could be a control motive involved, albeit not one that is part of a general pattern of coercive control. One partner may simply find that the argument is not going well for him or her, and decide that one way to win this is to get physical.

The critical distinctions among types of violence have to do with general patterns of power and control, not with the ostensible motives for specific incidents of violence. Thus, many of the separate violent incidents of situational couple violence may look exactly like those involved in intimate terrorism or violent resistance. The difference is in the general power and control dynamic of the relationship, not in the nature of

any one assault. If it appears that neither partner is generally trying to control the other—i.e., the relationship does not involve the use of a range of control tactics by one or both of the partners—then we are dealing with situational couple violence. It is simply that one or more disagreements have resulted in violence. The violence may even be frequent, if the situation that provokes the violence is recurring, as when one partner frequently feels that the other is flirting, and the confrontations over that issue regularly lead one or the other of them to lash out. And the violence may be quite severe, including even homicide. What makes it situational couple violence is that it is rooted in the events of a particular situation rather than in a relationshipwide attempt to control.

Mutual Violent Control

Finally, in a very small number of cases, both members of the couple are violent and controlling, each behaving in a manner that would identify him or her as an intimate terrorist if it weren't for the fact that their partner also seems to be engaged in the same sort of violent attempt to control the relationship. We know very little about the dynamics of such relationships other than that they seem to involve the "mutual combat" that researchers have for decades attributed to any relationship in which both partners reported that they had been violent. In most such cases, however, that so-called mutual violence was a product of intimate terrorism with violent resistance, or situational couple violence in which both partners had been violent. With mutual violent control, we have the true mutuality of two people fighting for general control over the relationship. . . .

Not Asking the Right Questions: The Battered Husband Fiasco

In 1977, in one of the first publications to come out of the groundbreaking 1975 National Family Violence Survey, Suzanne Steinmetz ignited a decades-long and not-yet-dead debate about the nature of partner violence. Her article, "The Battered Husband Syndrome," argued that there were as many battered husbands in U.S. families as there were battered wives.[9] Her article was immediately answered with intense criticism, a great scholarly debate ensued, and over the years hundreds of studies have addressed the issue of gender symmetry in partner violence.[10] While we have amassed a great deal of scientific evidence that men are far and away more likely than women to be perpetrators of domestic violence,[11] there also appears to be considerable evidence that women are just as likely as men to attack their partners.[12] The debate on this issue has been so acrimonious that, in the late 1990s, I was unable to persuade the protagonists to take part in a panel discussion of the issue at scholarly meetings, the parties basically refusing to be in the same room with each other. How did we come to have two groups of renowned scholars presenting ostensibly credible evidence for their obviously contradictory positions regarding the simplest possible question about partner violence: "Who does it?"?

The answer is that a terrible mistake characterized research on partner violence from the beginning of its development in the early 1970s. No one was thinking about distinguishing among types of partner violence. Researchers assumed that "violence was violence," that although there might be differences in how often and how severely partners assaulted each other, intimate partner violence was essentially one phenomenon. There were two major groups of social scientists doing this early research, but doing it from quite different perspectives and using different sources of data.[13] The "family violence scholars" were interested in violence between parents and their children and between siblings, as well as violence between spouses. Violence was seen as an outcome of family conflict. They did large-scale surveys, interviewing large numbers of U.S. husbands and wives, and were distressed to find that family conflict led many spouses, siblings, and parents to assault other family members in the privacy of their own homes.[14] The "feminist scholars" were focused more specifically on wife abuse. They studied agency data from the police, courts, emergency rooms, and shelters, and they interviewed women who had come to these agencies for help. Violence was seen as a product of patriarchal family traditions and general male dominance in the society. They were appalled at the number of women who were terrorized in their own homes.[15] The two groups of scholars did, however, have at least one thing in common: they each thought that their own research identified the true nature of partner violence. They have been at an impasse over the gender issue for almost thirty years.

The simple solution to this dilemma (simple once you see it) is that the two groups are studying different kinds of partner violence.[16] How can this be? In general, the studies that demonstrate the predominance of male violence involve agency data (courts, police agencies, hospitals, and shelters), while the studies that show gender symmetry involve the "representative" samples of large-scale survey research. Both of these research strategies are heavily biased, the former through its use of biased sampling frames (agency client lists), the latter through refusals. Although the biases of agency data are generally taken to be obvious,[17] representative sample surveys are mistakenly assumed to be unbiased. In fact, the final samples of so-called random sample surveys are *not* random—due to refusals. I have estimated, for example, that the refusal rate in the National Family Violence Surveys was approximately 40 percent rather than the 18 percent usually reported.[18] Could there be two qualitatively different forms of partner violence, one gender-symmetric and overrepresented in general surveys, the other male-perpetrated and overrepresented in agency samples?

In my early work (1995) on this question, I identified a number of agency-based studies and general surveys that used the same set of questions to assess the nature of partner violence.[19] My conclusion from comparing these findings was that the two sampling strategies identify partner violence that differs not only in gender symmetry, but also in a variety of other important ways. Agency samples identify partner violence that is more frequent, more likely to escalate, more severe, less likely to be mutual, and perpetrated almost entirely by men. This gender-asymmetric pattern resonated for me with feminist analyses of partner violence as one tactic in a general pattern of controlling behaviors used by some men to exercise general control over "their" women.[20] The asymmetry of such control contrasted dramatically, it seemed to me, with the family violence perspective's predominantly symmetric image of partner violence as a matter of conflict. I hypothesized that there were two qualitatively different forms/patterns of partner violence—one part of a general strategy of power and control (intimate terrorism), the other involving violence that is not part of a general pattern of control, probably a product of the escalation of couple conflict into violence (situational couple violence).[21] I argued that each research group was unknowingly studying only one of these two types of violence. Couples involved in situational couple violence are unlikely to become agency clients, because such situationally provoked violence does not, in most cases, call for police intervention, emergency room visits, Protection from Abuse orders, an escape to a shelter, or a divorce. Couples involved in intimate terrorism are unlikely to agree to participate in general surveys—the victims out of fear of reprisal from the batterer, the batterers out of fear of exposing themselves to intervention by the police or other agencies. Although these arguments seemed reasonable enough, my 1995 paper provides no direct evidence of their validity because, at that time, no one had made such distinctions among types of violence.

Here is the evidence. The data come from a unique study designed by Irene Frieze in the 1970s. The women she interviewed came from a variety of sources, including agencies (courts and shelters) and a general sample. Thus, if my theory

was correct, her sample was likely to include both situational couple violence and intimate terrorism (and its response, violent resistance). One source of respondents was a flyer placed in laundromats. The second source was a shelter sample of women who had sought help at one of the Pittsburgh area shelters for battered women. Another group consisted of women who had filed for a Protection from Abuse order (PFA) in the courts. The fourth source was women who lived on the same block as the women in each of the first three groups; i.e., this group had not been selected because of violence and, therefore, probably was quite similar to the typical general survey sample.

From the lengthy interview protocols, I chose one question to determine whether the husband and/or wife had been violent, as reported by the wife: "Has he (Have you) ever actually slapped or pushed you (him) or used other physical force with you (him)?" I also selected eleven questions tapping control tactics that did not involve violence toward one's partner. From them, I constructed a coercive control scale and split it into a high-control group and a low-control group. The information regarding the violence and control of both partners was then used to designate each spouse as either nonviolent or involved in one of the four types of partner violence. Given my initial interest in the gender debate, my first question was whether the Pittsburgh data supported my idea that (a) the violence in general survey samples consists mostly of situational couple violence, while the violence in agency samples is mostly intimate terrorism and violent resistance, and (b) situational couple violence is gender-symmetric, intimate terrorism is mostly male-perpetrated, with violent resistors therefore mostly women.

First, let's nail down the sampling argument. Do general survey samples tap primarily situational couple violence, while agency samples give access primarily to intimate terrorism (and violent resistance)? Looking first at male violence, Table 11.2 shows that in the Pittsburgh

TABLE 11.2

MEN'S VIOLENCE IN DIFFERENT SAMPLES

	Survey sample (n = 37)	Court sample (n = 35)	Shelter sample (n = 50)
Mutual violent control	0%	11%	2%
Intimate terrorism	11%	46%	66%
Violent resistance	3%	6%	4%
Situational couple violence	86%	37%	28%

TABLE 11.3

WOMEN'S VIOLENCE IN DIFFERENT SAMPLES

	Survey sample (n = 29)	Court sample (n = 29)	Shelter sample (n = 38)
Mutual violent control	0%	14%	3%
Intimate terrorism	3%	7%	5%
Violent resistance	10%	41%	61%
Situational couple violence	86%	31%	32%

study's general sample (a type of sample that is typical of family violence research), the violent men are involved mostly in situational couple violence, with only 11 percent of their violence being intimate terrorism. In the agency samples, intimate terrorism is much more typical, representing 46 percent of the men's violence in the court data and 66 percent in the shelter data. Table 11.3 presents the data regarding women's violence, which are the other side of the same picture. Situational couple violence dominates the women's violence in the survey sample, while violent resistance is the largest category in the shelter sample, with the court data being intermediate.

Before we move on, let's think about this for a moment. The results for the general sample are much as predicted: targets of intimate terrorism are evidently not willing to participate in general surveys, and we can reasonably assume that any findings from general surveys apply to situational couple violence, not to intimate terrorism. The data from the courts and the shelter, however, surprised me. I had expected agency data to be heavily dominated by men's intimate terrorism and women's violent resistance, but there are considerably more cases of situational couple violence than I had thought there would be. Where did I go wrong? I had mistakenly assumed that only intimate terrorism would frighten women enough to send them to the courts for a Protection from Abuse order, or to a shelter for support or temporary housing. I hadn't paid close enough attention to my own statements that even situational couple violence can be quite frequent and/or severe. And I

TABLE 11.4

GENDER SYMMETRY OF TYPES OF VIOLENCE

	Husbands	Wives	(n)
Intimate terrorism	89%	11%	(81)
Violent resistance	15%	85%	(61)
Situational couple violence	55%	45%	(167)
Mutual violent control*	50%	50%	(16)

*Mutual violent control is symmetrical by definition in heterosexual relationships.

hadn't taken seriously enough the evidence from general surveys (thus dealing with situational couple violence) that men's situational couple violence is much more likely than women's to produce injuries.[22] Shelters and courts are places that women turn to when they fear for their safety. Although intimate terrorism is certainly the type of violence that is most likely to produce such a reaction, situational couple violence involving a man assaulting a woman can also be severe enough or frequent enough to be quite frightening. Thus, although the relatively large number of cases of situational couple violence in the shelter and court samples was somewhat surprising, in retrospect the pattern makes sense.[23] General samples involve almost entirely cases of situational couple violence, while agency samples involve a mix of intimate terrorism and the most frightening cases of situational couple violence.[24]

The data in Tables 11.2 and 11.3 establish that the different sampling strategies do, indeed, tap different kinds of violence. Are the gender differences in violence type such that those biases could have created the gender debate? The answer clearly is "Yes," as you can see from Table 11.4. Eighty-nine percent of the intimate terrorists in the Pittsburgh data were men.[25] Of course, it follows that in this sample of heterosexual couples almost all of the violent resistance comes from women (85 percent). In dramatic contrast to the clear gendering of intimate terrorism and violent

resistance is situational couple violence, which is close to gender-symmetric, at least by the crude criterion of prevalence. . . . Mutual violent control, which is very rare, is gender-symmetric by definition in heterosexual couples, because it is defined by both partners' being violent and controlling.[26]

That explains the gender fiasco, doesn't it? Men and women are equally involved only in situational couple violence.[27] When someone goes on television or publishes a paper to pronounce that the survey evidence proves that women are as violent as men in intimate relationships, they are suggesting that women are as likely as men to be batterers and abusers—intimate terrorists. And the suggestion is not subtle. They tell stories about some of the few women who are, indeed, intimate terrorists,[28] or they are on a talk show in which the panel consists of "girls who beat up their boyfriends" or "men who are afraid of their wives." But we have just shown that *survey* data about violence are only about situational couple violence, not intimate terrorism. Intimate terrorism is in fact perpetrated almost entirely by men.

And situational couple violence isn't anything like intimate terrorism. Here are some data about the violence perpetrated by the men from the Pittsburgh study. The violence in men's intimate terrorism is quite frequent; the modal number of incidents in these marriages is one hundred.[29] The modal number of violent events in men's situational couple violence is one. Intimate terrorism escalated in severity of violence in 72 percent of the cases; situational couple violence escalated in only 29 percent. In terms of injuries, the violence of intimate terrorism was severe in 67 percent of the cases, compared to 29 percent of the cases of situational couple violence. These data do not leave much doubt that intimate terrorism and situational couple violence are not the same phenomenon.[30] We need to make these distinctions.

■ Review Questions

1. How does what Johnson calls "intimate terrorism" differ from what he calls "situational couple violence"?
2. Why do surveys find many more reports of the "situational" form of violence than of the "terrorism" form?

ENDNOTES

1. R. Emerson Dobash and Russell P. Dobash, *Violence against Wives: A Case against Patriarchy* (New York: Free Press, 1979), 94.
2. I have avoided using the term "perpetrator" here because it implies that the violent resister is the primary initiator of the violence in the relationship. That certainly is not the case for violent resistance. A violent resister is, however, a perpetrator in the sense of having committed a violent act, and should that violence come to the attention of the criminal justice system, "perpetrator" is the term that would be applied.
3. Ellen Pence and Michael Paymar, *Education Groups for Men Who Batter: The Duluth Model* (New York: Springer, 1993).
4. I am going to use gendered pronouns here because, as I will show later, the vast majority of intimate terrorists are men terrorizing female partners. That does not mean that women are never intimate terrorists. There are a small number of women who do terrorize their male partners, and there are also women in same-sex relationships who terrorize their partners. I will discuss both of these situations later. Suzanne K. Steinmetz, "The Battered Husband Syndrome," *Victimology* 2, no. 3-sup-4 (1977–78); Claire M. Renzetti, *Violent Betrayal: Partner Abuse in Lesbian Relationships* (Thousand Oaks, Calif.: Sage, 1992).
5. Catherine Kirkwood, *Leaving Abusive Partners: From the Scars of Survival to the Wisdom for Change* (Newbury Park, Calif.: Sage, 1993).
6. Once again, I will use gendered pronouns because most violent resisters are women in heterosexual relationships. There certainly are also violent resisters in same-sex relationships and in the small number of cases in which a woman is able to terrorize her male partner.
7. Lenore E. Walker, "Legal Self-Defense for Battered Women," in *Battering and Family Therapy: A Feminist Perspective,* ed. Marsali Hansen and Michele Harway (Thousand Oaks, Calif.: Sage, 1993); Lenore E. Walker, *Terrifying Love: Why Battered Women Kill and How Society Responds* (New York: Harper & Row, 1989).
8. Linda L. Ammons, "Dealing with the Nastiness: Mixing Feminism and Criminal Law in the Review of Cases of Battered Incarcerated Women—a Tenth-Year Reflection," *Buffalo Criminal Law Review* 4 (2001).
9. Steinmetz, "The Battered Husband Syndrome."
10. Elizabeth Pleck et al., "The Battered Data Syndrome: A Comment on Steinmetz's Article," *Victimology* 2 (1978).
11. Russell P. Dobash et al., "The Myth of Sexual Symmetry in Marital Violence," *Social Problems* 39, no. 1 (1992).
12. John Archer, "Sex Differences in Aggression between Heterosexual Partners: A Meta-Analytic Review," *Psychological Bulletin* 126, no. 5 (2000).
13. I use the word "groups" here loosely. Although some of the scholars within each group have collaborated with each other, these groups are identified primarily by the theoretical frameworks that drive their work and the sources from which they generally gather

their information. Michael P. Johnson, "Patriarchal Terrorism and Common Couple Violence: Two Forms of Violence against Women," *Journal of Marriage and the Family* 57, no. 2 (1995); Demie Kurz, "Social Science Perspectives on Wife Abuse: Current Debates and Future Directions," *Gender & Society* 3, no. 4 (1989): 489–505.

14. Richard J. Gelles, "Violence in the Family: A Review of Research in the Seventies," *Journal of Marriage & the Family* 42, no. 4 (1980); Murray A. Straus, "A General Systems Theory Approach to a Theory of Violence between Family Members," *Social Science Information* 12, no. 3 (1973); Murray A. Straus, Richard J. Gelles, and Suzanne K. Steinmetz, *Behind Closed Doors: Violence in the American Family* (Garden City, N.Y.: Doubleday, 1980).

15. Dobash and Dobash, *Violence against Wives;* Dell Martin, *Battered Wives* (New York: Pocket Books, 1976); Mildred Daley Pagelow, *Woman-Battering: Victims and Their Experiences* (Newbury Park, Calif.: Sage, 1981); Maria Roy, ed., *Battered Women: A Psychosociological Study of Domestic Violence* (New York: Van Nostrand Reinhold, 1977); Lenore E. Walker, *The Battered Woman* (New York: Harper & Row, 1979).

16. Johnson, "Patriarchal Terrorism and Common Couple Violence."

17. Murray A. Straus, "Injury and Frequency of Assault and the 'Representative Sample Fallacy' in Measuring Wife Beating and Child Abuse," in *Physical Violence in American Families.*

18. Johnson, "Patriarchal Terrorism and Common Couple Violence."

19. Much of the gender debate in the literature has centered on the inadequacies of these questions, called the Conflict Tactics Scales or CTS, as a means to assess partner violence. Dobash et al., "The Myth of Sexual Symmetry in Marital Violence"; Straus, "The Conflict Tactics Scales." Whatever the inadequacies of the CTS may be, it is the most widely used instrument for assessing level of partner violence. Comparing studies that all used the CTS eliminated this potential source of bias.

20. Dobash and Dobash, *Violence against Wives;* Pence and Paymar, *The Duluth Model;* Evan Stark and Anne Flitcraft, *Women at Risk: Domestic Violence and Women's Health* (Thousand Oaks, Calif.: Sage, 1996).

21. The terminology I use has changed somewhat over the years, although the definitions have remained the same. My 1995 paper refers to "patriarchal terrorism" and "common couple violence." I soon abandoned the former term because it begs the question of men's and women's relative involvement in this form of controlling violence. It also implies that all such intimate terrorism is somehow rooted in patriarchal structures, traditions, or attitudes. I still believe that intimate terrorism is perpetrated primarily by men in heterosexual relationships and that in such cases the violence is, indeed, rooted in patriarchal traditions. However, it is clear that there are women who are intimate terrorists in both heterosexual and same-sex relationships. Renzetti, *Violent Betrayal.* Furthermore, it is not necessarily the case that all intimate terrorism, even men's, is rooted in patriarchal ideas or structures. With regard to "common couple violence," I abandoned it in favor of "situational couple violence" because the former terminology implies to some readers that I feel that such violence is acceptable. I also prefer the new terminology because it more clearly identifies the roots of this violence in the situated escalation of conflict.

22. Jan E. Stets and Murray A. Straus, "Gender Differences in Reporting Marital Violence and Its Medical and Psychological Consequences," in *Physical Violence in American Families.*

23. It is also possible that there is a measurement error issue involved in this finding. The difference between situational couple violence (SCV) and intimate terrorism (IT) amounts to being on one side or the other of a cutoff between "low" and "high" on the Coercive Control Scale. The choice of cutoff is somewhat arbitrary, and there are likely to be some low-control cases that may actually involve intimate terrorism. This is one of those areas in social science where I am convinced that a reasonably well designed qualitative interview could give us better information than can an "objective" scale. In fact, there is even a quantitative approach, called cluster analysis, that I believe does a better job of identifying the types; when I use that approach, the Pittsburgh data look a little more as expected. Only 29 percent of the male violence in the court sample is identified as situational couple violence (compared to 37 percent with the arbitrary cutoff); 19 percent is identified

as situational couple violence in the shelter sample (compared to 28 percent with the arbitrary cutoff). Michael P. Johnson, "Conflict and Control: Symmetry and Asymmetry in Domestic Violence," in *Couples in Conflict,* ed. Alan Booth, Ann C. Crouter, and Mari Clements (Mahwah, N.J.: Lawrence Erlbaum, 2001), 102.

24. Looking, for example, at the frequency of violence from male partners involved in situational couple violence, we see that the average number of violent incidents is one in the general Pittsburgh sample, fifteen in the court sample, and twelve in the shelter sample. Similarly, situational couple violence involves serious injury to the woman in 19 percent of the cases in the general sample, 64 percent in the court sample, and 50 percent in the shelter sample.

25. If I use the cluster analysis approach, intimate terrorism is 97 percent male perpetrated. Situational couple violence is 56 percent male perpetrated. Johnson, "Conflict and Control," 100.

26. Nevertheless, the debate about gender symmetry continues, and there is very little published empirical work that addresses the issue in terms of the gender symmetry of intimate terrorism versus situational couple violence. There is one study (done in England) that quite closely replicates my findings. Graham-Kevan and Archer (2003) used control measures completely different from those I constructed from the Pittsburgh data and a sample that included 43 women shelter clients, 4 male batterer intervention participants, 104 students (mixed gender), and 97 male prisoners (not selected for domestic violence). They found that 87 percent of the intimate terrorists were men and 90 percent of the violent resisters were women, while situational couple violence was 45 percent male and 55 percent female. Their data also confirm the sampling pattern, with 75 percent of the men's violence in their nonselected sample being situational couple violence, as compared with 10 percent in their shelter sample. Nicola Graham-Kevan and John Archer, "Intimate Terrorism and Common Couple Violence: A Test of Johnson's Predictions in Four British Samples," *Journal of Interpersonal Violence* 18, no. 11 (2003): 1256, 1260.

There are also two recent studies that raise some questions about the gender distribution of intimate terrorism, finding intimate terrorism to be roughly gender symmetric. Nicola Graham-Kevan and John

Archer, "Using Johnson's Domestic Violence Typology to Classify Men and Women in a Non-Selected Sample," unpublished (2005); Denis Laroche, "Aspects of the Context and Consequences of Domestic Violence: Situational Couple Violence and Intimate Terrorism in Canada," report, Government of Québec, Institut de la statistique du Québec, 2005. However, both of these studies use general samples. The problem with a general sample is that, as Graham-Kevan and Archer, and I, have shown, such samples include very little intimate terrorism. Because we have no well-defined criterion for the level of control required to identify intimate terrorism, authors generally resort to a cluster analysis approach. In a sample with little or no intimate terrorism, the cluster analysis will still identify a high-control cluster, but it is likely to consist mostly of situational couple violence, perhaps with a few cases of intimate terrorism. Thus, the gender distribution for the so-called intimate terrorism will be more like that of situational couple violence.

27. And mutual violent control, which is very rare.

28. Steinmetz, "The Battered Husband Syndrome."

29. I must admit, I used the mode here in part for dramatic effect, although it is true that 11 percent of the intimate terrorists are reported to have been violent one hundred times, and 32 percent of the men involved in situational common violence had been violent only once. The modal figure of one hundred reported by wives for intimate terrorists is certainly inflated, because it is up in the range where women would not be giving precise estimates, but choosing numbers that approximated their experiences. The means and medians may not provide as dramatic a picture, but the differences are still clear. The means for intimate terrorism and situational couple violence are forty-four and ten, respectively. The medians are nineteen and three, respectively.

30. Remember that the types are defined in terms of control context, not the frequency or severity of the violence. The hypothesized differences in frequency and severity of the violence are derived from theory. It is assumed that attempts by husbands to exert general control over their wives will be met by considerable resistance in the United States, where marriage is seen by most women as a partnership. Thus, the intimate terrorist will in some cases turn to violence repeatedly and may escalate its severity in order to gain control.

READING 11-2

Controversies Surrounding Mandatory Arrest Policies and the Police Response to Intimate Partner Violence

Amy Leisenring

INTRODUCTION

Understandings of and responses to violence against women by an intimate partner have changed drastically in the last several decades in the USA. While in the 1960s, intimate partner violence was primarily understood as a personal and private issue and was largely ignored by the police and criminal justice system, it is now viewed as a major social problem and is taken much more seriously. Pressure from feminist groups and battered women's advocates has led to numerous reforms within the criminal justice system. One of the most significant reforms has been the implementation of policies that encourage or mandate the arrest of offenders, often referred to as "mandatory arrest policies." (Many jurisdictions have also adopted "no-drop" prosecution policies that encourage or mandate the prosecution of offenders but a discussion of such policies is beyond the scope of this paper.) Mandatory arrest policies have been the source of much controversy and debate; researchers, activists, victim's advocates, policy-makers, and law enforcement officials disagree about the effectiveness of such policies and the ultimate effects that they have on the lives of the women that they were designed to protect. . . .

Mandatory and pro-arrest (or presumptive) policies are common today in the majority of jurisdictions in the USA. A mandatory arrest law

Amy Leisenring, "Controversies Surrounding Mandatory Arrest Policies and the Police Response to Intimate Partner Violence," *Sociology Compass* 2/2 (2008): 451–466. Reprinted with permission.

requires the police to arrest an offender if there is probable cause to believe that intimate partner violence has occurred (Schneider 2000). Pro-arrest policies or presumptive policies encourage arrest but allow officers a bit more discretion. In the last two decades, numerous districts have adopted aggressive arrest policies: currently, 31 states have passed mandatory arrest laws (American Civil Liberties Union 2007). Such laws and policies remove the decision to press charges from the victim. They also reduce the likelihood that responding officers will use their own judgment to decide whether or not to make an arrest, which in the past, often resulted in inaction by many police officers. Policies that mandate or encourage arrest of abusers are seen as sending a message to police officers to "take domestic assaults seriously; treat them criminally" (Gosselin 2000, 316). However, these policies have been the subject of much controversy and debate.

DEBATES OVER REFORMS

Mandatory arrest polices have been highly controversial, both in and outside of feminist circles. At issue are a number of questions, mainly: (i) Who should have control over what happens when the police respond to an intimate partner violence case: the state, the police, or the victim? (ii) Are mandatory arrest policies in the best interest of all victims? (iii) Do mandatory arrest policies have an impact on the behavior of perpetrators? In this section, I will review the central debates surrounding each of these questions and discuss what the research shows surrounding these issues.

Mandatory Arrest Policies and Issue of Control

A central issue surrounding mandatory arrest policies is the issue of control. Because these policies either mandate or encourage police officers who respond to intimate partner violence calls to arrest the perpetrator, ostensibly the decision-making power about what happens to an offender is removed from both the victim and police and rests with the state. Many argue that this is a good thing and favor mandatory arrest policies because they help the state to send a uniform message to the community that intimate partner violence is a serious crime and is a matter of public concern instead of a private issue between the two people involved (Schneider 2000). Battered women's advocates in favor of mandatory arrest laws argue that such laws hold agents of the state such as police officers responsible for fulfilling the government's responsibility to protect its citizens (Stark 2004). Furthermore, as Stark (1993) states, "making battering the only crime in which police discretion is removed acknowledges a special social interest in redressing the legacy of discriminatory treatment of women by law enforcement" (p. 662).

Others argue that removing or lessening responding police officers decision-making powers through mandatory arrest policies is positive (see Stark 1993 for discussion). Such policies control the behavior of police officers and hold them accountable for taking action. Many feminists and battered women's activists see this as beneficial given the typical police response of minimal or no action when they have responded to intimate partner violence calls in the past. Indeed, as Stark (1993) points out, arrests for assaults rose 70% from 1984 to 1989 due to the implementation of mandatory arrest laws.

Finally, some have also argued that having policies that mandate the arrest of abusers is helpful to victims because it takes the pressure off of victims to make the decision whether or not to arrest their batterer (see Stewart 2001 for discussion). This makes it less likely that batterers will hold victims responsible for their arrest and thus retaliate at a later date. Mandating arrest also helps to ensure that the offender will be arrested for breaking a law regardless of the wishes of the victim. Indeed, a study conducted by Buzawa and Austin (1993) revealed that the actions taken by police officers who respond to intimate partner violence calls were largely influenced by victims'

preferences for what they wanted to have happen to their abusers. The officers were more likely to arrest a perpetrator if this is what the victim desired and less likely to arrest a perpetrator if it went against the victim's wishes. Supporters of mandatory arrest policies argue that these policies will help to ensure that all offenders of intimate partner violence are arrested.

Even though mandatory arrest policies are supposed to remove the discretion of police officers who respond to intimate partner violence calls and diminish the likelihood that police will respond negatively to victims, current research demonstrates that gender bias within the system still exists and that many female victims continue to have negative experiences with the police. For example, Stephens and Sinden (2000) found that the majority of battered women in their study who had more than one encounter with law enforcement officials for intimate partner violence reported that police officers commonly minimized the seriousness of their situation, doubted their story, conveyed attitudes of nonchalance and indifference, and/or were rude and condescending. Similarly, a study by Belknap and Hartman (2000) of victim advocates' reports found that while some advocates reported favorable police behaviors and responses, many believe that there are still a "significant" portion of cases in which police response is unfavorable or even hostile.

Finally, not everyone believes that taking away control from battered women during the police response to intimate partner violence calls is a good thing; some argue that removing victims from major-decision-making roles in their cases is not always in the best interest of the women who experience intimate partner violence (Dasgupta 2003; Ford 1991; Hilton 1993; Mills 2003). Some researchers and battered women's advocates argue that mandatory arrest policies disempower women because they limit women's agency and ability to act in their own best interests, ignore their opinions, and revictimize them through forced submittal to state power (Ferraro and Pope 1993; Ford 1991; McLeod 1983). Many women who call the police do not want their batterer arrested (Ferraro and Pope 1993; Stewart 2001). There are multiple reasons a woman may not want her batterer to be arrested and/or jailed: she may depend on him for income and/or housing for herself and/or her children, she may be afraid he will be even angrier when he gets out of jail and his violence against her will escalate, she may not trust the system, she may prefer he receive counseling and support instead of prosecution and punishment, and/or she may not want to end her relationship with him. As Gelles (1993) argues, some women who do not wish their abuser to be arrested use their call to the police and/or the resulting police visit as a means of controlling their abuser's behavior. Because mandatory arrest policies remove this option from women, some have argued that they also remove power from abused women. And, as Rajah et al. (2006) point out, some see the removal of control from female victims as particularly problematic because "women who are denied decision-making power in mandatory arrest encounters may be dissatisfied with the criminal justice response to intimate partner violence and discouraged from calling the police in future domestic disputes" (p. 899).

What does research show about how victimized women themselves view mandatory arrest policies and the amount of control they have in the police response to violence perpetrated against them? Studies indicate that there is mixed support from battered women for such policies. Smith (2001) surveyed 93 battered women staying at emergency shelters and found that while the majority of the women were supportive of mandatory policies, their support varied by race, marital status, and the extent of their injuries, suggesting that some women desire more control over the outcomes of their cases. For example, while 79% of the white women in her sample were supportive of the adoption of mandatory arrest policies, only 53% of the black women in her study were supportive of such policies, suggesting that "Black women prefer more power and control over the arrest decision than White

women" (p. 102). Single and divorced women were more supportive of mandatory arrest policies than married or separated women. Smith concludes that her findings lend support to the claim that universalistic policies are not likely the best means of addressing the individual needs of victims. Similarly, Bohmer et al. (2002), who conducted focus groups with both victims of intimate partner violence and service providers for intimate partner violence victims, found that while support for mandatory policies was mixed among the providers, clients were even less likely to support such policies. The foremost concern of the clients was "their future financial and personal well-being" and they saw the criminal justice system as "being an impediment to that future rather than a source of help" (p. 84). As one victim in this study stated of her abuser: "Well I need him to pay the bills more than I need him to pay for the violence" (p. 82). Such findings have led to broader questions about whether or not mandatory arrest policies serve the best interests of all battered women.

Mandatory Arrest Policies and Victims' Best Interests

Again, many argue that because mandatory arrest policies have led to police officers taking intimate partner violence more seriously, they are beneficial to battered women. The findings from a study conducted by Jones and Belknap (1999) suggest that the implementation of a pro-arrest policy in one jurisdiction served to improve the likelihood of a "strong" police response to intimate partner violence. Epstein (1999) discusses a study conducted in 1990 in the District of Columbia that found that police officers who responded to intimate partner violence calls were arresting accused batterers in only 5% of all cases; furthermore, they failed to arrest in over 80% of cases where the victim had visible injuries. After the city implemented a mandatory arrest law, the rate of arrest of offenders by responding police officers rose from 5% to 41%. Epstein (1999) argues that mandatory arrest policies appear to benefit those victims who desire the arrest of their abusers. Furthermore, research also demonstrates that under mandatory arrest policies more intimate partner violence victims are reporting the violence that they experience to the police (Cho and Wilke 2005).

A number of critics of mandatory arrest policies have argued that these policies are not in the best interest of all abused women. A major argument stems from the recognition that abused women's experiences are diverse and multifaceted—there is no one universal victimized woman's experience. Some critics see uniform responses to intimate partner violence as problematic because such responses fail to take into account the diversity of women's situations based on structural factors such as race, culture, and class and individual factors such as different women's desires and needs (Crenshaw 1994; Dasgupta 2003; Mills 1996). For example, Epstein (1999) makes the argument that the recent reforms to immigration law in the USA may lead abused immigrant women to reject the criminal justice system as a means of addressing the violence in their lives because of fear that their abuser will be deported.

Similarly, some have argued that using arrest as the main means of addressing intimate partner violence exacerbates problems in minority and/ or poor communities where police have often demonstrated inappropriate behavior and women may be mistrustful of the police (Sparks 1997). For example, Crenshaw (1994) argues that some women of color may be reluctant to call the police because they do not want to subject their abuser to a criminal justice system that has historically discriminated against men of color. Research on this topic has been mixed. One study cited by Epstein (1999) found that African American abused women worried that reporting abusers to the police "could further contribute to the social stereotyping of black men as particularly violent" (p. 137). However, a 2000 study by Rennison and Welchans (as cited in Stark 2004) found that some women of color actually report their victimization at higher rates (67% for black

women and 65% for Hispanic women) than other groups, including white women (50%).

Still others who argue that mandatory arrest policies are not always in victimized women's best interests point to the increasing number of studies showing that a growing number of women are arrested under these policies. Evidence suggests that in some jurisdictions after mandatory arrest policies were implemented the number of women arrested for intimate partner violence substantially increased (Hirschel and Buzawa 2002; Miller 2001). For example, female aggregate felony intimate partner violence arrest rates increased more than 500% in California from 1987 to 1997 (DeLeon-Granados et al. 2006). Dual arrests—where women are arrested along with their male partners and ex-partners—appear to be the most common scenario under which women are arrested for intimate partner violence (Finn and Bettis 2006). While a possible explanation for the rise in women's arrest rates for intimate partner violence is that their use of violence has increased (DeLeon-Granados et al. 2006), many scholars and battered women's advocates argue that this is not the case. For example, while acknowledging that some women who are arrested for intimate partner violence do actually assault their partners, Osthoff (2002) argues that many women are wrongly arrested for engaging in acts of self-defense or when their abusers falsely accuse them of violence.

Indeed, a study conducted by Finn and Bettis (2006) that explored police officers' justifications for using dual arrest did find that even though police officers are required by law to fully investigate the context in which an act of intimate partner violence occurs, many are hesitant to do so. Finn and Bettis state that the officers "for the most part, fail to take into consideration factors that would help [them] distinguish an assault that was part of an ongoing pattern of battering from one that was not" (p. 282). This is tied to a criticism of mandatory arrest policies that centers on what Stark (2004) terms the "incident-specific understanding" of battering held by the criminal justice system (p. 1321). Under current practice, when police respond to an intimate partner violence call, they are required to make an arrest based on whether or not an incident of violence has occurred; thus, they often fail to take into consideration the context in which the abuse has occurred and the continuous cycle of control and abuse that is common to many abusive relationships.

Mandatory Arrest Policies and Effect on Offenders' Behavior

Debate also exists surrounding if/how mandatory arrest policies impact the behavior of offenders and whether or not these policies actually prevent intimate partner violence. Once again, research examining the effectiveness of mandatory arrest policies in deterring future violence has produced contradictory results (Belknap 2001; Schmidt and Sherman 1996). In the 1980s Sherman and Berk's (1984) Minneapolis experiment showed that arresting batterers helped to serve as a deterrent to future violence and resulted in the implementation of mandatory arrest policies all around the USA (Schmidt and Sherman 1996). However, in the 1990s, replication studies of the Minneapolis experiment in six other cities reflected both deterrent and backfiring effects of arrest (Schmidt and Sherman 1996). For example, based on the replication studies, researchers concluded that (i) arrest reduces intimate partner violence in some cities but increases it in others; (ii) arrest reduces intimate partner violence among employed people but increases it among unemployed people; and (iii) arrest reduces intimate partner violence in the short term but may increase it in the long run (Sherman 1992). These replication studies paint a very muddy and confusing picture regarding the effectiveness of arrest in deterring intimate partner violence. Sherman (1992) himself has retracted the importance of the results of his original Minneapolis experiment and argues that mandatory arrest laws should be repealed.

Other studies examining the success of mandatory arrest policies also have produced mixed

results. Maxwell et al. (2002) found that while in general arrest is associated with a decrease in subsequent intimate partner violence, 40% of victims in their sample experienced repeat victimizations. They conclude that "arresting suspects, although effective on average, is not a panacea for all victims of intimate partner violence" (p. 72). Simpson et al. (2006) argue that research on the impact of mandatory arrest policies on police actions and behavior is somewhat limited and the results are contradictory. They found that in the state of Maryland there was a significant and positive impact of legislation encouraging arrest on the likelihood of police officers to arrest offenders in intimate partner violence cases.

Some research suggests that mandatory arrest policies are not executed uniformly across all populations and that racial and class disparities exist surrounding responding police officers' decisions about who to arrest. For example, Avakame and Fyfe (2001) found that police are more likely to arrest an offender if the victim is a wealthy, white, older, suburban female. They also found that the police are more likely to arrest if the offender is African American, if the offender is under the influence of drugs and alcohol, if the assault occurred in a suburban or rural area (as opposed to an urban area), and if there was injury to the victim. The study of Maxwell et al. (2002) showed that according to official arrest records more men of color were likely to reoffend but if victim interviews were consulted then white men were more likely to reoffend. The authors argue that this discrepancy may be due to a greater willingness of African American women to call the police and a greater likelihood of police officers to arrest African American offenders. In their study, Simpson et al. (2006) found that the implementation of a mandatory arrest policy did not differentially impact the arrest probabilities for African Americans and whites.

Data from the Bureau of Justice Statistics indicate that the rate of nonfatal incidents of intimate partner violence dropped from 5.8 per 1,000 residents in 1993 to 2.6 per 1,000 residents in 2004

(Catalano 2006). These data also show a 26% decline between 1993 and 2004 in the number of females murdered by an intimate partner and a 45% decline in the number of males murdered by an intimate partner (Catalano 2006). Because many battered women end up killing their batterer in self-defense when they believe that the state has failed to protect them (Belknap 2001; Schneider 2000), it is possible that the decrease in the number of males murdered by an intimate partner is a sign that increased intervention by the criminal justice system has provided battered women with the resources they need to safely exit their abusive relationship without having to kill their abuser. However, these trends also may be the function of the increased efforts of the battered women's and shelter movement over the past several decades which have aided women in safely exiting violent relationships. As some critics have pointed out, the exact relationship between criminal justice reforms and the decrease in intimate partner violence is unclear (Dasgupta 2003). Thus, drawing specific conclusions from trends about the success or failure of criminal justice reforms such as mandatory arrest policies is risky at best. A study conducted by the National Institute of Justice determined that "no one policy affects all groups the same way in terms of decreasing violence" (as cited in Dasgupta 2003, 9).

FUTURE DIRECTIONS

How are we to make sense of the conflicting and contradictory findings of the numerous studies that examine mandatory arrest policies and their impact on victims and offenders? Given that the findings of most of these studies are not consistent, how can we determine whether or not mandatory arrest policies are successful in preventing intimate partner violence and whether they are beneficial to the victims of such violence? Returning to Johnson's (2005, 2006) argument that there are different types of intimate partner violence is useful when trying to answer these questions. The existence of different types

of intimate partner violence likely helps to explain the lack of consistent findings surrounding the effects of mandatory arrest policies: the impact of arrest on perpetrators and/or victims may differ depending upon the type of intimate partner violence that exists in a relationship. Johnson and Ferraro (2000) argue, "Partner violence cannot be understood without acknowledging important distinctions among types of violence, motives of perpetrators, the social locations of both partners, and the cultural contexts in which violence occurs" (p. 948). And obviously, if we cannot understand partner violence we cannot develop a response that will successfully reduce and eradicate partner violence.

Clearly, a more aggressive police response to intimate partner violence by the criminal justice system has helped to solidify the message that such violence is not socially acceptable. Evidence suggests that policies that encourage the arrest and prosecution of abusers help some victimized women in some instances. However, the creation of laws and policies that treat all intimate partner violence cases uniformly are problematic if they fail to recognize the various types of domestic violence; place too much emphasis on particular incidents of violence; and fail to understand victim's experiences with violence in the context of their entire relationship (Mahoney 1994; Wittner 1998). Uniform policies appear unable to account for and address the complex nature of intimate partner violence and the diversity of abused women's needs, desires, and experiences. A growing number of studies seem to suggest that mandatory law enforcement policies do not always serve the best interests of all victimized women, nor do they appear to be the sole solution to stopping intimate partner violence and guaranteeing the safety of women who are abused. Research indicates that in some cases (such as those in which victimized women are arrested), mandatory arrest policies may do more harm for abused women than good.

Thus, it seems that if as a society we truly are invested in the idea of stopping intimate partner violence, several things are necessary. First, we need more research that looks at how the needs and desires of the victims of various types of intimate partner violence may differ and how these needs may be best met. Similarly, we need research that examines if/how mandatory arrest policies differently impact the various types of intimate partner violence. For example, research is needed to answer questions such as whether or not arrest is more effective for those who perpetrate situational couple violence than for those men who perpetrate intimate terrorism. Second, there needs to be more training for agents of the criminal justice system such as police officers to help them better understand and recognize the different types of violence and the dynamics and patterns of abuse that exist in violent relationships. As Johnson (2005) points out, the response and intervention strategies that are most successful in eradicating intimate partner violence will likely vary depending on the type of violence. Finally, we must question the value of mandatory policies that dictate the uniform treatment of all intimate partner violence cases and acknowledge that such policies have had many unintended consequences. Instead of uniform policies, we should encourage responses that recognize the complexity of intimate partner violence and victims' experiences. These are challenging tasks, for sure, but they are neccessary in order to ensure the safety of all victims of intimate partner violence.

■ Review Questions

1. Why do some advocates think that it is necessary to require the police to arrest a batterer even if the victim does not want him to be arrested?
2. In what situations do you think that mandatory arrests would be justified?

CHAPTER 12

Divorce

The experience of having one's parents divorce is now common in childhood. Perhaps 40 percent of American children under age 18 will witness their parents' divorce. The process is often very difficult. Nearly all children are upset when they first learn of the separation, although a minority who are in highly conflicted families also may feel some relief. For the first year or two, commonly referred to in the literature as the "crisis period," difficulties are likely to persist. What is the longer-term picture?

This chapter presents two perspectives on this topic. The first is by Sara McLanahan, a sociologist. She focuses on the social and economic consequences: the chances of dropping out of high school, having a child outside of marriage, or having trouble finding a job. Her reading of the literature is that most children adequately adjust to divorce and avoid serious long-term problems but that the risk of undesirable outcomes increases. She also addresses questions such as the following: Do some of the apparent effects of divorce actually reflect conditions that were present in the family prior to the divorce? Why exactly does father absence make a difference?

And what policies might be adopted to reduce divorce and its harmful effects?

The second selection is by two psychologists, Joan B. Kelly and Robert E. Emery. They focus on the psychological outcomes of divorce, such as behavior problems, anxiety, and depression. Like McLanahan, they conclude that divorce raises the risk of experiencing problems but that most children do not experience serious problems as a result of their parents' divorce. But why, they then ask, do we commonly hear that most children are harmed by divorce in the long-term? The answer, they argue, is that many adults whose parents divorced can function well in life but still have painful memories of the divorce and its aftermath. When we ask them about their family lives, they can easily call up these memories. Nevertheless, most such people go about their lives without much difficulty. We should not minimize the painful reflections they have, say the authors; but we should not make the mistake of confusing their pain with pathology. They may have painful reflections, but their adult lives are not compromised by antisocial behavior, depression, or the inability to hold a job.

Life without Father

What Happens to the Children?

Sara McLanahan

Over half of all children born in the United States today will, if current trends continue, live apart from at least one of their biological parents—usually the father—before they reach adulthood. A substantial proportion (about one-fifth) will never live with their fathers. These families are economically vulnerable and they disproportionately represent ethnic minorities. As almost all Americans have either experienced divorce or are close to people who have, the consequences of divorce are of personal as well as social interest.

The conventional wisdom on the issue of father absence has shifted dramatically over the past four decades. During the 1960s, most people viewed divorce and out-of-wedlock childbearing as leading inevitably to delinquency, school failure, and other social problems. During the 1970s, the pendulum swung in the opposite direction. Leading sociologists argued that single motherhood was just another lifestyle reflecting women's growing economic independence and freedom to leave unhappy marriages. Since the mid-1980s, a new consensus holds that although most children of divorced parents do all right, growing up without a father increases the risk of numerous undesirable outcomes. Whether these outcomes are caused by the divorce itself, as opposed to something else about the family, remains controversial.

THE SCOPE OF THE PROBLEM

Children raised apart from a biological parent are disadvantaged in numerous ways. They are more

Sara McLanahan, "Life without Father: What Happens to the Children?" *Contexts*, Vol. 1, No. 1, 2002: 35–44.

likely to drop out of high school, less likely to attend college, and less likely to graduate from college than children raised by both biological parents. Girls from father-absent families are more likely to become sexually active at a younger age and to have a child outside of marriage. Boys who grow up without their fathers are more likely to have trouble finding (and keeping) a job in young adulthood. Young adult men and women from one-parent families tend to work at low-paying jobs.

The popular perception of these effects is subjective. High school graduation is one example. Some argue that the effects of father absence are small, noting that most children living apart from their fathers graduate from high school (80 percent, as compared with 90 percent for children in two-parent families). Others argue that the effects are large, noting that dropout rates double (from 10 percent to 20 percent) when fathers are gone. Most of the outcomes described above follow this pattern and therefore are subject to these two conflicting interpretations.

Although father absence is much more common among ethnic minorities and low-income families, the penalties associated with single parenthood appear to be more or less similar for children from all socioeconomic backgrounds. Where differences do exist, the costs tend to be higher for children from white and middle-class backgrounds than for children from more disadvantaged backgrounds. In other words, children from advantaged backgrounds seem to lose more when their fathers leave. Possible explanations are that living without a father is more common in poorer communities, or children from middle-class families have more to lose. In most instances, children of widowed mothers fare better than children of divorced and never-married mothers, perhaps because widows experience less economic insecurity (they are eligible for social security benefits) or because a father's death disrupts a child's family and friendship ties less than a divorce does. Also, a child is less likely to feel rejected by a parent who dies than a parent who is absent by choice.

Some believe that children of never-married mothers fare worse than children raised by divorced mothers. The evidence suggests otherwise. Once differences in parents' economic circumstances are taken into account, these two groups of children do equally well. What about children who grow up in stable cohabiting unions? Unfortunately, social scientists can say little about whether a child born to unmarried parents who stay together is disadvantaged relative to a child born to married parents who stay together. Since cohabitation was relatively rare until recently, and since long-term cohabiting unions are still very rare, we know little about the long-term effects on children of this family arrangement.

Remarriage is another instance where general perceptions are distorted. Children in stepfamilies fare no better than children in single-parent families and in some instances fare worse. Frank Furstenberg and Andrew Cherlin, two leading family sociologists, attribute this finding to the lack of established societal guidelines about how stepfamilies should operate. Parents and children therefore constantly negotiate over their rights and responsibilities. Other researchers claim that biological parenthood benefits children more than step-parenthood for genetic reasons.

DOES FATHER ABSENCE CAUSE POOR OUTCOMES IN CHILDREN?

While most researchers agree that father absence is associated with adverse outcomes among children, they disagree over whether it causes those outcomes. Many think that parental conflict is the source of the problem. We know that conflict is bad for children, and we also know that parents who divorce experience more conflict than parents who stay together. Conflict is not the whole story, however. Many couples that divorce do not experience high levels of conflict.

Other scholars argue that the negative outcomes associated with father absence are due to flaws in the character or genes of one or both of the parents. Alcoholism and depression, for example, can cause both family instability as well as poor outcomes in children. One way to test this theory is to look at children before and after their parents separate. If the "flawed individual" argument is correct, we would expect the children in these families to be doing poorly even before their parents' divorce. Andrew Cherlin and his colleagues have taken this approach, using a large study that followed children born in England in 1958. They found that some, but not all, of the harm suffered by children whose fathers were absent could be explained by conditions that preceded the divorce.

The economist Jonathan Gruber has taken a different approach. Noting that parents (irrespective of their flaws) are less likely to divorce in states that make divorce more difficult, he compared children in these two types of states. Gruber found that those who grew up in states with easy access to divorce obtained less education and had lower incomes as adults than children who grew up in states that discouraged divorce.

Yet another way to assess whether divorce causes children to do worse is to compare children who have the same parents (or parent) but experience different family structures. Sibling differences can occur if the parents divorce after the first child grows up but before the last child leaves home, or if a single mother remarries, has a second child, and remains married to the second husband. Researchers find that in families like these, both siblings fare worse than children raised by two parents, suggesting that the problem is the parents (or parent) rather than the divorce itself.

In sum, the evidence is mixed with respect to whether divorce causes children to have problems or whether the problems associated with divorce are due to poor parenting or even poor genes.

WHY DOES FATHER ABSENCE MAKE A DIFFERENCE?

Three general factors account for the disadvantages associated with father absence: economic deprivation, poor parenting and lack of social support. Economic insecurity is probably the most important reason why children who live apart from their fathers tend to be less successful. In the United States, where childrearing is primarily a private rather than a public responsibility, parental income is significant. It determines the quality of child care and health care that children receive, and it also determines the quality of their education. School quality is closely related to where parents live, with the best schools typically found in more expensive neighborhoods. According to the U.S. Census Bureau, in 1995, the median income of two-parent families with children under age 18 was just over $50,000, as compared with just under $18,000 for female-headed families. Half of families headed by single mothers live below the poverty line, as compared with 10 percent of two-parent families. Of course, many single-mother families were poor even before the father left the household, but in most instances, the departure of the father reduced their economic prospects even further.

Income cannot account for all of the disadvantages of children without fathers, however. The fact that children in stepfamilies do just as poorly as children in single-mother families tells us that something other than financial deprivation is at work. The most obvious problem is that a father's absence reduces a child's access to parental attention. Interacting with the estranged mother and building a new relationship with the child can be a difficult and painful experience for a nonresident father, and many men respond by disengaging from the children.

A father's absence may also affect the quality of the mother-child relationship. The economic hardship and insecurity of single parenthood can bring on depression and psychological distress, thereby interfering with good mothering. Even among middle-class families, the departure of the father from the household can trigger disruptions in household routines such as meals and bedtimes, and undermine discipline. With their time, energy, and spirit stretched thin, some single mothers become too lenient and others

become too rigid or strict. Neither mothering style bodes well for children.

The loss of social support is the third reason why father absence matters. The sustaining web of facilities, programs, people, and care providers that back up parents' efforts is likely to decline when families are forced to move, which is often the case after divorce (and remarriage). The longer a family resides in the same community or neighborhood, the more likely the parent is to know about opportunities for the child. The mother is more likely to know about after-school programs and the names of the best teachers, and to have the connections and influence to access these resources. Even children who do not move may lose touch with people and other valuable resources. For example, many children lose access to their father's family and friends, and they may also be cut off from their mother's family and friends if she is too stressed and weary to maintain old relationships.

WHAT CAN BE DONE?

The United States is not the only country that has experienced increases in divorce and nonmarital childbearing in the past four decades. Indeed, although divorce is more common in the United States, bearing children out of wedlock is more common in the Scandinavian countries. Yet the conditions that single mothers face there are very different. For example, the poverty rate—measured as having income below 50 percent of median income—for single-mother families is 55 percent in the United States, 52 percent in Canada, 24 percent in the Netherlands, 46 percent in the U.K. and 7 percent in Sweden. Although part of this difference is due to differences in who becomes a single mother (single mothers in the United States are younger, less educated and more likely to be nonwhite than single mothers in other countries), most of the difference is due to welfare-state policies. Whereas in the United States, government assistance reduces poverty rates by about 15 percent, in Sweden public support reduces poverty by 90 percent.

Given that poverty rates among single mothers are much lower in other nations than in the United States, the effects of single motherhood might be expected to be much more benign elsewhere. Yet this is not always the case. Although children in single-mother families fare better in Sweden, where their poverty rates are low, they also appear to do well in Canada, where poverty rates are high. And, somewhat surprisingly, they do poorly in the U.K. and the Netherlands, where poverty rates are lower than in the United States. So the cross-national picture is something of a puzzle and suggests (once again) that economic deprivation is not the whole story.

Aside from easing the economic problems of children without fathers, we can try to reduce their risks more directly. First, we can make sure that parents are informed about the potential risks associated with the father's departure and the ways in which they can minimize the risks. While information alone is not likely to have a huge effect on divorce (or nonmarital childbearing), it may encourage some parents to try to rebuild their marriage and it may encourage others to work harder at maintaining a cooperative relationship after divorce.

Second, we can make sure that social policies do not discourage marriage. Although this point may seem obvious to most people, our current tax and transfer system is not neutral. Rather, it contains numerous "marriage penalties" that discourage permanent unions for couples at all income levels. These penalties include categorical restrictions that limit benefits to certain groups of parents (e.g., single mothers) as well as "income tests" and tax schedules that favor one-parent families over two-parent families in some instances.

For instance, take a couple in which both parents have little education and both work for low wages. This couple must choose between living together and getting very little help from the government or living apart and getting a great deal of help, including cash assistance, child care subsidies and health care subsidies. If the mother believes that the father's employment prospects are poor,

she may decide that living alone is more beneficial economically than living with her child's father.

Working-class families also face a "marriage penalty." One of the most popular (and fastest growing) programs in the United States is the Earned Income Tax Credit, a program that provides a subsidy to parents with low incomes. A single mother earning $12,000 a year can receive an additional $3,000 from the government. If she lives with a man who earns $15,000, however, the family receives nothing. One way to deal with the disincentives inherent in income-tested programs is to make the individual, rather than the family, the basis for determining taxes and transfers. If we followed this course, people's taxes and transfers would not be affected by their decisions to marry or cohabit. Of course, such an approach would be very expensive because more families would qualify for benefits. But it would probably also increase the incidence of marriage.

A third way to minimize the potential harm associated with a father's departure is to insist that fathers support their children even when they live elsewhere. This means establishing paternity for children born outside wedlock and enforcing child-support obligations for all children with an absent father. Unlike our welfare and tax systems, which discourage marriage, child-support enforcement reduces divorce and nonmarital childbearing. It not only prevents fathers from leaving but also mitigates the negative effects of their going by reducing the economic insecurity of single mothers. In short, child-support enforcement is a win-win policy, which is one reason why it has received broad bipartisan support in Congress. Unfortunately for low-income children, the situation is not quite so rosy. Since welfare benefits are reduced by one dollar for each dollar of child support a mother receives, child-support collections do not improve the economic status of children in welfare households. This policy saves welfare dollars, but it does not benefit children's welfare. It may even harm children by increasing tension and conflict between low-income parents.

What about joint custody and visitation? Real joint custody is hard to sustain, and moderate levels of visitation do not appear to help children much. What does seem to help is a close father-child relationship, which depends on the parents' ability to minimize conflict after divorce. Because of this finding, some states have started to mandate parent workshops and counseling sessions at the time of divorce to inform parents of the benefits (to their children) of maintaining a positive coparenting relationship and to increase their communication skills.

Finally, if we are serious about keeping fathers and their children together, we should be doing much more for "fragile families," defined as unmarried parents who are raising a child together. Not only is this group of families growing much faster than divorcing families, in most instances, the parents in these families have high hopes for a future together at the time their child is born. Yet because of their marginal financial circumstances, these parents face many barriers to achieving a stable family life, including potentially harmful government policies. Helping these families form and maintain a stable union is not a matter of changing the minds of parents who no longer want to be together. Rather, it is a matter of helping them achieve their goals. Policies that strengthen fragile families should appeal both to conservatives who want to promote marriage and to liberals who want to increase the "marriageability" of low-income parents.

■ Review Questions

1. How can it be true that most children of divorced parents do all right *and* that divorce raises the risks of undesirable outcomes?
2. What specific aspects of father absence appear detrimental to children after divorce?

READING 12-2

Children's Adjustment Following Divorce
Risk and Resilience Perspectives

Joan B. Kelly

Robert E. Emery

DIVORCE AS RISK FOR CHILDREN

A large body of empirical research confirms that divorce increases the risk for adjustment prob-

Joan B. Kelly and Robert E. Emery, "Children's Adjustment Following Divorce: Risk and Resilience Perspectives," *Family Relations* Vol. 52, No. 4 (2003): 352–362. Reprinted by permission of the publisher.

lems in children and adolescents (for reviews, see Amato, 2000; Emery, 1999; Hetherington, 1999; Kelly, 2000; McLanahan, 1999; Simons et al., 1996). Children of divorce were significantly more likely to have behavioral, internalizing, social, and academic problems when compared with children from continuously married families. The extent of risk is at least twice that of children in continuously married families (Hetherington, 1999; McLanahan; Zill, Morrison, & Coiro, 1993). Although 10% of children in continuously married families also have serious psychological and social problems, as measured on objective tests, estimates are that 20–25% of children from divorced families had similar problems (Hetherington & Kelly, 2002; Zill & Schoenborn, 1990). The largest effects are seen in externalizing symptoms, including conduct disorders, antisocial behaviors, and problems with authority figures and parents. Less robust differences are found with respect to depression, anxiety, and self-esteem. Whereas preadolescent boys were at greater risk for these negative outcomes than girls in several studies (see Amato, 2001; Hetherington, 1999), no gender differences specifically linked to divorce were found in other studies (Sun, 2001; Vandewater & Lansford, 1998). The complex interaction between gender, age at separation, preseparation adjustment, sex of custodial parent, quality of relationships with both parents, and extent of conflict confounds efforts to clarify findings regarding gender.

Children in divorced families have lower academic performance and achievement test scores compared with children in continuously married families. The differences are modest and decrease, but do not disappear, when income and socioeconomic status are controlled (for review, see McLanahan, 1999). Children from divorced families are two to three times more likely to drop out of school than are children of intact families, and the risk of teenage childbearing is doubled. However, it appears that youngsters are already at risk for poorer educational performance and lowered expectations well before separation. For example, the risk for school dropout is associated with poverty or low income prior to separation, and this may be exacerbated by the further decline in economic resources following separation (Pong & Ju, 2000). Further, in looking at parental resources available to children prior to separation, parents provided less financial, social, human, and cultural capital to their children compared with parents who remained married (Sun & Li, 2001), and parent-child relationships were less positive (Sun, 2001). Adolescents from divorced families scored lower on tests of math and reading both prior to and after parental separation compared with adolescents in married families, and their parents were less involved in their adolescents' education (Sun & Li, 2002).

The increased risk of divorced children for behavioral problems is not diminished by remarriage. As with divorce, children in stepfamily homes are twice as likely to have psychological, behavioral, social, and academic problems than are children in nondivorced families (Bray, 1999; Hetherington & Kelly, 2002; Zill, 1998; Zill & Schoenborn, 1990).

Children from divorced families have more difficulties in their intimate relationships as young adults. Compared with young adults in continuously married families, young adults from divorced families marry earlier, report more dissatisfaction with their marriages, and are more likely to divorce (Amato, 1999, 2000; Chase-Lansdale, Cherlin, & Kierman, 1995). Relationships between divorced parents and their adult children also are less affectionate and supportive than those in continuously married families (Amato & Booth, 1996; Zill et al., 1993). When divorced parents denigrated the other parent in front of the children, young adults were more likely to report angry and less close relationships with the denigrating parents (Fabricius & Hall, 2000). Somewhat surprising is the finding that young adults whose parents had low-conflict marriages and then divorced had more problems with intimate relationships, less social support of friends and relatives, and lower psychological well-being compared with children whose high-conflict parents divorced (Booth & Amato, 2001). Parents in low-conflict marriages who divorced differed in certain dimensions, including less integration in the community and more risky behaviors, and this may place their children at greater risk. Further research is needed to understand the aspects of parenting and parent-child relationships in these low-conflict marriages that negatively affect the later relationships of their offspring.

Higher divorce rates for children of divorced families compared with those in still-married families are substantiated in a number of studies (Amato, 1996; McLanahan & Sandefur, 1994; Wolfinger, 2000). The risk of divorce for these young adults is related to socioeconomic factors, as well as life course decisions such as cohabitation, early marriage, and premarital childbearing; attitudes toward marriage and divorce; and interpersonal behaviors, all of which are associated with marital instability (Amato, 1996, 2000). The number and cumulative effect of family structure transitions is linked to the higher probability of divorce; three or more transitions (divorce, remarriage, redivorce) greatly increase the risk of offspring divorce (Wolfinger).

PROTECTIVE FACTORS REDUCING RISK FOR CHILDREN OF DIVORCE

In the last decade, researchers have identified a number of protective factors that may moderate the risks associated with divorce for individual children and that contribute to the variability in outcomes observed in children of divorce. These include specific aspects of the psychological adjustment and parenting of custodial parents, the type of relationships that children have with their nonresident parents, and the extent and type of conflict between parents.

Competent Custodial Parents and Parenting

Living in the custody of a competent, adequately functioning parent is a protective factor associated with positive outcomes in children. Overall, one of the best predictors of children's psychological functioning in the marriage (Cummings & Davies, 1994; Keitner & Miller, 1990) and after divorce (Emery et al., 1999; Hetherington, 1999; Johnston, 1995; Kaiter et al., 1989; Kline et al., 1990) is the psychological adjustment of custodial parents (usually mothers) and the quality of parenting provided by them. A particular cluster of parenting behaviors following divorce is an important protective factor as well. When custodial parents provide warmth, emotional support, adequate monitoring, discipline authoritatively, and maintain age-appropriate expectations, children and adolescents experience positive adjustment compared with children whose divorced custodial parents are inattentive,

less supportive, and use coercive discipline (Amato, 2000; Buchanan et al., 1996; Hetherington, 1999; Krishnakumar & Buehler, 2000; Maccoby & Mnookin, 1992).

Nonresident Parents

There is a potential protective benefit from the timely and appropriate parenting of nonresident parents. Frequency of visits between fathers and children generally is not a reliable predictor of children's outcomes, because frequency alone does not reflect the quality of the father-child relationship. In one study, boys and younger children, but not girls or older children, were better adjusted with frequent and regular contact with their fathers (Stewart, Copeland, Chester, Malley, & Barenbaum, 1997). In the context of low conflict, frequent visits between fathers and children is associated with better child adjustment, but where interparental conflict is intense, more frequent visits were linked to poorer adjustment, presumably because of the opportunities for more direct exposure of the children to parental aggression and pressures (Amato & Rezac, 1994; Hetherington & Kelly, 2002; Johnston, 1995).

Frequency of contact also has beneficial effects when certain features of parenting are present in nonresident parents. A meta-analysis of 57 studies found that children who had close relationships with their fathers benefited from frequent contacts when their fathers remained actively involved as parents (Amato & Gilbreth, 1999). When fathers helped with homework and projects, provided authoritative parenting, and had appropriate expectations for their children, the children had more positive adjustment and academic performance than did those with less involved fathers. More paternal involvement in children's schooling was also associated with better grades and fewer repeated grades and suspensions (Nord, Brimhall, & West, 1997). The combination of fathers engaging in activities with their children and providing financial support was associated with increased probability of completing high school and entering college compared with activities alone or activities combined with very low financial support (Menning, 2002). Indeed, when both parents engage in active, authoritative, competent parenting, adolescent boys from divorced families had no greater involvement in delinquent behavior than did those in continuously married families (Simons and Associates, 1996).

New reports about joint custody, compared with sole custody, also suggest a protective effect for some children. A meta-analysis of 33 studies of sole- and joint-physical custody studies reported that children in joint-custody arrangements were better adjusted on multiple objective measures, including general adjustment, emotional and behavioral adjustment, and academic achievement compared with children in sole-custody arrangements (Bausermann, 2002). In fact, children in joint custody were better adjusted regardless of the level of conflict between parents, and they did not differ in adjustment from the children in still-married families. Although the joint-custody parents had less conflict prior to separation and after divorce than did sole-custody parents, these differences did not affect the advantage of joint custody. Lee (2002) also reported positive effects of dual residence on children's behavioral adjustment, although the effects were suppressed by high interparental conflict and children's sadness.

In sharp contrast to the 1980s, some findings suggest that between 35% and 40% of children may now have at least weekly contacts with their fathers, particularly in the first several years after divorce (Brayer & O'Connell, 1998; Hetherington, 1999; Seltzer, 1991, 1998). This may reflect changes in legal statutes and social contexts that now encourage shared legal decision-making, less restrictive views of paternal time with children, and greater opportunities for interested fathers to engage more fully in active parenting. Mothers also are more satisfied with higher levels of paternal involvement than they were 20 years ago (King & Heard, 1999), possibly reflecting changing cultural and work-related trends and

the increased role of the father in raising children (Doherty, 1998; Pleck, 1997).

Diminished Conflict between Parents Following Divorce

Low parental conflict is a protective factor for children following divorce. Although we know little about the thresholds at which conflict becomes a risk factor following divorce in different families, some conflict appears to be normative and acceptable to the parties (King & Heard, 1999). Young adults whose parents had low conflict during their earlier years were less depressed and had fewer psychological symptoms compared with those whose parents had continued high conflict (Amato & Keith, 1991; Zill et al., 1993). When parents have continued higher levels of conflict, protective factors include a good relationship with at least one parent or caregiver; parental warmth (Emery & Forehand, 1994; Neighbors, Forehand, & McVicar, 1993; Vandewater & Lansford, 1998); and the ability of parents to encapsulate their conflict (Hetherington, 1999). Several studies found no differences in the amount of conflict between parents in sole- or joint-custody arrangements (Braver & O'Connell, 1998; Emery et al., 1999; Maccoby & Mnookin, 1992), although results from a meta-analysis found more conflict in sole-custody families prior to and after divorce (Bausermann, 2002).

Most parents diminish their conflict in the first 2–3 years after divorce as they become disengaged and establish their separate (or remarried) lives. Studies indicate that between 8% and 12% of parents continue high conflict 2–3 years after divorce (Hetherington, 1999; King & Heard, 1999; Maccoby & Mnookin, 1992). The relatively small group of chronically contentious and litigating parents are more likely to be emotionally disturbed, character-disordered men and women who are intent on vengeance and/or on controlling their former spouses and their parenting (Johnston & Campbell, 1988; Johnston & Roseby, 1997). Such parents use disproportionate resources and time in family courts, and their children are more likely to be exposed to parental aggression. When one or both parents continue to lash out during transitions between households, mediation experience indicates that children can be protected from this exposure through access arrangements that incorporate transfers at neutral points (e.g., school, day care).

Related to the level of conflict between parents postdivorce is the effect of the coparental relationship. Research shows that between 25% and 30% of parents have a cooperative coparental relationship characterized by joint planning, flexibility, sufficient communication, and coordination of schedules and activities. However, more than half of parents engage in parallel parenting, in which low conflict, low communication, and emotional disengagement are typical features. Although there are distinct advantages of cooperative coparenting for children, children thrive as well in parallel parenting relationships when parents are providing nurturing care and appropriate discipline in each household (Hetherington, 1999; Hetherington & Kelly, 2002; Maccoby & Mnookin, 1992; Whiteside & Becker, 2000).

RESILIENCE OF CHILDREN OF DIVORCE

Despite the increased risk reported for children from divorced families, the current consensus in the social science literature is that the majority of children whose parents divorced are not distinguishable from their peers whose parents remained married in the longer term (Amato, 1994, 2001; Chase-Lansdale et al., 1995; Emery, 1999; Emery & Forehand, 1994; Furstenberg & Kiernan, 2001; Hetherington, 1999; Simons and Associates, 1996; Zill et al., 1993). There is considerable overlap between groups of children and adolescents in married and postdivorce families, with some divorced (and remarried) children functioning quite well in all dimensions, and some children in married families experiencing severe psychological, social, and academic difficulties (Amato, 1994, 2001; Hetherington, 1999). Whereas a slight widening of the differences

between children from married and divorced families is found in studies in the 1990s, the magnitude of the differences remains small (Amato, 2001). Both large-scale studies with nationally representative samples and multimethod longitudinal studies using widely accepted psychological and social measures and statistics indicate that the majority of children of divorce continue to fall within the average range of adjustment (Amato, 2001; Hetherington & Kelly, 2002; Zill et al., 1993).

Not to minimize the stresses and risk to children that separation and divorce create, it is important to emphasize that approximately 75–80% of children and young adults do not suffer from major psychological problems, including depression; have achieved their education and career goals; and retain close ties to their families. They enjoy intimate relationships, have not divorced, and do not appear to be scarred with immutable negative effects from divorce (Amato, 1999, 2000; Laumann-Billings & Emery, 2000; McLanahan, 1999; Chase-Lansdale et al., 1995). In fact, Amato (1999) estimated that approximately 42% of young adults from divorced families in his study had well-being scores above the average of young adults from nondivorced families.

As we indicated here, the differences in children's lives that determine their longer-term outcomes are dependent on many circumstances, among them their adjustment prior to separation, the quality of parenting they received before and after divorce, and the amount of conflict and violence between parents that they experienced during marriage and after divorce. Children from high-conflict and violent marriages may derive the most benefit from their parents' divorces (Amato, Loomis, & Booth, 1995; Booth & Amato, 2001) as a result of no longer enduring the conditions that are associated with significant adjustment problems in children in marriages. Once freed from intense marital conflict, these findings suggest that parenting by custodial parents improves, although research is needed to explain more specifically what aspects of parent-child relationships and family functioning facilitate recovery in these youngsters. Clearly, the links between level of marital conflict and outcomes for children are complex. For children whose parents reported marital conflict in the midrange, divorce is associated with only slightly lower psychological well-being (Booth & Amato, 2001). If this midrange marital conflict represents approximately 50% of the families that divorce, as others have found, then the large number of resilient children seen in the years following divorce is not surprising.

UNDERSTANDING CONTRADICTORY FINDINGS ON ADULT CHILDREN OF DIVORCE

These broadly based findings of long-term resiliency are at odds with the 25-year longitudinal study that has received widespread attention. In *The Unexpected Legacy of Divorce* (Wallerstein, Lewis, & Blakeslee, 2000), the authors report that children of divorce, interviewed in young adulthood, do not survive the experience of divorce and that the negative effects are immutable. These young adults are described as anxious, depressed, burdened, failing to reach their potential, and fearful of commitment and failure.

What accounts for these enormously disparate findings? Many of these differences can be traced to methodological issues and may relate as well to the clinical interpretations of participant interviews about their experiences as divorced young adults. An essential methodological concern is that this study (Wallerstein & Kelly, 1980; Wallerstein & Blakeslee, 1989; Wallerstein et al., 2000) was a qualitative study, used a clinical sample, and no comparison group of married families existed from the start. The data were collected in clinical interviews by experienced therapists, and no standardized or objective measures of psychological adjustment, depression, anxiety, self-esteem, or social relationships were used. The goal of the study, initiated in 1969 when information about children of divorce was

extremely limited, was to describe in detail the responses of children and parents to the initial separation and divorce, and then to see how they fared over the first 5 years in comparison with their initial reports and behaviors (Wallerstein & Kelly). . . .

Aside from sampling and methodological concerns, another explanation for the marked divergence in longer-term outcomes of divorced offspring may be a confusion of pain and pathology. Like young adults participating in more objective assessments of pain, participants in the Wallerstein study may have reported considerable distress in reflecting upon their parents' divorce. However, painful reflections on a difficult past are not the same as an inability to feel and function competently in the present.

PAINFUL MEMORIES AS LONGER-TERM RESIDUES OF DIVORCE

A third perception of the short- and longer-term effects of divorce may be a useful complement and balance to risk and resilience perspectives. Painful memories and experiences may be a lasting residue of the divorce (and remarriage) process for many youngsters and young adults. However, it is important to distinguish pain or distress about parental divorce from longer-term psychological symptoms or pathology. Clearly, divorce can create lingering feelings of sadness, longing, worry, and regret that coexist with competent psychological and social functioning. Substantial change and relationship loss, when compounded for some by continuing conflict between parents, represents an ongoing unpleasant situation over which the child or adolescent may have no control. Research that includes standardized and objective measures of both psychological adjustment and painful feelings is useful in disentangling differences in long-term outcomes reported in young adults from divorced families. Such research may help to explain some of the apparent conflict between studies using clinical and quantitative methods.

A decade after divorce, well-functioning college students reported continued pain and distress about their parents' divorces (Laumann-Billings & Emery, 2000). Compared with students in still-married families, they reported more painful childhood feelings and experiences, including worry about such things as their parents attending major events and wanting to spend more time with their fathers. They did not blame themselves for parental divorce, and 80% thought that the divorce was right for their parents. Feelings of loss were the most prevalent of the painful feelings, and the majority reported they missed having their father around. Many questioned whether their fathers loved them. Despite these painful feelings and beliefs, these young adults did not differ on standardized measures of depression or anxiety from a comparison sample of students in still-married families. These findings were replicated in a second sample of low-income young adults who were not college students. Among factors associated with more pain among children from divorced families were living in sole mother or father custody, rather than a shared custody arrangement, and higher levels of postdivorce parental conflict. When children's parents continued their high conflict, these young adults reported greater feelings of loss and paternal blame and were more likely to view their lives through the filter of divorce (Laumann-Billings & Emery). Young adults in both samples also reported lower levels of loss when they had lived in joint physical custody and were less likely to see life through the filter of divorce. As would be expected, there is no question that divorce impacted the lives of many of these young adults and that parental attitudes and behavior affected the degree of painful feelings lingering after divorce. Although tempting, this impact should not be confused with or portrayed as poor psychological adjustment.

Feelings of loss also were reported by half of 820 college students a decade after divorce in another study (Fabricius & Hall, 2000). Subjects indicated that they had wanted to spend more time with their fathers in the years after divorce.

They reported that their mothers were opposed to increasing their time with fathers. When asked which of nine living arrangements would have been best for them, 70% chose "equal time" with each parent, and an additional 30% said a "substantial" number of overnights with their fathers, preferences that were similar in a sample of young adults in nondivorced families. The typical amount of contact reported in this and other studies between children and their fathers was every other weekend. One can infer from these findings that for many years, many of these students experienced some degree of painful longing for the absent parent that might have been alleviated with more generous visiting arrangements. An analysis of the amount of contact and closeness to fathers indicated that with each increment of increased contact between these children and their fathers, there was an equal increase in young adults reporting closeness to their fathers and a corresponding decrease in anger toward their fathers. Further, the increased feelings of closeness toward fathers did not diminish their reported closeness to mothers (see Fabricius, 2003). Further, increasing increments of father contact were linked to incremental amounts of support paid by fathers for their children's college (Fabricius, Braver, & Deneau, 2003). In fact, students who perceived their parents as opposed to or interfering with contact with the nonresident parent were more angry and less close to those parents than were students who reported their parents as more supportive of contact with the nonresident parents.

Another source of pain may be the extent to which adult children feel that they had no control over their lives following divorce. As indicated earlier, the majority of children and adolescents are not adequately informed about the divorce and its implications for their lives (Dunn et al., 2001). They also are not consulted for their ideas regarding access arrangements and how they are working for them, both emotionally and practically (Kelly, 2002; McIntosh, 2000; Smart & Neale, 2000). The young adults cited earlier who longed to spend increased time with their fathers either perceived that they had no control over this arrangement or in reality did not have control. In lacking a voice in these divorce arrangements, not only did they miss their fathers over an extended period, but they were left with lingering doubts as to whether their fathers loved them. The substantial presence of involved nonresident parents in children's lives after divorce may be an important indicator to many children that they are valued and loved.

Transitions between two households constitute another arena where many children do not have sufficient input and control, particularly as they move into adolescence, and this may cause lingering angry or painful feelings. Whereas 25% of youngsters had *some* to *many* negative feelings about transitions between households, 73% had *some* to *many* positive feelings about the transitions. There was a significant association between positive feelings about transitions and being given a voice or role in some decision-making about the arrangements (Dunn et al., 2001). Although some research calls attention to the importance of children having a voice in formulating or shaping postdivorce parenting plans, there is the danger of burdening children with decisions that the adults cannot make. Giving children the right to be heard, if not done with sensitivity and care, may give children the responsibility for making an impossible choice between their two parents. There is a distinction between providing children with the possibility of input regarding their access arrangements and the inherent stresses of decision-making—a

distinction with which children themselves seem quite familiar and comfortable (Kelly, 2002; McIntosh, 2000; Smart & Neale, 2000).

IMPLICATIONS FOR PRACTICE AND INTERVENTIONS

There are a number of important implications for practice and intervention that derive from this analysis of children's adjustment following divorce. Rather than communicating a global or undifferentiated view of the impact of divorce, research has begun to identify particular factors that increase children's risk following divorce and, equally important, those that are protective and promote resiliency in children and adolescents. Understanding this literature is central to promoting policies and developing and assessing services that have the potential to help mitigate family problems so that adjustment problems among children from divorced families are diminished. There are few better examples than the importance of adopting a systems approach (including family systems and broader social and legal systems) to helping these children. Whatever its specific nature or focus, interventions are more likely to benefit children from divorced families if they seek to contain parental conflict, promote authoritative and close relationships between children and *both* of their parents, enhance economic stability in the postdivorce family, and, when appropriate, involve children in effective interventions that help them have a voice in shaping more individualized and helpful, access arrangements (Kelly, 2002). . . .

■ Review Questions

1. What is the difference between having painful memories and having long-term psychological problems?
2. What "protective factors" reduce the risk that children will have serious problems after their parents get a divorce?

CHAPTER 13

Stepfamilies

It is common today for adults to have two or more cohabiting relationships and marriages over their lifetimes. When neither partner already has children, life in a second or third partnership can be very similar to life in a first partnership. To be sure, the partners tend to be older, more established, and more set in their preferences about personal life, but the basic day-to-day interaction isn't all that different. However, when one or both partners has children from a previous marriage or relationship, then the new partnership creates a stepfamily. The new stepparent must adjust to the immediate presence of the children of the other partner. This adjustment can be difficult, not just for the stepparent but for the biological parent and the stepchildren as well. If the stepchildren have contact with their noncustodial biological parent (who is usually their father), they create links with other households as they make visits to him. In this situation, it can be difficult for the new couple to forge a strong, viable partnership because of the tugs and pulls of stepchildren, biological children, and former spouses.

Moreover, family law and policy tend to ignore stepparents. In many states, they have few rights and responsibilities and cannot even sign a stepchild's permission form to go on a field trip. Mary Ann Mason argues in the first selection that this situation needs to change. She advocates modifications of law and public policy that would recognize the contribution of stepparents and more clearly define their position. But it's not easy to decide what changes would be best. Sometimes giving more responsibility to stepparents, such as requiring them to contribute to the support of their stepchildren, could make it easier for noncustodial biological parents to shirk their responsibilities. Mason thoughtfully considers these complications, describes the various positions legal observers take, and makes her recommendations.

There is great variation in the roles that stepparents play in their stepchildren's lives. Some are heavily involved and become virtually indistinguishable from biological parents. Others invest little time and energy into building relationships with the stepchildren and never function as much more than a parent's partner. Perhaps more common is an in-between role in which the stepparent becomes a friend, a source of support, or even a confidant—somewhat like a favorite uncle or aunt. The kind of relationship that develops depends on many factors, including how old the stepchild was at the time the new relationship was formed, whether the stepparent resides in the same household as the stepchild full-time, and how involved the biological parent from the previous relationship is with the stepchild.

The task of becoming a valued stepparent is more difficult for stepmothers than for stepfathers. That's because of the typical custody arrangements after a marriage or relationship ends. Children typically remain in the household of their mother and the new stepfather. A stepmother only enters the picture if the noncustodial father starts a new partnership. The stepchildren may see her only when they spend time at their father's home, which might be once a week or less often. In most cases, the stepmother can't aspire to be a mother to the children, because they still have a full-time mother. Learning how stepmothers and stepchildren build relationships in these precarious circumstances can help us understand the complexities of stepfamily life. In the second reading, Helen M. Crohn reports on the enormous range of stepmother–stepdaughter ties that were described to her by young women in the New York City area.

READING 13-1

The Modern American Stepfamily
Problems and Possibilities

Mary Ann Mason

Cinderella had one, so did Snow White and Hansel and Gretel. Our traditional cultural myths are filled with the presence of evil stepmothers. We learn from the stories read to us as children that stepparents, particularly stepmothers, are not to be trusted. They may pretend to love us in front of our biological parent, but the moment our real parent is out of sight they will treat us cruelly and shower their own children with kindnesses. Few modern children's tales paint stepparents so harshly, still the negative image of stepparents lingers in public policy. While the rights and obligations of biological parents, wed or unwed, have been greatly strengthened in recent times, stepparents have been virtually ignored. At best it is fair to say that as a society we have a poorly formed concept of the role of stepparents and a reluctance to clarify that role.

Indeed, the contrast between the legal status of stepparents and the presumptive rights and obligations of natural parents is remarkable. Child support obligations, custody rights, and inheritance rights exist between children and their natural parents by virtue of a biological tie alone, regardless of the quality of social or emotional bonds between parent and child, and regardless of whether the parents are married. In recent years policy changes have extended the rights and obligations of natural parents, particularly in regard to unwed and divorced parents, but have not advanced with regard to

stepparents. Stepparents in most states have no obligation during the marriage to support their stepchildren, nor do they enjoy any right of custody or control. Consistent with this pattern, if the marriage terminates through divorce or death, they usually have no rights to custody or even visitation, however longstanding their relationship with their stepchildren. Conversely, stepparents have no obligation to pay child support following divorce, even if their stepchildren have depended on their income for many years. In turn, stepchildren have no right of inheritance in the event of the stepparent's death (they are, however, eligible for Social Security benefits in most cases).[1]

Policymakers who spend a great deal of time worrying about the economic and psychological effects of divorce on children rarely consider the fact that about 70 percent of mothers are remarried within six years. Moreover, about 28 percent of children are born to unwed mothers, many of whom eventually marry someone who is not the father of their child. In a study including all children, not just children of divorce, it was estimated that one-fourth of the children born in the United States in the early 1980s will live with a stepparent before they reach adulthood.[2] These numbers are likely to increase in the future, at least as long as the number of single-parent families continues to grow. In light of these demographic trends, federal and state policies affecting families and children, as well as policies governing private-sector employee benefits, insurance, and other critical areas of everyday life, may need to be adapted to address the concerns of modern stepfamilies. . . .

STEPFAMILIES IN LAW AND PUBLIC POLICY

Both state and federal law set policies that affect stepfamilies. Overall, these policies do not reflect a coherent policy toward stepparents and stepchildren. Two competing models are roughly evident. One, a "stranger" model, followed by

Mary Ann Mason, "The Modern American Stepfamily: Problems and Possibilities" in Mary Ann Mason, Arlene Skolnik, Stephen D. Sugarman (eds.), *All Our Families,* Oxford University Press, Chapter 5, pp. 96–97, 102–116. © 2003. Used by permission of Oxford University Press.

most states, treats the residential stepparent as if he or she were a legal stranger to the children, with no rights and no responsibilities. The other, a "dependency" model, most often followed by federal policymakers, assumes the residential stepfather is, in fact, supporting the stepchildren and provides benefits accordingly. But there is inconsistency in both state and federal policy. Some states lean at times toward a dependency model and require support in some instances, and the federal government sometimes treats the stepparent as if he or she were a stranger to the stepchildren, and ignores them in calculating benefits.

State law governs the traditional family matters of marriage, divorce, adoption, and inheritance, while federal law covers a wide range of programs and policies that touch on the lives of most Americans, including stepfamilies. As the provider of benefits through such programs as Temporary Aid for Needy Families (TANF) and Social Security, the federal government sets eligibility standards that affect the economic well-being of many stepfamilies. In addition, as the employer of the armed forces and civil servants, the federal government establishes employee benefits guidelines for vast numbers of American families. And in its regulatory role, the federal government defines the status of stepfamilies for many purposes ranging from immigration eligibility to tax liability.

Not covered in this chapter or, to my knowledge, yet systematically investigated are the wide range of private employee benefit programs, from medical and life insurance through educational benefits. These programs mostly take their lead from state or federal law. Therefore, it is fair to guess that they suffer from similar inconsistencies.

State Policies

State laws generally give little recognition to the dependency needs of children who reside with their stepparent; they are most likely to treat the stepparent as a stranger to the children, with no

rights or obligations. In contrast to the numerous state laws obligating parents to support natural children born out of wedlock or within a previous marriage, only a few states have enacted statutes which specifically impose an affirmative duty on stepparents. The Utah stepparent support statute, for example, provides simply that "A stepparent shall support a stepchild to the same extent that a natural or adoptive parent is required to support a child."[3] This duty of support ends upon the termination of the marriage. Most states are silent on the obligation to support stepchildren.[4]

A few states rely on common law, the legal tradition stemming from our English roots. The common law tradition leans more toward a dependency model. It dictates that a stepparent can acquire the rights and duties of a parent if he or she acts *in loco parentis* (in the place of a parent). Acquisition of this status is not automatic; it is determined by the stepparent's intent. A stepparent need not explicitly state the intention to act as a parent; he or she can "manifest the requisite intent to assume responsibility by actually providing financial support or by taking over the custodial duties."[5] Courts, however, have been reluctant to grant *in loco* parental rights or to attach obligations to unwilling stepparents. In the words of one Wisconsin court, "A good Samaritan should not be saddled with the legal obligations of another and we think the law should not with alacrity conclude that a stepparent assumes parental relationships to a child."[6]

At the extreme, once the status of *in loco parentis* is achieved, the stepparent "stands in the place of the natural parent, and the reciprocal rights, duties, and obligations of parent and child subsist." These rights, duties, and obligations include the duty to provide financial support, the right to custody and control of the child, immunity from suit by the stepchild, and, in some cases, visitation rights after the dissolution of the marriage by death or divorce.

Yet stepparents who qualify as *in loco parentis* are not always required to provide support in all circumstances. A subset of states imposes obligation only if the stepchild is in danger of becoming dependent on public assistance. For example, Hawaii provides that

> A stepparent who acts in loco parentis is bound to provide, maintain, and support the stepparent's stepchild during the residence of the child with the stepparent if the legal parents desert the child or are unable to support the child, thereby reducing the child to destitute and necessitous circumstances.[7]

Just as states do not regularly require stepparents to support their stepchildren, they do not offer stepparents the parental authority of custody and control within the marriage. A residential stepparent generally has fewer rights than a legal guardian or a foster parent. According to one commentator, a stepparent "has no authority to make decisions about the child—no authority to approve emergency medical treatment or even to sign a permission slip for a field trip to the fire station."[8]

Both common law and state statutes almost uniformly terminate the stepparent relationship upon divorce or the death of the custodial parent. This means that the support obligations, if there were any, cease, and that the stepparent has no rights to visitation or custody. State courts have sometimes found individual exceptions to this rule, but they have not created any clear precedents. Currently only a few states authorize stepparents to seek visitation rights, and custody is almost always granted to a biological parent upon divorce. In the event of the death of the stepparent's spouse, the noncustodial, biological parent is usually granted custody even when the stepparent has, in fact, raised the child. In one such Michigan case, *Henrickson v. Gable*,[9] the children, aged nine and ten when their mother died, had lived with their stepfather since infancy and had rarely seen their biological father. In the ensuing custody dispute, the trial court left the children with their stepfather, but an appellate court, relying upon a state law that created a strong preference for biological parents, reversed this decision and turned the children over to their biological father.

Following the stranger model, state inheritance laws, with a few complex exceptions, do not recognize the existence of stepchildren. Under existing state laws, even a dependent stepchild whose stepparent has supported and raised the child for many years is not eligible to inherit from the stepparent if there is no will. California provides the most liberal rule for stepchild recovery when there is no will, but only if the stepchild meets relatively onerous qualifications. Stepchildren may inherit as the children of a deceased stepparent only if "it is established by clear and convincing evidence that the stepparent would have adopted the person but for a legal barrier."[10] Very few stepchildren have been able to pass this test. Similarly a stepchild cannot bring a negligence suit for the accidental death of a stepparent. In most instances, then, only a biological child will inherit or receive legal compensation when a stepparent dies.

Federal Policies

The federal policies that concern us here are of two types: federal benefit programs given to families in need, including TANF and Supplemental Security Income (SSI), and general programs not based on need, including Social Security as well as civil service and military personnel employee benefits. Most of these programs follow the dependency model. They go further than do most states in recognizing or promoting the actual family relationship of residential stepfamilies. Many of them (although not all) assume that residential stepparents support their stepchildren and accordingly make these children eligible for benefits equivalent to those afforded to other children of the family.

Despite the fact that federal law generally recognizes the dependency of residential stepchildren, it remains wanting in many respects. There is a great deal of inconsistency in how the numerous federal programs and policies treat the stepparent-stepchild relationship, and the very definitions of what constitutes a stepchild are often quite different across programs. Most of the programs strive for a dependency-based definition, such as living with or receiving 50 percent of support from a stepparent. However, some invoke the vague definition, "actual family relationship," and some do not attempt any definition at all, thus potentially including nonresidential stepchildren among the beneficiaries. In some programs the category of stepchild is entirely absent or specifically excluded from the list of beneficiaries for some programs.

Even where program rules permit benefits for dependent stepchildren as for natural children, the benefits to stepchildren are typically severed by death or divorce.[11] While Social Security does cover dependent stepchildren in the event of death, several programs specifically exclude stepchildren from eligibility for certain death benefits. Under the Federal Employees' Retirement System, stepchildren are explicitly excluded from the definition of children in determining the default beneficiary, without concern for the stepchild's possible dependency. All stepchildren are similarly excluded from eligibility for lump-sum payments under the Foreign Service Retirement and Disability System and the CIA Retirement and Disability program.[12]

Stepchildren are even more vulnerable in the event of divorce. Here the stranger model is turned to. As with state law, any legally recognized relationship is immediately severed upon divorce in nearly all federal programs. The children and their stepparents become as strangers. Social Security does not provide any cushion for stepchildren if the deceased stepparent is divorced from the custodial parent. Under Social Security law, the stepparent-stepchild relationship is terminated immediately upon divorce and the stepchild is no longer eligible for benefits even if the child has in fact been dependent on the insured stepparent for the duration of a very long marriage.[13] If the divorce were finalized the day before the stepparent's death, the child would receive no benefits.

In sum, current federal policy goes part way toward defining the role of the stepparent by assuming a dependency model in most programs, even when state law does not, and providing benefits to stepchildren based on this assumption of stepparent support. However, as described, existing federal stepparent policy falls short in several critical areas. And state laws and policies fall far short of federal policies in their consideration of stepfamilies, for the most part treating stepparents as strangers with regard to their stepchildren.

NEW POLICY PROPOSALS

Proposals for policy reform regarding stepfamilies are scant in number and, so far, largely unheard by policymakers. Most of the proposals come from legal scholars, a few from social scientists. Stepparents have not been organized to demand reform, nor have child advocates. All the reforms have some disagreements with the existing stranger and dependency models, but few offer a completely new model.

All of the proposals I review base their arguments to a greater or lesser degree on social science data, although not always the same data. The proposers may roughly be divided into three camps. The first, and perhaps smallest camp, I call *negativists.* These are scholars who view stepfamilies from a sociobiological perspective, and find them a troublesome aberration to be actively discouraged. The second, and by far largest group of scholars, I term *voluntarists.* This group acknowledges both the complexity and the often distant nature of stepparent relationships, and largely believes that law and policy should leave stepfamilies alone, as it does now. If stepparents wish to take a greater role in their stepchildren's lives, they should be encouraged to do so, by adoption or some other means. The third camp recognizes the growing presence of stepfamilies as an alternate family form and believes they should be recognized and strengthened in some important ways. This group, I call them *reformists,* believes the law should take the lead in providing more rights or obligations to stepparents. The few policy initiatives from this group range from small specific reforms regarding such issues as inheritance and visitation to my own proposal for a full-scale redefinition of stepparents' rights and obligations.

The negativist viewpoint on stepparenting, most prominently represented by sociologist David Popenoe, relies on a sociobiological theory of reproduction. According to this theory, human beings will give unstintingly to their own biological children, in order to promote their own genes, but will be far less generous to others. The recent rise in divorce and out-of-wedlock births, according to Popenoe, has created a pattern of essentially fatherless households that cannot compete with the two-biological-parent families.

Popenoe believes the pattern of stepparent disengagement revealed by many researchers is largely based on this biological stinginess.

> If the argument . . . is correct, and the family is fundamentally rooted in biology and at least partly activated by the "genetically selfish" activities of human beings, childbearing by non relatives is inherently problematic. It is not that unrelated individuals are unable to do the job of parenting, it is just that they are not as likely to do the job well. Stepfamily problems, in short, may be so intractable that the best strategy for dealing with them is to do everything possible to minimize their occurrence.

Moreover, Popenoe cites researchers on the greatly increased incidence of child abuse by stepfathers over natural fathers, who suggest that "stepchildren are not merely 'disadvantaged' but imperiled."[14] This argument is not so farfetched, he claims, in fact it is the stuff of our folk wisdom. Snow White and Hansel and Gretel had it right; stepparents are not merely uncaring, they may be dangerous.

Popenoe goes beyond the stranger model, which is neutral as to state activity, and suggests an active discouragement of stepparent families. He believes the best way to obstruct stepfamilies is to encourage married biological two-parent families. Premarital and marital counseling, a longer waiting period for divorce, and a redesign

of the current welfare system so that marriage and family are empowered rather than denigrated are among his policy recommendations. He is heartened by what he calls the "new familism," a growing recognition of the need for strong social bonds, which he believes can best be found in the biological two-parent family.[15]

The second group of scholars, whom I call voluntarists, generally believe that the stepparent relationship is essentially voluntary and private and the stranger model most clearly reflects this. The legal bond formed by remarriage is between man and wife—stepchildren are incidental; they are legal strangers. Stepparents may choose, or not choose, to become more involved with everyday economic and emotional support of their stepchildren; but the law should not mandate this relationship, it should simply reflect it. These scholars recognize the growth of stepfamilies as a factor of modern life and neither condone nor condemn this configuration. Family law scholar David Chambers probably speaks for most scholars in this large camp when he says,

> In most regards, this state of the law nicely complements the state of stepparent relationships in the United States. Recall the inescapable diversity of such relationships—residential and non-residential, beginning when the children are infants and when they are teenagers, leading to comfortable relationships in some cases and awkward relationships in others, lasting a few years and lasting many. In this context it seems sensible to permit those relationships to rest largely on the voluntary arrangements among stepparents and biologic parents. The current state of the law also amply recognizes our nation's continuing absorption with the biologic relationship, especially as it informs our sensibilities about enduring financial obligations.[16]

Chambers is not enthusiastic about imposing support obligations on stepparents, either during or following the termination of a marriage, but is interested in promoting voluntary adoption. He would, however, approve some middle ground where biological parents are not completely cut off in the adoption process.

Other voluntarists are attracted by the new English model of parenting, as enacted in the Children Act of 1989. Of great attraction to American voluntarists is the fact that under this model a stepparent who has been married at least two years to the biological parent may voluntarily petition for a residence order for his or her spouse's child. With a residence order the stepparent has parental responsibility toward the child until the age of sixteen. But this order does not extinguish the parental responsibility of the noncustodial parent.[17] In accordance with the Children Act of 1989, parents, biological or otherwise, no longer have parental rights, they have only parental responsibilities, and these cannot be extinguished upon the divorce of the biological parents. In England, therefore, it is possible for three adults to claim parental responsibility. Unlike biological parental responsibility, however, stepparent responsibility does not usually extend following divorce. The stepparent is not normally financially responsible following divorce, but he or she may apply for a visitation order.

The third group, whom I call reformists, believe that voluntary acts on the part of stepparents are not always adequate, and that it is necessary to reform the law in some way to more clearly define the rights and responsibilities of stepparents. The American Bar Association Family Law Section has been working for some years on a proposed Model Act to suggest legislative reforms regarding stepparents' obligations to provide child support and rights to discipline, visitation, and custody. A Model Act is not binding anywhere; it is simply a model for all states to consider. Traditionally, however, Model Acts have been very influential in guiding state legislative reform. In its current form, the ABA Model Act would require stepparents to assume a duty of support during the duration of the remarriage only if the child is not adequately supported by the custodial and noncustodial parent. The issue is ultimately left to the discretion of the family court, but the Model Act does not require that the stepparent would need to have a close relationship with a stepchild before a support duty is imposed. The Model Act, however, does not describe what the rule should be if the stepparent and the custodial parent divorce.

The proposed statute is rather more complete in its discussion of stepparent visitation or custody rights following divorce. It takes a two-tiered approach, first asking if the stepparent has standing (a legal basis) to seek visitation and then asking if the visitation would be in the best interests of the child. The standing question is to be resolved with reference to five factors, which essentially examine the role of the stepparent in the child's life (almost an *in loco parentis* question), the financial support offered by the stepparent, and the detriment to the child from denying visitation. The court, if it finds standing, then completes the analysis with the best interests standard of the jurisdiction. The Model Act's section on physical custody also requires a two-tiered test, requiring standing and increasing the burden on the stepparent to present clear and convincing proof that he or she is the better custodial parent.

The ABA Model Act is a worthwhile start, in my opinion, but it is little more than that. At most it moves away from a stranger model and provides a limited concept of mandatory stepparent support during a marriage, acknowledging that stepchildren are at least sometimes dependent. It also gives a stepparent a fighting chance for visitation or custody following a divorce. It fails to clarify stepparents' rights during the marriage, however, and does not deal with the issue of economic support at the period of maximum vulnerability, the termination of the marriage through death and divorce. Moreover, the Model Act, and, indeed, all the existing reform proposals, deal only with traditional legal concepts of parenthood defined by each state and do not consider the vast range of federal programs, or other public and private programs, that define the stepparent-stepchild relationship for purposes of benefits, insurance, or other purposes.

I propose, instead, a new conceptualization of stepparent rights and responsibilities, a de facto parent model, that will cover all aspects of the stepparent-stepchild relationship and will extend to federal and private policy as well. My first concern in proposing a new framework is the welfare of the stepchildren, which is not adequately dealt with in either the stranger or the dependency model. The failure of state and, to a lesser extent, federal policy to address coherently the financial interdependencies of step relationships, described earlier in this chapter, means that children dependent upon a residential stepparent may not receive adequate support or benefits from that parent during the marriage, and they may not be protected economically in the event of divorce or parental death.

The longitudinal studies of families described earlier in this chapter suggest that the most difficult periods for children are those of marital transition, for example, divorce and remarriage. Families with a residential stepfather have a much higher family income than mother-headed single families; indeed, their household incomes look much like nuclear families.[18] However, research demonstrates that stepfamilies are fragile and are more likely to terminate in divorce than biological families. The event of divorce can quite suddenly pull the resources available for the children back to the single-parent level. Currently children are at least financially cushioned by child support following the divorce of their biological parents, but have no protective support following the breakup of their stepfamily. Nor are they protected in the event of the death of the stepparent, which is certainly another period of vulnerability (as discussed earlier, only a small minority continue to receive support from non-custodial parents).

A second reason for proposing a new framework is to strengthen the relationship of the stepparent and stepchildren. While research generally finds that stepparents are less engaged in parenting than natural parents, research studies do not explain the causes; others must do so. In addition to the sociobiologists' claim for stingy, genetically driven behavior, sociologists have posited the explanation of "incomplete institutionalization."[19] This theory is based on the belief that, by and large, people act as they are expected to act by society. In the case of stepfamilies, there are unclear or absent societal norms and standards for how to define the remarried family, especially the role of the stepparent in relation to the stepchild.

Briefly, my new model requires, first of all, dividing stepparents into two subclasses: those who are de facto parents and those who are not. De facto parents would be defined as "those stepparents legally married to a natural parent who primarily reside with their stepchildren, or who provide at least 50 percent of the stepchild's financial support." Stepparents who do not meet the de facto parent requirements would, in all important respects, disappear from policy.

For the purposes of federal and state policy, under this scheme, a de facto parent would be treated virtually the same as a natural parent during the marriage. The same rights, obligations, and presumptions would attach vis-à-vis their stepchildren, including the obligation of support. These rights and duties would continue in some form, based on the length of the marriage, following the custodial parent's death or divorce from the stepparent, or the death of the stepparent. In the event of divorce the stepparent would have standing to seek custody or visitation but the stepparent could also be obligated for child support of a limited duration. Upon the death of a stepparent, a minor stepchild would be treated for purposes of inheritance and benefits as would a natural child.

So far this proposal resembles the common law doctrine of *in loco parentis,* described earlier, where the stepparent is treated for most purposes (except inheritance) as a parent on the condition that he or she voluntarily agrees to support the child. In the de facto model, however, support is mandatory, not voluntary, on the grounds both that it is not fair to stepchildren to be treated by the law in an unequal or arbitrary manner, and that child welfare considerations are best met by uniform support of stepchildren. Furthermore, in the traditional common law *in loco parentis* scenario, the noncustodial parent had died and was not a factor to be reckoned with. Under this scheme, creating a de facto parent category for stepparents would not invalidate the existing rights and obligations of a noncustodial biological parent. Rather, this proposal would empower a stepparent as an additional parent.

Multiple parenting and the rights and obligations of the stepparent and children following divorce or death are controversial and difficult policy matters that require more detailed attention than the brief exposition that can be offered here. Multiple parenting is the barrier upon which many family law reform schemes, especially in custody and adoption, have foundered. It is also one of the reasons that there has been no consistent effort to reformulate the role of stepparents. Working out the details is critical. For instance, mandating stepparent support raises a central issue of fairness. If the stepparent is indeed required to support the child, there is a question about the support obligations of the noncustodial parent. Traditionally, most states have not recognized the stepparent contribution as an offset to child support.[20] While this policy promotes administrative efficiency, and may benefit some children, it may not be fair to the noncustodial parent. An important advance in recognizing the existence of multiple parents in the nonlinear family is to recognize multiple support obligations. The few states that require stepparent obligation have given limited attention to apportionment of child support obligations, offering no clear guidelines. I propose that state statutory requirements for stepparent obligation as de facto parents also include clear guidelines for apportionment of child support between the noncustodial natural parent and the stepparent.

Critics of this proposal may say that if the custodial parent's support is reduced, the child will have fewer resources. For some children, this may be true, but as discussed earlier in this chapter, only about 25 percent of all stepchildren

receive child support and the average amount is less than $2000 per year.[21] Therefore, a reduction of this small amount of support to a minority of stepchildren would not have a large overall effect compared with the increased resources of living with a stepparent that most stepchildren enjoy. And, certainly, the additional safety net of protection in the event of the death of the stepparent or divorce from the custodial parent would benefit all stepchildren. In addition, under the de facto scheme, the reduction of the support payment for the noncustodial parent may help to sweeten the multiple parenting relationship.

Let us apply this model to the Jones-Hutchins family introduced earlier. If Ray Jones, the noncustodial parent, were paying $6000 a year support for his two children (on the high end for noncustodial parents according to the National Survey for Children and Families), his payments could be reduced by as much as half, since Sam Hutchins's income is $50,000 per year and he has no other dependents. It should be emphasized, however, that in most stepfamilies there would be no reduction in support, because the noncustodial parent is paying no support. In the Jones-Hutchins family the $3000 relief would certainly be welcome to Ray, who is also now living with and helping to support his new wife's child. The relief would likely make him somewhat friendlier toward Sam, or at least more accepting of his role in his children's lives. It also might make him more likely to continue support past eighteen, since he would not feel as financially pinched over the years. More important, while the children would lose some support, they would have the security that if Sam died they would be legal heirs and default beneficiaries to his life insurance. They could also ask for damages if his death were caused by negligence or work-related events. And if he and their mother divorced, they could continue for a time to be considered dependents on his health and other benefits and to receive support from him.

Another facet of multiple parenting is legal authority. If stepparents are required to accept parental support obligations, equal protection and fairness concerns dictate that they must also be given parental rights. Currently, state laws, as noted earlier, recognize only natural or adoptive parents; a stepparent currently has no legal authority over a stepchild, even to authorize a field trip. If stepparents had full parental rights, in some cases, as when the parents have shared legal custody, the law would be recognizing the parental rights of three parents, rather than two. While this sounds unusual, it is an accurate reflection of how many families now raise their children. Most often, however, it would be only the custodial parent and his or her spouse, the de facto parent, who would have authority to make decisions for the children in their home.

In the Jones-Hutchins family this policy would give Sam more recognition as a parent. Schools, camps, hospitals, and other institutions that require parental consent or involvement would now automatically include him in their consideration of the children's interests. Since Sam is the more day-to-day parent, their biological father, Ray, may not mind at all. If he did mind, the three of them would have to work it out (or in an extreme event, take it to mediation or family court). In fact, since only a minority of noncustodial dads see their children on a regular basis, three-parent decision making would be unusual.

Critics of this scheme may argue that adoption, not the creation of the legal status of de facto parent, is the appropriate vehicle for granting a stepparent full parental rights and responsibilities.[22] If, as discussed earlier, nearly three-quarters of stepchildren are not being supported by their noncustodial parents, policy initiatives could be directed to terminating the nonpaying parents' rights and promoting stepparent adoption. Adoption is not possible, however, unless the parental rights of the absent natural parent have been terminated—a difficult procedure against a reluctant parent. Normally, the rights of a parent who maintains contact with his or her child cannot be terminated even if that parent is not contributing child support. And when parental rights are terminated, visitation rights are terminated as well in most states. It is by no means clear that it is in the best interests of children to terminate contact with a natural parent, even if the parent is not meeting his or her obligation to support.[23] As discussed earlier, a large percentage (another 25 percent or so) of noncustodial parents continue some contact with their children, even when not paying support.[24] And while stepparent adoption should be strongly encouraged when it is possible, this solution will not resolve the problem of defining the role of stepparents who have not adopted.

Extending, in some form, the rights and obligations following the termination of the marriage by divorce or death is equally problematical. Currently, only a few courts have ruled in favor of support payments following divorce, and these have been decided on an individual basis. Only one state, Missouri, statutorily continues stepparent support obligations following divorce.[25] It would clearly be in the best interests of the child to experience continued support, since a significant number of children may sink below the poverty line upon the dissolution of their stepfamily.[26]

Since the de facto model is based on dependency, not blood, a fair basis for support following divorce or the death of the custodial parent might be to require that a stepparent who qualified as a de facto parent for at least one year must contribute child support for half the number of years of dependency until the child reached majority. If a child resided with the stepparent for four years, the stepparent would be liable for support for two years. If the biological noncustodial parent were still paying support payments, the amount could be apportioned. While it may be said that this policy would discourage people from becoming stepparents by marrying, it could also be said to discourage divorce once one has become a stepparent. Stepparents might consider working harder at maintaining a marriage if divorce had some real costs.

Conversely, stepparents should have rights as well as responsibilities following divorce or the death of the custodial parent. Divorced or widowed stepparents should be able to pursue visitation or custody if they have lived with and supported the child for at least one year. Once again, multiple parent claims might sometimes be an issue, but these could be resolved, as they are now, under a primary caretaker, or a best interest standard.

The death of a stepparent is a particular period of vulnerability for stepchildren for which they are unprotected by inheritance law. While Social Security and other federal survivor benefits are based on the premise that a stepchild relies on the support of the residential stepparent and will suffer the same hardship as natural children if the stepparent dies, state inheritance laws, notoriously archaic, decree that only biology, not dependency, counts. State laws should assume that a de facto parent would wish to have all his dependents receive a share of his estate if he died without a will. If the stepchildren are no longer dependent, that assumption would not necessarily prevail. The same assumption should prevail for insurance policies and compensation claims following an accidental death. A dependent stepchild, just as a natural child, should have the right to sue for loss of support.

On the federal front, a clear definition of stepparents as de facto parents would eliminate the inconsistencies regarding stepparents which plague current federal policies and would clarify the role of the residential stepparent. For the duration of the marriage, a stepchild would be treated as a natural child for purposes of support and the receipt of federal benefits. This treatment would persist in the event of the death of the stepparent. The stepchild would receive all the survivor and death benefits that would accrue to a natural child.[27]

In the case of divorce, the issue of federal benefits is more complicated. Stepchildren and natural children should not have identical coverage for federal benefits following divorce, again, but neither is it good policy to summarily cut off children who have been dependent, sometimes

for many years, on the de facto parent. A better policy is to extend federal benefits for a period following divorce, based on a formula that matches half the number of years of dependency, as earlier suggested for child support. For instance, if the stepparent resided with the stepchild for four years, the child would be covered by Social Security survivor benefits and other federal benefits, including federal employee benefits, for a period of two years following the divorce. This solution would serve children by at least providing a transitional cushion. It would also be relatively easy to administer. In the case of the death of the biological custodial parent, benefits could be similarly extended, or continued indefinitely if the child remains in the custody of the stepparent.

All other private benefits programs would similarly gain from the application of a clear definition of the rights and obligations of residential stepparents. While these nongovernmental programs, ranging from eligibility for private health and life insurance and annuities to access to employee child care, are not reviewed in this chapter, they almost surely reflect the same inconsistencies or silences evident in federal and state policies.

Ultimately, state law defines most of these stepfamily relationships, and it is difficult, if not impossible to achieve uniform reform on a state-by-state basis. In England it is possible to pass a single piece of national legislation, such as the Children Act of 1989, which completely redefines parental roles. In America, the process of reform is slower and less sure. Probably the first step in promoting a new policy would be for the federal government to insist all states pass stepparent general support obligation laws requiring stepparents acting as de facto parents (by my definition) to support their stepchildren as they do their natural children. This goal could be accomplished by making stepparent general support obligation laws a prerequisite for receiving federal welfare grants. Federal policy already assumes this support in figuring eligibility in many programs, but it has not insisted that states change their laws. Precedent for this strategy has been set by the Family Support Acts of 1988 in which the federal government mandated that states set up strict child support enforcement laws for divorced parents and unwed fathers at TANF levels in order to secure AFDC funding.[28] The second, larger step would be to require limited stepparent support following divorce, as described previously. Once the basic obligations were asserted, an articulation of basic rights would presumably follow.

CONCLUSION

Stepfamilies compose a large and growing sector of American families that is largely ignored by public policy. Social scientists tell us that these families have problems. Stepparent-stepchildren relationships, poorly defined by legal and social norms, are not as strong or nurturing as those in non-divorced families, and stepchildren do not do as well in school and in other outside settings. Still, stepfamily relationships are important in lifting single-parent families out of poverty. When single or divorced mothers marry, the household income increases by more than three-fold, rising to roughly the same level as nuclear families. A substantial portion of these families experiences divorce, however, placing the stepchildren at risk of falling back into poverty. It makes good public policy sense then, both to strengthen these stepfamily relationships and to cushion the transition for stepchildren should the relationship end.

■ Review Questions

1. Give an example of how the law follows the "stranger model" of stepparenting.
2. Should stepparents have the same obligation to support the children in their families as biological parents do?

ENDNOTES

1. Mary Ann Mason and David Simon, "The Ambiguous Stepparent: Federal Legislation in Search of a Model," *Family Law Quarterly* 29:446–448, 1995.
2. E. Mavis Heatherington and Kathleen M. Jodl, "Stepfamilies as Settings for Child Development," in Alan Booth and Judy Dunn (eds.), *Stepfamilies: Who Benefits? Who Does Not?* (Hillsdale, N.J.: L. Erlbaum 1994), 55; E. Mavis Heatherington, "An Overview of the Virginia Longitudinal Study of Divorce and Remarriage: A Focus on Early Adolescence," *Journal of Family Psychology* 7:39–56, 1993.
3. Utah Code Ann. 78-45-4.1.
4. Margaret Mahoney, *Stepfamilies and the Law* (Ann Arbor: University of Michigan Press, 1994), 13–47.
5. Miller v. United States, 123 F.2d 715, 717 (8th Cir. 1941).
6. Niesen v. Niesen, 157 N.W.2d 660, 664 (Wis. 1968).
7. Hawaii Revised Stat. Ann., Title 31, Sec. 577-4.
8. David Chambers, "Stepparents, Biologic Parents, and the Law's Perceptions of 'Family' after Divorce," in S. Sugarman and H. H. Kay (eds.), *Divorce Reform at the Crossroads* (New Haven: Yale University Press, 1990), 102–129.
9. Henrickson v. Gable.
10. Cal. Prob. Code, Sec. 6408.
11. Mason and Simon, "The Ambiguous Stepparent: Federal Legislation in Search of a Model," 449.
12. Ibid., pp. 460–466.
13. 42 U.S.C. sec. 416(e), 1994.
14. M. Daly and M. Wilson, *Homicide* (New York: Aldine de Gruyter, 1988), 230.
15. Barbara Whitehead, "A New Familism?" *Family Affairs,* Summer, 1992.
16. Chambers, "Stepparents, Biologic Parents, and the Law's Perceptions of 'Family' after Divorce," 26.

17. Mark A. Fine, "Social Policy Pertaining to Stepfamilies: Should Stepparents and Stepchildren Have the Option of Establishing a Legal Relationship?" in Booth and Dunn (eds.), *Stepfamilies,* 199.

18. Mary Ann Mason and Jane Mauldon, "The New Stepfamily Needs a New Public Policy," *Journal of Social Issues* 52(3):5, Fall 1996.

19. Andrew Cherlin, "Remarriage as an Incomplete Institution," *American Journal of Sociology* 84:634–649, 1978.

20. S. Ramsey and J. Masson, "Stepparent Support of Stepchildren: A Comparative Analysis of Policies and Problems in the American and British Experience," *Syracuse Law Review* 36:649–666, 1985.

21. Mason and Mauldon, "The New Stepfamily," 7.

22. Joan Hollinger (ed.) et al., *Adoption Law and Practice* (New York: Matthew Bender, 1988).

23. Katherine Bartlett, "Re-thinking Parenthood as an Exclusive Status: The Need for Alternatives When the Premise of the Nuclear Family Has Failed," *Virginia Law Review* 70:879–903, 1984.

24. Mason and Mauldon, "The New Stepfamily," 5.

25. Vernon's Ann. Missouri Stats. 453.400, 1994.

26. Mason and Mauldon, "The New Stepfamily," 5.

27. Mason and Simon, "The Ambiguous Stepparent," 471.

28. 100 P.L. 485; 102 Stat. 2343 (1988).

READING 13-2

Five Styles of Positive Stepmothering from the Perspective of Young Adult Stepdaughters

Helen M. Crohn

INTRODUCTION

Having a stepmother is not a recent phenomenon. A comparatively more recent experience is to have a stepmother *and* a living mother. After a marital dissolution, mothers tend to retain custody of the children (Buchanon, Maccoby & Dornbush, 1996; Clarke-Stewart & Bailey, 1989). When a father remarries, many children visit, or spend significant periods of time with their fathers, and more than 11 million women who are "part-time" or "nonresidential" stepmothers in the United States (Nielson, 1999).

Studies indicate that children of divorce and children in stepfamilies are at somewhat greater risk for academic, behavioral and emotional problems than children in nuclear families (Bray, 1988; Dawson, 1991; Garnefski & Diekstra, 1997; Hetherington, 1992; Spruijt & Goede,

1997). Girls in stepfamilies, particularly girls who have stepmothers, are said to have distinct adjustment problems that girls in nuclear families do not experience (Brand & Clingempeel, 1987; Hoffman & Johnson, 1998; Lee, Burkham, Zimilies & Ladewski, 1994; Needle, Su & Doherty, 1990; Suh, Schutz & Johansson, 1996).

Hetherington, Bridges and Insabella (1998) reported that the risk for negative outcomes in children's adjustment resulting from divorce and remarriage may be mediated by resources that engender resiliency. A good relationship with an adult, be it a parent, teacher or friend, is considered an external resource that promotes resiliency in children at risk (Doyle, Wolchik & Dawson-McClure, 2003; Martinez & Forgatch, 2002).

One such resource is a positive relationship between a child and her custodial parent (Cartwright & Seymour, 2003; Kurdek, 1987; Kurtz, 1995; Porter & O'Leary, 1980; Shaw & Emery, 1987; Stolberg, Camplear, Currier & Wells, 1987). Another potential resource may be a good relationship between a girl and her nonresidential stepmother.

This study sought to examine the factors which are associated with positive relationships between daughter/divorced mother and stepdaughter/stepmother in the same divorced-remarried family system. The purpose of this study was to add to the literature concerning long-term well-functioning stepfamilies, an area in which studies are sparse. . . . Secondarily, this study sought to determine whether there are any characteristics which are *unique* to a positive stepmother/stepdaughter relationship when compared with the divorced mother/daughter relationship. There is a continued need to understand stepmother/stepdaughter relationships that "work," so that such information may be used by family educators and therapists. This report will present part of the findings of this study: five styles of positive stepmothering based on the perceptions of these young women. . . .

METHOD

The primary theoretical framework which informed this study was the "strengths perspective" (Saleeby, 2002). Research using the strengths perspective, known as "empowerment research," is defined as an inquiry that contributes to knowledge while empowering people by identifying conceptual tools, action guidelines and useful information for professionals and clients (Holmes, 1992, p. 158). The outcome of empowerment research is to contribute to a body of knowledge concerning human creativity and wellness. Perceptions and narratives of the participants form the database of strengths-based studies.

Participants

Recruitment. A purposive sample of nineteen young women who self-identified as having positive relationships with their mothers and stepmothers was used. The participants were recruited through flyers that were posted around the New York City Metropolitan area.

Demographics. The nineteen participants were middle class and white. They ranged in age from 19 to 25, with the mean age being 23.10 (SD = 1.69) years. One participant was married, and one self-identified as partnered; the rest of the participants were single. Five of the participants were employed, the rest were undergraduate and graduate students.

Length of time in a stepfamily. The ages of the participants when their birth parents permanently separated and/or divorced ranged from 1.5 to 10 years, with the mean age of 5.52 . . . years. The ages of the participants when their fathers married their stepmothers ranged from two years to twenty years, with the mean age of 10.21 . . . years. Four of the fathers were divorced a second time and one of the fathers had married a third time.

Siblings. Out of the nineteen participants, fifteen had full siblings, fourteen had half siblings by their fathers' and/or mothers' remarriages and ten had stepsiblings.

Custody/Visitation. Sixteen of the participants described a custody arrangement in which their mothers had primary custody and they visited their fathers' and stepmothers' households. Four of these young women lived with their fathers and stepmothers during adolescence and young adulthood for various periods of time. Three young women described the custody as split evenly, fifty percent of the time in each birth parent's household.

Procedure

Interviewing was selected as the method of obtaining data because it is considered as a useful means of accessing the perceptions of participants and the meanings they have attached to events and relationships (Taylor & Bogdan, 1998, 98). The semi-standardized in-depth interview was used (Berg, 2001; McCracken, 1988). The interviews lasted between forty-five minutes and an hour and fifteen minutes. The researcher conducted two interviews with each participant in order to gather information on two separate occasions to increase the credibility of data. The interviews were audiotaped and transcribed. . . .

Findings were grouped into three categories: (1) findings concerning the mother/daughter relationship, (2) findings concerning the stepmother/stepdaughter relationship, and (3) findings concerning the influence of other family members. This report is limited to some of the findings concerning the stepmother/stepdaughter relationship.

RESULTS

Five styles of stepmothering were reported by the stepdaughters. No matter what style described the stepmother, *all* the young women reported that the stepmothers did not attempt to usurp the mothers. The participants consistently named this as a primary ingredient in perceiving the relationship with their stepmothers as positive. For example:

> B: My stepmom has always been very careful not to be intruding on my mother's territory. She didn't try to become a parent figure when she came into my life. Two parents, who needs more?

> (Barbara, age 20, student, parents separated at age 2, father remarried at age 5)

As the literature attests, the participants did not describe the same intensity of connection, closeness, availability and focus from their stepmothers that they described from their mothers (Pruett, Calsyn & Jensen, 1993), but many clearly felt supported emotionally, and sometimes instrumentally.

When the participants tried to give a name to their stepmothers' roles in their lives, they used descriptive phrases such as "friend," "fun girlfriend," "girlfriend," "cool babysitter," "good friend," "like a sister," "like an aunt," "like a cousin" and like "another mom to me." The most disengaged stepmother was described as "my father's wife." These different role perceptions were characterized by different amounts and types of warmth from the stepmother, variations in control functions, different degrees of attachment from the participants to the stepmothers, different perceived status (equal or unequal), and different degrees of openness in communication. The continuum of perceived roles of stepmothers, as described by the participants, was (1) My Father's Wife, (2) A Peer-Like Girlfriend, (3) An Older Friend, (4) A Type of Kin, and (5) Like Another Mother.

These categories represent some major configurations of trends as described by the participants. Stepmothers sometimes manifested more than one style. These are loose topologies and are presented as possible directions for further investigation.

My Father's Wife (2 participants)   While not hostile, these stepmothers were perceived as disengaged. Visits tended to include the father only. All communication took place with the father; communication with the stepmother tended to be incidental. Support from the stepmother consisted of ritualized gift-giving and informational support. Being together was cordial. Status was perceived by the participant as equal. The stepmother fulfilled no or minimal parent-like roles; only the father exerted parental authority. Stepdaughter to stepmother self-disclosure was infrequent, and topic avoidance was pronounced. For example, Dotty said of her third stepmother:

> H: Do you have contact with your stepmother?

> D: Not separately. I mean I'm always real polite to her. During the year we see her maybe once or twice . . . I would drive down and have breakfast with my dad, and usually she wouldn't come. . . . I mean, she's polite to me.

> (Dotty, age 23, married, parents separated at age 7, father remarried at age 8)

One participant stated that her relationship with her stepmother was positive, not for what it *was,* but for how bad it *could* have been:

> K: I definitely can't complain because I've heard so many horror stories about stepmothers. So I feel like in comparison to that, I have such a piece of cake . . . there's things I don't like about it. But also, like, there's a lot of absence of bad things too! You know what I mean?

> (Kathie, age 25, employed, parents separated at age 7, father remarried at age 10)

A Peer-Like Girlfriend (3 participants)   The stepmothers who were described as peer-like girlfriends were significantly younger than the biological parents. Nine of the remarriages in this study were these so-called May-December relationships, but not all the younger stepmothers took this role.

These stepmother/stepdaughter relationships were perceived as somewhat close. There was tangible support from the stepmother in the form of gifts and a number of perceived commonalities such as music and preferences in (junk) food. The time with the stepmother was characterized by fun activities such as shopping, and by sharing interests in fashion and cosmetics.

These stepmothers tended to confide in the participants about their problems. The participants provided emotional support to the stepmothers. Possibly in reaction to the stepmothers' self-disclosures, which made the participant-receivers feel uncomfortable, the participants tended not to self-disclose as readily to these stepmothers, in order to attempt to draw a privacy boundary.

The peer-like stepmothers did not take on control functions, which were the domain of the father. Status was perceived by the participants as equal. Communication between the participants and the stepmothers had a "girlfriend" quality. For instance, Lucy described her stepmother as a peer-like friend:

> *L:* I'd say we're just like friends way more like friends. . . . She calls me to gossip and you know and we gossip or like she wants to show me the cool clothes she got or something like that. . . .

(Lucy, age 24, employed, parents separated at age 4, father remarried at age 7)

An Older Close Friend (8 participants)   Just as stepparents describe themselves as older friends to their stepchildren (Fine, Coleman & Ganong, 1998), the stepmother as a friend was a theme described by these stepchildren participants. In contrast to the peer-like girlfriend/stepmothers, the participants reported a more intense connection with their older friend/stepmothers. None of these stepmothers were perceived as giving a mother's unconditional love, but they

were affectionate and loving towards the participants. Katy described the love from her stepmother as "different":

> *K:* My mother is really, when I'm home, a mom to me, she feels like the mom I've always known. But Alice, my stepmother, when she does things like that it feels real special. It's almost more special because it comes from a love that she has for me as a person. 'Cause my parents love me since I was born, but my stepmother has grown to love me. Not just as part of my father but for who I am. It's special; it's different.

(Katy, age 24, graduate student, parents separated at age 7, father remarried at age 8)

Unlike with peer-like stepmothers, a generational boundary was clearly demarcated between the stepmother and stepdaughter. These older friend/stepmothers did not confide in their stepdaughters about their problems. The participants received emotional support from these stepmothers as well as informational support (e.g., advice), and belongingness support (e.g., helping the participant feel like part of the family) (Pruett, Calsyn & Jensen, 1993). One stepmother was very generous financially. Several other stepmothers taught their stepdaughters skills or how to dress fashionably. Some participants mentioned that their stepmothers filled a role which the mother didn't fulfill or enjoy. For example, one mother was weak in money management, but the stepmother was able to teach the participant how to manage her finances.

The participants self-disclosed to these older friend/stepmothers, sometimes about topics they did not discuss with their mothers, particularly about sexual activity and sometimes about acting-out behavior. Some adult friend stepmothers also counseled and guided these participants when necessary. For example, Rachel's stepmother was well aware of her teenage stepdaughter's rebellious behavior:

> *R:* Whenever I got caught for doing things wrong, usually Molly was the one to catch me . . . so she always caught me in the act. She grounded me a

few times, you know. . . . Caught me when I snuck out a few times, and was very stern, not like my mom. My mom, I felt, was a little bit of a pushover. Molly wasn't like that. She was sterner, firm, strong-minded. . . . But we definitely have a very strong friendship (now).

(Rachel, age 23, graduate student, parents separated at age 10, father remarried at age 11)

Like the other stepmother styles, adult friend/stepmothers tended not to exert control, leaving that to the biological parent(s). If the stepmothers needed to discipline or enforce rules, they did so in a suggestive, non-authoritarian manner:

B: She (stepmother) would sometimes say, 'Did you get your homework done?' But she would never say 'Barbara, you have to get your homework done before you go out!' or anything like that.

(Barbara, age 20, student, parents separated at age 2, father remarried at age 5)

A Type of Kin (5 participants) The role of these stepmothers, as perceived by the participants, was similar to the stepmothers who were described as an older friend. However, kinship words such as "a cousin," "older sister," "sister" or "aunt" were used to describe their stepmothers' role. For example:

A: I almost view my stepmother as a sibling 'cause I have a very close relationship with her. Or a cousin, like someone who is close but not always there.

(Abby, age 25, graduate student, parents separated at age 1.5, father remarried at age 4)

Sister said:

She was always nice and fun and whatever, and. . . . she was more like an older sister, and I think that's one of the reasons why we got as close as we did 'cause I think I would have been offended if she tried to be another mother and you know 'cause I have a mother that I love. . . .

(Sister #2, age 21, student, parents separated at age 5, father remarried at age 7 and divorced at age 13)

Like older friend/stepmothers, kin-like stepmothers did not tend to discipline, leaving that to the father. Sister went on to say:

S: She (stepmother) let my father handle everything involving rearing, you know, at the household like she never got involved in any like curfew or anything like that. . . . and I can't even remember really a time of tension.

An interesting finding was that some of the older friend and kin-like stepmothers took the role of a wise guide or mentor. Several participants appreciated the strong encouragement they felt they got from their stepmothers. These stepmothers were described as less worried about the participants than the birth mothers. They perceived their stepmothers as the ones supporting them to make bold choices such as to leave their home towns to pursue an education or a career.

Like Another Mother (1 participant) This participant stated that her stepmother took a very nurturing role, giving a great deal of esteem support and tangible support in the form of cooking and providing personalized thoughtful gifts. This childless stepmother was reported to be proud when outsiders thought she was the real mother. The participant was pleased with her stepmother as a nurturer, as her own career-minded birth mother did not like to nurture in this way and was less available. Judy stated:

J: I'd call her (stepmother) on Mother's Day. That became a thing. Maybe at some point in college, I started realizing that she is another mother to me.

(Judy, age 24, employed, parents separated at age 7, father remarried at age 9)

DISCUSSION

. . . The five styles of stepmothering reported by the stepdaughter/participants, overlap with stepmother styles, as reported in the literature from the adults' perspectives. This overlap gives more credibility to the styles suggested by the current scholar. There also was an overlap between these styles, and the one typology developed from the children's perspectives (Gross, 1987).

These styles were characterized by different amounts and types of warmth, control functions, attachment, perceived status (more or less equal), and topic avoidance and self-disclosure. These variations support the importance of paying attention to in-group differences in stepmother/stepdaughter relations, and to understand the diversity *and* similarities in well-functioning stepmother/stepdaughter relationships. Such knowledge may help family practitioners widen their perceptions of healthy step relations.

Some of the younger stepmothers related to their stepdaughters as a peer-like friend. In the stepmother literature, there is no mention of this type of role. Many stepmother studies interview the stepmothers only, who may not perceive themselves as peer-like with their stepdaughters. In addition, stepmother studies tend to primarily include residential (full-time) stepmothers, who would be less inclined to take on such a role. Full-time stepmothers generally need to take on control functions and duties, which peer-like stepmothers do not take on. Certainly this style deserves further investigation, to ascertain if it is common in May-December relationships, or merely an artifact of this study. Knowledge of this style may help new and young stepmothers, who believe they "should" relate to their adolescent and young adult stepchildren in a "parental" manner, and be more comfortable in a peer-like role.

Church (1999) defined a couple model of kinship which dovetails with "My Father's Wife." A detached style is cited in the literature as one that can "work" for stepfathers, and does not seem to harm stepchildren (Coleman, Ganong & Fine, 2000). In the literature, this style has a negative tinge when applied to stepmothers (self-involved women who don't like children). Further studies may fruitfully examine which children are satisfied with a detached style of stepmothering, and whether or not this style is harmful to stepchildren. Such an investigation may help support stepmothers in taking this

role, and indicate how, in certain circumstances, a detached style may be preferable.

One participant described her stepmother as "Another Mother." This participant reported that she had always wanted a more "gushy" mother. This stepmother took a role that stepmothers usually take when the birth mother has died, has abandoned, or is minimally involved with her child. Usually the children reside full-time with the stepmother and father. Orchard and Solberg (1999) referred to this style as "the additional mother"; Church (1999) referred to this style as the "nuclear model" of kinship, and Berger (1998) called such a family as an "invented" stepfamily. In the current study, unlike Church's "nuclear model" stepmother role, "Like Another Mother" did not consider the birth mother a "poor parent" (Church, 1999). . . . This stepmother openly admired and praised the birth mother. Further studies should look at when and how an "additional mother" style of stepmothering is functional, and if it is one that other non-residential stepmothers may successfully adopt, even when there is a strong, close, and positive custodial mother/daughter relationship.

Variations in stepmother styles is an area in which study should continue; it is important to continue to refine the definitions of these styles and to recognize this diversity of successful stepmothering from the perspective of the stepchildren and the stepmother.

Unlike the stepfamilies in which the birth mother has died or is not involved with her children, the stepmothers in the current study were unlikely candidates for a maternal role because of the presence of a caring mother. It is possible that when the participants realized that their stepmothers were not trying to take the place of their mothers, they were able to relax about liking the stepmother, thereby reducing the much mentioned loyalty conflicts that children are said to experience between their same sex parent and stepparent (Sager et al., 1983).

It appears that the amount of information and education that new stepmothers have available to them has made a difference. In 1979, the Vishers put forth the notion that most stepmothers have "unrealistic expectations" of their roles. New stepmothers believed they should act like mothers, expect to be appreciated like mothers, and expect themselves to feel "instant love" for and from their stepchildren. The current study and others have refuted the idea of unrealistic expectations and instant bonding, which may be related to new stepmothers being more informed about workable, stepmother roles, through the amount of public information available. What women who become stepmothers in the twenty-first century expect from themselves in contrast to stepmothers in the seventies, eighties, and nineties may be a fruitful line of inquiry, indicating whether or not a true shift in expectations has taken place.

■ Review Questions

1. What is a "nonresidential stepmother"?
2. Describe the range of relationships that stepdaughters have with nonresidential stepmothers.

Part Six

Family and Society

CHAPTER 14

The Family, the State, and Social Policy

In 1996, the U.S. Congress passed the most sweeping changes since the Great Depression in the program that provides cash assistance to poor families with children. President Bill Clinton, who had promised in his 1992 campaign to "end welfare as we know it," overcame misgivings about the bill and signed it. With the stroke of his pen, "welfare," as the program is commonly called, was transformed from an open-ended source of income to a program that required work and limited the amount of time that families could spend on the rolls.

What was the effect of "welfare reform," as it was called? The number of people enrolled in the main welfare program, now renamed Temporary Assistance for Needy Families, or TANF, has declined by more than two-thirds. Many of the former recipients found work at least some of the time. Others are in stable partnerships or marriages in which their partners work. But some are neither working, nor receiving TANF, nor even in a household in which someone else is working. These women and their children are disconnected from both work and welfare as sources of income. They tend to have problems that make finding and holding a job difficult, such as learning disabilities, depression, physical ailments, and drug problems. In the first reading, Rebecca M. Blank estimates that perhaps 20 to 25 percent of low-income single mothers could be classified as "disconnected." She discusses the reasons they are not working, and she proposes a new program to assist them.

When the welfare reform legislation was reauthorized in 2006, there was much debate about whether to include funds to promote marriage. (The final bill did include these funds.) Indeed, marriage had emerged as a public-policy issue in the 2000s. But while attention first focused on promoting heterosexual marriage among the poor, the legalization of same-sex marriage in Massachusetts in 2004 and in several other states thereafter focused attention on whether same-sex marriage, or even same-sex domestic partnerships, should be allowed. It is a divisive issue with passionate supporters and opponents. Some opponents see it as a moral issue, while some supporters see it as a civil rights issue. In the second selection, William Meezan and Jonathan Rauch analyze same-sex marriage as a family policy issue. Legalizing same-sex marriage, the authors say, could make same-sex parenting (even among nonmarried gay men and lesbians) more widely accepted socially. So it is reasonable to ask what the consequences of growing up with gay or lesbian parents are for children. If the consequences are negative, some policymakers might oppose same-sex marriage even if they have no moral objections; and if there are no negative consequences, more observers might favor it. The authors review the evidence and comment on its implications.

READING 14-1

Improving the Safety Net for Single Mothers Who Face Serious Barriers to Work

Rebecca M. Blank

Welfare reform efforts during the mid-1990s led all fifty states to increase the scope of welfare-to-work programs and require more welfare recipients to participate in them. Although most of the adult caseload entered employment during the years following reform, some women continue to receive welfare benefits—through the Temporary Assistance for Needy Families (TANF) program—while remaining jobless. Although recent changes in welfare reform law will intensify the demand that women receiving TANF move toward work, not all the unemployed women now on TANF will be able to make the transition to work. And a fast-growing share of single mothers has already left welfare (either voluntarily or involuntarily) but is not working. By my estimate, 20 to 25 percent of all low-income single mothers (those with household income below 200 percent of the official poverty level) fit in this latter category in 2004.

In this article I examine the issues faced by women who have multiple barriers to work and for whom substantial work, at least in the short run, is difficult. These hard-to-employ women are increasingly being moved off TANF in response to growing demands that welfare recipients begin work. They are largely not eligible for disability assistance through the Supplemental Security Income (SSI) program, because although their ability to work is seriously impaired, they do

not meet SSI's strict disability requirements. An increasing number of highly disadvantaged single mothers thus cannot access either welfare support or SSI.

To meet the needs of these women, I propose that states design a Temporary and Partial Work Waiver Program to assess family needs, set realistic and limited work requirements (providing at least partial support), and link these women to other services that can help them address the issues that limit their access to employment.

The new program would be more flexible than either TANF or SSI and would serve highly disadvantaged women both on and off welfare. Recognizing that some women cannot move into full-time employment, it would allow for partial work waivers, while continuing to demand that women work as much as they are able to. Recognizing that barriers to work can change over time, it would make waivers temporary and would regularly reassess the women's ability to work. The program would cost about $5,200 per woman served, though precise costs would depend heavily on the nature and availability of special services (such as job training, mental health programs, or substance abuse programs). Assuming that the program operated in all fifty states and that it were used by one-fourth of the low-income single mothers who appear to have difficulty finding work (a maximal participation assumption), it would cost around $2.8 billion a year. Only a portion of that estimate represents new spending; some of these women would receive funding through TANF, and some of the services that would be provided through the new program are already funded from other sources.

The new program would provide services to women and children in some of the nation's poorest families—families that are increasingly disconnected from public support of any kind. It would enable states that wish to provide some type of safety net for these families to balance ongoing work requirements with the recognition that at least some single mothers face formidable barriers to work.

Rebecca M. Blank. 2007. "Improving the Safety Net for Single Mothers Who Face Serious Barriers to Work." *The Future of Children,* 17 (no. 2): 183-197. From *The Future of Children,* a collaboration of The Woodrow Wilson School of Public and International Affairs at Princeton University and the Brookings Institution.

WELFARE REFORM, REDUCED CASELOADS, AND INCREASED WORK—BY SOME

As shown in Figure 14.1 welfare caseloads plummeted during the 1990s. Between 1994 and 2004, the number of adults on welfare fell 60 percent, from 5 million to 2 million. Case-loads began falling even before passage of the 1996 welfare reform law. The decline slowed during the early 2000s, when economic growth slowed and unemployment rose, but to many people's surprise it has continued, though many families remain on welfare and only about one-third of these families' adult heads met work requirements in 2003.

The remaining TANF caseload includes at least three groups, only one of which is seriously disconnected from work. One group includes long-term and short-term TANF recipients who are working relatively steadily, especially in states with lower benefit reduction rates (the rate at which benefits are reduced as earnings increase) where women can combine welfare benefits with low-wage work. Another group includes short-term nonworking TANF recipients who use benefits after some economic disruption in their lives, but then leave welfare relatively quickly.

The third group—longer-term recipients who are not working or working only sporadically—is of most concern. Experts estimate that these longer-term (and typically non-working) welfare recipients make up 40–45 percent of the caseload.[1]

In addition to long-term TANF participants, in some states there are certain families who have been moved off TANF and into special state programs (SSPs). As of 2003, thirty states had created SSPs as a way to avoid counting these families toward their TANF welfare goals. Participants in SSPs are not included in the TANF caseload because they are funded by state dollars rather than the TANF block grant, even though they typically receive benefits on the same formula as those receiving TANF. In 2003, an estimated 320,000 women—14.6 percent of adult welfare recipients—were in an SSP for part or all of the year, although in some states the share is much higher.[2]

The substantial declines in TANF caseloads since the mid-1990s might lead one to expect that the remaining caseload would be more and more heavily populated by the more disadvantaged and longer-term recipients. But though this group represents a large share of the caseload, its share does not seem to have increased.[3] The explanation appears to be that more disadvantaged women have left welfare at about the same rate as more work-ready women. Since the 1996 law was passed, more and more women are being

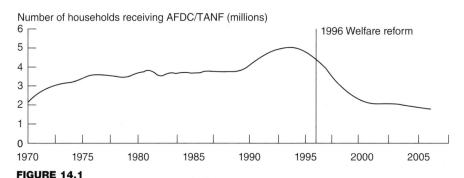

FIGURE 14.1

Total AFDC/TANF Caseloads. (*Note:* 2006 data are through March. *AFDC* Is the acronym for Aid to Families with Dependent Children, it was the precursor to TANF.). (*Source:* Agency for Children and Families, Department of Health and Human Services (www.acf.dhhs.gov).)

involuntarily terminated from welfare, either through sanctions or through time limits. All states have imposed sanctions on women who do not follow program rules (for example, if they do not show up for welfare-to-work programs). And since states implemented their TANF plans, a federal sixty-month time limit has applied to the majority of the caseload, with about one-fourth of the states imposing even stricter limits. Many studies have noted that more disadvantaged women (those with the characteristics of long-term welfare recipients) are more likely than others to be sanctioned or time limited.[4]

HOW MANY WOMEN ARE NEITHER WORKING NOR ON WELFARE?

Because of the time limits and sanctions that cause women to leave welfare, and because not all women who leave welfare for employment are able to keep their jobs, the share of women who neither work nor receive welfare has been rising. One recent study concludes that six years after welfare reform, as many as 18 percent of former welfare recipients were disconnected from both work and welfare.[5] The well-being of this group of "disconnected" welfare leavers is of increasing concern.[6]

Table 14.1 shows that these disconnected mothers are becoming a greater and greater share of all low-income single mothers. In the first column, disconnected mothers are defined as those who report no work and no welfare income over the entire past year and do not report "schooling" as a primary activity. In the second column, disconnected mothers are defined more expansively: they are not in school, and they report less than $2,000 in earnings and less than $1,000 in public assistance over the past year.

Under both definitions, the share of disconnected mothers has risen sharply since the early 1990s. The share reporting no work and no welfare income rose 69 percent, from 11.6 percent to 19.6 percent, between 1995 and 2004. The share reporting only limited work or welfare income rose 56 percent, from 16.2 percent to 25.3 percent. As of 2004, between 1.4 million (by the first definition) and 1.7 million (by the second) low-income single mothers qualified as disconnected. Similar increases in the number of women not at

TABLE 14.1

SHARE OF DISCONNECTED LOW-INCOME SINGLE MOTHERS AMONG ALL LOW-INCOME SINGLE MOTHERS, 1990–2004

Percent

Year	Definition 1[a]	Definition 2[b]
1990	10	14.8
1995	11.6	16.2
2000	13.7	18.8
2001	16.4	21.7
2002	17.3	22.9
2003	16.5	21
2004	19.6	25.3

[a]Definition 1: Mother has no welfare or work income reported in the previous year. In 2004, this group numbered 1.35 million.
[b]Definition 2: Mother reports no more than $2,000 in earnings and no more than $1,000 in public assistance income over the previous year. In 2004, this group numbered 1.73 million.
Source: Data tabulated by the author from the March Supplement of the Current Population Survey. Includes all single mothers, ages eighteen to fifty-four, living with children aged eighteen or younger, in households where total income is less than 200 percent of the official poverty line.

work and not on welfare have also been reported in the national Survey of Income and Program Participation and in state-specific surveys.

Who are these disconnected mothers? Table 14.2 describes their characteristics as reported in 2004, using the same two definitions. Again, whether they report occasional or very low rates of work and welfare use or report being completely disconnected, the two groups look very similar. About half live in households with other adults: 23 percent with their parents, 18 percent with unrelated men. It is perhaps surprising that the share living with other adults, who may provide potential sources of income, is

so low (though it is high relative to less disadvantaged adults). Fully half of these disconnected women have no other adults in the household to provide additional income. (However, while some observers argue that only single women living without other adults are truly "disconnected," one should note that some single women may have difficulty holding jobs *because* they live with other adults who need care and attention.)

In 2003 these women's personal income averaged around $4,300 (in 2000 dollars). Even though many resided with other adults, their average total household income was less than $20,000. Median incomes were well below

TABLE 14.2

CHARACTERISTICS OF DISCONNECTED LOW-INCOME SINGLE MOTHERS IN 2004

Percent, except as indicated

Characteristic	Definition 1	Definition 2
Domestic arrangement		
Living with other adults	50.1	49.9
With a parent	23.5	23.6
With unrelated male	18.2	18.2
Average number of children	1.8	1.8
Income (2003)		
Average self (in 2000 dollars)	4,435	4,287
Average household (in 2000 dollars)	19,607	19,437
Median household (in 2000 dollars)	12,934	12,379
Share with household income below poverty	72.6	73.2
Work		
Labor force participation last year[a]	13.0	28.9
Current labor force participation[b]	20.5	30.0
Race/ethnicity		
White or other non-Hispanic	42.6	44.2
African American, non-Hispanic	28.0	28.6
Hispanic	25.4	23.3
Education		
Less than high school degree	35.2	35.5
High school degree only	37.4	36.7
Disability		
Receiving disability income	3.7	3.1
Disability as reason for not working last year	31.9	31.9

[a]Employed or searching for employment at some point in 2003.
[b]Employed or searching for employment last week.
Source: See Table 1 for source and definitions.

average incomes, and for at least half of these women total household income was less than $13,000. Nearly 75 percent had household income below the poverty level. By contrast, 43 percent of "connected" low-income single mothers (that is, those who are working or on welfare) are below the poverty line, while their average household income is more than $27,000. In short, disconnected women live in very poor households, even taking into account their high likelihood of living with another adult. Even if they are receiving additional (unreported) economic help from family and friends outside their household, their resources are so low that they are still likely to be quite poor.

Fewer than half of these disconnected women are white, non-Hispanic, more than one-quarter are African American; another quarter, Hispanic. More than 70 percent have only a high school degree or less. Although only 3 to 4 percent report some sort of disability-related income, around 30 percent report disability or illness as the reason for not working, which suggests that a significant minority have some serious health problems.

By my estimate, there are approximately 1.7 million disconnected single mothers, based on the more expansive definition above. The estimated 40 percent of the single-mother TANF caseload that are long-term cases (I exclude child-only cases in this calculation) and the single mothers in SSP programs together add about another 500,000 disconnected mothers. These rough calculations suggest that some 2.2 million women who head families do not support themselves either with welfare or with their own earnings. That is not a trivial number. If these women have, on average, 1.8 children, almost 4 million children live in these severely economically challenged families.

WHY AREN'T THESE WOMEN WORKING?

A growing research literature has been trying to determine why some women can successfully enter work and why others either do not move

into work or do begin to work but cannot hold a stable job. The findings suggest unambiguously that women who do not move into stable employment are disadvantaged along a number of dimensions. Researchers have identified six primary barriers to work.[7]

First, women who stay on welfare or cannot find stable employment have less education—and more learning disabilities—than those who find and keep work. Second, these women are more likely to have past or current problems with substance abuse.[8] Third, they have higher rates of depression and other forms of mental illness, as well as more physical health problems.[9] Fourth, they tend to have younger children or larger families, or both, and they are more likely to be caring for someone with health issues, either a child or another relative. Fifth, they are more likely to report a history of domestic violence or a current relationship that involves domestic violence.[10] Finally, many live in central cities, where welfare caseloads have fallen less than in other parts of the country.[11]

Most welfare leavers who have trouble finding or keeping employment face one or more of these problems. One study finds that more than half—57 percent—had multiple barriers to work, compared with only 17 percent of those who had found work.[12] A series of in-depth assessments of a small group of single mothers who were about to exceed time limits in one county in Minnesota found that all had some combination of serious cognitive limits, mental and physical health issues, a lack of community and social networks, and limited management and decisionmaking skills.[13] Such evidence explains why these long-term TANF recipients have not moved into employment and suggests why they are likely to be jobless after their TANF benefits end.

The success of welfare reform, together with the growth in the number of disconnected women, may be compared to deinstitutionalization and the growth of homelessness during the early 1980s. As Christopher Jencks has suggested, efforts during the 1970s to stop the warehousing of mentally disabled adults in substandard state hospitals appeared at first to be "successful" because the disabled were initially taken in or helped by families.[14] But over time such help became harder to maintain, and homelessness rose within this population. Likewise, the initial success of efforts to move low-skilled single women out of welfare and into employment may not have been sustainable for the more disadvantaged welfare leavers. Over time, families may grow less willing to provide help to single mothers who cannot keep jobs, and disadvantaged women who initially find jobs (for example, in a very strong economy in the late 1990s) are not able to keep them. The result could be an erosion of employment gains among disadvantaged welfare leavers and a rise in the share of women disconnected from both work and welfare. This particular story remains to be proven, but it provides one interpretation for the rising numbers of disconnected women in recent years.

A GROWING POLICY CONCERN

Recent changes in federal legislation will increase states' attention to women on welfare who have not successfully transitioned into employment. In January 2006 Congress passed revisions to the TANF legislation that require states to have 50 percent of their current welfare caseloads at work or in work-related programs. Although the original 1996 law also had a 50 percent work requirement, it reduced the share of the caseload required to work in states whose caseloads fell over time. For example, if the caseload fell 25 percent in a given state, that state's work requirement would be 25 percent (50 percent minus 25 percent). Because all states experienced caseload declines, their work requirements declined and, over time, the required share was much lower than the 50 percent standard. The reauthorizing legislation sets the 50 percent work requirement on current caseloads, thereby eliminating previous

caseload declines from the work requirement calculation. It also requires states to include women who are in SSPs in their welfare caseloads. States that do not meet this new work requirement will lose part of their federal block grant.[15]

Virtually no state now meets the 50 percent work requirement; some are far from meeting it. Using the counting rules in the new legislation, the average state participation rate—the share of the caseload meeting the work requirement—in 2003 would have been 30 percent.[16] States that do not want to face financial sanctions must find a way to move more of their nonworking caseload, both in TANF and in SSPs, into work.

These new requirements create a strong incentive for states to remove disadvantaged women from the caseload through time limits and sanctions, so that more women on welfare can hold at least part-time work. An increasing share of hard-to-employ women may thus lose TANF benefits and join the already growing group of women who are not on welfare and not working.

A PROPOSED POLICY RESPONSE

Public attention over the past fifteen years has focused on moving women into work. It has not yet adequately addressed the reality that some women are not making this transition. It is time to rethink policy for women who face such serious disadvantages, and often so many of them, that full-time and steady employment is not possible. As noted, increasingly these women are losing access to welfare. Many have already left TANF, in part because of sanctions and time limits, and recent changes in the law will only accelerate this process.

Most women in this group also lack access to SSI, the primary federal low-income disability program (the poor elderly do qualify for SSI). During the 1990s, states made a concerted effort to move as many women (or their children) as possible onto SSI, in part because the program is funded primarily by federal dollars, whereas nearly half of welfare dollars are paid by states. To receive SSI, one must meet low-income eligibility standards, have a medical disability that will last at least twelve months, and be unable to engage in "substantial gainful activity" (as defined by a monthly earnings amount). Essentially, an SSI applicant has to prove that she is largely unable to work. Although SSI participants are encouraged to work if they can, not surprisingly a very small share of the SSI caseload does work.[17]

Policy analysts have increasingly been recognizing the need for some sort of temporary or partial disability system that allows people to receive partial support (for problems that limit work but do not create complete disability) or temporary support (for problems that may not be permanent but that limit work in the short term).[18] Such an approach is widely used in European social welfare systems and in private disability systems in the United States. The current public U.S. disability system for low-income people does not recognize that "disability is a dynamic process rather than a static classifications."[19] I propose that states create a Temporary and Partial Work Waiver Program to assist hard-to-employ low-income mothers.

States must address the needs of the growing population of disconnected mothers and their children who are receiving support neither from TANF nor from SSI. Women who are not receiving TANF benefits are less likely to receive other services for their children or themselves, including food stamps and Medicaid.[20] States must also address the needs of long-term TANF recipients who need more help in moving to employment than most short-term job search programs can provide. Helping these women deal effectively with their barriers to employment can move them toward greater economic self-sufficiency and reduce the need for states to impose time limits or sanctions. In short, my proposed program could serve both disadvantaged women in the TANF caseload and women outside TANF who have not found stable employment. (Some other low-income family heads who are not

single mothers might need and be eligible for the services provided by this program. For convenience, I discuss the program as if it were available solely to single mothers; in reality, it is likely to be used primarily by them.)

A state Temporary and Partial Work Waiver Program would, like TANF, demand that its clients work as much as possible, but it would provide economic stability and support to highly disadvantaged families. It would have more flexibility than TANF. For example, it would recognize that many of these women may be able to work part time or irregularly even if they cannot work full time; that the circumstances that create work barriers may change, necessitating changes in levels of support; and that these families must be linked with medical and economic supports both to prevent extreme poverty and to ease the severity and duration of the barriers that keep the mothers from work.

What would such a state program look like? It would begin by assessing (and later, as appropriate, reassessing) the family's health problems, the mother's personal and skill limitations, and the family's overall economic situation. Then, if TANF or SSI support was not feasible, it would determine eligibility. Two key questions would be how much work could realistically be expected and how long support should be provided before a reassessment is in order. The program would determine whether barriers to work should be considered full time or partial and would provide support for the family (at the level of TANF monthly benefits) accordingly. For example, a woman whose work barrier is judged to require a 50 percent work waiver would be eligible for 50 percent of the TANF benefit, based on the assumption that she is able to work part time. The program would then refer the mother to other available services, such as mental health services, substance abuse services, counseling on domestic violence, job training, and subsidized child care. Caseworkers would also assist families in applying for programs such as food stamps, the federal nutrition program for infants and children, or Medicaid. Finally the program would involve case management. A caseworker would regularly assess how the family is doing with regard to employment, child well-being, and the use of services.

A client could enter the program in many ways. The TANF system could refer its more disadvantaged clients who have not found jobs. It could also refer people who have lost TANF eligibility either through time limits or through sanctions. Some states may want to refer some new TANF applicants to this program, rather than enrolling them in TANF. The SSI program could refer people turned down for SSI assistance who are not on TANF. People not connected to any public assistance programs could also request help. Some of these clients might receive support in the program through TANF block grant funds and some could be funded out of other dollars.

I would propose setting up the program as a separate funding and program stream that states would administer as part of their TANF-related programs. On the one hand, program participants would be outside the standard TANF caseload counts; they would not be subject to TANF rules on time limits once they had a waiver, and they would not be counted as part of the state's caseload that is subject to forty-hour work requirements. On the other hand, participants would continue to face work requirements (either current and part-time or forthcoming at the end of their waiver) and could be sanctioned if they do not participate in mental health or counseling services to which they are assigned or if they do not fulfill their (part-time) job search or employment expectations.

Three examples will show how various clients might interact with this system. In the first, a mother who is caring for a partly disabled preschooler is initially given a full work waiver. Once the child reaches school age, the mother is given a partial work waiver and expected to find work that allows her to be home outside school hours.

In the second, a mother who was sanctioned off TANF a year ago but has not been steadily employed is initially assessed and found to have a history of substance abuse. States with substance abuse programs may want to refer her to such a program and to reassess when she has completed it. Some states may be willing to provide a partial waiver but require part-time work. Other states may link her with food stamps and Medicaid and make sure the children are adequately cared for, but refuse additional help given her earlier TANF sanctions.

In the third, a mother who left TANF with a job but has since worked only sporadically is initially assessed and found to have depression and low cognitive functioning. A caseworker might want to make sure she receives medical services for her depression. She may receive a temporary partial work waiver, providing at least part-time support, but face reassessment of her employability after receiving treatment for depression.

Clearly, different state responses are possible in each of these situations, depending on funding capability and the availability of other services. Not all low-income single mothers will be employable in the short run or even in the long run. Some may best be served by being placed in the 20 percent of the TANF caseload that can be waived from time limits. But even highly disadvantaged women can be encouraged to work at least part-time and as regularly as possible. Some women may receive partial benefits over an extended period, with a partial work waiver under this program.

The primary advantage of this system is that it would provide states with flexibility to respond to families for whom current welfare-to-work efforts are not adequate. The system recognizes that not all family heads are able to move into full-time employment and supports them even in some circumstances where TANF funds cannot be used. It recognizes that family circumstances change over time and that women who have trouble holding a full-time job this month might be able to do so in the future. It also allows states to assist and recognize disabilities that are less permanent and severe than those covered by SSI. . . .

CONCLUSION

A public conversation about women for whom welfare-to-work efforts have failed is long overdue. These women do not always evoke public sympathy. They are likely to live in poor neighborhoods, to have a history of drug abuse or sexual abuse, and to face ongoing mental or physical health problems. Public willingness to help them would be low if they lived on their own—just as there is little public interest in helping low-income men with these same problems. But these women are also mothers whose economic instability, poverty, and joblessness affect their children's life opportunities. Policymakers' concerns about this population are evident in the growing interest in research and demonstration projects aimed at the hard-to-employ. As findings from evaluations of the demonstration projects become available, they should be used to inform the design and implementation of new programs such as the one proposed here.

The relative lack of information about this population creates policy challenges. High on the policy agenda must be a database that provides better national information on the extent of long-term welfare use and the problems faced by the more disadvantaged women who leave welfare. The growing number of women who report no work and no welfare support is particularly troublesome. To develop effective policy prescriptions, it is essential to know more about who these women are and how they and their children are coping and surviving.

The success of welfare reform over the past ten years demonstrates that low-income women want to work and provide better futures for their children. A surprisingly large share of women has left welfare and entered the labor force, far greater than even the strongest supporters of welfare reform predicted in 1996. Yet some parents require more assistance than others. Although short-term job search assistance has been effective for many former welfare recipients, it is not effective for all. Greater attention must be given to the needs of mothers who face serious barriers in entering the workforce and whose need for ongoing support may continue even if they are successful in finding low-wage work.

■ Review Questions ■

1. What is a disconnected single mother?
2. What are the barriers that these women often face to achieving stable employment?

ENDNOTES

1. The share of long-term recipients in 2003 is estimated at 40 percent in Michael Wiseman, "Three Views of Welfare Turnover" (George Washington University, 2003). The share of the caseload in long-term spells is 45 percent (based on data from the mid- to late 1990s) in Lashawn Richburg-Hayes and Stephen Freeman, "A Profile of Families Cycling On and Off Welfare," report from MDRC to the Office of the Assistant Secretary for Planning and Evaluation, U.S. Department of Health and Human Services (April 2004).
2. Michael Wiseman, "Another Look at Turnover," Research Memorandum, Human Services Policy Division, Office of the Assistant Secretary for Planning and Evaluation, U.S. Department of Health and Human Services (December 2005).
3. Sheila R. Zedlewski, "Work and Barriers to Work among Welfare Recipients in 2002," *Snapshots of America's Families* 3, no. 3 (Washington: Urban Institute, 2003).
4. A review of this evidence is in Richard Fording, Sanford F. Schram, and Joe Soss, "Devolution, Discretion, and Local Variation in TANF Sanctioning," Discussion Paper Series 2006–04 (University of Kentucky Center for Poverty Research, February 2006); see also LaDonna Pavetti, Michelle K. Derr, and Heather Hesketh,

"Review of Sanction Policies and Research Studies," report from Mathematica Policy Research, Inc., to the Office of the Assistant Secretary for Planning and Evaluation, U.S. Department of Health and Human Services (March 2003).

5. Lesley J. Turner, Sheldon Danziger, and Kristin Seefeldt, "Failing the Transition from Welfare to Work: Women Chronically Disconnected from Employment and Cash Welfare," *Social Science Quarterly* 87, no. 2 (June 2006): 227–49.

6. See Gregory Acs and Pamela Loprest, *Leaving Welfare: Employment and Well-Being of Families That Left Welfare in the Post-Entitlement Era* (Kalamazoo, Mich.: W. E. Upjohn Institute, 2004); and Sheila R. Zedlewski and Sandi Nelson, "Families Coping without Earnings or Government Cash Assistance," Assessing the New Federalism, Occasional Paper 64 (Washington: Urban Institute, 2003).

7. Papers that discuss these multiple barriers include Sandra K. Danziger and others, "Barriers to the Employment of Welfare Recipients," in *Prosperity for All? The Economic Boom and African Americans,* edited by Robert Cherry and William Rogers (New York: Russell Sage, 2000); Robert Moffitt and others, "The Characteristics of Families Remaining on Welfare," Welfare, Children, and Families Study, Policy Brief 02-2 (Johns Hopkins University, 2002); Matthew Stagner, Katherine Kortenkamp, and Jane Reardon-Anderson, "Work, Income, and Well-Being among Long-Term Welfare Recipients: Findings from a Survey of California's 'Precarious Families,'" Assessing the New Federalism, Discussion Paper 02-10 (Washington: Urban Institute, 2002); Kristin S. Seefeldt and Sean M. Orzol, "Watching the Clock Tick: Factors Associated with TANF Accumulation," National Poverty Center Working Paper Series 04-9, revised (Ann Arbor: University of Michigan, May 2005); and Ellen Meara and Richard G. Frank, "Welfare Reform, Work Requirements, and Employment Barriers," Working Paper 12480 (Cambridge, Mass.: National Bureau of Economic Research, 2006).

8. A particularly good discussion of this issue is in Lisa R. Metsch and Harold Pollack, "Welfare Reform and Substance Abuse," *Milbank Quarterly* 83, no. 1 (2005): 65–99.

9. A good summary of the research literature on health limitations among disadvantaged single mothers is in Mark Nadel, Steve Wamhoff, and Michael Wiseman, "Disability, Welfare Reform, and Supplemental Security Income," *Social Security Bulletin* 65, no. 3 (2003–04): 14–30.

10. A summary of the recent research is in Stephanie Riger, Susan L. Staggs, and Paul Schewe, "Intimate Partner Violence as an Obstacle to Employment among Mothers Affected by Welfare Reform," *Journal of Social Issues* 60, no.4 (2004): 801–18.

11. See the discussion in Margy Waller and Alan Berube, "Timing Out: Long-Term Welfare Caseloads in Large Cities and Counties" (Center on Urban and Metropolitan Policy, Brookings, September 2002).

12. Pamela Loprest, "Disconnected Welfare Leavers Face Serious Risks," *Snapshots of America's Families* 3, no. 7 (Washington: Urban Institute, 2003).

13. LaDonna A. Pavetti and Jacqueline Kauff, "When Five Years Is Not Enough: Identifying and Addressing the Needs of Families Nearing the TANF Time Limit in Ramsey County, Minnesota," Lessons from the Field (Princeton, N.J.: Mathematica Policy Research, March 2006).

14. Christopher Jencks, *The Homeless* (Harvard University Press, 1994).

15. For more information on these legislative changes, see Center for Best Practices, "The Wait Is Over, the Work Begins: Implementing the New TANF Legislation," issue brief (National Governors' Association, June 14, 2006).

16. Mark Greenberg, "Conference TANF Agreement Requires States to Increase Work Participation by 69 Percent, but New Funding Meets Only a Fraction of New Costs" (Washington: Center for Law and Social Policy, January 11, 2006).

17. For an excellent discussion of the SSI program, see Mary C. Daly and Richard V. Burkhauser, "The Supplemental Security Income Program," in *Means-Tested Transfer Programs in the United States,* edited by Robert A. Moffitt (University of Chicago Press, 2003).

18. For instance, see David Wittenburg and Pamela J. Loprest, "A More Work-Focused Disability Program? Challenges and Options" (Washington: Urban Institute, November 2003); and U.S. General Accounting Office, "SSA Disability: Other Programs May Provide Lessons for Improving

Return-to-Work Efforts," testimony before the Subcommittee on Social Security, Committee on Ways and Means, U.S. House of Representatives, GAO/T-HEHS-00-151 (January 2001).

19. Richard V. Burkhauser and Mary C. Daly, "U.S. Disability Policy in a Changing Environment,"

Journal of Economic Literature 15, no.1 (Winter 2002): 219.

20. Sheila Zedlewski and others, "Is There a System Supporting Low-Income Working Families?" Low-Income Working Families Paper 4 (Washington: Urban Institute, February 2006).

READING 14-2

Gay Marriage, Same-Sex Parenting, and America's Children

William Meezan

Jonathan Rauch

Although Americans are deeply divided over same-sex marriage, on one point most would agree: the issue has moved from the obscure fringes to the roiling center of the family-policy debate in a startlingly brief time. In May of 1970, Jack Baker and Mike McConnell applied for a marriage license in Hennepin County, Minnesota. They were turned down. For a generation, subsequent efforts in other venues met the same fate. In the 1990s, Hawaii's state supreme court seemed, for a time, likely to order same-sex marriage, but a state constitutional amendment preemptively overruled the court. Vermont's civil-union program, adopted in 2000 by order of Vermont's high court, offered state (though not federal) benefits to same-sex couples. That program, however, was seen as a substitute for full-fledged marriage. No state, it seemed, was prepared to grant legal matrimony to same-sex couples.

William Meezan and Jonathan Rauch, "Gay Marriage, Same-Sex Parenting, and America's Children," *The Future of Children*, Vol. 15, No. 2, Fall 2005, pp. 98–107, 110. *From The Future of Children*, a collaboration of The Woodrow Wilson School of Public and International Affairs at Princeton University and The Brookings Institution.

Last year [2004], that taboo broke. Under order of its state supreme court, Massachusetts began offering marriage licenses to same-sex couples. More than forty states, by contrast, have enacted laws or, in some cases, constitutional amendments declaring they would *not* recognize same-sex marriage—a trend that escalated in 2004 when thirteen states passed constitutional amendments banning same-sex marriage.[1] The issue pits left against right and, perhaps more significant, old against young: Americans over age forty-four oppose same-sex marriage by a decisive majority, but a plurality of Americans under age thirty support it.[2] Today, across generations and geography, the country is divided over the meaning of marriage as it has not been since the days when states were at odds over interracial marriages and no-fault divorces—if then.

For many of its advocates, same-sex marriage is a civil rights issue, plain and simple. For many of its opponents, it is just as simply a moral issue. In reality, it is both, but it is also a family-policy issue—one of the most important, yet least studied, family-policy issues on the American scene today. The most controversial of its family-policy aspects is the question: how might same-sex marriage affect the well-being of American children?

COUNTING THE CHILDREN

To begin thinking about gay marriage and children, it is useful to pose another question: which children? Consider three groups of children. First, there are those who are now being raised, or who would in the future be raised, by same-sex couples even if same-sex marriage were unavailable. No one knows just how many American children are being raised by same-sex couples today. The 2000 census counted about 594,000 households headed by same-sex couples, and it found children living in 27 percent of such households.[3] The census did not, however, count the number of children in each home. So all we can say is that, conservatively, at least 166,000 children are being raised by gay and lesbian couples.[4] Many of these children, whatever their number, would be directly affected by the introduction of same-sex marriage—a point we will return to later in this article.

On the obverse is a second group that is much larger but on which the effects, if any, of same-sex marriage are entirely unclear: children *not* being raised by same-sex couples—which is to say, children being raised by opposite-sex couples, married or unmarried, or by single parents. How might same-sex marriage affect these children? Or, to put it another way, how (if at all) might homosexual marriage affect heterosexual behavior? Some opponents, such as the journalist Maggie Gallagher and Massachusetts Governor Mitt Romney, argue that same-sex marriage will signal governmental indifference to whether families contain both a mother and a father.[5] Such legal and cultural indifference, they fear, would further erode the norm of childrearing by both biological parents; more children would end up in fatherless homes. On the other hand, some advocates, such as Jonathan Rauch, argue that same-sex marriage will signal the government's (and society's) preference for marriage over other family arrangements, reinforcing marriage's status at a time when that status is under strain.[6] Same-sex marriage, in this view, would encourage marriage over nonmarriage and thus would benefit adults and children alike. Still others believe that same-sex marriage will have little or no effect of any sort on heterosexual families, if only because the number of gay and lesbian couples is small. There is, however, no evidence at all that bears directly on this question, at least in the American context,

because until last year same-sex marriage had never been tried in the United States.[7]

In principle, a third class of children might be affected by same-sex marriage: additional children, so to speak, who might grow up with same-sex couples as a direct or indirect result of the legalization of same-sex marriage. Although even many opponents of same-sex marriage believe that gay and lesbian people should be allowed to foster and adopt children under certain circumstances, they worry that legalizing same-sex marriage would send an irrevocable cultural signal that same-sex parenting and opposite-sex parenting are interchangeable, when in fact they may not be equally good for children. In any case, the advent of same-sex marriage would probably make same-sex parenting easier legally and more widely accepted socially, particularly for couples adopting children from the child welfare system. It is thus not surprising that questions about same-sex parenting come up time and again in discussions of same-sex marriage. To those questions we turn next.

WHAT ARE SAME-SEX FAMILIES?

To speak of same-sex parenting is, almost by definition, to bundle together an assortment of family arrangements. Most children of opposite-sex parents got there the old-fashioned way, by being the biological children of both parents. Because same-sex couples cannot conceive together, their children arrive by a multiplicity of routes into families that assume a variety of shapes. In many cases (no one knows just how many), children living with gay and lesbian couples are the biological offspring of one member of the couple, whether by an earlier marriage or relationship, by arrangement with a known or anonymous sperm donor (in the case of lesbian couples), or by arrangement with a surrogate birth mother (in the case of male couples). Though, again, numbers are unavailable, male couples seem more likely than female couples to adopt children who are not biologically related to either custodial parent.

It is worth noting that these different paths to parenthood lead to disparate destinations. The family dynamics of a female couple raising one partner's biological son from a previous marriage may be quite different from the dynamics of, say, a male couple raising a biologically unrelated son adopted from foster care.

Legal arrangements vary, too. Nonbiological parents in same-sex couples who seek to be legally recognized as parents must adopt, and the rules that govern adoption are as diverse as the state legislatures that pass adoption laws, the state agencies that promulgate adoption regulations, and the state courts that interpret them. All the states allow married couples to apply jointly—as couples—for adoption (but marriage is no guarantee that the adoption will be approved); and all the states allow unmarried individuals to apply for adoption. Only one state, Utah, denies adoption to unmarried couples (heterosexual and homosexual). And so marriage and adoption, though intertwined, are treated as distinct matters by the law and the courts.

Beyond that point, the rules diverge, especially for same-sex couples. Florida, uniquely, bans homosexual individuals from adopting. Mississippi explicitly bans adoption by same-sex couples. At the other end of the spectrum, as of mid-2004 nine states and the District of Columbia permitted same-sex couples to apply jointly for adoption, meaning that both members of the couple could be simultaneously granted parental status. In almost two dozen other states, courts in either the whole state or in some jurisdictions allow "second-parent" adoptions, under which one gay or lesbian partner can petition to become the second parent of the first partner's biological or previously adopted child. (For instance, a gay man could first adopt as a single parent, and then his partner could apply to become the child's other legal parent.) In the remaining states, same-sex couples are not eligible for either joint or second-parent adoption, which means that any children they might be raising are legally related to only one custodial parent.[8]

To study same-sex parenting, then, is to study not one phenomenon but many. As of this writing, indeed, the many same-sex couples whom researchers have studied share just one common trait: not one of them was legally married.[9] So—with suitable caveats about the diversity of same-sex family relationships and structures—what can we say about same-sex parenting and its impact on children? As it happens, the literature on same-sex parenting and its effects on children is significant and growing. For the present article, we reviewed most of it: more than fifty studies, many literature reviews, and accounts of a number of dissertations and conference papers dating back to the 1970s.

WHY SAME-SEX PARENTING IS HARD TO STUDY

This body of research grew partly out of court cases in which lesbian and gay parents (or coparents) sought to defend or obtain custody of children.[10] Many researchers approached the subject with a sympathetic or protective attitude toward the children and families they studied. Critics have accused researchers of downplaying differences between children of gay and straight parents, especially if those differences could be interpreted unfavorably—a charge that has been debated in the field.[11] We will not enter that debate here, beyond noting that the best defense against bias is always to judge each study, whatever its author's motivation, critically and on its merits.

More significant, we believe, are the daunting methodological challenges that the researchers faced, especially at first.

Difficulty Finding Representative Samples

Perhaps the most important such challenge is that researchers have no complete listing of gay and lesbian parents from which to draw representative samples (probability samples, as researchers call them). To find study participants, they

have often had to rely on word-of-mouth referrals, advertisements, and other recruiting tools
that may produce samples not at all like the full
population of gay and lesbian parents. All but
one of the studies we examined employed samples composed of either totally or predominantly
white participants. Almost all the participants
were middle- to upper-middle-class, urban, well
educated, and "out." Most were lesbians, not
gay men. Participants were often clustered in a
single place. It may be that most same-sex parents *are* white, relatively affluent lesbians, or it
may be merely that these parents are the easiest
for researchers to find and recruit, or both may
be partly true. No one knows. Absent probability
samples, generalizing findings is impossible.

Small Sample Sizes

Gay- and lesbian-headed families can be difficult to locate, and funding for this research has
been sparse.[12] Those factors and others have
forced researchers to deal with the challenge
of small samples. Most studies describing the
development of children raised in gay or lesbian
homes report findings on fewer than twenty-five
children, and most comparative studies compare
fewer than thirty children in each of the groups
studied. Other things being equal, the smaller
the number of subjects in the groups studied, the
harder it is to detect differences between those
groups.[13]

Comparison Groups

The question is often not just how well same-sex
parents and their children fare, but compared with
whom? Should a single lesbian mother be compared with a single heterosexual mother? If so,
divorced or never married? Should a two-mother
family be compared with a two-biological-parent
family, a mother-father family headed by one
biological parent and one stepparent, or a single-
parent family? It all depends on what the
researcher wants to know. Identifying appropriate comparison groups has proved vexing, and
no consistent or wholly convincing approach has

emerged. Many studies mix family forms in both
their homosexual and heterosexual groups, blur-
ring the meaning of the comparison being made.
Some studies do not use comparison groups at all
and simply describe children or adults in same-
sex households. Some, in fact, have argued that
comparing gay and straight families, no matter
how closely matched the groups, is inappropriate
inasmuch as it assumes a "heterosexual norm"
against which same-sex parents and their children should be judged.[14]

Subject-Group Heterogeneity

As we noted, families headed by same-sex parents are structurally very different from one
another. That fact presents researchers with
another challenge, because studies are most
accurate when each of the groups being examined or compared is made up of similar individuals or families. When the pool of potential
subjects is small, as it is for same-sex parents,
assuring within-group homogeneity is often difficult. Thus some studies use "mixed" groups of
lesbian-headed households, yielding results that
are difficult to interpret. For example, partnered
lesbians are often included with single lesbians,
with all called "single" by the author; children
who live both in and outside the home are discussed as a single group; children born into
homes that originated both as heterosexual marriages and as lesbian households are included
in the same sample; and separated and divorced
women are mixed with never-married women
and called "single." In at least one of the studies
reviewed, children of transsexuals and lesbians,
children who are both biological and adopted,
and parents who are both biological and adopters
are treated as a single group.

Measurement Issues

Another challenge is to gauge how well children are faring. Few studies collect data from
the children directly, and even fewer observe
the children's behavior—the gold standard for
research of this kind, but more expensive and

time-consuming than asking parents and children to evaluate themselves. Some studies use nonstandardized measures, while others use either measures with poor reliability and validity or measures whose reliability and validity were either not known or not reported.

Another measurement issue arises from the sometimes dated content of the measures used. In one 1986 study, for example, dressing in pants and wanting to be a doctor or lawyer were considered masculine for girls, and seeking leadership roles was considered a display of dominance.[15] Those classifications look rather quaint today.

Statistical Issues

To some extent, researchers can compensate for heterogeneous samples and nonequivalent comparison groups by using statistical methods that control for differences, particularly in studies with larger samples. Not all studies have done so, especially in the era before today's advanced software made statistical work considerably easier. Some studies thus did not perform appropriate statistical analyses when that was possible. Others did not report the direction of the significant relationships that they found, leaving unclear which group of children fared better. Most failed to control for potentially confounding factors, such as divorce stress or the status of a current relationship with a former partner.

Putting the Research Challenges in Perspective

This is an imposing catalog of challenges and shortcomings, and it needs to be seen in context. The challenges we describe are by no means unique to the research on same-sex parenting, and neither are the flaws that result.[16] Studying small, hard-to-locate populations is inherently difficult, especially if the subject pool is reticent. One of us, Meezan, has been conducting and reviewing field research on foster and adoptive families since the 1970s; he finds that the studies reviewed here are not under par by the standards of their discipline at the time they were conducted.

WHAT THE EVIDENCE SHOWS—AND MEANS

So what do the studies find? Summarizing the research, the American Psychological Association concluded in its July 2004 "Resolution on Sexual Orientation, Parents, and Children,"

> There is no scientific basis for concluding that lesbian mothers or gay fathers are unfit parents on the basis of their sexual orientation. . . . On the contrary, results of research suggest that lesbian and gay parents are as likely as heterosexual parents to provide supportive and healthy environments for their children. . . . Overall, results of research suggest that the development, adjustment, and well-being of children with lesbian and gay parents do not differ markedly from that of children with heterosexual parents.[17]

Our own review of the evidence is consistent with that characterization. Specifically, the research supports four conclusions.

First, lesbian mothers, and gay fathers (about whom less is known), are much like other parents. Where differences are found, they sometimes favor same-sex parents. For instance, although one study finds that heterosexual fathers had greater emotional involvement with their children than did lesbian co-mothers, others find either no difference or that lesbian co-mothers seem to be more involved in the lives of their children than are heterosexual fathers.[18]

Second, there is no evidence that children of lesbian and gay parents are confused about their gender identity, in either childhood or adulthood, or that they are more likely to be homosexual. Evidence on gender behavior (as opposed to identification) is mixed; some studies find no differences, whereas others find that girls raised by lesbians may be more "masculine" in play and aspirations and that boys of lesbian parents are less aggressive.[19] Finally, some interesting differences have been noted in sexual behavior and attitudes (as opposed to orientation). Some studies report that children, particularly daughters, of lesbian parents adopt more accepting and open attitudes toward various sexual identities and are more willing to question their own sexuality. Others report that young women raised in lesbian-headed families are more likely to have homosexual friends and to disclose that they have had or would consider having same-sex sexual relationships.[20] (Just how to view such differences in behavior and attitude is a matter of disagreement. Where conservatives may see lax or immoral sexual standards, liberals may see commendably open-minded attitudes.)

Third, in general, children raised in same-sex environments show no differences in cognitive abilities, behavior, general emotional development, or such specific areas of emotional development as self-esteem, depression, or anxiety. In the few cases where differences in emotional development are found, they tend to favor children raised in lesbian families. For example, one study reports that preschool children of lesbian mothers tend to be less aggressive, bossy, and domineering than children of heterosexual mothers. Another finds more psychiatric difficulties and a greater number of psychiatric referrals among children of heterosexual parents.[21] The only negative suggestion to have been uncovered about the emotional development of children of same-sex parents is a fear on the part of the children—which seems to dissipate during adolescence when sexual orientation is first expressed—that they might be homosexual.[22]

Finally, many gay and lesbian parents worry about their children being teased, and children often expend emotional energy hiding or otherwise controlling information about their parents, mainly to avoid ridicule. The evidence is mixed, however, on whether the children have heightened difficulty with peers, with more studies finding no particular problems.[23]

The significance of this body of evidence is a matter of contention, to say the least. Steven Nock, a prominent scholar reviewing the literature in 2001 as an expert witness in a Canadian court case, found it so flawed methodologically that the "only acceptable conclusion at this point is that the literature on this topic does not constitute a solid body of scientific evidence," and that "all of the articles I reviewed contained at least one fatal flaw of design or execution. . . . Not a single one was conducted according to generally accepted standards of scientific research."[24] Two equally prominent scholars, Judith Stacey and Timothy Biblarz, vigorously disputed the point: "He is simply wrong to say that all of the studies published to date are virtually worthless and unscientific. . . . If the Court were to accept Professor Nock's primary criticisms of these studies, it would have to dismiss virtually the entire discipline of psychology."[25]

We believe that both sides of that argument are right, at least partially. The evidence provides a great deal of information about the particular families and children studied, and the children now number more than a thousand.[26] They are doing about as well as children normally do. What the evidence does not provide, because of the methodological difficulties we outlined, is much knowledge about whether those studied are typical or atypical of the general population of children raised by gay and lesbian couples. We do not know how the *normative* child in a same-sex family compares with other children. To make the same point a little differently, those who say the evidence shows that many same-sex parents do an excellent job of parenting are right. Those who say the evidence falls short of showing that same-sex parenting is equivalent to opposite-sex parenting (or better, or worse) are also right.

Fortunately, the research situation is improving, so we may soon have clearer answers. Over the past several decades researchers have worked to improve their methods, and the population of gay and lesbian parents has become easier to study. Studies using larger samples are appearing in the literature, the first long-term study following the same group of people over time has been published, and studies using representative, population-based samples have appeared. More studies now use standardized instruments with acceptable reliability and validity. Recent studies are much more likely to match comparison groups closely and are also more likely to use statistical methods to control for differences both within and between the study groups.

We identified four studies—all comparatively recent (dating from 1997)—that we believe represent the state of the art, studies that are as rigorous as such research could today reasonably be expected to be (see table). Their conclusions do not differ from those of the main body of research.

FOUR STRONG STUDIES

How do children of lesbian or gay parents fare and compare? Following are summaries of four methodologically rigorous studies.

Wainwright, Russell, and Patterson (2004)

Methodology: Drawing on a nationally representative sample of more than 12,105 adolescents in the National Study of Adolescent Health, the authors compared forty-four adolescents being raised by female same-sex couples with forty-four raised by heterosexual couples. The comparison groups were matched child for child (not on group averages) on many traits, and the study samples did not differ on numerous demographic characteristics from the national sample of 12,105. Metrics were mostly standardized instruments with good reliability and validity, and many were the most commonly used measures in the field. Multivariate analysis was used to determine the impact of family type, controlling for other demographic and social factors.

Findings: "No differences in adolescents' psychosocial adjustment," including depressive symptoms, anxiety, and self-esteem; no differences in grade-point averages or problems in school. Adolescents with same-sex parents reported feeling more connected to school. The authors found that "it was the qualities of adolescent-parent relationships rather than the structural features of families (for example, same- versus opposite-sex parents) that were significantly associated with adolescent adjustment. . . . Across a diverse array of assessments, we found that the personal, family, and school adjustment of adolescents living with same-sex parents did not differ from that of adolescents living with opposite-sex parents."

Golombok and Others (2003)

Methodology: In southwest England, researchers drew on a geographic population study of almost 14,000 mothers and their children to identify eighteen lesbian-mother families (headed both by lesbian couples and single mothers) and then added twenty-one lesbian mothers identified through personal referrals, a lesbian mothers' support organization, and advertisements. The twenty-one supplementary subjects were "closely comparable" to the eighteen drawn from the population study. The resulting sample of thirty-nine "cannot be deemed truly representative of the population of lesbian-mother families" but "constitutes the closest approximation achieved so far." Those families were compared with seventy-four families headed by heterosexual couples and sixty families headed by single heterosexual mothers. Standardized measures were administered and interview data were coded by personnel blind to the family's type and structure and were checked for reliability.

Findings: "Children reared by lesbian mothers appear to be functioning well and do not experience negative psychological consequences arising from the nature of their family environment." After the authors controlled for initial differences between groups (age of children, number of siblings) and the number of statistical comparisons made, "the only finding that remained significant . . . was greater smacking of children by fathers than by co-mothers." Also, "boys and girls in lesbian-mother families were not found to differ in gender-typed behavior from their counterparts from heterosexual homes." Children did better psychologically with two parents, regardless of whether the parents were same-sex or opposite-sex couples, than with a single mother.

Chan, Raboy, and Patterson (1998)

Methodology: Using a sample drawn from people who used the same sperm bank (in California), and thus controlling for the effects of biological relatedness, the researchers compared four family structures: lesbian couples (thirty-four), lesbian single mothers (twenty-one), heterosexual couples (sixteen), and single heterosexual mothers (nine). Participation rates were significantly higher for lesbian couples than for others. Though education and income levels were above average for all groups, lesbian parents had completed more education, and lesbian and coupled families had higher

(*continued*)

FOUR STRONG STUDIES (*continued*)

---

incomes; otherwise, group demographics were similar. Information on children's adjustment was collected from parents and teachers, using standardized measures with good reliability and validity.

Findings: "Children's outcomes were unrelated to parental sexual orientation," for both single-parent and coupled families. "On the basis of assessments of children's social competence and behavior problems that we collected, it was impossible to distinguish children born to and brought up by lesbian versus heterosexual parents." Sample size was large enough to detect large or medium effects but not small ones, so family structure had either small or nonexistent effects.

Brewaeys and Others (1997)
Methodology: Using a sample drawn from the fertility clinic at Brussels University Hospital, thirty lesbian-couple families who conceived through donor insemination (DI) were compared with thirty-eight heterosexual families who conceived through DI and thirty heterosexual families who conceived naturally. Response rates were generally good, but better for lesbian co-mothers than for heterosexual fathers. Statistical analysis controlled for demographic differences between comparison groups and for number of comparisons made, and good metrics were used.

Findings: Children's emotional and behavior adjustment "did not differ" between lesbian and opposite-sex families, and "boys and girls born in lesbian mother families showed similar gender-role behaviour compared to boys and girls born in heterosexual families." The quality of parents' relationship with each other did not differ across the two family types, nor did the quality of interaction between children and biological parents. "However, one striking difference was found between lesbian and heterosexual families: social mothers [that is, nonbiological lesbian parents] showed greater interaction with their children than did fathers."

Sources: Jennifer L. Wainwright, Stephen T. Russell, and Charlotte J. Patterson, "Psychosocial Adjustment, School Outcomes, and Romantic Relationships of Adolescents with Same-Sex Parents," *Child Development* 75, no. 6 (December 2004): 1886–98, quotes pp. 1892, 1895; Susan Golombok and others, "Children with Lesbian Parents: A Community Study," *Developmental Psychology* 39, no. 1 (January 2003): 20–33, quotes pp. 30, 31; Raymond Chan, Barbara Raboy, and Charlotte J. Patterson, "Psychosocial Adjustment among Children Conceived via Donor Insemination by Lesbian and Heterosexual Mothers," *Child Development* 69, no. 2 (April 1998): 443–57, quotes p. 453; A. Brewaeys and others, "Donor Insemination: Child Development and Family Functioning in Lesbian Mother Families," *Human Reproduction* 12, no. 6 (1997): 1349–59, quotes pp. 1356, 1357.

It bears emphasizing that the issue of same-sex parenting is directly relevant to same-sex marriage only to the extent that the latter extends the scope of the former. Gay and lesbian couples make up only a small share of the population, not all of those couples have or want children, and many who do have or want children are likely to raise them whether or not same-sex marriage is legal. The number of additional children who might be raised by same-sex couples as a result of same-sex marriage is probably small. Moreover, an important question, where family arrangements are concerned, is always, "Compared with what?" We doubt that same-sex marriage would shift any significant number of children out of the homes of loving heterosexual parents and into same-sex households; and, to the extent that same-sex marriage helps move children out of foster care and into caring adoptive homes, the

prospect should be welcomed. If the past several decades' research establishes anything, it is that the less time children spend in the public child welfare system, the better. Put simply, research shows that the state makes a poor parent for many of the children in its custody, particularly compared with stable, loving, developmentally appropriate environments.

AN OPPORTUNITY TO LEARN

It is important, we think, to recognize that social science cannot settle the debate over same-sex marriage, even in principle. Some people believe the United States should have same-sex marriage as a matter of basic right even if the change proves deleterious for children; others believe the country should reject same-sex marriage as a matter of morality or faith even if the change would benefit kids. Consequential factors are but one piece of a larger puzzle; and, as is almost always the case, social research will for the most part follow rather than lead the national debate.

Both authors of this paper are openly gay and advocates of same-sex marriage, a fact that readers should weigh as they see fit. In any case, our personal judgments about the facts presented here are no better than anyone else's. Two points, however, seem to us to be both incontrovertible and important.

First, whether same-sex marriage would prove socially beneficial, socially harmful, or trivial is an empirical question that cannot be settled by any amount of armchair theorizing. There are plausible arguments on all sides of the issue, and as yet there is no evidence sufficient to settle them.

Second, the costs and benefits of same-sex marriage cannot be weighed if it cannot be tried—and, preferably, compared with other alternatives (such as civil unions). Either a national constitutional ban on same-sex marriage or a national judicial mandate would, for all practical purposes, throw away the chance to collect the information the country needs in order to make a properly informed decision.

As it happens, the United States is well situated, politically and legally, to try same-sex marriage on a limited scale—without, so to speak, betting the whole country. As of this writing, one state (Massachusetts) is marrying same-sex couples, two others (Vermont and Connecticut) offer civil unions, and several more (notably California) offer partner-benefit programs of one sort or another. Most other states have pre-emptively banned gay marriage, and some have banned civil unions as well. The upshot is that the nation is running exactly the sort of limited, localized experiment that can repay intensive study.

In particular, the clustering in four neighboring states of all three kinds of arrangement—same-sex marriage in Massachusetts, civil unions in Vermont and Connecticut, and neither in New Hampshire—offers a near-ideal natural laboratory. A rigorous study of how children fare when they are raised in these various arrangements and environments would not be easy to design and execute, and it would require a considerable amount of time and money; but the knowledge gained would make the debate over gay marriage better lit and perhaps less heated, to the benefit of all sides of the argument.

■ Review Questions ■

1. Why has it been so difficult to study the consequences for children of growing up in gay and lesbian families?
2. What do the studies, limited though they may be, find?

ENDNOTES

1. The thirteen were Arkansas, Georgia, Kentucky, Louisiana, Michigan, Mississippi, Missouri, Montana, North Dakota, Oklahoma, Ohio, Oregon, and Utah.
2. *Los Angeles Times* poll, March 27–30, 2004. Among respondents under age thirty, 44 percent supported same-sex marriage and 31 percent supported civil unions; 22 percent favored neither.
3. U.S. Census Bureau, *Married-Couple and Unmarried-Partner Households: 2000* (February 2003). See also Gary J. Gates and Jason Ost, *The Gay and Lesbian Atlas* (Washington: Urban Institute, 2004), p. 45.
4. Because same-sex couples, especially those with children, may be reluctant to identify themselves to census takers, and because small populations are inherently difficult to count, this number is likely to be an undercount. See Gates and Ost,

The Gay and Lesbian Atlas (see note 3). Other estimates range much higher. See, for example, Frederick W. Bozett, "Gay Fathers: A Review of the Literature," in *Psychological Perspectives on Lesbian and Gay Male Experiences,* edited by Linda Garnets and Douglas Kimmel (Columbia University Press, 1993), pp. 437–57.

5. See, for example, Maggie Gallagher, "What Is Marriage For?" *Weekly Standard,* August 4–11, 2003; and Mitt Romney, testimony before the U.S. Senate Judiciary Committee, June 22, 2004.

6. Jonathan Rauch, *Gay Marriage: Why It Is Good for Gays, Good for Straights, and Good for America* (New York: Times Books, 2004).

7. As of this writing, the Netherlands, Belgium, and several Canadian provinces had adopted same-sex marriage, but only recently. The effects, if any, on the welfare of children and families are both unclear and disputed. See, for example, Stanley Kurtz, "The End of Marriage in Scandinavia," *Weekly Standard,* February 2, 2004; and in rebuttal, M. V. Lee Badgett, *Will Providing Marriage Rights to Same-Sex Couples Undermine Heterosexual Marriage? Evidence from Scandinavia and the Netherlands,* Discussion Paper (Council on Contemporary Families and Institute for Gay and Lesbian Strategic Studies, July 2004). Also in rebuttal, William N. Eskridge, Darren R. Spedale, and Hans Ytterberg, "Nordic Bliss? Scandinavian Registered Partnerships and the Same-Sex Marriage Debate," *Issues in Legal Scholarship,* Article 4, available at www.bepress .com/ils/iss5/art4/.

8. The authors are indebted to the Human Rights Campaign, the Lambda Legal Defense and Education Fund, and the National Adoption Information Clearinghouse for information on state adoption policies. Because adoption policies are often set by courts on a case-by-case basis, adoption rules are in flux and vary within as well as between states. The summary counts presented here are subject to interpretation and may have changed by the time of publication.

9. At this writing, same-sex marriage was too new in Massachusetts to have generated any research results.

10. "A third perspective from which [research] interest in lesbian and gay families with children has arisen is that of the law. . . . Because judicial and legislative bodies in some states have found lesbians and gay men unfit as parents because of their sexual orientation, lesbian mothers and gay fathers have often been denied custody or visitation with their children following divorce." Charlotte Patterson, "Lesbian Mothers, Gay Fathers, and Their Children," in *Lesbian, Gay and Bisexual Identities over the Lifespan: Psychological Perspectives,* edited by Anthony R. D'Augelli and Charlotte Patterson (Oxford University Press, 1995), p. 264.

11. Judith Stacey and Timothy J. Biblarz examine twenty-one studies and find that "researchers frequently downplay findings indicating difference regarding children's gender and sexual preferences and behavior." Judith Stacey and Timothy Biblarz, "(How) Does the Sexual Orientation of Parents Matter?" *American Sociological Review* 66 (April 2001): 159–83. Golombok and others reply that it is Stacey and Biblarz who "have overemphasized the differences that have been reported between children with lesbian and heterosexual parents." Susan Golombok and others, "Children with Lesbian Parents: A Community Study," *Developmental Psychology* 39, no. 1 (January 2003): 21.

12. For example, as best we can discern, none of the studies reviewed for this article was funded by the federal government, the major source of social science research funding in the United States.

13. For example, Tasker and Golombok note that there was only a 51 percent chance of detecting a moderate effect size in their sample, and an even lower possibility (if any at all) of detecting a small effect size. See Fiona Tasker and Susan Golombok, *Growing Up in a Lesbian Family* (New York: Guilford Press, 1997).

14. From the perspective of gay men, Gerald Mallon states, "Usually, explorations of gay parenting focus on the differences between gay and straight parents. [I] approach this topic through a gay-affirming lens, meaning that I do not take heterosexuality as the norm and then compare gay parenting to that model and discuss how it measures up. In most cases heterosexually oriented men become fathers for different reasons and in different ways than do gay men. Comparisons of gay fathers to heterosexual fathers are therefore inappropriate." Gerald Mallon, *Gay Men Choosing*

Parenthood (Columbia University Press, 2004), p. xii. From a lesbian perspective, Victoria Clarke states, "In the rush to prove. . . . our similarities to heterosexual families, oppressive norms of femininity, masculinity, and heterosexuality are reinforced. The use of sameness arguments suppresses feminist critiques of the family as a prime site of hetero-patriarchal oppression. . . . By taking mainstream concerns seriously, lesbian and gay psychologists inadvertently invest them with validity and reinforce the anti-lesbian agendas informing popular debates about lesbian parenting." Victoria Clarke, "Sameness and Differences in Lesbian Parenting," *Journal of Community and Applied Social Psychology* 12 (2002): 218.

15. Richard Green and others, "Lesbian Mothers and Their Children: A Comparison with Solo Parent Heterosexual Mothers and Their Children," *Archives of Sexual Behavior* 15, no. 2 (1986): 167–83.

16. For example, similar issues arise in the study of transracial adoption: "Study findings that support greater use of transracial adoption as a placement option . . . are fraught with conceptual and methodological limitations. . . . For instance, many have small sample sizes and no—or inappropriate—comparison groups. While they tend to be cross-sectional, those that are longitudinal are potentially biased from sample attrition." Devon Brooks and Richard P. Barth, "Adult Transracial and Inracial Adoptees: Effects of Race, Gender, Adoptive Family Structure, and Placement History on Adjustment Outcomes," *American Journal of Orthopsychiatry* 69 (January 1999): 88.

17. Available at www.apa.org/pi/lgbc/.

18. A. Brewaeys and others, "Donor Insemination: Child Development and Family Functioning in Lesbian Mother Families," *Human Reproduction* 12 (1997): 1349–59; David K. Flaks and others, "Lesbians Choosing Motherhood: A Comparative Study of Heterosexual Parents and Their Children," *Developmental Psychology* 31 (1995): 105–14; Golombok and others, "Children with Lesbian Parents" (see note 11), pp. 20–33; Katrien Vanfraussen, Ingrid Ponjaert-Kristoffersen, and Anne Brewaeys, "Family Functioning in Lesbian Families Created by Donor Insemination," *American Journal of Orthopsychiatry* 73, no. 1 (January 2003): 78–90.

19. Green and others, "Lesbian Mothers and Their Children" (see note 15); Beverly Hoeffer, "Children's Acquisition of Sex Role Behavior in Lesbian-Mother Families," *American Journal of Orthopsychiatry* 51, no. 3 (1981): 536–44; Ailsa Steckel, "Psychosocial Development of Children of Lesbian Mothers," in *Gay and Lesbian Parents,* edited by Frederick W. Bozett (New York: Praeger, 1987), pp. 75–85.

20. Lisa Saffron, *"What about the Children?" Sons and Daughters of Lesbian and Gay Parents Talk about Their Lives* (London: Cassell, 1996); Tasker and Golombok, *Growing Up in a Lesbian Family* (see note 13). It is unclear whether the young women are more likely to *engage* in same-sex relations, more likely to *disclose* them, or some combination of the two.

21. Steckel, "Psychosocial Development of Children of Lesbian Mothers" (see note 19); Susan Golombok, Ann Spencer, and Michael Rutter, "Children in Lesbian and Single-Parent Households: Psychosexual and Psychiatric Appraisal," *Journal of Child Psychology and Psychiatry* 24, no. 4 (1983): 551–72.

22. Karen G. Lewis, "Children of Lesbians: Their Point of View," *Social Work* 25 (May 1980): 198–203; Ann O'Connell, "Voices from the Heart: The Developmental Impact of Mother's Lesbianism on Her Adolescent Children," *Smith College Studies in Social Work* 63, no. 3 (June 1993): 281–99; S. J. Pennington, "Children of Lesbian Mothers," in *Gay and Lesbian Parents,* edited by Bozett (see note 19), pp. 58–74.

23. Phillip A. Belcastro and others, "A Review of Data Based Studies Addressing the Effects of Homosexual Parenting on Children's Sexual and Social Functioning," *Journal of Divorce and Remarriage* 20, nos. 1–2 (1993): 105–22; Frederick W. Bozett, "Children of Gay Fathers," *Gay and Lesbian Parents,* edited by Bozett (see note 19), pp. 39–57; Margaret Crosbie-Burnett and Lawrence Helmbrecht, "A Descriptive Empirical Study of Gay Male Stepfamilies," *Family Relations* 42 (1993): 256–62; Nanette Gatrell and others, "The National Lesbian Family Study: Interviews with Mothers of Five-Year-Olds," *American Journal of Orthopsychiatry* 70, no. 4 (October 2000): 542–48; Tamar D. Gershon, Jeanne M. Tschann, and John M. Jemerin,

"Stigmatization, Self-Esteem, and Coping among the Adolescent Children of Lesbian Mothers," *Journal of Adolescent Health* 24, no. 6 (June 1999): 437–45; Golombok, Spencer, and Rutter, "Children in Lesbian and Single-Parent Households" (see note 21); Golombok and others, "Children with Lesbian Parents" (see note 11); Jan Hare, "Concerns and Issues Faced by Families Headed by a Lesbian Couple," *Families in Society* 75 (1994): 27–35; Ghazala Afzal Javaid, "The Children of Homosexual and Heterosexual Single Mothers," *Child Psychiatry and Human Development* 24 (1993): 235–48; Suzanne M. Johnson and Elizabeth O'Connor, *The Gay Baby Boom: The Psychology of Gay Parenthood* (New York University Press, 2002); Lewis, "Children of Lesbians" (see note 22); O'Connell, "Voices from the Heart" (see note 22); Pennington, "Children of Lesbian Mothers" (see note 22); Tasker and Golombok, *Growing Up in a Lesbian Family* (see note 13); Norman Wyers, "Homosexuality and the Family: Lesbian and Gay Spouses," *Social Work* 32 (1987): 143–48.

24. Steven L. Nock, affidavit in the superior court of Ontario, Canada, *Halpern et al. v. Canada* and *MCCT v. Canada* (2001), at items 141 (p. 47) and 115 (p. 39).

25. Judith Stacey and Timothy Biblarz, affidavit in the superior court of Ontario, Canada, *Halpern et al. v. Canada* and *MCCT v. Canada* (2001), at items 4 (p. 3) and 14 (p. 7).

26. Anderssen and others' review of the literature up until 2000, which did not cover all of the studies through that date, puts the number of children studied at 615. Norman Anderssen, Christine Amlie, and Erling Andre Ytteroy, "Outcomes for Children with Lesbian or Gay Parents: A Review of Studies from 1978 to 2000," *Scandinavian Journal of Psychology* 43 (2002): 335–51. Since that time, larger-scale studies, some with samples larger than 200, have been undertaken. Stacey and Biblarz, in their affidavit (see note 25) at item 41 (p. 19), cite more than 1,000 children, and 500 observed in "22 of the best studies."

References

CHAPTER 1

Reading 1-2

Almond, Richard. 1977. "Character, Role and Self: Evolution in Personality Styles." Unpublished manuscript. Palo Alto, California.

Bellah, Robert; Richard Madsen; William Sullivan; Ann Swidler; and Steven Tipton. 1985. *Habits of the Heart.* Berkeley: University of California Press.

Campbell, Angus; Philip Converse; and Willard L. Rodgers. 1976. *The Quality of American Life.* New York: Russell Sage.

Cancian, Francesca, and Bonnie Ross. 1981. "Mass Media and the Women's Movement." *Journal of Applied Behavioral Science* 17:9–26.

Carden, Maren L. 1974. *The New Feminist Movement.* New York: Russell Sage Foundation.

Chafe, William H. 1972. *The American Woman.* New York: Oxford University Press.

Cherlin, Andrew. 1981. *Marriage, Divorce, Remarriage.* Cambridge, Massachusetts: Harvard University Press.

Clecak, Peter. 1983. *America's Quest for the Ideal Self.* New York: Oxford University Press.

Degler, Carl N. 1980. *At Odds: Women and the Family in America from the Revolution to the Present.* New York: Oxford University Press.

Duncan, Otis Dudley; Howard Schuman; and Beverly Duncan. 1973. *Social Change in a Metropolitan Community.* New York: Russell Sage.

Easterlin, Richard A. 1980. *Birth and Fortune.* New York: Basic Books.

Elder, Glen. 1974. *Children of the Great Depression.* Chicago: University of Chicago Press.

Fass, Paula S. 1977. *The Damned and the Beautiful.* New York: Oxford University Press.

Filene, Peter. 1974. *Him/Her/Self: Sex Roles in Modern America.* New York: Harcourt Brace Jovanovich.

Flexner, Eleanor. 1974. *Century of Struggle.* New York: Atheneum.

Freeman, Jo. 1975. *The Politics of Women's Liberation.* New York: David McKay.

Friedan, Betty. 1963. *The Feminine Mystique.* New York: Norton.

Gecas, V. 1979. "The Influence of Social Class on Socialization." In W. Burr et al. (eds.), *Contemporary Theories about the Family,* Vol. I. New York: Free Press.

Gratton, Lynda C. 1980. "Analysis of Maslow's Need Hierarchy with Three Social Class Groups." *Social Indicators Research* 7:463–76.

Gurin, Gerald; J. Veroff; and S. Feld. 1960. *Americans View Their Mental Health.* New York: Basic Books.

Hantover, Jeffrey P. 1980. "The Boy Scouts and the Validation of Masculinity." In Elizabeth Pleck and Joseph Pleck, *The American Man.* Englewood Cliffs, New Jersey: Prentice Hall.

Harris, Louis, and Associates. 1979. *The Playboy Report on American Men.* Playboy Inc.

Harris, William H., and Judith Levy (eds.). 1975. *The New Columbia Encyclopedia.* New York: Columbia University Press.

Heer, David M., and Amyra Grossbard-Shechtman. 1981. "The Impact of the Female Marriage Squeeze and the Contraceptive Revolution on Sex Roles and the Women's Liberation Movement in the U.S. 1960–1975." *Journal of Marriage and the Family* 43:49–65.

Hicks, Mary W., and Marilyn Platt. 1970. "Marital Happiness and Stability: A Review of Research in the Sixties." *Journal of Marriage and the Family* 32:553–74.

Hole, J., and E. Levine. 1971. *The Rebirth of Feminism.* New York: Quadrangle.

Johns-Heine, Patrick, and Hans Gerth. 1949. "Values in Mass Periodical Fiction, 1921–1940." *Public Opinion Quarterly* 13:105–13.

Kidd, Virginia. 1974. "Happy Ever After and Other Relationship Styles." Ph.D. Dissertation. Department of Speech, University of Minnesota.

———. 1975. "Happily Ever After and Other Relationship Styles: Advice on Interpersonal Relations in Popular Magazines, 1951–1973." *Quarterly Journal of Speech* 61:31–39.

Kohn, Melvin. 1969. *Class and Conformity: A Study in Values.* Homewood, Illinois: Dorsey Press.

Komarovsky, Mirra. 1962. *Blue-Collar Marriage.* New York: Random House.

Lasch, Christopher. 1977. *Haven in a Heartless World.* New York: Basic Books.

———. 1978. *The Culture of Narcissism: American Life in an Age of Diminishing Expectations.* New York: Norton.

Lebergott, Stanley. 1976. *The American Economy.* Princeton, New Jersey: Princeton University Press.

Lederer, William, and Don Jackson. 1974. "Do People Really Marry for Love?" *Reader's Digest,* January.

Luker, Kristin. 1984. *Abortion and the Politics of Motherhood.* Berkeley: University of California Press.

Lynd, Robert S., and Helen Lynd. 1937. *Middletown in Transition.* New York: Harcourt, Brace and Co.

Maslow, Abraham. 1970. *Motivation and Personality.* 2nd ed. New York: Harper and Row.

Mason, Karen; John Czajka; and Sara Arber. 1976. "Change in U.S. Women's Sex-Role Attitudes, 1969–1974." *American Sociological Review* 41:573–96.

Maurois, Andre. 1940. "The Art of Marriage." *Ladies' Home Journal,* April.

Miller, Ruth Scott. 1925. "Masterless Wives and Divorce." *Ladies' Home Journal,* January.

Newcomb, Theodore. 1937. "Recent Change in Attitudes Toward Sex and Marriage." *American Sociological Review* 1:659–67.

O'Neil, William. 1978. "Divorce in the Progressive Era." In M. Gordon (ed.), *The American Family in Social-Historical Perspective,* pp. 140–51. New York: St. Martin's Press.

Oppenheimer, Valerie Kincade. 1973. "Demographic Influence on Female Employment and the Status of Women." *American Journal of Sociology* 78:946–61.

Osmond, Marie W., and Patricia Y. Martin. 1975. "Sex and Sexism." *Journal of Marriage and the Family* 37:744–59.

Pahl, J. M., and R. E. Pahl. 1971. *Managers and Their Wives.* London: Allen Love and Penguin Press.

Parelius, Ann P. 1975. "Emerging Sex-Role Attitudes, Expectations and Strains among College Women." *Journal of Marriage and the Family* 37:146–54.

Pleck, Joseph. 1985. *Working Wives, Working Husbands.* New York: Sage.

Quinn, Naomi. 1982. "'Commitment' in American Marriage: A Cultural Analysis." *American Ethnologist* 9:775–98.

Roper, Brent S., and Emily Labeff. 1977. "Sex Roles and Feminism Revisited: An Intergenerational Attitude Comparison." *Journal of Marriage and the Family* 39:113–20.

Rothman, Sheila M. 1978. *Women's Proper Place: A History of Changing Ideals and Practices 1870 to the Present.* New York: Basic Books.

Rubin, Lillian. 1976. *Worlds of Pain.* New York: Basic Books.

Ryan, Mary. 1979. *Womanhood in America (From Colonial Times to the Present).* 2nd ed. New York: New Viewpoints.

Swidler, Ann. 1982. "Ideologies of Love in Middle Class America." Paper read at Annual Meeting of Pacific Sociological Association, San Diego.

Thornton, Arland; Duane Alwin; and Donald Camburn. 1983. "Causes and Consequences of Sex-Role Attitudes and Attitude Change." *American Sociological Review* 48:211–27.

Turner, Ralph. 1976. "The Real Self: From Institution to Impulse." *American Journal of Sociology* 81:789–1016.

U.S. Bureau of the Census. 1976. *The Statistical History of the United States.* New York: Basic Books.

U.S. Bureau of the Census. 1982. Current Population Reports, Series P-20, No. 367 and No. 371.

Vahanian, Tilla, and Sally Olds. 1978. "How Good Is Your Marriage?" *Ladies' Home Journal,* January.

Veroff, Joseph; Elizabeth Douran; and Richard Kulka. 1981. *The Inner American: A Self-Portrait from 1957 to 1976.* New York: Basic Books.

Yankelovich, Daniel. 1974. *The New Morality.* New York: McGraw-Hill.

———. 1981. *New Rules.* New York: Random House.

Zaretsky, Eli. 1976. *Capitalism, the Family and Personal Life.* New York: Harper Colophon.

Zelnik, Melvin, and John Kantner. 1980. "Sexual Activity, Contraceptive Use and Pregnancy." *Family Planning Perspectives* 12:230–37.

Zube, Margaret. 1972. "Changing Concepts of Morality: 1948–1969." *Social Forces* 50:385–96.

CHAPTER 3

Reading 3-1

Berger, Joseph; Bernard P. Cohen; and Morris Zelditch, Jr. 1972. "Status Characteristics and Social Interaction." *American Sociological Review* 37:241–55.

Berger, Joseph; Thomas L. Conner; and M. Hamit Fisek, eds. 1974. *Expectation States Theory: A Theoretical Research Program.* Cambridge: Winthrop.

Berger, Joseph; M. Hamit Fisek; Robert Z. Norman; and Morris Zelditch, Jr. 1977. *Status Characteristics and Social Interaction: An Expectation States Approach.* New York: Elsevier.

Bernstein, Richard. 1986. "France Jails 2 in Odd Case of Espionage." *New York Times* (May 11).

Blackwood, Evelyn. 1984. "Sexuality and Gender in Certain Native American Tribes: The Case of Cross-Gender Females." *Signs: Journal of Women in Culture and Society* 10:27–42.

Bourne, Patricia G., and Norma J. Wikler. 1978. "Commitment and the Cultural Mandate: Women in Medicine." *Social Problems* 25:430–40.

Chodorow, Nancy. 1978. *The Reproduction of Mothering: Psychoanalysis and the Sociology of Gender.* Los Angeles: University of California Press.

Connell, R. W. 1983. *Which Way Is Up?* Sydney: Allen & Unwin.

———. 1985. "Theorizing Gender." *Sociology* 19:260–72.

Cucchiari, Salvatore. 1981. "The Gender Revolution and the Transition from Bisexual Horde to Patrilocal Band: The Origins of Gender Hierarchy." pp. 31–79 in *Sexual Meanings: The Cultural Construction of Gender and Sexuality,* edited by S. B. Ortner and H. Whitehead. New York: Cambridge.

Firestone, Shulamith. 1970. *The Dialectic of Sex: The Case for Feminist Revolution.* New York: William Morrow.

Fishman, Pamela. 1978. "Interaction: The Work Women Do." *Social Problems* 25:397–406.

Garfinkel, Harold. 1967. *Studies in Ethnomethodology.* Englewood Cliffs, NJ: Prentice Hall.

Gerson, Judith M., and Kathy Peiss. 1985. "Boundaries, Negotiation, Consciousness: Reconceptualizing Gender Relations." *Social Problems* 32:317–31.

Goffman, Erving. 1976. "Gender Display." *Studies in the Anthropology of Visual Communication* 3:69–77.

———.1977. "The Arrangement Between the Sexes." *Theory and Society* 4:301–31.

Henley, Nancy M. 1985. "Psychology and Gender." *Signs: Journal of Women in Culture and Society* 11:101–119.

Heritage, John. 1984. *Garfinkel and Ethnomethodology.* Cambridge: Polity Press.

Hill, W. W. 1935. "The Status of the Hermaphrodite and Transvestite in Navaho Culture." *American Anthropologist* 37:273–79.

Hochschild, Arlie R. 1973. "A Review of Sex Roles Research." *American Journal of Sociology* 78:1011–29.

Hughes, Everett C. 1945. "Dilemmas and Contradictions of Status." *American Journal of Sociology* 50:353–59.

Humphreys, Paul, and Joseph Berger. 1981. "Theoretical Consequences of the Status Characteristics Formulation." *American Journal of Sociology* 86:953–83.

Jaggar, Alison M. 1983. *Feminist Politics and Human Nature.* Totowa, NJ: Rowman & Allanheld.

Kessler, S.; D. J. Ashendon; R. W. Connell; and G. W. Dowsett. 1985. "Gender Relations in Secondary Schooling." *Sociology of Education* 58:34–48.

Kessler, Suzanne J., and Wendy McKenna. 1978. *Gender: An Ethnomethodological Approach.* New York: Wiley.

Kollock, Peter; Philip Blumstein; and Pepper Schwartz. 1985. "Sex and Power in Interaction." *American Sociological Review* 50:34–46.

Komarovsky, Mirra. 1946. "Cultural Contradictions and Sex Roles." *American Journal of Sociology* 52:184–89.

———. 1950. "Functional Analysis of Sex Roles." *American Sociological Review* 15:508–16.

Linton, Ralph. 1936. *The Study of Man.* New York: Appleton-Century.

Lopata, Helen Z., and Barrie Thorne. 1978. "On the Term 'Sex Roles'." *Signs: Journal of Women in Culture and Society* 3:718–21.

Lorber, Judith. 1984. *Women Physicians: Careers, Status and Power.* New York: Tavistock.

———. 1986. "Dismantling Noah's Ark." *Sex Roles* 14:567–80.

Martin, M. Kay, and Barbara Voorheis. 1975. *Female of the Species.* New York: Columbia University Press.

Mead, Margaret. 1963. *Sex and Temperament.* New York: Dell.

———. 1968. *Male and Female.* New York: Dell.

Mithers, Carol L. 1982. "My Life as a Man." *The Village Voice* 27 (October 5):1ff.

Money, John. 1968. *Sex Errors of the Body.* Baltimore: Johns Hopkins.

———. 1974. "Prenatal Hormones and Postnatal Sexualization in Gender Identity Differentiation." pp. 221–95 in *Nebraska Symposium on Motivation,* Vol. 21, edited by J. K. Cole and R. Dienstbier. Lincoln: University of Nebraska Press.

——— and John G. Brennan. 1968. "Sexual Dimorphism in the Psychology of Female Transsexuals." *Journal of Nervous and Mental Disease* 147:487–99.

——— and Anke A. Ehrhardt. 1972. *Man and Woman/Boy and Girl.* Baltimore: Johns Hopkins.

——— and Charles Ogunro. 1974. "Behavioral Sexology: Ten Cases of Genetic Male Intersexuality with Impaired Prenatal and Pubertal Androgenization." *Archives of Sexual Behavior* 3:181–206.

——— and Patricia Tucker. 1975. *Sexual Signatures.* Boston: Little, Brown.

Morris, Jan. 1974. *Conundrum.* New York: Harcourt Brace Jovanovich.

Parsons, Talcott. 1951. *The Social System.* New York: Free Press.

——— and Robert F. Bales. 1955. *Family, Socialization and Interaction Process.* New York: Free Press.

Raymond, Janice G. 1979. *The Transsexual Empire.* Boston: Beacon.

Richards, Renee (with John Ames). 1983. *Second Serve: The Renee Richards Story.* New York: Stein and Day.

Rossi, Alice. 1984. "Gender and Parenthood." *American Sociological Review* 49:1–19.

Rubin, Gayle. 1975. "The Traffic in Women: Notes on the 'Political Economy' of Sex." pp. 157–210 in *Toward an Anthropology of Women,* edited by R. Reiter. New York: Monthly Review Press.

Sacks, Harvey. 1972. "On the Analyzability of Stories by Children." pp. 325–45 in *Directions in Sociolinguistics,* edited by J. J. Gumperz and D. Hymes. New York: Holt, Rinehart & Winston.

Schutz, Alfred. 1943. "The Problem of Rationality in the Social World." *Economics* 10:130–49.

Stacey, Judith, and Barrie Thorne. 1985. "The Missing Feminist Revolution in Sociology." *Social Problems* 32:301–16.

Thorne, Barrie. 1980. "Gender . . . How Is It Best Conceptualized?" Unpublished manuscript.

Tresemer, David. 1975. "Assumptions Made About Gender Roles." pp. 308–39 in *Another Voice: Feminist Perspectives on Social Life and Social Science,* edited by M. Millman and R. M. Kanter. New York: Anchor/Doubleday.

West, Candace. 1984. "When the Doctor Is a 'Lady': Power, Status and Gender in Physician-Patient Encounters." *Symbolic Interaction* 7:87–106.

——— and Bonita Iritani. 1985. "Gender Politics in Mate Selection: The Male-Older Norm." Paper presented at the Annual Meeting of the

American Sociological Association, August, Washington, DC.

——— and Don H. Zimmerman. 1983. "Small Insults: A Study of Interruptions in Conversations Between Unacquainted Persons." pp. 102–17 in *Language, Gender, and Society,* edited by B. Thorne, C. Kramarae, and N. Henley. Rowley, MA: Newberry House.

Wieder, D. Lawrence. 1974. *Language and Social Reality: The Case of Telling the Convict Code.* The Hague: Mouton.

Williams, Walter L. 1986. *The Spirit and the Flesh: Sexual Diversity in American Indian Culture.* Boston: Beacon.

Wilson, Thomas P. 1970. "Conceptions of Interaction and Forms of Sociological Explanation." *American Sociological Review* 35:697–710.

Zimmerman, Don H., and D. Lawrence Wieder. 1970. "Ethnomethodology and the Problem of Order: Comment on Denzin." pp. 287–95 in *Understanding Everyday Life,* edited by J. Denzin. Chicago: Aldine.

Reading 3-2

Adams, Natalie, and Pamela Bettis. 2003. "Commanding the Room in Short Skirts: Cheering as the Embodiment of Ideal Girlhood." *Gender and Society* 17: 73–91.

Adams, Natalie, Alison Schmitke, and Amy Franklin. 2005. "Tomboys, Dykes, and Girly Girls: Interrogating the Subjectivities of Adolescent Female Athletes." *Women's Studies Quarterly* 33: 17–34.

Adler, Patricia A., and Peter Adler. 1995. "Dynamics of Inclusion and Exclusion in Preadolescent Cliques." *Social Psychology Quarterly* 58(3): 145–162.

Adler, Patricia A., and Peter Adler. 1998. *Peer Power: Preadolescent Culture and Identity.* New Brunswick, NJ: Rutgers University Press.

Allison, M. T. 1991. "Role Conflict and the Female Athlete: Preoccupations with Little Grounding." *Journal of Applied Sport Psychology* 3: 49–60.

Bettie, Julie. 2003. *Women Without Class: Girls, Race, and Identity.* Berkeley, CA: University of California Press.

Broad, K. L. 2001. "The Gendered Unapologetic: Queer Resistance in Women's Sport." *Sociology of Sport Journal* 18(2): 181–204.

Burn, Shawn Meghan. 2000. "Heterosexuals' Use of 'Fag' and 'Queer' to Deride One Another:

A Contributor to Heterosexism and Stigma." *Journal of Homosexuality* 40: 1–11.

Canada, Geoffrey. 1998. *Reaching Up for Manhood: Transforming the Lives of Boys in America.* Boston: Beacon Press.

Chambers, Deborah, Estella Tincknell, and Joost Van Loon. 2004. "Peer Regulation of Teenage Sexual Identities." *Gender and Education* 16: 397–415.

Cockburn, Cynthia, and Gill Clarke. 2002. " 'Everybody's Looking at You!': Girls Negotiating the 'Femininity Deficit' They Incur in Physical Education." *Women's Studies International Forum* 25: 651–665.

Connell, R. W. 1987. *Gender and Power: Society, the Person, and Sexual Politics.* Stanford, CA: Stanford University Press.

Deutsch, Francine M. 2007. "Undoing Gender." *Gender & Society* 21(1): 106–127.

Eder, Donna, Catherine Colleen Evans, and Stephen Parker. 1995. *School Talk: Gender and Adolescent Culture.* New Brunswick, NJ: Rutgers University Press.

Enke, Janet. 2005. "Athleticism and Femininity on a High School Basketball Team: An Interpretive Approach." *Sociological Studies of Children and Youth* 11: 115–152.

Eitzen, D. S. 1990. *Fair and Foul: Beyond the Myths and Paradoxes of Sports.* Lanham, MD: Rowman & Littlefield.

Fine, Gary Alan. 2004. "Adolescence as Cultural Toolkit: High School Debate and the Repertoires of Childhood and Adulthood." *Sociological Quarterly* 45(1): 1–20.

Froyum, Carissa. 2007. "At Least I'm Not Gay: Heterosexual Identity Making among Poor Black Teens." *Sexualities* 10(5): 605–624.

Gerson, Kathleen. 2002. "Moral Dilemmas, Moral Strategies, and the Transformation of Gender." *Gender & Society* 16(1): 8–28.

Hurrelmann, Klaus, and Stephen F. Hamilton. 1996. *Social Problems and Social Contexts in Adolescence.* New York: Aldine de Gruyter.

Kehily, Mary Jane, and Anoop Nayak. 1997. " 'Lads and Laughter': Humour and the Production of Heterosexual Hierarchies." *Gender & Education* 9: 69–88.

Kling, Kristen C., Janet Shibley Hyde, Carolin J. Showers, and Brenda N. Buswell. 1999. "Gender

Differences in Self-Esteem: A Meta-Analysis." *Psychological Bulletin* 125(4): 470–500.

Klomsten, Anne Torhild, Herb W. Marsh, and Einar M. Skaalvik. 2005. "Adolescents' Perceptions of Masculine and Feminine Values in Sport and Physical Education: A Study of Gender Differences." *Sex Roles: A Journal of Research* 52: 625–636.

Krane, Vikki. 2001. "We Can Be Athletic and Feminine, But Do We Want To? Challenging Hegemonic Femininity in Women's Sport." *Quest* 53: 115–133.

Krane, Vikki, Precilla Y. L. Choi, Shannon M. Baird, Christine M. Aimar, and Kerrie J. Kauer. 2004. "Living the Paradox: Female Athletes Negotiate Femininity and Muscularity." *Sex Roles: A Journal of Research* 50: 315–329.

Lemish, Dafna. 1998. "Spice Girls' Talk: A Case Study in the Development of Gendered Identity." Pp. 145–167 in *Millennium Girls: Today's Girls around the World,* edited by Sherri A. Inness. Lanham, MD: Rowman & Littlefield.

Mahaffy, Kimberly A. 2004. "Girls' Low Self-Esteem: How Is It Related to Later Socioeconomic Achievements?" *Gender & Society* 18(3): 309–327.

Malcom, Nancy L. 2003. "Constructing Female Athleticism: A Study of Girls' Recreational Softball." *American Behavioral Scientist* 46(10): 1387–1404.

Nayak, Anoop, and Mary Jane Kehily. 1996. "Playing It Straight: Masculinities, Homophobias and Schooling." *Journal of Gender Studies* 5: 211–231.

Pascoe, C. J. 2003. "Multiple Masculinities? Teenage Boys Talk about Jocks and Gender." *American Behavioral Scientist* 46: 1423–1438.

———. 2005. "'Dude, You're a Fag': Adolescent Masculinity and the Fag Discourse." *Sexualities* 8(3): 329–346.

———. 2007. *Dude, You're a Fag: Masculinity and Sexuality in High School.* Berkeley, CA: University of California Press.

Peterson, Anne, Rainer K. Silbereisen, and Silvia Sorenson. 1996. "Adolescent Development: A Global Perspective." Chapter 1 in *Social Problems and Social Contexts in Adolescence,* edited by K. Hurrelmann and S. F. Hamilton. New York: Aldine de Gruyter.

Phoenix, Ann, Stephen Frosh, and Rob Pattman. 2003. "Producing Contradictory Masculine Subject Positions: Narratives of Threat, Homophobia and Bullying in 11–14 Year Old Boys." *Journal of Social Issues* 59(1): 179–195.

Plummer, David C. 2001. "The Quest for Modern Manhood: Masculine Stereotypes, Peer Cultures and the Social Significance of Homophobia." *Journal of Adolescence* 24: 15–23.

Sutton-Smith, Brian. 1982. "A Performance Theory of Peer Relations." Pp. 65–77 in *The Social Life of Children in a Changing Society,* edited by K. Borman. Hillsdale, NJ: Lawrence Erlbum Associates.

Swidler, Ann. 1986. "Culture in Action: Symbols and Strategies." *American Sociological Review* 51(2): 273–286.

Talbani, Aziz. 2003. "Keeping Up Appearances: Multicultural Education in Postmodern Society," *Education and Society* 21(2): 5–18.

Thome, Barrie. 1993. *Gender Play: Girls and Boys in School.* New Brunswick, NJ: Rutgers University Press.

Visser, Irene. 1996. "The Prototypicality of Gender: Contemporary Notions of Masculine and Feminine." *Women's Studies International Forum* 19(6): 589–600.

Wellman, David T. 1993. *Portraits of White Racism,* 2nd ed. New York: Cambridge University Press.

West, Candace, and Donald Zimmerman. 1987. "Doing Gender." *Gender & Society* 1: 125–151.

CHAPTER 4

Reading 4-1

Amato, P. R., Booth, A., Johnson, D. R., & Rogers, S. J. (2007). *Alone together: How marriage in America is changing.* Cambridge, MA: Harvard University Press.

Autor, D. H., Katz, L. F., & Kearney, M. (2006). The polarization of the U.S. Labor market. *American Economic Review, 96,* 189–194.

Cherlin, A. J., Cross-Barnet, C, Burton, L. M, & Garrett-Peters, R. (2008). Promises they can keep: Low-income women's attitudes toward motherhood, marriage, and divorce. *Journal of Marriage and Family, 70,* 919–933.

Connelly, A. (2007, June 21). 15 days for sparrows point, *Baltimore Sun.*

Edin, K., & Kefalas, M. J. (2005). *Promises I can keep: Why poor women put motherhood before marriage.* Berkeley: University of California Press.

Ellwood, D. T., & Jencks, C. (2004). The uneven spread of single-parent families: What do we know? Where do we look for answers? In K. M. Neckerman (Ed.), *Social inequality* (pp. 3–118). New York: Russell Sage Foundation.

Fallows, J. (2007). China makes, the world takes. *The Atlantic.*

Kennedy, S., & Bumpass, L. L. (2007). Cohabitation and children's living arrangements: New estimates from the United States. (Working Paper 2007–20). Center for Demography and Ecology, Madison, WI.

LeMasters, E. E. (1975). *Blue-collar aristocrats: Life-styles at a working-class tavern.* Madison, WI: University of Wisconsin Press.

Levy, F. (1998). *The new dollars and dreams: American incomes and economic change.* New York: Russell Sage Foundation.

Martin, S. P. (2004). Women's education and family timing: Outcomes and trends associated with age at marriage and first birth. In K. M. Neckerman (Ed.), *Social inequality* (pp. 79–118). New York: Russell Sage Foundation.

Martin, S. P. (2006). Trends in marital dissolution by women's education in the United States. *Demographic Research, 15,* 537–560.

Oppenheimer, V. K. (2003). Cohabiting and marriage during young men's career-development process. *Demography, 40,* 127–149.

Raley, R. K., & Bumpass, L. L. (2003). The topography of the divorce plateau: Levels and trends in union stability in the United States after 1980. *Demographic Research, 8,* 245–259.

Reutter, M. (2001, October 19). Shadow of steel's lost empire, *Baltimore Sun.*

Richer, E., Frank, A., Greenberg, M., Savner, S., & Turetsky, V. (2003). Boom times a bust: Declining employment among less-educated young men Retrieved December 4, 2008, from http://www.clasp.org/publications/Boom Times.pdf

Rubin, L. B. (1994). *Families on the fault line.* New York: Harper Collins.

Smock, P. J., Manning, W. D., & Porter, M. (2005). "Everything's there except money": How money shapes decisions to marry among cohabitors. *Journal of Marriage and Family, 67,* 680–696.

U.S. Bureau of the Census. (2007). Statistical abstract of the United States: 2007 Retrieved July 1, 2007, from http://www.census.gov/compendia/statab/2007/2007edition.html

Reading 4-2

Aries, Philippe. 1962. *Centuries of Childhood: A Social History of the Family.* Translated by R. Baldick. London: Cape.

Bourdieu, Pierre. 1976. "Marriage Strategies as Strategies of Social Reproduction." pp. 117–44 in *Family and Society,* edited by R. Forster and O. Ranum. Baltimore, MD: Johns Hopkins University Press.

———. 1984. *Distinction: A Social Critique of the Judgment of Taste.* Cambridge, MA: Harvard University Press.

———. 1986. "The Forms of Capital." pp. 241–58 in *Handbook of Theory and Research for the Sociology of Education,* edited by J. C. Richardson. New York: Greenwood.

———. 1989. *The State Nobility: Elite Schools in the Field of Power.* Stanford, CA: Stanford University Press.

Bronfenbrenner, Urie. 1966. "Socialization and Social Class through Time and Space." pp. 362–77 in *Class, Status and Power,* edited by R. Bendix and S. M. Lipset. New York: Free Press.

Burawoy, Michael; Alice Burton; Ann Arnett Ferguson; and Kathryn J. Fox, eds. 1991. *Ethnography Unbound: Power and Resistance in the Modern Metropolis.* Berkeley: University of California Press.

Chidekel, Dana. 2002. *Parents in Charge.* New York: Simon and Schuster.

Conley, Dalton. 1999. *Being Black, Living in the Red: Race, Wealth, and Social Policy in America.* Berkeley: University of California Press.

Corsaro, William A. 1997. *The Sociology of Childhood.* Thousand Oaks, CA: Pine Forge.

Donzelot, Jacques. 1979. *The Policing of Families.* Translated by R. Hurley. New York: Pantheon.

Epstein, Joyce. 2001. *Schools, Family, and Community Partnerships.* Boulder, CO: Westview.

Erikson, Robert, and John H. Goldthorpe. 1993. *The Constant Flux: A Study of Class Mobility in Industrial Societies.* Oxford, England: Clarendon.

Fordham, Signithia, and John U. Ogbu. 1986. "Black Students' School Success: Coping with the 'Burden of Acting White'." *The Urban Review* 18:176–206.

Gordon, Linda. 1989. *Heroes of Their Own Lives: The Politics and History of Family Violence.* New York: Penguin.

Halbfinger, David M. 2002. "A Hockey Parent's Life: Time, Money, and Yes, Frustration." *New York Times,* January 12, p. 29.

Hart, Betty, and Todd Risley. 1995. *Meaningful Differences in the Everyday Experience of Young American Children.* Baltimore, MD: Paul Brooks.

Hays, Sharon. 1996. *The Cultural Contradictions of Motherhood.* New Haven, CT: Yale University Press.

Heimer, Carol A., and Lisa Staffen. 1998. *For the Sake of the Children: The Social Organization of Responsibility in the Hospital and at Home.* Chicago: University of Chicago Press.

Hochschild, Jennifer L. 1995. *Facing Up to the American Dream.* Princeton, NJ: Princeton University Press.

Kingston, Paul. 2000. *The Classless Society.* Stanford, CA: Stanford University Press.

Kohn, Melvin, and Carmi Schooler, eds. 1983. *Work and Personality: An Inquiry into the Impact of Social Stratification.* Norwood, NJ: Ablex.

Kropp, Paul. 2001. *I'll Be the Parent, You Be the Child.* New York: Fisher Books.

Lamont, Michele. 2000. *The Dignity of Working Men: Morality and the Boundaries of Race, Class, and Immigration.* Cambridge, MA: Harvard University Press.

Lareau, Annette. 2000. *Home Advantage: Social Class and Parental Intervention in Elementary Education.* 2d ed. Lanham, MD: Rowman and Littlefield.

———. 2002. "Doing Multi-Person, Multi-Site 'Ethnographic' Work: A Reflective, Critical Essay." Department of Sociology, Temple University, Philadelphia, PA. Unpublished manuscript.

———. 2003. *Unequal Childhood: Class, Race, and Family Life.* Berkeley: University of California Press.

Massey, Douglas, and Nancy Denton. 1993. *American Apartheid.* Cambridge, MA: Harvard University Press.

McLanahan, Sara, and Gary Sandefur. 1994. *Growing Up with a Single Parent: What Hurts, What Helps.* Cambridge, MA: Harvard University Press.

Newman, Kathleen. 1993. *Declining Fortunes: The Withering of the American Dream.* New York: Basic Books.

Pattillo-McCoy, Mary. 1999. *Black Picket Fences: Privilege and Peril among the Black Middle-Class.* Chicago: University of Chicago Press.

Sandberg, John F., and Sandra L. Hofferth. 2001. "Changes in Children's Time with Parents, U.S., 1981–1997." *Demography* 38:423–36.

Tatum, Beverly Daniel. 1997. *Why Are All the Black Kids Sitting Together in the Cafeteria? And Other Conversations about Race.* New York: Basic Books.

Van Ausdale, Debra, and Joe R. Feagin. 1996. "Using Racial and Ethnic Concepts: The Critical Case of Very Young Children." *American Sociological Review* 61:779–93.

Waters, Mary C. 1999. *Black Identities: West Indian Immigrant Dreams and American Realities.* New York: Russell Sage Foundation.

Wright, Erik Olin. 1997. *Class Counts: Comparative Studies in Class Analysis.* Cambridge: Cambridge University Press.

Wrigley, Julia. 1989. "Do Young Children Need Intellectual Stimulation? Experts' Advice to Parents, 1900–1985." *History of Education* 29:41–75.

Zelizer, Vivianna. 1985. *Pricing the Priceless Child: The Changing Social Value of Children.* New York: Basic Books.

CHAPTER 5

Reading 5-1

Allen, W. R. 1978. The search for applicable theories of black family life. *Journal of Marriage and the Family* 40, no. 1: 117–129.

Amato, P. R. 2004. Tension between institutional and individual views of marriage. *Journal of Marriage and Family* 66 (November): 959–965.

Anderson, E. 1990. *Streetwise: Race, class, and change in an urban community.* Chicago: University of Chicago Press.

———. 1999. *Code of the street: Decency, violence, and the moral life of the inner city.* New York: Norton.

Billingsley, A. 1968. *Black families in white America.* Englewood Cliffs, N.J.: Prentice-Hall.

———. 1992. *Climbing Jacob's ladder: The enduring legacy of African-American families.* New York: Simon & Schuster.

Blassingame, J. W. 1972. *The slave community: Plantation life in the antebellum south.* New York: Oxford University Press.

Blee, K. M., and A. R. Tickamyer. 1995. Racial differences in men's attitudes about women's gender roles. *Journal of Marriage and the Family* 57, no. 1: 21–30.

Bobo, L., J. R. Kluegel, and R. A. Smith. 1997. Laissez-faire racism: The crystallization of a kinder, gentler, antiblack ideology. In S. A. Tuch and J. K. Martin, eds., *Racial attitudes in the 1990s: Continuity and change,* 15–42. Westport, Conn.: Praeger.

Booker, C. B. 2000. *"I will wear no chain!" A social history of African American males.* Westport, Conn.: Praeger.

Bridges, J. S., and A. M. Orza. 1996. Black and white employed mothers' role experience. *Sex Roles* 35, nos. 5–6: 337–385.

Browne, I., and I. Kennelly. 1995. Stereotypes and realities: Images of black women in the labor market. In I. Brown, ed., *Latinas and African American women at work: Race, gender, and economic inequality,* 302–326. New York: Russell Sage.

Caldwell, J. C. 1996. The demographic implications of West African family systems. *Journal of Comparative Family Studies* 27: 331–352.

Cherlin, A. J. 2008. *Public and private families: An introduction.* New York: McGraw Hill.

Collins, P. H. 1999. Moving beyond gender: Intersectionality and scientific knowledge. In M. M. Ferree, J. Lorber, and B. B. Hess, eds., *Revisioning gender,* 261–284. Thousand Oaks, Calif.: Sage.

Conrad, C. A., and M. C. King. 2005. Single-mother families in the black community: Economic context and policies. In C. A. Conrad, J. Whitehead, P. Mason, and J. Stewart, eds., *African Americans in the U.S. Economy,* 163–174. Lanham, Md.: Rowman & Littlefield.

Coontz, S. 2005. *Marriage, a history: From obedience to intimacy, or how love conquered marriage.* New York: Viking Penguin.

Dabel, J. E. 2002. African American women and household composition in New York City, 1827–1877. In J. L. Conyers Jr., ed., *Black cultures and race relations,* 60–72. Chicago: Burnham.

Davis, A., and R. J. Havighurst. 1946. Social class and color differences in child-rearing. *American Sociological Review* 2: 698–710.

Dill, B. T. 1988. Our mothers' grief: Racial ethnic women and the maintenance of families. *Journal of Family History* 13, no. 4: 415–431.

Dunaway, W. A. 2003. *The African American family in slavery and emancipation.* New York: Cambridge University Press.

Edin, K. 2000. What do low-income single mothers say about marriage? *Social Problems* 47, no. 1: 112–113.

Ellwood, D. T., and C. Jencks. 2004. The spread of single-parent families in the United States since 1960. In D. P. Moynihan, T. M. Smeeding, and L. Rainwater, eds., *Future of the family,* 25–65. New York: Russell Sage Foundation.

Fitch, C. A., and S. Ruggles. 2000. Historical trends in marriage formation: The United States 1850–1990. In L. J. Waite, C. Bachrach, M. Hindin, E. Thomson, and A. Thornton, eds., *The ties that bind: Perspectives on marriage and cohabitation.* New York: Aldine de Gruyter.

Frankel, N. 1999. *Freedom's women: Black women and families in Civil War-era Mississippi.* Bloomington: Indiana University Press.

Franklin, D. L. 1997. *Ensuring inequality: The structural transformation of the African-American family.* New York: Oxford University Press.

Frazier, E. F. 1957. *The Negro in the United States.* New York: Macmillan.

Genovese, E. D. 1974. *Roll, Jordan, roll: The world the slaves made.* New York: Pantheon.

Giddings, P. 1984. *When and where I enter: The impact of black women on race and sex in America.* New York: Bantam.

Goodwin, P. Y. 2003. African American and European American women's marital well-being. *Journal of Marriage and the Family* 65 (August): 550–560.

Gutman, H. G. 1976. *The black family in slavery and freedom, 1750–1925.* New York: Pantheon.

Hall, R. L. 2002. E. Franklin Frazier and the Chicago school of sociology. In J. E. Teele, ed., *E. Franklin Frazier and the black bourgeoisie,* 47–67. Columbia: University of Missouri Press.

Harknett, K., and S. S. McLanahan. 2004. Racial and ethnic differences in marriage after the birth of a child. *American Sociological Review* 69 (December): 790–811.

Hawkins, D., and A. Booth. 2005. Unhappily ever after: Effects of long-term, low-quality marriages on well-being. *Social Forces* 84, no. 1: 451–471.

Higginbothan, E. B. 1993. *Righteous discontent: The women's movement in the black Baptist church, 1880–1920.* Cambridge, Mass.: Harvard University Press.

Hill, R. B. 1972. *The strengths of black families.* New York: Emerson Hall.

Hill, S. A. 2005. *Black intimacies: A gender perspective on families and relationships.* Walnut Creek, Calif.: AltaMira.

———. 2006. Marriage among African Americans: A gender perspective. *Journal of Comparative Family Studies* 37, no. 3: 421–440.

Hughes, M., and M. E. Thomas. 1998. The continuing significance of race revisited: A study of race, class and quality of life in America, 1972 to 1996. *American Sociological Review* 63 (December): 785–795.

Huston, T. L., and H. Melz. 2004. The case for (promoting) marriage: The devil is in the details. *Journal of Marriage and Family* 66 (November): 943–958.

Jayakody, R., and N. Cabrera. 2002. What are the choices for low-income families? Cohabitation, marriage, and remaining single. In A. Booth and A. C. Crounter, eds., *Just living together: Implications of cohabitation on families, children, and social policy*, 85–95. Mahwah, N.J.: Erlbaum.

John, D., and B. A. Shelton. 1997. The production of gender among black and white women and men: The case of household labor. *Sex Roles* 36, nos. 3–4: 171–193.

Kardiner, A., and L. Ovesey. 1951. *The mark of oppression: Explorations in the personality of the American Negro*. New York: Meridian.

Koball, H. 1998. Have African American men become less committed to marriage? Explaining the twentieth century racial cross-over in men's marriage timing. *Demography* 35, no. 2: 251–258.

Landry, B. 2000. *Black working wives: Pioneers of the American family revolution*. Berkeley: University of California Press.

Lichter, D. T., D.R. Graefe, and J.B. Brown. 2003. Is marriage a panacea? Union formation among economically disadvantaged unwed mothers. *Social Problems* 50, no. 1: 60–86.

Marks, C. 1989. *Farewell—we're good and gone: The great black migration*. Bloomington: Indiana University Press.

Massey, D. S., and N. A. Denton. 1993. *American apartheid: Segregation and the making of the underclass*. Cambridge, Mass.: Harvard University Press.

Moss, P., and C. Tilly. 1996. "Soft" skills and race: An investigation of black men's employment problems. *Work and Occupations* 23, no. 3: 252–276.

Moynihan, D. P. 1965. *The Negro family: The case for national action*. Washington, D.C.: Office of Policy Planning and Research.

Murray, C. 1984. *Losing ground: American social policy, 1950–1980*. New York: Basic Books.

Nobles, W. W. 1974. Africanity: Its role in black families. *Black Scholar* 5, no. 9: 10–17.

Ruggles, S. 1994. The origins of African-American family structure. *American Sociological Review* 59 (February): 136–151.

Scanzoni, J. 1977. *The black family in modern society: Patterns of stability and security*. Chicago: University of Chicago Press.

Schwalm, L. A. 1997. *A hard fight for we: Women's transition from slavery to freedom in South Carolina*. Urbana: University of Illinois Press.

Scott, R. J. 1985. The battle over the child: Child apprenticeship and the freedmen's bureau in North Carolina. In N. R. Hiner and J. M. Hawes, eds., *Growing up in America: Children in historical perspective*, 193–207. Chicago: University of Chicago Press.

Sigle-Rushton, W., and S. McLanahan. 2004. Father absence and child well-being: A critical review. In D. P. Moynihan, T. M. Smeeding, and L. Rainwater, eds., *Future of the family*, 116–155. New York: Russell Sage Foundation.

Stack, C. 1974. *All our kin: Strategies for survival in a black community*. New York: Harper & Row.

Thomas, G., M. P. Farrell, and G. M. Barnes. 1996. The effects of single-mother families and nonresident fathers on delinquency and substance abuse in black and white adolescents. *Journal of Marriage and the Family* 58 (November): 884–894.

U.S. Department of Labor, Bureau of Labor Statistics. Household data and annual averages. Retrieved January 25, 2008, from www.bls.gov/cps/cpsaat24.pdf.

Waite, L. 1995. Does marriage matter? *Demography* 32, no. 4: 483–507.

Waite, L., and M. Gallagher. 2000. *The case for marriage: Why married people are happier, healthier, and better off financially*. New York: Doubleday.

Western, B., and K. Beckett. 1999. How unregulated is the U.S. labor market? The penal system as a labor market institution. *American Journal of Sociology* 104, no. 4: 1030–1060.

Wilson, W. J. 1978. *The declining significance of race: Blacks and changing American institutions*. Chicago: University of Chicago Press.

———. 1987. *The truly disadvantaged*. Chicago: University of Chicago Press.

Young, V. H. 1970. Family and childhood in a southern Negro community. *American Anthropologist* 72, no. 2: 269–288.

CHAPTER 6

Reading 6-1

Blumstein, Philip, and Pepper Schwartz. 1983. *American Couples: Money, Work, Sex.* New York: William Morrow.

Buss, D. 1994. *The Evolution of Desire: Strategies of Human Mating.* New York: Basic Books.

———. 1995. "Psychological Sex Differences: Origins through Sexual Selection." *American Psychologist* 50:164–68.

D'Emilio, John, and Estelle B. Freedman. 1988. *Intimate Matters: A History of Sexuality in America.* New York: Harper and Row.

Dutton, D., and A. Aron. 1974. "Some Evidence for Heightened Sexual Attraction under Conditions of High Anxiety." *Journal of Personality and Social Psychology* 30:510–17.

Fisher, H. E. 1992. *Anatomy of Love: The Natural History of Monogamy, Adultery, and Divorce.* New York: Norton.

Foucault, M. 1978. *A History of Sexuality: Vol. 1. An Introduction.* New York: Pantheon.

Greenhalgh, S. 1977. "Hobbled Feet, Hobbled Lives: Women in Old China." *Frontiers* 2:7–21.

Malthus, T. R. [1798] 1929. *An Essay on the Principle of Population as It Affects the Future Improvement of Society.* New York and London: Macmillan.

Sexuality Information and Education Council of the United States. 1995. *A Report on Adolescent Sexuality.* New York: SIECUS.

Valins, S. 1966. "Cognitive Effects of False Heart-Rate Feedback." *Journal of Personality and Social Psychology* 4:400–8.

Reading 6-2

Aharons, C. R., and Rodgers, R. H. 1987. *Divorced Families: A Multidisciplinary Developmental View.* New York: Norton.

Befolkningsförändringar [Population Changes] (1968) Stockholm: Statistiska Central-byrån.

Befolkningsstatistik [Population Statistics] (1995) Stockholm: Statistiska Central-byrån.

Booth, A., and Amato, P. R. 2001. "Parental Pre-Divorce Relations and Offspring Post-Divorce Well-Being." *Journal of Marriage and Family* 63(1):197–212.

Caradec, V. 1996. "Les Formes de la vie conjugale des 'jeunes' couple 'âgés.' *Population* 51:897–928.

Furstenberg, F. F., and Kiernan, K. E. 2001. "Delayed Parental Divorce: How Much Do Children Benefit?" *Journal of Marriage and Family* 63(2):446–57.

Giddens, A. 1994. *Intimitetens forandring* [Intimacy in Change]. Copenhagen: Hans Reitzels forlag.

Heimdal, K. R., and Houseknecht, S. K. 2003. "Cohabiting and Married Couples' Income Organisation: Approaches in Sweden and the United States." *Journal of Marriage and Family* 65(3):539–49.

Historisk statistik (1967) Stockholm: Statistiska Central-byrån.

Hopper, J. 2001. "The Symbolic Origins of Conflict in Divorce." *Journal of Marriage and Family* 63(2):446–57.

Kamp Dush, C. M., Cohan, C. L., and Amato, P. R. 2003. "The Relationship Between Cohabitation and Marital Quality and Stability: Change Across Cohorts?" *Journal of Marriage and Family* 65(3):539–49.

Levin, I. 1993. "Family as Mapped Realities." *Journal of Family Issues* special issue "Rethinking Family as a Social Form" 14(1):82–91.

———. 1994. *Stefamilien—variasjon og mangfold.* Oslo: Aventura.

——— and Trost, J. 1992. "Understanding the Concept of Family." *Family Relations* 41:348–51.

——— and Trost, J. 1996. *Å forstå hverdagen—med et symbolsk interaksjonistisk perspektiv* [To Understand Everyday Life: With a Symbolic Interactionist Perspective]. Oslo: Tano Aschehoug.

——— and Trost, J. 1999. "Living Apart Together." *Community, Work and Family* 2(3):279–93.

———. 2001. "Barns perspektiv på skilsmisse— ett eller flere fenomen?" (Children's Perspective of Family—One or More Perspectives?) In K. Moxnes, I. Kvaran, H. Kaul, and I. Levin (eds.), *Skilsmissens mange ansikter.* Kristiansand: Norwegian Academic Press.

——— and Trost, J. 2003. *Særbo—ett par to hjem.* Oslo: Damm and Søn forlag.

Lewis, J., and Meredith, B. 1989. *Daughters Who Care.* London: Routledge.

Moxnes, K. 1990. *Kjernesprengning i familien.* Oslo: Universitetesforlaget.

———. 2001. "Skilsmissens virkning på barna." In K. Moxnes, I. Kvaran, H. Kaul, and I. Levin (eds.), *Skilsmissens mange ansikter,* pp. 17–32. Kristiansand: Norwegian Academic Press.

Schneider, N. F. 1996. "Partnerschaften mit getrennten Haushalten in den neuen und alten Bundesländern." In W. Bien (ed.), *Familie an der Schwelle zum neuen Jahrtausend,* pp. 88–97. Opladen: Leske und Budrich.

Sogner, S., and Dupâquir, J. 1981. "Marriage and Remarriage in Populations of the Past." *International Colloquium on Historical Demography 1979 in Kristiansand.* London: Academic Press.

Stryker, S. 1980. *Symbolic Interaction: A Social-Structural Version.* Menlo Park, CA: Cummings.

Sundt, E. 1975. *Om giftermaal i Norge.* Oslo: Gyldendal norsk forlag. (Orig. pub. 1855)

Trost, J. 1979. *Unmarried Cohabitation.* Västerås: International Library.

———. 1993. *Familjen i Sverige* [The Family in Sweden]. Stockholm: Liber.

———. 1995. "Ehen und andere dyadische Beziehungen." In B. Nauck and C. Onnen-Isemann (eds.), *Familie im Brennpunkt von Wissenschaft und Forschung,* pp. 343–56. Berlin: Luchterhand.

———. 1997. *Kvalitativa intervjuer* [Qualitative Interviews]. 2nd ed. Lund: Studentlitteratur.

———. 1998. "LAT Relationships Now and in the Future." In K. Matthijs (ed.), *The Family: Contemporary Perspectives and Challenges; Festschrift in Honor of Wilfried Dumon,* pp. 209–220. Leuven: Leuven University Press.

Wallerstein, J. S., and Kelly, J. B. 1980. *Surviving the Breakup.* New York: Basic Books.

Winfield, F. E. 1985. *Commuter Marriage: Living Together, Apart.* New York: Columbia University Press.

CHAPTER 7

Reading 7-1

Bumpass, L., and Lu, H. 2000. Trends in cohabitation and implications for children's family contexts. *Population Studies* 54:29–41.

———, and Sweet, J. A. 2001. Marriage, divorce, and intergenerational relationships. In A. Thornton (ed.), *The well-being of children and families: Research and data needs* (pp. 295–313). Ann Arbor: University of Michigan Press.

Casper, L., and Bianchi, S. 2002. *Continuity and change in the American family.* Thousand Oaks, CA: Sage.

Cherlin, A. J. 2004. The deinstitutionalization of American marriage. *Journal of Marriage and Family* 66:848–61.

Clarkberg, M. E. 1999. The price of partnering: The role of economic well-being in young adults' first union experiences. *Social Forces* 77:945–68.

———, Stolzenberg, R. M., and Waite, L. J. 1995. Attitudes, values, and entrance into cohabitational versus marital unions. *Social Forces* 74:609–34.

Clark-Nicolas, P., and Gray-Little, B. 1991. Effect of economic resources on marital quality in African American married couples. *Journal of Marriage and Family* 53:645–55.

Conger, R. D., Elder, G., Lorenz, F., Conger, K., Simons, R., Whitbeck, L., Huck, S., and Melby, J. 1990. Linking economic hardship to marital quality and stability. *Journal of Marriage and Family* 52:643–56.

Edin, K. 2000. What do low-income single mothers say about marriage? *Social Problems* 47:112–33.

Ellwood, D., and Jencks, C. 2001. *The growing difference in family structure: What do we know? Where do we look for answers?* Retrieved June 8, 2005, from http://www.russellsage.org/programs/other/inequality/050221.100862/download

Fields, J., and Casper, L. 2001. *America's families and living arrangements: Population characteristics* (Current Population Reports No. P20-537). Washington, DC: U.S. Government Printing Office.

Fox, G. L., and Chancey, D. 1998. Sources of economic distress: Individual and family outcomes. *Journal of Family Issues* 19:725–49.

Furstenberg, F. F. 1995. Fathering in the inner city: Paternal participation and public policy. In W. Marsiglio (ed.), *Fatherhood: Contemporary theory, research, and social policy* (pp. 119–47). Thousand Oaks, CA: Sage.

Gibson, C., Edin, K., and McLanahan, S. 2003. *High hopes but even higher expectations: The retreat from marriage among low income couples.* Center for Research on Child Wellbeing Working Paper 03-06-FF, Princeton, NJ.

Hughes, M. E. 2003. Home economics: Metropolitan labor and housing markets and domestic arrangements in young adulthood. *Social Forces* 81:1300–429.

Johnson, D., and Booth, A. 1990. Rural economic decline and marital quality: A panel study of farm marriages. *Family Relations* 39:159–65.

Landale, N. S., and Forste, R. 1991. Patterns of entry into cohabitation and marriage among mainland Puerto Rican women. *Demography* 28:587–607.

Lichter, D. T., Graefe, D. R., and Brown, J. B. 2003. Is marriage a panacea? Union formation among economically disadvantaged unwed mothers. *Social Problems* 50:60–86.

Lin, A. C. 1998. Bridging positivist and interpretivist approaches to qualitative methods. *Policy Studies Journal* 26:162–80.

Manning, W. 2002. The implications of cohabitation for children's well-being. In A. Booth and A. C. Crouter (eds.), *Just living together: Implications for children, families, and public policy* (pp. 121–52). Mahwah, NJ: Erlbaum.

Manning, W. D., and Smock, P. J. 1995. Why marry? Race and the transition to marriage among cohabitors. *Demography* 32:509–20.

Mead, G. H. 1934. *Mind, self, and society: From the standpoint of a social behaviorist.* Chicago: University of Chicago Press.

Oppenheimer, V. 2003. Cohabiting and marriage during young men's career development process. *Demography* 40:127–49.

Rubin, L. B. 1976. *Worlds of pain: Life in the working-class family.* New York: Basic Books.

Sassler, S. 2004. The process of entering into cohabiting unions. *Journal of Marriage and Family* 66:491–505.

——— and McNally, J. 2003. Cohabiting couples' economic circumstances and union transitions: A re-examination using multiple imputation techniques. *Social Science Research* 32:553–78.

Smock, P. J. 2004. The wax and wane of marriage: Prospects for marriage in the 21st century. *Journal of Marriage and Family* 66:966–73.

——— and Manning, W. D. 1997. Cohabiting partners' economic circumstances and marriage. *Demography* 34:331–41.

Stryker, S. 1972. Symbolic interaction theory: A review and some suggestions for comparative family research. *Journal of Comparative Family Studies* 3:17–32.

Thornton, A., Axinn, W., and Teachman, J. 1995. The influence of school enrollment and accumulation on cohabitation and marriage in early adulthood. *American Sociological Review* 60:762–74.

Thornton, A., Fricke, T., Axinn, W., and Alwin, D. 2001. Values and beliefs in the lives of children and families. In A. Thornton (ed.), *The well-being of children and families: Research and data needs* (pp. 215–43). Ann Arbor: University of Michigan Press.

Thornton, A., and Young-Demarco, L. 2001. Four decades of trends in attitudes toward family issues in the United States: The 1960s through the 1990s. *Journal of Marriage and Family* 63:1009–37.

Waite, L. 1995. Does marriage matter? *Demography* 32:483–507.

———. 2000. Trends in men's and women's well-being in marriage. In L. Waite, C. Bachrach, M. Hindin, E. Thomson, and A. Thornton (eds.), *The ties that bind: Perspectives on marriage and cohabitation* (pp. 368–92). New York: Aldine de Gruyter.

Weiss, R. S. 1994. *Learning from strangers: The art and method of qualitative interview studies.* New York: Free Press.

Weitzman, E. 1999. Analyzing qualitative data with computer software. *Health Services Research* 34:1241–63.

Xie, Y., Raymo, J., Goyette, K., and Thornton, A. 2003. Economic potential and entry into marriage and cohabitation. *Demography* 40:351–67.

CHAPTER 8

Reading 8-2

Albelda, R., and C. Cosenza. 2000. *Choices and trade-offs: The parent survey on childcare in Massachusetts.* Boston: Parents United for Child Care.

Appelbaum, E., T. Bailey, P. Berg, and A.L. Kalleberg. 2001. *Shared work, valued care: New norms for organizing market work and unpaid care work.* Washington, D.C.: Economic Policy Institute.

Blair-Loy, M., and A. Wharton. 2004. Mothers in finance: Surviving and thriving. *Annals of the American Academy of Political and Social Science* 596:151–71.

California Labor Code. § § 230.7, 230.8, 233, 513. 2006.

Chicago Transit Authority. Case no. 96–080. Goldstein 1997.

Chicago Transit Authority. Case no. 97–0166. Hayes 1999.

Clearinghouse on International Developments in Child, Youth, and Family Policies at Columbia University. 2002. *Mother's Day: More than* candy and flowers, working parents need paid time-off. http://www.childpolicyintl.org/issuebrief/issuebrief5.pdf

Crittenden, A. 2001. *The price of motherhood: Why the most important job in the world is still the least valued.* New York: Metropolitan Books.

Dye, J.L. 2008. *U.S. Census Bureau, Fertility of American women: 2006, Population, Charateristic.* http://www.census.gov/prod/2008pubs/p20-558.pdf.

European Union Online. n.d. European Union Council Directive 93/104/EC concerning certain aspects of the organization of working time. *Official Journal of the European Union* L 307, 13.12.1993 and European Union Council Directive 97/81/EC concerning the Framework agreement on part-time work. *Official Journal of the European Union* 20.1.98 L14/9-11.

Glass, J. 2004. Blessing or curse? Work-family policies and mother's wage growth over time. *Work and Occupations* 31: 367–406.

Golden, L., and H. Jorgensen. 2002. *Time after time: Mandatory overtime in the U.S. economy.* January. WPI Briefing Paper No. 120. http://www.epi.org/publications/entry/briefingpapers_bp120/

Golden, L., and B. Wiens-Tuers. 2005. Mandatory overtime work in the United States: Who, where, and what? *Labor Studies Journal* 30: 1–25.

Goldin, C. 2004. The long road to the fast track: Career and family. *Annals of the American Academy of Political and Social Science* 596: 20–35.

Gornick, J.C., and M.K. Meyers. 2003. *Families that work: policies for reconciling parenthood and employment.* New York: Russell Sage Foundation.

Grossman, K. 2001. Getting off supermom track. *Chicago Sun Times,* May 27, 17.

GTE California, Inc. Case no. 11-91-86. Miller 1992.

Hays, S. 1996. *The cultural contradictions of motherhood.* New Haven: Yale University Press.

Hewlett, S. A., and C.B. Luce, P. Shiller, and S. Southwell. 2005. *The hidden brain drain: Off-ramps and on-ramps in women's careers.* Boston: Harvard Business School Publishing.

Heymann, J. 2000. *The widening gap: Why America's working families are in jeopardy and what can be done about it.* New York: Basic Books.

Interlake Material Handling Div., Interlake Conveyors Inc. 113 LA 1120. Lalka 2000.

International Labour Organization. 2003a. *Yearbook of labour statistics, 2003.* Geneva: ILO.

ITT Industries, NightVision Roanoke Plant. 118 LA 1504. Cohen 2003.

Jacobs, J.A., and K. Gerson. 2004. *The time divide: Work, family, and gender inequality.* Cambridge: Harvard University Press.

Jacobs, J.A., and S. Winslow. 2004. Overworked faculty: Job stresses and family demands. *Annals of the American Academy of Political and Social Science* 596: 104–29.

Kamerman, S.B. 2005. Europe advanced while the United States lagged. In *Unfinished work: Building equality and democracy in an era of working families,* ed. J. Heymann and C. Beem, 309–47. New York: New Press.

Knauf Fiber Glass. 81 LA 333. Abrams 1983.

Kornbluh, K. 2003. The parent trap. *Atlantic Monthly,* January-February, 111–14.

Lareau, Annette. 2002. Invisible inequality: Social class and childrearing in black families and white families. *American Sociological Review* 67: 747–76.

Lewis, K.R. 2005. Want better work-life balance? Negotiate reduced hours. *Newhouse News Service,* August 24.

Marcus, R. 2006. The family as firing offense. *Washington Post,* May 14, B1.

Presser, H.B. 2003. *Working in a 24/7 economy: Challenges for American families.* New York: Russell Sage Foundation.

Rose, S.J., and H.I. Hartmann. 2004. *Still a man's labor market: The long-term earnings gap.* http://www.iwpr.org/pdf/C355.pdf#search=%22Rose%2C%20Stephen%20and%20Heidi%20Hartmann%20still%20a%20man's%20labor%20market%22

Skocpol, T., and R.C. Leone. 2001. *The missing middle: Working families and the future of American social policy.* New York: W.W. Norton.

Skolverket. n.d. *Child care in Sweden.* http://www.skolverket.se/content/1/c4/09/44/00-531.pdf.

Social Security Administration, Westminster Teleservice Ctr. 93 LA 687. Feigenbaum 1990.

State of New York, Rochester Psychiatric Center. 87 LA 725. Babiskin 1986.

Tenneco Packaging Burlington Container Plant. 112 LA 761. Kessler 1999.

U.S. Bureau of the Census. 2006a. *Current population survey: 2006 March supplement.* Washington, D.C.: Bureau of the Census.

U.S. Steel Corp. 95 LA 610. Das 1990.

Wachovia. n.d. *If you're from Venus, why get your financial advice from Mars?* http://www.wachovia.com/personal/pag/0,505_513_1091_1252,00.html

Warner, J. 2005. *Perfect madness: Motherhood in the age of anxiety.* New York: Riverhead Books.

Wenger, J. 2001. *The continuing problems with part-time jobs.* EPI Issue brief No. 155. Washington, D.C.: Economic Policy Institute.

Williams, J.C. 2000. *Unbending gender: Why family and work conflict and what to do about it.* New York: Oxford University Press.

Williams, J.C. 2006. *One sick child away from being fired: When "opting out" is not an option.* San Francisco: WorkLife Law, University of California Hastings College of Law.

CHAPTER 9

Reading 9-1

Anderson, E. 1989. Sex codes and family life among poor inner city youths. *The Annals of the American Academy of Political and Social Science* 501:59–78.

Becker, Gary S. 1981. *A treatise on the family.* Cambridge, MA: Harvard University Press.

Bennett, Neil G., David E. Bloom, and Cynthia K. Miller. 1995. The influence of nonmarital childbearing on the formation of first marriages. *Demography* 32:47–62.

Bzostek, Sharon, Mareia Carlson, and Sara McLanahan. 2006. Does mother know best? A comparison of biological and social fathers after a nonmarital birth. Working Paper no. 2006–27-FF, Center for Research on Child Wellbeing, Princeton, NJ.

Carlson, Mareia J., and Frank F. Furstenberg. 2006. The prevalence and correlates of multipartnered fertility among urban U.S. parents. *Journal of Marriage and Family* 68:718–32.

———. 2007. The consequences of multi-partnered fertility for parental involvement and relationships. Working Paper no. 2006–28-FF, Center for Research on Child Wellbeing, Princeton, NJ.

Carlson, Mareia, Sara McLanahan, and Jeanne Brooks-Gunn. Forthcoming. Co-parenting and nonresident fathers' involvement with young children after a nonmarital birth. *Demography.*

Carlson, Mareia, Sara McLanahan, and Paula England. 2004. Union formation in fragile families. *Demography* 41:237–61.

Chase-Lansdale, Lindsay P., Kathleen Kieman, and Ruth J. Friedman, eds. 2004. *Human development across lives and generations: The potential for change.* New York: Cambridge University Press.

Coleman, James S. 1988. Social capital in the creation of human capital. *American Journal of Sociology* 94:S95–S120.

Coontz, Stephanie. 1997. *The way we really are: Coming to terms with America's changing families.* New York: Basic Books.

Coontz, Stephanie, and Nancy Folbre. 2002. Marriage, poverty and public policy. Discussion Paper from the Council on Contemporary Families (CCF), Prepared for the Fifth Annual CCF Conference, New York.

Cooper, Carey, Sara McLanahan, Sarah Meadows, and Jeanne Brooks-Gunn. 2007. Family structure transitions and maternal parenting stress. Working Paper no. 2007–16-FF, Center for Research on Child Wellbeing, Princeton, NJ.

Cowan, Carolyn P., and Philip A. Cowan. 1992. *When partners become parents: The big life change for couples.* New York: Basic Books. (Republished by Lawrence Erlbaum Associates, Mahwah, NJ, 2000)

DeKlyen, Michelle, Jeanne Brooks-Gunn, Sara McLanahan, and Jean Knab. 2006. The mental health of married, cohabiting, and non-coresident parents with infants. *American Journal of Public Health* 96:1836–41.

Eggebeen, David J. 1992. Family structure and intergenerational exchanges. *Research on Aging* 14: 427–47.

The frequency and correlates of mothers' residential mobility. 2007. Fragile Families Research Brief no. 40, Center for Research on Child Wellbeing, Princeton, NJ.

Furstenberg, Frank F., Kay E. Sherwood, and Mercer L. Sullivan. 1992. Daddies and fathers: Men who do for their children and men who don't. In *Report on parents' fair share demonstration,* 34–56. New York: Manpower Development Research Corporation.

Garfinkel, Irwin, and Sara McLanahan. 2003. Strengthening fragile families. In *One percent for the kids: New policies, brighter futures for Americas children,* ed. I. Sawhill, 76–92. Washington, DC: Brookings Institution.

Garfinkel, Irwin, Sara McLanahan, and Thomas L. Hanson. 1998. A patchwork portrait of non-resident fathers. In *Fathers under fire: The revolution in child support enforcement,* ed. Irwin Garfinkel, Sara McLanahan, Daniel Meyer, and Judith Seltzer, 31–60. New York: Russell Sage Foundation.

Garfinkel, Irwin, Sarah Meadows, Sara McLanahan, and R. Mincy. 2008. Unmarried fathers' earnings trajectories. Manuscript, Princeton University, Princeton, NJ.

Geller, Amanda, Irwin Garfinkel, and Bruce Western. 2006. The effects of incarceration on employment and wages: An analysis of the Fragile Families Survey. Working Paper no. 2006–01-FF, Center for Research on Child Wellbeing, Princeton, NJ.

Gibson-Davis, Christina, Kathryn Edin, and Sara McLanahan. 2005. High hopes, but even higher expectations: The retreat from marriage among low-income couples. *Journal of Marriage and Family* 67:1301–12.

Gove, Walter R., Michael Hughes, and Carolyn Briggs Style. 1983. Does marriage have positive effects on the psychological well-being of individuals? *Journal of Health and Social Behavior* 24:122–31.

Harknett, Kristen, and Jean Knab. 2007. More kin, less support: Multipartnered fertility and kin support among new mothers. *Journal of Marriage and the Family* 69:237–53.

Harknett, Kristen, and Sara S. McLanahan. 2004. Racial and ethnic differences in marriage after the birth of a child. *American Sociological Review* 6:790–811.

Johnson, Waldo E. 2001. Paternal involvement among unwed fathers. *Children and Youth Services Review* 23:513–36.

Massey, Douglas S. 2007. *Categorically unequal: The American stratification system.* New York: Russell Sage Foundation.

McLanahan, Sara. 2004. Diverging Destinies: How Children Are Faring Under the Second Demographic Transition. *Demography* 41:607–627

McLanahan, Sara, and Gary Sandefur. 1994. *Growing up with a single parent: What hurts, what helps.* Cambridge, MA: Harvard University Press.

Meadows, Sarah. 2007. Family structure and fathers' well-being: Trajectories of physical and mental health. Working Paper no. 2007–19-FF, Center for Research on Child Wellbeing, Princeton, NJ.

Meadows, Sarah O., Sara S. McLanahan, and Jeanne Brooks-Gunn. 2007. Parental depression and anxiety and early childhood behavior problems across family types. *Journal of Marriage and the Family* 69:1162–77.

Monte, Lindsay. 2007. Blended but not the Bradys: Navigating unmarried multiple partner fertility. In *Unmarried couples with children,* ed. Paula England and Kathryn Edin, 183–203. New York: Russell Sage Foundation.

Moynihan, Daniel Patrick. 1965. *The Negro family: The case for national action.* Washington, DC: U.S. Department of Labor, Office of Policy Planning and Research.

Murray, Charles. 1984. *Losing ground: American social policy, 1950–1980.* New York: Basic Books.

Nepomnyaschy, Lenna, and Irwin Garfinkel. 2006. Child support enforcement and fathers' contributions to their non-marital children. Working Paper no. 2006–09-FF, Center for Research on Child Wellbeing, Princeton, NJ.

Nock, Steven L. 1998. The consequences of premarital fatherhood. *American Sociological Review* 63: 250–63.

Osborne, Cynthia, and Sara McLanahan. 2007. Partnership instability and child wellbeing. *Journal of Marriage and the Family* 69:1065–83.

Rainwater, Lee, and William L. Yancey. 1967. *The Moynihan Report and the politics of controversy.* Boston: MIT Press.

Reichman, Nancy E., Julien O. Teitler, Irwin Garfinkel, and Sara McLanahan. 2001. Fragile Families: Sample and design. *Children and Youth Services Review* 23:303–26.

Rendall, Michael S., Lynda Clarke, H. Elizabeth Peters, Nalini Ranjit, and Georgia Verropoulou. 1999. Incomplete reporting of men's fertility in the United States and Britain: A research note. *Demography* 36:135–44.

Ryan, William. 1976. *Blaming the victim.* New York: Vintage Books.

Seltzer, Juditha A. 1991. Relationships between fathers and children who live apart. *Journal of Marriage and the Family* 53:79–101.

Stacey, Judith. 1998. *Brave new families: Stories of domestic upheaval in late twentieth century America.* Berkeley: University of California Press.

Stack, Carol B. 1974. *All our kin: Strategies for survival in a black community.* New York: Harper & Row.

Sullivan, M. L. 1989. Absent fathers in the inner city. *The Annals of the American Academy of Political and Social Science* 501:59–78.

Swisher, Raymond, and Maureen Waller. Forthcoming. Confining fatherhood: Incarceration and paternal involvement among unmarried white, African-American and Latino fathers. *Journal of Family Issues.*

Turney, Kristin, and Kristen Harknett. 2007. Neighborhood disadvantage, residential stability, and perceptions of instrumental support among new mothers. Working Paper no. WP07–08-FF, Center for Research on Child Wellbeing, Princeton, NJ.

Waite, Linda J. 1995. Does marriage matter? *Demography* 32:535–51.

Waller, Maureen R. 2002. *My baby's father: Unmarried parents and paternal responsibility.* Ithaca, NY: Cornell University Press.

Waller, Maureen R., and Sara S. McLanahan. 2005. "His" and "her" marriage expectations: Determinants and consequences. *Journal of Marriage and the Family* 67:53–67.

Waller, Maureen R., and Raymond Swisher. 2006. Fathers' risk factors in fragile families: Implications for "healthy" relationships and father involvement. *Social Problems* 53:392–420.

Western, Bruce. 2007. *Punishment and inequality in America.* New York: Russell Sage Foundation.

Willis, Robert. 2000. The economics of fatherhood. *American Economic Review* 90:378–82.

Wilson, James Q. 2002. *The marriage problem: How our culture has weakened families.* New York: HarperCollins.

Wilson, William Julius. 1987. *The truly disadvantaged: The inner city, the underclass, and public policy.* Chicago: University of Chicago Press.

Reading 9-2

Dale, Kerry J. 2001. "Deconstructing Family Time: From Ideology to Lived Experience." *Journal of Marriage and Family* 63: 283–294.

Hochschild, Arlie R. 1999. *The Time Bind: When Work Becomes Home and Home Becomes Work.* New York: Metropolitan Books.

Roy, Kevin M., Carolyn Y. Tubbs, and Linda M. Burton. 2004. "Don't Have No Time: Daily Rhythms and the Organization of Time for Low-Income Families." *Family Relations* 53: 168–178.

Thorpe, Kate, and Kerry Daly. 1999. "Children, Parents, and Time: The Dialectics of Control." *Contemporary Perspectives on Family Research* 1: 199–223.

CHAPTER 10

Reading 10-1

Ahrons, C. R. 1994. *The good divorce.* New York: Harper Collins.

Amato, P., and Booth, A. 1997. *A generation at risk: Growing up in an era of family upheaval.* Cambridge, MA: Harvard University Press.

Bengtson, V. L. 1975. Generations and family effects in value socialization. *American Sociological Review* 40:358–71.

———. 1993. Is the "contract across generations" changing? Effects of population aging on obligations and expectations across age groups. In V. L. Bengtson and W. A. Achenbaum (eds.), *The changing contract across generations* (pp. 3–24). New York: Aldine de Gruyter.

———. 1996. Continuities and discontinuities in intergenerational relationships over time. In V. L. Bengtson (ed.), *Adulthood and aging: Research on continuities and discontinuities.* New York: Springer.

Bengtson, V. L., and Allen, K. R. (1993). The life course perspective applied to families over time. In P. Boss, W. Doherty, R. LaRossa, W. Schumm, and S. Steinmetz (eds.), *Sourcebook of family theories and methods: A contextual approach* (pp. 469–98). New York: Plenum Press.

Bengtson, V. L., Biblarz, T., Clarke, E., Giarrusso, R., Roberts, R. E. L., Richlin-Klonsky, J., and Silverstein, M. 2000. Intergenerational relationships and aging: Families, cohorts, and social change. In J. M. Claire and R. M. Allman (eds.), *The gerontological prism: Developing interdisciplinary bridges.* Amityville, NY: Baywood.

Bengtson, V. L., Biblarz, T. L., and Roberts, R. E. L. (2002). *How families still matter: A longitudinal study of youth in two generations.* New York: Cambridge University Press.

Bengtson, V. L., and Harootyan, R. (eds.). 1994. *Intergenerational linkages: Hidden connections in American society.* New York: Springer.

Bengtson, V. L., and Kuypers, J. A. 1971. Generational difference and the "developmental stake." *Aging and Human Development* 2:249–60.

Bengtson, V. L., and Mangen, D. J. 1988. Family intergenerational solidarity revisited. In D. J. Mangen, V. L. Bengtson, and P. H. Landry (eds.), *Measurement of intergenerational relations* (pp. 222–38). Newbury Park, CA: Sage.

Bengtson, V. L., and Putney, N. 2000. Who will care for the elderly? Consequences of population aging in East and West. In K. D. Kim, V. L. Bengtson, G. C. Meyers, and K. S. Eun (eds.), *Aging in East and West: Families, states and the elderly.* New York: Springer.

Bengtson, V. L., Rosenthal, C. J., and Burton, L. M. 1990. Families and aging: Diversity and heterogeneity. In R. Binstock and L. George (eds.), *Handbook of aging and the social sciences* (3rd ed., pp. 263–87). New York: Academic Press.

Bengtson, V. L., Rosenthal, C. J., and Burton, L. M. 1995. Paradoxes of families and aging. In R. H. Binstock and L. K. George (eds.), *Handbook of aging and the social sciences* (4th ed., pp. 253–82). San Diego, CA: Academic Press.

Bengtson, V. L., and Schrader, S. S. 1982. Parent-child relations. In D. Mangen and W. Peterson (eds.), *Handbook of research instruments in social gerontology* (Vol. 2, pp. 115–85). Minneapolis: University of Minnesota Press.

Bumpass, L. L., Sweet, J., and Martin, C. 1990. Changing patterns of remarriage. *Journal of Marriage and the Family* 52:747–56.

Burgess, E. W. 1916. *The function of socialization in social evolution.* Chicago: University of Chicago Press.

———. 1926. The family as a unity of interacting personalities. *The Family* 7:3–9.

Burton, L. 1995. Intergenerational patterns of providing care in African-American families with teenage childbearers: Emergent patterns in an ethnographic study. In V. L. Bengtson, K. W. Schaie, and L. M. Burton (eds.), *Adult intergenerational relations* (pp. 79–97). New York: Springer.

Burton, L. M., and Bengtson, V. L. 1985. Black grandmothers: Issues of timing and continuity in roles. In V. Bengtson and J. Robertson (eds.), *Grandparenthood* (pp. 304–38). Beverly Hills, CA: Sage.

Cherlin, A. J. 1992. *Marriage, divorce, remarriage* (rev. and enlarged ed.). Cambridge, MA: Harvard University Press.

———. 1999. *Public and private families.* Boston: McGraw-Hill.

Clarke, E., Preston, M., Raskin, J., and Bengtson, V. L. 1999. Types of conflicts and tensions between older parents and adult children. *Gerontologist* 39:261–70.

Collins, P. H. 1990. *Black feminist thought.* New York: Routledge.

Coontz, S. 1991. *The way we never were.* New York: Basic Books.

Davis, K. 1941. Family structure and functions. *American Sociological Review* 8:311–20.

Elder, G. H., Rudkin, L., and Conger, R. D. 1994. Intergenerational continuity and change in rural America. In K. W. Schaie, V. Bengtson, and L. Burton (eds.), *Societal impact on aging: Intergenerational perspectives.* New York: Springer.

Farkas, J., and Hogan, D. 1995. The demography of changing intergenerational relationships. In V. L. Bengtson, K. W. Schaie, and L. M. Burton (eds.), *Adult intergenerational relations: Effects of societal change* (pp. 1–19). New York: Springer.

Furstenberg, F., and Cherlin, A. 1991. *Divided families: What happens to children when parents part.* Cambridge, MA: Harvard University Press.

Giarrusso, R., Stallings, M., and Bengtson, V. L. 1995. The "intergenerational stake" hypothesis revisited: Parent-child differences in perceptions of relationships 20 years later. In V. L. Bengtson, K. W. Schaie, and L. M. Burton (eds.), *Adult intergenerational relations: Effects of societal change* (pp. 227–63). New York: Springer.

Goldscheider, F. K. 1990. The aging of the gender revolution: What do we know and what do we need to know? *Research on Aging* 12:531–45.

Goldscheider, F. K., and Goldscheider, C. 1993. *Leaving home before marriage: Ethnicity, familism, and generational relationships.* Madison: University of Wisconsin Press.

Hagestad, G. O. 1996. On-time, off-time, out of time? Reflections on continuity and discontinuity from an illness process. In V. L. Bengtson (ed.), *Adulthood and aging: Research on continuities and discontinuities* (pp. 204–22). New York: Springer.

Harris, S. C. 2000. *Grandmothers raising grandchildren: An ethnography of family life and life in "The System."* Dissertation in progress, University of Southern California, Los Angeles.

Harris, S. C., and Pedersen, H. L. 1997, October. *Grandparents who parent.* Paper presented at the American Association for Marriage and Family Therapists, Atlanta, GA.

Hayward, M. D., and Heron, M. 1999. Racial inequality in active life among adult Americans. *Demography* 36:77–91.

Johnson, C. L., and Barer, B. M. 1987. Marital instability and the changing kinship networks of grandparents. *Gerontologist* 27:330–35.

King, V. 1994. Variation in the consequences of nonresident father involvement for children's well-being. *Journal of Marriage and the Family* 56:963–72.

King, V., and Elder, G. H., Jr. 1997. The legacy of grandparenting: Childhood experiences with grandparents and current involvement with grandchildren. *Journal of Marriage and the Family* 59:848–59.

Kurdek, L. A., and Schmidt, J. P. 1987. Perceived emotional support from family and friends in members of homosexual, married, and heterosexual cohabiting couples. *Journal of Homosexuality* 14:57–68.

Laslett, P. 1976. Societal development and aging. In R. Binstock and E. Shanas (eds.), *Handbook of aging and the social sciences* (pp. 87–116). New York: Van Nostrand Reinhold.

Lee, G. R., Netzer, J. K., and Coward, R. T. 1994. Filial responsibility expectations and patterns of intergenerational assistance. *Journal of Marriage and the Family* 56:559–65.

Mangen, D. J., Bengtson, V. L., and Landry, P. H., Jr. (eds.). 1988. *The measurement of intergenerational relations.* Beverly Hills, CA: Sage.

Marshall, V. W., Matthews, S. H., and Rosenthal, C. J. 1993. Elusiveness of family life: A challenge for the sociology of aging. In G. L. Maddox and M. P. Lawton (eds.), *Kinship, aging, and social change. Annual review of gerontology and geriatrics, Vol. 13* (pp. 39–74). New York: Springer.

McGarry, K., and Schoeni, R. F. 1995. Transfer behavior in the health and retirement study. *Journal of Human Resources* 30 (Suppl.): S184–S226.

McLanahan, S. S. 1983. Family structure and stress: A longitudinal comparison of two-parent and female-headed families. *Journal of Marriage and the Family* 45:347–57.

———. 1994. The consequences of single motherhood. *American Prospect* 18:94–58.

McLanahan, S. S., and Sandefur, G. 1994. *Growing up with a single parent: What helps, what hurts.* Cambridge, MA: Harvard University Press.

Minkler, M., and Rowe, J. 1993. *Grandparents as caregivers.* Newbury Park, CA: Sage.

Myers, G. 1990. Demography of aging. In R. Binstock and L. George (eds.), *Handbook of aging and the social sciences* (3rd ed., pp. 19–44). New York: Academic Press.

Ogburn, W. F. 1932. The family and its functions. In W. F. Ogburn, *Recent social trends.* New York: McGraw-Hill.

Osmond, M. W., and Thorne, B. 1993. Feminist theories: The social construction of gender in families and society. In P. G. Boss, W. J. Doherty, R. La Rossa, W. R. Schumm, and S. K. Steinmetz, *Sourcebook of family methods and theories* (pp. 591–623). New York: Plenum Press.

Parsons, T. 1944. The social structure of the family. In R. N. Anshen (ed.), *The family: Its function and destiny* (pp. 173–201). New York: Harper.

Popenoe, D. 1993. American family decline, 1960–1990: A review and appraisal. *Journal of Marriage and the Family* 55:527–55.

———. 1996. *Life without father: Compelling new evidence that fatherhood and marriage are indispensable for the good of children and society.* New York: Free Press.

Riley, M. W., and Riley, J. W. 1993. Connections: Kin and cohort. In V. L. Bengtson & W. A. Achenbaum (eds.), *The changing contract across generations.* New York: Aldine de Gruyter.

Roberts, R. E. L., and Bengtson, V. L. 1990. Is intergenerational solidarity a unidimensional construct? A second test of a formal model. *Journal of Gerontology: Social Sciences* 45: S12–S20.

Roberts, R. E. L., Richards, L. N., and Bengtson, V. L. 1991. Intergenerational solidarity in families: Untangling the ties that bind. In S. K. Pfeifer and M. B. Sussman (eds.), *Marriage and Family Review, Vol. 16* (pp. 11–46). Binghamton, NY: Haworth Press.

Rossi, A., and Rossi, P. 1990. *Of human bonding: Parent-child relations across the life course.* New York: Aldine de Gruyter.

Silverstein, M., and Litwak, E. 1993. A task-specific typology of intergenerational family structure in later life. *Gerontologist* 33:256–64.

Silverstein, M., Giarrusso, R., and Bengtson, V. L. 1998. Intergenerational solidarity and the grandparent role. In M. Szinovacz (ed.), *Handbook on grandparenthood* (pp. 144–58). Westport, CT: Greenwood Press.

Silverstein, M., Parrott, T. M., and Bengtson, V. L. 1995. Factors that predispose middle-aged sons and daughters to provide social support to older parents. *Journal of Marriage and the Family* 57:465–75.

Skolnick, A. 1991. *Embattled paradise: The American family in an age of uncertainty.* New York: Basic Books.

Smock, P. J., and Manning, W. D. 1997. Nonresident parents' characteristics and child support. *Journal of Marriage and the Family* 59:798–808.

Soldo, B. J., and Hill, M. S. 1993. Intergenerational transfers: Economic, demographic, and social perspectives. *Annual Review of Gerontology and Geriatrics* 13:187–216.

Stacey, J. 1990. *Brave new families: Stories of domestic upheaval in late twentieth century America.* New York: Basic Books.

———. 1993. Is the sky falling? *Journal of Marriage and the Family* 55:555–59.

———. 1996. *In the name of the family: Rethinking family values in the postmodern age.* Boston: Beacon Press.

Stacey, J., and Biblarz, T. (2001). How does the sexual orientation of parents matter? *American Sociological Review* 66(2):159–83.

Stack, C. 1974. *All our kin: Strategies for survival in a Black community.* New York: Harper and Row.

Szinovacz, M. 1998. *Handbook on grandparenthood.* Westport, CT: Greenwood Press.

Thorne, B., and Yalom, M. 1992 *Rethinking the family: Some feminist questions.* Boston: Northeastern University Press.

Treas, J. 1995a. Commentary: Beanpole or beanstalk? Comments on "The Demography of Changing Intergenerational Relations." In V. L. Bengtson, K. W. Schaie, and L. M. Burton (eds.), *Adult intergenerational relations* (pp. 26–29). New York: Springer.

———. 1995b. Older Americans in the 1990s and beyond. *Population Bulletin* 50:2–46.

Uhlenberg, P. 1996. Mutual attraction: Demography and life-course analysis. *Gerontologist* 36:226–29.

Wachter, K. W. 1997. Kinship resources for the elderly. *Philosophical transactions of the Royal Society of London* 352:1811–17.

Walker, A. J., and McGraw, L. A. 2000. Who is responsible for responsible fathering? *Journal of Marriage and the Family* 62:563–69.

CHAPTER 11

Reading 11-2

American Civil Liberties Union. 2007. *Domestic Violence: Protective Orders and the Role of Police Enforcement.* http://www.aclu.org/womensrights/protectiveorders.pdf (last accessed 15 April 2007)

Avakame, Edem F. and James J. Fyfe. 2001. "Differential Police Treatment of Male-on-Female Spousal Violence: Additional Evidence on the Leniency Thesis." *Violence against Women* 7:22–45.

Belknap, Joanne. 2001. *The Invisible Woman: Gender, Crime, and Justice* (2nd ed.). Belmont, CA: Wadsworth.

Belknap, Joanne and Jennifer L. Hartman. 2000. "Police Responses to Woman Battering: Victim Advocates' Reports." *International Review of Victimology* 1–3:159–77.

Bohmer, Carol, Jennifer Brandt, Denise Bronson and Helen Hartnett. 2002. "Domestic Violence Law Reforms: Reactions from the Trenches." *Journal of Sociology and Social Welfare* 29:71–87.

Buzawa, Eve S. and Thomas Austin. 1993. "Determining Police Response to Domestic Violence Victims: The Role of Victim Preference." *American Behavioral Scientist* 36:610–23.

Catalano, Shannon. 2006. *Intimate Partner Violence in the United States.* Washington, DC: US Department of Justice, Bureau of Justice Statistics. http://www.ojp.usdoj.gov/bjs/intimate/ipv.htm (last accessed 15 April 2007)

Cho, Hyunkag and Dina J. Wilke. 2005. "How Has the Violence Against Women Act Affected the Response of the Criminal Justice System to Domestic Violence?" *Journal of Sociology and Social Welfare* 32:125–39.

Crenshaw, Kimberle W. 1994. "Mapping the Margins: Intersectionality, Identity Politics, and Violence against Women of Color." pp. 93–118 in *The Public Nature of Private Violence,* edited by Martha A. Fineman and Roxanne Mykitiuk. New York: Routledge.

Dasgupta, Shamita D. 2003. *Safety & Justice for All: Examining the Relationship between the Women's Anti-Violence Movement and the Criminal Legal System.* New York: Ms. Foundation. http://www.ms.foundation.org/user-assets/PDF/Program/safety_justice.pdf (last accessed 15 April 2007)

DeLeon-Granados, William, William Wells and Ruddyard Binsbacher. 2006. "Arresting Developments: Trends in Female Arrests for Domestic Violence and Proposed Explanations." *Violence against Women* 12:355–71.

Epstein, Deborah. 1999. "Redefining the State's Response to Domestic Violence: Past Victories and

Future Challenges." *Georgetown Journal of Gender and the Law* 1. 127–43.

Ferraro, Kathleen J. and Lucille Pope. 1993. "Irreconcilable Differences: Battered Women, Police and the Law." pp. 96–123 in *Legal Responses to Wife Assault: Current Trends and Evaluations,* edited by N. Zoe Hilton. Newbury Park, CA: Sage Publications.

Finn, Mary A. and Pamela Bettis. 2006. "Punitive Action or Gentle Persuasion: Exploring Police Officers' Justifications for Using Dual Arrest in Domestic Violence Cases." *Violence against Women* 12:268–87.

Ford, David A. 1991. "Prosecution as a Victim Power Resource: A Note on Empowering Women in Violent Conjugal Relationships." *Law and Society Review* 25:313–34.

Gelles, Richard J. 1993. "Constraints Against Family Violence: How Well Do They Work?" *American Behavioral Scientist* 36:575–85.

Gosselin, Denise K. 2000. *Heavy Hands: An Introduction to the Crimes of Family Violence* (2nd ed.). Upper Saddle River, NJ: Prentice Hall.

Hilton, N. Zoe. 1993. "Introduction." pp. 3–8 in *Legal Responses to Wife Assault: Current Trends and Evaluations,* edited by N. Zoe Hilton. Newbury Park, CA: Sage Publications.

Hirschel, J. David and Eve Buzawa. 2002. "Understanding the Context of Dual Arrest with Directions for Future Research." *Violence against Women* 81: 1449–73.

Johnson, Michael P. 2005. "Domestic Violence: It's Not about Gender—Or Is It?" *Journal of Marriage and Family* 67:1126–30.

Johnson, Michael P. 2006. "Conflict and Control: Gender Symmetry and Asymmetry in Domestic Violence." *Violence against Women* 12: 1003–18.

Johnson, Michael P. and Kathleen J. Ferraro. 2000. "Research on Domestic Violence in the 1990s: Making Distinctions." *Journal of Marriage and the Family* 62:948–63.

Jones, Dana A. and Joanne Belknap. 1999. "Police Responses to Battering in a Progressive Pro-Arrest Jurisdiction." *Justice Quarterly* 16:249–73.

Mahoney, Martha R. 1994. "Victimization or Oppression? Women's Lives, Violence, and Agency." pp. 59–92 in *The Public Nature of Private Violence,* edited by Martha A. Fineman and Roxanne Mykituk. New York, NY: Routledge.

Maxwell, Christopher D., Joel H. Garner and Jeffrey Fagan. 2002. "The Preventive Effects of Arrest on Intimate Partner Violence: Research, Policy, and Theory." *Criminology and Public Policy* 2:51–80.

McLeod, Maureen. 1983. "Victim Noncooperation in the Prosecution of Domestic Assault." *Criminology* 21:395–416.

Mills, Linda G. 1996. "Empowering Women Transnationally: The Case for Postmodern Interventions." *Social Work* 41:261–68.

Mills, Linda G. 2003. *Insult to Injury: Rethinking Our Responses to Intimate Abuse.* Princeton, NJ: Princeton University Press.

Miller, Susan L. 2001. "The Paradox of Women Arrested for Domestic Violence: Criminal Justice Professionals and Service Providers Respond." *Violence against Women* 7:1339–76.

Osthoff, Sue. 2002. "But, Gertrude, I Beg to Differ, a Hit Is Not a Hit Is Not a Hit." *Violence against Women* 8:1521–44.

Rajah, Valli, Victoria Frye and Mary Haviland. 2006. "Aren't I a Victim? Notes on Identity Challenges Relating to Police Action in a Mandatory Arrest Jurisdiction." *Violence against Women* 12: 897–916.

Schmidt, Janell D. and Lawrence W. Sherman. 1996. "Does Arrest Deter Domestic Violence?" pp. 43–53 in *Do Arrests and Restraining Orders Work?* edited by Eve S. Buzawa and Carl G. Buzawa. Thousand Oaks, CA: Sage Publications.

Schneider, Elizabeth M. 2000. *Battered Women and Feminist Lawmaking.* New Haven, CT: Yale University Press.

Sherman, Lawrence W. 1992. *Policing Domestic Violence: Experiments and Dilemmas.* New York: Free Press.

Sherman, Lawrence W. and Richard A. Berk. 1984. "The Specific Deterrent Effects of Arrest for Domestic Assault." *American Sociological Review* 49:261–72.

Simpson, Sally S., Leana Allen Bouffard, Joel Garner and Laura Hickman. 2006. "The Influence of Legal Reform on the Probability of Arrest in Domestic Violence Cases." *Justice Quarterly* 23: 297–316.

Smith, Alisa. 2001. "Domestic Violence Laws: The Voices of Battered Women." *Violence and Victims* 16:91–111.

Sparks, Anne. 1997. "Feminists Negotiate the Executive Branch: The Policing of Male Violence." pp. 35–52 in *Feminists Negotiate the State: The*

Politics of Domestic Violence, edited by Cynthia R. Davies. Lanham, MD: University Press of America.

Stark, Evan. 1993. "Mandatory Arrest of Batterers: A Reply to Its Critics." *American Behavioral Scientist* 36:651–79.

Stark, Evan. 2004. "Insults, Injury, and Injustice: Rethinking State Intervention in Domestic Violence Cases." *Violence against Women* 10:1302–30.

Stephens, B. Joyce and Peter G. Sinden. 2000. "Victims' Voices: Domestic Assault Victim's Perceptions of Police Demeanor." *Journal of Interpersonal Violence* 15:534–47.

Stewart, Anna. 2001. "Policing Domestic Violence: An Overview of Emerging Issues." *Police Practice and Research* 2:447–59.

Wittner, Judith. 1998. "Reconceptualizing Agency in Domestic Violence Court." pp. 81–104 in *Community Activism and Feminist Politics: Organizing Across Race, Class, and Gender,* edited by Nancy Naples. New York: Routledge.

CHAPTER 12

Reading 12-2

Amato, P. R. (1994). Life-span adjustment of children to their parents' divorce. *Future of Children: Children and Divorce, 4,* 143–164.

Amato, P. (1996). Explaining the intergenerational transmission of divorce. *Journal of Marriage and the Family, 58,* 628–640.

Amato, P. (1999). Children of divorced parents as young adults. In E. M. Hetherington (Ed.), *Coping with divorce, single parenting, and remarriage* (pp. 147–164). Mahwah, NJ: Erlbaum.

Amato, P. (2000). The consequences of divorce for adults and children. *Journal of Marriage and Family, 62,* 1269–1287.

Amato, P. R. (2001). Children of divorce in the 1990s: An update of the Amato and Keith (1991) meta-analysis. *Journal of Family Psychology, 15,* 355–370.

Amato, P., & Booth, A. (1996). A prospective study of divorce and parent-child relationships. *Journal of Marriage and the Family, 58,* 356–365.

Amato, P., & Gilbreth, J. (1999). Nonresident fathers and children's well-being: A meta-analysis. *Journal of Marriage and the Family, 61,* 557–573.

Amato, P., & Keith, B. (1991). Parental divorce and adult well-being: A meta-analysis. *Journal of Marriage and the Family, 53,* 43–58.

Amato, P. R., Loomis, L., & Booth, A. (1995). Parental divorce, parental marital conflict, and offspring well-being during early adulthood. *Social Forces, 73,* 895–916.

Amato, P. R., & Rezac, S. (1994). Contact with residential parents, interparental conflict, and children's behavior. *Journal of Family Issues, 12,* 578–599.

Bausermann, R. (2002). Child adjustment in joint-custody versus sole-custody arrangements: A meta-analytic review. *Journal of Family Psychology, 16,* 91–102.

Booth, A., & Amato, P. R. (2001). Parental predivorce relations and offspring postdivorce well-being. *Journal of Marriage and Family, 63,* 197–212.

Braver, S. L., & O'Connell, E. (1998). *Divorced dads: Shattering the myths.* New York: Tarcher, Putnam.

Bray, J. H. (1999). From marriage to remarriage and beyond: Findings from the Developmental Issues in StepFamilies research project. In E. M. Hetherington (Ed.), *Coping with divorce, single parenting, and remarriage: A risk and resiliency perspective* (pp. 253–272). Mahwah, NJ: Erlbaum.

Buchanan, C., Maccoby, E., & Dornbusch, S. (1991). Caught between parents: Adolescents' experience in divorced homes. *Child Development, 62,* 1008–1029.

Chase-Lansdale, P. L., Cherlin, A. J., & Kierman, K. E. (1995). The long-term effects of parental divorce on the mental health of young adults: A developmental perspective. *Child Development, 66,* 1614–1634.

Cummings, E., & Davies, P. (1994). *Children and marital conflict.* New York: Guilford Press.

Doherty, W. J. (1998). Responsible fathering: An overview and conceptual framework. *Journal of Marriage and the Family, 60,* 277–292.

Dunn, J., Davies, L., O'Connor, T., & Sturgess, W. (2001). Family lives and friendships: The perspectives of children in step-, single-parent, and non-stop families. *Journal of Family Psychology, 15,* 272–287.

Emery, R. E. (1999). *Marriage, divorce, and children's adjustment* (2nd ed.). Thousand Oaks, CA: Sage.

Emery, R. E., & Forehand, R. (1994). Parental divorce and children's well-being: A focus on resilience.

In R. J. Haggerty, L. Sherred, N. Garmezy, & M. Rutter (Eds.), *Risk and resilience in children* (pp. 64–99). London: Cambridge University Press.

Emery, R. E., Kitzmann, K. M., & Waldron, M. (1999). Psychological interventions for separated and divorced families. In E. M. Hetherington (Ed.), *Coping with divorce, single parenting, and remarriage* (pp. 323–344). Mahwah, NJ: Erlbaum.

Fabricius, W. V. (2003). Listening to divorce: New findings that diverge from Wallerstein, Lewis, and Blakeslee. *Family Relations, 52,* 385–396.

Fabricius, W. V., Braver, S. L., & Deneau, K. (2003). Divorced parents' financial support of their children's college expenses. *Family Court Review, 41,* 224–241.

Fabricius, W. V., & Hall, J. (2000). Young adults' perspectives on divorce: Living arrangements. *Family and Conciliation Courts Review, 38,* 446–461.

Furstenberg, F. F., & Kiernan, K. E. (2001). Delayed parental divorce: How much do children benefit? *Journal of Marriage and Family, 63,* 446–457.

Hetherington, E. M. (1999). Should we stay together for the sake of the children? In E. M. Hetherington (Ed.), *Coping with divorce, single parenting, and remarriage* (pp. 93–116). Mahwah, NJ: Erlbaum.

Hetherington, E. M., & Kelly, J. (2002). *For better or for worse.* New York: Norton.

Johnston, J. R. (1995). Research update: Children's adjustment in sole custody compared to joint custody families and principles for custody decision making. *Family and Conciliation Courts Review, 33,* 415–425.

Johnston, J. R., & Campbell, L. (1988). *Impasses of divorce: The dynamics and resolution of family conflict.* New York: Free Press.

Johnston, J. R., & Roseby, V. (1997). *In the name of the child. A developmental approach to understanding and helping children of conflict and violent divorce.* New York: Free Press.

Kalter, N., Kloner, A., Schreiser, S., & Okla, K. (1989). Predictors of children's post-divorce adjustment. *American Journal of Orthopsychiatry, 59,* 605–618.

Keitner, G. I., & Miller, I. W. (1990). Family functioning and major depression: An overview. *American Journal of Psychiatry, 147,* 1128–1137.

Kelly, J. B. (2000). Children's adjustment in conflicted marriage and divorce: A decade review of research. *Journal of Child and Adolescent Psychiatry, 39,* 963–973.

Kelly, J. B. (2002). Psychological and legal interventions for parents and children in custody and access disputes: Current research and practice. *Virginia Journal of Social Policy and Law, 10,* 129–163.

King, V., & Heard, H. E. (1999). Nonresident father visitation, parental conflict, and mother's satisfaction: What's best for child well-being? *Journal of Marriage and the Family, 61,* 385–396.

Kline, M., Johnston, J., & Tschann, J. (1990). The long shadow of marital conflict: A model of children's postdivorce adjustment. *Journal of Marriage and the Family, 53,* 297–309.

Krishnakamur, A., & Buehler, C. (2000). Interparental conflict and parenting behaviors: A meta-analytic review. *Family Relations, 49,* 25–44.

Laumann-Billings, L., & Emery, R. E. (2000). Distress among young adults in divorced families. *Journal of Family Psychology, 14,* 671–687.

Lee, M.-Y. (2002). A model of children's postdivorce behavioral adjustment in maternal and dual-residence arrangements. *Journal of Family Issues, 23,* 672–697.

Maccoby, E., & Mnookin, R. (1992). *Dividing the child.* Cambridge, MA: Harvard University Press.

McIntosh, J. (2000). Child-inclusive divorce mediation: Report on a qualitative research study. *Mediation Quarterly, 18,* 55–70.

McLanahan, S. S. (1999). Father absence and children's welfare. In E. M. Hetherington (Ed.), *Coping with divorce, single parenting, and remarriage: A risk and resiliency perspective* (pp. 117–146). Mahwah, NJ: Erlbaum.

McLanahan, S. S., & Sandefur, G. (1994). *Growing up with a single parent.* Cambridge, MA: Harvard University Press.

Menning, C. L. (2002). Absent parents are more than money: The joint effects of activities and financial support on youths' educational attainment. *Journal of Family Issues, 23,* 648–671.

Neighbors, B., Forehand, R., & McVicar, D. (1993). Resilient adolescents and interparental conflict. *American Journal of Orthopsychiatry, 63,* 462–471.

Nord, C. W., Brimhall, D., & West, J. (1997). *Fathers' involvement in their children's schools.* Washington, DC: National Center for Education Statistics.

Pleck, J. H. (1997). Paternal involvement: Level, sources, and consequences. In M. E. Lamb (Ed.), *The role of the father in child development* (3rd ed.; pp. 66–103). New York: Wiley.

Pong, S.-L., & Ju, D.-B. (2000). The effects of change in family structure and income on dropping out of middle and high school. *Journal of Family Issues, 21,* 147–169.

Seltzer, J. (1991). Relationships between fathers and children who live apart: The father's role after separation. *Journal of Marriage and the Family, 53,* 79–101.

Seltzer, J. (1998). Father by law: Effects of joint legal custody on nonresident fathers' involvement with children. *Demography, 35,* 135–146.

Simons, R. L., & Associates (1996). *Understanding differences between divorced and intact families: Stress, interaction, and child outcome.* Thousand Oaks, CA: Sage.

Smart, C., & Neale, B. (2000). "It's my life too"—Children's perspectives on post-divorce parenting. *Family Law, 30,* 163–169.

Stewart, A., Copeland, A., Chester, N., Malley, J., & Barenbaum, N. (1997). *Separating together: How divorce transforms families.* New York: Guilford.

Sun, Y. (2001). Family environment and adolescents' well-being before and after parents' marital disruption: A longitudinal analysis. *Journal of Marriage and Family, 63,* 697–713.

Sun, Y., & Li, Y. (2001). Marital disruption, parental investment, and children's academic achievement. *Journal of Family Issues, 22,* 27–62.

Sun, Y., & Li, Y. (2002). Children's well-being during parents' marital disruption process: A pooled time-series analysis. *Journal of Marriage and Family, 64,* 472–488.

Vandewater, E., & Lansford, J. (1998). Influences of family structure and parental conflict on children's well-being. *Family Relations, 47,* 323–330.

Wallerstein, J. S., & Blakeslee, S. (1989). *Second chances: Men, women and children a decade after divorce.* New York: Ticknor & Fields.

Wallerstein, J. S., & Kelly, J. B. (1980). *Surviving the breakup: How children and parents cope with divorce.* New York: Basic Books.

Wallerstein, J. S., Lewis, J. M., & Blakeslee, S. (2000). *The unexpected legacy of divorce: A 25 year landmark study.* New York: Hyperion.

Whiteside, M. F., & Becker, B. J. (2000). Parental factors and young child's postdivorce adjustment: A meta-analysis with implications for parenting arrangements. *Journal of Family Psychology, 14,* 5–26.

Wolfinger, N. H. (2000). Beyond the intergenerational transmission of divorce: Do people replicate the patterns of marital instability they grew up with? *Journal of Family Issues, 21,* 1061–1086.

Zill, N. D. (1988). Behavior, achievement, and health problems among children in stepfamilies: Findings from a national survey of child health. In E. M. Hetherington & J. D. Arasteh (Eds.), *Impact of divorce, single parenting, and stepparenting on children* (pp. 325–363). Hillsdale, NJ: Erlbaum.

Zill, N., Morrison, D., & Coiro, M. (1993). Long-term effects of parental divorce on parent-child relationships, adjustment, and achievement in young adulthood. *Journal of Family Psychology, 7,* 91–103.

Zill, N., & Schoenborn, C. A. (1990). *Developmental, learning, and emotional problems: Health of our nation's children, United States, 1988.* Advance data from Vital and Health Statistics, No. 190. Washington, DC: National Center for Health Statistics.

CHAPTER 13

Reading 13-2

Berg, B. L. (2001). Qualitative research methods for the social sciences. Boston: Allyn & Bacon.

Berger, R. (1998). Stepfamilies: A multidimensional perspective. New York: Haworth Press.

Brand, E. & Clingempeel, W. G. (1987). Interdependencies of marital and stepparent-stepchild relationships and children's psychological adjustment: Research findings and clinical implications. *Family Relations, 36,* 140–145.

Bray, J. H. (1988). Children's development during early remarriage. In B. M. Hetherington & J. Arasteh (Eds.), *The impact of divorce, single parenting and stepparenting on children* (pp. 279–298). Hillsdale, NJ: Erlbaum.

Buchanon, C. M., Maccoby, E. E. & Dornbusch, S. M. (1996). Adolescents after divorce. Cambridge, MA: Harvard University Press.

Cartwright, C. & Seymour, F. (2002). Young adults' perceptions of parents' responses in stepfamilies:

What hurts? What helps? *Journal of Divorce & Remarriage,* 37(3/4), 123–141.

Church, E. (1999). Who are the people in your family? Stepmothers' diverse notions of kinship. *Journal of Divorce & Remarriage,* 31(1/2), 83–105.

Clarke-Stewart, K. A. & Bailey, B. L. (1989). Adjustment to divorce: Why do men have it easier? *Journal of Divorce,* 13(2), 75–94.

Coleman, M., Ganong, L. H. & Fine, M. (2000). Reinvestigating remarriage: Another decade of progress. *Journal of Marriage and the Family,* 62(4), 1288–1308.

Dawson, D. (1991). Family structure and children's health and well-being: Data from the 1988 national health interview survey on child health. *Journal of Marriage and the Family,* 53, 573–584.

Doyle, K. W., Wolchik, S. A. Dawson-McClure & Sandler, I. N. (2003). Positive events as a stress buffer for children and adolescents in families in transition. *Journal of Clinical Child and Adolescent Psychology,* 32(4), 536–545.

Fine, M. A., Coleman, M. & Ganong, L. H. (1998). Consistency in perceptions of the stepparent role among stepparents, parents and stepchildren. *Journal of Social and Personal Relationships,* 15, 810–828.

Garnefski, N. & Diekstra, F. W. (1997). Adolescents from one-parent, stepparent and intact families: Emotional problems and suicide attempts. *Journal of Adolescence,* 20, 201–208.

Gross, P. (1987). Defining post-divorce remarriage families: A typology based on the subjective perceptions of children. *Journal of Divorce,* 10(1/2), 208–219.

Hetherington, E. M. (1992). Coping with marital transitions: A family systems perspective. *Monograph of the Society for Research in Child Development,* 57(2/3), 1–14.

Hetherington, E. M., Bridges, M. & Insabella, G. M. (1998). What matters? What does not? *The American Psychologist,* 53(2), 167–177.

Hoffman, J. P. & Johnson, R. A. (1998). A national portrait of family structure and adolescent drug use. *Journal of Marriage and the Family,* 60, 633–645.

Holmes, P. P. (1992). *Research from a strengths perspective.* In D. Saleeby (Ed.) The strengths perspective in social work practice. NY: Longman.

Kurdek, L. A. (1987). Children's adjustment to parental divorce: An ecological perspective. In J. P. Vincent

(Ed.). *Advances in family intervention and theory* (Volume 4) (pp. 1–31). Greenwich, CT: JAI Press.

Kurtz, L. (1995). The relation between parental coping strategies and children's adaptive processes in divorced and intact families. *Journal of Divorce & Remarriage,* 24(3/4), 89–110.

Lee, V.E., Burkham, D. T., Zimilies, H. & Ladewski, B. (1994). Family structure and its effects on behavioral and emotional problems in young adolescents. *Journal of Research on Adolescence,* 4, 405–437.

Martinez, C. R. & Forgatch, M. S. (2002). Adjusting to change: Linking family structure transitions with parenting and boys' adjustment. *Journal of Family Psychology,* 16(2), 107–116.

McCracken, G. (1988). The long interview: Qualitative research methods, Volume 13. Newbury Park, CA: Sage.

Needle, R.H., Su, S. S. & Doherty, W. J. (1990). Divorce, remarriage and adolescent substance abuse: A prospective longitudinal study. *Journal of Marriage and the Family,* 52, 157–169.

Nielson, L. (1999). Stepmothers: Why so much stress? A review of the research. *Journal of Divorce & Remarriage,* 30(1/2), 115–148.

Orchard, A. L. & Solberg, K. B. (1999). Expectations of the stepmother's role. *Journal of Divorce & Remarriage,* 31(1/2), 107–123.

Porter, B. & O'Leary, D. (1980). Marital discord and childhood behavioral problems. *Journal of Abnormal Child Psychology,* 8(3), 287–295.

Pruett, C. L., Calsyn, R. J. & Jensen, F. M. (1993). Social support received by children in stepmother, stepfather and intact families. *Journal of Divorce & Remarriage,* 19, 165–179.

Sager, C., Brown, H., Crohn, H. M., Engel, T., Rodman, E. & Walker, L. (1983). Treating the remarried family. NY: Brunner/Mazel.

Saleeby, D. (Ed.) (2002). The strengths perspective in social work practice. Boston: Allyn & Bacon.

Shaw, D. S. & Emery, R. E. (1987). Parental conflict and other correlates of the adjustment of school-age children whose parents have separated. *Journal of Abnormal Child Psychology,* 15(21), 269–281.

Spruit, E. & Goede, M. (1997). Transitions in family structure and adolescent well-being. *Adolescence,* 15, 897–902.

Stolberg, A. L., Camplear, C., Currier, K. & Wells, M.J. (1987). Individual, familial and environmental determinants of children's post-divorce adjustment and maladjustment. *Journal of Divorce,* 11(1), 51–70.

Sun, T., Schutz, C. G. & Johanson, C. E. (1996). Family structure and initiating non-medical drug use among adolescents. *Journal of Child & Adolescent Substance Abuse,* 5, 21–36.

Taylor, S. & Bogdan, R. (1998). Introduction to qualitative research methods (3rd ed.). NY: Wiley.

Visher, E. B. & Visher, J. S. (1979). Stepfamilies: A guide to working with stepparents and stepchildren. NY: Brunner/Mazel.

Credits

Reading 12-1: Sara McLanahan, "Life without Father: What Happens to the Children?" *Contexts*, Vol. 1, No. 1, 2002: 35–44. © 2002, The American Sociological Association. Used by permission. All rights reserved.

Reading 12-2: Joan B. Kelly and Robert E. Emery, "Children's Adjustment Following Divorce: Risk and Resilience Perspectives." *Family Relations*, Vol. 52, No. 4, 2003, pp. 352–362.

Reading 13-1: Mary Ann Mason, "The Modern American Stepfamily: Problems and Possibilities" in Mary Ann Mason, Arlene Skolnik, Stephen D. Sugarman (eds.), *All Our Families,* Oxford University Press, Chapter 5, pp. 96–97, 102–116. © 2003. Used by permission of Oxford University Press.

Reading 13-2: Helen M. Crohn. 2006. "Five Styles of Positive Stepmothering from the Perspective of Young Adult Stepdaughters." *Journal of Divorce and Remarriage* 46: 119–134.

Reading 14-1: From *The Future of Children*, a collaboration of The Woodrow Wilson School of Public and International Affairs at Princeton University and the Brookings Institution.

Reading 14-2: William Meezan and Jonathan Rauch, "Gay Marriage, Same-Sex Parenting, and America's Children," *The Future of Children*, Vol. 15, No. 2, Fall 2005, pp. 98–107, 110. From *The Future of Children*, a publication of The Woodrow Wilson School of Public and International Affairs at Princeton University and The Brookings Institution.